CLASSIC TEXTS SERIES

PROBLEMS IN

CALCULUS OF ONE VARIABLE

CLASSIC TEXTS SERIES

PROBLEMS IN CALCULUS OF ONE VARIABLE

IA MARON

ARIHANT PRAKASHAN (Series), MEERUT

卐 **Administrative & Production Offices**

Regd. Office

'Ramchhaya' 4577/15, Agarwal Road, Darya Ganj, New Delhi -110002
Tele: 011- 47630600, 43518550

卐 **Head Office**

Kalindi, TP Nagar, Meerut (UP) - 250002
Tel: 0121-7156203, 7156204

卐 **Sales & Support Offices**

Agra, Ahmedabad, Bengaluru, Bareilly, Chennai, Delhi, Guwahati, Hyderabad, Jaipur, Jhansi, Kolkata, Lucknow, Nagpur & Pune.

卐 **PRICE** ₹275.00

卐 **PO No :** TXT-59-T069246-2-26

Published by Arihant Publications (India) Ltd.

For further information about the books published by Arihant, log on to www.arihantbooks.com or e-mail at info@arihantbooks.com

Follow us on   

CONTENTS

FROM THE AUTHOR

In fond memory of my Parents

This text book on mathematical analysis is based on many years' experience of lecturing at a higher technical college. Its aim is to train the students in active approach to mathematical exercises, as is done at a seminar.

Much attention is given to problems improving the theoretical background. Therefore standard computational exercises are supplemented by examples and problems explaining the theory, promoting its deeper understanding and stimulating precise mathematical thinking. Some counter-examples explaining the need for certain conditions in the formulation of basis theorems are also included.

The book is designed along the following lines. Each section opens with a concise theoretical introduction containing the principal definitions, theorems and formulas. Then follows a detailed solution of one or more typical problems. Finally, problems without solution are given, which are similar to those solved but contain certain peculiarities. Some of them are provided with hints.

Each chapter (except Chap. IV and V) closes with a separate section of supplementary problems and questions aimed at reviewing and extending the material of the chapter. These sections should prove of interest to the inquiring student, and possibly also to lecturers in selecting material for class work or seminars.

The full solutions developed in the text pursue two aims: (1) to provide lecturers with a time-saver, since they can refer the students to the textbook for most of the standard exercises of a computational character and concentrate mainly on the solution of more sophisticated problems, thus gaining time for more rewarding work; and (2) to meet the needs of those who are working on their own or following correspondence courses, providing a substitute for the oral explanations given to full-time students.

The student will find the book most useful if he uses it actively, that is to say, if he studies the relevant theoretical material carefully before going on to the worked-out solutions are finally reinforces the newly-acquired knowledge by solving the problems given for independent work. The best results will be obtained when the student, having mastered the theoretical part, immediately attacks the unsolved problems without referring to the text solutions unless in difficulty.

Isac Maron

The [illegible] solutions developed in the book pursue two aims: (1) to provide the learner with [illegible] knowledge of the [illegible] text, [illegible] most of its standard [illegible] of [illegible] and [illegible] [illegible] in the solution of more separate [illegible] problems [illegible] in the line of [illegible] [illegible] and (2) to meet the needs of those who [illegible] [illegible] providing [illegible] the [illegible] equations [illegible].

[illegible]

1 Introduction to Mathematical Analysis

1.1. Real Numbers

The Absolute Value of a Real Number

Any decimal fraction, terminating or nonterminating, is called a *real* number.

Periodic decimal fractions are called *rational* numbers. Every rational number may be written in the form of a ratio, $\frac{p}{q}$, of two integers p and q, and vice versa.

Nonperiodic decimal fractions are called *irrational* numbers.

If X is a certain set of real numbers, then the notation $x \in X$ means that the number x belongs to X, and the notation $x \notin X$ means that the numbers x does not belong to X.

A set of real numbers x satisfying the inequalities $a < x < b$, where a and b are fixed numbers, is called an *open interval* (a, b). A set of real numbers x satisfying the inequalities $a \le x \le b$ is called a *closed interval* $[a, b]$. A set of real numbers x, satisfying the inequalities $a \le x < b$ or $a < x \le b$, is called a *half-open interval* $[a, b)$ or $(a, b]$. Open, closed, and half-open intervals are covered by a single term *interval*.

Any real number may be depicted as a certain point on the coordinate axis which is called a *proper point*. We may also introduce two more, so-called *improper points* $+\infty$ and $-\infty$ infinitely removed from the origin of coordinates in the positive and negative directions, respectively. By definition, the inequalities $-\infty < x < +\infty$ hold true for any real number x.

The interval $(a - \varepsilon, a + \varepsilon)$ is called the ε-*neighbourhood* of the number of a.

The set of real numbers $x > M$ is called the *M-neighbourhood* of the improper point $+\infty$.

The set of real number $x < M$ is called the *M-neighbourhood* of the improper point $-\infty$.

The *absolute value* of a number x (denoted $|x|$) is a number that satisfies the conditions

$$|x| = -x \text{ if } x < 0;$$
$$|x| = x \text{ if } x \ge 0.$$

The properties of absolute values are :

(1) the inequality $|x| \le \alpha$ means that $-\alpha \le x \le \alpha$;

(2) the inequality $|x| \ge \alpha$ means that $x \ge \alpha$ or $x \le -\alpha$;

(3) $|x \pm y| \le |x| + |y|$;

(4) $|x \pm y| \ge ||x| - |y||$;

(5) $|xy| = |x||y|$;

(6) $\left|\frac{x}{y}\right| = \frac{|x|}{|y|}$ $(y \ne 0)$.

1.1.1. Prove that the number

$$0.1010010001\ldots\underbrace{1000\ldots01}_{n}\ldots$$

is irrational.

Solution To prove this, it is necessary to ascertain that the given decimal fraction is not a periodic one. Indeed, there are n zeros between the nth and $(n + 1)$th unities, which cannot occur in a periodic fraction.

1.1.2. Prove that any number, with zeros standing in all decimal places numbered 10^n and only in these places, is irrational.

1.1.3. Prove that the sum of, or the difference between, a rational number α and an irrational number β is an irrational number.

Solution Consider the sum of α and β. Suppose $\alpha + \beta = \gamma$ is a rational number, then $\beta = \gamma - \alpha$ is also a rational number, since it is the difference between two rational numbers, which contracts the condition. Hence, the supposition is wrong and the number $\alpha + \beta$ is irrational.

1.1.4. Prove that the product $\alpha\beta$ and the quotient α/β of a rational number $\alpha \ne 0$ and an irrational number β is an irrational number.

1.1.5. (a) Find all rational values of x at which $y = \sqrt{x^2 + x + 3}$ is a rational number.

Solution (a) Suppose x and $y = \sqrt{x^2 + x + 3}$ are rational numbers. Then the difference $y - x = q$ is also a rational number. Let us now express x through q

$$y - x = \sqrt{x^2 + x + 3} - x = q,$$

$$\sqrt{x^2 + x + 3} = q + x,$$

$$x^3 + x + 3 = q^2 + 2qx + x^2,$$

$$x = \frac{q^2 - 3}{1 - 2q}$$

By a direct check it is easy to ascertain that $q \ne \frac{1}{2}$.

Prove the reverse, namely, $y = \sqrt{x^2 + x + 3}$ is a rational number if $x = \frac{q^2 - 3}{1 - 2q}$, where q is any rational number not equal to $\frac{1}{2}$.

$$y = \sqrt{x^2 + x + 3} = \sqrt{\frac{(q^2 - 3)^2}{(1 - 2q)^2} + \frac{q^2 - 3}{1 - 2q} + 3}$$

$$= \sqrt{\frac{q^4 - 2q^3 + 7q^2 - 6q + 9}{(1 - 2q)^2}}$$

$$= \sqrt{\frac{(q^2 - q + 3)^2}{(1 - 2q)^2}} = \frac{q^2 - q + 3}{|1 - 2q|} \left(q \neq \frac{1}{2}\right)$$

The latter expression is rational at any rational q not equal to $\frac{1}{2}$.

(b) Prove that $\sqrt{2}$ is an irrational number.

1.1.6. Prove that the sum $\sqrt{3} + \sqrt{2}$ is an irrational number.

Solution Assume the contrary, *ie*, that the number $\sqrt{3} + \sqrt{2}$ is rational. Then the number

$$\sqrt{3} - \sqrt{2} = \frac{1}{\sqrt{3} + \sqrt{2}}$$

is also rational, since it is the quotient of two rational numbers. Whence the number

$$\sqrt{2} = \frac{1}{2}[(\sqrt{3} + \sqrt{2}) - (\sqrt{3} - \sqrt{2})]$$

is rational, which contradicts the irrational nature of the number $\sqrt{2}$ (sec Problem **1.1.5**). Hence, the supposition is wrong and the number $\sqrt{3} + \sqrt{2}$ is irrational.

1.1.7. Prove that for every positive rational number r satisfying the condition $r^2 < 2$ one can always find a larger rational number $r + h\,(h > 0)$ for which $(r + h)^2 < 2$.

Solution We may assume $h < 1$. Then $h^2 < h$ and $(r + h)^2 < r^2 + 2rh + h$. That is why it is sufficient to put $r^2 + 2rh + h = 2$, *ie*, $h = (2 - r^2)/(2r + 1)$.

1.1.8. Prove that for every positive rational number s satisfying the condition $s^2 > 2$ one can always find a smaller rational number $s - k\,(k > 0)$ for which $(s - k)^2 > 2$.

1.1.9. Solve the following inequalities :

(a) $|2x - 3| < 1$; (b) $(x - 2)^2 \geq 4$;

(c) $x^2 + 2x - 8 \leq 0$; (d) $|x^2 - 7x + 12| > x^2 - 7x + 12$.

Solution (a) The inequality $|2x - 3| < 1$ is equivalent to the inequalities

$$-1 < 2x - 3 < 1,$$

whence $2 < 2x < 4$ and $1 < x < 2$.

(d) The given inequality is valid for those values of x at which $x^2 - 7x + 12 < 0$, whence $3 < x < 4$.

1.1.10. Find out whether the following equations have any solutions :

(a) $|x| = x + 5$; (b) $|x| = x - 5$?

Solution (a) At $x \geq 0$ we have $x = x + 5$. Hence, there are no solutions. At $x < 0$ we have $-x = x + 5$, whence $x = -5/2$. This value satisfies the initial equation.

(b) At $x \geq 0$ we have $x = x - 5$, Hence, there are no solutions. At $x < 0$ we have $-x = x - 5$, whence $x = 5/2$, which contradicts our supposition ($x < 0$). Thus, the equation has no solution.

1.1.11. Determine the values of x satisfying the following equalities:

(a) $\left|\dfrac{x-1}{x+1}\right| = \dfrac{x-1}{x+1}$; (b) $|x^2 - 5x + 6| = -(x^2 - 5x + 6)$.

1.1.12. Determine the values of x satisfying the following equalities:

(a) $|(x^2 + 4x + 9) + (2x - 3)| = |x^2 + 4x + 9| + |2x - 3|$;

(b) $|(x^4 - 4) - (x^2 + 2)| = |x^4 - 4| - |x^2 + 2|$.

Solution (a) The equality $|a + b| = |a| + |b|$ is valid if and only if both summands have the same sign. Since

$$x^2 + 4x + 9 = (x + 2)^2 + 5 > 0$$

at any values of x, the equality is satisfied at those values of x at which $2x - 3 \geq 0$, *ie*, at $x \geq 3/2$.

(b) The equality $|a - b = |a| - |b|$ holds true if and only if a and b have the same sign and $|a| \geq |b|$.

In our case the equality will hold true for the values of x at which

$$x^4 - 4 \geq x^2 + 2.$$

Whence $x^2 - 2 \geq 1$; $|x| \geq \sqrt{3}$.

1.1.13. Solve the inequalities:

(a) $|3x - 5| - |2x + 3| > 0$;

(b) $|x^2 - 5x| > |x^2| - |5x|$.

1.1.14. Find the roots of the following equations :

(a) $|\sin x| = \sin x + 1$;

(b) $x^2 - 2|x| - 3 = 0$.

Solution (a) This equation will hold true only for those values of x at which $\sin x < 0$, that is why we may rewrite it in the following way :

$$-\sin x = \sin x + 1 \quad \text{or} \quad \sin x = -\frac{1}{2};$$

whence $x = \pi k - (-1)^k \dfrac{\pi}{6}$ $(k = 0, \pm 1, \pm 2, \ldots)$.

(b) This equation can be solved in a regular way by considering the cases $x \geq 0$ and $x \leq 0$. We may also solve this equation re-writing it in the form

$$|x|^2 - 2|x| - 3 = 0.$$

Substituting y for $|x|$, we obtain

$$y^2 - 2y - 3 = 0,$$

whence $y_1 = 3$, $y_2 = -1$. Since $y = |x| \geq 0$, the value $y_2 = -1$ does not fit in. Hence

$$y = |x| = 3,$$

ie, $$x_1 = -3,\ x_2 = 3.$$

1.2. Function. Domain of Definition

The independent variable x is defined by a set X of its values. If to each value of the independent variable $x \in X$ there corresponds one definite value of another variable y, then y is called the *function* of x with a *domain of definition*(or *domain*) X or, in functional notation, $y = y(x)$ or $y = f(x)$, or $y = \varphi(x)$, and so forth. The set of values of the function $y(x)$ is called the *range* of the given function.

In particular, the functions defined by the set of natural numbers 1, 2, 3, ..., are called *numerical sequences.* They are written in the following way : $x_1, x_2, \ldots, x_n, \ldots$ or $\{x_n\}$.

1.2.1. Given the function $f(x) = (x + 1)/(x - 1)$.

Find $f(2x), 2f(x), f(x^2), [f(x)]^2$.

Solution $f(2x) = \dfrac{2x+1}{2x-1}$; $2f(x) = 2\dfrac{x+1}{x-1}$;

$$f(x^2) = \frac{x^2+1}{x^2-1};\ [f(x)]^2 = \left(\frac{x+1}{x-1}\right)^2.$$

1.2.2. (a) Given the function

$$f(x) = \log\frac{1-x}{1+x}.$$

Show that at $x_1, x_2 \in (-1, 1)$ the following identity holds true :

$$f(x_1) + f(x_2) = f\left(\frac{x_1 + x_2}{1 + x_1x_2}\right).$$

Solution At $x \in (-1, 1)$ we have $(1 - x)/(1 + x) > 0$ and hence

$$f(x_1) + f(x_2) = \log\frac{1-x_1}{1+x_1} + \log\frac{1-x_2}{1+x_2} = \log\frac{(1-x_1)(1-x_2)}{(1+x_1)(1+x_2)}. \quad ...(1)$$

On the other hand,

$$f\left(\frac{x_1 + x_2}{1 + x_1x_2}\right) = \log \frac{1 - \dfrac{x_1 + x_2}{1 + x_1x_2}}{1 + \dfrac{x_1 + x_2}{1 + x_1x_2}}$$

$$= \log \frac{1 + x_1x_2 - x_1 - x_2}{1 + x_1x_2 + x_1 + x_2}$$

$$= \log \frac{(1 - x_1)(1 - x_2)}{(1 + x_1)(1 + x_2)},$$

which coincides with the right-hand member of expression (1).

(b) Given that function $f(x) = (a^x + a^{-x})/2 \ (a > 0)$. Show that

$$f(x + y) + f(x - y) = 2f(x)f(y).$$

1.2.3. Given the function $f(x) = (x + 1)/(x^3 - 1)$. Find

$$f(-1);\ f(a + 1);\ f(a) + 1.$$

1.2.4. Given the function $f(x) = x^3 - 1$. Find

$$\frac{f(b) - f(a)}{b - a}\ (b \neq a) \quad \text{and} \quad f\left(\frac{a + h}{2}\right).$$

1.2.5. Given the function

$$f(x) = \begin{cases} 3^{-x} - 1, & -1 \le x < 0, \\ \tan(x/2), & 0 \le x < \pi, \\ x/(x^2 - 2), & \pi \le x \le 6. \end{cases}$$

Find $f(-1)$, $f(\pi/2)$, $f(2\pi/3)$, $f(4)$, $f(6)$.

Solution The point $x = -1$ lies within the interval $[-1, 0)$.

Hence $$f(-1) = 3^{-(-1)} - 1 = 2.$$

The points $x = \pi/2$, $x = 2\pi/3$ belong to the interval $[0, \pi)$.

Hence $$f(\pi/2) = \tan(\pi/4) = 1;$$
$$f(2\pi/3) = \tan(\pi/3) = \sqrt{3}.$$

The points $x = 4, x = 6$ belong to the interval $[\pi, 6]$. Hence $f(4) = \dfrac{4}{16 - 2} = \dfrac{2}{7}$; $f(6) = \dfrac{6}{36 - 2} = \dfrac{3}{17}$.

1.2.6. The function $f(x)$ is defined over the whole number scale by the following law :

$$f(x) = \begin{cases} 2x^3 + 1, & \text{if } x \le 2, \\ 1/(x - 2), & \text{if } 2 < x \le 3, \\ 2x - 5, & \text{if } x > 3. \end{cases}$$

Find : $f(\sqrt{2})$, $f(\sqrt{8})$, $f(\sqrt{\log_2 1024})$.

1.2.7. In the square $ABCD$ with side $AB = 2$ a straight line MN is drawn perpendicularly to AC. Denoting the distance from the vertex A to the line MN as x, express through x the area S of the triangle AMN cut off from the square by the straight line MN. Find this area at $x = \sqrt{2}/2$ and at $x = 2$ (Fig. 1).

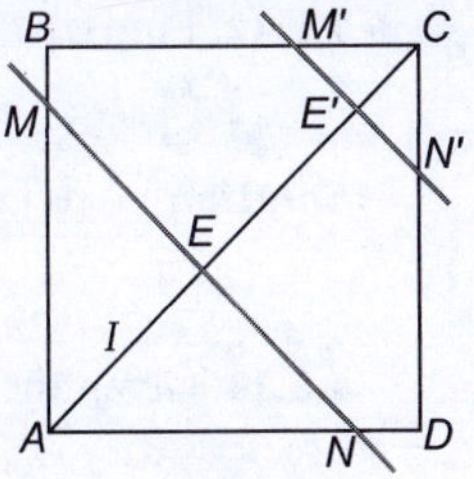

Fig. 1

Solution Note that $AC = 2\sqrt{2}$.

Hence $0 \le x \le 2\sqrt{2}$. If $x \le \sqrt{2}$,

$$S(x) = S_{\Delta\, AMN} = x^2.$$

If $x > \sqrt{2}$, then

$$S(x) = 4 - (2\sqrt{2} - x)^2 = -x^2 + 4x\sqrt{2} - 4.$$

Thus, $S(x) = \begin{cases} x^2, & 0 \le x \le \sqrt{2}, \\ -x^2 + 4x\sqrt{2} - 4 & \sqrt{2} < x \le 2\sqrt{2}. \end{cases}$

Since $\sqrt{2}/2 < \sqrt{2}, S(\sqrt{2}/2) = (\sqrt{2}/2)^2 = \dfrac{1}{2}$.

Since $2 > \sqrt{2}$,

$$S(2) = -4 + 8\sqrt{2} - 4 = 8(\sqrt{2} - 1).$$

1.2.8. Bring the number a_n, which is equal to the nth decimal place in the expansion of $\sqrt{2}$ into a decimal fraction, into correspondence with each natural number n. This gives us a certain function $\alpha_n = \varphi(n)$. Calculate $\varphi(1), \varphi(2), \varphi(3), \varphi(4)$.

Solution Extracting a square root, we find $\sqrt{2} = 1.4142....$

Hence $\varphi(1) = 4;\ \ \varphi(2) = 1;\ \ \varphi(3) = 4;\ \ \varphi(4) = 2.$

1.2.9. Calculate $f(x) = \dfrac{49}{x^2} + x^2$ at the points for which $\dfrac{7}{x} + x = 3$.

Solution $f(x) = \dfrac{49}{x^2} + x^2 = (7/x + x)^2 - 14$, but $\dfrac{7}{x} + x = 3$, hence $f(x) = 9 - 14 = -5$.

1.2.10. Find a function of the form $f(x) = ax^2 + bx + c$, if it is known that $f(0) = 5; f(-1) = 10; f(1) = 6$.

Solution $f(0) = 5 = a \cdot 0^2 + b \cdot 0 + c,$

$$f(-1) = 10 = a - b + c,$$

$$f(1) = 6 = a + b + c.$$

Determine the coefficients a, b, c from the above system. we have : $a = 3; b = -2; c = 5$; hence $f(x) = 3x^2 - 2x + 5$.

1.2.11. Find a function of the form

$$f(x) = a + bc^x\ (c > 0),$$

if $f(0) = 15; f(2) = 30; f(4) = 90.$

1.2.12. Find $\varphi[\psi(x)]$ and $\psi[\varphi(x)]$ if

$$\varphi(x) = x^2 \quad \text{and} \quad \psi(x) = 2^x.$$

Solution $\varphi[\psi(x)] = [\psi(x)]^2 = (2^x)^2 = 2^{2x}$,

$$\psi[\varphi(x)] = 2^{\psi(x)} = 2^{x^2}.$$

1.2.13. Given the function

$$f(x) = \frac{5x^2 + 1}{2 - x}.$$

Find $f(3x); f(x^3); 3f(x); [f(x)]^3$.

1.2.14. Let $f(x) = \begin{cases} 3^x & \text{at} \quad -1 < x < 0, \\ 4 & \text{at} \quad 0 \le x < 1, \\ 3x - 1 & \text{at} \quad 1 \le x \le 3. \end{cases}$

Find $f(2)$, $f(0)$, $f(0.5)$, $f(-0.5)$, $f(3)$.

1.2.15. Prove that if for an exponential function $y = a^x$ $(a > 0; a \ne 1)$ the values of the argument $x = x_n (n = 1, 2, \ldots)$ form an arithmetic progression, then the corresponding values of the function $y_n = a^{x_n} (n = 1, 2, \ldots)$ form a geometric progression.

1.2.16. $f(x) = x^2 + 6, \varphi(x) = 5x$. Solve the equation $f(x) = |\varphi(x)|$.

1.2.17. Find $f(x)$ if

$$f(x + 1) = x^2 - 3x + 2.$$

1.2.18. Evaluate the functions

$$f(x) = x^2 + \frac{1}{x^2} \quad \text{and} \quad \varphi(x) = x^4 + \frac{1}{x^4}$$

for the points at which $\frac{1}{x} + x = 5$.

1.2.19. $f(x) = x + 1; \varphi(x) = x - 2$; solve the equation

$$|f(x) + \varphi(x)| = |f(x)| + |\varphi(x)|.$$

1.2.20. A rectangle with altitude x is inscribed in a triangle ABC with the base b and altitude h. Express the perimeter P and area S of the rectangle as function of x.

1.2.21. Find the domains of definition of the following functions :

(a) $f(x) = \sqrt{x - 1} + \sqrt{6 - x}$;

(b) $f(x) = \sqrt{x^2 - x - 2} + \dfrac{1}{\sqrt{3 + 2x - x^2}}$;

(c) $f(x) = \dfrac{x}{\sqrt{x^2 - x - 2}}$;

(d) $f(x) = \sqrt{\sin x - 1}$;

(e) $f(x) = \sqrt{\log \frac{5x - x^2}{4}}$;

(f) $f(x) = \log_x 5$;

(g) $f(x) = \log \frac{x^2 - 5x + 6}{x^2 + 4x + 6}$;

(h) $f(x) = \arcsin \frac{x - 3}{2} - \log(4 - x)$;

(i) $f(x) = \frac{1}{\log(1 - x)} + \sqrt{x + 2}$;

(j) $f(x) = \log \cos x$;

(k) $f(x) = \arccos \frac{3}{4 + 2\sin x}$;

(l) $y = \frac{1}{\sqrt{|x| - x}}$.

Solution (a) The domain of definition of the given function consists of those values of x at which both items take on real values. To ensure this the following two conditions must be satisfied :

$$\begin{cases} x - 1 \geq 0, \\ 6 - x \geq 0. \end{cases}$$

By solving the inequalities we obtain $x \geq 1$; $x \leq 6$. Hence, the domain of definition of the function will be the segment [1, 6].

(e) The function is defined for the values of x for which

$$\log \frac{5x - x^2}{4} \geq 0.$$

This inequality will be satisfied if

$$\frac{5x - x^2}{4} \geq 1 \quad \text{or} \quad x^2 - 5x + 4 \leq 0.$$

Solving the latter inequality, we find $1 \leq x \leq 4$. Thus, the segment [1, 4] is the domain of definition of the function.

(f) The function is defined for all positive x different from unity, which means that the domain of definition of the function consists of the intervals (0, 1) and $(1, +\infty)$.

(k) The function is defined for the values of x for which

$$-1 \leq \frac{3}{4 + 2\sin x} \leq 1.$$

Since $4 + 2\sin x > 0$ at any x, the problem is reduced to solving the inequality

$$\frac{3}{4 + 2\sin x} \leq 1.$$

Whence

$$3 \le 4 + 2\sin x, \quad ie, \quad \sin x \ge -\frac{1}{2}.$$

By solving the latter inequality we obtain

$$-\frac{\pi}{6} + 2k\pi \le x \le \frac{7\pi}{6} + 2k\pi \ (k = 0, \pm 1, \pm 2, \ldots).$$

(l) The function is defined for the values of x for which $|x| - x > 0$, whence $|x| > x$. This inequality is satisfied at $x < 0$. Hence, the function is defined in the interval $(-\infty, -0)$.

1.2.22. Find the domains of definition of the following functions :

(a) $f(x) = \sqrt{\arcsin(\log_2 x)}$;

(b) $f(x) = \log_2 \log_3 \log_4 x$;

(c) $f(x) = \dfrac{1}{x} + 2^{\arcsin x} + \dfrac{1}{\sqrt{x-2}}$;

(d) $f(x) = \log|4 - x^2|$;

(e) $f(x) = \sqrt{\cos(\sin x) + \arcsin \dfrac{1 + x^2}{2x}}$.

Find the ranges of the following functions :

(f) $y = \dfrac{1}{2 - \cos 3x}$;

(g) $y = \dfrac{x}{1 + x^2}$.

Solution (a) For the function $f(x)$ to be defined the following inequality must be satisfied

$$\arcsin(\log_2 x) \ge 0,$$

whence $0 \le \log_2 x \le 1$ and $1 \le x \le 2$.

(b) The function $\log_2 \log_3 \log_4 x$ is defined for $\log_3 \log_4 x > 0$, whence $\log_4 x > 1$ and $x > 4$. Hence, the domain of definition is the interval $4 < x < +\infty$.

(c) The given function is defined if the following inequalities are satisfied simultaneously :

$$x \ne 0; -1 \le x \le 1 \quad \text{and} \quad x > 2,$$

but the inequalities $-1 \le x \le 1$ and $x > 2$ are incompatible, that is why the function is not defined for any value of x.

(e) The following inequalities must be satisfied simultaneously :

$$\cos(\sin x) \ge 0 \quad \text{and} \quad \left|\frac{1 + x^2}{2x}\right| \le 1.$$

The first inequality is satisfied for all values of x, the second, for $|x| = 1$. Hence, the domain of definition of the given function consists only of two points $x = \pm 1$.

Since
$$\cos 3x = \frac{2y-1}{y}.$$

$-1 \le \cos 3x \le 1$, we have $-1 \le \dfrac{2y-1}{y} \le 1.$

Whence, taking into account that $y > 0$, we obtain
$$-y \le 2y - 1 \le y \quad \text{or} \quad \frac{1}{3} \le y \le 1.$$

(g) Solving with respect to x, we obtain
$$x = \frac{1 \pm \sqrt{1-4y^2}}{2y}.$$

The range of the function y will be determined from the relation
$$1 - 4y^2 \ge 0.$$

Whence,
$$-\frac{1}{2} \le y \le \frac{1}{2}.$$

1.2.23. Solve the equation
$$\text{arc tan} \sqrt{x(x+1)} + \text{arc sin} \sqrt{x^2 + x + 1} = \frac{\pi}{2}.$$

Solution Let us investigate the domain of definition of the function on the left side of the equation. This function will be defined for
$$x^2 + x \ge 0, \quad 0 \le x^2 + x + 1 \le 1.$$

Whence,
$$x^2 + x = 0.$$

Thus, the left member of the equation attains real values only at $x_1 = 0$ and $x_2 = -1$. By a direct check we ascertain that they are the roots of the given equation.

This problem shows that a study of domains of definition of a function facilitates the solution of equations, inequalities, *etc.*

1.2.24. Find the domains of definition of the following functions :

(a) $y = \dfrac{2x-3}{\sqrt{x^2+2x+3}}$; (b) $y = \log \sin (x-3) + \sqrt{16 - x^2}$;

(c) $y = \sqrt{3-x} + \text{arc cos} \dfrac{x-2}{3}$; (d) $y = \dfrac{x}{\log(1+x)}$.

1.2.25. The function $f(x)$ is defined on the interval [0, 1]. What are the domains of definition of the following functions :

(a) $f(3x^2)$; (b) $f(x-5)$; (c) $f(\tan x)$?

Solution The given functions are functions of functions, or *super positions* of functions, *ie*, *composite* functions.

(a) Let us introduce an intermediate argument $u = 3x^2$. Then the function $f(3x^2) = f(u)$ is defined if $0 \le u \le 1$, *ie*, $0 \le 3x^2 \le 1$,

whence, $-\frac{1}{\sqrt{3}} \le x \le \frac{1}{\sqrt{3}}$.

(c) Similarly : $0 \le \tan x \le 1$, whence

$$k\pi \le x \le \frac{\pi}{4} + k\pi \ (k = 0, \pm 1, \pm 2, \ldots).$$

1.2.26. The function $f(x)$ is defined on the interval [0, 1]. What are the domains of definition of the functions

(a) $f(\sin x)$; (b) $f(2x + 3)$?

1.3. Investigation of Functions

A function $f(x)$ defined on the set X is said to be *non-decreasing* on this set (respectively, *increasing, non-increasing, decreasing*), if for any numbers $x_1, x_2 \in X$, $x_1 < x_2$, the inequality $f(x_1) \le f(x_2)$ (respectively, $f(x_1) < f(x_2)$, $f(x_1) \ge f(x_2)$, $f(x_1) > f(x_2)$) is satisfied. The function $f(x)$ is said to be monotonic on the set X if it possesses one of the four indicated properties. The function $f(x)$ is said to be *bounded above* (or below) on the set X if there exists a number M (or m) such that $f(x) \le M$ for all $x \in X$ (or $m \le f(x)$ for all $x \in X$). The function $f(x)$ is said to be bounded on the set X if it is bounded above and below.

The function $f(x)$ is called *periodic* if there exists a number $T > 0$ such that $f(x + T) = f(x)$ for all x belonging to the domain of definition of the function (together with any point x the point $x + T$ must belong to the domain of definition). The least number T possessing this property (if such a number exists) is called the *period of the function* $f(x)$. The function $f(x)$ takes on the *maximum value* at the point $x_0 \in X$ if $f(x_0) \ge f(x)$ for all $x \in X$, and the *minimum value* if $f(x_0) \le f(x)$ for all $x \in X$. A function $f(x)$ defined on a set X which is symmetric with respect to the origin of coordinates is called *even* if $f(-x) = f(x)$, and *odd* if $f(-x) = -f(x)$.

In analysing the behaviour of a function it is advisable to determine the following :

1. The domain of definition of the function.
2. Is the function even, odd, periodic ?
3. The zeros of the function.
4. The sign of the function in the intervals between the zeros.
5. Is the function bounded and what are its minimum and maximum values ?

The above items do not exhaust the analysis of a function, and later on their scope will be increased.

1.3.1. Find the intervals of increase and decrease of the function $f(x) = ax^2 + bx + c$, and its minimum and maximum values.

Solution Isolating a perfect square from the square trinomial, we have

$$f(x) = a\left(x + \frac{b}{2a}\right)^2 + \frac{4ac - b^2}{4a}.$$

If $a > 0$, then the function $f(x)$ will increase at those values of x satisfying the inequality $x + \frac{b}{(2a)} > 0$, *ie*, at $x \geq \frac{b}{(2a)}$, and decrease when $x + \frac{b}{(2a)} < 0$, *ie*, at $x < -\frac{b}{(2a)}$. Thus, if $a > 0$, the function $f(x)$ decreases in the interval $\left(-\infty, -\frac{b}{2a}\right)$ and increases in the interval $\left(-\frac{b}{(2a)}, +\infty\right)$. Obviously, at $x = -b/(2a)$ the function $f(x)$ assumes the minimum value

$$f_{\min} = f\left(-\frac{b}{2a}\right) = \frac{4ac - b^2}{4a}.$$

At $a > 0$ the function has no maximum value.

Similarly, at $a < 0$ the function $f(x)$ will increase in the interval $\left(-\infty, -\frac{b}{2a}\right)$ and decrease in the interval $\left(-\frac{b}{(2a)}, \infty\right)$; at $x = -\frac{b}{(2a)}$ the function $f(x)$ takes on the maximum value

$$f_{\max} = f\left(-\frac{b}{2a}\right) = \frac{4ac - b^2}{4a},$$

whereas it has no minimum value.

1.3.2. (a) Find the minimum value of the function

$$y = 3x^2 + 5x - 1.$$

(b) Find the rectangle with the maximum area from among all rectangles of a given perimeter.

Solution (a) Apply the results of Problem 1.3.1 : $a = 3 > 0, b = 5, c = -1$. The minimum value is attained by the function at the point $x = -\frac{5}{6}$

$$y_{\min} = \frac{4ac - b^2}{4a} = -\frac{37}{12}.$$

(b) We denote by $2p$ the length of the perimeter of the required rectangle, and by x the length of one of its sides; then the area S of the rectangle will be expressed as

$$S = x\,(p - x) \text{or } S = px - x^2.$$

Thus, the problem is reduced to the determination of the maximum value of the function $S(x) = -x^2 + px$. Apply the results of Problem 1.3.1; $a = -1 < 0, b = p, c = 0$. The maximum value is attained by the function at the point $x = -\frac{b}{(2a)} = \frac{p}{2}$. Hence, one of the sides of the desired rectangle is $\frac{p}{2}$, the other side being equal to $p - x = \frac{p}{2,}$ *ie*, the required rectangle is a square.

1.3.3. Show that

(a) the function $f(x) = x^3 + 3x + 5$ increases in the entire domain of its definition;

(b) the function $g(x) = \dfrac{x}{(1 + x^2)}$ decreases in the interval $(1, +\infty)$.

Solution The function is defined for all points of the number scale. Let us take arbitrary points x_1 and x_2, $x_1 < x_2$ on the number scale and write the following difference :

$$
\begin{aligned}
f(x_2) - f(x_1) &= (x_2^3 + 3x_2 + 5) - (x_1^3 + 3x_1 + 5) \\
&= (x_2 - x_1)(x_2^2 + x_1x_2 + x_1^2 + 3) \\
&= (x_2 - x_1)\left[\left(x_1 + \frac{1}{2}x_2\right)^2 + \frac{3}{4}x_2^2 + 3\right].
\end{aligned}
$$

Since $x_2 - x_1 > 0$ and the expression in the brackets is positive at all x_1 and x_2, then $f(x_2) - f(x_1) > 0$, *ie*, $f(x_2) > f(x_1)$, which means that the function $f(x)$ increases for all values of x.

1.3.4. Find the intervals of increase and decrease for the following functions :

(a) $f(x) = \sin x + \cos x$;

(b) $\tan\left(x + \dfrac{\pi}{3}\right)$

Solution (a) Using the familiar trigonometric formulas, we find

$$f(x) = \sqrt{2}\cos\left(x - \frac{\pi}{4}\right).$$

It is known that the function $\cos x$ decreases in the intervals

$$2n\pi \le x \le (2n + 1)\pi$$

and increases in the intervals

$$(2n - 1)\pi \le x \le 2n\pi \qquad (n = 0, \pm 1, \pm 2, \ldots).$$

Hence, the intervals of decrease of the function $f(x)$ are :

$$\frac{\pi}{4} + 2n\pi \le x \le \frac{\pi}{4} + (2n + 1)\pi \qquad (n = 0, \pm 1, \ldots),$$

and the intervals of increase of the same function are :

$$\frac{\pi}{4} + (2n - 1)\pi \le x \le \frac{\pi}{4} + 2n\pi \qquad (n = 0, \pm 1, \ldots).$$

1.3.5. Find the minimum and maximum values of the function

$$f(x) = a\cos x + b\sin x \ (a^2 + b^2 > 0).$$

Solution The given function can be represented as :

$$f(x) = \sqrt{a^2 + b^2}\cos(x - \alpha),$$

where $\cos\alpha = \dfrac{a}{\sqrt{a^2+b^2}}$, $\sin\alpha = \dfrac{b}{\sqrt{a^2+b^2}}$. Since, $|\cos(x-\alpha)| \le 1$, the maximum value of $f(x)$ equals $+\sqrt{a^2+b^2}$ (at $\cos(x-\alpha)=1$), the minimum value of $f(x)$ being equal to $-\sqrt{a^2+b^2}$ (at $\cos(x-\alpha)=-1$).

1.3.6. Find the minimum value of the function

$$f(x) = 3^{(x^2-2)^3+8}$$

Solution We denote by $\varphi(x)$ the exponent, *ie,*

$$\varphi(x) = (x^2-2)^3 + 8$$

The function $f(x) = 3^{\varphi(x)}$ takes on the minimum value at the same point as the function $\varphi(x)$.

Hence

$$\varphi(x) = x^6 - 6x^4 + 12x^2 = x^2\,[(x^2-3)^2+3].$$

Whence it is clear that the function $\varphi(x)$ attains the minimum value (equal to zero) at $x=0$. That is why the minimum value of the function $f(x)$ is equal to $3^0 = 1$.

1.3.7. Test the function

$$f(x) = \tan x + \cot x, \text{where } 0 < x < \frac{\pi}{2},$$

for increase and decrease.

1.3.8. Given : n numbers $a_1, a_2, \ldots, a_n$. Determine the value of x at which the function

$$f(x) = (x-a_1)^2 + (x-a_2)^2 + \ldots + (x-a_n)^2$$

takes on the minimum value.

Solution Rewrite the function $f(x)$ in the following way :

$$f(x) = nx^2 - 2(a_1+a_2+\ldots+a_n)\,x + (a_1^2+a_2^2+\ldots+a_n^2),$$

where from it is clear that $f(x)$ is a quadratic trinomial ax^2+bx+c, where $a=n>0$. Using the results of Problem **1.3.1,** we find that the function assumes the minimum value at $x=-b/(2a)$, *ie*, at $x=(a_1+a_2+\ldots+a_n)/n$.

Thus, the sum of the squares of deviations of the value of x from n given numbers attains the minimum value when x is the mean arithmetic value for these numbers.

1.3.9. Which of the given functions is (are) even, odd; and which of them is (are) neither even, nor odd ?

(a) $f(x) = \log(x+\sqrt{1+x^2})$; (b) $f(x) = \log\dfrac{1-x}{1+x}$;

(c) $f(x) = 2x^3 - x + 1$; (d) $f(x) = x\,\dfrac{a^x+1}{a^x-1}$.

Solution (a) It can be seen that $f(+x)+f(-x)=0$. Indeed,

$$f(+x)+f(-x)=\log(x+\sqrt{1+x^2})+\log(-x+\sqrt{1+x^2})$$
$$=\log(1+x^2-x^2)=0,$$

hence $f(x)=-f(-x)$ for all x, which means that the function is odd.

(b) $f(-x)=\log\dfrac{1+x}{1-x}=\log\left(\dfrac{1-x}{1+x}\right)^{-1}=-\log\dfrac{1-x}{1+x}$.

Thus, $f(-x)=-f(x)$ for all x from the domain of definition $(-1,1)$. Hence, the function is odd.

1.3.10. Which of the following functions is (are) even and which is (are) odd ?

(a) $f(x)=4-2x^4+\sin^2 x$;   (b) $f(x)=\sqrt{1+x+x^2}-\sqrt{1-x+x^2}$;

(c) $f(x)=\dfrac{1+a^{kx}}{1-a^{kx}}$;   (d) $f(x)=\sin x+\cos x$;

(e) $f(x)=\text{const}$.

1.3.11. Prove that if $f(x)$ is a periodic function with periodic T, then the function $f(ax+b)$, where $a>0$, is periodic with period $\dfrac{T}{a}$.

Solution Firstly,

$$f[a(x+T/a)+b]=f[(ax+b)+T]=f(ax+b),$$

since T is the period of the function $f(x)$. Secondly, let T_1 be a positive number such that

$$f[a(x+T_1)+b]=f(ax+b).$$

Let us the an arbitrary point x from the domain of definition of the function $f(x)$ and put $x'=(x-b)/a$. Then

$$f(ax'+b)=f\left(a\frac{x-b}{a}+b\right)=f(x)=f[a(x'+T_1)+b]$$
$$=f(ax'+b+aT_1)=f(x+aT_1).$$

Whence it follows that the period $T\le aT_1$, ie, $T_1\ge\dfrac{T}{a}$ and $\dfrac{T}{a}$ is the period of the function $f(ax+b)$.

Note. The periodic function $f(x)=A\sin(\omega x+\varphi)$, where A, ω, φ are constants, is called a *harmonic* with amplitude $|A|$, frequency ω and initial phase φ. Since, the function $\sin x$ has a period 2π, the function $A\sin(\omega x+\varphi)$ has a period $T=2\pi/\omega$.

1.3.12. Indicate the amplitude $|A|$, frequency ω initial phase φ and period T of the following harmonics :

(a) $f(x)=5\sin 4x$;   (b) $f(x)=4\sin(3x+\pi/4)$;

(c) $f(x)=3\sin(x/2)+4\cos(x/2)$.

1.3.13. Find the period for each of the following functions :

(a) $f(x) = \tan 2x$;

(b) $f(x) = \cot\left(\dfrac{x}{2}\right)$;

(c) $f(x) = \sin 2\pi x$.

Solution (a) Since, the function $\tan x$ has a period π, the function $\tan 2x$ has a period $\dfrac{\pi}{2}$.

1.3.14. Find the period for each of the following functions :

(a) $f(x) = \sin^4 x + \cos^4 x$;

(b) $f(x) = |\cos x|$.

Solution (a) $\sin^4 x + \cos^4 x = (\sin^2 x + \cos^2 x)^2 - 2\sin^2 x \cos^2 x$

$$= 1 - \frac{1}{2}\sin^2 2x = 1 - \frac{1}{4}(1 - \cos 4x) = \frac{3}{4} + \frac{1}{4}\sin\left(4x + \frac{\pi}{2}\right);$$

whence $$T = \frac{2\pi}{\omega} = \frac{2\pi}{4} = \frac{\pi}{2}.$$

(b) $f(x) = |\cos x| = \sqrt{\cos^2 x} = \sqrt{(1 + \cos 2x)/2}$; but the function $\cos 2x$ has a period $T = \pi$; hence, the given function has the same period.

1.3.15. Prove that the function $f(x) = \cos x^2$ is not a periodic one.

Solution Let us prove contrary. Suppose the function has a period T; then the identity $\cos (x + T)^2 \equiv \cos x^2$ is valid.

By the conditions of equality of cosines for a certain integer k we have

$$x^2 + 2Tx + T^2 \pm x^2 \equiv 2\pi k.$$

But this identity is impossible, since k may attain only integral values, and the left member contains a linear or quadratic function of the continuous argument x.

1.3.16. Find the greatest value of the function

$$f(x) = \frac{2}{\sqrt{2x^2 - 4x + 3}}.$$

1.3.17. Which of the following functions are even, and which are odd :

(a) $f(x) = \sqrt[3]{(1 - x)^2} + \sqrt[3]{(1 + x)^2}$;

(b) $f(x) = x^2 - |x|$;

(c) $f(x) = x\sin^2 x - x^3$;

(d) $f(x) = (1 + 2^x)^2 / 2^x$?

1.3.18. Find the period for each of the following functions :

(a) $f(x) = \arctan(\tan x)$;

(b) $f(x) = 2\cos\dfrac{x - \pi}{3}$.

1.3.19. Prove that the functions

(a) $f(x) = x + \sin x$; (b) $f(x) = \cos\sqrt{x}$ are non-periodic.

1.4. Inverse Functions

Let the function $y = f(x)$ be defined on the set X and have a range Y. If for each $y \in Y$ there exists a single value of x such that $f(x) = y$, then this correspondence defines a certain function $x = g(y)$ called inverse with respect to the given function $y = f(x)$. The sufficient condition for the existence of an inverse function is a strict monotony of the original function $y = f(x)$. If the function increases (decreases), then the inverse function also increases (decreases)

The graph of the inverse function $x = g(y)$ concides with that of the function $y = f(x)$ if the independent variable is marked off along the y-axis. If the independent variable is laid off along the x-axis, *ie*, if the inverse function is written in the form $y = g(x)$, then the graph of the inverse function will be symmetric to that of the function $y = f(x)$ with respect to the bisector of the first and third quadrants.

1.4.1. Find the inverse to the function $y = 3x + 5$.

Solution The function $y = 3x + 5$ is defined and increases throughout the number scale. Hence, an inverse function exists and increases. Solving the equation $y = 3x + 5$ with respect to x obtain $x = \frac{(y - 5)}{3}$.

1.4.2. Show that the function $y = \frac{k}{x}$ $(k \neq 0)$ is inverse to itself.

Solution The function is defined and monotonic throughout the entire number scale except $x = 0$. Hence, an inverse function exists. The range of the function is the entire number scale, except $y = 0$. Solving the equation $y = \frac{k}{x}$ with respect to x, we get $x = \frac{k}{y}$.

1.4.3. Find the inverse of the function

$$y = \log_a(x + \sqrt{x^2 + 1}), (a > 0, a \neq 1).$$

Solution The function $y = \log_a(x + \sqrt{x^2 + 1})$ is defined for all x, since $\sqrt{x^2 + 1} > |x|$, and is odd [see Problem **1.3.9** (a)]. It increases for positive values of x, hence, it increases everywhere and has an inverse function. Solving the equation

$$y = \log_a(x + \sqrt{x^2 + 1})$$

with respect to x, we find

$$a^y = x + \sqrt{x^2 + 1}; a^{-y} = -x + \sqrt{x^2 + 1},$$

whence

$$x = \frac{1}{2}(a^y - a^{-y}) = \sinh(y \ln a).$$

1.4.4. Show that the functions

$$f(x) = x^2 - x + 1, x \geq \frac{1}{2} \quad \text{and} \quad \varphi(x) = \frac{1}{2} + \sqrt{x - \frac{3}{4}}$$

are mutually inverse, and solve the equation

$$x^2 - x + 1 = \frac{1}{2} + \sqrt{x - \frac{3}{4}}.$$

Solution The function $y = x^2 - x + 1 = \left(x - \frac{1}{2}\right)^2 + \frac{3}{4}$ increases in the interval $\frac{1}{2} \le x < \infty$, and with x varying in the indicated interval we have $\frac{3}{4} \le y < \infty$. Hence, defined in the interval $\frac{3}{4} \le y < \infty$ is the inverse function $x = g(y)$, $x \ge \frac{1}{2}$, which is found from the equation

$$x^2 - x + (1 - y) = 0.$$

Solving the equation with respect to x, we obtain

$$x = g(y) = \frac{1}{2} + \sqrt{y - \frac{3}{4}} = \varphi(y)$$

Let us now solve the equation

$$x^2 - x + 1 = \frac{1}{2} + \sqrt{x - \frac{3}{4}}.$$

Since the graphs of the original and inverse functions can intersect only on the straight line $y = x$, solving the equation $x^2 - x + 1 = x$ we find $x = 1$.

1.4.5. Find the inverse of $y = \sin x$.

Solution The domain of definition of the function $y = \sin x$ is the entire number scale, the range of the function is the interval $[-1, 1]$. But the condition of existence of an inverse function is not fulfilled.

Divide the x-axis into intervals $n\pi - \frac{\pi}{2} \le x, \le n\pi + \frac{\pi}{2}$. If n is even, then the function increases on the intervals $n\pi - \frac{\pi}{2} \le x \le n\pi + \frac{\pi}{2}$; if n is odd, the function decreases on the intervals $n\pi - \frac{\pi}{2} \le x \le n\pi + \frac{\pi}{2}$. Hence, on each of the indicated intervals there exists an inverse function defined on the interval $[-1, 1]$.

In particular, for an interval $-\frac{\pi}{2} \le x \le \frac{\pi}{2}$ there exists an inverse function $x = \arcsin y$.

The inverse of the function $y = \sin x$ on the interval $n\pi - \frac{\pi}{2} \le x \le n\pi + \frac{\pi}{2}$ is expressed through arc sin y in the following way :

$$x = (-1)^n \arcsin y + n\pi \ (n = 0, \pm 1, \pm 2, \ldots).$$

1.4.6. Find the inverse of the given functions :

(a) $y = \sin(3x - 1)$ at $-\left(\dfrac{\pi}{6} + \dfrac{1}{3}\right) \le x \le \left(\dfrac{\pi}{6} + \dfrac{1}{3}\right)$;

(b) $y = \text{arc}\sin\left(\dfrac{x}{3}\right)$ at $-3 \le x \le 3$;

(c) $y = 5^{\log x}$;

(d) $y = 2^{x(x-1)}$.

1.4.7. Prove that the function $y = (1 - x)/(1 + x)$ is inverse to itself.

1.5. Graphical Representation of Functions

1.5.1. Sketch the graph of each of the following functions :

(a) $f(x) = x^4 - 2x^2 + 3$;

(b) $f(x) = \dfrac{2x}{1 + x^2}$;

(c) $f(x) = \sin^2 x - 2\sin x$;

(d) $f(x) = \text{arc}\cos(\cos x)$;

(e) $f(x) = \sqrt{\sin x}$;

(f) $f(x) = x^{1/\log x}$.

Solution (a) The domain of definition of the function $f(x)$ is the entire number scale. The function $f(x)$ is even, hence, its graph is symmetrical about the ordinate axis and it is sufficient to investigate the function at $x \ge 0$.

Let us single out a perfect square $f(x) = (x^2 - 1)^2 + 2$. Since, the first summand $(x^2 - 1)^2 \ge 0$, the minimum value of the function, equal to 2, is attained at the points $x = \pm 1$ (see Fig. 2).

Fig. 2

The function $f(x)$ decreases from 3 to 2 on the closed interval $0 \le x \le 1$ and increases unboundedly on the open interval $1 < x < \infty$.

(b) The domain of definition of the function $f(x)$ is the entire number scale. The function $f(x)$ is odd, therefore its graph is symmetrical about the origin of coordinates and it is sufficient to investigate the function at $x \ge 0$.

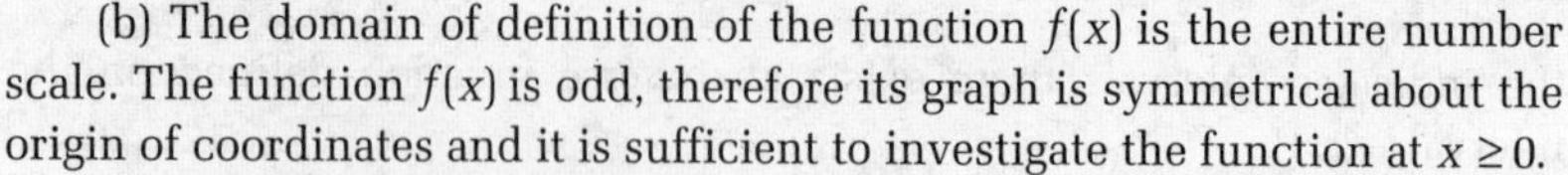

Since, $f(0) = 0$, the graph passes through the origin. It is abvious that there are no other points of intersection with the coordinate axes. Note that $|f(x)| \le 1$. Indeed, $(1 - |x|)^2 \ge 0$ or $1 + x^2 \ge 2|x|$,

whence
$$1 \ge \frac{2|x|}{1 + x^2} = |f(x)|.$$

Since, $f(x) \ge 0$ at $x \ge 0$ and $f(1) = 1$, in the interval $[0, \infty)$ the maximum value of the function $f(x)$ equals 1, the minimum value being zero (see Fig. 3).

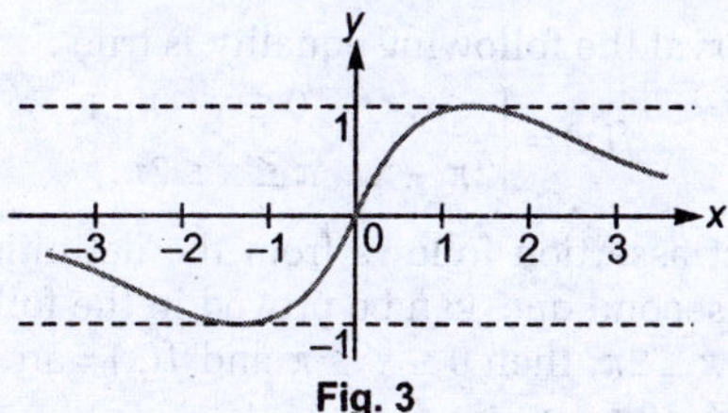

Fig. 3

Let us prove that the function increases on the closed interval $0 \le x \le 1$. Let $0 \le x_1 \le x_2 \le 1$. Then

$$f(x_2) - f(x_1) = \frac{2x_2}{1+x_2^2} - \frac{2x_1}{1+x_1^2}$$

$$= \frac{2x_2 + 2x_2x_1^2 - 2x_1 - 2x_1x_2^2}{(1+x_2^2)(1+x_1^2)}$$

$$= \frac{2(x_2 - x_1)(1 - x_1x_2)}{(1+x_2^2)(1+x_1^2)} \ge 0$$

and $$f(x_2) > f(x_1).$$

Similarly, we can show that on the interval $(1, \infty)$ the function decreases. Finally,

$$f(x) = 2x/(1+x^2) < 2x/x^2 = 2/x,$$

whence it is clear that $f(x)$ tends to zero with an increase in x.

(c) The domain of definition of the function $f(x)$ is the entire number scale. The function has a period 2π, that is why it is quite sufficient to investigate it on the interval $[0, 2\pi]$, where it becomes zero at the points $x = 0$; $x = \pi$; $x = 2\pi$.

Writing the given function in the form

$$f(x) = (1 - \sin x)^2 - 1,$$

we note that it increases with a decrease in the function $\sin x$ and decreases as $\sin x$ increases. Hence, the function $f(x)$ decreases on the intervals $\left[0, \frac{\pi}{2}\right]$ and $\left[\frac{3\pi}{2}, 2\pi\right]$, and increases on the interval $[\pi/2, 3\pi/2]$. Since $f(\pi/2) = -1$, and $f\left(\frac{3\pi}{2}\right) = 3$, the range of the function is $-1 \le f(x) \le 3$ (Fig. 4).

(d) The domain of definition of the function is the entire number scale. Indeed, $|\cos x| \le 1$ at any x, hence, arc $\cos(\cos x)$ has a meaning. The function $f(x)$ is a periodic one with the period 2π, hence, it is sufficient to sketch its graph on the interval $[0, 2\pi]$.

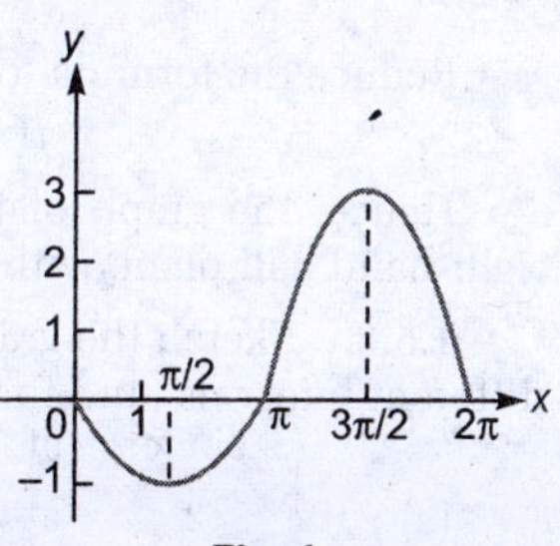

Fig. 4

But on this interval the following equality is true :

$$f(x) = \begin{cases} x, & 0 \le x \le \pi, \\ 2\pi - x, & \pi \le x \le 2\pi. \end{cases}$$

Indeed, the first assertion follows from the definition of the function arc cos x, while the second one can be proved in the following way. Let us put $x' = 2\pi - x, \pi \le x \le 2\pi$; then $0 \le x' \le \pi$ and $f(x) = \text{arc cos}\,[\cos(2\pi - x')]$ $= \text{arc cos}\,(\cos x') = x' = 2\pi - x$.

Taking all this into consideration, we draw the graph (see Fig. 5).

(e) The function $y = \sqrt{\sin x}$ is a periodic one with period 2π; that is why we may confine ourselves to the interval $[0, 2\pi]$. But the function is not

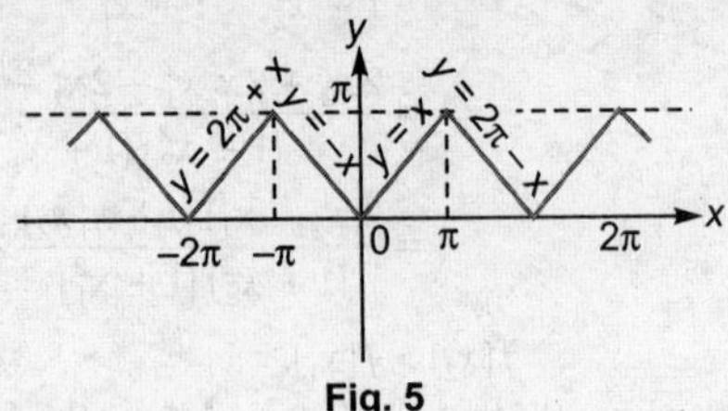

Fig. 5

defined in the whole interval $[0, 2\pi]$, it is defined only in the interval $[0, \pi]$, as in the interval $(\pi, 2\pi)$ the radicand is negative. The graph is symmetrical about the straight line $x = \dfrac{\pi}{2}$, as well as the graph $y = \sin x$ (see Fig. 6).

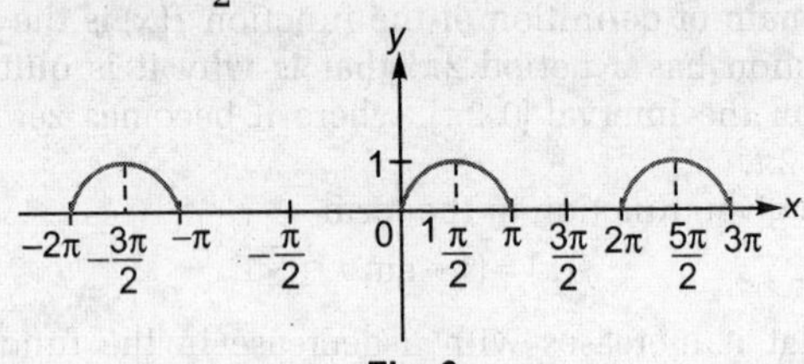

Fig. 6

Here we have an example of a periodic function which does not exist in the infinite set of intervals.

(f) The domain of definition of the function is

$$0 < x < 1 \text{ and } 1 < x < \infty.$$

Reduce the formula to the form

$$f(x) = x^{1/\log x} = x^{\log_x 10} = 10.$$

Hence, the graph of the given function is the half-line $y = 10$ in the right-hand half plane with the point $x = 1$ removed (see Fig. 7).

1.5.2. Sketch the graphs of functions defined by different formulas in different intervals (and in those reducible to them) :

$$\text{(a) } y = \begin{cases} \sin x & \text{at } -\pi \le x \le 0, \\ 2 & \text{at } 0 < x \le 1, \\ 1/(x-1) & \text{at } 1 < x \le 4; \end{cases}$$

(b) $y = \begin{cases} -2 & \text{at} \quad x > 0, \\ \dfrac{1}{2} & \text{at} \quad x = 0, \\ -x^3 & \text{at} \quad x < 0; \end{cases}$

(c) $y = x + \sqrt{x^2}$;

(d) $y = \dfrac{2}{(x + \sqrt{x^2})}$.

Fig. 7

Solution (a) The domain of definition of the function is the interval $[-\pi, 4]$. The graph of the function consists of a portion of the sinusoid $y = \sin x$ on the interval $-\pi \le x \le 0$, straight line $y = 2$ on the interval $(0, 1]$ and a part of the branch of the hyperbola $y = \dfrac{1}{(x-1)}$ on the interval $(1, 4]$ (see Fig. 8).

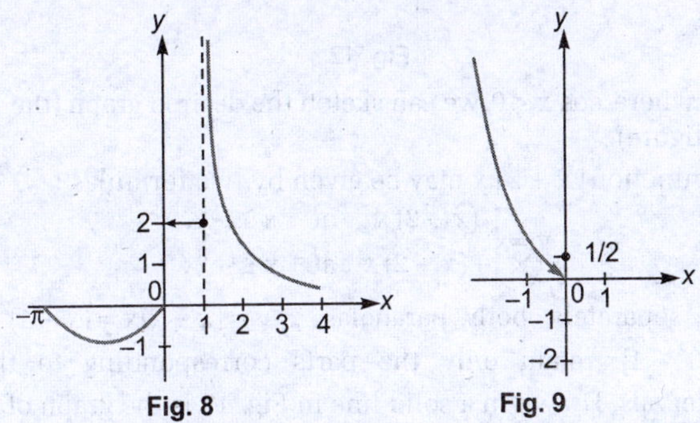

Fig. 8 Fig. 9

(b) The graph of the function consists of a portion of a cubic parabola an isolated point and a half-line (see Fig. 9).

(c) The function may be give by two formulas :

$$y = \begin{cases} 2x, & \text{if} \quad x \ge 0, \\ 0, & \text{if} \quad x < 0. \end{cases}$$

Thus, the graph of our function is a polygonal line (see Fig. 10).

(d) From (c) it follows that the function is defined only in the interval $(0, +\infty)$, y being equal to $\dfrac{1}{x}$ $(x > 0)$. Thus, the graph of our function is the right-hand part of an equilateral hyperbola (see Fig. 11).

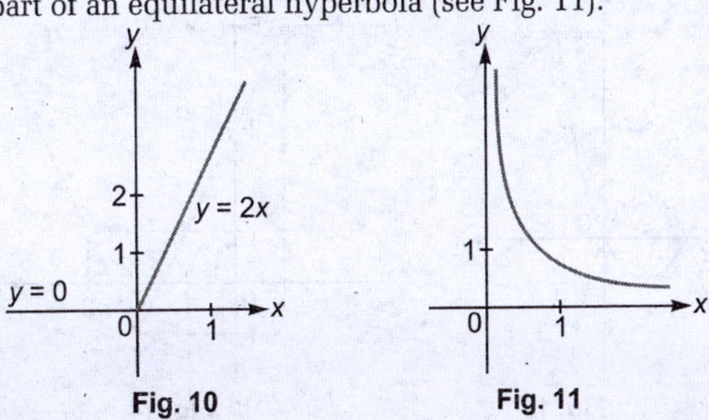

Fig. 10 Fig. 11

1.5.3. Sketch the graphs of the following functions :

(a) $y = \cos x + |\cos x|$;

(b) $y = |x + 2|\, x$.

Solution (a) $\cos x + |\cos x| = \begin{cases} 2\cos x & \text{at} \quad \cos x \geq 0, \\ 0 & \text{at} \quad \cos x < 0. \end{cases}$

Doubling the non-negative ordinates of the graph for the function $y = \cos x$ (the broken line in Fig. 12) and assuming $y = 0$

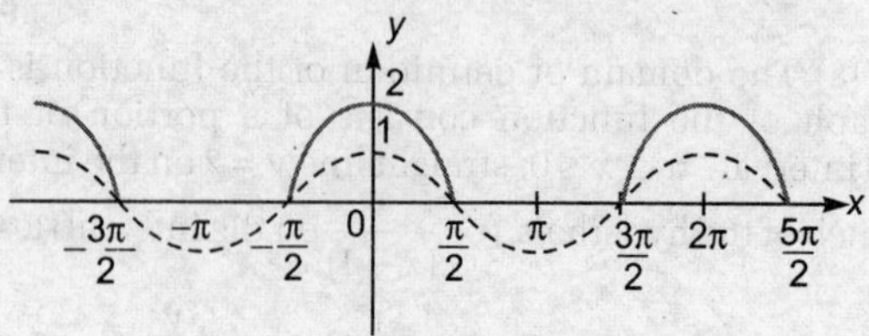

Fig. 12

at the points where $\cos x < 0$, we can sketch the desired graph (the solid line in the same figure).

(b) The function $|x + 2|\, x$ may be given by two formulas :

$$y = \begin{cases} (x + 2)\,x & \text{at} \quad x \geq -2, \\ -(x + 2)\,x & \text{at} \quad x \leq -2. \end{cases}$$

Plotting separately both parabolas : $y = (x + 2)x = (x + 1)^2 - 1$, and $y = -[(x + 10^2 - 1]$, retain only the parts corresponding to the above indicated intervals. Drawn in a solid line in Fig. 13 is the graph of the given function, the broken line showing the deleted parts of the constructed parabolas.

1.5.4. Sketch the graph of the function

$$y = 2|x - 2| - |x + 1| + x.$$

Solution At $x \geq 2$

$$y = 2(x - 2) - (x + 1) + x = 2x - 5.$$

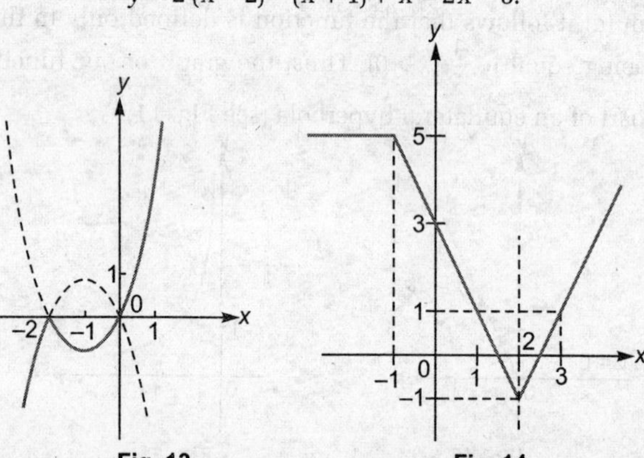

Fig. 13 **Fig. 14**

At $-1 \le x \le 2$

$$y = -2(x-2) - (x+1) + x = -2x + 3.$$

Finally, at $x \le -1$

$$y = -2(x-2) + (x+1) + x = 5.$$

Hence, the given function can be rewritten in the following way :

$$y = \begin{cases} 5, & x \le -1, \\ -2x+3, & -1 \le x \le 2, \\ 2x-5, & x \ge 2. \end{cases}$$

Therefore the graph is a polygonal line (see Fig. 14).

1.5.5. Sketch the graph of the function $y = 2^x - 2^{-x}$.

Solution Draw graphs for the functions $y_1 = 2^x$ and $y_2 = -2^{-x}$ (broken lines in Fig. 15), and add graphically their ordinates. In doing so bear in mind that $y_2 < y < y_1$, and that y_2 tends to zero with an increase in x, whereas y_1 tends to zero with a decrease in x (the solid line in Fig. 15).

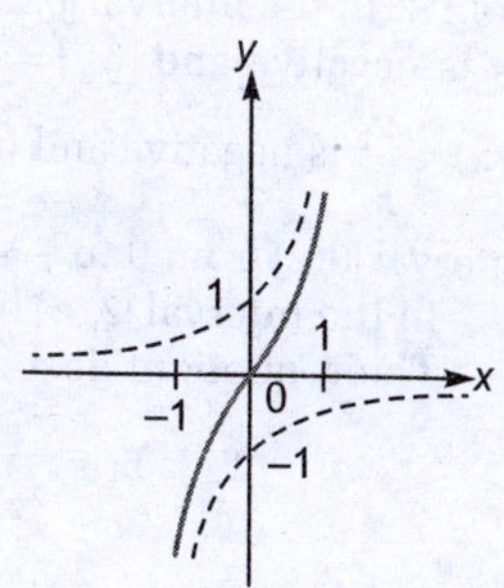

Fig. 15

1.5.6. Sketch the graph of the function

$$y = x \sin x.$$

Solution Being the product of two odd functions $y_1 = x$ and $y_2 = \sin x$, the function y is an even one, that is why we shall analyse it for $x \ge 0$.

We draw graphs for $y_1 = x$ and $y_2 = \sin x$ (the broken lines in Fig. 16).

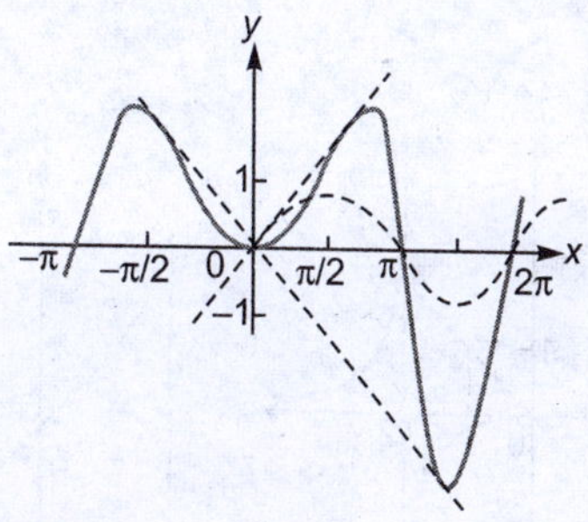

Fig. 16

At the points where $y_2 = \sin x = 0, y = y_1 \cdot y_2 = 0$, and at the points where $y_2 = \sin x = \pm 1, y = \pm y_1 = \pm x$. The latter equality indicates the expedience of graphing the auxiliary function $y_3 = -x$.

Marking the indicated points and joining them into a smooth curve, we obtain the required graph (the solid line in Fig. 16).

1.5.7. Sketch the graph o the function $y = x(x^2 - 1)$ by multiplying the ordinates of the graphs $y_1 = x$ and $y_2 = x^2 - 1$.

1.5.8. Graph the following functions :

(a) $y = x/(x^2 - 4)$,

(b) $y = 1/\text{arc cos } x$.

Solution (a) Since the function is odd, it is sufficient to investigate it for $x \geq 0$.

Let us consider it as the quotient of the two functions :

$$y_1 = x \text{ and } y_2 = x^2 - 4.$$

Since at $x = 2$ the denominator $y_2 = 0$, the function is not defined at the point 2. In the interval $[0, 2)$ the function y_1 increases from 0 to 2, the function y_2 is negative and $|y_2| = 4 - x^2$ decreases from 4 to 0; hence, the quotient $f(x) = \dfrac{y_1}{y_2}$ is negative and increases in absolute value, *ie*, $f(x)$ decreases in the interval $[0, 2)$ from 0 to $-\infty$.

In the interval $(2, \infty)$ both functions are positive and increasing. Their quotient decreases since from $2 \leq x_1 < x_2$ it follows that

$$y_2 - y_1 = \frac{x_2}{x_2^2 - 4} - \frac{x_1}{x_1^2 - 4} = \frac{(x_1 - x_2)(x_1 x_2 + 4)}{(x_2^2 - 4)(x_1^2 - 4)} < 0.$$

The indicated quotient tendfs to zero as $x \to \infty$, since $y = \dfrac{1/x}{1 - 4/x^2} \to 0$.

The general outline of the graph is presented in Fig. 17 (three solid lines).

(b) Denote $y_1 = \text{arc cos } x$. The domain of definition of this function $|x| \leq 1$. At $x = 1$ we have $y_1 = 0$, hence, $y = \dfrac{1}{y^1} \to \infty$ at $x \to 1$, *ie*, $x = 1$ is a vertical asymptote.

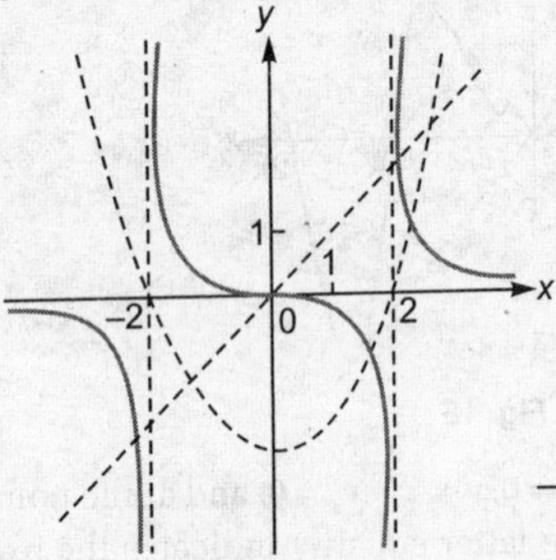

Fig. 17

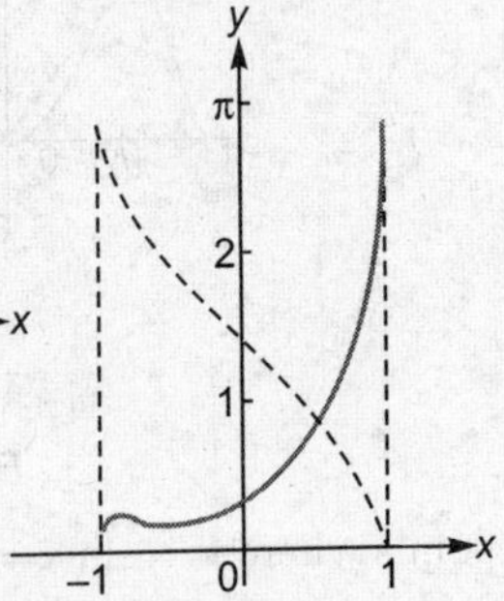

Fig. 18

The function y_1 decreases on the entire interval of definition $[-1, 1)$, hence $y = \dfrac{1}{y_1}$ increases. The maximum value $y_1 = \pi$ is attained at $x = -1$.

Accordingly, the minimum value of the function is $\frac{1}{\pi}$. The solid line in Fig. 18 represents the general outline of the graph.

Simple Transformations of Graphs

I. The graph of the function $y = f(x + a)$ is obtained from the graph of the function $y = f(x)$ by translating the latter graph along the x-axis by $|a|$ scale units in the direction opposite to the sign of a (see Fig. 19).

II. The graph $y = f(x) + b$ is obtained from the graph of the function $y = f(x)$ by translating the latter graph along the y-axis by $|b|$ scale units in the direction opposite to the sign of b (see Fig. 20).

III. The graph of the function $y = f(kx)$ $(k > 0)$ is obtained from the graph of the function $y = f(x)$ by "compressing" the latter graph against the y-axis in the horizontal direction k times at $k > 1$ and by "stretching" it in the horizontal direction from the y-axis $\frac{1}{k}$ times at $k < 1$ (see Fig. 21).

IV. The graph of the function $y = kf(x)$ $(k > 0)$ is obtained from the graph of function $y = f(x)$ by "stretching" it in the horizontal direction k times at $k > 1$ and "compressing" it against the x-axis (*ie*, vertically) $\frac{1}{k}$ times at $k < 1$ (see Fig. 21).

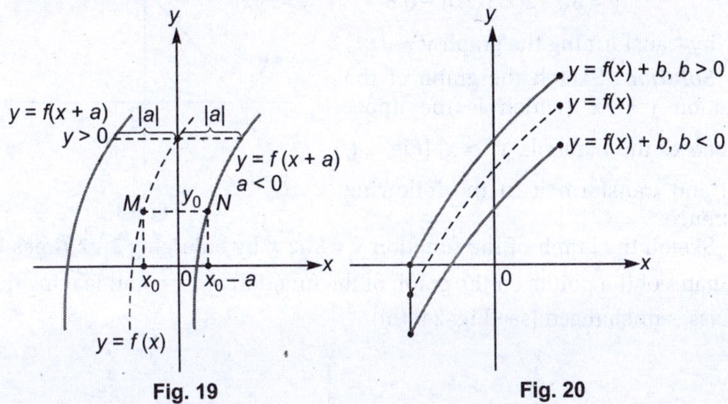

Fig. 19

Fig. 20

V. The graph of the function $y = -f(x)$ is symmetrical to that of the function $y = f(x)$ about the x-axis, while the graph of the function $y = f(-x)$ is symmetrical to that of the function $y = f(x)$ about the y-axis.

VI. The graph of the function $y = f(|x|)$ is obtained from the graph of the function $y = f(x)$ in the following way : for $x \geq 0$ the graph of the function $y = f(x)$ is retained, then this retained part of the graph is reflected symmetrically about the y-axis, thus determining the graph of the function for $x \leq 0$ (see Fig. 22).

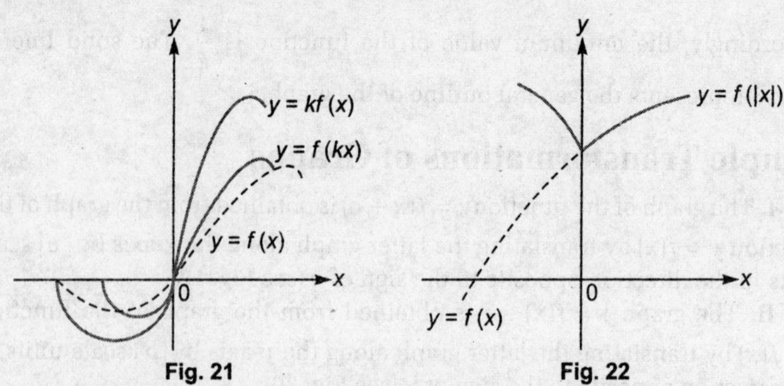

Fig. 21 Fig. 22

VII. The graph of the function $y = |f(x)|$ is constructed from the graph $y = f(x)$ in the following way; the portion of the graph of the function $y = f(x)$ lying above the x-axis remains unchanged. its other portion located below the x-axis being transformed symmetrically about the x-axis (see Fig. 23).

VIII. The graphs of the more complicated functions

$$y = \lambda f(kx + a) + b$$

are drawn from the graph of $y = f(x)$ applying consecutively transformations I to V.

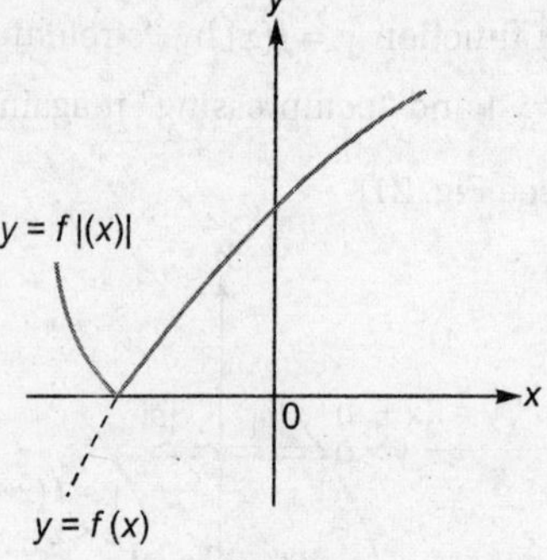

Fig. 23

1.5.9. Graph the function

$$y = 3\sqrt{-2(x+2.5)} - 0.8$$

by transforming the graph $y = \sqrt{x}$.

Solution Sketch the graph of the function $y = \sqrt{x}$ (which is the upper branch of the parabola $y^2 = x$) [Fig. 24, (a)], and transform it in the following sequence.

Sketch the graph of the function $y = 3\sqrt{2x}$ by enlarging $3\sqrt{2}$ times the ordinates of the points on the graph of the function $y = \sqrt{x}$ and leaving their abscissas unchanged (see Fig. 24, (b)).

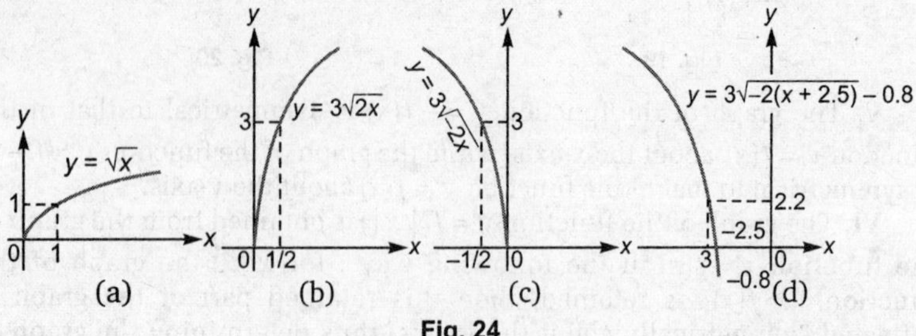

Fig. 24

Then sketch the graph of the function $y = 3\sqrt{-2x}$ which will be the mirror image of the preceding graph about the y-axis (see Fig. 24,(c)).

By shifting the obtained graph 2.5. scale units leftward and then 0.8 unit downward draw the desired graph of the function $y = 3\sqrt{-2(x + 2.5)} - 0.8$ (see Fig. 24, (d)).

1.5.10. Graph the function $y = 3\cos x - \sqrt{3}\sin x$ by transforming the cosine curve.

Solution Transform the given function

$$y = 3\cos x - \sqrt{3}\sin x = 2\sqrt{3}\left(\frac{\sqrt{3}}{2}\cos x - \frac{1}{2}\sin x\right)$$

$$= 2\sqrt{3}\cos\left(x + \frac{\pi}{6}\right).$$

Thus, we have to sketch the graph of the function

$$y = 2\sqrt{3}\cos\left(x + \frac{\pi}{6}\right),$$

which is the graph of the function $y = 2\sqrt{3}\cos x$ translated by $\pi/6$ leftward. The function has a period of 2π, hence it is sufficient to draw its graph for $-\pi \le x \le \pi$ (see Fig. 25).

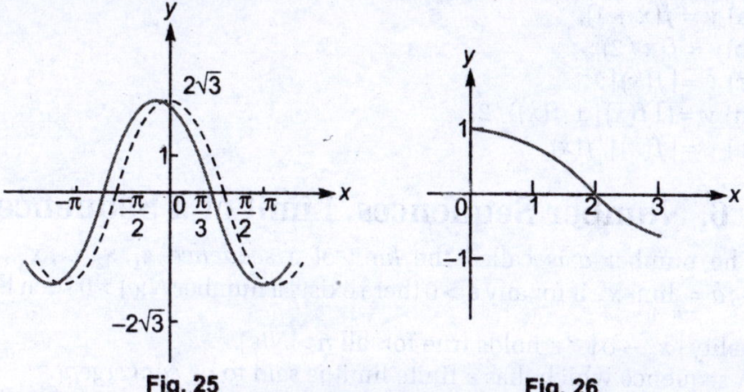

Fig. 25 Fig. 26

The graph of any function of the form $y = a\cos x + b\sin x$, where a and b are constants, is sketched in a similar way.

1.5.11. Graph the following functions :

(a) $y = \dfrac{x + 3}{x + 1}$;

(b) $y = \dfrac{1}{x^2 - 9}$;

(c) $y = \begin{cases} x^2 + x + 1, & \text{if } -1 \le x < 0, \\ \sin^2 x, & \text{if } 0 \le x \le \pi, \\ (x - 1)/(x + 1), & \text{if } \pi < x \le 5; \end{cases}$

(d) $y = x + \dfrac{1}{x}$;

(e) $y = x^2 - x^3$;

(f) $y = x + \sin x$;

(g) $y = \dfrac{1}{\cos x}$;

(h) $y = 3\sin(2x - 4)$;

(i) $y = 2\sqrt{-3(x + 1.5)} - 1.2$;

(j) $y = |x^2 - 2x - 1|$;

(k) $y = ||x| - 1|$;

(l) $y = \cos(\sin x)$;

(m) $y = |\sin x| + \sin x + \sin x$ on the interval $[0, 3\pi]$;

(n) $y = x^2 \operatorname{sign} x$, where $\operatorname{sign} x = \begin{cases} 1 & \text{at } x > 0, \\ 0 & \text{at } x = 0, \\ -1 & \text{at } x < 0. \end{cases}$

1.5.12. The function $y = f(x)$ is given graphically (Fig. 26). Sketch the graphs of the following functions :

(a) $y = f(x + 1)$;

(b) $y = f(x/2)$;

(c) $y = |f(x)|$;

(d) $y = (|f(x)| \pm f(x))/2$;

(e) $y = |f(x)|/f(x)$.

1.6. Number Sequences. Limit of a Sequence

The number a is called the *limit* of a *sequence* $x_1, x_2, \ldots, x_n, \ldots\ldots$ as $n \to \infty, a = \lim\limits_{n\to\infty} x_n$ if for any $\varepsilon > 0$ there exists a number $N(e) > 0$ such that the inequality $|x_n - a| < \varepsilon$ holds true for all $n > N(\varepsilon)$.

A sequence which has a finite limit is said to be *convergent*.

A sequence $\{x_n\}$ is called *infinitely small* if $\lim x_n = 0$, and *infinitely* large if $\lim x_n = \infty$.

1.6.1. Given the general term of the sequence $\{x_n\}$:

$$x_n = \frac{\sin(n\pi/2)}{n}.$$

Write the first five terms of this sequence.

Solution Putting consecutively $n = 1, 2, 3, 4, 5$ in the general term x_n, we obtain

$$x_1 = \frac{\sin(\pi/2)}{1} = 1;$$

$$x_2 = \frac{\sin(2\pi/2)}{2} = 0;$$

$$x_3 = \frac{\sin(3\pi/2)}{3} = -\frac{1}{3};$$

$$x_4 = \frac{\sin(4\pi/2)}{4} = 0;$$

$$x_5 = \frac{\sin(5\pi/2)}{5} = \frac{1}{5}.$$

1.6.2. Knowing the first several terms of the sequence, write one of the possible expressions for the general term:

(a) $\frac{2}{3}, \frac{5}{8}, \frac{10}{13}, \frac{17}{18}, \frac{26}{23};$

(b) $1, \frac{1}{2}, 2, \frac{1}{3}, 3, \frac{1}{4}, 4, \frac{1}{5}.$

Note. A knowledge of the first several terms of a sequence is not sufficient to define this sequence. That is why this problem should be understood as one of finding a certain simple inductive regularity compatible with the given terms.

Solution (a) Note that the numerator of each of the given terms of the sequence equals the square of the number of this term plus of the sequence equals the square of the number of this term plus unity, *ie*, $n^2 + 1$, while the denominators form the arithmetic progression 3, `8, 13, 18,... with the first term $a_1 = 3$ and the common difference $d = 5$. Hence,

$$a_n = a_1 + d(n-1) = 3 + 5(n-1) = 5n - 2,$$

thus, we have

$$x_n = \frac{n^2+1}{5n-2}.$$

(b) Here the general term of the sequence can be written with the aid of two formulas : one for the terms standing in odd places, the other for those in even places :

$$x_n = \begin{cases} k & \text{at } n = 2k-1, \\ 1/(k+1) & \text{at } n = 2k. \end{cases}$$

It is also possible to express the general term by one formula, which will be more complicated, for instance,

$$x_n = \frac{n+1}{4}[1-(-1)^n] + \frac{1}{n+2}[1+(-1)^n].$$

1.6.3. Find the first several terms of the sequence if the general term is given by one of the following formulas :

(a) $x_n = \sin\left(\frac{n\pi}{3}\right);$

(b) $x_n = 2^{-n}\cos n\pi;$

(c) $x_n = (1 + 1/n)^n.$

1.6.4. Using the definition of the limit of a sequence, prove that

(a) $\lim x_n = 1$ if $x_n = (2n-1)/(2n+1)$,

(b) $\lim x_n = 3/5$ if $x_n = (3n^2+1)/(5n^2-1)$. Beginning with which n is the inequality $|x_n - 3/5| < 0.01$ fulfilled ?

Solution (a) For any $\varepsilon > 0$ let us try to find a natural number $N(\varepsilon)$ such that for any natural number $n > N(\varepsilon)$ the inequality $|x_n - 1| < \varepsilon$ is fulfilled.

For this purpose let us find the absolute value of the difference

$$\left|\frac{2n-1}{2n+1} - 1\right| = \left|\frac{-2}{2n+1}\right| = \frac{2}{2n+1}.$$

Thus, the inequality $|x_n - 1| < \varepsilon$ is satisfied if $\frac{2}{2n+1} < \varepsilon$, whence $n > 1/\varepsilon - \frac{1}{2}$. Hence, the integral part of the number $\frac{1}{\varepsilon} - \frac{1}{2}$ may be taken as $N(\varepsilon)$, *ie*, $N = E\left(\frac{1}{\varepsilon} - \frac{1}{2}\right)$.

So, for each $\varepsilon > 0$ we can find a number N such that from the inequality $n > N$ it will follow that $|x_n - 1| < \varepsilon$, which means that

$$\lim_{n\to\infty} \frac{2n-1}{2n+1} = 1.$$

(b) Let us find the absolute value of the difference $|x_n - 3/5|$:

$$\left|\frac{3n^2+1}{5n^2-1} - \frac{3}{5}\right| = \frac{8}{5(5n^2-1)}.$$

Let $\varepsilon > 0$ be given. Choose n so that the inequality

$$\frac{8}{5(5n^2-1)} < \varepsilon,$$

is fulfilled.

Solving this inequality, we find

$$n^2 > \frac{8}{25\varepsilon} + \frac{1}{5}; \quad n > \frac{1}{5}\sqrt{\frac{8+5\varepsilon}{\varepsilon}}.$$

Putting

$$N = E\left(\frac{1}{5}\sqrt{\frac{8+5\varepsilon}{\varepsilon}}\right),$$

we conclude that at $n > N$

$$|x_n - 3/5| < \varepsilon,$$

which completes the proof.

If $\varepsilon = 0.01$, then

$$N = E\left(\frac{1}{5}\sqrt{\frac{8+5\varepsilon}{\varepsilon}}\right) = E\left(\frac{1}{5}\sqrt{805}\right) = 5,$$

and all terms of the sequence, beginning with the 6th, are contained in the interval $\left(\frac{3}{5}-0.01; \frac{3}{5}+0.01\right)$.

1.6.5. Given a sequence with the general term $x_n = \frac{3n-5}{9n+4}$. It is known that $\lim_{n\to\infty} x_n = \frac{1}{3}$. Find the number of points x_n lying outside the open interval

$$L = \left(\frac{1}{3} - \frac{1}{1000}; \frac{1}{3} + \frac{1}{1000}\right).$$

Solution The distance from the point x_n to the point $\frac{1}{3}$ is equal to

$$\left|x_n - \frac{1}{3}\right| = \left|-\frac{19}{3\,(9n+4)}\right| = \frac{19}{3\,(9n+4)}.$$

Outside the interval L there will appear those terms of the sequence for which this distance exceeds 0.001, *ie*,

$$\frac{19}{3\,(9n+4)} > \frac{1}{1000},$$

whence

$$1 \le n \le \frac{18988}{27} = 703\frac{7}{27}.$$

Hence, 703 points ($x_1, x_2, \ldots, x_{702}$) are found outside the interval L.

1.6.6. Prove that the number $l = 0$ is not the limit of a sequence with the general term $x_n = (n^2-2)/(2n^2-9)$.

Solution Estimate from below the absolute value of the difference

$$\left|\frac{n^2-2}{2n^2-9} - 0\right| = \frac{|n^2-2|}{|2n^2-9|}.$$

At $n \ge 3$ the absolute value of the difference remains greater than the constant number $\frac{1}{2}$; hence, there exists such $\varepsilon > 0$, say, $\varepsilon = \frac{1}{2}$, that the inequality

$$\left|\frac{n^2-2}{2n^2-9} - 0\right| > \frac{1}{2}$$

holds true for any $n \ge 3$.

The obtained inequality proves that $l = 0$ is not the limit of the given sequence.

1.6.7. Prove that the sequence

$$1, \frac{1}{2}, \frac{1}{3}, \frac{2}{3}, \frac{1}{5}, \frac{3}{4}, \frac{1}{7}, \frac{4}{5}, \ldots$$

with the general term

$$x_n = \begin{cases} 1/n, & \text{if } n = 2k-1, \\ n/(n+2), & \text{if } n = 2k, \end{cases}$$

has no limit.

Solution It is easy to show that the points x_n with odd numbers concentrate about the point 0, and the points x_n with even numbers, about the point 1. Hence, any neighbourhood of the point 0, as well as any neighbourhood of the point 1, contains in infinite set of points x_n. Let a be an arbitrary real number. We can always choose such a small $\varepsilon > 0$ that the ε-neighbourhood of the point a will not contain at least a certain neighbourhood of either pont 0 or point 1. Then an infinite set of numbers x_n will be found outside this neighbourhood, and that is why one cannot assert that all the numbers x_n, beginning with a certain one, will enter the ε-neighbourhood of the number a. This means, by definition, that the number a is not the limit of the given sequence. But a is an arbitary number, hence no number is the limit of this sequence.

1.6.8. Prove that $\lim x_n = 1$, if $x_n = (3^n + 1)/3^n$.

1.6.9. Prove that $\lim x_n = 2$, if $x_n = (2n+3)/(n+1)$. Find the number of the term beginning with which the inequality $|(2n+3)/(n+1) - 2| < \varepsilon$, where $\varepsilon = 0.1; 0.01; 0.001$, is fulfilled.

1.6.10. Prove that the sequence

$$\frac{1}{2}, \frac{1}{2}, \frac{3}{4}, \frac{1}{4}, \frac{7}{8}, \frac{1}{8}, \ldots,$$

with the general term $x_n = \begin{cases} 1 - \dfrac{1}{2^{(n+1)/2}} & \text{if } n \text{ is odd,} \\ \dfrac{1}{2^{n/2}} & \text{if } n \text{ is odd,} \end{cases}$

has no limit.

1.6.11. Prove that at any arbitrarily large $a > 0$ $\lim x_n = 0$ if $x_n = \dfrac{a^n}{n!}$.

Solution Let a natural number $k > 2a$. Then at $n > k$

$$\frac{a^n}{n!} = \frac{a}{1}\cdot\frac{a}{2}\ldots\frac{a}{n} = \left(\frac{a}{1}\cdot\frac{a}{2}\ldots\frac{a}{k}\right)\left(\frac{a}{k+1}\cdot\frac{a}{k+2}\ldots\frac{a}{n}\right) < a^k\left(\frac{1}{2}\right)^{n-k}$$

$$= (2a)^k\left(\frac{1}{2}\right)^n.$$

Since $\lim\left(\frac{1}{2}\right)^n = 0$ (prove it!), then at a sufficiently large n we have : $\left(\frac{1}{2}\right)^n < \dfrac{\varepsilon}{(2a)^k}$ and, hence, $\dfrac{a^n}{n!} < \varepsilon$, which means that $\lim\left(\dfrac{a^n}{n!}\right) = 0$.

1.6.12. Test the following sequences for limits;

(a) $x_n = \dfrac{1}{(2\pi)}$; (b) $x_n = \begin{cases} 1 & \text{for an even } n, \\ 1/n & \text{for an odd } n; \end{cases}$

(c) $x_n = \dfrac{1}{n}\cos\dfrac{n\pi}{2}$; (d) $x_n = n[1-(-1)^n]$.

1.6.13. Prove that the sequence with the general term

$$x_n = \frac{1}{n^k}\ (k>0)$$

is an infinitely small sequence.

Solution To prove that the sequence x_n is infinitely small is to prove that $\lim\limits_{n\to\infty} x_n = 0$.

Take an arbitrary $\varepsilon > 0$. Since $|x_n| = \dfrac{1}{n^k}$, we have to solve the inequality

$$\frac{1}{n^k} < \varepsilon,$$

whence $n > \sqrt[k]{\dfrac{1}{\varepsilon}}$. Hence, N may be expressed as the integral part of $\sqrt[k]{\dfrac{1}{\varepsilon}}$, *ie*, $N = E\left(\sqrt[k]{\dfrac{1}{\varepsilon}}\right)$.

1.6.14. Prove that the sequence with the general terms

(a) $x_n = \dfrac{1-(-1)^n}{n}$,

(b) $x_n = \dfrac{1}{n}\sin\left[(2n-1)\dfrac{\pi}{2}\right]$

are infinitely small as $n\to\infty$.

1.6.15. Show that the sequence with the general term $x_n = (-1)^n\, 2/(5\sqrt[3]{n}+1)$ is infinitely small as $n\to\infty$. Find a number N beginning with which the points x_n belong to the interval $\left(-\dfrac{1}{10}, \dfrac{1}{10}\right)$.

Solution Take an arbitrary $\varepsilon > 0$ and estimate $|x_n|$:

$$|x_n| = \frac{2}{5\sqrt[3]{n}+1} < \frac{2}{5\sqrt[3]{n}} < \frac{2}{2\sqrt[3]{n}} = \frac{1}{\sqrt[3]{n}}.$$

That is why $|x_n| < \varepsilon$ as soon as $n > \dfrac{1}{\varepsilon^2}$. Hence, $\lim\limits_{n\to\infty} x_n = 0$. *ie*, the sequence is infinitely small.

We take now $\varepsilon = \dfrac{1}{10}$. Since $|x_n| < 1/\sqrt[3]{n}$, x_n will necessarily be smaller than $\dfrac{1}{10}$ if $1/\sqrt[3]{n} < \dfrac{1}{10}$ or $n > 1000$. Hence, N may be taken equal to 1000. But we can obtain a more accurate result by solving the inequality

$$|x_n| = \frac{2}{5\sqrt[3]{n+1}} < \frac{1}{10}.$$

It holds true at $n > \left(\frac{19}{5}\right)^3 = 3.8^3 = 54.872$. Hence, N may be taken equal to $54 < 1000$.

1.6.16. It is known that if $x_n = a + \alpha_n$, where α_n is an infinitesimal as $n \to \infty$, then $\lim\limits_{n\to\infty} x_n = a$. Taking advantage of this rule, find the limits :

(a) $x_n = \dfrac{3^{n+1} + \sin(n\pi/4)}{3^n}$;

(b) $x_n = \dfrac{2^n + (-1)^n}{2^n}$.

Solution $x_n = \dfrac{3^{n+1} + \sin(n\pi/4)}{3^n} = 3 + \alpha_n$, where $\alpha_n = \dfrac{\sin(n\pi/4)}{3^n}$ is an infinitesimal as $n \to \infty$, hence, $\lim\limits_{n\to\infty} x_n = 3$.

1.6.17. Prove that $\lim\limits_{n\to\infty} \sqrt[n]{n} = 1$.

Solution Let us prove that the variable $\sqrt[n]{n}$ can be represented as the sum $1 + \alpha_n$, where α_n is an infinitesimal as $n \to \infty$.

Let us put $\sqrt[n]{n} = 1 + \alpha_n$. Raising to the nth power we obtain

$$n = (1+\alpha_n)^n = 1 + n\alpha_n + \frac{n(n-1)}{2!}\alpha_n^2 + \ldots + \alpha_n^n,$$

where from we arrive at the conclusion that for any $n > 1$ the following inequality holds true :

$$n > 1 + \frac{n(n-1)}{2!}\alpha_n^2$$

(Since all the terms on the right are non-negative). Transposing the unity to the left and reducing the inequality by $n - 1$ we obtain

$$1 > \frac{n}{2}\alpha_n^2,$$

whence it follows that $\frac{2}{n} > \alpha_n^2$ or $\sqrt{2/n} > \alpha_n > 0$. Since $\lim\limits_{n\to\infty} \sqrt{2/n} = 0$, $\lim\limits_{n\to\infty} \alpha_n$ also equals zero, *ie*, α_n is an infinitesimal. Hence it follows that

$$\lim_{n\to\infty} \sqrt[n]{n} = 1.$$

1.6.18. Prove that the sequence with the general term

$$x_n = 3^{\sqrt[3]{n}}$$

is inifinitely large as $n \to \infty$.

Solution Let us take an arbitrary positive number M and solve the inequality

$$3^{\sqrt[3]{n}} > M.$$

Taking the logrithm, we obtain

$$\sqrt[3]{n} > \log_3 M, n > (\log_3 M)^3.$$

If we now take $N = E(\log_3 M)^3$, then for all $n > N$ the inequality $|x_n| > M$ will be fulfilled, which means that the sequence is infinitely large.

1.6.19. Prove that

$$\lim_{n\to\infty} \sqrt[n]{a} = 1 \ (a > 0).$$

1.7. Evaluation of Limits of Sequences

If the sequence $\{x_n\}$ and $\{y_n\}$ are convergent, then

(1) $\lim(x_n \pm y_n) = \lim x_n \pm \lim y_n$;

(2) $\lim(x_n y_n) = \lim x_n \lim y_n$;

(3) $\lim \dfrac{x_n}{y_n} = \dfrac{\lim x_n}{\lim y_n}$ $(\lim y_n \neq 0)$.

If $x_n \leq y_n$ then $\lim x_n \leq \lim y_n$.

1.7.1. Find $\lim\limits_{n\to\infty} x_n$ if

(a) $x_n = \dfrac{3n^2 + 5n + 4}{2 + n^2}$; (b) $x_n = \dfrac{5n^3 + 2n^2 - 3n + 7}{4n^3 - 2n + 11}$;

(c) $x_n = \dfrac{4n^2 - 4n + 3}{2n^3 + 3n + 4}$; (d) $x_n = \dfrac{1^2 + 2^2 + \ldots + n^2}{5n^3 + n + 1}$;

(e) $x_n = \dfrac{1 + 2 + \ldots + n}{n^2}$.

Solution (a) $x_n = \dfrac{3 + \dfrac{5}{n} + \dfrac{4}{n^2}}{\dfrac{2}{n^2} + 1}$,

$$\lim_{n\to\infty} x_n = \frac{\lim\limits_{n\to\infty} (3 + 5/n + 4/n^2)}{\lim\limits_{n\to\infty} \left(\dfrac{2}{n^2} + 1\right)} = 3$$

(d) Recall that

$$1^2 + 2^2 + 3^2 + \ldots + n^2 = \frac{n(n+1)(2n+1)}{6}.$$

Hence $$x_n = \frac{n(n+1)(2n+1)}{6(5n^3 + n + 1)} = \frac{2n^3 + 3n^2 + n}{6(5n^3 + n + 1)} = \frac{2 + \dfrac{3}{n} + \dfrac{1}{n^2}}{30 + \dfrac{6}{n^2} + \dfrac{6}{n^3}},$$

$$\lim_{n\to\infty} x_n = \frac{1}{15}.$$

1.7.2. Find $\lim_{n\to\infty} x_n$, if

(a) $x_n = \left(\dfrac{3n^2 + n - 2}{4n^2 + 2n + 7}\right)^3$; (b) $x_n = \left(\dfrac{2n^3 + 2n^2 + 1}{4n^3 + 7n^2 + 3n + 4}\right)^4$;

(c) $x_n = \sqrt[n]{5n}$; (d) $x_n = \sqrt[n]{n^8}$;

(e) $x_n = \sqrt[n]{n^5}$; (f) $x_n = \sqrt[n]{6n + 3}$.

Solution (a) $\lim_{n\to\infty} \left(\dfrac{3n^2 + n - 2}{4n^2 + 2n + 7}\right)^3$

$$= \lim_{n\to\infty} \left(\frac{3n^2 + n - 2}{4n^2 + 2n + 7}\right)\left(\frac{3n^2 + n - 2}{4n^2 + 2n + 7}\right)\left(\frac{3n^2 + n - 2}{4n^2 + 2n + 7}\right)$$

$$= \left(\lim_{n\to\infty} \frac{3 + 1/n - 2/n^2}{4 + 2/n + 7/n^2}\right)^3 = \left(\frac{3}{4}\right)^3 = \frac{27}{64}.$$

(c) In solving this example, and also the rest of the examples of Problem **1.7.2**, take advantage of the following equalities (see Problems **1.6.17** and **1.6.19**) :

$$\lim_{n\to\infty} = \sqrt[n]{n} = 1 \text{ and } \lim_{n\to\infty} \sqrt[n]{a} = 1. \qquad \text{...(i)}$$

We have

$$\lim_{n\to\infty} x_n = \lim_{n\to\infty} \sqrt[n]{5n} = \lim_{n\to\infty} \sqrt[n]{5} \lim_{n\to\infty} \sqrt[n]{n},$$

but from (1) it follows that $\lim \sqrt[n]{5} = 1$ and $\lim \sqrt[n]{n} = 1$; hence, $\lim x_n = 1 \cdot 1 = 1$.

1.7.3. Find

$$\lim_{n\to\infty} \left(\frac{2n^3}{2n^2 + 3} + \frac{1 - 5n^2}{5n + 1}\right).$$

Solution Summing the fractions, we obtain

$$x_n = \frac{2n^3 - 13n^2 + 3}{10n^3 + 2n^2 + 15n + 3}.$$

Whence $$\lim_{n\to\infty} x_n = \lim_{n\to\infty} \frac{2n^3 - 13n^2 + 3}{10n^3 + 2n^2 + 15n + 3} = \frac{1}{5}.$$

Note. If we put

$$y_n = \frac{2n^3}{2n^2 + 3}; \; z_n = \frac{1 - 5n^2}{5n + 1},$$

then the limit of their sum $\lim (y_n + z_n) = \dfrac{1}{5}$, though each of the summands is an infinitely large quantity. Thus, from the convergence of a sum of sequences it does not, generally speaking, follow that the summands converge too.

1.7.4. Find $\lim\limits_{n\to\infty} x_n$ if

(a) $x_n = \sqrt{2n+3} - \sqrt{n-1}$;

(b) $x_n = \sqrt{n^2+n+1} - \sqrt{n^2-n+1}$;

(c) $x_n = n^2(n - \sqrt{n^2+1})$;

(d) $x_n = \sqrt[3]{n^2-n^3} + n$;

(e) $x_n = \dfrac{\sqrt{n^2+1}+\sqrt{n}}{\sqrt[4]{n^3+n}-\sqrt{n}}$;

(f) $x_n = \sqrt[3]{(n+1)^2} - \sqrt[3]{(n-1)^2}$;

(g) $x_n = \dfrac{1-2+3-4+5-6+\ldots-2n}{\sqrt{n^2+1}+\sqrt{4n^2-1}}$;

(h) $x_n = \dfrac{1}{1\cdot 2} + \dfrac{1}{2\cdot 3} + \dfrac{1}{3\cdot 4} + \ldots + \dfrac{1}{n(n+1)}$.

Solution (a) $x_n = \sqrt{n}\,(\sqrt{2+3/n} - \sqrt{1-1/n}) \to +\infty$ as $n\to\infty$, since the second multiplier has a positive limit.

(c) $x_n = \dfrac{n^2(n-\sqrt{n^2+1})}{1} = \dfrac{-n^2}{n+\sqrt{n^2+1}}$

$$= -n\cdot\frac{1}{1+\sqrt{1+\dfrac{1}{n^2}}} \to -\infty \text{ as } n\to\infty.$$

(d) $x_n = \dfrac{n^2}{(n^3-n^3)^{2/3} - n\sqrt[3]{n^2-n^3} + n^2}$

$$= \frac{1}{\left(\dfrac{1}{n}-1\right)^{2/3} - \left(\dfrac{1}{n}-1\right)^{1/3} + 1}.$$

It means $x_n \to \dfrac{1}{3}$.

(e) Factoring out the terms of the highest power in the numerator and denominator, we have :

$$x_n = \frac{\sqrt{n^2+1}+\sqrt{n}}{\sqrt[4]{n^3+n}-\sqrt{n}} = \frac{n\left(\sqrt{1+\dfrac{1}{n^2}}+\sqrt{\dfrac{1}{n}}\right)}{n^{3/4}\left(\sqrt{1+\dfrac{1}{n^2}}-\sqrt{\dfrac{1}{n}}\right)}$$

$$= n^{1/4}\frac{\sqrt{1+\dfrac{1}{n^2}}+\sqrt{\dfrac{1}{n}}}{\sqrt{1+\dfrac{1}{n^2}}-\sqrt{\dfrac{1}{n}}} \to +\infty \text{ as } n\to\infty.$$

1.7.5. Find $\lim\limits_{n\to\infty} x_n$ if

(a) $x_n = \dfrac{\sqrt{n}}{\sqrt{n+1}+\sqrt{n}}$;

(b) $x_n = \dfrac{\sqrt{n^2+4n}}{\sqrt[3]{n^3-3n^2}}$;

(c) $x_n = \sqrt[3]{1-n^3}+n$;

(d) $x_n = \dfrac{1}{2n}\cos n^3 - \dfrac{3n}{6n+1}$;

(e) $x_n = \dfrac{2n}{2n^2-1}\cos\dfrac{n+1}{2n-1} - \dfrac{n}{1-2n}\,\dfrac{n(-1)^n}{n^2+1}$;

(f) $x_n = \dfrac{1+\frac{1}{2}+\frac{1}{4}+\ldots+\frac{1}{2^n}}{1+\frac{1}{3}+\frac{1}{9}+\ldots+\frac{1}{3^n}}$.

1.8. Testing Sequences for Convergence

Bolzano-Weierstrass theorem. A monotonic bounded sequence has a finite limit.

Theorem on passing to the limit in inequalities. If $x_n \le y_n \le z_n$ and $\lim\limits_{n\to\infty} x_n = \lim\limits_{n\to\infty} z_n = c$, then $\lim\limits_{n\to\infty} y_n = c$ too (c is a number, $+\infty$ or $-\infty$ but not ∞).

1.8.1. Prove that the sequence with the general term $x_n = \dfrac{(2n-1)}{(3n+1)}$ is an increasing one.

Solution We have to prove that $x_{n+1} > x_n$ for any n, *ie*, to prove that

$$\frac{2n+1}{3n+4} > \frac{2n-1}{3n+1}.$$

The latter inequality is equivalent to the obvious inequality

$$6n^2+5n+1 > 6n^2+5n-4.$$

Hence, $$x_{n+1} > x_n$$

1.8.2. Given a sequence with the general term

$$x_n = \frac{10^n}{n!}.$$

Prove that this sequence decrease at $n \ge 10$.

Solution $x_{n+1} = \dfrac{10^{n+1}}{(n+1)!} = \dfrac{10^n}{n!}\cdot\dfrac{10}{n+1} = x_n\dfrac{10}{n+1}.$

Since $\dfrac{10}{n+1} < 1$ at $n \ge 10$, then $x_{n+1} < x_n$ beginning with this number, which means that the sequence decreases at $n \ge 10$.

1.8.3. Test the following sequences for boundedness :

(a) $x_n = \dfrac{5n^2}{n^2+3}$; (b) $y_n = (-1)^n \dfrac{2n}{n+1} \sin n$; (c) $z_n = n \cos \pi n$.

Solution (a) The sequence $\{x_n\}$ is bounded, since, it is obvious that $0 < \dfrac{5n^2}{n^2+3} < 5$ for all n.

(b) The sequence $\{y_n\}$ is bounded;

$$|y_n| = |(-1)^n| \frac{2n}{n+1} |\sin n| < \frac{2n}{n+1} < 2.$$

(c) The sequence $\{z_n\}$ is not bounded, since

$$|z_n| = |n \cos \pi n| = n.$$

1.8.4. Prove that the sequence

$$x_1 = \frac{x_0}{a+x_0};\ x_2 = \frac{x_1}{a+x_1};\ x_3 = \frac{x_2}{a+x_2};\ \ldots;\ x_n = \frac{x_{n-1}}{a+x_{n-1}};\ldots\ (a > 1,\ x_0 > 0)$$

converges.

Solution Let us prove that this sequence is monotonic and bounded. Firstly, $x_n < x_{n-1}$ as

$$x_n = \frac{x_{n-1}}{a+x_{n-1}} < x_{n-1}.$$

Hence, the given sequence is a decreasing one. Secondly, all its terms are positive (by condition $a > 0$ and $x_0 > 0$), which means that the sequence is bounded below. Thus, the given sequence is monotonic and bounded, hence, it has a limit.

1.8.5. Prove that the sequence with the general term

$$x_n = \frac{1}{5+1} + \frac{1}{5^2+1} + \frac{1}{5^3+1} + \ldots + \frac{1}{5^n+1}$$

$$\left(ie,\ x_1 = \frac{1}{5+1};\ x_2 = \frac{1}{5+1} + \frac{1}{5^2+1};\ x_3 = \frac{1}{5+1} + \frac{1}{5^2+1} + \frac{1}{5^3+1};\ldots \right)$$

converges.

Solution The sequence $\{x_n\}$ increases, since $x_{n+1} = x_n + \dfrac{1}{(5^{n+1}+1)}$ and hence, $x_{n+1} > x_n$. Besides, it is bounded above, since $\dfrac{1}{(5^n+1)} < \dfrac{1}{5^n}$ at any n and

$$x_n = \frac{1}{5+1} + \frac{1}{5^2+1} + \frac{1}{5^3+1} + \ldots + \frac{1}{5^n+1}$$

$$< \frac{1}{5} + \frac{1}{5^2} + \frac{1}{5^8} + \ldots + \frac{1}{5^n} = \frac{\frac{1}{5} - \frac{1}{5^{n+1}}}{1 - \frac{1}{5}} = \frac{1}{4}\left(1 - \frac{1}{5^n}\right) < \frac{1}{4}.$$

Hence, the sequence converges.

1.8.6. Taking advantage of the theorem on the existence of a limit of monotonic bounded sequence, prove that the following sequences are convergent :

(a) $x_n = \dfrac{n^2 - 1}{n^2}$; (b) $x_n = 2 + \dfrac{1}{2!} + \dfrac{1}{3!} + \ldots + \dfrac{1}{n!}$.

1.8.7. Prove that the following sequences converge and find their limits :

(a) $x_1 = \sqrt{2}$; $x_2 = \sqrt{2 + \sqrt{2}}$; $x_3 = \sqrt{2 + \sqrt{2 + \sqrt{2}}}$;...;

$$x_n = \underbrace{\sqrt{2 + \sqrt{2 + \ldots + 2}}}_{n \text{ radicals}};\ldots;$$

(b) $x_n = \dfrac{2^n}{(n+2)!}$;

(c) $x_n = \dfrac{E(ny)}{n}$;

(d) the sequence of successive decimal approximations 1; 1.4; 1.41; 1.414;... of the irrational number $\sqrt{2}$;

(e) $x_n = \dfrac{n!}{n^n}$.

Solution (a) It is obvious that $x_1 < x_2 < x_3 < \ldots < x_n < x_{n+1} < \ldots$, *ie*, the sequence is increasing. It now remains to prove that it is bounded.

We have $x_n = \sqrt{2 + x_{n-1}}$, $n = 2, 3, \ldots$

Since, $x_1 = \sqrt{2} < 2$, $x_2 = \sqrt{2 + x_1} < \sqrt{2 + 2} = 2$, $x_3 = \sqrt{2 + x_2} < \sqrt{2 + 2} = 2, \ldots$

Let it be proved that $x_{n-1} < 2$. Then $x_n = \sqrt{2 + x_{n-1}} < \sqrt{2 + 2} = 2$. Thus, with the aid of mathematical induction we have proved that $x_n < 2$, *ie*, the sequence is bounded. Hence, it has a finite limit. Let us find it. Denote

$$\lim_{n \to \infty} x_n = y.$$

Then, $x_n = \sqrt{2 + x_{n-1}}$; raising to the second power, we obtain

$$x_n^2 = 2 + x_{n-1}.$$

Passing to the limit, we can rewrite this equality as follows

$$\lim_{n \to \infty} x_n^2 = \lim_{n \to \infty} (2 + x_{n-1}), \text{or } y^2 + 2 + y.$$

The roots of the obtained quadratic equation are :

$$y_1 = 2; y_2 = -1.$$

The negative root does not suit not suit here, since, $x > 0$. Hence, $\lim_{n\to\infty} x_n = y_1 = 2$.

(c) We have $ny - 1 < E(ny) \le ny$ or $y - \frac{1}{n} < \frac{E(ny)}{n} \le y$. But the sequences $\left\{y - \frac{1}{n}\right\}$ and $\{y\}$ converge, their limit being y, that is why $\lim_{n\to\infty} x_n = y$.

(d) This sequence is non-decreasing, since each following term x_{n+1} is obtained from the preceding one x_n by adding one more significant digit to the decimal fraction. The sequence is bounded above, say, by the number 1.5. Hence, the sequence converges, its limit being $\sqrt{2}$.

(e) The sequence decreases monotonically. Indeed,

$$x_{n+1} = \frac{(n+1)!}{(n+1)^{n+1}} = \frac{n!}{(n+1)^n} = \frac{n!}{n^n} \cdot \frac{n^n}{(n+1)^n} = \frac{n^n}{(n+1)^n} x_n.$$

Since $\frac{n^n}{(n+1)^n} < 1$, $x_{n+1} < x_n$.

Then, since $x_n > 0$, the sequence is bounded below, hence $\lim_{n\to\infty} x_n$ exists. Let us denote it l. Obviously, $l = \lim_{n\to\infty} x_n \ge 0$. Now let us show that $l = 0$. Indeed,

$$\frac{(n+1)^n}{n^n} = \left(\frac{n+1}{n}\right)^n = \left(1 + \frac{1}{n}\right)^n \ge 1 + n\frac{1}{n} = 2.$$

Hence, $\frac{n^n}{(n+1)^n} < \frac{1}{2}$ and $x_{n+1} < \frac{1}{2} x_n$. Passing over to the limit, we obtain

$$l \le \frac{1}{2} l,$$

which, together with $l \ge 0$, brings us to the conclusion :

$$l = 0.$$

1.8.8. Find the limits of the sequences with the following general terms :

$$x_n = \frac{n}{\sqrt{n^2 + n}}; \; z_n = \frac{n}{\sqrt{n^2 + 1}};$$

$$y_n = \frac{1}{\sqrt{n^2 + 1}} + \frac{1}{\sqrt{n^2 + 2}} + \ldots + \frac{1}{\sqrt{n^2 + n}}.$$

Solution Let us prove that $\lim_{n\to\infty} x_n = 1$. Indeed

$$|x_n - 1| = \left|\frac{n}{\sqrt{n^2 + n}} - 1\right| = \left|\frac{n - \sqrt{n^2 + n}}{\sqrt{n^2 + n}}\right| = \frac{n}{\sqrt{n^2 + n}\,(n + \sqrt{n^2 + n})} < \frac{1}{2n}.$$

We can prove similarly that

$$\lim_{n\to\infty} z_n = 1.$$

Then, $$y_n < \underbrace{\frac{1}{\sqrt{n^2+1}} + \frac{1}{\sqrt{n^2+1}} + \ldots + \frac{1}{\sqrt{n^2+1}}}_{n} = \frac{n}{\sqrt{n^2+1}} = z_n.$$

On the other hand,
$$y_n > \underbrace{\frac{1}{\sqrt{n^2+n}} + \frac{1}{\sqrt{n^2+n}} + \ldots + \frac{1}{\sqrt{n^2+n}}}_{n} = \frac{n}{\sqrt{n^2+n}} = x_n.$$

Thus, $x_n < y_n < z_n$, $\lim\limits_{n\to\infty} x_n = \lim\limits_{n\to\infty} z_n = 1$,
and according to the theorem on passing to the limit in inequalities
$$\lim_{n\to\infty} y_n = 1.$$

1.8.9. Using the theorem on passing to the limit in inequalities prove
$$\lim_{n\to\infty} \sqrt[n]{a} = 1 \; (a > 0).$$

1.8.10. Prove the existence of the limit of the sequence $y_n = a^{\frac{1}{2^n}}$ $(a > 1)$ and calculate it.

1.8.11. Taking advantage of the theorem on the limit of a monotonic sequence, prove the existence of a finite limit of the sequence
$$x_n = 1 + \frac{1}{2^n} + \frac{1}{3^2} + \ldots + \frac{1}{n^2}.$$

1.8.12. Taking advantage of the theorem on passing to the limit in inequalities, prove that
$$\lim_{n\to\infty} x_n = 1 \text{ if } x_n = 2n(\sqrt{n^2+1} - n).$$

1.8.13. Prove that the sequence
$$x_1 = \sqrt{a};\; x_2 = \sqrt{a + \sqrt{a}};$$
$$x_3 = \sqrt{a + \sqrt{a + \sqrt{a}}};\; \ldots;\; x_n = \underbrace{\sqrt{a + \sqrt{a + \ldots + \sqrt{a}}}}_{n \text{ radicals}} \qquad (a > 0)$$
has the limits $b = (\sqrt{4a+1} + 1)/2$.

1.8.14. Prove that the sequence with the general term
$$x_n = \frac{1}{3+1} + \frac{1}{3^2+2} + \ldots + \frac{1}{3^n+n}$$
has a finite limit.

1.8.15. Prove that a sequence of lengths of perimeters of regular 2^n gons inscribed in a circle tends to a limit (called the length of circumference).

1.9. The Limit of a Function

A point a on the real axis is called the *limit point* of a set X if any neighbourhood of the point a contains points belonging to X which are different from a (a may be either a proper or an improper point).

Let the point a be the limit point of the domain of definition X of the function $f(x)$. The number A is called the *limit of the function* $f(x)$ as $x \to a$, $A = \lim_{x \to a} f(x)$, if for any neighbourhood V of the number A there exists a neighbourhood u of the number a such that for all $x \in X$ lying in u, $f(x) \in V$ (the definition of the limit of a function after Cauchy). The number A may be either finite or infinite. In particular, if the numbers A and a are finite we obtain the following definition.

A number A is called the limit of a function $f(x)$ as $x \to a$. $A = \lim_{x \to a} f(x)$, if for any $\varepsilon > 0$ there exists a number $\delta(\varepsilon) > 0$ such that for all x satisfying the inequality $0 < |x - a| < \delta$ and belonging to the domain of definition of the function $f(x)$ the inequality $|f(x) - A| < \varepsilon$ holds true (the "$\varepsilon - \delta$ definition").

If $a = +\infty$, the definition is as follows. A number A is called the limit of a function $f(x)$ as $x \to +\infty$, $A = \lim_{x \to +\infty} f(x)$, if for any $\varepsilon > 0$ there exists a number $M(\varepsilon) > 0$ such that for all x satisfying the inequality $x > M(\varepsilon)$ and belonging to the domain of definition of the function $f(x)$ the inequality $|f(x) - A| < \varepsilon$ holds true (the "ε-M definition").

The notation $\lim_{x \to a} f(x) = \infty$ means that $\lim_{x \to a} |f(x)| = +\infty$. The rest of the cases are considered similarly.

The definition of the limit of a function after Heine. The notation $\lim_{x \to a} f(x) = A$ means that for any sequence of values of x converging to the number a

$$x_1, x_2, \ldots, x_n, \ldots$$

(belonging to the domain of definition of the function and differing from a) the corresponding sequence of values of y

$$y_1 = f(x_1); y_2 = f(x_2); \ldots; y_n = f(x_n), \ldots$$

has a limit, which is the number A.

1.9.1. Taking advantage of the definition of the limit after Heine (*ie*, in terms of sequences) and of the theorems on the limits of sequences, prove that

$$\lim_{x \to 2} \frac{3x + 1}{5x + 4} = \frac{1}{2}.$$

Solution Let us consider any sequence $x_1, x_2, \ldots$ satisfying the following two conditions : (1) the numbers $x_1, x_2, \ldots$ belong to the domain of definition of the function $f(x) = (3x + 1)/(5x + 4)$ (*ie*, $x_n \neq -4/5$); (2) the sequence $\{x_n\}$ converges to the number 2, *ie*, $\lim_{n \to \infty} x_n = 2$.

To the sequence $\{x_n\}$ there corresponds the sequence of values of the function

$$\frac{3x_1 + 1}{5x_1 + 4}; \frac{3x_2 + 1}{5x_2 + 4}; \ldots;$$

proceeding from the theorem on the limits (■■1.7),

$$\lim_{n\to\infty} f(x_n) = \lim_{n\to\infty} \frac{3x_n + 1}{5x_n + 4} = \frac{\lim(3x_n + 1)}{\lim(5x_n + 4)} = \frac{6+1}{10+4} = \frac{1}{2}.$$

Thus, independently of the choice of a sequence $\{x_n\}$ which converges to the number $2(x_n \neq -4/5)$, the corresponding sequences of values of the function $f(x_n)$ converge to the number $\frac{1}{2}$, which , according to the definition of the limit of a function, means that

$$\lim_{n\to\infty} \frac{3x+1}{5x+4} = \frac{1}{2}.$$

Note. The definition of the limit after Heine is conveniently applied when we have to prove that a function $f(x)$ has no limit. For this it is sufficient to show that there exist two sequences $\{x'_n\}$ and $\{x''_n\}$ such that $\lim_{n\to\infty} x'_n = \lim_{n\to\infty} x''_n = a$, but the corresponding sequences $\{f(x'_n)\}$ and $\{f(x''_n)\}$ do not have identical limits.

1.9.2. Prove that the following limits do not exist :

(a) $\lim_{x\to 1} \sin\frac{1}{x-1}$; (b) $\lim_{x\to 0} 2^{1/x}$;

(c) $\lim_{x\to\infty} \sin x$.

Solution (a) Choose two sequences

$$x_n = 1 + \frac{1}{n\pi} \quad \text{and} \quad x'_n = 1 + \frac{2}{(4n+1)\pi} \; (n = 1, 2, \ldots),$$

for which

$$\lim_{n\to\infty} x_n = \lim_{n\to\infty} x'_n = 1.$$

The corresponding sequences of values of the function are :

$$f(x_n) = \sin\frac{1}{1 + 1/(n\pi) - 1} = \sin n\pi = 0$$

and

$$f(x'_n) = \sin\frac{1}{1 + 2/[(4n+1)\pi] - 1} = \sin\frac{4n+1}{2}\pi$$

$$= \sin\left(2n\pi + \frac{\pi}{2}\right) = 1.$$

Hence, $\lim_{x_n\to 1} f(x_n) = 0$ and $\lim_{x'_n\to 1} f(x'_n) = 1$,

ie, the sequences $\{f(x_n)\}$ and $\{f(x'_n)\}$ have different limits, whence it follows that $\lim_{x\to 1} \sin\frac{1}{x-1}$ does not exist.

(c) Choose two sequences, $x_n = \pi n$ and $x'_n = 2\pi n + \frac{\pi}{2}$ $(n = 1, 2, \ldots)$, for which $\lim_{n\to\infty} x_n = \lim_{n\to\infty} x'_n = \infty$. Since,

$$\lim_{n\to\infty} \sin x_n = \lim_{n\to\infty} \sin \pi n = 0,$$

and
$$\lim_{n\to\infty} \sin x'_n = \lim_{n\to\infty} \sin(2\pi n + \pi/2) = 1,$$

$\lim_{n\to\infty} \sin x$ does not exist.

Note. The above examples show that one cannot draw the conclusion about the existence of the limit of a function proceeding from the sequence of values of x of a particular form (for example, proceeding from $x_n = 1 + 2/((4n + 1)\pi)$ in the item (a) of this problem), but it is necessary to consider an arbitrary sequence $x_1, x_2, \ldots, x_n, \ldots$ having a given limit.

1.9.3. Proceeding from the definition of the limit of a function after Cauchy (*ie*, in the terms of "ε-δ"; "ε-*M*", etc.), prove that

(a) $\lim_{x\to 1} (3x - 8) = -5$;

(b) $\lim_{x\to +\infty} \frac{5x+1}{3x+9} = \frac{5}{3}$;

(c) $\lim_{x\to 1} \frac{1}{(1-x)^2} = +\infty$;

(d) $\lim_{x\to\infty} \log_a x = \infty$ $(a > 1)$;

(e) $\lim_{x\to\infty} \operatorname{arc\,tan} x = \frac{\pi}{2}$;

(f) $\lim_{x\to\frac{\pi}{6}} \sin x = \frac{1}{2}$.

Solution (a) According to the "ε-δ" definition we are to prove that for any $\varepsilon > 0$ there exists $\delta > 0$ such that from the inequality $|x - 1| < \delta$ it follows that $|f(x) - (-5)| = |f(x) + 5| < \varepsilon$.

In other words, it is necessary to solve the inequality

$$|3x - 8 + 5| = 3|x - 1| < \varepsilon.$$

The latter inequality shows that the required inequality $|f(x) + 5| < \varepsilon$ is fulfilled as soon as $|x - 1| < \frac{\varepsilon}{3} = \delta$. Hence, $\lim_{x\to 1} (3x - 8) = -5$.

(b) According to the "ε-*M*" definition of the limit one has to show that for any $\varepsilon > 0$ it is possible to find a number $M > 0$ such that for all $x > M$ the inequality

$$\left|\frac{5x+1}{3x+9} - \frac{5}{3}\right| < \varepsilon \qquad (*)$$

will be fulfilled.

Transforming this inequality, we obtain

$$\left|\frac{5x+1}{3x+9} - \frac{5}{3}\right| = \frac{14}{|3x+9|} < \varepsilon.$$

Since $x > 0$, it remains to solve the inequality

$$\frac{14}{3x+9} < \varepsilon,$$

whence $$x > \frac{14 - 9\varepsilon}{3\varepsilon};$$

hence $$M = \frac{14 - 9\varepsilon}{3\varepsilon}.$$

Thus, for $\varepsilon > 0$ we have found $M = \dfrac{14 - 9\varepsilon}{3\varepsilon}$ such that for all values of $x > M$ the inequality (*) is fulfilled, and this means that

$$\lim_{x \to +\infty} \frac{5x + 1}{3x + 9} = \frac{5}{3}.$$

Let, for the example, $\varepsilon = 0.01$; then $M = \dfrac{14 - 0.09}{0.03} = 463\dfrac{2}{3}$.

(c) We have to prove that for any $K > 0$ there exists $\delta > 0$ such that from the inequality

$$|x - 1| < \delta$$

three always follows the inequality

$$\left|\frac{1}{(1 - x)^2}\right| = \frac{1}{(1 - x)^2} > K.$$

Let us choose an arbitrary number $K > 0$ and solve the inequality

$$\frac{1}{(1 - x)^2} > K, \qquad (**)$$

whence $$|1 - x| < \frac{1}{\sqrt{K}} \ (K > 0).$$

Thus, if we put $\delta = \dfrac{1}{\sqrt{K}}$, then the inequality (**) holds true as soon as $|x - 1| < \delta$, which means that $\lim\limits_{x \to 1} \dfrac{1}{(1 - x)^2} = +\infty$.

(d) We have to prove that for any $K > 0$ there exists $M > 0$ such that from the inequality $x > M$ there always the inequality $\log_a x > K$. Let us choose an arbitrary number $K > 0$ and consider the inequality $\log_a x > K$. If we put $a^k = M$, then at $x > m$ the inequality $\log_a x > K$ holds true. Hence,

$$\lim_{x \to +\infty} \log_a x = +\infty.$$

1.9.4. Prove that $\lim\limits_{x \to \infty} \cos x$ does not exist.

1.9.5. Using the sequences of the roots of the equations $\sin\left(\dfrac{1}{x}\right) = 1$ and $\sin\left(\dfrac{1}{x}\right) = -1$, show that the function $f(x) = \sin\left(\dfrac{1}{x}\right)$ has no limit as $x \to 0$.

1.9.6. Proceeding from Cauchy's definition of the limit of a function prove that :

(a) $\lim\limits_{x\to 1}(3x-2)=1$;

(b) $\lim\limits_{x\to 1}\dfrac{x-1}{\sqrt{x}-1}=2$;

(c) $\lim\limits_{x\to 0}\sin x=0$;

(d) $\lim\limits_{x\to 0}\cos x=1$;

(e) $\lim\limits_{x\to+\infty}\dfrac{2x-1}{3x+2}=\dfrac{2}{3}$;

(f) $\lim\limits_{x\to+\infty}a^x=+\infty\,(a>1)$;

(g) $\lim\limits_{x\to\infty}\dfrac{\sin x}{x}=0$.

1.10. Calculation of Limits of Functions

I. If the limits $\lim\limits_{x\to a}u(x)$ and $\lim\limits_{x\to a}v(x)$ exist, then the following theorems hold true :

(1) $\lim\limits_{x\to a}[u(x)\pm v(x)]=\lim\limits_{x\to a}u(x)\pm\lim\limits_{x\to a}v(x)$;

(2) $\lim\limits_{x\to a}[u(x)\cdot v(x)]=\lim\limits_{x\to a}u(x)\cdot\lim\limits_{x\to a}v(x)$;

(3) $\lim\limits_{x\to a}\dfrac{u(x)}{v(x)}=\dfrac{\lim\limits_{x\to a}u(x)}{\lim\limits_{x\to a}v(x)}\,(\lim\limits_{x\to a}v(x)\neq 0)$.

II. For all main elementary functions at any point of their domain of definition the equality $\lim\limits_{x\to a}f(x)=f(\lim\limits_{x\to a}x)=f(a)$ holds true.

III. If for all values of x in a certain neighbourhood of a point a (except for, perhaps, $x=a$) the functions $f(x)$ and $\varphi(x)$ are equal and one of them has a limit as x approaches a, then the other one has the same limit.

IV. The following limits are frequently used :

(1) $\lim\limits_{x\to 0}\dfrac{\sin x}{x}=1$;

(2) $\lim\limits_{x\to\infty}(1+1/x)^x=\lim\limits_{\alpha\to 0}(1+\alpha)^{1/\alpha}=e=2.71828\ldots$;

(3) $\lim\limits_{x\to 0}\dfrac{\log_a(1+x)}{x}=\log_a e\,(a>0;\,a\neq 1)$;

(4) $\lim\limits_{x\to 0}\dfrac{\ln(1+x)}{x}=1$;

(5) $\lim\limits_{x\to 0}\dfrac{a^x-1}{x}=\ln a\,(a>0)$.

1.10.1. Find the limits :

(a) $\lim\limits_{x\to 1}\dfrac{4x^5+9x+7}{3x^6+x^3+1}$;

(b) $\lim\limits_{x\to 2}\dfrac{x^3+3x^2-9x-2}{x^3-x-6}$;

(c) $\lim\limits_{x\to -1}\dfrac{x+1}{\sqrt{6x^2+3}+3x}$;

(d) $\lim\limits_{x\to 1}\dfrac{x^p-1}{x^q-1}$ (p and q integers);

(e) $\lim\limits_{x\to 0}\dfrac{\sqrt{9+5x+4x^2}-3}{x}$; (f) $\lim\limits_{x\to 2}\dfrac{\sqrt[3]{10-x}-2}{x-2}$;

(g) $\lim\limits_{x\to 0}\dfrac{\sqrt{x+7}-3\sqrt{2x-3}}{\sqrt[3]{x+6}-2\sqrt[3]{3x-5}}$; (h) $\lim\limits_{x\to 3}\left[\log_a\dfrac{x-3}{\sqrt{x+6}-3}\right]$;

(i) $\lim\limits_{x\to 1}\dfrac{x^3-x^2-x+1}{x^3-3x+2}$; (j) $\lim\limits_{x\to 1}\dfrac{\sqrt{x+8}-\sqrt{8x+1}}{\sqrt{5-x}-\sqrt{7x-3}}$.

Solution (a) Since there exist limits of the numerator and denominator and the limit of the denominator is different from zero, we can use the theorem on the limit of a quotient :

$$\lim_{x\to 1}\frac{4x^5+9x+7}{3x^6+x^3+1}=\frac{\lim\limits_{x\to 1}(4x^5+9x+7)}{\lim\limits_{x\to 1}(3x^6+x^3+1)}=\frac{4+9+7}{3+1+1}=4.$$

(b) The above theorem cannot be directly used here, since the limit of the denominator equals zero as $x\to 2$. Here the limit of the numerator also equals zero as $x\to 2$. Hence, we have the indeterminate form $\frac{0}{0}$. For $x\neq 2$ we have

$$\frac{x^3+3x^2-9x-2}{x^3-x-6}=\frac{(x-2)(x^2+5x+1)}{(x-2)(x^2+2x+3)}=\frac{x^2+5x+1}{x^2+2x+3}.$$

Thus in any domain which does not contain the point $x=2$ the functions

$$f(x)=\frac{x^3+3x^2-9x-2}{x^3-x-6}\quad\text{and}\quad \varphi(x)=\frac{x^2+5x+1}{x^2+2x+3}$$

are equal; hence, their limits are also equal. The limit of the function $\varphi(x)$ is found directly :

$$\lim_{x\to 2}\varphi(x)=\lim_{x\to 2}\frac{x^2+5x+1}{x^2+2x+3}=\frac{15}{11};$$

hence,

$$\lim_{x\to 2}f(x)=\lim_{x\to 2}\frac{x^3+3x^2-9x-2}{x^3-x-6}=\frac{15}{11}.$$

(c) Just as in (b), we remove the indeterminate form $\frac{0}{0}$ by transforming

$$\lim_{x\to -1}\frac{x+1}{\sqrt{6x^2+3}+3x}=\lim_{x\to -1}\frac{(x+1)(\sqrt{6x^2+3}-3x)}{3-3x^2}$$

$$=\lim_{x\to -1}\frac{\sqrt{6x^2+3}-3x}{3(1-x)}=1.$$

1.10.2. Find the limits :

(a) $\lim\limits_{x\to\infty}\left(\dfrac{x^3}{3x^2-4}-\dfrac{x^2}{3x+2}\right)$;

(b) $\lim\limits_{x\to+\infty}(\sqrt{9x^2+1}-3x)$;

(c) $\lim\limits_{x\to 1}\dfrac{2\sqrt{x}+3\sqrt[3]{x}+5\sqrt[5]{x}}{\sqrt{3x-2}+\sqrt[3]{2x-3}}$;

(d) $\lim\limits_{x\to-\infty}(\sqrt{2x^2-3}-5x)$;

(e) $\lim\limits_{x\to+\infty}x(\sqrt{x^2+1}-x)$;

(f) $\lim\limits_{x\to+\infty}\dfrac{\sqrt{2x^2+3}}{4x+2}$ and $\lim\limits_{x\to-\infty}\dfrac{\sqrt{2x^2+3}}{4x+2}$;

(g) $\lim\limits_{x\to\infty}5^{2x/(x+3)}$.

Solution (a) $\lim\limits_{x\to\infty}\left(\dfrac{x^3}{3x^2-4}-\dfrac{x^2}{3x+2}\right)$.

Here we have the indeterminate form $\infty-\infty$; let us subtract the fractions

$$\lim_{x\to\infty}\left(\frac{x^3}{3x^2-4}-\frac{x^2}{3x+2}\right)=\lim_{x\to\infty}\frac{2x^3+4x^2}{9x^3+6x^2-12x-8}$$

$$=\lim_{x\to\infty}\frac{2+\dfrac{4}{x}}{9+\dfrac{6}{x}-\dfrac{12}{x^2}-x^2-\dfrac{8}{x^3}}=\frac{2}{9}.$$

Note. We see that in such examples the limit is equal to the ratio of the coefficients at the superior power of x (provided the polynomials are of the same degree).

(b) $$\lim_{x\to+\infty}\frac{(\sqrt{9x^2+1}-3x)}{1}=\lim_{x\to+\infty}\frac{1}{\sqrt{9x^2+1}+3x}=0.$$

(c) In handing such examples bear in mind that the function $f(x)=\sqrt[m]{p_n(x)}$, where $p_n(x)$ is a polynomial of degree n, tending to infinity in the same way as the function $\sqrt[m]{x^n}$. This allows us to single out the superior power of x and divide both the numerator and denominator by this power of x. In the given example the divisor is $\sqrt{x}$; then we obtain :

$$\lim_{x\to+\infty}\frac{\sqrt[2]{x}+3\sqrt[3]{x}+5\sqrt[5]{x}}{\sqrt{3x-2}+\sqrt[3]{2x-3}}=\lim_{x\to+\infty}\frac{2+3/\sqrt[6]{x}+5/\sqrt[10]{x^3}}{\sqrt{3-2/x}+\sqrt[6]{4/x-12/x^2+9/x^3}}$$

$$=\frac{2}{\sqrt{3}}.$$

(d) Since the sum of two positive infinitely large quantities is also an infinitely large quantity, then

$$\lim_{x\to-\infty}(\sqrt{2x^2-3}-5x)=\lim_{x\to-\infty}[\sqrt{2x^2-3}+(-5x)]=+\infty.$$

(f) At $x>0$ we have $\sqrt{x^2}=x$, therefore

$$\lim_{x\to+\infty}\frac{\sqrt{x^2(2+3/x^2)}}{x(4+2/x)}=\lim_{x\to+\infty}\frac{x\sqrt{2+3/x^2}}{x(4+2/x)}=\frac{\sqrt{2}}{4}.$$

At $x<0$ we have $\sqrt{x^2}=-x$ and, hence,

$$\lim_{x\to-\infty}\frac{\sqrt{x^2(2+3/x^2)}}{x(4+2/x)}=\lim_{x\to-\infty}\frac{-x\sqrt{2+3/x^2}}{x(4+2/x)}=-\frac{\sqrt{2}}{4}.$$

Note. From this it follows, incidentally, that $\lim\limits_{x\to\infty}\dfrac{\sqrt{2x^2+3}}{4x+2}$ does not exist.

(g) $\lim\limits_{x\to1}5^{2x/(x+3)}=5^{\lim\limits_{x\to\infty}2x/(x+3)}=5^2=25.$

1.10.3. Find the limits :

(a) $\lim\limits_{x\to1}\dfrac{2x-2}{\sqrt[3]{26+x}-3}$;

(b) $\lim\limits_{x\to-1}\dfrac{x+1}{\sqrt[4]{x+17}-2}$;

(c) $\lim\limits_{x\to-1}\dfrac{1+\sqrt[3]{x}}{1+\sqrt[5]{x}}$;

(d) $\lim\limits_{x\to0}\dfrac{\sqrt[k]{1+x}-1}{x}$ (k positive integer);

(e) $\lim\limits_{x\to\pi/6}\dfrac{\sin(x-\pi/6)}{\sqrt{3}-2\cos x}$;

(f) $\lim\limits_{x\to\pi/2}\dfrac{\cos x}{\sqrt[3]{(1-\sin x)^2}}$;

(g) $\lim\limits_{x\to\pi/6}\dfrac{2\sin^2x+\sin x-1}{2\sin^2x-3\sin x+1}$.

Solution (*method of substitution*). (a) Let us put $26+x=z^3$. Then $x=z^3-26$ and $z\to3$ as $x\to1$; hence

$$\lim_{x\to1}\frac{2x-2}{\sqrt[3]{26+x}-3}=\lim_{z\to3}\frac{2z^3-54}{z-3}=\lim_{z\to3}\frac{2(z-3)(z^2+3z+9)}{z-3}$$

$$=\lim_{z\to3}2(z^2+3z+9)=54.$$

(d) Let us put $1+x=z^k$; then $x=z^k-1$ and $z\to1$ as $x\to0$.

Hence, $\lim\limits_{x\to 0}\dfrac{\sqrt[k]{1+x}-1}{x}=\lim\limits_{z\to 1}\dfrac{z-1}{z^k-1}=\dfrac{1}{k}$ (see Problem **1.10.1.** (d)).

(e) Let us put $x-\dfrac{\pi}{6}=z$; then $x=z+\dfrac{\pi}{6}$ and $z\to 0$ as $x\to\dfrac{\pi}{6}$. On substituting we obtain

$$\lim_{x\to\pi/6}\frac{\sin(x-\pi/6)}{\sqrt{3}-2\cos x}=\lim_{z\to 0}\frac{\sin z}{\sqrt{3}-2\cos(z+\pi/6)}$$

$$=\lim_{z\to 0}\frac{\sin z}{\sqrt{3}-\sqrt{3}\cos z+\sin z}$$

$$=\lim_{z\to 0}\frac{2\sin(z/2)\cos(z/2)}{\sqrt{3}\sin^2(z/2)+2\sin(z/2)\cos(z/2)}$$

$$=\lim_{z\to 0}\frac{\cos(z/2)}{\sqrt{3}\sin(z/2)+\cos(z/2)}=1.$$

1.10.4. Find the limits :

(a) $\lim\limits_{x\to 0}\dfrac{1-\cos x}{x^2}$; (b) $\lim\limits_{x\to 0}\dfrac{\tan x-\sin x}{x^3}$;

(c) $\lim\limits_{x\to 1}\dfrac{\cos(\pi x/2)}{1-x}$.

Solution (a) $\lim\limits_{x\to 0}\dfrac{1-\cos x}{x^2}=\lim\limits_{x\to 0}\dfrac{2\sin^2(x/2)}{x^2}$

$$=\frac{1}{2}\lim_{x\to 0}\left(\frac{\sin(x/2)}{x/2}\right)^2=\frac{1}{2};$$

(b) $\lim\limits_{x\to 0}\dfrac{\tan x-\sin x}{x^3}=\lim\limits_{x\to 0}\dfrac{\sin x(1-\cos x)}{\cos x\cdot x^3}$

$$=\lim_{x\to 0}\frac{1}{\cos x}\cdot\frac{\sin x}{x}\cdot\frac{1-\cos x}{x^2}=\frac{1}{2};$$

(c) Let us put $1-x=z$. Then $x=1-z$ and $z\to 0$ as $x\to 1$. Hence,

$$\lim_{x\to 1}\frac{\cos\frac{\pi}{2}x}{1-x}=\lim_{z\to 0}\frac{\cos\left(\frac{\pi}{2}-\frac{\pi}{2}z\right)}{z}$$

$$=\lim_{x\to 0}\frac{\sin\frac{\pi}{2}z}{z}=\frac{\pi}{2}.$$

Note. For a simple method of solving similar problem see **1.12.**

1.10.5. Find the limits :

(a) $\lim\limits_{x\to\infty}(1+1/x)^{7x}$; (b) $\lim\limits_{x\to 0}(1+x)^{1/(3x)}$;

(c) $\lim\limits_{x\to\infty}\left(\dfrac{x}{1+x}\right)^x$; (d) $\lim\limits_{x\to\infty}(1+k/x)^{mx}$;

(e) $\lim_{x\to 0} \dfrac{\ln(1+x)}{3^x - 1}$; (f) $\lim_{x\to 0} \dfrac{e^{4x}-1}{\tan x}$;

(g) $\lim_{x\to 0} \dfrac{\ln(a+x) - \ln a}{x}$; (h) $\lim_{x\to 0} \dfrac{e^x - e^{-x}}{\sin x}$;

(i) $\lim_{x\to e} \dfrac{\ln x - 1}{x - e}$.

Solution (a) $\lim_{x\to\infty}\left(1+\dfrac{1}{x}\right)^{7x} = \lim_{x\to\infty}\left[\left(1+\dfrac{1}{x}\right)^{x}\right]^7 = \left[\lim_{x\to\infty}\left(1+\dfrac{1}{x}\right)^{x}\right]^7 = e^7$;

(e) $\lim_{x\to 0} \dfrac{\ln(1+x)}{3^x - 1} = \lim_{x\to 0}\left[\dfrac{\ln(1+x)}{x}\cdot\dfrac{x}{3^x-1}\right] = \dfrac{1}{\ln 3}$.

(i) Put $x/e - 1 = z$; then $x = e(z+1)$; $z \to 0$ as $x \to e$.
On substituting we obtain

$$\lim_{x\to e}\frac{\ln x - 1}{x - e} = \lim_{x\to\infty}\frac{\ln(x/e)}{e(x/e-1)}$$
$$= \frac{1}{e}\lim_{z\to 0}\frac{\ln(1+z)}{z} = \frac{1}{e}.$$

1.10.6. Find

$$\lim_{x\to\infty}\left(1+\frac{1}{x^2}\right)^x.$$

Solution $\lim_{x\to\infty}\left(1+\dfrac{1}{x^2}\right)^x = \lim_{x\to\infty}\left[\left(1+\dfrac{1}{x^2}\right)^{x^2}\right]^{1/x} = e^0 = 1.$

1.10.7. Find the limits :

(a) $\lim_{x\to 1}\left(\dfrac{1+x}{2+x}\right)^{(1-\sqrt{x})/(1-x)}$;

(b) $\lim_{x\to\infty}\left(\dfrac{x^2+2x-1}{2x^2-3x-2}\right)^{(2x+1)/(x-1)}$.

Solution (a) Denote :

$$f(x) = (1+x)/(2+x);$$
$$\varphi(x) = \frac{1-\sqrt{x}}{1-x};$$
$$\lim_{x\to 1} f(x) = \lim_{x\to 1}\frac{1+x}{2+x} = \frac{2}{3};$$
$$\lim_{x\to\infty}\varphi(x) = \lim_{x\to 1}\frac{1-\sqrt{x}}{1-x} = \frac{1}{2}.$$

But at finite limits $\lim_{x\to a} f(x) = A > 0$, $\lim_{x\to a}\varphi(x) = B$ the following relation holds true :

$$\lim_{x\to a}[f(x)]^{\varphi(x)} = e^{\lim\limits_{x\to a}\phi(x)\ln f(x)} = e^{B\ln A} = A^B.$$

Hence,

$$\lim_{x\to 1}\left(\frac{1+x}{2+x}\right)^{(1-\sqrt{x})/(1-x)} = \left(\frac{2}{3}\right)^{1/2} = \sqrt{\frac{2}{3}}.$$

Note. If in handing example of the form $\lim\limits_{x\to a}[f(x)]^{\varphi(x)}$ it turns out that $\lim\limits_{x\to a} f(x) = 1$ and $\lim\limits_{x\to a}\phi(x) = \infty$, then the following transformation may be recommended :

$$\lim_{x\to a}[f(x)]^{\varphi(x)} = \lim_{x\to a}\{1+[f(x)-1]\}^{\varphi(x)}$$

$$= \lim_{x\to a}\{[1+(f(x)-1)]^{1/(f(x)-1)}\}^{\varphi(x)[f(x)-1]}$$

$$= e^{\lim\limits_{x\to a}\varphi(x)[f(x)-1]} \qquad (*)$$

1.10.8. Find the limits :

(a) $\lim\limits_{x\to\infty}\left(\dfrac{2x^2+3}{2x^2+5}\right)^{8x^2+3}$;

(b) $\lim\limits_{x\to 0}\left(\dfrac{1+\tan x}{1+\tan x}\right)^{1/\sin x}$;

(c) $\lim\limits_{x\to 1}(1+\sin\pi x)^{\cot\pi x}$;

(d) $\lim\limits_{x\to 1}\left(\dfrac{\sin x}{\sin a}\right)^{1/(x-a)}$ $(a \neq k\pi$, with k integer).

Solution (a) Let us denote :

$$f(x) = \frac{2x^2+3}{2x^2+5};\ \phi(x) = 8x^2+3;$$

$$\lim_{x\to\infty} f(x) = \lim_{x\to\infty}\frac{2x^2+3}{2x^2+5} = 1;$$

$$\lim_{x\to\infty}\varphi(x) = \lim_{x\to\infty}(8x^2+3) = \infty.$$

Use the formula (*) :

$$\lim_{x\to\infty}\left(\frac{2x^2+3}{2x^2+5}\right)^{8x^2+3} = e^{\lim\limits_{x\to\infty}\varphi(x)[f(x)-1]};$$

$$f(x)-1 = \frac{2x^2+3}{2x^2+5} - 1 = -\frac{2}{2x^2+5};$$

$$\lim_{x\to\infty}\varphi(x)[f(x)-1] = -\lim_{x\to\infty}\frac{2(8x^2+3)}{2x^2+5} = -8.$$

Therefore $$\lim_{x\to\infty}\left(\frac{2x^2+3}{2x^2+5}\right)^{8x^2+3} = e^{-8}.$$

1.10.9. The function $f(x)$ is given with the aid of the limit

$$f(x) = \lim_{n\to\infty}\frac{x^{2n}-1}{x^{2n}+1}.$$

Investigate this function and graph it.

Solution Consider three cases :

(1) $|x| > 1$. Since in this case $\lim\limits_{n\to\infty} x^{2n} = \infty$, then

$$f(x) = \lim_{n\to\infty}\frac{1-1/x^{2n}}{1+1/x^{2n}} = 1.$$

(2) $|x| < 1$. In this case $\lim\limits_{n\to\infty} x^{2n} = 0$; therefore $f(x) = -1$.

(3) $x = \pm 1$. In this case $x^{2n} = 1$ at any n, and therefore $f(x) = 0$. Thus, the function under consideration can be written in the following way :

$$f(x) = \begin{cases} 1, & \text{if } |x| > 1 \\ -1, & \text{if } |x| < 1 \\ 0, & \text{if } x = \pm 1 \end{cases}$$

or, briefly, $f(x) = \text{sign}\,(|x| - 1)$ (see Problem **1.5.11** (n)).

The graph of this function is shown in Fig. 27.

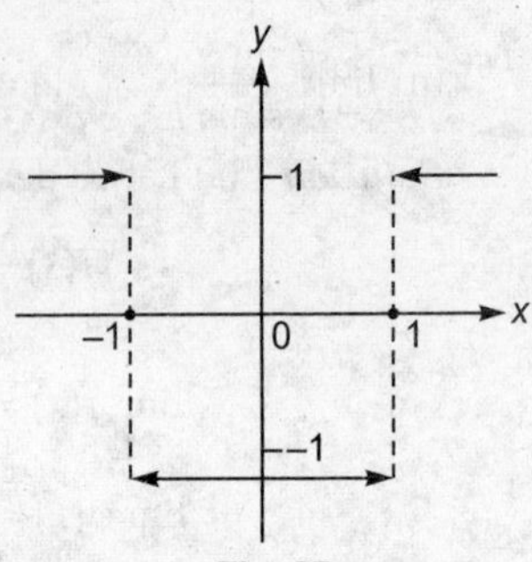

Fig. 27

1.10.10. The population of a country increases by 2% per year. By how many times does it increase in a century ?

Solution If we denote the initial number of inhabitants of a given country as A, then after a year the total population will amount to

$$A + \frac{A}{100}\cdot 2 = \left(1 + \frac{1}{50}\right)A.$$

After two years the population will amount to $A\left(1+\frac{1}{50}\right)^2$. After 100 years it will reach the total of $A\left(1+\frac{1}{50}\right)^{100}$, *ie*, it will have increased $\left[\left(1+\frac{1}{50}\right)^{50}\right]^2$ times.

Taking into account that $\lim\limits_{n\to\infty}\left(1+\frac{1}{n}\right)^n = e$, we can approximately consider that $\left(1+\frac{1}{50}\right)^{50} \approx e$. Hence, after 100 years the population of the country will have increased $e^2 \approx 7.39$ times.

Of course, this estimation is very approximate, but it gives an idea as to the order of the increase in the population; (the quantity $\left(1+\frac{1}{50}\right)^{100}=7.245$ to within three decimal place.

1.10.11. Find the limits :

(a) $\lim\limits_{x\to 0}\dfrac{\cos x+4\tan x}{2-x-2x^4}$; (b) $\lim\limits_{x\to -2}\dfrac{2x^2+5x-7}{3x^2-x-2}$;

(c) $\lim\limits_{x\to 1}\dfrac{\sqrt{5-x}-2}{\sqrt{2-x}-1}$; (d) $\lim\limits_{x\to \infty}\dfrac{2x^2-5x+4}{5x^2-2x-3}$;

(e) $\lim\limits_{x\to \infty}(\sqrt{x^2+1}-\sqrt{x^2-1})$; (f) $\lim\limits_{x\to a}\left(\dfrac{1-2x}{\sqrt[3]{1+8x^3}}+2^{-x}\right)$.

1.10.12. Find the limits :

(a) $\lim\limits_{x\to 0}\dfrac{\sqrt{x+4}-2}{\sin 5x}$; (b) $\lim\limits_{x\to 1}\dfrac{\sin(1-x)}{\sqrt{x}-1}$;

(c) $\lim\limits_{\alpha\to \pi}\dfrac{\sin\alpha}{1-\alpha^2/\pi^2}$; (d) $\lim\limits_{x\to \pi/4}\tan 2x\tan(\pi/4-x)$;

(e) $\lim\limits_{x\to \pi/3}\dfrac{\tan^3 x-3\tan x}{\cos(x+\pi/6)}$.

1.10.13. Find the limits :

(a) $\lim\limits_{x\to \infty}\left(1+\dfrac{4}{x}\right)^{x+3}$; (b) $\lim\limits_{x\to 0}\dfrac{e^{-x}-1}{x}$;

(c) $\lim\limits_{x\to 0}\dfrac{a^{2x}-1}{x}$; (d) $\lim\limits_{x\to 0}(1+3\tan^2 x)^{\cot^2 x}$;

(e) $\lim\limits_{x\to \pi/4}(\sin 2x)^{\tan^2 2x}$; (f) $\lim\limits_{x\to \infty}\left(\dfrac{2x-1}{2x+1}\right)^{x}$;

(g) $\lim\limits_{x\to \pi/2}(\tan x)^{\tan 2x}$; (h) $\lim\limits_{x\to \pi/2}(\sin x)^{\tan x}$;

(i) $\lim\limits_{x\to \infty}\left(\dfrac{3x^2+2x+1}{x^2+x+2}\right)^{(6x+1)/(3x+2)}$; (j) $\lim\limits_{x\to \infty}\left(\dfrac{1+3x}{2+3x}\right)^{(1-\sqrt{x})/(1-x)}$;

(k) $\lim\limits_{x\to 0}\dfrac{e^{\alpha x}-e^{\beta x}}{x}$.

1.10.14. Find the limits :

(a) $\lim\limits_{x\to 0}\dfrac{\arccos(1-x)}{\sqrt{x}}$; (b) $\lim\limits_{x\to \pi/4}\dfrac{\ln\tan x}{1-\cot x}$;

(c) $\lim\limits_{x\to 0}\dfrac{1}{\sin x}\ln(1+a\sin x)$.

1.11. Infinitesimal and Infinite Functions. Their Definition and Comparison

The function $\alpha(x)$ is called *infinitesimal* as $x \to a$ or as $x \to \infty$ if $\lim\limits_{x \to a} \alpha(x) = 0$ or $\lim\limits_{x \to \infty} \alpha(x) = 0$.

The function $f(x)$ is called *infinite* as $x \to a$ or as $x \to \infty$ if $\lim\limits_{x \to a} f(x) = \infty$ or $\lim\limits_{x \to \infty} f(x) = \infty$.

A quantity inverse to an infinite quantity is called an *infinitesimal.*

Infinitesimal functions possess the following properties :

(1) The sum and the product of any definite number of infinitesimal functions as $x \to a$ are also infinitesimals as $x \to a$.

(2) The product of an infinitesimal function by a bounded function is an infinitesimal.

Comparison of Infinitesimals. Let the functions $\alpha(x)$ and $\beta(x)$ be infinitesimal as $x \to a$. If

$$\lim_{x \to a} \frac{\alpha(x)}{\beta(x)} = c,$$

where c is a certain finite number different from zero, then the functions $\alpha(x)$ and $\beta(x)$ are called infinitesimals of the *same order,* If $c = 1$, then the functions $\alpha(x)$ and $\beta(x)$ are called *equivalent ;* notation : $\alpha(x) \sim \beta(x)$.

If $c = 0$, then the function $\alpha(x)$ is called an infinitesimal of a *higher order* relative to $\beta(x)$, which is written thus : $\alpha(x) = 0(\beta(x))$, and $\beta(x)$ is called an infinitesimal of a *lower order* with respect to $\alpha(x)$.

If $\lim\limits_{x \to a} \dfrac{\alpha(x)}{[\beta(x)]^n} = c$, where $0 < |c| < +\infty$, then the function $\alpha(x)$ is called an infinitesimal of the *nth order* as compared with the function $\beta(x)$. The concept of infinite functions of various orders is introduced similarly.

1.11.1. Prove that the functions

(a) $f(x) = \dfrac{2x - 4}{x^2 + 5}$ as $x \to 2$;

(b) $f(x) = (x - 1)^2 \sin^3 \dfrac{1}{x - 1}$ as $x \to 1$ are infinitesimals.

Solution (a) It is sufficient to find the limit

$$\lim_{x \to 2} f(x) = \lim_{x \to 2} \frac{2x - 4}{x^2 + 5} = 0.$$

(b) Firstly, the function $\varphi(x) = (x - 1)^2$ is infinitesimal as $x \to 1$; indeed, $\lim\limits_{x \to 1}(x - 1)^2 = 0$. Secondly, the function

$$\psi(x) = \sin^3 \frac{1}{x - 1}; x \neq 1,$$

is bounded :

$$\left|\sin^3 \frac{1}{x-1}\right| \le 1.$$

Hence, the given function $f(x)$ represents the product of the bonded function $\psi(x)$ by the infinitesimal $\varphi(x)$, which means that $f(x)$ is an infinitesimal function as $x \to 1$.

1.11.2. Prove that the functions

(a) $f(x) = \dfrac{3x-12}{2x^2+7}$ as $x \to 4$;

(b) $f(x) = \dfrac{\sin x}{x}$ as $x \to \infty$ are infinitesimal.

1.11.3. Find $\lim\limits_{x\to 0} x \sin(1/x)$.

Solution Since x is an infinitesimal as $x \to 0$ and the function $\sin(1/x)$ is bounded, the product $x\sin(1/x)$ is an infinitesimal, which means that $\lim\limits_{x\to 0} x\sin(1/x) = 0$.

1.11.4. Compare the following infinitesimal functions (as $x \to 0$) with the infinitesimal $\varphi(x) = x$:

(a) $f_1(x) = \tan x^3$;

(b) $f_3(x) = \sqrt[3]{\sin^2 x}$;

(c) $f_3(x) = \sqrt{9+x} - 3$.

Solution (a) We have

$$\lim_{x\to 0} \frac{\tan x^3}{x} = \lim_{x\to 0}\left[\frac{\tan x^3}{x^3}\, x^2\right]$$

$$= \lim_{x\to 0} \frac{\tan x^3}{x^3} \lim_{x\to 0} x^2 = 0.$$

Hence, $\tan x^3$ is an infinitesimal of a higher order relative to x.

(b) We have

$$\lim_{x\to 0} \frac{\sqrt[3]{\sin^2 x}}{x} = \lim_{x\to 0}\left[\sqrt[3]{\frac{\sin^2 x}{x^2}}\, \frac{1}{\sqrt[3]{x}}\right] = \infty.$$

Hence, $\sqrt[3]{\sin^2 x}$ is an infinitesimal of a lower order as compared with x.

(c) We have

$$\lim_{x\to 0} \frac{\sqrt{9+x}-3}{x} = \lim_{x\to 0} \frac{1}{\sqrt{9+x}+3} = \frac{1}{6}.$$

Hence, the infinitesimals $\sqrt{9+x} - 3$ and x are of the same order.

1.11.5. Determine the order of smallness of the quantity β with respect to the infinitesimal α.

(a) $\beta = \cos\alpha - \cos 2\alpha$;

(b) $\beta = \tan\alpha - \sin\alpha$.

Solution (a) $\beta = \cos\alpha - \cos 2\alpha = 2\sin\frac{3}{2}\alpha\sin\frac{\alpha}{2}$.

Whence $$\lim_{\alpha\to 0}\frac{\beta}{\alpha^2} = \lim_{\alpha\to 0}\frac{2\sin(3\alpha/2)\sin(\alpha/2)}{\alpha^2} = \frac{3}{2}.$$

Hence, β is an infinitesimal of the same order as α^2, *ie*, of the second one with respect to α.

1.11.6. Assuming $x\to\infty$, compare the following infinitely large quantities :

(a) $f(x) = 3x^2 + 2x + 5$ and $\varphi(x) = 2x^3 + 2x - 1$;

(b) $f(x) = 2x^2 + 3x$ and $\varphi(x) = (x+2)^2$;

(c) $f(x) = \sqrt[3]{x+a}$ and $\varphi(x) = \sqrt[3]{x}$.

Solution (a) The infinite function $3x^2 + 2x + 5$ is of a lower order as compared with the infinite function $2x^3 + 2x - 1$, since

$$\lim_{x\to\infty}\frac{3x^2 + 2x + 5}{2x^3 + 2x - 1} = \lim_{x\to\infty}\frac{3/x + 2/x^2 + 5/x^3}{2 + 2/x^2 - 1/x^3} = 0.$$

1.11.7. Prove that the infinitesimals $\alpha = x$ and $\beta = x\cos(1/x)$ (as $x\to 0$) are not comparable, *ie*, their ratio has no limit.

Solution Indeed, $\lim_{x\to 0}\frac{x\cos(1/x)}{x} = \lim_{x\to 0}\cos(1/x)$ does not exist (prove it!), which means that these infinitesimal functions are not comparable.

1.11.8. If $x\to 0$, then which of the following infinitesimals is (are) of a higher order than x; of a lower order than x; of the same order as x?

(a) $100x$; (b) x^2;

(c) $6\sin x$; (d) $\sin x^3 x$;

(e) $\sqrt[3]{\tan^2 x}$.

1.11.9 Let $x\to 0$. Determine the orders of the following infinitesimal functions with respect to x:

(a) $2\sin^4 x - x^5$; (b) $\sqrt{\sin^2 x + x^4}$;

(c) $\sqrt{1+x^3} - 1$; (d) $\sin 2x - 2\sin x$;

(e) $1 - 2\cos\left(x + \frac{\pi}{3}\right)$; (f) $2\sqrt{\sin x}$;

(g) $\frac{x}{x-1}$; (h) $\tan x + x^2$;

(i) $\cos x - \sqrt[3]{\cos x}$; (j) $e^x - \cos x$.

1.11.10. Assuming the side of a cube to be an infinitesimal, determine the order of smallness of the diagonal of the cube (d); of the area of its surface (S); of its volume (V).

1.12. Equivalent Infinitesimals.

Application to Finding Limits

If the functions $\alpha(x)$ and $\beta(x)$ are infinitesimal as $x \to a$ and if $\alpha(x) \sim \gamma(x), \beta(x) \sim \delta(x)$, then

$\lim\limits_{x \to a} \frac{\alpha(x)}{\beta(x)} = \lim\limits_{x \to a} \frac{\gamma(x)}{\delta(x)}$ *replacing an infinitesimal by an equivalent one*).

If $$\lim_{x \to a} f(x) = k,\ 0 < |k| < \infty,$$
then $$f(x)\alpha(x) \sim k\alpha(x).$$
If $$\alpha(x) \sim \gamma(x).$$
$$\beta(x) \sim \gamma(x),$$
then $$\alpha(x) \sim \beta(x).$$

For the infinitesimal functions to be equivalent it is necessary and sufficient that their difference be an infinitesimal of a higher order as compared with each of the two.

Listed below are infinitesimal function :

($\alpha(x)$ is an infinitesimal as $x \to 0$)

(1) $\sin\alpha(x) \sim \alpha(x)$; (2) $\tan\alpha(x) \sim \alpha(x)$;

(3) $1 - \cos\alpha(x) \sim [\alpha(x)]^2/2$;

(4) $\arcsin\alpha(x) \sim \alpha(x)$; (5) $\arctan\alpha(x) \sim \alpha(x)$;

(6) $\ln[1 + \alpha(x)] \sim \alpha(x)$; (7) $a^{\alpha(x)} - 1 \sim \alpha(x)\ln a$

$(a > 0)$, in particular, $e^{\alpha(x)} - 1 \sim \alpha(x)$;

(8) $[1 + \alpha(x)]^P - 1 \sim P\alpha(x)$, in particular, $\sqrt[n]{1 + \alpha(x)} - 1 \sim \frac{\alpha(x)}{n}$.

1.12.1. Prove that as $x \to 0$

(a) $1 - \frac{1}{\sqrt{1 + x}} \sim \frac{1}{2}x$; (b) $1 - \frac{1}{1 + x} \sim x$;

(c) $\sin\sqrt{x\sqrt{x}} \sim \sqrt{x^2 + \sqrt{x^3}}$.

Solution (a) By formula (8) at $P = \frac{1}{2}$ we have

$$1 - \frac{1}{\sqrt{1 + x}} = \frac{1}{\sqrt{1 + x}}(\sqrt{1 + x} - 1) \sim 1 \cdot \frac{1}{2}x.$$

(c) By formula (1) we have

$$\sin\sqrt{x\sqrt{x}} \sim \sqrt{x\sqrt{x}} = x^{3/4},$$

$$\sqrt{x^2 + \sqrt{x^3}} = x^{3/4}\sqrt{1 + x^{1/2}} \sim x^{3/4},$$

whence $\sin\sqrt{x\sqrt{x}} \sim \sqrt{x^2 + \sqrt{x^3}}$.

1.12.2. Replace each of the following infinitesimals with an equivalent one :

(a) $3\sin\alpha - 5\alpha^3$; (b) $(1-\cos\alpha)^2 + 16\alpha^3 + 5\alpha^4 + 6\alpha^5$.

Solution (a) Note that the sum of two infinitesimals α and β of different orders is equivalent to the summand of the lower order, since the replacement to an infinitesimal with one equivalent to it is tantamount to the rejection of an infinitesimal of a higher order. In our example the quantity $3\sin\alpha$ has the order of smallness 1, $(-5\alpha^3)$ – the order of smallness 3, hence

$$3\sin\alpha + (-5\alpha^3) \sim 3\sin\alpha \sim 3\alpha.$$

(b) $(1-\cos\alpha)^2 + 16\alpha^3 + 5\alpha^4 + 6\alpha^5 = 4\sin^4\frac{\alpha}{2} + 16\alpha^3 + 5\alpha^4 + 6\alpha^5.$

The summand $16\alpha^3$ is of the lower order, therefore

$$(1-\cos\alpha)^2 + 16\alpha^3 + 5\alpha^4 + 6\alpha^5 \sim 16\alpha^3.$$

1.12.3. With the aid of the principle of substitution of equivalent quantities find the limits :

(a) $\lim\limits_{x\to 0}\dfrac{\sin 5x}{\ln(1+4x)}$; (b) $\lim\limits_{x\to 0}\dfrac{1-\cos x}{1-\cos\frac{x}{2}}$;

(c) $\lim\limits_{x\to 0}\dfrac{\ln\cos x}{\sqrt[4]{1+x^2}-1}$; (d) $\lim\limits_{x\to 0}\dfrac{\sqrt{1+x+x^2}-1}{\sin 4x}$;

(e) $\lim\limits_{x\to 0}\dfrac{\sin 2x + \operatorname{arc\,sin}^2 x - \operatorname{arc\,tan}^2 x}{3x}$;

(f) $\lim\limits_{x\to 0}\dfrac{3\sin x - x^2 + x^3}{\tan x + 2\sin^2 x + 5x^4}$;

(g) $\lim\limits_{x\to 0}\dfrac{(\sin x - \tan x)^2 + (1-\cos 2x)^4 + x^5}{7\tan^7 x + \sin^6 x + 2\sin^5 x}$;

(h) $\lim\limits_{x\to 0}\dfrac{\sin\sqrt[3]{x}\,\ln(1+3x)}{(\operatorname{arc\,tan}\sqrt{x})^2\left(e^{5\sqrt[3]{x}}-1\right)}$;

(i) $\lim\limits_{x\to 0}\dfrac{1-\cos x + 2\sin x - \sin^3 x - x^2 + 3x^4}{\tan^3 x - 6\sin^2 x + x - 5x^3}$.

Solution (a) We have $\sin 5x \sim 5x$; $\ln(1+4x) \sim 4x$ (see the list of equivalent infinitesimals on page 72). Therefore

$$\lim_{x\to 0}\frac{\sin 5x}{\ln(1+4x)} = \lim_{x\to 0}\frac{5x}{4x} = \frac{5}{4}.$$

(c) $$\lim_{x\to 0}\frac{\ln\cos x}{\sqrt[4]{1+x^2}-1} = \lim_{x\to 0}\frac{\ln[1+(\cos x-1)]}{\frac{x^2}{4}}$$

$$= 4\lim_{x\to 0}\frac{\cos x - 1}{x^2} = -4\lim_{x\to 0}\frac{x^2/2}{x^2} = -2.$$

(d) From the list of equivalent infinitesimals we find :

$$\sqrt{1+x+x^2}-1 \sim (x+x^2)/2 \sim x/2, \sin 4x \sim 4x.$$

Therefore, $$\lim_{x\to 0}\frac{\sqrt{1+x+x^2}-1}{\sin 4x} = \lim_{x\to 0}\frac{x/2}{4x} = \frac{1}{8}.$$

(e) Using the list of equivalent infinitesimal functions given on page 72 we obtain

$$\sin 2x + \arcsin^2 x - \arctan^2 x \sim \sin 2x \sim 2x.$$

Hence, $$\lim_{x\to 0}\frac{\sin 2x + \arcsin^2 x - \arctan^2 x}{3x} = \lim_{x\to 0}\frac{2x}{3x} = \frac{2}{3}.$$

(h) $\sin\sqrt[3]{x} \sim \sqrt[3]{x}$; $\ln(1+3x) \sim 3x$;

$$\arctan\sqrt{x} \sim \sqrt{x}; e^{5\sqrt[3]{x}} - 1 \sim 5\sqrt[3]{x};$$

$$\lim_{x\to 0}\frac{\sin\sqrt[3]{x}\ \ln(1+3x)}{(\arctan\sqrt{x})^2\left(e^{5\sqrt[3]{x}}-1\right)} = \lim_{x\to 0}\frac{\sqrt[3]{x}\cdot 3x}{x\cdot 5\sqrt[3]{x}} = \frac{3}{5}.$$

1.12.4. Find the approximate values of the roots $\sqrt{1.02}$ and $\sqrt{0.994}$. Estimate the absolute error.

Solution Use the approximate formula

$$\sqrt{1+x} \sim 1 + x/2 \qquad (*)$$

(for x sufficiently close to zero). In our case

$$\sqrt{1+0.02} \sim 1 + \frac{0.02}{2} = 1.01;$$

$$\sqrt{1-0.006} \sim 1 - \frac{0.006}{2} = 0.997.$$

To estimate the error we note that

$$\frac{x}{2} - (\sqrt{1+x}-1) = \frac{1}{2}(x - 2\sqrt{1+x} + 2)$$

$$= \frac{1}{2}(x + 1 - 2\sqrt{x+1} + 1)$$

$$= \frac{1}{2}(\sqrt{x+1}-1)^2 \sim \frac{1}{2}\left(\frac{x}{2}\right)^2 = \frac{x^2}{8}.$$

Hence, the absolute error of the approximate formula (*) is estimated by the quantity $\frac{x^2}{8}$.

Using this estimate we find that the absolute error of the root $\sqrt{1.02} \approx 1.01$ is $\approx \frac{(0.02)^2}{8} = 0.00005$, and the absolute error of $\sqrt{0.994} \approx 0.997$ amounts to $\approx \frac{(0.006)^2}{8} \approx 0.000005$.

1.12.5. Prove that, as $x \to 0$,

(a) $\sqrt[3]{1+x} - 1 \sim \frac{1}{3} x$;

(b) $\arctan mx \sim mx$;

(c) $1 - \cos^3 x \sim \frac{3}{2} \sin^2 x$.

1.12.6. For $x \to 0$ determine the order of smallness, relative to the infinitesimal $\beta(x) = x$, of the following infinitesimals :

(a) $\sqrt{\sin^2 x + x^4}$; (b) $\frac{x^2(1+x)}{1+\sqrt[3]{x}}$.

1.12.7. For $x \to 2$ determine the order of smallness, relative to the infinitesimal $\beta(x) = x - 2$, of the following infinitesimals :

(a) $3(x-2)^2 + 2(x^2-4)$; (b) $\sqrt[3]{\sin \pi x}$.

1.12.8. Making use of the method of replacing an infinitesimal with an equivalent one, find the following limits :

(a) $\lim\limits_{x \to 0} \frac{\sin 3x}{\ln(1+5x)}$; (b) $\lim\limits_{x \to 0} \frac{\ln(1+\sin 4x)}{e^{\sin 5x} - 1}$;

(c) $\lim\limits_{x \to 0} \frac{e^{\sin 3x} - 1}{\ln(1+\tan 2x)}$; (d) $\lim\limits_{x \to 0} \frac{\arctan 3x}{\arcsin 2x}$;

(e) $\lim\limits_{x \to 0} \frac{\ln(2-\cos 2x)}{\ln^2(\sin 3x + 1)}$; (f) $\lim\limits_{x \to 0} \frac{\sqrt{1+\sin 3x} - 1}{\ln(1+\tan 2x)}$;

(g) $\lim\limits_{x \to 0} \frac{\ln(1+2x-3x^2+4x^3)}{\ln(1-x+2x^2-7x^3)}$; (h) $\lim\limits_{x \to 0} \frac{\sqrt{1+x^2} - 1}{1-\cos x}$.

1.12.9. Find an approximate value of the root $\sqrt[3]{1042}$.

1.13. One-Sided Limits

A number A is called the *limit to the right of the function* $f(x)$ as $x \to x_0$ $(A = \lim\limits_{x \to x_0 + 0} f(x) = f(x_0 + 0))$ if for any $\varepsilon > 0$ there exists $\delta(\varepsilon) > 0$ such that for all x satisfying the inequality $0 < x - x_0 < \delta(\varepsilon)$ and belonging to the domain of definition of the function $f(x)$ the inequality $|f(x) - A| < \varepsilon$ holds true. The limit to the left of the function $f(x_0 - 0)$ as $x \to x_0 - 0$ is defined in a similar way. If $x_0 = 0$, then we write simply $x \to +0$ or $x \to -0$ and, respectively, $f(+0)$ and $f(-0)$.

1.13.1. Find the one-sided limits of the functions :

(a) $f(x) = \begin{cases} -2x+3 & \text{if } x \le 1, \\ 3x-5 & \text{if } x > 1 \end{cases}$ as $x \to 1$;

(b) $f(x) = \frac{x^2-1}{|x-1|}$ as $x \to 1$;

(c) $f(x) = \frac{\sqrt{1-\cos 2x}}{x}$ as $x \to 0$;

(d) $f(x) = 3 + \dfrac{1}{1 + 7^{1/(1-x)}}$ as $x \to 1$;

(e) $f(x) = \cos\left(\dfrac{\pi}{x}\right)$ as $x \to 0$;

(f) $f(x) = 5/(x-2)^3$ as $x \to 2$.

Solution Let $x \le 1$. Then $f(x) = -2x + 3$. Hence, $f(1-0) = \lim\limits_{x \to 1-0} f(x) = 1$

is the limit to the left.

If $x > 1$, then $f(x) = 3x - 5$; hence, $f(1+0) = \lim\limits_{x \to 1+0} f(x) = -2$ is the limit to the right (see Fig. 28).

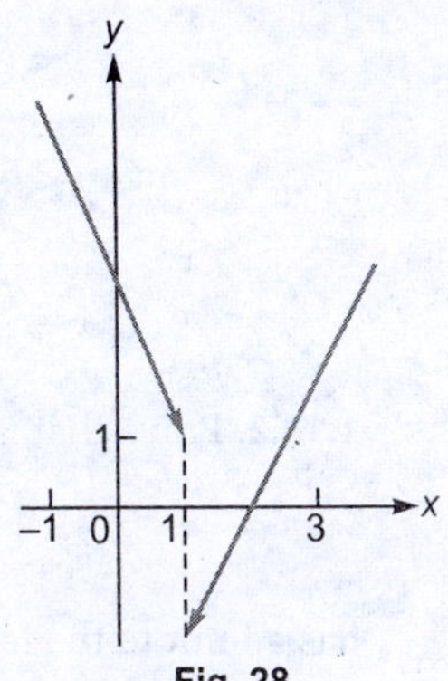

Fig. 28

(c) $f(x) = \dfrac{\sqrt{1-\cos 2x}}{x} = \dfrac{\sqrt{2\sin^2 x}}{x}$

$$= \frac{\sqrt{2}\,|\sin x|}{x},$$

but $|\sin x| = \begin{cases} \sin x, & \text{if } 0 < x < \pi/2, \\ -\sin x, & \text{if } -\pi/2 < x < 0. \end{cases}$

Hence,

$$f(-0) = \lim_{x \to -0} f(x) = \lim_{x \to -0}\left(-\sqrt{2}\frac{\sin x}{x}\right) = -\sqrt{2},$$

$$f(+0) = \lim_{x \to +0} f(x) = \lim_{x \to +0}\left(\sqrt{2}\frac{\sin x}{x}\right) = \sqrt{2}.$$

(d) The expression $1/(1-x)$ tends to $+\infty$, when x tends to 1, remaining less than 1, therefore

$$\lim_{x \to 1-0} 7^{1/(1-x)} = +\infty, \lim_{x \to 1-0} \frac{1}{1 + 7^{1/(1-x)}} = 0, f(1-0) = 3.$$

Further, as $x \to 1+0$ we have $1/(1-x) \to -\infty$. Therefore $\lim\limits_{x \to 1+0} 7^{1/(1-x)} = 0$,

$$f(1+0) = \lim_{x \to 1+0}\left(3 + \frac{1}{1 + 7^{1/(1-x)}}\right) = 3 + 1 = 4.$$

(e) Let us choose two sequence, $\{x_n\}$ and $\{x_n'\}$, with the general terms

$$x_n = \frac{1}{2n} \text{ and } x_n' = \frac{2}{2n+1} \; (n = 1, 2, \ldots)$$

respectively.

Then $\lim\limits_{n \to \infty} x_n = \lim\limits_{n \to 0} x_n' = 0$ and

$$\lim_{n \to \infty} f(x_n) = \lim_{n \to \infty} \cos 2\pi n = 1;$$

$$\lim_{n \to \infty} f(x'_n) = \lim_{n \to \infty} \cos(2n+1)\frac{\pi}{2} = 0.$$

Hence, the function $f(x)$ has no limit to the right at the point 0; taking into account that $f(x)$ is an even function, we conclude that it has no limit to the left either (see Fig. 29).

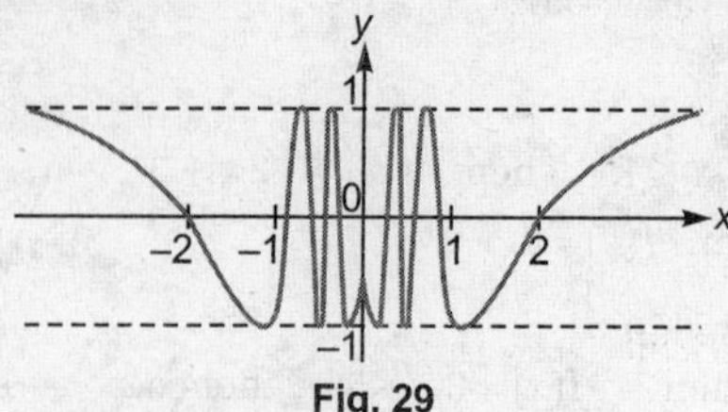

Fig. 29

1.13.2. Prove that, as $x \to 1$, the function

$$f(x) = \begin{cases} x+1 & \text{at } 0 \le x < 1, \\ 3x+2 & \text{at } 1 < x < 3, \end{cases}$$

has a limit to the left equal to 2 and a limit to the right equal to 5.

1.13.3. Find the one-sided limits of the following functions as $x \to 0$:

(a) $f(x) = \dfrac{1}{2 - 2^{1/x}}$;

(b) $f(x) = e^{1/x}$;

(c) $f(x) = \dfrac{|\sin x|}{x}$.

1.14. Continuity of a Function.

Points of Discontinuity and Their Classification

Let the function $y = f(x)$ be defined on the set X and let the point $x_0 \in X$ be the limit point of this set. The function $f(x)$ is said to be *continuous at the point* x_0 if $\lim\limits_{x \to x_0} f(x) = f(x_0)$. The latter condition is equivalent to the condition $\lim\limits_{\Delta x \to 0} \Delta y(x_0) = \lim\limits_{\Delta x \to 0} [f(x_0 + \Delta x) - f(x_0)] = 0$.

The function $f(x)$ is continuous at the point x_0 if and only if $f(x_0 - 0) = f(x_0 + 0) = f(x_0)$.

The function $f(x)$ is *continuous on the set* X if it is continuous at every point of this set.

Points of Discontinuity of the First Kind. Let the point x_0 be the limit point of the domain of definition X of the function $f(x)$. The pont x_0 is called a *discontinuity of the first kind* of the function $f(x)$ if there exist the limits to the right and to the left and they are finite. If $f(x_0 - 0) = f(x_0 + 0) \ne f(x_0)$, then x_0 is called a *removable discontinuity*. Further, if $f(x_0 - 0) \ne f(x_0 + 0)$, then x_0 is a non-removable discontinuity of the first kind, and the difference $f(x_0 + 0) - f(x_0 - 0)$ is called a *jump discontinuity* of the function $f(x)$ at the point x_0.

Points of Discontinuity of the Second Kind. If at least one of the limits of $f(x_0 - 0)$ and $f(x_0 + 0)$ is non-existent and infinite, then point x_0 is called a *discontinuity of the second kind* of the function $f(x)$.

1.14.1. Using only the definition prove discontinuity of the function $f(x) = 3x^4 + 5x^3 + 2x^2 + 3x + 4$ at any x.

Solution Let x_0 be an arbitrary point on the number scale. First find $\lim\limits_{x \to x_0} f(x)$:

$$\lim_{x \to x_0} f(x) = \lim_{x \to x_0} (3x^4 + 5x^3 + 2x^2 + 3x + 4)$$
$$= 3x_0^4 + 5x_0 + 2x_0^2 + 3x_0 + 4$$

Then compute the value of the function at the point x_0:

$$f(x_0) = 3x_0^4 + 5x_0^3 + 2x_0^2 + 3x_0 + 4.$$

Comparing the results thus obtained, we see that

$$\lim_{x \to x_0} f(x_0) = f(x_0).$$

Hence, the function $f(x)$ is continuous at the point x_0 by definition. Since x_0 is an arbitrary point on the number scale, we have proved continuity of the function for all values of x.

1.14.2. Given the functions :

(a) $$f(x) = \begin{cases} \frac{1}{5}(2x^2 + 3) & \text{for } -\infty < x \le 1, \\ 6 - 5x & \text{for } 1 < x < 3, \\ x - `3 & \text{for } 3 \le x < \infty; \end{cases}$$

(b) $$f(x) = \begin{cases} -2x^2 & \text{for } x \le 3, \\ 3x & \text{for } x > 3; \end{cases}$$

(c) $$f(x) = \frac{|2x - 3|}{2x - 3}.$$

Find the points of discontinuity (if any). Determine the jump discontinuities of the functions at the points of discontinuity of the first kind.

Solution (a) The domain of definition of the function is the entire number scale $(-\infty, \infty)$. In the open intervals $(-\infty, 1), (1, 3), (3, \infty)$ the function is continuous. Therefore discontinuities are possible only at the points $x = 1$, $x = 3$, at which analytic representation of the function is changed.

Let us find the one-sided limits of the function at the point $x = 1$:

$$f(1 - 0) = \lim_{x \to 1-0} \frac{1}{5}(2x^2 + 3) = 1;$$

$$f(1 + 0) = \lim_{x \to 1+0} (6 - 5x) = 1.$$

The value of the function at the point $x = 1$ is determined by the first analytic representation, *ie*, $f(1) = (2 + 3)/5 = 1$. Since

$$f(1 - 0) = f(1 + 0) = f(1),$$

the function is continuous at the point $x = 1$.

Consider the point $x = 3$:

$$f(3-0) = \lim_{x \to 3-0} (6 - 5x) = -9;$$

$$f(3+0) = \lim_{x \to 3+0} (x - 3) = 0.$$

We see that the right-hand and the left-hand limits, though finite, are not equal to each other, therefore the function has a discontinuity of the first kind at the point $x = 3$.

The jump of the function at the point of discontinuity is $f(3+0) - f(3-0) = 0 - (-9) = 9$.

(c) The function is defined and continuous throughout the entire number scale, except at the point $x = \frac{3}{2}$. Since $2x - 3 > 0$ for $x > \frac{3}{2}$ and $2x - 3 < 0$ for $x < \frac{3}{2}$,

$$f(x) = \begin{cases} 1 \text{ at } x > 3/2, \\ -1 \text{ at } x < 3/2. \end{cases}$$

Hence, $$f(3/2 + 0) = 1, f(3/2 - 0) = -1.$$

Therefore, at the point $x = \frac{3}{2}$ the function has a finite discontinuity of the first kind. The jump of the function at this point $f(3/2 + 0) - f(3/2 - 0)$ is equal to $1 - (-1) = 2$.

1.14.3. Test the following functions for continuity :

(a) $f(x) = \begin{cases} \dfrac{\sin x}{x} & \text{for } x \neq 0, \\ 1 & \text{for } x = 0; \end{cases}$

(b) $f(x) = \sin(1/x)$;

(c) $f(x) = \begin{cases} x\sin(1/x) & \text{for } x \neq 0, \\ 0 & \text{for } x = 0; \end{cases}$

(d) $f(x) = \begin{cases} 4 \cdot 3^x & \text{for } x < 0, \\ 2a + x & \text{for } x \geq 0; \end{cases}$

(e) $f(x) = \text{arc tan}(1/x)$; (f) $f(x) = (x^3 + 1)/(x + 1)$.

Solution (a) The function is continuous at all points $x \neq 0$. At the point $x = 0$ we have

$$f(0) = 1; \lim_{x \to -0} \frac{\sin x}{x} = \lim_{x \to +0} \frac{\sin x}{x} = 1.$$

Hence, at this point the function is continuous as well, which means that it is continuous for all values of x.

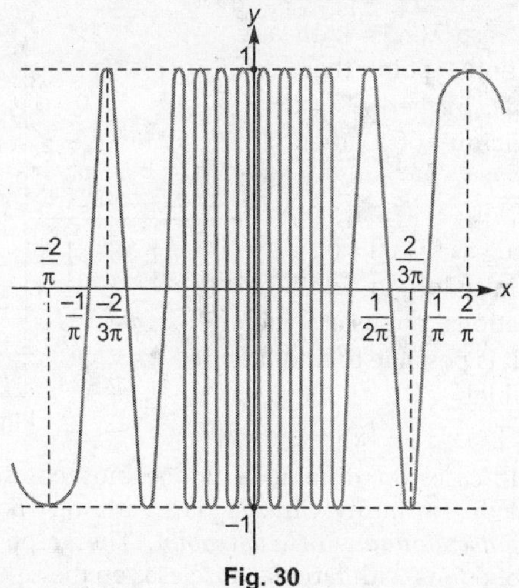

Fig. 30

(b) The function is defined and continuous for all $x \neq 0$. There are no one-sided limits at the point $x = 0$ (cf. Problem **1.13.1.** (e)). Therefore, at the point $x = 0$ the function suffers a discontinuity of the second kind. (see Fig. 30).

(d) $f(-0) = 4$, and $f(+0) = 2a$; the equality $f(-0) = f(+0) = f(0)$ will be fulfilled, *ie*, the function $f(x)$ will be continuous at the point $x = 0$ if we put $2a = 4, a = 2$.

(f) $f(-1-0) = f(-1+0) = \lim\limits_{x \to -1}(x^2 - x + 1) = 3$, *ie*, both one sided limits are finite and coincide. But at the point $x = -1$ the function is not defined and therefore, is not continuous. The graph of the function is the parabola $y = x^2 - x + 1$ with the point $M(-1, 3)$ removed. If we redefine the function putting $f(-1) = 3$, then it will become continuous. Thus, at $x = -1$ the function has a removable discontinuity.

1.14.4. Test the following functions for continuity :

(a) $f(x) = E(x)$. It should be borne in mind that the function $E(x)$ is defined as the maximum integer n contained in the number x, *ie*, as a number satisfying the inequality $n \leq x$.

(b) $\lambda(x) = \begin{cases} 1 \text{ if } x \text{ is rational,} \\ 0 \text{ if } x \text{ is irrational.} \end{cases}$

$\lambda(x)$ is called the *Dirichlet function*. For instance, $\lambda(0) = 1$; $\lambda(-1/2) = 1$; $\lambda(\sqrt{2}) = 0$; $\lambda(\pi) = 0$, etc.

Solution (a) The function $E(x)$ is defined throughout the entire number scale and takes on only integral values. This function is discontinuous at every integral value n of the independent variable, since $E(n-0) = n-1$; $E(n+0) = n$ (see Fig. 31).

(b) Let us choose an arbitrary point x_0 on the x-axis; two cases are possible : (1) the number x_0 is rational; (2) the number x_0 is irrational.

In the first case $\lambda(x_0) = 1$. In any vicinity of a rational point there are irrational points, where $\lambda(x) = 0$. Hence, in any vicinity of x_0 there are points x for which $|\Delta y| = |\lambda(x_0) - \lambda(x)| = 1$.

In the second case $\lambda(x_0) = 0$.

In any vicinity of an irrational point there are rational points at which $\lambda(x) = 1$. Hence, it is possible to find the values of x for which

$$|\Delta y| = |\lambda(x_0) - \lambda(x)| = 1.$$

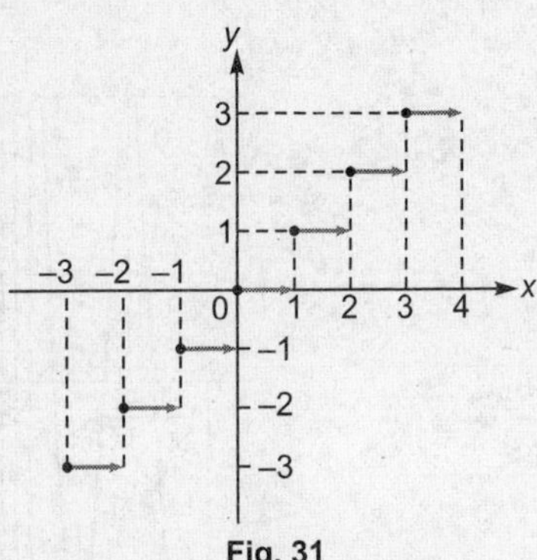

Fig. 31

Thus, in both cases the difference Δy does not tend to zero as $\Delta x \to 0$. Therefore, x_0 is a discontinuity. Since x_0 is an arbitrary point, the Dirichlet function $\lambda(x)$ is *discontinuous at each point*. The graph of this function consists of a set of points with rational abscissas on the x-axis and of a set of points with rational abscissas on the straight line $y = 1$, that is why it is impossible to sketch it.

1.14.5. Using the definition of continuity of a function in terms of "$\varepsilon - \delta$", test the following functions for continuity :

(a) $f(x) = ax + b \; (a \neq 0)$;

(b) $f(x) = \begin{cases} x^2 \text{ if } x \text{ is rational,} \\ -x^2 \text{ if } x \text{ is irrational.} \end{cases}$

Solution (a) Choose an arbitrary point x_0. According to the "$\varepsilon - \delta$" definition it is necessary to show that for any preassigned, arbitrarily small number $\varepsilon > 0$ it is possible to find a number $\delta > 0$ such that at $|x - x_0| < \delta$ the inequality $|f(x) - f(x_0)| < \varepsilon$ holds true.

Consider the absolute value of the difference

$$|f(x) - f(x_0)| = |(ax + b) - (ax_0 + b)|$$
$$= |ax + b - ax_0 - b| = |a||x - x_0|.$$

Let us require that $|f(x) - f(x_0)| < \varepsilon$. This requirement will be fulfilled for all x satisfying the inequality

$$|a||x - x_0| < \varepsilon \quad \text{or} \quad |x - x_0| < \varepsilon/|a| \, (a \neq 0).$$

Hence, if we take $\delta \leq \varepsilon/|a|$, then at $|x - x_0| < \delta$ the inequality $|f(x) - f(x_0)| < \varepsilon$ is fulfilled. Continuity is thus proved for any point $x = x_0$.

(b) Choose an arbitrary point x_0. If $\{x_n\}$ is a sequence of rational numbers tending to x_0, then $\lim\limits_{x_n \to x_0} f(x_n) = x_0^2$. If $\{x'_n\}$ is a sequence of irrational numbers tending to x_0, then $\lim\limits_{x'_n \to x_0} f(x'_n) = -x_0^2$. At $x_0 \neq 0$ the indicated limits are different and hence the function is discontinuous at all points $x \neq 0$.

On the other hand, let now $x = 0$. Find the absolute value of the difference $|f(x) - f(0)|$:

$$|f(x)-f(0)|=|\pm x^2-0|=x^2.$$

It is obvious that $x^2<\varepsilon$ at $|x|<\sqrt{\varepsilon}$. If $\varepsilon>0$ is given, then putting $\delta\le\sqrt{\varepsilon}$ and $|x-0|=|x|<\delta$, we obtain $|\Delta f(0)|=x^2<\varepsilon$.

Hence, at the point $x=0$ the function is continuous. And so, the point $x=0$ is the only point at which the function is continuous. Note that the function under consideration can be expressed through the Dirichlet function (see Problem **1.14.4.** (b)) : $f(x)=x^2[2\lambda(x)-1]$.

1.14.6. Determine which kind of discontinuity the following functions have at the point $x=x_0$:

(a) $f(x)=\begin{cases} x+2 \text{ for } x<2, \\ x^2-1 \text{ for } x\ge 2;\ x_0=2; \end{cases}$

(b) $f(x)=\text{arc tan}\dfrac{1}{x-5}$; $x_0=5$; (c) $f(x)=\dfrac{1}{1+2^{1/x}}$; $x_0=0$;

(d) $f(x)=\tan x$; $x_0=\pi/2$;

(e) $f(x)=\sqrt{x}-E(\sqrt{x})$; $x_0=n^2$, where n is a natural number.

Solution (a) Find the one-sided limits at the point $x_0=2$;

$$f(2-0)=\lim_{x\to 2-0}(x+2)=4;$$

$$f(2+0)=\lim_{x\to 2+0}(x^2-1)=3.$$

Here the limits to the right and to the left exist, are finite but do not coincide, therefore the function has a discontinuity of the first kind at the point $x_0=2$.

(e) The function $E(\sqrt{x})$ has discontinuities of the first kind at every point $x=n^2$, where n is a natural number (see Problem **1.14.4.** (a)), whereas the function $\sqrt{x}$ is continuous at all $x\ge 0$. Therefore the function $f(x)=\sqrt{x}-E(\sqrt{x})$ has discontinuities of the first kind at the points $1, 4, 9, \ldots, n^2, \ldots$

1.14.7. Test the following functions for continuity

(a) $f(x)=\dfrac{e^x-1}{x}$;

(b) $f(x)=\begin{cases} \dfrac{e^x-1}{x} & \text{for } x\ne 0, \\ 3 & \text{for } x=0; \end{cases}$

(c) $f(x)=\begin{cases} e^{1/x} & \text{for } x\ne 0, \\ 0 & \text{for } x=0; \end{cases}$

(d) $f(x)=\lim\limits_{n\to\infty}(\sin x)^{2n}$; (e) $f(x)=\dfrac{|\sin x|}{\sin x}$;

(f) $f(x)=E(x)+E(-x)$.

1.14.8. For each of the following functions find the points of discontinuity and determine the jumps of the function at these points :

(a) $f(x) = \dfrac{4}{x^2 - 2x + 1}$;

(b) $f(x) = x + \dfrac{x+2}{|x+2|}$;

(c) $f(x) = \dfrac{2|x-1|}{x^2 - x^3}$;

(d) $f(x) = \begin{cases} -x \text{ for } x \le 1, \\ \dfrac{2}{x-1} \text{ for } x > 1. \end{cases}$

1.14.9. Redefine the following functions at the point $x = 0$ so as to make them continuous :

(a) $f(x) = \dfrac{\tan x}{x}$; (b) $f(x) = \dfrac{5x^2 - 3x}{2x}$;

(c) $f(x) = \dfrac{\sqrt{1+x} - 1}{x}$; (d) $f(x) = \dfrac{\sin^2 x}{1 - \cos x}$.

1.15. Arithmetical Operations on Continuous Functions. Continuity of a Composite Function

If the functions $f(x)$ and $g(x)$ are continuous at the point $x = x_0$, then the functions

$$(1)\ f(x) \pm g(x);\ (2)\ f(x) \cdot g(x);\ (3)\ \frac{f(x)}{g(x)}\ (g(x_0) \ne 0)$$

are also continuous at this point.

If the function $u = \varphi(x)$ is continuous at the point $x = x_0$ and the function $y = f(u)$ is continuous at the point $u_0 = \varphi(x_0)$, then the composite function $y = f[\varphi(x)]$ is continuous at the point $x = x_0$.

1.15.1. Test the following functions for continuity :

(a) $f(x) = \dfrac{2x^5 - 8x^2 + 11}{x^4 + 4x^3 + 8x^2 + 8x + 4}$;

(b) $f(x) = \dfrac{3\sin^3 x + \cos^2 x + 1}{4\cos x - 2}$;

(c) $f(x) = \dfrac{x^3 \cos x + x^2 \sin x}{\cos(1/\sin x)}$.

Solution (a) A function representing a ratio of two continuous functions (polynomials in this case) is discontinuous only at points for which the denominator becomes zero. But in our case

$$x^4 + 4x^3 + 8x^2 + 8x + 4 = (x^2 + 2x + 2)^2,$$

and since $x^2 + 2x + 2 = (x+1)^2 + 1 > 0$ at any x, the denominator never becomes zero. Hence, the function $f(x)$ is continuous throughout the entire number scale.

(b) The function $f(x)$ suffers discontinuities only at points for which the denominator equals zero, *ie*, at points which are the roots of the equation

$$4\cos x - 2 = 0 \quad \text{or} \quad \cos x = 1/2,$$

whence $\quad x = x_n = \pm\,\pi/3 + 2\pi n\,(n = 0, \pm 1, \pm 2, \ldots)$.

Thus, the function $f(x)$ is continuous everywhere, except at the points x_n.

(c) Just as in the preceding example, the numerator is continuous throughout the entire number scale. As far as the denominator is concerned, according to the theorem on continuity of a composite function, it is continuous at points where the function $u = 1/\sin x$ is continuous, since the function $\cos u$ is continuous everywhere. Hence, the denominator is continuous everywhere, except at the points $x = k\pi$ (k an integer). Besides, we must exclude the points at which $\cos(1/\sin x) = 0$, *ie*, the points at which $1/\sin x = (2p+1)\,\pi/2$ (p an integer), or $\sin x = 2/[(2p+1)\pi]$. Thus, the function $f(x)$ is continuous everywhere except at the points $x = k\pi$ and $x = (-1)^n \arcsin \dfrac{2}{(2p+1)\,\pi} + n\pi$ $(k, p, n = 0, \pm 1, \pm 2, \ldots)$.

1.15.2. Test the following composite functions for continuity :

(a) $y = \cos x^n$, where n is a natural number;

(b) $y = \cos \log x$;

(c) $y = \sqrt{1/2 - \cos^2 x}$.

Solution (a) We have a composite function $y = \cos u$, where $u = x^n$. The function $y = \cos u$ is continuous at any point u, and the function $u = x^n$ is continuous at any value of x. Therefore, the function $y = \cos x^n$ is continuous throughout the entire number scale.

(c) Here $y = \sqrt{1/2 - u^2}$, where $u = \cos x$. The function $\sqrt{1/2 - u^2}$ is defined and continuous on the interval $|-\sqrt{2}/2, \sqrt{2}/2|$, the function $u = \cos x$ is continuous throughout the entire number scale. Therefore, the function $y = \sqrt{1/2 - \cos^2 x}$ is continuous at all values of x for which

$$|\cos x| \le \sqrt{2}/2, \textit{ie}, \begin{cases} \pi/4 + 2\pi n \le x \le 3\pi/4 + 2\pi n, \\ 5\pi/4 + 2\pi n \le x \le 7\pi/4 + 2\pi n. \end{cases}$$

1.15.3. For each of the following functions find the points of discontinuity and determine their character :

(a) $y = \dfrac{1}{u^2 + u - 2}$, where $u = \dfrac{1}{x-1}$;

(b) $y = u^2$, where $u = \begin{cases} x-1 \text{ for } x \ge 0, \\ x+1 \text{ for } x < 0; \end{cases}$

(c) $y = \frac{1-u^2}{1+u^2}$, where $u = \tan x$.

Solution (a) The function

$$u = \varphi(x) = \frac{1}{x-1}$$

suffers a discontinuity at the point $x = 1$. The function

$$y = f(u) = \frac{1}{u^2 + u - 2}$$

suffers a discontinuity at points where $u^2 + u - 2 = 0$, *ie*, $u_1 = -2$ and $u_2 = 1$. Using these values of u, find the corresponding values by$x$ by solving the equations :

$$-2 = \frac{1}{x-1}, 1 = \frac{1}{x-1};$$

whence $x = 1/2$ and $x = 2$.

Hence, the composite function is discontinuous at three points : $x_1 = 1/2$. $x_2 = 1$, $x_3 = 2$. Let us find out the character of discontinuities at these points.

$$\lim_{x \to 1} y = \lim_{u \to \infty} y = 0,$$

therefore $x_2 = 1$ is a removable discontinuity.

$$\lim_{x \to 1/2} y = \lim_{u \to -2} y = \infty; \ \lim_{x \to 2} y = \lim_{u \to 1} y = \infty;$$

hence, the points $x_1 = 1/2$, $x_3 = 2$ are discontinuities of the second kind.

1.15.4. Given the function $f(x) = 1/(1-x)$. Find the points of discontinuity of the composite function

$$y = f\{f[f(x)]\}.$$

Solution The point $x = 1$ is a discontinuity of the function $v = f(x) = \frac{1}{1-x}$.

If $x \neq 1$, then

$$u = f[f(x)] = \frac{1}{1 - 1/(1-x)} = \frac{x-1}{x}.$$

Hence, the point $x = 0$ is a discontinuity of the function $u = f[f(x)]$.
If $x \neq 0$, $x \neq 1$, then

$$y = f\{f[f(x)]\} = \frac{1}{1 - (x-1)/x} = x$$

is continuous everywhere.

Thus, the points of discontinuity of this composite function are $x = 0$, $x = 1$, both of them being removable.

1.16. The Properties of a Function Continuous on a Closed Interval. Continuity of an Inverse Function

I. The function $f(x)$, continuous on the interval $[a, b]$, possesses the following properties :

(1) $f(x)$ is bounded on $[a, b]$;

(2) $f(x)$ has the minimum and maximum values on $[a, b]$;

(3) If $m = \min_{a \le x \le b} f(x)$, $M = \max_{a \le x \le b} f(x)$, then for any A satisfying the inequalities $m \le A \le M$ there exists a point $x_0 \in [a, b]$ for which $f(x_0) = A$.

In particular, if $f(a) \cdot (b) < 0$, then we can find a point c $(a < c < b)$ such that $f(c) = 0$.

II. Continuity of an Inverse Function. If the function $y = f(x)$ is defined, continuous and strictly monotonic on the interval X, then there exists a single-valued inverse function $x = \varphi(y)$ defined, continuous and also strictly monotonic in the range of the function $y = f(x)$.

1.16.1. Does the equation $\sin x - x + 1 = 0$ have a root ?

Solution The function

$$f(x) = \sin x - x + 1$$

is continuous over the entire number scale. Besides, this function changes sign, since $f(0) = 1$, and $f(3\pi/2) = -3\pi/2$. Hence, by property (3) within the interval $[0, 3\pi/2]$ there is at least one root of the given equation.

1.16.2. Has the equation $x^5 - 18x + 2 = 0$ roots belonging to the interval $[-1, 1]$?

1.16.3. Prove that any algebraic equation of an odd power with real coefficients

$$a_0x^{2n+1} + a_1x^{2n} + \ldots + a_{2n}x + a_{2n+1} = 0 \qquad \ldots(*)$$

has at least one real root.

Solution Consider the function

$$f(x) = a_0x^{2n+1} + a_1x^{2n} + \ldots + a_{2n}x + a_{2n+1},$$

which is continuous throughout the number scale.

Let, for determinacy sake, $a_0 > 0$. Then

$$\lim_{x \to +\infty} f(x) = +\infty, \quad \text{and} \quad \lim_{x \to -\infty} f(x) = -\infty.$$

Hence, we can find numbers $a, b, a < b$ such that $f(a) < 0$; $f(b) > 0$. By property (3), between a and b there exists a number c such that $f(x) = 0$, which proves that the equation (*) has at least one real root.

1.16.4. Let the function $f(x)$ be continuous on $[a, b]$ and let the equation $f(x) = 0$ have a finite number of roots on the interval $[a, b]$. Arrange them in the ascending order :

$$a < x_1 < x_2 < x_3 < \ldots < x_n < b.$$

Prove that in each of the intervals

$$(a, x_1), (x_1, x_2), (x_2, x_3), \ldots, (x_n, b)$$

the function $f(x)$ retains the same sign.

Solution If the function changed its sign on a certain interval, then we could find one more root of the function, which contradicts the condition. To determine the sign of the function on any of the indicated intervals it is sufficient to compute the value of the function at an arbitrary point of the appropriate interval.

1.16.5. Given a function on the interval $[-2, +2]$:

$$f(x) = \begin{cases} x^2 + 2 & \text{if } -2 \le x < 0, \\ -x^2 + 2) & \text{if } 0 \le x \le 2. \end{cases}$$

Is there a point on this closed interval at which $f(x) = 0$?

Solution At the end-points of the interval $[-2, +2]$ the given function has different signs :

$$f(-2) = +6; \; f(+2) = -6.$$

But it is easy to notice that it does not become zero at any point of the interval $[-2, +2]$. Indeed, $x^2 + 2 > 0$ and $-(x^2 + 2) < 0$ at any x; this is due to the fact that $f(x)$ has a discontinuity at the point $x = 0$.

1.16.6. Does the function

$$f(x) = x^3/4 - \sin \pi x + 3$$

take on the value $2\frac{1}{3}$ within the interval $[-2, 2]$?

Solution The function $f(x) = x^3/4 - \sin \pi x + 3$ is continuous within the intervals $[-2, 2]$. furthermore, at the end-points of this interval it attains the values

$$f(-2) = 1; \; f(2) = 5.$$

Since $1 < 2\frac{1}{3} < 5$, then by property (3), within the interval $[-2, 2]$ there exists at least one point x such that $f(x) = 2\frac{1}{3}$.

1.16.7. Show that the function

$$f(x) = \begin{cases} 2^x + 1 \text{ for } -1 \le x < 0, \\ 2^x \text{ for } x = 0, \\ 2^x - 1 \text{ for } 0 < x \le 1, \end{cases}$$

defined and bounded on the interval $[-1, 1]$, has neither maximum, nor minimum values.

Solution In there interval $[-1, 0)$ the function increases from $\frac{3}{2}$ to 2 and in $(0, 1]$ it increases from 0 to 1, it does not attain either the value 2 or 0.

Therefore the function is bounded but never reaches its upper and lower bounds. This is because there is a discontinuity at the point $x = 0$.

1.16.8. Show that on any interval $[a, b]$ of length greater than unity the function $f(x) = x - E(x)$ attains its minimum value but never reaches its maximum.

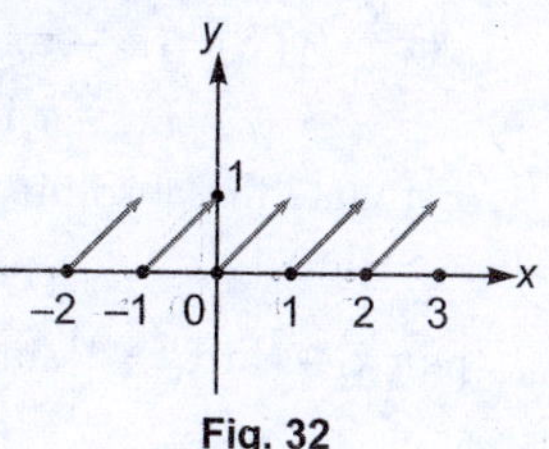

Fig. 32

Solution In any interval $[n, n+1)$, where n is an integer, the given function $f(x)$ increases from 0 to 1, never attaining the maximum. Hence, $0 \le f(x) < 1$ for any x. Since on the interval $[a, b]$ we can find at least one internal integral point n, then $f(n) = 0$ and $\lim_{x \to n-0} f(x) = 1$, but $f(x) \ne 1$ for any x. It means that the function reaches its minimum value but never reaches its maximum. This is because there is a discontinuity at the point $x = n$ (see Fig. 32).

1.16.9. Prove that function $y = \sqrt[2n+1]{x}$ (n a natural number) is continuous throughout the number scale, considering it as a function inverse to $y = x^{2n+1}$.

Solution The function $y = x^{2n+1}$ is continuous and increases from $-\infty$ to ∞ over the entire number scale. Hence, the inverse function $x = \sqrt[2n+1]{y}$ is defined for all y, continuous and increasing. Denoting the independent variable again as x, we find that the function $y = \sqrt[2n+1]{x}$ possesses the required properties.

1.16.10. Prove that for any function of the form

$$y = a_0 x^{2n+1} + a_1 x^{2n-1} + a_2 x^{2n-3} + \ldots + a_n x + a_{n+1}, \qquad \ldots(*)$$

where $a_0, a_1, a_2, \ldots, a_n, a_{n+1}$ are positive numbers, there exists an inverse function increasing and continuous throughout the number scale.

Solution As is known, the functions $x, x^3, x^5, \ldots, x^{2n+1}$ increase throughout the entire number scale. Then, since the coefficients $a_i (i = 0, 1, \ldots, n+1)$ are positive, the function $f(x) = a_0 x^{2n+1} + a_1 x^{2n-1} + \ldots + a_n x + a_{n+1}$ also increases. Furthermore, it is continuous. Therefore, for a function of the form (*) there exists an inverse function increasing and continuous over the entire number scale.

Note. This example establishes only the existence of an inverse function $x = g(y)$, but gives no analytic expression for it. It is not always possible to express it in radicals. The problems of the existence of an inverse function and of expressing it analytically should not be confused.

1.16.11. Prove that there exists only one continuous function $x = x(y)$ $(-\infty < y < \infty)$ which satisfies the *Kepler equation* :

$$x - \varepsilon \sin x = y \; (0 < \varepsilon < 1).$$

Solution Let us show that $y(x)$ is an increasing function. Let $x_1 < x_2$ be arbitrary points on the number scale. Then

$$y(x_2) - y(x_1) = (x_2 - \varepsilon \sin x_2) - (x_1 - \varepsilon \sin x_1)$$
$$= (x_2 - x_1) - \varepsilon (\sin x_2 - \sin x_1).$$

Estimate the absolute value of the difference $|\sin x_2 - \sin x_1|$:

$$|\sin x_2 - \sin x_1| = 2\left|\sin \frac{x_2 - x_1}{2}\right|\left|\cos \frac{x_2 + x_1}{2}\right|$$
$$\le 2\left|\sin \frac{x_2 - x_1}{2}\right| \le 2\frac{|x_2 - x_1|}{2}.$$
$$= |x_2 - x_1| = (x_2 - x_1).$$

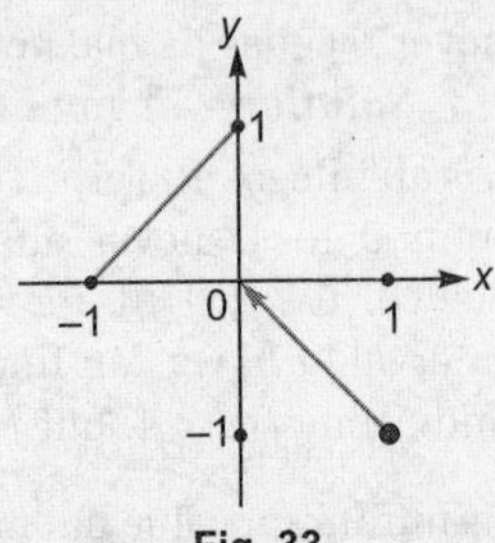

Fig. 33

Since $0 < \varepsilon < 1$,
$\varepsilon |\sin x_2 - \sin x_1| < (x_2 - x_1)$.
Whence $(x_2 - x_1) - \varepsilon (\sin x_2 - \sin x_1) = y(x_2) - y(x_1) > 0$.

Since $y(x)$ is a continuous function in the interval $(-\infty, \infty)$, the inverse function x is a angle-valued and continuous function of y.

1.16.12. Show that the equation $x^3 - 3x + 1 = 0$ has one root on the interval $[1, 2]$. Calculate this root approximately to within two decimal places.

1.16.13. The function $f(x)$ is defined on the interval $[a, b]$ and has values of the same sign on its end-points. Can one assert that there is no point on $[a, b]$ at which the function becomes zero ?

1.16.14. Prove that the function

$$f(x) = \begin{cases} x + 1 & \text{at } -1 \le x \le 0, \\ -x & \text{at } 0 < x \le 1, \end{cases}$$

is discontinuous at the point $x = 0$ and still has the maximum and the minimum value on $[-1, 1]$ (see Fig. 33).

1.17. Additional Problems

1.17.1. Prove the inequalities :

(a) $n! < \left(\frac{n+1}{2}\right)^n$ for a natural $n > 1$;

(b) $\frac{1}{2} \cdot \frac{3}{4} \cdot \frac{5}{6} \cdots \frac{2n-1}{2n} < \frac{1}{\sqrt{2n+1}}$.

1.17.2. Prove the inequalities :

(a) $202^{303} > 303^{202}$; (b) $200! < 100^{200}$.

1.17.3. Solve the inequalities :

(a) $||x| - 2| \le 1$; (b) $||2 - 3x| - 1| > 2$;

(c) $(x - 2)\sqrt{x^2 + 1} > x^2 + 2$.

1.17.4. Can a sum, difference, product or quotient of irrational numbers be a rational number ?

1.17.5. Do the equations

(a) $|\sin x| = \sin x + 3$; (b) $|\tan x| = \tan x + 3$ have any roots ?

1.17.6. Prove the identity $\left(\frac{x+|x|}{2}\right)^2 + \left(\frac{x-|x|}{2}\right)^2 = x^2$.

1.17.7. Prove that Bernoulli inequality

$$(1 + x_1)(1 + x_2)\dots(1 + x_n) \geq 1 + x_1 + x_2 + \dots + x_n,$$

where $x_1, x_2, \dots, x_n$ are numbers of like sign, and $1 + x_i > 0 (i = 1, 2, \dots, n)$.

1.17.8. Find the domains of definition of the following functions :

(a) $f(x) = \sqrt{x^3 - x^2}$;

(b) $f(x) = \sqrt{\sin\sqrt{x}}$;

(c) $f(x) = \sqrt{-\sin^2 \pi x}$;

(d) $f(x) = \frac{1}{\sqrt{|x| - x}}$ and $g(x) = \frac{1}{\sqrt{x - |x|}}$;

(e) $f(x) = \arcsin(|x| - 3)$;

(f) $f(x) = \arccos\frac{1}{\sin x}$.

1.17.9. Are the following functions identical ?

(a) $f(x) = \frac{x}{x}$ and $\varphi(x) = 1$;

(b) $f(x) = x$ and $\varphi(x) = (\sqrt{x})^2$;

(c) $f(x) = 1$ and $\varphi(x) = \sin^2 x + \cos^2 x$;

(d) $f(x) = \log(x - 1) + \log(x - 2)$ and $\varphi(x) = \log(x - 1)(x - 2)$.

1.17.10. In what interval are the following functions identical ?

(a) $f(x) = x$ and $\varphi(x) = 10^{\log x}$;

(b) $f(x) = \sqrt{x}\sqrt{x-1}$ and $\varphi(x) = \sqrt{x(x-1)}$.

1.17.11. An isosceles triangle of a given perimeter $2p = 12$ revolves about its base. Write the function $V(x)$, where V is the volume of the solid of revolution thus obtained and x is the length of the lateral side of the triangle.

1.17.12. Investigating the domain of definition of functions,

(a) Solve the inequality

$$\sqrt{x+2} + \sqrt{x-5} \geq \sqrt{5-x};$$

(b) Prove that the inequality

$$\log_{2-x}(x - 3) \geq -5$$

has no solution.

1.17.13. The function $y = \operatorname{sign} x$ was defined in Problem **1.5.11** (n). Show that

(a) $|x| = x$ sign; (b) $x = |x| \operatorname{sign} x$;

(c) $\operatorname{sign}(\operatorname{sign} x) = \operatorname{sign} x$.

1.17.14. Prove that if for a linear function

$$f(x) = ax + b$$

the values of the argument $x = x_n (n = 1, 2, \dots)$ from an arithmetic progression, then the corresponding values of the function

$$y_n = f(x_n)\ (n = 1, 2, \dots)$$

also form an arithmetic progression.

1.17.15. Prove that the product of two even or two odd functions is an even function, whereas the product of ane even and an odd function is an odd function.

1.17.16. Prove that if the domain of definition of the function $f(x)$ is symmetrical with respect to $x = 0$, then $f(x) + f(-x)$ is an even function and $f(x) - f(-x)$ is an odd one.

1.17.17. Prove that any function $f(x)$ defined in a symmetrical interval $(-l, l)$ can be presented as a sum of an even and an odd function. Rewrite the following functions in the form of a sum of an even and an odd function :

(a) $f(x) = \dfrac{x + 2}{1 + x^2}$; (b) $y = a^x$.

1.17.18. Extend the function $f(x) = x^2 + x$ defined on the interval $[0, 3]$ onto the interval $[-3, 3]$ in an even and an odd way.

1.17.19. The function $\{x\} = x - E(x)$ is a fractional part of a number x. Prove that it is a periodic function with period 1.

1.17.20. Sketch the graph of a periodic function with period $T = 1$ defined on the half-open interval $(0, 1]$ by the formula $y = x^2$.

1.17.21. Let us have two periodic functions $f(x)$ and $\varphi(x)$ defined on a common set. Prove that if the periods of these functions are commensurate, then their sum and product are also periodic function.

1.17.22. Prove that the Drichlet function $\lambda(x)$ (see Problem **1.14.4 (b)**) is a periodic one but has no period.

1.17.23. Prove that if the function

$$f(x) = \sin x + \cos ax$$

is periodic, then a is a rational number.

1.17.24. Test the following functions for monotony :

(a) $f(x) = |x|$; (b) $f(x) = |x| - x$.

1.17.25. Prove that the sum of two functions increasing on a certain open interval is a function monotonically increasing on this interval. Will the difference of increasing functions be a monotonic function ?

1.17.26. Give an example of a non-monotonic function that has an inverse.

1.17.27. Determine the inverse function and its domain of definition if

(a) $y = \tan h\, x$; (b) $y = \begin{cases} x & \text{if } -\infty < x < 1, \\ x^2 & \text{if } 1 \le x \le 4, \\ 2^x & \text{if } 4 < x < \infty. \end{cases}$

1.17.28. Show that the equation $x^2 + 2x + 1 = -1 + \sqrt{x}$ has no real roots.

1.17.29. Construct the graph of the function

$$y = f(x - l) + f(x + l),$$

where
$$f(x) = \begin{cases} k(1 - |x|/l) \text{ at } |x| \le l, \\ 0 \quad \text{at } |x| > l. \end{cases}$$

1.17.30. Knowing the graph of the function $y = f(x)$, sketch the graphs of the following functions :

(a) $y = f^2(x)$; (b) $y = \sqrt{f(x)}$;

(c) $y = f[(x)]$.

1.17.31. Prove that the graphs of the functions $y = \log_a x$ and $y = \log_{a^n} x$ can be derived from each other by changing all ordinates in the ratio $1 : 1/n$.

1.17.32. Prove that if the graph of the function $y = f(x)$, defined throughout the number scale, is symmetrical about two vertical axes $x = a$ and $x = b$ $(a < b)$, then this function is a periodic one.

1.17.33. Let the sequence x_n converge and the sequence y_n diverge. What can be said about convergence of the sequences

(a) $x_n + y_n$; (b) $x_n y_n$?

1.17.34. Let the sequences x_n and y_n diverge. Can one assert that the sequences $x_n + y_n$, $x_n y_n$ diverge too ?

1.17.35. Let α_n be an interior angle of a regular n-gon $(n = 3, 4, \ldots)$. Write the first several terms of the sequence α_n. Prove that lime $a_n = \pi$.

1.17.36. Prove that from $\lim\limits_{n\to\infty} x_n = a$ it follows that $\lim\limits_{n\to\infty} |x_n| = |a|$. Is the converse true ?

1.17.37. If a sequence has an infinite limit, does it mean that this sequence is unbounded ? And if a sequence is unbounded, does it mean that it has infinite limit ? Prove that $x_n = n^{(-1)^n}$ is an unbounded but not an infinite function.

1.17.38. Prove that the sequence $\{\alpha_n\}$, where α_n is the nth digit of an arbitrarily chosen irrational number, cannot be monotonic.

1.17.39. Prove that if the sequence $\{a_n/b_n\}$ $(b_n > 0)$ is monotonic, then the sequence

$$\left\{\frac{a_1 + a_2 + \ldots + a_n}{b_1 + b_2 + \ldots + b_n}\right\}$$

will also be monotonic.

1.17.40. Prove the existence of limits of the following sequences and find them.

(a) $\sqrt{2}, \sqrt{2\sqrt{2}}, \sqrt{2\sqrt{2\sqrt{2}}} \ldots$;

(b) $x_n = c^n/\sqrt[k]{n!}$ $(c > 0, k > 0)$;

(c) $x_n = \alpha_n/n$, where α_n is the nth digit of the number π.

1.17.41. Prove that at an arbitrarily chosen x the sequence $\left\{\frac{E(nx)}{n}\right\}$ is bounded.

1.17.42. Prove that the sequence

$$\left\{\frac{E(x)+E(2x)+\ldots+E(nx)}{n^2}\right\}$$

has the limit $x/2$.

1.17.43. Prove that

$$\lim_{h\to 0} a^h = 1 \ (a > 0).$$

1.17.44. Given the function

$$f(x) = \begin{cases} 1 + x & \text{for} \quad x \neq 0, \\ 0 & \text{for} \quad x = 0. \end{cases}$$

Prove that

$$\lim_{x\to 0} f(x) = 1.$$

1.17.45. Let $P(x) = \dfrac{a_0x^n + a_1x^{n-1} + \ldots + a_n}{b_0x^m + b_1x^{m-1} + \ldots + b_m}$ $(a_0 \neq 0;\ b_0 \neq 0)$.

Prove that
$$\lim_{x\to\infty} P(x) = \begin{cases} \infty, & \text{if } n > m, \\ a_0/b_0, & \text{if } n = m, \\ 0, & \text{if } n < m. \end{cases}$$

1.17.46. Find the constants a and b from the condition :

(a) $\lim\limits_{x\to\infty}\left(\dfrac{x^2+1}{x+1} - ax - b\right) = 0;$

(b) $\lim\limits_{x\to-\infty}\left(\sqrt{x^2 - x + 1} - ax - b\right) = 0.$

1.17.47. Sketch the graphs of the following functions :

(a) $f(x) = \lim\limits_{n\to\infty} \sqrt[n]{1 + x^n}\,(x \geq 0);$

(b) $f(x) = \lim\limits_{n\to\infty} \sin^{2n} x.$

1.17.48. Prove that

$$\lim_{n\to\infty}[(1+x)(1+x^2)(1+x^4)\ldots(1+x^{2^n})] = \frac{1}{1-x}\,(|x|<1).$$

1.17.49. Can one replace infinitesimal summands by equivalent infinitesimals in computing a limit ?

1.17.50. Determine the order of smallness of the chord of an infinitely small circular arc relative to the sagitta of the same arc.

1.17.51. Determine the order of smallness of the difference of the perimeters of an inscribed and circumscribed regular n-gons relative to an infinitely small side of the inscribed n-gon.

1.17.52. The volumetric expansion coefficient of a body is considered to be approximately equal to the triple coefficient of linear expansion. On equivalence of what infinitesimals is it based ?

1.17.53. Does the relation $\log(1 + x) \sim x$ hold true as $x \to 0$?

1.17.54. Will the sum of two functions $f(x) + g(x)$ be necessarily discontinuous at a given point x_0 if :

(a) the function $f(x)$ is continuous and the function $g(x)$ is discontinuous at $x = x_0$,

(b) both functions are discontinuous at $x = x_0$? Give some examples.

1.17.55. Is the product of two functions $f(x)\,g(x)$ necessarily discontinuous at a given point x_0 if :

(a) the function $f(x)$ is continuous and the function $g(x)$ is discontinuous at this point;

(b) both functions $f(x)$ and $g(x)$ are discontinuous at $x = x_0$? Give some examples.

1.17.56. Can one assert that the square of a discontinuous function is also a discontinuous function ? Given an example of a function discontinuous everywhere whose square is a continuous function.

1.17.57. Determine the points of discontinuity of the following functions and investigate the character of these points if :

(a) $f(x) = \dfrac{1}{1 - e^{x/(1-x)}}$;

(b) $f(x) = 2^{-2^{1/(1-x)}}$;

(c) $\varphi(x) = x[1 - 2\lambda(x)]$, where $\lambda(x)$ is the Dirichlet function (see Problem **1.14.4** (b)).

1.17.58. Test the following functions for continuity and sketch their graphs :

(a) $y = x - E(x)$;

(b) $y = x^2 + E(x^2)$;

(c) $y = (-1)^{E(x^2)}$;

(d) $y = \lim\limits_{n \to \infty} \dfrac{x}{1 + (2 \sin x)^{2n}}$.

1.17.59. Investigate the functions $f[g(x)]$ and $g[f(x)]$ for continuity if $f(x) = \text{sign}\, x$ and $g(x) = x(1 - x^2)$.

1.17.60. Prove that the function

$$f(x) = \begin{cases} 2x & \text{at } -1 \le x \le 0, \\ x + \dfrac{1}{2} & \text{at } \quad 0 < x \le 1 \end{cases}$$

is discontinuous at the point $x = 0$ and nonetheless has both maximum and minimum values on $[-1, 1]$.

1.17.61. Given the function

$$f(x) = \begin{cases} (x+1)\,2^{-(1/|x|+1/x)} & \text{if } x \neq 0, \\ 0 & \text{if } x = 0. \end{cases}$$

Ascertain that on the interval $[-2, 2]$ the function takes on all intermediate values from $f(-2)$ to $f(2)$ although it is discontinuous (at what point ?).

1.17.62. Prove that if the function $f(x)$: (1) is defined and monotonic on the interval $[a, b]$; (2) traverses all intermediate values between $f(a)$ and $f(b)$, then it is continuous on the interval $[a, b]$.

1.17.63. Let the function $y = f(x)$ be continuous on the interval $[a, b]$, its range being the same interval $a \leq y \leq b$. Prove that on this closed interval there exists at least one point x such that $f(x) = x$. Explain this geometrically.

1.17.64. Prove that if the function $f(x)$ is continuous on the interval (a, b) and $x_1, x_2, \ldots, x_n$ are any values from this open interval, then we can find among them a number ξ such that

$$f(\xi) = \frac{1}{n}[f(x_1) + f(x_2) + \ldots + f(x_n)].$$

1.17.65. Prove that the equation $x\,2^x = 1$ has at least one positive root which is less than unity.

1.17.66. Prove that if a polynomial of an even degree attains at least one value the sign of which is opposite to that of the coefficient at the superior power of x of the polynomial, then the latter has at least two real roots.

1.17.67. Prove that the inverse of the discontinuous function $y = (1 + x^2)$ sing x is a continuous function.

2 Differentiation of Functions

2.1. Definition of the Derivative

The derivative $f'(x)$ of the function $y = f(x)$ at a given point x is defined by the equality

$$f'(x) = \lim_{\Delta x \to 0} \frac{\Delta y}{\Delta x} = \lim_{\Delta x \to 0} \frac{f(x + \Delta x) - f(x)}{\Delta x}.$$

If this limit is finite, then the function $f(x)$ is called *differentiable* at the point x; and it is infallibly continuous at this point. Geometrically, the value of the derivative $f'(x)$ represents the slope of the line tangent to the graph of the function $y = f(x)$ at the point x.

The number

$$f'_{+}(x) = \lim_{\Delta x \to +0} \frac{f(x + \Delta x) - f(x)}{\Delta x}$$

is called the *right-side* derivative at the point x

The number

$$f'_{-}(x) = \lim_{\Delta x \to -0} \frac{f(x + \Delta x) - f(x)}{\Delta x}$$

is called the *left-side* derivative at the point x.

The necessary and sufficient condition for the existence of the derivative $f'(x)$ is the existence of the finite right-side and left-side derivatives, and also of the equality $f'_{-}(x) = f'_{+}(x)$.

If $f'(x) = \infty$, the function $f(x)$ is said to have an infinite derivative at the point x. In this case the line tangent to the graph of the function $y = f(x)$ at the point x is perpendicular to the x-axis.

2.1.1. Find the increment Δy and the ratio, $\frac{\Delta y}{\Delta x}$ for the following functions :

(a) $y = \sqrt{x}$ at $x = 0$ and $\Delta x = 0.0001$;

(b) $y = \dfrac{1}{x^2 + x - 6}$ at $x = 1$ and $\Delta x = 0.2$.

Solution (a) $\Delta y = \sqrt{x + \Delta x} - \sqrt{x} = \sqrt{0.0001} = 0.01$;

$$\frac{\Delta y}{\Delta x} = \frac{0.01}{0.0001} = 100.$$

2.1.2. Using the definition of the derivative, find the derivatives of the following functions :

(a) $y = \cos ax$; (b) $y = 5x^2 - 2x$.

Solution (a) $\Delta y = \cos a(x + \Delta x) - \cos ax$

$$= -2 \sin\left(ax + \frac{a}{2}\Delta x\right) \sin \frac{a}{2} x;$$

$$\frac{\Delta y}{\Delta x} = \frac{-2 \sin\left(ax + \frac{a}{2}\Delta x\right) \sin \frac{a}{2}\Delta x}{\Delta x};$$

$$y' = \lim_{\Delta x \to 0} \frac{\Delta y}{\Delta x} = -2 \lim_{\Delta x \to 0} \sin\left(ax + \frac{a}{2}\Delta x\right) \lim_{\Delta x \to 0} \frac{\sin \frac{a}{2}\Delta x}{\Delta x} = -a \sin ax.$$

In particular, if $a = 1$, then $y = \cos x$ and $y' = -\sin x$.

2.1.3. Show that the following functions have no finite derivatives at the indicated points :

(a) $y = \sqrt[5]{x^3}$ at the point $x = 0$;

(b) $y = \sqrt[3]{x-1}$ at the point $x = 1$;

(c) $y = 3|x| + 1$ at the point $x = 0$.

Solution (a) $\Delta y = \sqrt[5]{(x + \Delta x)^3} - \sqrt[5]{x^3}$.

At $x = 0$ we have $\Delta y = \sqrt[5]{\Delta x^3}$, $\frac{\Delta y}{\Delta x} = \frac{\sqrt[5]{\Delta x^3}}{\Delta x}$

$= \frac{1}{\sqrt[5]{\Delta x^2}}$; hence, $y'(0) = \lim_{\Delta x \to 0} \frac{1}{\sqrt[5]{\Delta x^2}} = \infty$,

ie, there is no finite derivative.

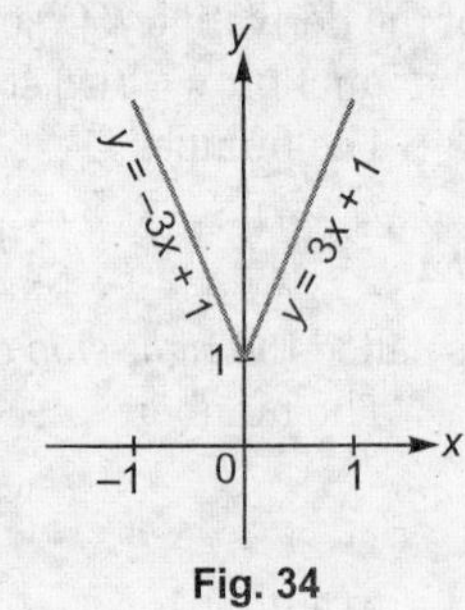

Fig. 34

(c) At $\Delta x > 0$ the increment of the function Δy at $x = 0$ will be: $\Delta y = 3(0 + \Delta x) + 1 - 1 = 3\Delta x$. Therefore

$$\lim_{\Delta x \to +0} \frac{\Delta y}{\Delta x} = 3.$$

At $\Delta x < 0$ the increment of the function Δy will be

$$\Delta y = -3(0 + \Delta x) + 1 - 1 = -3\Delta x,$$

hence,
$$\lim_{\Delta x \to -0} \frac{\Delta y}{\Delta x} = -3.$$

Since the one-sided limits are different, there is no derivative at the point $x = 0$. (see Fig. 34).

2.1.4. Investigate the function $y = |\ln x|$ for differentiability at the point $x = 1$.

Solution At $x = 1$

$$\Delta y = |\ln(1 + \Delta x)| - |\ln 1| = |\ln(1 + \Delta x)|,$$

ie, $$\Delta y = |\ln(1+\Delta x)| = \begin{cases} \ln(1+\Delta x) \text{ at } \Delta x \geq 0, \\ -\ln(1+\Delta x) \text{ at } \Delta x < 0. \end{cases}$$

Therefore $$\frac{\Delta y}{\Delta x} = \begin{cases} \dfrac{\ln(1+\Delta x)}{\Delta x} \text{ at } \Delta x > 0, \\ -\dfrac{\ln(1+\Delta x)}{\Delta x} \text{ at } \Delta x < 0, \end{cases}$$

whence

$$\lim_{\Delta x \to +0} \frac{\Delta y}{\Delta x} = +1 \quad \text{and} \quad \lim_{\Delta x \to -0} \frac{\Delta y}{\Delta x} = -1.$$

Since the one-sided limits are different, there is no derivative. Hence, the function $y = |\ln x|$ is not differentiable at the point $x = 1$ (see Fig. 35).

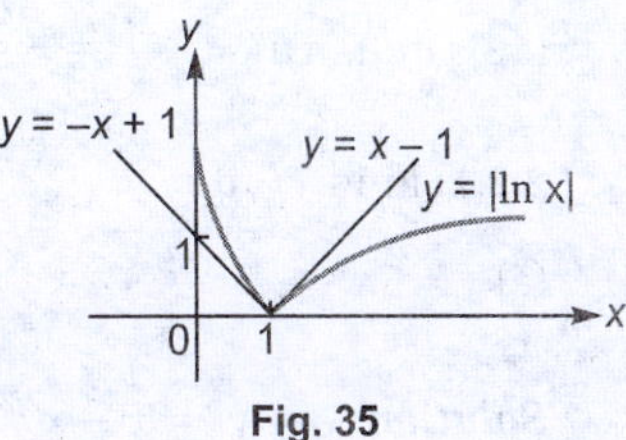

Fig. 35

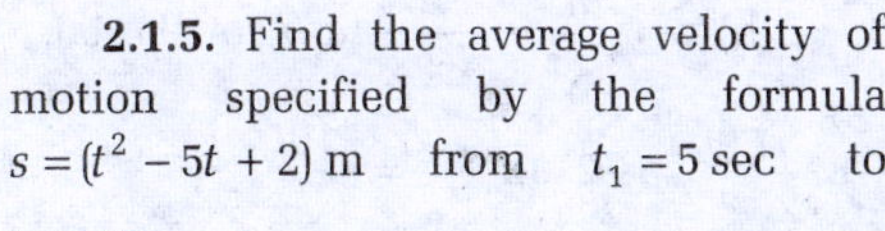

2.1.5. Find the average velocity of motion specified by the formula $s = (t^2 - 5t + 2)$ m from $t_1 = 5$ sec to $t_2 = 15$ sec.

2.1.6. Using the definition of the derivative, find the derivatives of the following functions :

(a) $y = x^3$; (b) $y = 1/x^2$.

2.1.7. Investigate the function $y = |\cos x|$ for differentiability at the points $x = \dfrac{\pi}{2} + n\pi$ (n an integer).

2.2. Differentiation of Explicit Functions

I. Basic Rules of Differentiation

(1) $c' = 0$;

(2) $(u \pm v)' = u' \pm v'$;

(3) $(cu)' = cu'$;

(4) $(uv)' = u'v + uv'$, the product rule;

(5) $\left(\dfrac{u}{v}\right)' = \dfrac{u'v - uv'}{v^2}$ $(v \neq 0)$, the quotient rule.

Here $c =$ const, and u and v are functions of x which have derivatives at a corresponding point.

(6) If the function $u = \varphi(x)$ is differentiable at the point x_0, and the function $y = f(u)$ is differentiable at the point $u_0 = \varphi(x_0)$, then the composite function $y = f(\varphi(x))$ is differentiable at the point x_0 and $y'_x(x_0) = y'_u(u_0)u'_x(x_0)$, the function of a function, or chain, rule.

II. Differentiation of Basic Elementary Functions

(1) $(u^n)' = nu^{n-1}u'$; (2) $(\sin u)' = \cos u \cdot u'$;

(3) $(\cos u)' = -\sin u \cdot u'$;

(4) $(\tan u)' = \dfrac{u'}{\cos^2 u}$; (5) $(\cot u)' = -\dfrac{u'}{\sin^2 u}$;

(6) $(\ln u)' = \dfrac{u'}{u}$;

(7) $(a^u)' = a^u \ln a \cdot u'$; (8) $(e^u)' = e^u u'$;

(9) $(\sinh u)' = \cosh u \cdot u'$;

(10) $(\cosh u)' = \sinh u \cdot u'$;

(11) $(\text{arc} \sin u)' = \dfrac{u'}{\sqrt{1-u^2}} = -(\text{arc} \cos u)'$;

(12) $(\text{arc} \tan u)' = \dfrac{u'}{1+u^2} = -(\text{arc} \cot u)'$.

2.2.1. Find y', if :

(a) $y = 5x^{2/3} - 3x^{5/2} + 2x^{-3}$; (b) $y = \dfrac{a}{\sqrt[3]{x^2}} - \dfrac{b}{x\sqrt[3]{x}}$ (a, b constants).

Solution (a) $y' = 5 \cdot \dfrac{2}{3} x^{2/3-1} - 3 \cdot \dfrac{5}{2} x^{5/2-1} - 2 \cdot 3x^{-3-1} = \dfrac{10}{3\sqrt[3]{x}}$

$$-\frac{15}{2} x\sqrt{x} - \frac{6}{x^4}.$$

2.2.2. Find y', if :

(a) $y = 3\cos x + 2\sin x$; (b) $y = \dfrac{\sin x + \cos x}{\sin x - \cos x}$;

(c) $y = (x^2 + 1) \text{ arc} \tan x$; (d) $y = x^3 \text{arc} \sin x$.

Solution (a) $y' = 3(\cos x)' + 2(\sin x)' = -3\sin x + 2\cos x$;

(b) $y' = \dfrac{(\sin x + \cos x)'(\sin x - \cos x) - (\sin x - \cos x)'(\sin x + \cos x)}{(\sin x - \cos x)^2}$

$$= \frac{(\cos x - \sin x)(\sin x - \cos x) - (\cos x + \sin x)(\sin x + \cos x)}{(\sin x - \cos x)^2}$$

$$= -\frac{2}{(\sin x - \cos x)^2};$$

(d) $y' = (x^3)' \text{arc} \sin x + (\text{arc} \sin x)' x^3 = 3x^2 \text{ arc} \sin x + \dfrac{x^3}{\sqrt{1-x^2}}$.

2.2.3. Find the derivative of the given function and then compute the particular value of the derivative at the indicated value of the argument :

(a) $f(x) = 1 - \sqrt[3]{x^2} + 16/x$ at $x = -8$;

(b) $f(x) = (1 - \sqrt{x})^2/x$ at $x = 0.01$;

(c) $f(t) = (\cot t)/(1 - \sin t)$ at $t = \dfrac{\pi}{6}$.

Solution (a) $f'(x) = -\frac{2}{3}x^{-1/3} - 16x^{-2} = -\frac{2}{3\sqrt[3]{x}} - \frac{16}{x^2}.$

Putting $x = -8$, we obtain

$$f'(-8) = -\frac{2}{3\sqrt[3]{-8}} - \frac{16}{(-8)^2} = \frac{1}{12};$$

(c) $f'(t) = \frac{-\sin t\,(1 - \sin t) + \cos^2 t}{(1 - \sin t)^2} = \frac{1}{1 - \sin t}.$

Whence $f'(\pi/6) = 2$.

2.2.4. Taking advantage of the differentiation formulas, find the derivatives of the following functions :

(a) $y = 2x^3 + 3x - 5;$ (b) $y = \sqrt{x} + \frac{1}{\sqrt{x}} + 0.1x^{10};$

(c) $y = \frac{2x^2 + x + 1}{x^2 - x + 1};$ (d) $y = \frac{x + \sqrt{x}}{x - 2\sqrt[3]{x}};$

(e) $y = \frac{\cos\varphi + \sin\varphi}{1 - \cos\phi};$ (f) $y = 2e^x + \ln x;$

(g) $y = e^x(\cos x + \sin x);$ (h) $y = \frac{e^x + \sin x}{xe^x}.$

2.2.5. Taking advantage of the rule for differentiation of a composite function find the derivatives of the following function :

(a) $y = \sin^3 x;$ (b) $y = \ln\tan x;$

(c) $y = 5^{\cos x};$ (d) $f = \ln\sin(x^3 + 1);$

(e) $y = \arcsin\sqrt{1 - x^2};$ (f) $y = \ln^5(\tan 3x);$

(g) $y = \sin^2\sqrt{1/(1 - x)}.$

Solution (a) Here the role of the external function is played by the power function : sin x is raised to the third power. Differentiating this power function with respect to the intermediate argument (sin x), we obtain

$$(\sin^3 x)_{\sin x} = 3\sin^2 x;$$

but the intermediate argument sin x is a function of an independent variable x; therefore we have to multiply the obtained result by the derivative of sin x with respect to the independent variable x. Thus, we obtain

$$y'_x = (\sin^3 x)_{\sin x}(\sin x)'_x = 3\sin^2 x\cos x;$$

(b) $y'_x = (\ln\tan x)_{\tan x}(\tan x)'_x = \frac{1}{\tan x\cos^2 x} = \frac{2}{\sin 2x};$

(c) $y'_x = (5^{\cos x})'_{\cos x}(\cos x)'_x = 5^{\cos x}\ln 5\,(-\sin x) = -5^{\cos x}\sin x\ln 5;$

(d) $y'_x = [\ln\sin(x^3 + 1)]_{\sin(x^3+1)}[\sin(x^3 + 1)]_{x^3+1}[x^3 + 1]'_x$

$$= \frac{1}{\sin(x^3 + 1)}\cdot\cos(x^3 + 1)\cdot 3x^2 = 3x^2\cot(x^3 + 1);$$

(e) $y'_x = (\arc \sin \sqrt{1-x^2})'_{\sqrt{1-x^2}} (\sqrt{1-x^2})'_{1-x^2} (1-x^2)'_x$

$$= \frac{1}{\sqrt{1-(1-x^2)}} \cdot \frac{1}{2\sqrt{1-x^2}} \cdot (-2x) = -\frac{x}{|x|\sqrt{1-x^2}} \quad (x \neq 0).$$

2.2.6. Find the derivatives of the following functions :

(a) $y = (1 + 3x + 5x^2)^4$; (b) $y = (3 - \sin x)^3$;

(c) $y = \sqrt[3]{\sin^2 x + 1/\cos^2 x}$; (d) $y = \sqrt[3]{2e^x + 2^x + 1 + \ln^5 x}$;

(e) $y = \sin 3x + \cos (x/5) + \tan \sqrt{x}$; (f) $y = \sin (x^2 - 5x + 1) + \tan (a/x)$;

(g) $y = \arc \cos \sqrt{x}$; (h) $y = \arc \tan (\ln x) + \ln (\arc \tan x)$;

(i) $y = \ln^2 \arc \tan (x/3)$; (j) $y = \sqrt{x + \sqrt{x + \sqrt{x}}}$.

Solution (a) $y' = 4(1 + 3x + 5x^2)^3 (1 + 3x + 5x^2)'$

$$= 4(1 + 3x + 5x^2)^3 (3 + 10x);$$

(g) $$y' = -\frac{1}{\sqrt{1-(\sqrt{x})^2}} (\sqrt{x})' = -\frac{1}{\sqrt{1-x}} \frac{1}{2\sqrt{x}} = -\frac{1}{2\sqrt{x(1-x)}};$$

(j) $$y' = \frac{1}{2\sqrt{x + \sqrt{x + \sqrt{x}}}} \left[1 + \frac{1}{2\sqrt{x + \sqrt{x}}} \left(1 + \frac{1}{2\sqrt{x}}\right)\right].$$

2.2.7. Find the derivative of the function

$$y = \arc \sin \frac{2x}{1 + x^2}.$$

We have

$$y' = \frac{1}{\sqrt{1 - \left(\frac{2x}{1+x^2}\right)^2}} \frac{2(1+x^2) - 4x^2}{(1+x^2)^2}$$

$$= \frac{2(1-x^2)}{\sqrt{(1-x^2)^2}\,(1+x^2)} = \frac{2(1-x^2)}{|1-x^2|(1+x^2)},$$

ie, $$y' = \begin{cases} \dfrac{2}{1+x^2} & \text{at } |x| < 1, \\ -\dfrac{2}{1+x^2} & \text{at } |x| > 1, \end{cases}$$

At $|x| = 1$ the derivative is non-existent.

2.2.8. Find the derivatives of the following functions :

(a) $y = \sinh 5x \cosh (x/3)$;

(b) $y = \coth (\tan x) - \tanh (\cot x)$;

(c) $y = \arc \cos (\tanh x) + \sinh (\sin 6x)$;

(d) $y = \sinh^2 x^3 + \cosh^3 x^2$;

(e) $$y = \frac{e^{\sinh ax}}{\sinh bx - \cosh bx}.$$

Solution $y' = (\sinh 5x)' \cosh \frac{x}{3} + \sinh 5x \left(\cosh \frac{x}{3}\right)'$

$$= 5 \cosh 5x \cosh \frac{x}{3} + \frac{1}{3} \sinh 5x \sinh \frac{x}{3};$$

(c) $y' = -\frac{(\tanh x)'}{\sqrt{1 - \tanh^2 x}} + \cosh(\sin 6x)(\sin 6x)'$

$$= -\frac{1/\cosh^2 x}{\sqrt{(\cosh^2 x - \sinh^2 x)/\cosh^2 x}}$$

$$+ 6 \cos 6x \cos\text{h} (\sin 6x) = -\frac{1}{\cosh x} + 6 \cos 6x \cosh(\sin 6x).$$

2.2.9. Find the derivatives of the following functions :

(a) $y = \sqrt[3]{\frac{x^3(x^2+1)}{\sqrt[5]{5-x}}}$; (b) $y = [u(x)]^{v(x)} (u(x) > 0)$;

(c) $y = \sqrt[3]{x^2} \frac{1-x}{1+x^2} \sin^3 x \cos^2 x$; (d) $y = (\sqrt{\tan x})^{x+1}$.

Solution (a) Apply the method of logarithmic differentiation. Consider, instead of y, the function

$$z = \ln|y| = \ln \sqrt[3]{\frac{|x^3|(x^2+1)}{\sqrt[5]{|5-x|}}} = \ln|x| + \frac{1}{3} \ln(x^2+1) - \frac{1}{15} \ln|5-x|\cdot$$

Taking into account that $(\ln|u|)' = u'/u$, we have

$$z' = \frac{1}{x} + \frac{2x}{3(x^2+1)} + \frac{1}{15(5-x)} = \frac{-24x^3 + 125x^2 - 14x + 75}{15x(x^2+1)(5-x)}.$$

But $z' = (\ln|y|)' = y'/y$, whence

$$y' = yz' = \sqrt[3]{\frac{x^3(x^2+1)}{\sqrt[5]{5-x}}} \cdot \frac{-24x^3 + 125x^2 - 14x + 75}{15x(x^2+1)(5-x)}.$$

(b) Suppose the functions $u(x)$ and $v(x)$ have derivatives in the given domain of definition. Then the function

$$z = \ln y = v \ln u$$

also has a derivative in this domain, and

$$z' = (v \ln u)' = v' \ln u + v \frac{u'}{u}.$$

Hence, the function

$$y = e^{\ln y} = e^x$$

also has a derivative in the indicated domain, and

$$y' = e^z z' = yz'.$$

Thus, $y' = u^v \left(v' \ln u + v \frac{u'}{u}\right) = vu^{v-1}u' + u^v \ln v \cdot v'.$

2.2.10. Show that the function $y = xe^{-x^2/2}$ satisfies the equation

$$xy' = (1 - x^2)\, y.$$

Solution $y' = e^{-x^2/2} - x^{2^{-x^2/2}} = e^{x^2/2}(1 - x^2);$

$$xy' = xe^{-x^2/2}(1 - x^2).$$

Hence, $\quad xy' = y(1 - x^2).$

2.2.11. Show that the function $y = xe^{-x}$ satisfies the equation $xy' = (1 - x)\, y$.

2.2.12. Investigate the following functions for differentiability :

(a) $y = arc \sin(\cos x)$; (b) $y = \sqrt{1 - \sqrt{1 - x^2}}$.

Solution (a) $y' = \dfrac{(\cos x)'}{\sqrt{1 - \cos^2 x}} = -\dfrac{\sin x}{\sqrt{\sin^2 x}} = -\dfrac{\sin x}{|\sin x|}$.

Hence, $y' = -1$ at points where $\sin x > 0$; $y' = 1$ at points where $\sin x < 0$. At points where $\sin x = 0$, *ie*, at the points $x = k\pi$ $(k = 0, \pm 1, \pm 2, \ldots)$ the function, though continuous, is not differentiable.

(b) The domain of definition of this function is the interval $-1 \le x \le 1$.

$$y' = \frac{1}{2\sqrt{1 - \sqrt{1 - x^2}}} \cdot \frac{-1}{2\sqrt{1 - x^2}}(-2x)$$

at $\quad x \ne 0 \;$ and $\; x \ne \pm 1.$

As $x \to 1 - 0$ or $x \to -1 + 0$ we have $y' \to +\infty$. Let us find out whether the derivative y' exists at the point $x = 0$, *ie*, whether $\lim\limits_{\Delta x \to 0} \dfrac{\sqrt{1 - \sqrt{1 - \Delta x^2}}}{\Delta x}$ exists.

Since $\sqrt{1 - \Delta x^2} - 1 \sim -\dfrac{1}{2}\Delta x^2$, then

$$\lim_{\Delta x \to 0} \frac{\sqrt{1 - \sqrt{1 - \Delta x^2}}}{\Delta x} = \lim_{\Delta x \to 0} \frac{\sqrt{\frac{1}{2}\Delta x^2}}{\Delta x} = \begin{cases} \dfrac{1}{\sqrt{2}} & \text{as } \Delta x \to +0 \\[2ex] -\dfrac{1}{\sqrt{2}} & \text{as } \Delta x \to -0 \end{cases}$$

Thus, $y'_-(0) \ne y'_+(0)$, which means that the function under consideration has no derivative at the point $x = 0$, though it is continuous at this point.

Note. There are cases of failure of existence of $f'(x)$ and even of $f'_+(x)$ and $f'_-(x)$ at a given point, *ie*, when the graph of the function has neither a right-side, nor a left-side tangent at the given point. For instance, the function

$$f(x) = \begin{cases} x \sin\left(\dfrac{1}{x}\right) & \text{at } x \ne 0, \\ 0 & \text{at } x = 0 \end{cases}$$

is continuous at the point $x = 0$, but does not have even one-sided derivatives, since $\dfrac{\Delta f(x)}{\Delta x} = \sin \dfrac{1}{\Delta x}$.

2.2.13. Find the derivatives of the following functions :

(a) $f(x) = \sinh\left(\frac{x}{2}\right) + \cosh\left(\frac{x}{2}\right)$;

(b) $f(x) = \ln[\cosh x]$; (c) $f(x) = 2\sqrt{\cosh x - 1}$;

(d) $f(x) = \arcsin[\tanh x]$;

(e) $f(x) = \sqrt{1 + \sinh^2 4x}$;

(f) $f(x) = e^{ax}(\cosh bx + \sinh bx)$.

2.2.14. Applying logrithmic differentiation find the derivatives of the following functions :

(a) $y = (\cos x)^{\sin x}$; (b) $y = \sqrt[3]{\frac{\sin 3x}{1 - \sin 3x}}$;

(c) $y = \frac{\sqrt{x-1}}{\sqrt[3]{(x+2)^2}\sqrt{(x+3)^3}}$.

2.2.15. $f(x) = \frac{\cos^2 x}{1 + \sin^2 x}$;

show that

$$f\left(\frac{\pi}{4}\right) - 3f'\left(\frac{\pi}{4}\right) = 3$$

2.2.16. Show that the function

$$y = \frac{x - e^{-x^2}}{2x^2}$$

satisfies the differential equation

$$xy' + 2y = e^{-x^2}.$$

2.2.17. Find the derivatives of the following functions :

(a) $y = \ln\cos\sqrt{\arcsin 3^{-2x}}$ $(x > 0)$;

(b) $y = \sqrt[3]{\arctan\sqrt[5]{\cos\ln^3 x}}$.

2.3. Successive Differentiation of Explicit Functions. Leibnitz Formula

If the derivative of the $(n-1)$th order of a function $y = f(x)$ is already found, then the derivative of the nth order is determined by the equality

$$y^{(n)}(x) = [y^{(n-1)}(x)]'.$$

In particular, $y''(x) = [y'(x)]'$, $y'''(x) = [y''(x)]'$, and so on.

If u and v are functions differentiable n times, then for their linear combination $c_1u + c_2v$ (c_1, c_2 constants) we have the following formula :

$$(c_1u + c_2v)^{(n)} = c_1u^{(n)} + c_2v^{(n)}$$

and for their product uv the Leibnitz formula (or rule)

$$(uv)^{(n)} = u^{(n)}v + nu^{(n-1)}v' + \frac{n(n-1)}{1\cdot 2}u^{(n-2)}v^{n} + \ldots + uv^{(n)} = \sum_{k=0}^{n} C_n^k\, u^{(n-k)}v^{(k)},$$

where $u^{(0)} = u, v^{(0)} = v$ and $C_n^k = \dfrac{n(n-1)\ldots(n-k+1)}{1\cdot 2\cdot 3\ldots k} = \dfrac{n!}{k!(n-k)!}$ are binomial coefficients. Here are the basic formulas :

(1) $(x^m)^{(n)} = m(m-1)\ldots(m-n+1)\,x^{m-n}$.

(2) $(a^x)^{(n)} = a^x \ln^n a\ (a>0)$. In particular, $(e^x)^{(n)} = e^x$.

(3) $(\ln x)^{(n)} = (-1)^{n-1}\dfrac{(n-1)!}{x^n}$.

(4) $(\sin x)^{(n)} = \sin\left(x + \dfrac{n\pi}{2}\right)$.

(5) $(\cos x)^{(n)} = \cos\left(x + \dfrac{n\pi}{2}\right)$.

2.3.1. Find the derivatives of the nth order of the following functions :

(a) $y = \ln x$; (b) $y = e^{kx}$;

(c) $y = \sin x$; (d) $y = \sin 5x \cos 2x$;

(e) $y = \sin x \cos x$; (f) $y = \sin 3x \cos^2 x$;

(g) $y = \ln(x^2 + x - 2)$.

Solution (a) $y' = \dfrac{1}{x} = x^{-1}; y'' = (-1)\,x^{-2}; y'' = 1\cdot 2x^{-3}$;

$$y^{(4)} = -1\cdot 2\cdot 3x^{-4};\ldots; y^{(n)} = (-1)^{n-1}(n-1)!\,x^{-n} = \frac{(-1)^{n-1}(n-1)!}{x^n}.$$

(c) $y' = \cos x = \sin\left(x + \dfrac{\pi}{2}\right)$;

$$y'' = \cos\left(x + \frac{\pi}{2}\right) = \sin\left(x + \frac{2\pi}{2}\right)$$

In general, if we assume that for a given $n = k$

$$y^{(k)} = \sin\left(x + k\frac{\pi}{2}\right),$$

then it will turn out that

$$y^{(k+1)} = \cos\left(x + k\frac{\pi}{2}\right) = \sin\left[(k+1)\frac{\pi}{2} + x\right].$$

Whence, by virtue of mathematical induction we conclude that for any natural n

$$y^{(n)} = \sin\left(x + n\frac{\pi}{2}\right).$$

(d) $y = \sin 5x \cos 2x = \frac{1}{2}[\sin 7x + \sin 3x]$.

Therefore

$$y^{(n)} = \frac{1}{2}\left[7^n \sin\left(7x + n\frac{\pi}{2}\right) + 3^n \sin\left(3x + n\frac{\pi}{2}\right)\right].$$

(g) $y' = \frac{2x+1}{x^2 + x - 2}$.

To simplify the computations let us transform the obtained function :

$$y' = \frac{2x+1}{x^2+x-2} = \frac{(x+2)+(x-1)}{(x-1)(x+2)} = \frac{1}{x-1} + \frac{1}{x+2} = (x-1)^{-1} + (x+2)^{-1}.$$

Whence

$$y'' = -1\,(x-1)^{-2} - 1\,(x+2)^{-2};$$

$$y''' = 1\cdot 2\,(x-1)^{-3} + 1\cdot 2\,(x+2)^{-3};$$

....

$$y^{(n)} = (-1)^{n-1}(n-1)!\,[(x-1)^{-n} + (x+2)^{-n}]$$

$$= (-1)^{n-1}(n-1)!\left[\frac{1}{(x-1)^n} + \frac{1}{(x+2)^n}\right].$$

2.3.2. $y = \frac{ax+b}{cx+d}$; find $y^{(n)}$.

Solution Transform the given expression in the following way:

$$y = \frac{ax+b}{cx+d} = \frac{a}{c} + \frac{bc-ad}{c\,(cx+d)} = \frac{a}{c} + \frac{bc-ad}{c}(cx+d)^{-1}.$$

Whence

$$y' = (-1)\frac{bc-ad}{c}\,c\,(cx+d)^{-2},$$

$$y'' = (-1)(-2)\frac{bc-ad}{c}\,c^2\,(cx+d)^{-3},$$

$$y''' = (-1)(-2)(-3)\frac{bc-ad}{c}\,c^3\,(cx+d)^{-4},$$

....

$$y^{(n)} = (-1)^n n!\frac{bc-ad}{c}c^n(cx+d)^{-(n+1)}$$

$$= (-1)^n\frac{n!\,c^{n-1}}{(cx+d)^{n+1}}(bc-ad).$$

2.3.3. $y = \frac{x}{(x^2-1)}$; find $y^{(n)}$.

Solution Transform the given expression

$$y = \frac{x}{x^2 - 1} = \frac{1}{2}\left[\frac{1}{x+1} + \frac{1}{x-1}\right],$$

therefore (see Problem **2.3.2**) :

$$y^{(n)} = \frac{(-1)^n\, n!}{2}\left[\frac{1}{(x+1)^{n+1}} + \frac{1}{(x-1)^{n+1}}\right].$$

2.3.4. Using the Leibnitz formula, find the derivatives of the indicated orders for the following functions :

(a) $y = x^2 \sin x$; find $y^{(25)}$;

(b) $y = e^x (x^2 - 1)$; find $y^{(24)}$;

(c) $y = e^{\alpha x} \sin \beta\, x$; find $y^{(n)}$.

Solution (a) $y^{(25)} = (\sin x \cdot x^2)^{(25)} = (\sin x)^{(25)} x^2 + 25 (\sin x)^{(24)} (x^2)'$ $+ \dfrac{25 \cdot 24}{2} (\sin x)^{23} (x^2)^n$, since the subsequent summands equal zero. Therefore

$$y^{(25)} = x^2 \sin\left(x + 25\,\frac{\pi}{2}\right) + 50\, x \sin\left(x + 24\,\frac{\pi}{2}\right) + 600 \sin\left(x + 23\,\frac{\pi}{2}\right)$$

$$= (x^2 - 600) \cos x + 50\, x \sin x.$$

2.3.5. Compute the value of the *n*th derivative of the function $y = \dfrac{3x + 2}{x^2 - 2x + 5}$ at the point $x = 0$.

Solution By hypothesis we have $y(x)(x^2 - 2x + 5) = 3x + 2$. Let us differentiate this identity *n* times using the Leibnitz formula; then (for $n \geq 2$) we obtain

$$y^n (x) (x^2 - 2x + 5) + ny^{(n-1)} (x) (2x - 2) + \frac{n(n-1)}{2}\, y^{(n-2)}(x) \cdot 2 = 0$$

Putting $x = 0$, we get

$$5y^{(n)}(0) - 2ny^{(n-1)}(0) + n(n-1)\, y^{(n-2)}(0) = 0$$

Whence

$$y^{(n)}(0) = \frac{2}{5}\, ny^{(n-1)}(0) - \frac{n(n-1)}{5}\, y^{(n-2)}(0).$$

We have obtained a recurrence relation for determining the *n*th derivative at the point $x = 0$ $(n \geq 2)$. The values $y(0)$ and $y'(0)$ are found immediately : $y(0) = \dfrac{2}{5}$;

$$y'(x) = \frac{-3x^2 - 4x + 19}{(x^2 - 2x + 5)^2}; \qquad y'(0) = \frac{19}{25}.$$

Then, successively putting $n = 2, 3, 4, \ldots$, find the values of the derivatives of higher orders with the aid of the recurrence relation.

For example,

$$y''(0) = \frac{2}{5} \cdot 2 \cdot \frac{19}{25} - \frac{2 \cdot 1}{5} \cdot \frac{2}{5} = \frac{56}{125},$$

$$y'''(0) = \frac{2}{5} \cdot 3 \cdot \frac{56}{125} - \frac{3 \cdot 2}{5} \cdot \frac{19}{25} = -\frac{234}{625}.$$

2.3.6. Find the derivatives of the second order of the following functions :

(a) $y = x\sqrt{1 + x^2}$; (b) $y = \dfrac{\arcsin x}{\sqrt{1 - x^2}}$;

(c) $y = e^{-x^2}$.

2.3.7. Given the function

$$y = C_1 e^{2x} + C_2 x e^{2x} + e^x.$$

Show that this function satisfies the equation

$$y'' - 4y' + 4y = e^x$$

2.3.8. Using the Leibnitz formula give the derivatives of the indicated orders for the following functions :

(a) $y = x^3 \sin x$; find $y^{(20)}$;

(b) $y = e^{-x} \sin x$; find y''';

(c) $y = e^x (3x^2 - 4)$; find $y^{(n)}$;

(d) $y = (1 - x^2) \cos x$; find $y^{(2n)}$.

2.3.9. Using the expansion into a linear combination of simpler functions find the derivatives of the 100th order of the functions :

(a) $y = \dfrac{1}{x^2 - 3x + 2}$; (b) $y = \dfrac{1 + x}{\sqrt{1 - x}}$.

2.3.10. Show that the function

$$y = x^n [C_1 \cos(\ln x) + C_2 \sin(\ln x)]$$

(C_1, C_2, n constants) satisfies the equation

$$x^2 y'' + (1 - 2n) xy' + (1 + n^2) y = 0.$$

2.3.11. Prove that if $f(x)$ has a derivative of the nth order, then

$$[f(ax + b)]^{(n)} = a^n f^{(n)}(ax + b).$$

2.4. Differentiation of Inverse, Implicit and Parametrically Represented Functions

1. The Derivative of an Inverse Function. If a differentiable function $y = f(x)$, $a < x < b$ has a single-valued continuous inverse function $x = g(y)$ and $y'_x \neq 0$, then there exists also

$$x'_y = \frac{1}{y'_x}.$$

For the derivative of the second order we have

$$x''_{yy} = -\frac{y''_{xx}}{(y'_x)^3}.$$

2. The Derivative of an Implicit Function. If a differentiable function $y = y(x)$ satisfies the equation $F(x, y) = 0$, then we have to differentiate it with respect to x, considering y as a function of x, and solve the obtained equation $\frac{d}{dx}F(x, y) = 0$ with respect to y'_x. To find y''_x, the equation shoud be twice differentiated with respect to x, and so on.

3. The Derivative of a Function Represented Parametrically. If the system of equations

$$x = \varphi(t), \qquad y = \psi(t), \qquad \alpha < t < \beta,$$

where $\varphi(t)$ and $\psi(t)$ are differentiable functions and $\varphi'(t) \neq 0$, defines y as a single-valued continuous function of x, then there exists a derivative y'_x and

$$y'_x = \frac{\psi'_t(t)}{\varphi'_t(t)} = \frac{y'_t}{x'_t}$$

The derivatives of higher orders are computed successively :

$$y''_{xx} = \frac{(y'_x)'_t}{x'_t}; \qquad y'''_{xxx} = \frac{(y''_{xx})'_t}{x'_t}, \text{ and so on}$$

In particular, for the second derivative the following formula is true :

$$y''_{xx} = \frac{x'_t\, y''_{tt} - x''_{tt}\, y'_t}{(x'_t)^3}.$$

2.4.1. For the function :

(a) $y = 2x^3 + 3x^5 + x;$ find $x'_y;$

(b) $y = 3x - \frac{(\cos x)}{2};$ find $x''_{yy};$

(c) $y = x + e^x;$ find $x''_{yy}.$

Solution (a) We have $y'_x = 6x^2 + 15x^4 + 1$, hence

$$x'_y = \frac{1}{y'_x} = \frac{1}{6x^2 + 15x^4 + 1}.$$

(c) $y'_x = 1 + e^x$, $y''_{xx} = e^x$, hence

$$x'_y = \frac{1}{1 + e^x}, \; x''_{yy} = -\frac{e^x}{(1 + e^x)^3}.$$

2.4.2. Using the rule for differentiation of an inverse function, find the derivative y'_x for the following functions :

(a) $y = \sqrt[3]{x};$ (b) $y = \text{arc sin}\sqrt{x};$

(c) $y = \ln\sqrt{1 + x^2}.$

Solution (a) The inverse function $x = y^3$ has the derivative $x'_y = 3y^2$.

Hence,

$$y'_x = \frac{1}{x'_y} = \frac{1}{3y^2} = \frac{1}{3\sqrt[3]{x^2}}$$

(c) At $x > 0$ the inverse function $x = \sqrt{e^{2y} - 1}$ has the derivative $x'_y = \frac{e^{2y}}{\sqrt{e^{2y} - 1}}$. Hence

$$y'_x = \frac{1}{x'_y} = \frac{\sqrt{e^{2y} - 1}}{e^{2y}} = \frac{\sqrt{x^2}}{x^2 + 1} = \frac{x}{x^2 + 1}.$$

2.4.3. For each of the following functions represented parametrically find the derivative of the first order of y with respect to x :

(a) $x = a(t - \sin t)$, $\quad y = a(1 - \cos t)$;
(b) $x = k \sin t - \sin kt$, $\quad y = k \cos t + \cos kt$;
(c) $x = 2 \ln \cot t$, $\quad y = \tan t + \cot t$;
(d) $x = e^{ct}$, $\quad y = e^{-ct}$.

Solution (a) Find the derivatives of x and y with respect to the parameter t :

$$x'_t = a(1 - \cos t); \qquad y'_t = a \sin t.$$

Whence $\quad \dfrac{dy}{dx} = \dfrac{a \sin t}{a(1 - \cos t)} = \cot \dfrac{t}{2} \; (t \neq 2k\pi).$

(c) $\dfrac{dx}{dt} = \dfrac{-2 \operatorname{cosec}^2 t}{\cot t} = -\dfrac{4}{\sin 2t}$;

$$\frac{dy}{dt} = \sec^2 t - \operatorname{cosec}^2 t = -\frac{4 \cos 2t}{\sin^2 2t};$$

$$\frac{dy}{dx} = \frac{4 \cos 2t \sin 2t}{4 \sin^2 2t} = \cot 2t \left(t \neq \frac{k\pi}{2}\right).$$

2.4.4. The functions are defined parametrically.

(a) $\begin{cases} x = a \cos^3 t, \\ y = b \sin^3 t; \end{cases}$ $\qquad$ (b) $\begin{cases} x = t^3 + 3t + 1, \\ y = t^3 - 3t + 1; \end{cases}$

(c) $\begin{cases} x = a(\cos t + t \sin t), \\ y = a(\sin t - t \cos t); \end{cases}$ $\qquad$ (d) $\begin{cases} x = e^t \cos t, \\ y = e^t \sin t. \end{cases}$

Find for them the second derivative of y with respect to x.

Solution (a) First find y'_x,

$$y'_t = 3b \sin^2 t \cos t; \quad x'_t = -3a \cos^2 t \sin t;$$

$$y'_t = -\frac{3b \sin^2 t \cos t}{3a \cos^2 t \sin t} = -\frac{b}{a} \tan t \left(t \neq (2k + 1)\frac{\pi}{2}\right).$$

Then we shall find y''_{xx} using the formula

$$y''_{xx} = \frac{(y'_x)'_t}{x'_t};$$

where $(y'_x)'_t = -\dfrac{b}{a\cos^2 t}$.

whence $$y''_{xx} = -\frac{b}{a\cos^2 t\,(-3a\cos^2 t\sin t)} = \frac{b}{3a^2\cos^4 t\sin t}.$$

(d) $$x'_t = e^t\cos t - e^t\sin t = e^t(\cos t - \sin t);$$

$$y'_t = e^t\sin t + e^t\cos t = e^t(\cos t + \sin t);$$

$$y'_x = \frac{\cos t + \sin t}{\cos t - \sin t};$$

$$y''_{xx} = \frac{(y'_x)'_t}{x'_t} = \frac{\left(\dfrac{\cos t + \sin t}{\cos t - \sin t}\right)'}{e^t(\cos t - \sin t)}$$

$$= \frac{2}{e^t(\cos t - \sin t)^3}.$$

2.4.5. Find y'''_{xxx} :

(a) $x = e^{-t}; y = t^3;$ (b) $x = \sec t; y = \tan t.$

Solution (a) First find

$$x'_t = -e^{-t};\ y'_t = 3t^2,$$

whence $$y'_x = -\frac{3t^2}{e^{-t}} = -3e^t t^2.$$

Then find the second derivative

$$y''_{xx} = \frac{(y'_x)'_t}{x'_t} = \frac{-(3e^t t^2 + 6te^t)}{-e^{-t}} = 3\,te^{2t}(t+2).$$

And finally, find the third derivative

$$y''_{xxx} = \frac{(y''_{xx})'_t}{x'_t} = \frac{3e^{2t}\,[2(t^2+2t) + 2t + 2]}{-e^{-t}}$$

$$= -6e^{3t}(t^2 + 3t + 1).$$

2.4.6. Find the derivative y'_x of the following implicit functions :

(a) $x^3 + x^2y + y^2 = 0;$

(b) $\ln x + e^{-y/x} = c;$

(c) $x^2 + y^2 - 4x - 10y + 4 = 0;$

(d) $x^{2/3} + y^{2/3} = a^{2/3}.$

Solution (a) Differentiate with respect to x, considering y as a function of x; we get :

$$3x^2 + 2xy + x^2y' + 2yy' = 0.$$

Solving this equation with respect to y' find

$$y' = -\frac{3x^2 + 2xy}{x^2 + 2y}.$$

2.4.7. Find y''_{xx} if :

(a) $\text{arc tan } y - y + x = 0$;

(b) $e^x - e^y = y - x$;

(c) $x + y = e^{x-y}$.

Solution (a) Differentiate with respect to x, considering y as a function of x and determine y' :

$$\frac{y'}{1+y^2} - y' + 1 = 0,$$

Whence $$y' = \frac{1+y^2}{y^2} = y^{-2} + 1.$$

Differentiate once again with respect to x :

$$y'' = -2y^{-3}y'$$

Substituting the value of y' thus found, we finally get

$$y''_{xx} = -\frac{2(1+y^2)}{y^3}.$$

2.4.8. Find the value of y'' at the point $x = 1$ if

$$x^3 - 2x^2y^2 + 5x + y - 5 = 0 \quad \text{and } y|_{x=1} = 1.$$

Solution Differentiating with respect to x, we find that

$$3x^2 - 4xy^2 - 4x^2yy' + 5 + y' = 0$$

Putting $x = 1$ and $y = 1$, obtain the value of y' at $x = 1$;

$$3 - 4 - 4y' + 5 + y' = 0; \qquad y' = \frac{4}{3}.$$

Differentiate once again with respect to x :

$$6x - 4y^2 - 8xyy' - 8xyy' - 4x^2y'^2 - 4x^2yy'' + y'' = 0.$$

Putting $x = 1$; $y = 1$ and $y' = \frac{4}{3}$, find the value of y'' at $x = 1$:

$$6 - 4 - \frac{64}{3} - \frac{64}{9} - 3y'' = 0, \qquad y'' = -8\frac{22}{27}.$$

2.4.9. Find y'_x for the following implicit functions :

(a) $x + \sqrt{xy} + y = a$;

(b) $\text{arc tan}\left(\frac{y}{x}\right) = \ln\sqrt{x^2 + y^2}$;

(c) $e^x \sin y - e^{-y} \cos x = 0$;

(d) $e^y + xy = e$; find y'_x at the point (0, 1).

2.4.10. Find y''_{xx} of the following implicit functions :

(a) $y = x + \arctan y$;

(b) $x^2 + 5xy + y^2 - 2x + y - 6 = 0$; find y'' at the point (1, 1).

2.4.11. For each the following functions represented parametrically find the indicated derivatives :

(a) $x = \dfrac{a \sin t}{1 + b \cos t}$, $y = \dfrac{c \cos t}{1 + b \cos t}$; find y'_x;

(b) $x = \ln(1 + t^2)$, $y = t - \arctan t$; find y'_x ;

(c) $x = t^2 + 2$, $y = \dfrac{t^3}{3} - t$; find y''_{xx};

(d) $x = e^{-t^2}$, $y = \arctan(2t + 1)$; find y'_x;

(e) $x = 4 \tan^2\left(\dfrac{t}{2}\right)$, $y = a \sin t + b \cos t$; find y'_x ;

(f) $x = \arcsin(t^2 - 1)$, $y = \arccos 2t$; find y'_x;

(g) $x = \arcsin t$, $y = \sqrt{1 - t^2}$; find y''_{xx}.

2.4.12. Show that the function $y = f(x)$, defined by the parametric equations $x = e^t \sin t, y = e^t \cos t$, satisfies the relation $y''(x + y)^2 = 2(xy' - y)$.

2.5. Applications of the Derivative

The equation of the line tangent to the curve of a differentiable function $y = y(x)$ at a point $M(x_0, y_0)$, where $y_0 = y(x_0)$, has the form

$$y - y_0 = y'(x_0)(x - x_0).$$

A straight line passing through the point of contact perpendicularly to the tangent line is called the *normal to the curve.* The equation of the normal at the point M will be

$$y - y_0 = -\frac{1}{y'(x_0)}(x - x_0),$$

$$y'(x_0) \neq 0.$$

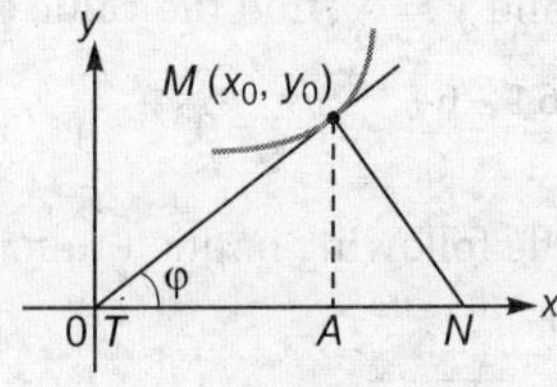

Fig. 36

The segments AT, AN are called the subtangent and the subnormal, respectively and the lengths MT and MN are the so-called segment of the tangent and the segment of the normal, respectively (see Fig. 36). The lengths of the four indicated segments are expressed by the following formulas :

$$AT = \left|\frac{y}{y'}\right|; \qquad AN = |yy'|; \qquad MT = \left|\frac{y}{y'}\right|\sqrt{1+(y')^2};$$

$$MN = |y|\sqrt{1+(y')^2};$$

2.5.1. Write the equations of the tangent line and the normal :

(a) to the curve $y = x^3 - 3x + 2$ at the point $(2, 4)$,

(b) to the parabola $y = 2x^2 - x + 5$ at $x = -0.5$;

(c) to the curve $y = x^4 + 3x^2 - 16$ at the points of intersection with the parabola $y = 3x^2$.

Solution (a) Find the derivative at the point $x = 2$:

$$y' = 3x^2 - 3, \qquad y'(2) = 9.$$

The equation of the tangent line has the following form :

$$y - 4 = 9(x - 2) \qquad \text{or} \qquad 9x - y - 14 = 0.$$

The equation of the normal is of the form :

$$y - 4 = -\frac{1}{9}(x - 2) \qquad \text{or} \qquad x + 9y - 38 = 0.$$

(c) Solving the system of equations

$$\begin{cases} y = x^3 + 3x^2 - 16, \\ y = 3x^2, \end{cases}$$

we shall find the points of intersection of the curves

$$x_1 = -2, \quad x_2 = 2, \quad y_1 = y_2 = 12.$$

Now we find the derivatives at the points $x = -2$ and $x = 2$: $y' = 4x^3 + 6x$, $y'(-2) = -44$, $y'(2) = 44$,

Therefore, the equations of the tangent lines have the form

$$y - 12 = -44(x + 2), \; y - 12 = 44(x - 2)$$

The equations of the normals have the form

$$y - 12 = \frac{1}{44}(x + 2), \quad y - 12 = -\frac{1}{44}(x - 2).$$

2.5.2. Find the points on the curve $y = x^3 - 3x + 5$ at which the tangent line :

(a) is parallel to the straight line $y = -2x$;

(b) is perpendicular to the straight line $y = -\dfrac{x}{9}$;

(c) forms an angle of 45° with the positive direction of the x-axis.

Solution To find the required points we take into consideration that at the point of tangency the slope of the tangent is equal to the derivative $y' = 3x^2 - 3$ computed at this point.

(a) By the condition of parallelism

$$3x^2 - 3 = -2,$$

whence $x_1 = -\frac{1}{\sqrt{3}}$, $x_2 = \frac{1}{\sqrt{3}}$. The required points are

$$M_1\left(-\frac{1}{\sqrt{3}}, 5+\frac{8\sqrt{3}}{9}\right),\quad M_2\left(\frac{1}{\sqrt{3}}, 5-\frac{8\sqrt{3}}{9}\right).$$

(b) By the condition of perpendicularity

$$3x^2 - 3 = 9,$$

whence $x_1 = -2$, $x_2 = 2$. The required points :

$$M_1\ (-2, 3),\quad M_2\ (2, 7).$$

2.5.3. Find the angles at which the following lines intersect :

(a) the straight line $y = 4 - x$ and the parabola $y = 4 - \frac{x^2}{2}$;

(b) the sinusoid $y = \sin x$ and the cosine curve $y = \cos x$.

Solution (a) Recall that the angles between two curves at the point of their intersection is defined as the angle formed by the lines tangent to these curves and drawn at this point. Find the points of intersection of the curves by solving the system of equations

$$\begin{cases} y = 4 - x, \\ y = 4 - \dfrac{x^2}{2}, \end{cases}$$

Whence $\qquad M_1\ (0, 4);\quad M_2\ (2, 2).$

Determine then the slopes of the lines tangent to the parabola at the points M_1 and M_2 :

$$y'(0) = 0,\qquad y'(2) = -2.$$

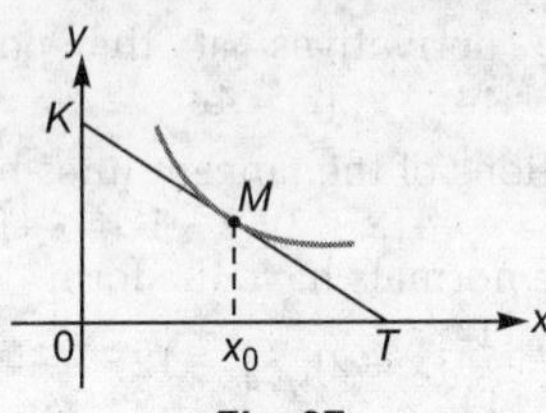

Fig. 37

The slope of a straight line is constant for all its points; in our case it equals −1. Finally, determine the angle between the two straight lines :

$$\tan\varphi_1 = 1;\qquad \varphi_1 = 45°;$$

$$\tan\varphi_2 = \frac{-1+2}{1+2} = \frac{1}{3};\qquad \varphi_2 = \text{arc tan}\,\frac{1}{3} \approx 18.5°.$$

2.5.4. Prove that the segment of the tangent to the hyperbola $y = \frac{c}{x}$ which is contained between the coordinate axes is bisected at the point of tangency.

Solution We have $y' = -\frac{c}{x^2}$; hence, the value of the subtangent for the tangent at the point $M(x_0, y_0)$ will be

$$\left|\frac{y}{y'}\right| = |x'_0|,$$

ie, $Ox_0 = x_0T$ (Fig. 37), which completes the proof.

Whence follows a simple method of constructing a tangent to the hyperbola $y = \frac{c}{x}$; lay off the x-intercept $OT = 2x_0$. Then MT will be the desired tangent.

2.5.5. Prove that the ordinate of the catenary $y = a\cosh\left(\frac{x}{a}\right)$ is the geometric mean of the length of the normal and the quantity a.

Solution Compute the length of the normal. Since

$$y' = \sinh\left(\frac{x}{a}\right)$$

the length of the normal will be

$$MN = |y|\sqrt{1 + (y')^2} = y\sqrt{1 + \sinh^2\left(\frac{x}{a}\right)} = y\cosh\left(\frac{x}{a}\right) = \frac{y^2}{a},$$

whence $y^2 = a \cdot MN$, and $y = \sqrt{a \cdot MN}$, which completes the proof.

2.5.6. Find the slope of the tangent to the curve,

$$\begin{cases} x = t^2 + 3t - 8, \\ y = 2t^2 - 2t - 5 \end{cases}$$

at the point $M(2, -1)$.

Solution First determine the value of t corresponding to the given values of x and y. This value must simultaneously satisfy the two equations.

$$\begin{cases} t^2 + 3t - 8 = 2 \\ 2t^2 - 2t - 5 = -1 \end{cases}.$$

The roots of the first equation are $t_1 = 2$; $t_2 = -5$, the roots of the second equation $t_1 = 2; t_2 = -1$. Hence, to the given point there corresponds the value $t = 2$. Now determine the value of the derivative at the point M:

$$y'|_{x=2} = \left(\frac{y'_t}{x'_t}\right)_{t=2} = \left(\frac{4t - 2}{2t + 3}\right)_{t=2} = \frac{6}{7}.$$

And so, the slope of the tangent at the point $M(2, -1)$ is equal to $\frac{6}{7}$.

2.5.7. Prove that the tangent to the lemniscate $\rho = a\sqrt{\cos 2\theta}$ at the point corresponding to the value $\theta_0 = \frac{\pi}{6}$ is parallel to the x-axis.

Solution Write in the parametric form the equation of the lemniscate :

$$x = \rho \cos \theta = a\sqrt{\cos 2\theta}\cos \theta,$$

$$y = \rho \sin \theta = a\sqrt{\cos 2\theta}\sin \theta.$$

Whence
$$x'_\theta = -\frac{a \cos \theta \sin 2\theta}{\sqrt{\cos 2\theta}} - a\sqrt{\cos 2\theta}\sin \theta,$$

$$y'_\theta = -\frac{a \sin \theta \sin 2\theta}{\sqrt{\cos 2\theta}} + a\sqrt{\cos 2\theta}\cos \theta,$$

$$x_\theta\left(\frac{\pi}{6}\right) = -a\sqrt{2}, \qquad y_\theta\left(\frac{\pi}{6}\right) = 0.$$

Thus, the slope $k = \dfrac{y'_\theta\left(\frac{\pi}{6}\right)}{x'_\theta\left(\frac{\pi}{6}\right)} = 0$. Consequently, the line tangent to the lemniscate at the point with $\theta_0 = \dfrac{\pi}{6}$ and $\rho_0 = a\sqrt{\cos 2\theta_0} = \dfrac{a}{\sqrt{2}}$ is parallel to the x-axis.

2.5.8. Find the equations of the tangent and the normal to the following curves :

(a) $4x^3 - 3xy^2 + 6x^2 - 5xy - 8y^2 + 9x + 14 = 0$ at the point $(-2, 3)$;

(b) $x^5 + y^5 - 2xy = 0$ at the point $(1, 1)$.

Solution (a) Differentiate the implicit function :

$$12x^2 - 3y^2 - 6xyy' + 12x - 5y - 5xy' - 16yy' + 9 = 0.$$

Substitute the coordinates of the point $M(-2, 3)$;

$$48 - 27 + 36y' - 24 - 15 + 10y' - 48y' + 9 = 0;$$

Whence
$$y' = -\frac{9}{2}.$$

Thus the equation of the tangent line is

$$y - 3 = -\frac{9}{2}(x + 2)$$

and the equation of the normal

$$y - 3 = \frac{2}{9}(x + 2).$$

2.5.9. Through the point $(2, 0)$, which does not belong to the curve $y = x^4$, draw tangents to the latter.

Solution Let (x_0, x_0^4) be the point of tangency; then the equation of tangent will be of the form :

$$y - x_0^4 = y'(x_0)(x - x_0)$$

$$y - x_0^4 = 4x_0^3(x - x_0).$$

By hypothesis the desired tangent line passes through the point (2, 0), hence the coordinates of this point satisfy the equation of the tangent line :

$$-x_0^4 = 4x_0^3(2 - x_0);\ 3x_0^4 - 8x_0^3 = 0,$$

whence $x_0 = 0;\ x_0 = \frac{8}{3}$. Thus, there are two points of tangency : $M_1\,(0, 0), M_2\left(\frac{8}{3}, \frac{4096}{81}\right)$.

Accordingly, the equations of the tangent lines will be

$$y = 0,\ y - \frac{4096}{81} = \frac{2048}{27}\left(x - \frac{8}{3}\right).$$

2.5.10. $f(x) = 3x^5 - 15x^3 + 5x - 7$. Find out at which of the points x the rate of change of the function is minimal.

Solution The rate of change of a function at a certain point is equal to the derivative of the function at this point

$$f'(x) = 15x^4 - 45x^2 + 5 = 15\left[\left(x^2 - \frac{1}{2}\right)^2 + \frac{1}{12}\right].$$

The minimum value of $f'(x)$ is attained at $x = \pm\frac{1}{\sqrt{2}}$. Hence, the minimum rate of change of the function $f(x)$ is at the point $x = \pm\frac{1}{\sqrt{2}}$ and equals $\frac{5}{4}$.

2.5.11. A point is in motion along a cubic parabola $12y = x^3$. Which of its coordinates changes faster ?

Solution Differentiating both members of the given equation with respect to t we get the relation between the rates of change of the coordinates :

$$12\,y_t' = 3x^2 \cdot x'_t$$

or

$$\frac{y'_t}{x'_t} = \frac{x^2}{4}.$$

Hence,

(1) at $-2 < x < 2$ the ratio $y'_t : x'_t$ is less than unity, *ie*, the rate of change of the ordinate is less than that of the abscissa;

(2) at $x = \pm\,2$ the ratio $y'_t : x'_t$ is equal to unity, *ie*, at these points the rates of change of the coordinates are equal ;

(3) at $x < -2$ or $x > 2$ the ratio $y'_t : x'_t$ is greater than unity, *ie*, the rate of change of the ordinate exceeds that of the abscissa.

2.5.12. A body of mass 6g is in rectilinear motion according to the law $s = -1 + \ln(t + 1) + (t + 1)^3$ (s is in centimetres and t, in seconds). Find the kinetic energy $\left(\frac{mv^2}{2}\right)$ of the body one second after it begins to move.

Solution The velocity of motion is equal to the time derivative of the distance :

$$v(t) = s'_t = \frac{1}{t+1} + 3\,(t+1)^2.$$

Therefore

$$v(1) = 12\,\frac{1}{2} \text{ and } \frac{mv^2}{2} = \frac{6}{2}\left(12\,\frac{1}{2}\right)^2 = 468\,\frac{3}{4} \text{ (erg)}.$$

2.5.13. The velocity of rectilinear motion of a body is proportional to the square root of the distance covered (s), (as, for example, in free fall of a body). Prove that the body moves under the action of a constant force.

Solution By hypothesis we have

$$v = s'_t = \alpha\sqrt{s} \ (\alpha = \text{const});$$

whence

$$s''_{tt} = v'_t = \alpha = \frac{1}{2\sqrt{s}}\,s'_t = \frac{\alpha^2}{2}\cdot$$

But according to Newton's law the force

$$F = ks''_{tt} \ (k = \text{const}).$$

Hence,

$$F = k\,\frac{\alpha^2}{2} = \text{const}.$$

2.5.14. A raft is pulled to the bank by means of a rope which is wound on a drum, at a rate of 3/m/min. Determine the speed of the raft at the moment when it is 25/m distant from the bank if the drum is situated on the bank 4m above water level.

Solution Let s denote the length of the rope between the drum and the raft and x the distance from the raft to the bank. By hypothesis

$$s^2 = x^2 + 4^2.$$

Differentiating this relation with respect to t, find the relationship between their speeds :

$$2ss'_t = 2xx'_t,$$

whence,

$$x'_t = \frac{s}{x}\,s'_t\,.$$

Taking into consideration that

$$s'_t = 3;\ x = 25;\ s = \sqrt{25^2 + 4^2} \approx 25.3,$$

we obtain

$$x'_t = \frac{\sqrt{25^2 + 4^2}}{25}\cdot 3 \approx 3.03 \text{ (m/min)}.$$

2.5.15. (a) Find the slope of the tangent to the cube parabola $y = x^3$ at the point $x = \sqrt{\frac{3}{3}}$.

(b) Write the equations of the tangents to the curve $y = \frac{1}{(1 + x^2)}$ at the points of its intersection with the hyperbola $y = \frac{1}{(x + 1)}$.

(c) Write the equation of the normal to the parabola $y = x^2 + 4x + 1$ perpendicular to the line joining the origin of coordinates with the vertex of the parabola.

(d) At what angle does the curve $y = e^x$ intersect the y-axis ?

2.5.16. The velocity of a body in rectilinear motion is determined by the formula $v = 3t + t^2$. What acceleration will the body have 4s after the start ?

2.5.17. The law of rectilinear motion of a body with a mass of 100 kg is $s = 2t^2 + 3t + 1$. Determine the kinetic energy $\left(\frac{mv^2}{2}\right)$ of the body 5s after the start.

2.5.18. Show that if the law of motion of a body is $s = ae^t + be^{-t}$, then its acceleration is numerically equal to the distance covered.

2.5.19. A body is thrown vertically with an initial velocity of a m/sec. What altitude will it reach in t seconds ? Find the velocity of the body. In how many seconds and at what distance from the ground will the body reach the highest point ?

2.5.20. Artificial satellites move round. The Earth in elliptical orbits. The distance r of a satellite from the centre of the Earth as a function of time t can be approximately expressed by the following equation :

$$r = a\left[1 - \varepsilon \cos M - \frac{\varepsilon^2}{2}(\cos 2M - 1)\right]$$

where $$M = \frac{2\pi}{P}(t - t_n)$$

t = time parameter

a = semi-major axis of the orbit

ε = eccentricity of the orbit

P = period of orbiting

t_n = time of passing the perigee[1] by the satellite.

Here a, ε, P and t_n are constants.

Find the rate of change in the distance r from the satellite to the centre of the Earth (*ie*, find the so-called radial velocity of the satellite.

[1]The perigee of the satellite orbit is the shortest distance from the satellite to the centre of the Earth.

2.6. The Differential of a Function. Application to Approximate Computations.

If the increment Δy of the function $y = f(x)$ can be expressed as :

$$\Delta y = f(x + \Delta x) - f(x) = A(x)\Delta x + \alpha\,(x, \Delta x)\,\Delta x,$$

where

$$\lim_{\Delta x \to 0} \alpha\,(x, \Delta x) = 0,$$

then such a function is called differentiable at the point x. The principal linear part of this increment $A(x)\,\Delta x$ is called the differential and is denoted $df(x)$ or dy. By definition, $dx = \Delta x$.

For the differential of the function $y = f(x)$ to exist it is necessary and sufficient that there exist a finite derivative $y' = A(x)$. The differential of a function can be written in the following way :

$$dy = y'\,dx = f'(x)\,dx$$

For a composite function $y = f(u), u = \phi(x)$ the differential is retained in the form

$$dy = f'(u)\,du$$

(the invariance of the form of the differential).

With an accuracy up to infinitesimals of a higher order than Δx the approximate formula $\Delta y \approx dy$ takes place. Only for a linear function $y = ax + b$ do we have $\Delta y = dy$.

Differentials of higher orders of the function $y = f(x)$ are successively determined in the following way :

$$d^2y = d(dy); d^3y = d(d^2y), \ldots, d^ny = d(d^{n-1}\,y).$$

If $y = f(x)$ and x is an independent variable, then

$$d^2y = y''\,(dx)^2; d^3y = y'''\,(dx)^2, \ldots, d^ny = y^{(n)}\,dx)^n.$$

But if $y = f(u)$, where $u = \phi(x)$, then $d^2y = f''(u)\,du^2 + f'(u)\,d^2u$, and so on.

2.6.1. Find the differential of the function

$$y = \ln(1 + e^{10x}) + \text{arc}\,\tan e^{5x}.$$

Calculate dy at $x = 0$; $dx = 0.2$.

Solution $dy = \left[\dfrac{(1 + e^{10x})'}{1 + e^{10x}} - \dfrac{(e^{5x})'}{1 + e^{10x}}\right] dx = \dfrac{5e^{5x}\,(2e^{5x} - 1)}{1 + e^{10x}}\,dx.$

Substituting $x = 0$ and $dx = 0.2$, we get

$$dy\,|_{x = 0;\, dx = 0.2} = \frac{5}{2} \cdot 0.2 = 0.5.$$

2.6.2. Find the increment and the differential of the function

$$y = 3x^3 + x - 1$$

at the point $x = 1$ at $\Delta x = 0.1$.

Find the absolute and relative errors allowed when replacing the increment of the function with its differential.

Solution $\Delta y = [3(x + \Delta x)^3 + (x + \Delta x) - 1]$

$$- (3x^3 + x - 1) = 9x^2 \Delta x + 9x \Delta x^2 + 3\Delta x^3 + \Delta x,$$

$$dy = (9x^2 + 1) \Delta x.$$

whence $\Delta y - dy = 9x \Delta x^2 + 3\Delta x^3$

At $x = 1$ and $\Delta x = 0.1$ we get

$$\Delta y - dy = 0.09 + 0.003 = 0.093,$$

$$dy = 1; \Delta y = 1.093.$$

The absolute error $|\Delta y - dy| = 0.093$, the relative error $\left|\frac{\Delta y - dy}{\Delta y}\right| = \frac{0.093}{1.093} \approx = 0.085$ or 8.5%.

2.6.3. Calculate approximately the increment, of the function

$$y = x^3 - 7x^2 + 8$$

as x changes from 5 to 5.01.

2.6.4. Using the concept of the differential, find the approximate value of the function

$$y = \sqrt[5]{\frac{2 - x}{2 + x}} \text{ at } x = 0.15.$$

Solution Notice that from $\Delta y = y(x + \Delta x) - y(x)$ we get

$$y(x + \Delta x) = y(x) + \Delta y,$$

or, putting $\Delta y \approx dy$,

$$y(x + \Delta x) \approx y(x) + dy$$

In our problem let us put $x = 0$ and $\Delta x = 0.15$. Then

$$y' = \frac{1}{5}\sqrt[5]{\left(\frac{2 + x}{2 - x}\right)^4} \cdot \frac{(-4)}{(2 + x)^2};$$

$$y'(0) = -\frac{1}{5}, dy = -\frac{1}{5} \cdot 0.15 = -0.03.$$

Hence, $y(0.15) \approx y(0) + dy = 1 - 0.03 = 0.97$.
The true value of $y(0.15) = 0.9702$ (accurate to 10^{-4}).

2.6.5. Find the approximate value of :

(a) cos 31°; (b) log 10.21; (c) $\sqrt[5]{33}$; (d) cot 45°10′.

Solution (a) In solving this problem we shall use the formula (*) of the preceding problem. Putting $x = \frac{\pi}{6}, \Delta x = \frac{\pi}{180}$, we compute;

$$y(x) = \cos\frac{\pi}{6} = \frac{\sqrt{3}}{2};$$

$$y'(x) = -\sin\frac{\pi}{6} = -\frac{1}{2};$$

$$\cos 31° = \cos\left(\frac{\pi}{6} + \frac{\pi}{180}\right) \approx \frac{\sqrt{3}}{2} - \frac{1}{2}\frac{\pi}{180} = 0.851$$

(c) Put $x = 32; \Delta x = 1$. By formula (*) we get

$$\sqrt[5]{33} \approx \sqrt[5]{32} + (\sqrt[5]{x})_{x=32}, 1 = 2 + \frac{1}{5\sqrt[5]{32^4}} = 2 + \frac{1}{80} = 2.0125.$$

2.6.6. All faces of a copper cube with 5 cm sides were uniformly ground down. As a result the weight of the cube was reduced by 0.96 g. Knowing the specific weight of copper (8) find the reduction the cube size, *ie,* the amount by which its side was reduced.

Solution The volume of the cube $v = x^3$, where x is the length of the side. The volume is equal to the weight divided by the density: $v = \frac{p}{d}$; the change in cube's volume $\Delta v = \frac{0.96}{8} = 0.12$ (cm^3). Since, Δv approximately equals dv and taking into consideration that $dv = 3x^2\, dx$ we shall have $0.12 = 3 \times 5^2 \times \Delta x$, whence

$$\Delta x = \frac{0.12}{3.25} = 0.0016 \text{ cm}.$$

Thus, the side of the cube was reduced by 0.0016 cm.

2.6.7. Find the expressions for determining the absolute errors in the following function through the absolute errors in their arguments :

(a) $y = \ln x$; (b) $y = \log x$;

(c) $y = \sin\left(0 < x < \frac{\pi}{2}\right)$; (d) $y = \tan x \left(0 < x < \frac{\pi}{2}\right)$;

(e) $y = \log(\sin x)\left(0 < x < \frac{\pi}{2}\right)$; (f) $y = \log(\tan x)\left(0 < x < \frac{\pi}{2}\right)$.

Solution If the function $f(x)$ is differentiable at a point x and the absolute error of the argument Δ_x is sufficiently small, then the absolute error in the function y can be expressed by the number $\Delta_y = |\, y'_x \,|\, \Delta x$.

(a) $\Delta_y = |(\ln x)'|_x \Delta_x = \frac{\Delta_x}{x}$, *ie,* the absolute error of a natural logarithm is equal to the relative error in its argument;

(b) $\Delta_y = (\log x)' \Delta_x = \frac{M}{x}\Delta_x$, where $M = \log e = 0.43429$;

(e) $\Delta_y = |[\log(\sin x)]'|\,\Delta_x = M\,|\cot x|\,\Delta_x$;

(f) $\Delta_y = |[\log(\tan x)]'|\,\Delta_x = \frac{2M}{|\sin 2x|}\Delta_x$.

From (e) and (f) it follows that the absolute error in log tan x is always more than that in log sin x (for the same x and Δ_x).

2.6.8. Find the differentials dy and d^2y of the function

$$y = 4x^5 - 7x^2 + 3,$$

assuming that :

(1) x is an independent variable;

(2) x is a function of another independent variable.

Solution By virtue of the invariance of its form the differential of the first order dy is written identically in both cases :

$$dy = y'\,dx = (20x^4 - 14x)\,dx.$$

But in the first case dx is understood as the increment of the independent variable Δx ($dx = \Delta x$), and in the second, as the differential of x as of a function (dx may not be equal to Δx).

Since differentials of higher orders do not possess the property of invariance, to find d^2y we have to consider the following two cases.

(1) Let x be an independent variable; then

$$d^2y = y''\,dx^2 = (80x^3 - 14)\,dx^2.$$

(2) Let x be a function of some other variable. In this case

$$d^2y = (80x^3 - 14)\,dx^2 + (20x^4 - 14x)\,d^2x.$$

2.6.9. Find differentials of higher orders (x an independent variable) :

(a) $y = 4^{-x^2}$; find d^2y;

(b) $y = \sqrt{\ln^2 x - 4}$; find d^2y;

(c) $y = \sin^2 x$; find d^3y.

2.6.10. $y = \ln \dfrac{1 - x^2}{1 + x^2}$; find d^2y if : (a) x is an independent variable, (b) x is a function of another variable. Consider the particular case when $x = \tan t$.

2.6.11. The volume V of a sphere of radius r is equal to $\frac{4}{3}\pi r^3$. Find the increment and differential of the volume and explain their geometrical meaning.

2.6.12. The law of the free fall of a material point is $s = gt^2/2$. Find the increment and differential of the distance at a moment t and elucidate their mechanical meaning.

2.7. Additional Problems

2.7.1. Given the functions : (a) $f(x) = |x|$ and (b) $\phi(x) = |x^3|$. Do derivaties of these functions exist at the point $x = 0$?

2.7.2. Show that the curve $y = e^{|x|}$ cannot have a tangent line at the point $x = 0$. What is the angle between the one-sided tangents to this curve at the indicated point ?

2.7.3. Show that the function

$$f(x) = |x - a|\, \phi(x),$$

where $\phi(x)$ is a continuous function and $\phi(a) \neq 0$, has no derivative at the point $x = a$. Find the one-sided derivatives $f'_-(A)$ and $f'_+(a)$.

2.7.4. Given the function

$$f(x) = \begin{cases} x^2 \sin(1/x) & \text{at} \quad x \neq 0, \\ 0 & \text{at} \quad x = 0. \end{cases}$$

Use this example to show that the derivative of a continuous function is not always a continuous function.

2.7.5. Let

$$f(x) = \begin{cases} x^2, & \text{if} \quad x \leq x_0, \\ ax + b, & \text{if} \quad x > 0. \end{cases}$$

Find the coefficients a and b at which the function is continuous and has a derivative at the point x_0.

2.7.6. By differentiating the formula $\cos 3x = \cos^3 x - 3 \cos x \sin^2 x$ deduce the formula $\sin 3x = 3 \cos^2 x \sin x - \sin^3 x$.

2.7.7. From the formula for the sum of the geometric progression

$$1 + x + x^2 + \ldots + x^n = \frac{1 - x^{n+1}}{1 - x} \quad (x \neq 1)$$

deduce the formulas for the following sums :

(a) $1 + 2x + 3x^2 + \ldots. + nx^{n-1}$;

(b) $1^2 + 2^2 x + 3x^2 x^2 + \ldots + n^2 x^{n-1}$.

2.7.8. Prove the identity

$$\cos x + \cos 3x + \ldots + \cos(2n - 1)\, x = \frac{\sin 2nx}{2 \sin x}, \; x \neq k\pi$$

and deduce from it the formula for the sum

$$\sin x + 3 \sin 3x + \ldots + (2n - 1) \sin (2n - 1)\, x.$$

2.7.9. Find y' if :

(a) $y = f(\sin^2 x) + f(\cos^2 x)$; (b) $y = f(e^x)\, e^{f(x)}$;

(c) $y = \log_{\phi(x)} \psi(x)$ $(\phi(x) > 0;\ \psi(x) > 0)$.

2.7.10. Is it reasonable to assert that the product $F(x) = f(x)\, g(x)$ has no derivative at the point $x = x_0$ if :

(a) the function $f(x)$ has a derivative at the point x_0, and the function $\phi(x)$ has no derivative at this point ?

(b) neither function has a derivative at the point x_0 ?

Consider the examples : (1) $f(x) = x, g(x) = |x|$;

(2) $f(x) = |x|, g(x) = |x|$.

Is it reasonable to assert that the sum $F(x) = f(x) + g(x)$ has no derivative at the point $x = x_0$ if :

(c) the function $f(x)$ has a derivative at the point x_0, and the function $g(x)$ has no derivative at this point ?

(d) neither function has a derivative at the point x_0 ?

2.7.11. Prove that the derivative of a differentiable even function is an odd function, and the derivative of an odd function is an even function. Give a geometric explanation to these facts.

2.7.12. Prove that the derivative of a periodic function with period T is a periodic function with period T.

2.7.13. Find $F'(x)$ if

$$F(x) = \begin{vmatrix} x & x^2 & x^3 \\ 1 & 2x & 3x^2 \\ 0 & 2 & 6x \end{vmatrix}.$$

2.7.14. Find the derivative of the function $y = x`|x|$. Sketch the graphs of the given function and its derivative.

2.7.15. Suppose we have a composite function $y = f(u)$, where $u = \varphi(x)$. Among what points should we look for points at which the composite function may have no derivative ?

Does the composite function always have no derivative at these points ? Consider the function $y = u^2, u = |x|$.

2.7.16. Find y'' for the following functions :

(a) $y = |x^3|$; (b) $y = \begin{cases} x^2 \sin\left(\dfrac{1}{x}\right), & x \neq 0, \\ 0 \text{ at} & x = 0. \end{cases}$

Is there $y''(0)$?

2.7.17. (a) $f(x) = x^n$; show that

$$f(1) + \frac{f'(1)}{1!} + \frac{f^{(2)}(1)}{2!} + \ldots + \frac{f^{(n)}(1)}{n!} = 2^n;$$

(b) $f(x) = x^{n-1} e^{1/x}$; show that

$$[f(x)]^{(n)} = (-1)^n \frac{f(x)}{x^{2n}} \quad (n = 1, 2, \ldots).$$

2.7.18. $y = x^2 e^{-x/a}$; show that

$$f^{(n)}(0) = \frac{(-1)^n n(n-1)}{a^{n-2}} \, (n \geq 2).$$

2.7.19. Show that the function $y = \arcsin x$ satisfies the relation $(1 - x^2) y'' xy'$. Find $y^{(n)}(0)$ $(n \geq 2)$ by applying the Leibnitz formula to both members of this identity.

2.7.20. Prove that the Chebyshev polynomials

$$T_n(x) = \frac{1}{2^{n-1}} \cos (n \arccos x) \ (n = 1, 2, \ldots)$$

satisfy the equation

$$(1 - x^2)\, T''_n(x) - xT'_n(x) + n^2 T_n(x) = 0.$$

2.7.21. The derivative of the nth order of the function e^{-x^2} has the form

$$(e^{-x^2})^{(n)} = e^{-x^2} H_n(x),$$

where $H_n(x)$ is a polynomial of degree n called the *Chebyshev- Hermite polynomial.*

Prove that the recurrence relation

$$H_{n+1}(x) - 2xH_n(x) + 2nH_{n-1}(x) = 0 \ (n = 1, 2, \ldots)$$

is valid.

2.7.22. Show that there exists a single-valued function $y = y(x)$ defined by the equation $y^3 + 3y = x$, and find its derivative y_x.

2.7.23. Single out the single-valued continuous branches of the inverse function $x = x(y)$ and find their derivatives if $y = 2x^2 - x^4$.

2.7.24. $u = \frac{1}{2} \ln \frac{1+v}{1-v}$; check the relation $\frac{du}{dv} \frac{dv}{du} = 1.$

2.7.25. Inverse trigonometric functions are continuous at all points of the domain of definition. Do they have a finite derivative at all points of the domain ? Indicate the points at which the following functions have no finite derivatives :

(a) $y = \arccos \frac{x+1}{2}$; (b) $y = \arcsin \frac{1}{x}$.

2.7.26. Show that the function $y = y(x)$, defined parametrically: $x = 2t - |t|$, $y = t^2 + t\,|t|$, is differentiable at $t = 0$ but its derivative cannot be found by the usual formula.

2.7.27. Determine the parameters a, b, c in the equation of the parabola $y = ax^2 + bx + c$ so that it becomes tangent to the straight line $y = x$ at the point $x = 1$ and passes through the point $(-1, 0)$.

2.7.28. Prove that the curves $y_1 = f(x)$ $(f(x) > 0)$ and $y_2 = f(x) \sin ax$, where $f(x)$ is a differentiable function, are tangent to each other at the common points.

2.7.29. Show that for any point $M(x_0, y_0)$ of the equilateral hyperbola $x^2 - y^2 = a^2$ the segment of the normal from the point M to the point of intersection with the abscissa is equal to the radius vector of the point M.

2.7.30. Show that for any position of the generating circle the tangent line and the normal to the cycloid $x = a(t - \sin t)$, $y = a(1 - \cot t)$ pass through the highest $(at, 2a)$ and the lowest $(at, 0)$ points of the circle, respectively.

2.7.31. Show that two cardioids $\rho = a(1 + \cos \phi)$ and $\rho = (a(1 - \cos \phi)$ intersect at right angles.

2.7.32. Let $y = f(u)$, where $u = \varphi(x)$. Prove the validity of the equality

$$d^3y = f'''(u)\,du^3 + 3f''(u)\,du\,d^2u + f'(u)\,d^3u.$$

2.7.33. Let $y = f(x)$, where $x = \varphi(t)$; the functions $f(x)$ and $\varphi(t)$ are twice differentiable and $dx \neq 0$. Prove that

$$y''_{xx} = \frac{d^2y dx - dy d^2x}{dx^3},$$

where the differentials forming the right member of the relation are differentials with respect to the variable t.

2.7.34. How will the expression

$$(1 - x^2)\frac{d^2y}{dx^2} - x\frac{dy}{dx} + y$$

be transformed (where y is a twice differentiable function of x) if we introduce a new independent variable t, putting $x = \cos t$?

2.7.35. In determining an electric current by means of a tangent galvanometer use is made of the formula

$$I = k \tan \varphi,$$

where I = current

k = factor of proportionality (depending on the instrument)

φ = angle of pointer deflection.

Determine the relative error of the result which depends on the inaccuracy in reading the angle φ. At what position of the pointer can one obtain the most reliable results ?

3

Application of Differential Calculus to Investigation of Functions

3.1. Basic Theorems on Differentiable Functions

Fermat's Theorem. Let a function $y = f(x)$ be defined on a certain interval and have a maximum or a minimum value at an interior point x_0 of the interval.

If there exists a derivative $f'(x_0)$ at the point x_0, then $f'(x_0) = 0$.

Rolle's Theorem. If a function $f(x)$ is continuous in the interval $[a, b]$, has a finite derivative at all interior points of this interval, and $f(a) = f(b)$, then inside $[a, b]$ there exists a point $\xi \in (a, b)$ such that $f'(\xi) = 0$.

Lagrange's Theorem. If a function $f(x)$ is continuous in the interval $[a, b]$ and has a finite derivative at all interior points of the interval, then there exists a point $\xi \in (a, b)$ such that

$$f(b) - f(a) = (b - a) f'(\xi).$$

Test for the Constancy of a Function. If at all points of a certain interval $f'(x) = 0$, then the function $f(x)$ preserves a constant value within this interval.

Cauchy's Theorem. Let $\varphi(x)$ and $\psi(x)$ be two functions continuous in the interval $[a, b]$ and have finite derivatives at all interior points of the interval. If these derivatives do not vanish simultaneously and $\varphi(a) \neq \varphi(b)$, then there exists $\xi \in (a, b)$ such that

$$\frac{\psi(b) - \psi(a)}{\varphi(b) - \varphi(a)} = \frac{\psi'(\xi)}{\varphi'(\xi)}.$$

3.1.1. Does the function $f(x) = 3x^2 - 1$ satisfy the condition of the Fermat theorem in the interval $[1, 2]$?

Solution The given function does not satisfy the condition of the Fermat theorem, since it increases monotonically on the interval $[1, 2]$, and, consequently, takes on the minimum value at $x = 1$ and the maximum one at $x = 2$, *ie*, not at interior points of the interval. Therefore, the Fermat theorem is not applicable; in other words, we cannot assert that $f'(1) = f'(2) = 0$. Indeed, $f'(1) = 6$, $f'(2) = 12$.

3.1.2. Do the following functions satisfy the conditions of the Rolle theorem ?

(a) $f(x) = 1 - \sqrt[3]{x^2}$ in $[-1, 1]$; (b) $f(x) = \ln \sin x$ in $[\pi/6, 5\pi/6]$;

(c) $f(x) = 1 - |x|$ in $[-1, 1]$.
If they do not, explain why.

Solution (a) The function is continuous in the interval $[-1, 1]$; furthermore, $f(-1) = f(1) = 0$. Thus, two conditions of the Rolle theorem are satisfied. The derivative $f'(x) = -2/(3\sqrt[3]{x})$ exists at at all points except $x = 0$. Since this point is an interior one, the third condition of the theorem is not satisfied. Therefore the Rolle theorem is not applicable to the given function. Indeed, $f'(x) \neq 0$ in $[-1, 1]$

3.1.3. Prove that the equation

$$3x^5 + 15x - 8 = 0$$

has only one real root.

Solution (a) The existence of at least one real root follows from the fact that the polynomial $f(x) = 3x^5 + 15x - 8$ is of an odd power. Let us prove the uniqueness of such a root by reduction and absurdum. Suppose there exist two roots $x_1 < x_2$. Then in the interval $[x_1, x_2]$ the function $f(x) = 3x^5 + 15x - 8$ satisfies all conditions of the Rolle theorem : It is continuous, vanishes at the end points and has a derivative at all points. Consequently, at some point ξ; $x_1 < \xi < x_2$, $f'(\xi) = 0$. But $f'(x) = 15(x^4 + 1) > 0$. This contradiction proves that the equation in question has only one real root.

3.1.4. Does the function $f(x) = 3x^2 - 5$ satisfy the conditions of the Lagrange theorem in the interval $[-2, 0]$? If it does, then find the point ξ which figures in the Lagrange formula $f(b) - f(a) = f'(\xi)(b - a)$.

Solution The function satisfies the conditions of the Lagrange theorem, since it is continuous in the interval $[-2, 0]$ and has a finite derivative at all interior points of the interval. The point ξ is found from the Lagrange formula :

$$f'(\xi) = 6\xi = \frac{f(0) - f(-2)}{0 - (-2)} = \frac{-5 - 7}{2} = -6,$$

whence $\xi = -1$

3.1.5. Apply the Lagrange formula to the function $f(x) = \ln x$ in the interval $[1, e]$ and find the corresponding value of ξ.

3.1.6. Ascertain that the functions $f(x) = x^2 - 2x + 3$ and $g(x) = x^3 - 7x^2 + 20x - 5$ satisfy the condition of the Cauchy theorem in the interval $[1, 4]$ and find the corresponding value of ξ.

Solution The given functions $f(x)$ and $g(x)$ are continuous everywhere, and hence, in the interval $[1, 4]$ as well ; their derivatives $f'(x) = 2x - 2$ and $g'(x) = 3x^2 - 14x + 20$ are finite everywhere; in addition, $g'(x)$ does not vanish at any real value of x.

Consequently, the Cauchy formula is applicable to the given functions:

$$\frac{f(4) - f(1)}{g(4) - g(1)} = \frac{f'(\xi)}{g'(\xi)},$$

ie, $$\frac{11-2}{27-9} = \frac{2\xi - 2}{3\xi^2 - 14\xi + 20} \quad (1 < \xi < 4).$$

Solving the latter equation, we find two values of $\xi : \xi_1 = 2$ and $\xi_2 = 4$. Of these two values only $\xi_1 = 2$ is an interior point of the interval.

3.1.7. Do the functions $f(x) = e^x$ and $g(x) = \dfrac{x^2}{1+x^2}$ satisfy the conditions of the Cauchy theorem in the interval $[-3, 3]$?

3.1.8. On the curve $y = x^3$ find the point at which the tangent line is parallel to the chord through the points $A(-1, -1)$ and $B(2, 8)$.

Solution In the interval $[-1, 2]$, whose end-points are the abscissas of the points A and B, the function $y = x^3$ is continuous and has a finite derivative; therefore the Lagrange theorem is applicable. According to this theorem there will be, on the arc AB, at least one point M, at which the tangent is parallel to the chord AB. Let us write the Lagrange formula for the given function

$$f(2) - f(-1) = f'(\xi)\,[2 - (-1)],$$

or

$$8 + 1 = 3\xi^2 \cdot 3;$$

whence

$$\xi_1 = -1, \xi_2 = 1.$$

The obtained values of ξ are the abscissas of the desired points (as we see, there exists two such points). Substituting ξ_1 and ξ_2 in the equation of the curve, we find the corresponding ordinates

$$y_1 = \xi_1^3 = 1\,;\; y_2 = \xi_2^3 = -1.$$

Thus, the required points are : $M_1(1, 1)$ and $M_2(-1, -1)$, of which only the former is an interior point on the arc AB.

Note. This problem can be solved without using the Lagrange theorem ; write the equation of the chord as a straight line passing through two given points, and then find the point on the curve at which the tangent is parallel to the chord.

3.1.9. Taking advantage of the test for the constancy of a function, deduce the following formulas known from elementary mathematics :

(a) $\arcsin x + \arccos x = \pi/2$;

(b) $\sin^2 x = (1 - \cos 2x)/2$;

(c) $\arccos \dfrac{1-x^2}{1+x^2} = 2 \arctan x$ at $0 \le x < \infty$;

(d) $$\arcsin \frac{2x}{1+x^2} = \begin{cases} \pi - 2\arctan x & \text{at} \quad x \ge 1, \\ 2\arctan x & \text{at} \quad -1 \le x \le 1, \\ -\pi - 2\arctan x & \text{at} \quad x \le -1. \end{cases}$$

Solution (a) Let us consider the function

$$f(x) = \arcsin x + \arccos x,$$

defined in the interval [−1, 1]. The derivative of the indicated function inside this interval equals zero :

$$f'(x) = \frac{1}{\sqrt{1-x^2}} - \frac{1}{\sqrt{1-x^2}} \equiv 0 \; (-1 < x < 1).$$

According to the test for the constancy of a function $f(x) = \text{const}$, *ie*, arc sin x + arc cos $x = C \; (-1 < x < 1)$.

To determine the constant C let us put, for instance, $x = 0$; then we have $\pi/2 = -C$, whence

$$\arcsin x + \arccos x = \frac{\pi}{2} \; (-1 < x < 1).$$

The validity of this equality at the points $x = \pm 1$ is verified directly.

(b) Let us take the function

$$f(x) = \sin^2 x + \frac{1}{2}\cos 2x$$

defined throughout the number scale : $-\infty < x < \infty$. The derivative of this function is everywhere equal to zero :

$$f'(x) = 2\sin x \cos x - \sin 2x \equiv 0.$$

According to the test for the constancy of a function

$$\sin^2 x + \frac{1}{2}\cos 2x = C.$$

To determine C put, for instance, $x = 0$; then we get $1/2 = C$. Whereform

$$\sin^2 x + \frac{1}{2}\cos 2x = \frac{1}{2},$$

or

$$\sin^2 x = \frac{1-\cos 2x}{2}.$$

(c) Let us introduce the function

$$f(x) = \arccos\frac{1-x^2}{1+x^2} - 2\arctan x,$$

determined along the entire number scale, since $\left|\dfrac{1-x^2}{1+x^2}\right| \le 1.$

The derivative of the function $f(x)$ is zero for all $x > 0$:

$$f'(x) = \frac{1}{\sqrt{1-\left(\dfrac{1-x^2}{1+x^2}\right)^2}} \frac{-4x}{(1+x^2)^2} - \frac{2}{1+x^2} = \frac{4x}{2x(1+x^2)} - \frac{2}{1+x^2} \equiv 0.$$

According to the test for the constancy of a function

$$\arccos\frac{1-x^2}{1+x^2} - 2\arctan x = C \text{ at } x > 0.$$

To determine C let us put, say, $x = 1$, which gives $C = \arccos 0 - 2$ arc tan $1 = 0$.

The validity of the proved formula at $x = 0$ is verified directly.

Note. At $x = 0$ of the function $\text{arc cos}\,\dfrac{1-x^2}{1+x^2}$ has no derivative. At $x < 0$ its derivative is

$$\left(\text{arc cos}\,\frac{1-x^2}{1+x^2}\right)' = -\frac{2}{1+x^2}$$

which enables us to derive the formula

$$\text{across}\,\frac{1-x^2}{1+x^2} = -2\,\text{arc tan}\,x\,(x < 0).$$

The latter formula can be obtained on the strength of the fact that $\text{arc cos}\,\dfrac{1-x^2}{1+x^2}$ is an even function, and 2 arc tan x is an odd one.

3.1.10. As is known, $(e^x)' = e^x$ for all x. Are there any more functions that coincide with their derivatives everywhere ?

Solution Let the function $f(x)$ be such that $f'(x) = f(x)$ everywhere.

Let us introduce the function

$$\varphi(x) = \frac{f(x)}{e^x} = f(x)\,e^{-x}.$$

The derivative of this function equals zero everywhere :

$$\varphi'(x) = f'(x)\,e^{-x} - e^{-x} f(x) \equiv 0$$

By the test for the constancy of a function $f(x)/e^x = C$, whence $f(x) = ce^x$.

And so, we have proved that the group of functions for which $f'(x) = f(x)$ is covered by the formula $f(x) = Ce^x$.

3.1.11. Prove the inequality

$$\text{arc tan}\,x_2 - \text{arc tan}\,x_1 < x_2 - x_1,$$

where $x_2 > x_1$.

Solution To the function $f(x) = \text{arc tan}\,x$ on the interval $[x_1, x_2]$ apply the Lagrange formula :

$$\text{arc tan}\,x_2 - \text{arc tan}\,x_1 = \frac{1}{1+\xi^2}(x_2 - x_1),$$

where $x_1 < \xi < x_2$.

Since

$$0 < \frac{1}{1+\xi^2} < 1 \quad \text{and} \quad x_2 - x_1 > 0,$$

then

$$\text{arc tan}\,x_2 - \text{arc tan}\,x_1 < x_2 - x_1.$$

In particular, putting $x_1 = 0$ and $x_2 = x$, we get

$$\text{arc tan}\,x < x\;(x > 0).$$

3.1.12. Show that the square roots of two successive natural numbers greater than N^2 differ by less than $1/(2N)$.

Solution To the function $f(x) = \sqrt{x}$ on the interval $[n, n+1]$ apply the Lagrange formula :

$$f(n+1) - f(n) = \sqrt{n+1} - \sqrt{n} = \frac{1}{2\sqrt{\xi}},$$

where $n < \xi < n+1$.

If $n > N^2$, then $\xi > N^2$, hence $1/(2\sqrt{\xi}) < 1/(2N)$, whence

$$\sqrt{n+1} - \sqrt{n} < \left(\frac{1}{2N}\right).$$

3.1.13. Using the Rolle theorem prove that the derivative $f'(x)$ of the function

$$f(x) = \begin{cases} x \sin\frac{\pi}{x} & \text{at} \quad x > 0, \\ 0 & \text{at} \quad x = 0 \end{cases}$$

vanishes on an infinite set of points of the interval $(0, 1)$.

Solution The function $f(x)$ vanishes at points where

$$\sin(\pi/x) = 0,\ \pi/x = k\pi,\ x = 1/k,$$
$$k = 1, 2, 3, \ldots$$

Since the function $f(x)$ has a derivative at any interior point of the interval $[0, 1]$, the Rolle theorem is applicable to anyone of the intervals $[1/2, 1], [1/3, 1/2], \ldots, [1/(k+1), 1/k], \ldots$ Consequently, inside each of the intervals of the sequence, there is a point $\xi_k \cdot 1/(k+1) < \xi_k < 1/k$, at which the derivative $f'(\xi_k) = 0$.

And so we have shown that the derivative vanishes on an infinite set of point (see Fig. 38).

3.1.14. The *Legendre polynomial* is a polynomial defined by the following formula (Rodrigues formula) :

$$P_n(x) = \frac{1}{2^n n!} \cdot \frac{d^n}{dx^n}(x^2 - 1)^n$$
$$(n = 0, 1, 2, \ldots)$$

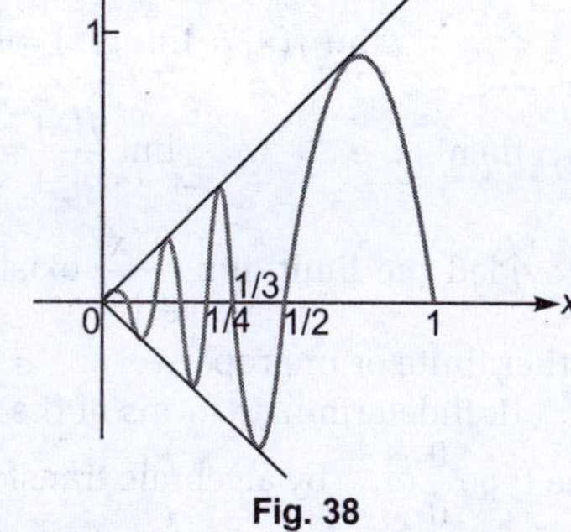

Fig. 38

Using the Rolle theorem, prove that the Legendre polynomial $P_n(x)$ has n different real roots, all of them found between -1 and $+1$.

Solution Consider the function $f(x) = (x^2 - 1)^n = (x-1)^n(x+1)^n$

This function and its $n-1$ successive derivatives vanish at the points $x = \pm 1$ (use the Leibnitz formula for higher derivatives of the product of two functions). It follows from $f(1) = f(-1) = 0$ that inside the interval $[-1, 1]$ a point ξ_1 can be found at which $f'(\xi_1) = 0$ *ie*, $x = \xi_1$ will be the root of the first derivative. Now apply the Rolle theorem once again to the function $f'(x)$ on the intervals $[-1, \xi_1]$, $[\xi_1, 1]$. We find that besides +1 and −1, the function $f''(x)$ has two more roots on the interval [−1, 1]. Reasoning as before. we will show that, apart from +1 and −1, the $(n-1)$ th derivative has $(n-1)$ more roots on the interval [−1, 1], *ie*, the function $f^{(n-1)}(x)$ has all in all $n+1$ roots on the interval [−1, 1], which divide this interval into n parts. Applying the Rolle theorem once again, we ascertain that the function $f^{(n)}(x)$, and hence, the function $P_n(x) = \frac{1}{2^n n!} f^{(n)}(x)$, has n different roots on the interval [−1, 1].

3.1.15. Check whether the Lagrange formula is applicable to the following functions :

(a) $f(x) = x^2$ on [3, 4] ;

(b) $f(x) = \ln x$ on [1, 3] ;

(c) $f(x) = 4x^3 - 5x^2 + x - 2$ on [0, 1];

(d) $f(x) = \sqrt[5]{x^4(x-1)}$ on [−1/2, 1/2].

If it is, find the values of ξ appearing in this formula.

3.1.16. Using the Lagrange theorem estimate has value $\ln(1+e)$

3.1.17. Using the Lagrange formula prove the inequality

$$\frac{x}{1+x} < \ln(1+x) < x \text{ at } x > 0.$$

3.2. Evaluation of Indeterminate Forms L'Hospital's Rule

I. Indeterminate forms of the type $\frac{0}{0}, \frac{\infty}{\infty}$. If the functions $f(x)$ and $g(x)$ are differentiable in a certain neighbourhood of the point a, except, may be, at the point a itself, and $g'(x) \neq 0$, and if

$$\lim_{x \to a} f(x) = \lim_{x \to a} g(x) = 0 \text{ or } \lim_{x \to a} f(x) = \lim_{x \to a} g(x) = \infty,$$

then
$$\lim_{x \to a} \frac{f(x)}{g(x)} = \lim_{x \to a} \frac{f'(x)}{g'(x)}$$

provided the limit $\lim_{x \to a} \frac{f'(x)}{g'(x)}$ exists (*L'Hospital's rule*). the point a may be either finite or improper $+\infty$ or $-\infty$.

II. Indeterminate forms of the type $0.\infty$ or $\infty - \infty$ are reduced to forms of the type $\frac{0}{0}$ or $\frac{\infty}{\infty}$ by algebraic transformations.

III. Indeterminate forms of the type 1^∞, ∞^0 or 0^0 are reduced to forms of the type $0.\infty$ by taking logarithms or by the transformation $[f(x)]^{\varphi(x)} = e^{\varphi(x) \cdot \ln f(x)}$.

3.2.1. Applying the L'Hospital rule, find the limits of the following functions :

(a) $\lim\limits_{x \to 0} \dfrac{e^{ax} - e^{-2ax}}{\ln(1+x)}$; (b) $\lim\limits_{x \to -1} \dfrac{\sqrt[3]{1+2x}+1}{\sqrt{2+x}+x}$;

(c) $\lim\limits_{x \to 0} \dfrac{e^{x} - e^{-x} - 2x}{x - \sin x}$; (d) $\lim\limits_{x \to 0} \dfrac{\ln(1+x^2)}{\cos 3x - e^{-x}}$;

(e) $\lim\limits_{x \to 0} \dfrac{\sin 3x^2}{\ln\cos(2x^2 - x)}$; (f) $\lim\limits_{x \to \infty} \dfrac{e^{1/x^2} - 1}{2\arctan x^2 - \pi}$.

Solution (a) Here both functions $f(x) = e^{ax} - e^{-2ax}$ and $g(x) = \ln(1+x)$ are infinitesimals in the neighbourhood of zero, since

$$\lim_{x \to 0} f(x) = 1 - 1 = 0\,;\ \lim_{x \to 0} g(x) = \ln 1 = 0\,.$$

Furthermore $f'(x)$ and $g'(x)$ exist in any neighbourhood of the point $x = 0$ that does not contain the point $x = -1$, and

$$g'(x) = \frac{1}{1+x} \neq 0\ (x > -1).$$

Finally, there exists a limit of the ratio of the derivatives :

$$\lim_{x \to 0} \frac{f'(x)}{g'(x)} = \lim_{x \to 0} \frac{ae^{ax} + 2ae^{-2ax}}{1/(1+x)} = 3a.$$

Therefore the L'Hospital rule is applicable :

$$\lim_{x \to 0} \frac{e^{ax} - e^{-2ax}}{\ln(1+x)} = \lim_{x \to 0} \frac{ae^{ax} + 2ae^{-2ax}}{1/(1+x)} = 3a. \qquad \ldots(*)$$

Note. When the limit of the ratio is computed according to the L'Hospital rule the result is usually written directly as shown in (*). Whether the desired derivatives and limits exists is ascertained in the course of calculation. In case the ratio of the derivatives $\dfrac{f'(x)}{g'(x)}$ again represents an indeterminate from, the L'Hospital rule should be applied for a second time, and so on until the indeterminacy is removed or until it becomes clear that the required limits do not exist. Therefore, henceforward we write only the necessary transformations, leaving to the reader the task of checking whether the conditions of their applicability are fulfilled.

(b) $$\lim_{x \to -1} \frac{\sqrt[3]{1+2x}+1}{\sqrt{2+x}+x} = \lim_{x \to -1} \frac{2/(3\sqrt[3]{(1+2x)^2})}{1/(2\sqrt{2+x})+1} = \frac{4}{9};$$

(e) $$\lim_{x \to 0} \frac{\sin 3x^2}{\ln\cos(2x^2 - x)} = \lim_{x \to 0} \frac{-6x\cos 3x^2 \cos(2x^2 - x)}{(4x-1)\sin(2x^2 - x)}$$

$$= -6 \lim_{x \to 0} \frac{\cos 3x^2 \cos(2x^2 - x)}{4x - 1} \lim_{x \to 0} \frac{x}{\sin(2x^2 - x)}.$$

The limit of the first factor is computed directly, the limit of the second one, which represents an indeterminate form of the type $\frac{0}{0}$ is found with the aid of the L'Hospital rule.

$$-6 \lim_{x \to 0} \frac{\cos 3x^2 \cos(2x^2 - x)}{4x - 1} \lim_{x \to 0} \frac{x}{\sin(2x^2 - x)}$$

$$= -6 \cdot \frac{1 \cdot 1}{-1} \lim_{x \to 0} \frac{1}{(4x - 1)\cos(2x^2 - x)} = 6 \cdot \frac{1}{-1 \cdot 1} = -6$$

3.2.2. It is known that, as $x \to +\infty$, the functions $x^k (k > 0)$; $\log_a x$; $a^x (a > 1)$ are infinitely large quantities. Applying the L'Hospital rule, compare these quantities.

Solution 1. $\lim\limits_{x \to +\infty} \dfrac{\log_a x}{x^k} = \lim\limits_{x \to +\infty} \dfrac{\frac{1}{x} \log_a e}{kx^{k-1}} = \log_a e \lim\limits_{x \to +\infty} \dfrac{1}{kx^k} = 0$;

2. $\lim\limits_{x \to +\infty} \dfrac{x^m}{a^x} = \lim\limits_{x \to +\infty} \dfrac{mx^{m-1}}{a^x \ln a} = \ldots. = \lim\limits_{k \to +\infty} \dfrac{m!}{a^x (\ln a)^m} = 0.$

Hence, the power function x^k $(k > 0)$ increases more repidly than the logarithmic function $\log_a x (a > 1)$, and the exponential function a^x with the base exceeding unity increases more rapidly than the power function x^m.

3.2.3. Find the limits :

(a) $\lim\limits_{x \to 1} \left(\dfrac{1}{\ln x} - \dfrac{1}{x - 1} \right)$; (b) $\lim\limits_{x \to 0} \left(\cot x - \dfrac{1}{x} \right)$;

(c) $\lim\limits_{x \to 0} \left(\dfrac{1}{x} - \dfrac{1}{e^x - 1} \right)$.

Solution (a) We have an indeterminate form of the type $\infty - \infty$. Let us reduce it to an indeterminate form of the type $\frac{0}{0}$ and then apply the L'Hospital rule :

$$\lim_{x \to 1} \left(\frac{1}{\ln x} - \frac{1}{x - 1} \right) = \lim_{x \to 1} \frac{x - 1 - \ln x}{(x - 1)\ln x} = \lim_{x \to 1} \frac{1 - 1/x}{\ln x + 1 - 1/x}$$

$$= \lim_{x \to 1} \frac{x - 1}{x \ln x + x - 1} = \lim_{x \to 1} \frac{1}{\ln x + 2} = \frac{1}{2}.$$

3.2.4. Find the limits :

(a) $\lim\limits_{x \to 0} x^n \ln x \, (n > 0)$;

(b) $\lim\limits_{x \to 0} [\ln(1 + \sin^2 x) \cot \ln^2 (1 + x)]$.

Solution (a) We have an indeterminate form of the type $0 . \infty$.

Let us transform it to $\frac{\infty}{\infty}$, and then apply the L'Hospital rule :

$$\lim_{x \to 0} x^n \ln x = \lim_{x \to 0} \frac{\ln x}{x^{-n}} = \lim_{x \to 0} \frac{1/x}{-nx^{-n-1}} = -\frac{1}{n} \lim_{x \to 0} x^n = 0, \text{ since } n > 0.$$

(b) We have an indeterminate form of the type $0.\,\infty$:

$$\lim_{x \to 0} [\ln (1 + \sin^2 x) \cot \ln^2 (1 + x)] = \lim_{x \to 0} \frac{\ln (1 + \sin^2 x)}{\tan \ln^2 (1 + x)}$$

$$= \lim_{x \to 0} \frac{\dfrac{1}{1 + \sin^2 x} \sin 2x}{2 \{1 + \tan^2 [\ln^2 (1 + x)]\} \cdot \ln (1 + x) \cdot \dfrac{1}{1 + x}}$$

$$= \lim_{x \to 0} \frac{\sin x}{\ln (1 + x)} = \lim_{x \to 0} \frac{\cos x}{\dfrac{1}{1 + x}} = 1.$$

3.2.5. Find the limits :

(a) $\lim\limits_{x \to +0} (1/x)^{\sin x}$; (b) $\lim\limits_{x \to +0} x^{1/\ln (e^x - 1)}$.

Solution (a) We have an indeterminate form of the type ∞^0.
Let $y = (1/x)^{\sin x}$; then

$$\ln y = \sin x \ln (1/x),$$

$$\lim_{x \to +0} \ln y = \lim_{x \to +0} \sin x \ln (1/x) \text{ (indeterminate form of the type } 0.\,\infty \text{).}$$

Let us transform it to $\frac{\infty}{\infty}$ and apply the L'Hospital rule :

$$\lim_{x \to +0} \ln y = \lim_{x \to +0} \frac{-\ln x}{1/\sin x} = \lim_{x \to 0} \frac{-1/x}{-(\cos x)/\sin^2 x} = \lim_{x \to 0} \frac{\sin^2 x}{x \cos x} = 0.$$

Hence, $\lim\limits_{x \to +0} y = e^0 = 1.$

3.2.6. Find the limits :

(a) $\lim\limits_{x \to \pi/2} (\sin x)^{\tan x}$; (b) $\lim\limits_{x \to 0} x^x$.

3.2.7. Compute

$$\lim_{x \to +\frac{\pi}{2} - 0} (\tan x)^{\cot x}.$$

Solution Let us take advantage of the identity

$$(\tan x)^{\cot x} = e^{\cot x \ln \tan x},$$

but

$$\lim_{x \to +\pi/2 - 0} \cot x \ln \tan x$$

$$= \lim_{x \to +\frac{\pi}{2} - 0} \frac{\ln \tan x}{\tan x}$$

$$= \lim_{y = \tan x \to +\infty} \frac{\ln y}{y} = 0.$$

Whence $\lim\limits_{x \to +\pi/2 - 0} (\tan x)^{\cot x} = e^0 = 1.$

3.2.8. Ascertain the existence of the following limits :

(a) $\lim\limits_{x \to 0} \dfrac{x^2 \sin (1/x)}{\sin x}$; (b) $\lim\limits_{x \to \infty} \dfrac{2 + 2x + \sin 2x}{(2x + \sin 2x)e^{\sin x}}$;

(c) $\lim\limits_{x \to \pi/2} \dfrac{\tan x}{\sec x}$.

Can the L'Hospital rule be applied in computing them ?
Does its formal application lead to the correct answer ?

Solution (a) The limit exists and equals zero. Indeed,

$$\lim_{x \to 0} \frac{x^2 \sin (1 x)}{\sin x} = \lim_{x \to 0} \frac{x}{\sin x} \lim_{x \to 0} x \sin \frac{1}{x} = 1 \cdot 0 = 0.$$

But the limit of the ratio of the derivatives does not exist. Indeed,

$$\lim_{x \to 0} \frac{2x \sin (1/x) - \cos (1/x)}{\cos x} = 0 - \lim_{x \to 0} \cos \frac{1}{x},$$

but $\lim\limits_{x \to 0} \cos (1/x)$ does not exist, hence the L'Hospital rule is not applicable here.

(b) The limit of the ratio of the functions does not exist :

$$\lim_{x \to \infty} \frac{2 + 2x + \sin 2x}{(2x + \sin 2x)\, e^{\sin x}} = \lim_{x \to \infty} \left(1 + \frac{2}{2x + \sin 2x}\right) e^{-\sin x}$$

but $\lim\limits_{x \to \infty} e^{-\sin x}$ does not exist, since the function $e^{-\sin x}$ traverses the values from $1/e$ to e infinitely many times.

Now we will show that the limit of the ratio of derivatives exists :

$$\lim_{x \to \infty} \frac{2 + 2 \cos 2x}{[2 + 2 \cos 2x + (2x + \sin 2x) \cos x]\, e^{\sin x}}$$

$$= \lim_{x \to \infty} \frac{4 \cos^2 x}{4 \cos^2 x + (2x + \sin 2x) \cos x} e^{-\sin x}$$

$$= \lim_{x \to \infty} \frac{4 \cos x}{2x + 4 \cos x + \sin 2x} e^{-\sin x} = 0,$$

since the function $e^{-\sin x}$ is bounded, and $\dfrac{4 \cos x}{2x + 4 \cos x + \sin 2x} \to 0.$

Here $\cos x$, which vanishes for an infinite set of values of x, has been cancelled out. It is the presence of this multiplier that makes the L'Hospital rule inapplicable in this case, since it simultaneously nullifies the derivatives of the functions being compared.

(c) $$\lim_{x \to \pi/2} \frac{\tan x}{\sec x} = \lim_{x \to \pi/2} \frac{\sec^2 x}{\sec x \tan x} = \lim_{x \to \frac{\pi}{2}} \frac{\sec x}{\tan x} = \lim_{x \to \pi/2} \frac{\tan x}{\sec x} = \ldots.$$

Here application of the L'Hospital rule gives no useful result, though there exists a limit :

$$\lim_{x \to \pi/2} \frac{\tan x}{\sec x} \lim_{x \to \pi/2} \frac{\sin x \cos x}{\cos x} = \lim_{x \to \pi/2} \sin x = 1.$$

3.2.9. Using the L'Hospital rule find limits of the following functions:

(a) $\lim\limits_{x \to 2} \dfrac{\ln (x^2 - 3)}{x^2 - 3x - 10}$; (b) $\lim\limits_{x \to 1} \dfrac{a^{\ln x} - x}{\ln x}$;

(c) $\lim\limits_{x \to 0} \dfrac{\tan x - x}{x - \sin x}$; (d) $\lim\limits_{x \to 1} \dfrac{1 - 4 \sin^2 (\pi x/6)}{1 - x^2}$;

(e) $\lim\limits_{x \to a} \arcsin \dfrac{x - a}{a} \cot (x - a)$; (f) $\lim\limits_{x \to +\infty} (\pi - 2 \arctan x) \ln x$;

(g) $\lim\limits_{x \to +0} \left(\dfrac{1}{x}\right)^{\tan x}$; (h) $\lim\limits_{x \to \infty} (a^{1/x} - 1)\, x \; (a > 0)$;

(i) $\lim\limits_{x \to 0} (\cos mx)^{n/x^2}$; (j) $\lim\limits_{x \to a} \left(2 - \dfrac{x}{a}\right)^{\tan (\pi x/(2a))}$;

(k) $\lim\limits_{x \to 1} \left(\dfrac{1}{\ln x} - \dfrac{x}{\ln x}\right)$; (l) $\lim\limits_{x \to 0} x^{1/\ln (e^x - 1)}$;

(m) $\lim\limits_{x \to 0} \left(\dfrac{1}{x^2} - \cot^2 x\right)$; (n) $\lim\limits_{x \to \infty} \left[x - x^2 \ln \left(1 + \dfrac{1}{x}\right)\right]$;

(o) $\lim\limits_{x \to \infty} x^2 \left[\cosh \dfrac{a}{x} - 1\right]$; (p) $\lim\limits_{x \to 0} \left(\dfrac{5}{2 + \sqrt{9 + x}}\right)^{1/\sin x}$;

(q) $\lim\limits_{x \to +0} (\ln \cot x)^{\tan x}$; (r) $\lim\limits_{x \to \infty} \dfrac{e^{1/x^2} - 1}{2 \arctan x^2 - \pi}$.

3.3. Taylor's Formula. Application to Approximate Calculations

If the function $f(x)$ is continuous and has continuous derivatives through order $n - 1$ on the interval $[a, b]$, and has a finite derivative of the nth order at every interior point of the interval then at $x \in [a, b]$ the following formula holds true :

$$f(x) = f(a) + f'(a)(x - a) + f''(a)\frac{(x-a)^2}{2!} + f'''(a)\frac{(x-a)^3}{3!} + \dots + f^{(n-1)}(a)\frac{(x-a)^{n-1}}{(n-1)!} + f^{(n)}(\xi)\frac{(x-a)^n}{n!},$$

where $\xi = a + \theta(x - a)$ and $0 < \theta < 1$.

It is called Taylor's formula of the function $f(x)$.

If in this formula we put $a = 0$, we obtain Maclaurin's formula :

$$f(x) = f(0) + f'(0)\,x + f''(0)\frac{x^2}{2!} + \dots + f^{(n-1)}(0)\frac{x^{n-1}}{(n-1)!} + f^{(n)}(\xi)\frac{x^n}{n!},$$

where $\xi = \theta x$, $-0 < \theta < 1$.

The last term in the Taylor formula is called the remainder in Lagrange's form and is denoted $R_n(x)$:

$$R_n(x) = \frac{f^{(n)}[a + \theta(x - a)]}{n!}\, x^n (x - a)^n;$$

3.3.1. Expand the polynomial $P(x) = x^5 - 2x^4 + x^3 - x^2 + 2x - 1$ in powers of the binomial $x - 1$ using the Taylor formula.

Solution To solve the problem it is necessary to find the value of the polynomial and its derivatives at the point $x = 1$. The relevant calculations are given below.

$$P\,(1) = 0, \quad P'\,(1) = 0,$$
$$P''\,(1) = 0, \quad P'''\,(1) = 0,$$
$$P^{(4)}\,(1) = 72, \quad P^{(5)}\,(1) = 120,$$
$$P^{(n)}\,(x) = 0\;(n \geq 6)$$

at any x.

Substituting the values thus found into the Taylor formula, we get

$$P(x) = \frac{18}{3!}(x-1)^3 + \frac{72}{4!}(x-1)^4 + \frac{120}{5!}(x-1)^5;$$
$$P(x) = 3\,(x-1)^3 + 3\,(x-1)^4 + (x-1)^5.$$

3.3.2. Applying the Maclaurin formula, expand in powers of x (up to x^9, inclusive) the function

$$f(x) = \ln\,(1 + x),$$

defined on the interval [0; 1]. Estimate the error due to deleting the remainder.

Solution $f(0) = \ln 1 = 0.$

The derivatives of any order of the given function (see ξ 2.3):

$$f^{(n)}\,(x) = (-1)^{n-1}\frac{(n-1)!}{(1+x)^n},$$
$$f^{(n)}\,(0) = (-1)^{n-1}\,(n-1)!\,(n = 1, 2, 3, \ldots).$$

Substituting the derivatives into the Maclaurin formula, we get

$$\ln\,(1 + x) = x - \frac{x^2}{2} + \frac{x^3}{3} - \ldots + \frac{x^9}{9} + R_{10}\,(x),$$

where the remainder $R_{10}(x)$ in the Lagrange form will be written as follows :

$$R_{10}\,(x) = \frac{f^{(10)}\,(\xi)}{10!}\,x^{10} = -\frac{9!}{10!\,(1+\xi)^{10}}\,x^{10} = -\frac{x^{10}}{10\,(1+\xi)^{10}}\;(0 < \xi < x).$$

Let us estimate the absolute value of the remainder $R_{10}(x)$; keeping in mind that $0 \leq x \leq 1$ and $\xi > 0$, we have

$$|\,R_{10}\,(x)\,| = \left|\frac{-x^{10}}{10\,(1+\xi)^{10}}\right| < \frac{1}{10}.$$

3.3.3. How many terms in the Maclaurin formula should be taken for the function $f(x) = e^x$ so as to get a polynomial representing this function on the interval $[-1, 1]$, accurate to there decimal place?

Solution The function $f(x) = e^x$ has a derivative of any order

$$f^{(n)}\,(x) = e^x.$$

Therefore, the Maclaurin formula is applicable to this function. Let us compute the values of the function e^x and its first $n-1$ derivatives at the point $x=0$, and the value of the nth derivative at the point $\xi = \theta x$ $(0<\theta<1)$. We will have

$$f(0) = f'(0) = f''(0) = \ldots = f^{(n-1)}(0) = 1;$$

$$f^{(n)}(\xi) = e^{\xi} = e^{\theta x}.$$

Whence

$$f(x) = 1 + \frac{x}{1!} + \frac{x^2}{2!} + \ldots + \frac{x^{n-1}}{(n-1)!} + R_n(x),$$

where

$$R_n(x) = \frac{x^n}{n!} e^{\theta x}.$$

Since, by hypothesis, $|x| \le 1$ and $0 < \theta < 1$, then

$$|R_n(x)| = \frac{|x|^n}{n!} e^{\theta x} < \frac{1}{n!} e < \frac{3}{n!}.$$

Hence, if the inequality

$$\frac{3}{n!} \le 0.001 \qquad (*)$$

is fulfilled, then the inequality

$$|R_n(x)| \le 0.001$$

will be fulfilled apriori. To this end it is sufficient to take $n \ge 7$ $(7! = 5040)$. Hence, 7 terms in the Maclaurin formula will suffice.

3.3.4. At what values of x will the approximate formula

$$\cos x \approx 1 - \frac{x^2}{2!} + \frac{x^4}{4!}$$

have an error less than 0.00005 ?

Solution The right member of the approximate equation represent the first six terms in the Maclaurin formula for the function cos x (the second, fourth and sixth terms are equal to zero. Check it)

Let us estimate $R_6(x)$. Since, $(\cos x)^{(6)} = -\cos x$, then

$$|R_6(x)| = \left|\frac{-\cos\theta x}{6!} x^6\right| \le \frac{|x|^6}{6!}.$$

For the error to be less than 0.00005, choose the values of x that satisfy the inequality

$$\frac{|x|^6}{6!} < 0.00005.$$

Solving this inequality, we get $|x| < 0.575$

3.3.5. Compute the approximate values of

(a) $\cos 5°$; (b) $\sin 20°$;

accurate to five decimal places.

Solution (a) Into the Maclaurin formula

$$\cos x = 1 - \frac{x^2}{2!} + \frac{x^4}{4!} - \ldots + (-1)^n \frac{x^{2n}}{(2n)!} + R_{2n+2}$$

Substitute $x = \pi/36$; since

$$\frac{x^2}{2!} = \frac{\pi^2}{2.36^2} = 0.003808, \quad \frac{x^4}{4!} = \frac{1}{6}\left(\frac{x^2}{2}\right)^2 = 2.4 \cdot 10^{-5},$$

we confine ourselves to the following terms :

$$\cos x \approx 1 - x^2/2,$$

the error being estimated at

$$|R_4(x)| = \left|\frac{\cos \theta x}{4!} x^4\right| \le \frac{|x|^4}{4!} < 2.5 \cdot 10^{-6}.$$

And so, within the required accuracy

$$\cos 5^\circ = \cos \frac{\pi}{35} = 1 - 0.00381 = 0.99619.$$

3.3.6. Compute the approximate value of $\sqrt[4]{83}$ accurate to six decimal places.

3.3.7. Prove the inequalities

(a) $x - x^2/2 < \ln(1 + x) < x$ at $x > 0$;

(b) $\tan x > x + x^3/3$ at $0 < x < \pi/2$;

(c) $1 + \frac{1}{2}x - \frac{x^2}{8} < \sqrt{1 + x} < 1 + \frac{1}{2}x$ at $0 < x < \infty$.

Solution According to the Maclaurin formula with the remainder $R_2(x)$ we have

$$\ln(1 + x) = x - \frac{x^2}{2(1 + \xi)^2},$$

where $0 < \xi < x$.

According to the same formula with the remainder $R_3(x)$ we have

$$\ln(1 + x) = x - \frac{x^2}{2} + \frac{x^3}{3(1 + \xi_1)^3},$$

where $0 < \xi_1 < x$.

Since $\frac{x^2}{2(1 + \xi)^2} > 0$ and $\frac{x^3}{3(1 + \xi_1)^3} > 0$ at $x > 0$, it follows that

$$x - x^2/2 < \ln(1 + x) < x.$$

3.3.8. Show that $\sin(a + h)$ differs from $\sin \alpha + h \cos \alpha$ by not more than $h^2/2$.

Solution By Taylor's formula

$$\sin(\alpha + h) = \sin \alpha + h \cos \alpha - \frac{h^2}{2} \sin \xi;$$

whence $|\sin(\alpha + h) - (\sin \alpha + h \cos \alpha)| = \frac{h^2}{2} |\sin \xi| \le \frac{h^2}{2}.$

3.4. Application of Taylor's Formula to Evaluation of Limits

The expression

$$f(x) = f(a) + \frac{f'(a)}{1!}(x-a) + \frac{f''(a)}{2!}(x-a)^2 + \dots + \frac{f^{(n)}(a)}{n!}(x-a)^n + o(|x-a|^n)$$

is the *Taylor formula* with the remainder in Peano's form where $\varphi(x) = o[\psi(x)]$ means that, as $x \to a$, the function $\varphi(x)$ has a higher order of smallness than the function $\psi(x)$, *ie*, $\lim\limits_{x \to a} \frac{\varphi(x)}{\psi(x)} = 0$.

In particular, at $a = 0$ we have

$$f(x) = f(0) + \frac{f'(0)}{1!}x + \frac{f''(0)}{2!}x^2 + \dots + \frac{f^{(n)}(0)}{n!}x^n + o(|x|^n).$$

Peano's form of the remainder for Taylor's formula shows that, when substituting the Taylor polynomial of degree n for $f(x)$ in the neighbourhood of the point a, we introduce an error which is an infinitesimal of a higher order than $(x-a)^n$ as $x \to a$.

The following five expansions are of greatest importance in solving practical problems :

$$e^x = 1 + x + \frac{x^2}{2!} + \dots + \frac{x^n}{n!} + o(x^n);$$

$$\sin x = x - \frac{x^3}{3!} + \dots + (-1)^{n-1}\frac{x^{2n-1}}{(2n-1)!} + o(x^{2n});$$

$$\cos x = 1 - \frac{x^2}{2!} + \frac{x^4}{4!} + \dots + (-1)^n\frac{x^{2n}}{(2n)!} + o(x^{2n+1});$$

$$(1+x)^\alpha = 1 + \alpha x + \frac{\alpha(\alpha-1)}{2!}x^2 + \dots + \frac{\alpha(\alpha-1)\dots(\alpha-n+1)}{n!}x^n + o(x^n);$$

$$\ln(1+x) = x - \frac{x^2}{2} + \frac{x^3}{3} + \dots + (-1)^{n-1}\frac{x^n}{n} + o(x^n).$$

3.4.1. Expand the function $f(x) = \sin^2 x - x^2 e^{-x}$ in positive integral powers of x up to the terms of the fourth order of smallness with respect to x.

Solution We have

$$f(x) = \left[x - \frac{x^3}{6} + o(x^4)\right]^2 - x^2\left[1 - x + \frac{x^2}{2} + o(x^2)\right]$$

$$= x^2 - \frac{x^4}{3} + o(x^5) - x^2 + x^3 - \frac{x^4}{2} + o(x^4) = x^3 - \frac{5}{6}x^4 + o(x^4).$$

3.4.2. Expand the following functions :

(a) $f(x) = x\sqrt{1-x^2} - \cos x \ln(1+x)$;

(b) $f(x) = \ln(1 + \sin x)$;

in positive integral powers of x up to the terms of the fifth order of smallness with respect to x.

3.4.3. Applying the Taylor formula with the remainder in Peano's form, compute the limits :

(a) $\lim\limits_{x\to 0} \dfrac{1-\sqrt{1+x^2}\cos x}{\tan^4 x}$;

(b) $\lim\limits_{x\to 0} \dfrac{\sqrt[3]{1+3x} - \sqrt{1+2x}}{x^2}$;

(c) $\lim\limits_{x\to 0} \dfrac{\cos x - e^{-x^2/2}}{x^4}$;

(d) $\lim\limits_{x\to 0} \dfrac{e^x \sin x - x(1+x)}{x^3}$;

(e) $\lim\limits_{x\to 0} \dfrac{e^x + e^{-x} - 2}{x^2}$.

Solution (a) Retaining the terms up to the fourth order with respect to x in the denominator and the numerator, we get

$$\lim_{x\to 0} \frac{1-\sqrt{1+x^2}\cos x}{\tan^4 x} = \lim_{x\to 0} \frac{1-(1+x^2)^{1/2}\cos x}{x^4}$$

$$= \lim_{x\to 0} \frac{1-\left[1+\frac{1}{2}x^2 + \frac{1/2(-1/2)}{2}x^4 + o(x^4)\right]\left[1-\frac{x^2}{2}+\frac{x^4}{24}+o(x^5)\right]}{x^4}$$

$$= \lim_{x\to 0} \frac{\frac{1}{4}x^4 + \frac{1}{8}x^4 - \frac{1}{24}x^4 + o(x^4)}{x^4} = \lim_{x\to 0}\left[\frac{1}{3} + \frac{o(x^4)}{x^4}\right] = \frac{1}{3}.$$

3.4.4. Expand the following function in positive integral powers of the variable x up to the terms of the indicated order, inclusive

(a) $f(x) = e^{2x-x^2}$ up to the terms containing x^5;

(b) $\ln \cos x$ up to the terms containing x^6

(c) $\dfrac{x}{e^x - 1}$ up to the terms containing x^4.

3.5. Testing a Function for Monotonicity

Let a continuous function $f(x)$ be defined on the interval $[a, b]$ and have a finite derivative inside this segment. Then :

(1) For $f(x)$ to be non-decreasing (non-increasing) on $[a, b]$ it is necessary and sufficient that $f'(x) \geq 0$ ($f'(x) \leq 0$) for all x in (a, b).

(2) For $f(x)$ to increasing (decreasing) on $[a,b]$ it is sufficient to fulfil the condition $f'(x)>0$ ($f'(x)<0$) for all x in (a,b).

3.5.1. Determine the intervals of monotonicity for the following functions

(a) $f(x)=2x^2-\ln x$;

(b) $f(x)=2x^3-9x^2-24x+7$;

(c) $f(x)=x^2e^{-x}$;

(d) $f(x)=\ln|x|$;

(e) $f(x)=4x^3-21x^2+18x+20$;

(f) $f(x)=e^x+5x$.

Solution The Solution of this problem is reduced to finding the intervals in which the derivative preserves its sign. If the function $f(x)$ has a continuous derivative in the interval (a,b) and has in it a finite number of stationary points $x_1, x_2, \ldots, x_n (a<x_1<x_2<\ldots<x_n<b)$, where $f'(x_k)=0$ $(k=1,2,\ldots,n)$, then $f'(x)$ preserves its sign in each of the intervals $(a, x_1), (x_1, x_2), \ldots (x_{n-1}, x_n), (x_n, b)$.

(a) The function is defined at $x>0$.

Let us find the derivative

$$f'(x)=4x-1/x.$$

The function increases if $4x-1/x>0$, *ie*, $x>1/2$.

The function decreases if $4x-1/x<0$, *ie*, $x<1/2$.

And so, the function decreases in the interval $0<x<1/2$ and increases in the interval $1/2<x<+\infty$.

(b) Evaluate the derivative

$$f'(x)=6x^2-18x-24=6(x^2-3x-4).$$

It vanishes at the points $x=-1$ and $x=4$. Since $f'(x)$ is a quadratic trinomial with a coefficient at its highest-power term $6<0$, then $f'(x)>0$ in the intervals $(-\infty,-1), (4,\infty)$ and $f'(x)<0$ in the interval $(-1, 4)$. consequently, $f(x)$ increases in the sequently, $f(x)$ increases in the first two intervals, whereas in $(-1, 4)$ it decreases.

(c) In this case the derivative $f'(x)=(2x-x^2)e^{-x}$ vanishes at the points $x=0$ and $x=2$. In the intervals $(-\infty, 0)$ and $(2,\infty)$ the derivative $f'(x)<0$ and the function decreases; in $(0, 2)$ the derivative $f'(x)>0$ and the function increases (see Fig. 39).

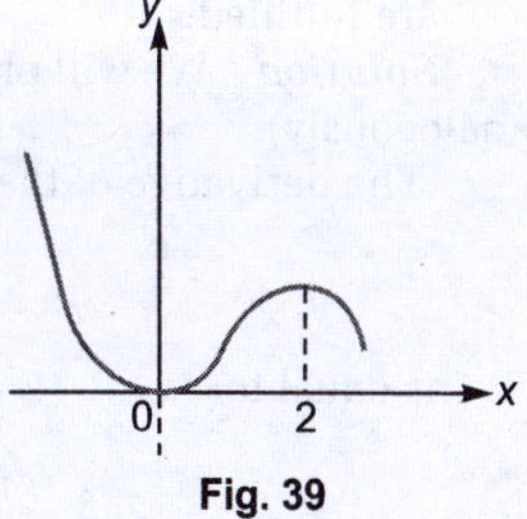

Fig. 39

3.5.2. Find the intervals of decreases and increases for the following functions :

(a) $f(x)=\cos(\pi/x)$;

(b) $f(x)=\sin x+\cos x$ on $[0, 2\pi]$.

(a) The function $y = \cos(\pi/x)$ is defined and differentiable throughout the number scale, except at the point $x = 0$;

$$y' = \frac{\pi}{x^2} \sin \frac{\pi}{x}.$$

As is obvious, the sign of y' coincides with that of the multiplier $\sin(\pi/x)$.

(1) $\sin(\pi/x) > 0$ if

$$2k\pi < \pi/x < (2k+1)\pi \ (k = 0, \pm 1, \pm 2, \ldots);$$

(2) $\sin(\pi/x) < 0$ if

$$(2k+1)\pi < \pi/x < 2(k+1)\pi.$$

Hence, the function increases in the intervals

$$\left(\frac{1}{2k+1}, \frac{1}{2k}\right)$$

and decreases in the intervals

$$\left(\frac{1}{2k+2}, \frac{1}{2k+1}\right).$$

3.5.3. Investigate the behaviour of the function $f(x) = 2\sin x + \tan x - 3x$ in the interval $(-\pi/2, \pi/2)$.

Solution The derivative

$$f'(x) = 2\cos x + \frac{1}{\cos^2 x} - 3 = \frac{(1-\cos x)(1+\cos x - 2\cos^2 x)}{\cos^2 x}$$

$$= \frac{4\sin^3(x/2)\sin(3x/2)}{\cos^2 x}$$

is positive in the intervals $(-\pi/2, 0)$ and $(0, \pi/2)$ and vanishes only at $x = 0$. Hence, in $(-\pi/2, \pi/2)$ the function $f(x)$ increases.

3.5.4. Prove that at $0 < x \le 1$ the inequalities

$$x - x^3/3 < \arctan x < x - x^3/6$$

are fulfilled.

Solution We will prove only the right inequality (the left one is proved analogously).

The derivative of the function

$$f(x) = \arctan x - x + \frac{x^3}{6}$$

is equal to

$$f'(x) = \frac{1}{1+x^2} - 1 + \frac{x^2}{2} = \frac{x^2(x^2-1)}{2(1+x^2)}.$$

The function $f(x)$ is continuous throughout the entire number scale, in particular, it is continuous in the interval $[0, 1]$, and inside this segment $f'(x) < 0$. Therefore, $f(x)$ decreases on the interval $[0, 1]$ and, consequently, for any point x, $0 < x \le 1$, the inequality $f(x) < f(0) = 0$ or

$$\text{arc tan } x - x + \frac{x^3}{6} < 0$$

is fulfilled, whence

$$\text{arc tan } x < x - \frac{x^3}{6}.$$

3.5.5. Prove the inequalities

$$x - x^3/6 < \sin x < x \text{ at } x > 0.$$

3.5.6. Prove that for $0 \le p \le 1$ and for any positive a and b the inequality $(a + b)^p \le a^p + b^p$ is valid.

Solution By dividing both sides of the inequality by b^p we get

$$\left(\frac{a}{b} + 1\right)^p \le \left(\frac{a}{b}\right)^p + 1$$

or

$$(1 + x)^p \le 1 + x^p, \qquad (*)$$

where $x = \frac{a}{b}$.

Let us show that the inequality (*) holds true at any positive x. Introduce the function

$$f(x) = 1 + x^p - (1 + x)^p;\ x \ge 0\,.$$

The derivative of this function

$$f'(x) = px^{p-1} - (1 + x)^{p-1} = p\left[\frac{1}{x^{1-p}} - \frac{1}{(1 + x)^{1-p}}\right]$$

is positive everywhere, since, by hypothesis, $1 - p \ge 0$ and $x > 0$. Hence, the function increases in the half-open interval $[0, \infty]$, *ie*, $f(x) = 1 + x^p - (1 + x)^p > f(0) = 0$, whence $1 + x^p > (1 + x)^p$, which completes the proof. If we put $p = 1/n$, then we obtain

$$\sqrt[n]{a + b} \le \sqrt[n]{a} + \sqrt[n]{b}\ (n \ge 1).$$

3.5.7. Prove that the function $y = x^5 + 2x^3 + x$ increases everywhere, and the function $y = 1 - x^3$ decreases everywhere.

3.5.8. Determine the intervals of increase and decrease for the following functions :

(a) $f(x) = x^3 + 2x - 5$; (b) $f(x) = \ln(1 - x^2)$;

(c) $f(x) = \cos x - x$; (d) $f(x) = \frac{1}{3}x^3 - \frac{1}{x}$;

(e) $f(x) = \frac{2x}{\ln x}$; (f) $f(x) = \frac{2x}{1 + x^2}$.

3.5.9. Prove the following inequalities :

(a) $\tan x > x + x^3/3$, if $(0 < x < \pi/2)$;

(b) $e^x \ge 1 + x$ for all values of x;

(c) $e^x > ex$ at $x > 1$.

3.5.10. At what values of the coefficient a does the function $f(x) = x^3 - ax$ increase along the entire number scale ?

3.5.11. At what value of b does the function

$$f(x) = \sin x - bx + c$$

decrease along the entire number scale ?

3.6. Maxima and Minima of Function

If a function $y = f(x)$ is defined on the interval X, then an interior point x_0 of this interval is called the point of maximum of the function $f(x)$ [the point of minimum of the function $f(x)$] if there exists a neighbourhood $U \in X$ of the point x_0, such that the inequality $f(x) \le f(x_0)$ [$f(x) \ge f(x_0)$] holds true within it.

The generic terms for points of maximum and minimum of a function are the points of extremum.

A Necessary Condition for the Existence of an Extremum. At points of extremum the derivative $f'(x)$ is equal to zero or does not exist.

The points at which the derivative $f'(x) = 0$ or does not exist are called *critical points*.

Sufficient Conditions for the Existence of an Extremum.

I. Let the function $f(x)$ be continuous in some neighbourhood of the point x_0.

1. If $f'(x) > 0$ at $x < x_0$ and $f'(X) < 0$ at $x > x_0$ (*ie*, if in moving from left to right through the point x_0 the derivative changes sign from plus to minus), then at the point x_0 the function reaches a maximum.

2. If $f'(x) < 0$ at $x < x_0$ and $f'(x) > 0$ at $x > x_0$ (*ie*, if in moving through the point x_0 from left to right the derivative changes sign from minus to plus), then the point x_0 the function reaches a minimum.

3. If the derivative does not change sign in moving through the point x_0, then there is no extremum.

II. Let the function $f(x)$ be twice differentiable (that is $f'(x_0) = 0$) at a critical point x_0. If $f''(x_0) < 0$, then at x_0 the function has a maximum; if $f''(x_0) > 0$, then at x_0 the function has a minimum ; but if $f''(x_0) = 0$, then the question of the existence of an extremum at this point remains open.

III. Let $f'(x_0) = f''(x_0) = \dots f^{(n-1)}(x_0) = 0$, but $f^{(n)}(x_0) \ne 0$. If n is even, then at $f^{(n)}(x_0) < 0$ there is a maximum at x_0, and at $f^{(n)}(x_0) > 0$, a minimum.

If n is odd, then there is no extremum at the point x_0.

IV. Let a function $y = f(x)$ be represented parametrically :

$$x = \varphi(t),\ y = \psi(t),$$

where the functions $\varphi(t)$ and $\psi(t)$have derivatives both of the first and second orders within a certain interval of change of the argument t, and $\varphi'(t) \ne 0$. Further, let, at $t = t_0$

$$\psi'(t) = 0.$$

Then :

(a) if $\psi''(t_0) < 0$, the function $y = f(x)$ has a maximum at $x = x_0 = \psi(t_0)$;

(b) if $\psi''(t_0) > 0$, the function $y = f(x)$ has a minimum at $x = x_0 = \varphi(t_0)$;

(c) if $\psi''(t_0) = 0$, the question of the existence of an extremum remains open.

The points at which $\varphi'(t)$ vanishes require a special study.

3.6.1. Using the first derivative, find the extrema of the following functions :

(a) $f(x) = \frac{3}{4}x^4 - x^3 - 9x^2 + 7;$

(b) $f(x) = x^4 - 8x^3 + 22x^2 - 24x + 12;$

(c) $f(x) = x(x+1)^3(x-3)^2;$

(d) $f(x) = \dfrac{x^2 - 3x + 2}{x^2 + 2x + 1}.$

Solution (a) The function is defined and differentiable over the entire number scale. Therefore, only the real roots of the derivative

$$f'(x) = 3x^3 - 3x^2 - 18x = 3x(x+2)(x-3)$$

are critical points. Equating this expression to zero, we find the critical points $x_1 = -2$, $x_2 = 0$, $x_3 = 3$ (they should always be arranged in an increasing order). Let us now investigate the sign of the derivative in the neighbourhood of each of these points. Since there are no critical points to the left of the point $x = -2$, the derivative at all the points $x < -2$ has one and the same sign : it is negative. Analogously, in the interval $(-2, 0)$ the derivative is positive, in the interval $(0, 3)$ it is negative, at $x > 3$ it is positive. Hence, at the points $x_1 = -2$ and $x_3 = 3$ we have minima $f(-2) = -9$ and $f(3) = -40\frac{1}{4}$, and at the point $x_2 = 0$, maximum $f(0) = 7$.

(c) Just as in item (a), the critical points are the roots of the derivative $f'(x)$, since the function is defined and differentiable throughout the number scale. Find $f'(x)$:

$$f'(x) = (x+1)^3(x-3)^2 + 3x(x+1)^2(x-3)^2 + 2x(x+1)^3 \times (x-3)$$
$$= 3(x+1)^2(x-3)(2x^2 - 3x - 1).$$

Equating this expression to zero, we find the critical points :

$$x_1 = -1,\ x_2 = (3 - \sqrt{17})/4,\ x_3 = (3 + \sqrt{17})/4,\ x_4 = 3.$$

Let us tabulate the signs of the derivative in the intervals between the critical points :

Intervals	$x < x_1$	$x_1 < x < x_2$	$x_2 < x < x_3$	$x_3 < x < x_4$	$x_4 < x$
Sign of $f'(x)$	–	–	+	–	+

As is seen from the table, there is no extremum at the point $x_1 = -1$, there is a minimum at the point x_2, a maximum at the point x_3, and a minimum at the point x_4.

3.6.2. Using the first derivative, find the extrema of the following functions :

(a) $f(x) = 3\sqrt[3]{x^2} - x^2;$ (b) $f(x) = \sqrt[3]{(x-1)^2} + \sqrt[3]{(x+1)^2}.$

Solution (a) The function is defined and continuous throughout the number scale.

Let us find the derivative :

$$f'(x) = 2\left(\frac{1}{\sqrt[3]{x}} - x\right).$$

From the equation $f'(x) = 0$ we find the roots of the derivative : $x = \pm 1$.

Furthermore, the derivative goes to infinity at the point $x = 0$. Thus, the critical points are $x_1 = -1$, $x_2 = 0$, $x_3 = 1$. The results of investigating the sign of the derivative in the neighbourhood of these points are given in Fig. 40. The investigation shows that the function has two maxima : $f(-1) = 2$; $f(1) = 2$ and a minimum $f(0) = 0$.

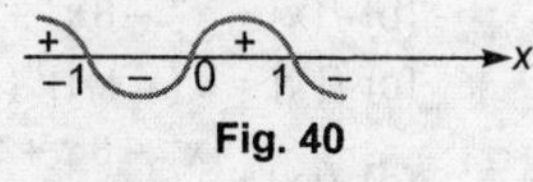

Fig. 40

3.6.3. Using the second derivative, find out the character of the extrema of the following functions :

(a) $y = 2\sin x + \cos 2x$;

(b) $f(x) = 2x^3 - 15x^2 - 84x + 8$.

Solution (a) Since the function is a periodic one we may confine ourselves to be interval $[0, 2\pi]$. Find the first and second derivatives :

$$y' = 2\cos x - 2\sin 2x = 2\cos x(1 - 2\sin x);$$
$$y'' = -2\sin x - 4\cos 2x$$

From the equation $2\cos x(1 - 2\sin x) = 0$ determine the critical points on the interval $[0, 2\pi]$:

$$x_1 = \pi/6,\ x_2 = \pi/2,\ x_3 = 5\pi/6,\ x_4 = 3\pi/2.$$

Now find the sign of th second derivative at each point :

$y''(\pi/6) = -3 < 0$; hence, we have a maximum $y(\pi/6) = 3/2$ at the point $x_1 = \pi/6$;

$y''(\pi/2) = 2 > 0$; hence, we have a minimum $y(\pi/2) = 1$ at the point $x_2 = \pi/2$

$y''(5\pi/6) = -3 < 0$; hence we have a maximum $y(5\pi/6) = 3/2$ at the point $x_3 = 5\pi/6$;

$y''(3\pi/2) = 6 > 0$; hence, we have a minimum $y(3\pi/2) = -3$ at the point $x_4 = 3\pi/2$ (sec Fig. 41).

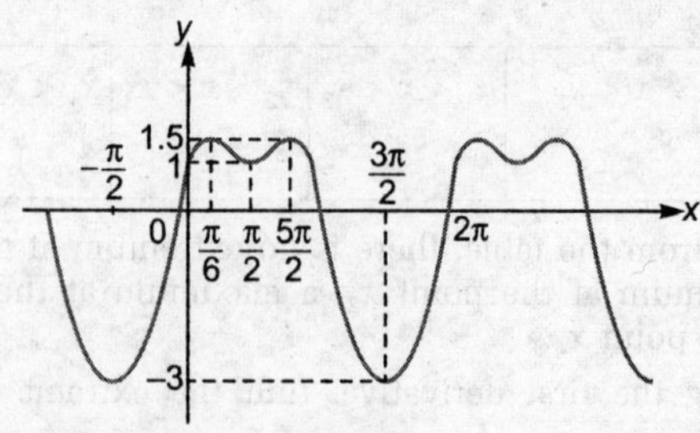

Fig. 41

3.6.4. Investigate the following functions for extrema :

(a) $f(x) = \begin{cases} -2x & (x < 0), \\ 3x + 5 & (x \geq 0); \end{cases}$

(b) $f(x) = \begin{cases} 2x^2 + 3 & (x \neq 0), \\ 4 & (x = 0). \end{cases}$

Solution (a) Though the derivative

$$f'(x) = \begin{cases} -2 \ (x < 0), \\ 3 \ (x > 0) \end{cases}$$

exists at all points, except the point $x = 0$ and changes sign from minus to plus when passing through the point $x = 0$, there is no minimum here :

$$f(0) = 5 > f(x) \text{ at } -1 < x < 0.$$

This is explained by the fact that the function is discontinuous at the point $x = 0$.

(b) Here the derivative $f'(x) = 4x \ (x \neq 0)$ also exists at all points, except at $x = 0$, and it changes sign from minus to plus when passing through the point $x = 0$. Nevertheless, we have here a maximum but not a minimum, which can readily be checked.

It is explained by the fact that the function is discontinuous at the point $x = 0$.

3.6.5. Find the extrema of the following functions :

(a) $f(x) = \dfrac{50}{3x^4 + 8x^3 - 18x^2 + 60}$;

(b) $f(x) = \sqrt{e^{x^2} - 1}$.

Solution (a) Here it is simpler to find the extrema of the function $f_1(x) = 3x^4 + 8x^3 - 18x^2 + 60$. Since

$$f'_1(x) = 12x^3 + 24x^2 - 36x = 12x\,(x^2 + 2x - 3),$$

$$f_1''(x) = 12\,(3x^2 + 4x - 3),$$

the critical points are

$$x_1 = -3,\ x_2 = 0,\ x_3 = 1,$$

and the character of the extrema is readily determined from the sign of the second derivative $f_1''(-3) < 0$; hence, at the point $x_1 = -3$ the function $f_1(x)$ has a minimum, and the given function $f(x)$ obviously has a maximum $f(-3) = -\frac{2}{3}$, $f_1''(0) < 0$; hence, at the point $x_2 = 0$ the function $f_1(x)$ has a maximum, and $f(x)$ a minimum $f(0) = 5/6$; $f_1''(1) > 0$; hence, at the point $x_3 = 1$ the function $f_1(x)$ has a minimum, and $f(x)$ a maximum $f(1) = 50/53$. (b) In this case it is easier to find the points of extremum of the redicand

$$f_1(x) = e^{x^2} - 1.$$

which coincide with the point of extremum of the function $f(x)$. Let us find the critical points of $f_1(x)$:

$f_1'(x) = 2xe^{x^2}$; $f_1'(x) = 0$ at the point $x = 0$. Determine the sign of the second derivative at the point $x = 0$;

$$f_1''(x) = 2e^{x^2}(1 + 2x^2),\ f_1''(0) = 2 > 0.$$

Therefore the point $x = 0$ is a minimum of the function $f_1(x)$; it will also be a minimum of the given function $f(x)$: $f(0) = 0$.

3.6.6. Investigate the character of the extremum of the function $y = \cosh x + \cos x$ at the point $x = 0$.

Solution The function y is an even one and apparently has an extremum at the point $x = 0$. To determine the character of the extremum let us evaluate the derivatives of this function at the point $x = 0$:

$$y' = \sinh x - \sin x,\ y'(0) = 0;$$
$$y'' = \cosh x - \cos x,\ y''(0) = 0$$
$$y''' = \sinh x + \sin x,\ y'''(0) = 0;$$
$$y^{(4)} = \cosh x + \cos x;\ y^{(4)}(0) = 2 > 0.$$

Since the first non-zero derivative at the point $x = 0$ is a derivative of an even order, which takes on a positive value, we have a minimum $y(0) = 2$ at this point.

3.6.7. Investigate the following functions for an extremum at the point $x = 0$:

(a) $y = \cos x - 1 + \dfrac{x^2}{2!} - \dfrac{x^3}{3!}$; (b) $y = \cos x - 1 + \dfrac{x^2}{2}$.

Solution (a) $y' = -\sin x + x - \dfrac{x^2}{2}$; $y'(0) = 0$;

$$y'' = -\cos x + 1 - x;\ y''(0) = 0;$$
$$y''' = \sin x - 1;\ y'''(0) = -1 \neq 0.$$

And so, the first non-zero derivative at the point $x = 0$ is a derivative of the third order, *ie*, of an odd order ; this means that there is no extremum at the point $x = 0$.

3.6.8. Investigate the following functions for extrema :

(a) $f(x) = x^4e^{-x^2}$; (b) $f(x) = \sin 3x - 3\sin x$.

Solution The function $f(x) = x^4e^{-x^2}$ is continuously differentiable everywhere. Equating the derivative

$$f'(x) = 4x^3e^{-x^2} - 2x^5e^{-x^2} = x^3e^{-x^2}(4 - 2x^2)$$

to zero, find the critical points :

$$x_1 = -\sqrt{2};\ x_2 = 0;\ x_3 = \sqrt{2}.$$

Compute the values of the second derivative at the critical points :

$$f''(x) = 12x^2e^{-x^2} - 8x^4e^{-x^2} - 10x^4e^{-x^2} + 4x^6e^{-x^2}$$
$$= 2x^2e^{-x^2}(6 - 9x^2 + 2x^4);$$
$$f''(0) = 0;\ f''(-\sqrt{2}) < 0;\ f''(\sqrt{2}) < 0.$$

Consequently, at the points $x_1 = -\sqrt{2}$ and $x_3 = +\sqrt{2}$ the function reaches a maximum $f(\pm\sqrt{2}) = 4e^{-2} = \frac{4}{e^2}$. As far as the critical point $x_2 = 0$ is concerned, nothing definite can be said as yet, we have to find derivatives of $f(x)$ of higher orders (up to the fourth order!). But this process is cumbersome, therefore we will turn to the first sufficient condition of an extremum : let us find the signs of the first derivative in the neighbourhood of the critical point $x_2 = 0$:

$$f'(-1) < 0 ; f'(1) > 0.$$

Hence, at the point $x = 0$ the function has a minimum $f(0) = 0$.

3.6.9. The function $y = f(x)$ is represented parametrically :

$$\begin{cases} x = \varphi(t) = t^5 - 5t^3 - 30t + 7, \\ y = \psi(t) = 4t^3 - 3t^2 - 18t + 3 \quad (-2 < t < 2). \end{cases}$$

Find the extrema of this function.

Solution We have

$$\varphi'(t) = 5t^4 - 15t^2 - 20.$$

In the interval $(-2, 2)$ $\varphi'(t) \neq 0$

Find $\psi'(t)$ and equate it to zero :

$$\psi'(t) = 12t^2 - 6t - 18 = 0.$$

Whence $t_1 = -1$ and $t_2 = 3/2$.

These roots are interior points of the considered interval of variation of the parameter t.

Furthermore

$$\psi''(t) = 24t - t ; \psi''(-1) = -30 < 0, \psi''(3/2) = 30 > 0.$$

Consequently, the function $y = f(x)$ has a maximum $y = 14$ at $t = -1$ (*ie*, at $x = 31$) and a minimum $y = -17.25$ at $t = 3/2$ (*ie*, at $x = 1033/32$).

3.6.10. Find the maxima and minima of the following functions :

(a) $f(x) - x^3e^{-x}$;

(b) $f(x) = \dfrac{4x}{x^2 + 4}$;

(c) $f(x) = -x^2\sqrt[5]{(x-2)^2}$;

(d) $f(x) = \dfrac{14}{x^4 - 8x^2 + 2}$;

(e) $f(x) = \sqrt[3]{2x^3 + 3x^2 - 36x}$;

(f) $f(x) = x^2 \ln x$;

(g) $f(x) = x \ln^2 x$.

3.6.11. Investigate the following functions for an extremum at the point $x = 0$:

(a) $f(x) = \sin x - x$;

(b) $f(x) = \sin x - x + x^3/3$;

(c) $f(x) = \sin x - x + \dfrac{x^3}{3!} - \dfrac{x^4}{4!}$;

(d) $f(x) = \begin{cases} e^{1/x}, & \text{if } x \neq 0, \\ 0, & \text{if } x = 0. \end{cases}$

3.7. Finding the Greatest and the Least Values of a Function

The greatest (least) value of a continuous function $f(x)$ on an interval $[a, b]$ is attained either at the critical points, or at the end-points of the interval. To find the greatest (least) value of the function we have to compute its values at all the critical points on the interval $[a, b]$, the values $f(a)$, $f(b)$ of the function at the end points of the interval and choose the greatest (least) one out of the numbers obtained.

If a function is defined and continuous in some interval, and if this interval is not a closed one, then it can have neither the greatest nor the least value.

3.7.1. Find the greatest and the least values of the following functions on the indicated intervals :

(a) $f(x) = 2x^3 - 3x^2 - 12x + 1$ on $[-2, 5/2]$;

(b) $f(x) = x^3 \ln x$ on $[1, e]$; (c) $f(x) = xe^{-x}$ on $[0, +\infty]$;

(d) $f(x) = \sqrt{(1 - x^2)(1 + 2x^2)}$ on $[-1, 1]$.

Solution Find the derivative $f'(x)$:

$$f'(x) = 6x^2 - 6x - 12.$$

It vanishes at two points : $x_1 = -1$ and $x_2 = 2$. They both lie in-side the indicated interval $\left[-2, \frac{5}{2}\right]$; consequently both of them must be taken into consideration. To find the extreme values of the function it is necessary to compute its values at the points x_1 and x_2, and also at the end-points of the segment :

$$f(-2) = -3, f(-1) = 8 \ ; f(2) = -19, f\left(\frac{5}{2}\right) = -16\frac{1}{2}\cdot$$

Hence, the greatest value is $f(-1) = 8$ and the least $f(2) = -19$.

(b) Find the critical points : $f'(x) = x(1 + 2 \ln x)$. The derivative $f'(x)$ does not vanish inside the given interval $[1, e]$. Therefore there are no critical points inside the indicated interval. It now remains to compute the values of the function at the end-points of the interval $[1, e]$.

$$f(1) = 0 \ ; f(e) = e^2.$$

Thus, $f(1) = 0$ is the least values of the function and $f(e) = e^2$ the greatest.

3.7.2. Find the greatest and the least values of the following functions on the indicated intervals:

(a) $y = \sin x \sin 2x$ on $(-\infty, \infty)$; (b) $y = \text{arc}\cos x^2$ on $[-\sqrt{2}/2, \sqrt{2}/2]$;

(c) $y = x + \sqrt{x}$ on $[0, 4]$.

Solution (a) Represent the function $y = \sin x \sin 2x$ in the form

$$y = \frac{\cos x - \cos 3x}{2},$$

whence it is seen that the function is an even one and has a period 2π. Hence, it is sufficient to seek the greatest and the least values among the extrema on the interval $[0, \pi]$. Find the derivative y':

$$y' = \frac{1}{2}(3 \sin 3x - \sin x).$$

In $[0, \pi]$ the derivative vanishes at the points

$$x_1 = 0,\ x_2 = \text{arc cos}\ \frac{1}{\sqrt{3}},\ x_3 = \text{arc cos}\left(-\frac{1}{\sqrt{3}}\right),\ x_4 = \pi.$$

Compute the values of the function at these points :

$$y(0) = y(\pi) = 0,\ y\left[\text{arc cos}\left(\pm\frac{1}{\sqrt{3}}\right)\right] = \pm\frac{4}{3\sqrt{3}}.$$

Hence, the least value of the function in the interval $(-\infty, \infty)$ is equal to $-4/(3\sqrt{3})$, and the greatest to $4/(3\sqrt{3})$.

3.7.3. The function

$$f(x) = ax + \frac{b}{x} \quad (a, b, x > 0)$$

consists of two summands : one summand is proportional to the independent variable x, the other inversely proportional to it.
Prove that this function takes on the least value at $x = \sqrt{b/a}$.

Solution Find the roots of the derivative $f'(x)$ in the interval $(0, \infty)$:

$$f'(x) = a - \frac{b}{x^2} = 0$$

at $x = \sqrt{b/a}(x > 0)$. Since $f''(x) = 2b/x^3 > 0$ for any $x > 0$ the function $f(x)$ reaches a minimum at this critical point. This is the only extremum (minimum) in the interval $(0, \infty)$. Hence, at $x = \sqrt{b/a}$ the function $f(x)$ attains the least value.

3.7.4. As a result of n measurements of an unknown quantity x the numbers $x_1, x_2, \ldots, x_n$ are obtained.
It is required to find at what value of x the sum of squares of the errors $f(x) = (x - x_1)^2 + (x - x_2)^2 + \ldots + (x - x_n)^2$ will be the least.

Solution Compute the derivative

$$f'(x) = 2(x - x_1) + 2(x - x_2) + \ldots + 2(x - x_n).$$

The only root of the derivative is

$$x = \frac{x_1 + x_2 + \ldots + x_n}{n}.$$

Then, for all x we have $f''(x) = 2n > 0$. Therefore, the function $f(x)$ has its minimum at the point

$$x = \frac{x_1 + x_2 + \ldots + x_n}{n}.$$

Being the only minimum, it coincides with the least value of the function (cf. Problem 1.3.8).

And so, the best (in the sense of "the principle of the minimum squares") approximate value of an unknown quantity x is the arithmetic mean of the values $x_1, x_2, \ldots, x_n$.

3.7.5. Find the largest term in the sequence

$$a_n = \frac{n^2}{n^3 + 200}.$$

Solution Consider the function $f(x) = \dfrac{x^2}{x^3 + 200}$ in the interval $[1, \infty)$.

Since the derivative

$$f'(x) = \frac{x(400 - x^3)}{(x^3 + 200)^2}$$

is positive at $0 < x < \sqrt[3]{400}$ and negative at $x > \sqrt[3]{400}$, the function $f(x)$ increases at $0 < x < \sqrt[3]{400}$ and decreases at $x > \sqrt[3]{400}$. From the inequality $7 < \sqrt[3]{400} < 8$ it follows that the largest term in the sequence can be either a_7, or a_8. Since $a_7 = 49/543 > a_8 = 8/89$, the largest term in the given sequence is

$$a_7 = \frac{49}{543}.$$

3.7.6. Find the greatest and the least values of the following functions on the indicated intervals :

(a) $f(x) = \frac{1}{4}x^4 - \frac{2}{3}x^3 - \frac{3}{2}x^2 + 2$ on $[-2, 4]$;

(b) $f(x) = \sqrt{4 - x^2}$ on $[-2, 2]$;

(c) $f(x) = \arctan x - \frac{1}{2}\ln x$ on $\left[\frac{1}{\sqrt{3}}, \sqrt{3}\right]$;

(d) $f(x) = 2\sin x + \sin 2x$ on $\left[0, \frac{3}{2}\pi\right]$;

(e) $f(x) = x - 2\ln x$ on $[1, e]$;

(f) $f(x) = \begin{cases} 2x^2 + \dfrac{2}{x^2} & \text{for } -2 \le x < 0; 0 < x \le 2, \\ 1 & \text{for } x = 0. \end{cases}$

3.8. Solving Problems in Geometry and Physics

3.8.1. The force of a circular electric current acting on a small magnet with the axis perpendicular to the plane of the circle and passing through its centre is expressed by the formula

$$F = \frac{Cx}{(a^2 + x^2)^{3/2}},$$

where a = radius of the circle
x = distance from the centre of the circle to the magnet $(0 < x < \infty)$
C = constant.
At what x will the value of F be the greatest ?

Solution The derivative

$$F'(x) = C\frac{a^2 - 2x^2}{(a^2 + x^2)^{3/2}}$$

has a single positive root $x = a/\sqrt{2}$. This solves the problem.

Note. It often happens that reasons of purely physical or geometric character make it unnecessary to resort to the differential methods in investigating a function for the greatest or the least value at he point under consideration.

3.8.2. Determine the most economical dimensions of an open-air swimming pool of volume 32 m^3 with a square bottom so that the facing of its walls and bottom require the least quantity of material.

Solution Let us denote the side of the bottom by x and the height by y. Then the volume V of the pool will be

$$V = x^2 y = 32, \qquad (*)$$

and the surface S to be faced

$$S = x^2 + 4xy.$$

Expressing y through x from the relation (*), we get

$$S = x^2 + 4x\frac{V}{x^2} = x^2 + \frac{128}{x}.$$

Investigate the function thus obtained for a minimum in the interval $(0, \infty)$:

$$S' = 2x - \frac{128}{x^2}; 2x - \frac{128}{x^2} = 0;\ x = 4.$$

The single point thus found will obviously yield the least value of the function S, since it has no greatest value (it increases unboundedly as $x \to 0$ and $x \to \infty$).

And so, the required dimensions of the pool are : $x = 4$ m, $y = 2$ m.

3.8.3. Inscribe into a given sphere a cylinder with the greatest lateral surface.

3.8.4. 20 m of wire is available for fencing off a flower-bed which should have the form of a circular sector. What must the radius of the circle be if we wish to have a flower-bed of the greatest possible surface area ?

Solution Let us denote the radius of the circle by x, and the length of the arc by y (see Fig. 42). Then

$$20 = 2x + y,$$

whence

$$y = 2(10 - x).$$

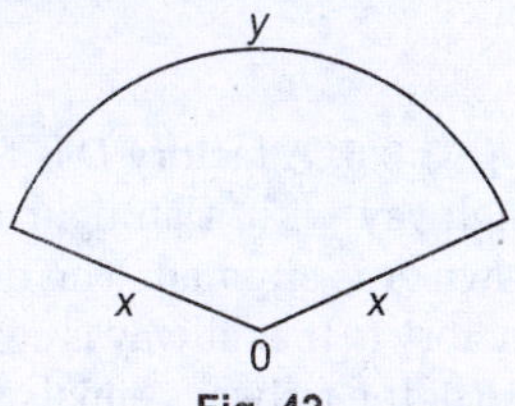

Fig. 42

The area of the circular sector

$$S = \frac{1}{2}xy = x(10 - x)\ (0 \le x \le 10).$$

The derivative $S'(x) = 10 - 2x$ has a root $x = 5$.

Since the lest value $S = 0$ is reached at the end-point of the interval $[0, 10]$, the obtained value $x = 5$ yields the greatest surface area S.

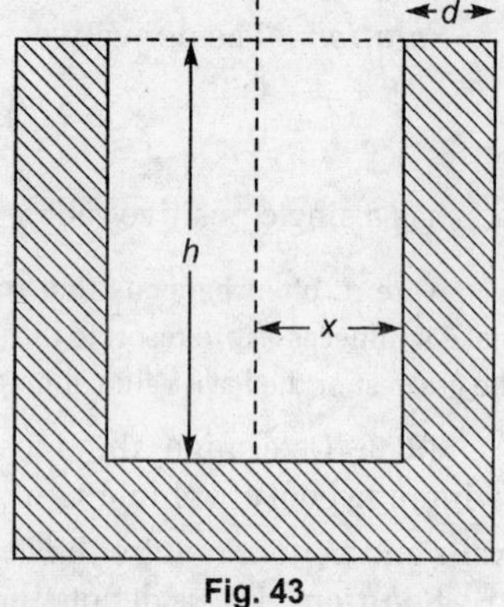

Fig. 43

3.8.5. It is required to construct an open cylindrical reservoir of capacity V_0. The thickness of the material is d. What dimension (the base radius and height) should the reservoir have so as to ensure the least possible expenditure of the material ?

Solution Figure 43 represents a longitudinal section of the reservoir, where the radius of the base of the inner cylinder is denoted by x and the height of the inner cylinder, by h. The volume of the bottom and the wall of the reservoir

$$V = \pi\,(x+d)^2 d + \pi\,[(x+d)^2 - x^2]\,h = \pi d(x+d)^2 + \pi h\,(2xd + d^2). \quad (*)$$

On the other hand, by hypothesis we must have

$$V_0 = \pi x^2 h$$

whence $h = \dfrac{V_0}{\pi x^2}$.

Substituting into (*), we get

$$V = \pi d\,(x+d)^2 + \frac{\pi V_0}{\pi x^2}(2xd + d^2) = \pi d\,(x+d)^2 + \frac{2V_0 d}{x} + \frac{V_0 d^2}{x^2}$$

Now we have to investigate the obtained function $V(x)$ for an extremum at $x > 0$

We have

$$V'(x) = 2\pi d(x+d) - \frac{2V_0 d}{x^2} - \frac{2V_0 d^2}{x^3} = \frac{2d\,(x+d)\,(\pi x^3 - V_0)}{x^3}$$

The only positive root of the derivative is the point $x = \sqrt[3]{V_0/\pi}$.

This solves the problem :

$$h = \frac{V_0\sqrt[3]{\pi^2}}{\pi\sqrt[3]{V_0^2}} = \sqrt[3]{\frac{V_0}{\pi}} = x.$$

3.8.6. A factory D is to be connected by a highway with a straight railway on which a town A is situated. The distance DB from the factory to the railway is equal to a, the segment AB of the railways equals l. Freight charges on the highway are m times higher than on the railway $(m > 1)$.

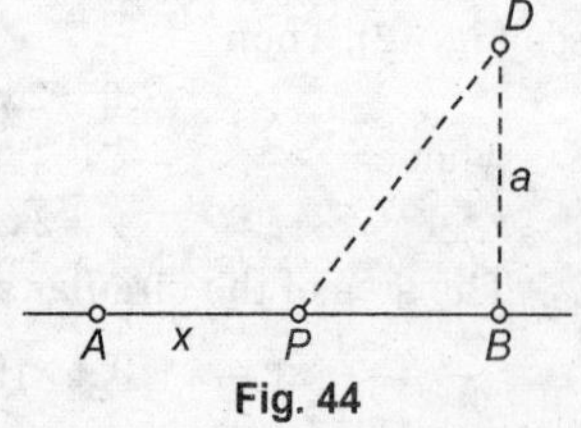

Fig. 44

How should the highway DP be connected with the railway so as to ensure the least freight charges from factory to town ?

Solution First let us make a drawing (see Fig. 44). It is absolutely clear that the highway must also be straight (a straight line is shorter than any curve connecting two given points!). Furthermore, the point P cannot lie either to the left of the point A or to the right of the point B. If we denote the distance AP by x, it will mean that $0 \leq x \leq l$.

Let the freight charges on the railways (per ton-kilometre) be k, then the freight charges on the highway will be km. The total freight charge N for transporting loads from D to A amounts to

$$N = kx + km\sqrt{a^2 + (l - x)^2}.$$

Hence, we have to find the least value of the function

$$f(x) = x + m\sqrt{a^2 + (x - l)^2}, 0 \leq x \leq l.$$

Take the derivative

$$f'(x) = 1 + \frac{m(x - l)}{\sqrt{a^2 + (x - l)^2}}.$$

It vanishes only at one point

$$x = l - \frac{a}{\sqrt{m^2 - 1}}.$$

If this point lies in the interval $[0, l]$, *ie*, if

$$l \geq \frac{a}{\sqrt{m^2 - 1}} \quad \text{or} \quad \frac{a}{l} \leq \sqrt{m^2 - 1},$$

then it yields the least freight charge (which is easy to check). If the indicated inequality is not observed, then $f(x)$ increases on $[0, l]$ and therefore the least freight charge is obtained at $x = 0$.

3.8.7. In constructing an a-c transformer it is important to insert into the coil a cross-shaped iron core of greatest possible surface area. Fig. 45 shows the cross-section of the core with appropriate dimension. Find the most suitable x and y if the radius of the coil is equal to a.

3.8.8. If the source of current is an electric cell, then the effect P (watts) obtained by cutting a resistance R (ohms) in the circuit is expressed by the formula

$$P = \frac{E^2 R}{(R + R_i)^2},$$

where E is electromotive force in volts and R_i the internal resistance in ohms.

Find the greatest effect which can be obtained at given E and R_i.

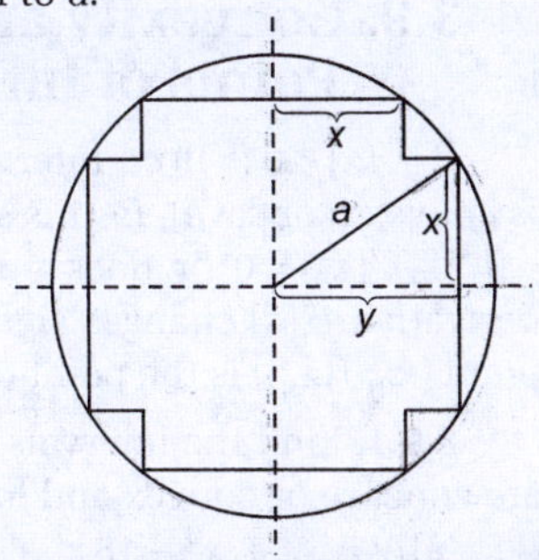

Fig. 45

3.8.9. A tin of a given volume V has the form of a cylinder. What must be the ratio of its height h to diameter $2R$ so as to use the least amount of material for its manufacture ?

3.8.10. In a given cone inscribe a cylinder having the greatest lateral surface so that the planes and centres of the base circles of the cylinder and cone coincide.

3.8.11. Given a point (1, 2) in the orthographic coordinates. Through this point drawn a straight line so that it forms, together with the positive semi-axis a triangle of the least area.

3.8.12. Given a point M on the axis of the parabola $y^2 = 2px$ at a distance a from its vertex. Find the abscissa of the point on the curve nearest to the given point.

3.8.13. The expenses sustained in one hour's sailing of a ship are expressed in roubles by an empirical formula of the form $a + bv^2$, where a and b are constants for a given ship, and v is the ship's speed in knots (one knot is equal to 1.85 km/hr). In this formula the constant part of the expenses a refers to depreciation and crew's upkeep, and the second term (bv^3) to the fuel cost. At what speed will the ship cover any required distance at the lowest cost ?

3.8.14. A trough is built from three boards of equal width. At what slope should the lateral boards be placed to ensure the largest cross-sectional area of the trough ?

3.8.15. A tank with a vertical wall of height h is installed on a horizontal plane. Determine the position of an orifice, at which the range of a liquid jet will be the greatest if the velocity of flow (according to Torricelli's law) is equal to $\sqrt{2gx}$, where x is the depth of the orifice.

3.8.16. Two aircraft are flying in a straight line and in the same plane at an angle of 120° to each other and with an equal speed of v km/hr. At a certain moment one aircraft reaches the point of intersection of their routes, while the second is at a distance of a km it. When will the distance between the aircraft be the least and what is the distance ?

3.9. Convexity and Concavity of a Curve. Points of Inflection

If $f''(x) < 0$ (> 0) on interval (a, b), then the curve $y = f(x)$ on this interval is convex (concave), *ie*, it is situated below (above) any of its tangent lines.

If $f''(x_0) = 0$ or does not exist but $f'(x_0)$ does exist and the second derivative $f''(x)$ changes sign when passing through the point x_0, then the point $(x_0, f(x_0))$ is the point of inflection of the curve $y = f(x)$.

3.9.1. Find the intervals in which the graphs of the following functions are concave or convex and locate the points of inflection :

(a) $y = x^4 + x^3 - 18x^2 + 24x - 12$;

(b) $y = 3x^4 - 8x^3 + 6x^2 + 12$;

(c) $y = \dfrac{x}{1+x^2}$;

(d) $y = x + x^{2/3}$;

(e) $y = 4\sqrt{(x-1)^5} + 20\sqrt{(x-1)^3}\ (x \geq 1)$;

(f) $y = \dfrac{\ln^2 x}{x}\ (x > 0)$;

(g) $y = x \sin(\ln x)\ (x > 0)$;

(h) $y = 2 - |x^5 - 1|$.

Solution. (a) Find the derivatives:

$$y' = 4x^3 + 3x^2 - 36x + 24,$$

$$y'' = 12x^2 + 6x - 36 = 12\left(x^2 + \frac{x}{2} - 3\right),$$

whence $y'' = 0$ at $x_1 = -2$, $x_2 = 3/2$.

Hence, $y'' > 0$ on the intervals $(-\infty, -2)$ and $(3/2, \infty)$; $y'' < 0$ on the interval $(-2, 3/2)$. The sign of the second derivative determines the convexity or concavity of the curve in a given interval.

This enables us to compile the following table :

x	$x < -2$	$-2 < x < \frac{3}{2}$	$x > \frac{3}{2}$
Sign of y''	+	−	+
Conclusion	Concavity	Convexity	Concavity

Since the second derivative changes its sign when passing through the points $x_1 = -2$ and $x_2 = 3/2$, the points $(-2, -124)$ and $\left(\frac{3}{2}, -8\frac{1}{16}\right)$ are points of inflection.

(d) Find the derivatives :

$$y' = 1 + \frac{5}{3}x^{2/3},\ y'' = \frac{10}{9\sqrt[3]{x}}.$$

The second derivative is non-zero everywhere and loses its meaning at the point $x = 0$. At $x < 0$ we have $y'' < 0$ and the curve is convex, at $x > 0$ we have $y'' > 0$ and the curve is concave.

At the point $x = 0$ the first derivative $y' = 1$, the second derivative changes sign when passing through the point $x = 0$. Therefore the point $(0, 0)$ is a point of inflection.

(g) Find the derivatives :

$$y' = \sin(\ln x) + \cos(\ln x),$$

$$y'' = \frac{1}{x}[\cos(\ln x) - \sin(\ln x)] = \frac{\sqrt{2}}{x}\sin\left(\frac{\pi}{4} - \ln x\right).$$

The second derivative vanishes at the points

$$x_k = e^{\pi/4 + k\pi}, k = 0, \pm 1, \pm 2, \ldots$$

The function $\sin(\pi/4 - \ln x)$, and together with it y'', changes sign when passing through each point x_k. Consequently, the points x_k are the abscissas of the points of inflection. In the intervals

$$(e^{2k\pi - 3\pi/4}, e^{2k\pi + \pi/4})$$

the curve is concave, and in the intervals

$$(e^{2k\pi + \pi/4}, e^{2k\pi + 5\pi/4})$$

it is convex.

(h) The given function can be written in the following way :

$$y = \begin{cases} 2 - (x^5 - 1), & x \geq 1, \\ 2 + (x^5 - 1), & x < 1. \end{cases}$$

Therefore

$$y' = \begin{cases} -5x^4, & x > 1, \\ 5x^4, & x < 1. \end{cases}$$

At the point $x = 1$ there is no derivative. Further.

$$y'' = \begin{cases} -20x^3, & x > 1, \\ 20x^3, & x < 1; \end{cases}$$

$y'' = 0$ at the point $x = 0$. Hence, we have to investigate three intervals : $(-\infty, 0), (0, 1), (1, \infty)$.

Compile a table of signs of y'' :

x	$x < 0$	$0 < x < 1$	$x > 1$
Sign of y''	–	+	–
Conclusion	Convexity	Concavity	Convexity

The point (0, 1) is a point of inflection, the point (1,, 2) being a corner point.

3.9.2. What conditions must the coefficients a, b, c satisfy for the curve $y = ax^4 + bx^3 + cx^2 + dx + e$ to have points of inflection ?

Solution Find the second derivative :

$$y'' = 12ax^2 + 6bx + 2c.$$

The curve has points of inflection if and only if the equation

$6ax^2 + 3bx + c = 0$

has different real roots, *ie*, when the discriminant $9b^2 - 24ac > 0$, or

$$3b^2 - 8ac > 0.$$

3.9.3. At what values of a will the curve

$$y = x^4 + ax^3 + + \frac{3}{2}x^2 + 1$$

be concave along the entire number scale ?

Solution Find y'':

$$y'' = 12x^2 + 6ax + 3.$$

The curve will be concave along the entire number scale if $y'' \geq 0$ for all values of x, *ie*, when

$$4x^2 + 2ax + 1 \geq 0 \quad \text{for all} \quad x.$$

For this it is necessary and sufficient that the inequality $4a^2 - 16 \leq 0$ be fulfilled; whence

$$|a| \leq 2.$$

3.9.4. Show that the curve $y = \dfrac{x+1}{x^2+1}$ has three points of inflection lying in a straight line.

Solution Find the derivatives :

$$y' = \frac{-x^2 - 2x + 1}{(x^2+1)^2}.$$

$$y'' = \frac{2x^3 + 6x^2 - 6x - 2}{(x^2+1)^3},$$

The second derivative becomes zero at three points, which are the roots of the equation

$$x^3 + 3x^2 - 3x - 1 = 0,$$

whence

$x_1 = -2 - \sqrt{3}$, $x_2 = -2 + \sqrt{3}$, $x_3 = 1.$

Let us compile the table of signs of y'':

x	$-\infty < x < -2 - \sqrt{-3}$	$-2 - \sqrt{3} < x < -2 + \sqrt{3}$	$-2 + \sqrt{3} < x < 1$	$1 < x < \infty$
Sign of y''	−	+	−	+
Conclusion	Convexity	Concavity	Convexity	Concavity

Hence, $\left(-2 - \sqrt{3} - \dfrac{\sqrt{3} - 1}{4}\right), \left(-2 + \sqrt{3}, \dfrac{1 + \sqrt{3}}{4}\right), (1, 1)$ are points of inflection. It is easy to ascertain that all of them lie in a straight line. Indeed the coordinates of these points satisfy the relation $\dfrac{-2 - \sqrt{3} - 1}{-2 + \sqrt{3} - 1} = \dfrac{(1 - \sqrt{3})/4 - 1}{(1 + \sqrt{3})/4 + 1}$.

3.9.5. Investigate the curves represented by the following equations for convexity (concavity) and locate points of inflection :

(a) $y = x - \sqrt[5]{(x-3)^2}$;

(b) $y = e^{\sin x}$ $(-\pi/2 \le x \le \pi/2)$.

3.9.6. Show that the points of inflection of the curve $y = x \sin x$ lie on the curve $y^2 (4 + x^2) = 4x^2$.

3.10. Asymptotes

A straight line is called an *asymptote* to the curve $y = f(x)$ if the distance from the variable point M of the curve to the straight line approaches zero as the point M recedes to infinity along some branch of the curve.

We will distinguish three kinds of asymptotes : vertical horizontal and inclined.

Vertical asymptotes. If at least one of the limits of the function $f(x)$ (at the point a on the right or on the left) is equal to infinity, then the straight line $x = a$ is a vertical asymptote.

Horizontal asymptotes. If $\lim\limits_{x \to \pm\infty} f(x) = A$, then the straight line $y = A$ is a horizontal asymptote (the right one as $x \to +\infty$) and the left one as $x \to -\infty$).

Inclined asymptotes. If the limits

$$\lim_{x \to +\infty} \frac{f(x)}{x} = k_1, \quad \lim_{x \to +\infty} [f(x) - k_1 x] = b_1$$

exist, then the straight line $y = k_1 x + b_1$ is an inclined (right) asymptote. If the limits

$$\lim_{x \to -\infty} \frac{f(x)}{x} = k_2$$

and

$$\lim_{x \to -\infty} [f(x) - k_2 x] = b_2$$

exist, then the straight line $y = k_2 x + b_2$ is an inclined (left) asymptote. A horizontal asymptote may be considered as a particular case of an inclined asymptote at $k = 0$.

3.10.1. Find the asymptotes of the following curves :

(a) $y = \frac{5x}{x-3}$; (b) $y = \frac{3x}{x-1} + 3x$; (c) $y = \frac{x}{x^2+1}$;

(d) $y = \frac{1}{x} + 4x^2$; (e) $y = xe^{\frac{1}{x}}$; (f) $y = \frac{3x}{2} \ln\left(e - \frac{1}{3x}\right)$;

(g) $y = \sqrt{1 + x^2} + 2x$; (h) $y = \sqrt{1 + x^2} \sin \frac{1}{x}$;

(i) $y = 2\sqrt{x^2 + 4}$.

Solution (a) The curve has a vertical asymptote $x = 3$, since

$$\lim_{x \to 3 \mp 0} y = \lim_{x \to 3 \mp 0} \frac{5x}{x-3} = \mp \infty$$

(the point $x = 3$ is a point of discontinuity of the second kind).
Find the horizontal asymptote :

$$\lim_{x \to \pm\infty} y = \lim_{x \to \pm\infty} \frac{5x}{x-3} = 5.$$

And so, the curve has a vertical asymptote $x = 3$ and a horizontal one $y = 5$.

(b) The curve has a vertical asymptote $x = 1$, since

$$\lim_{x \to 1-0} y = \lim_{x \to 1-0} \left(\frac{3x}{x-1} + 3x \right) = -\infty;$$

$$\lim_{x \to 1+0} y = \lim_{x \to 1+0} \left(\frac{3x}{x-1} + 3x \right) = +\infty;$$

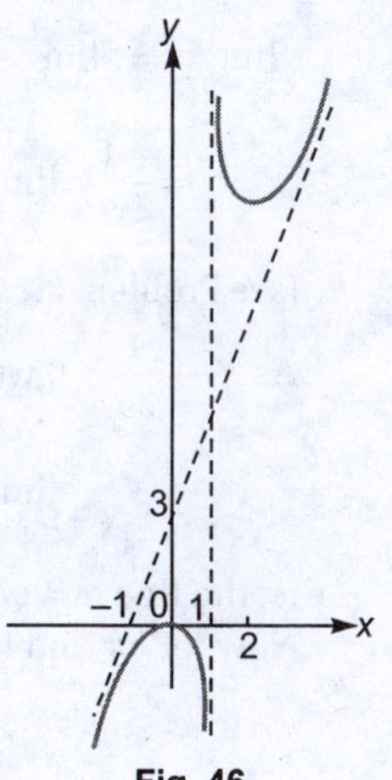

Fig. 46

Find the inclined asymptotes :

$$k = \lim_{x \to \pm\infty} \frac{y}{x} = \lim_{x \to \pm\infty} \left(\frac{3}{x-1} + 3 \right) = 3;$$

$$b = \lim_{x \to \pm\infty} (y - kx)$$

$$= \lim_{x \to \pm\infty} \left(\frac{3x}{x-1} + 3x - 3x \right) = 3$$

Thus, the straight line $y = 3x + 3$ is an inclined asymptote (see Fig . 46).

(e) The curve has a vertical asymptote $x = 0$, since

$$\lim_{x \to +0} y = \lim_{x \to +\infty} xe^{1/x} = \lim_{t = \frac{1}{x} \to +\infty} \frac{e^t}{t} = +\infty$$

(see Problem **3.2.2.**).
Find the inclined asymptotes:

$$k = \lim_{x \to \pm\infty} \frac{y}{x} = \lim_{x \to \pm\infty} e^{1/x} = e^0 = 1;$$

$$b = \lim_{x \to \pm\infty} (xe^{1/x} - x) = \lim_{x \to \pm\infty} \frac{e^{1/x} - 1}{1/x}$$

$$= \lim_{1/x = z \to 0} \frac{e^z - 1}{z} = 1,$$

Thus , the straight line $y = x + 1$ will be an inclined asymptote of the curve (see Fig. 47) . Note that

$$\lim_{x \to -0} y = \lim_{x \to -0} xe^{1/x} = 0.$$

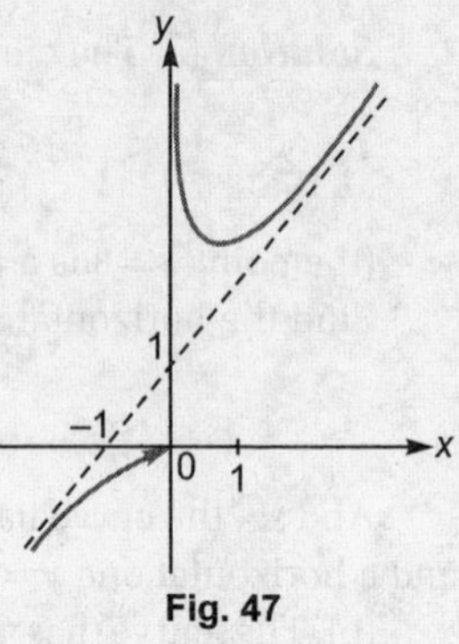

Fig. 47

(f) The function is defined and continuous at $e - \frac{1}{3x} > 0$, *ie*, at $x < 0$ and $x > \frac{1}{3e}$

Since the function is continuous at every point of the domain of definition, vertical asymptotes can exist only on finite boundaries of the domain of definition.

As $x \to -0$ we have

$$\lim_{x \to -0} y = \lim_{x \to -0} \frac{3x}{2} \ln\left(e - \frac{1}{3x}\right)$$

$$= -\frac{1}{2} \lim_{z \to +\infty} \frac{\ln(e+z)}{z} = 0 \left(z = -\frac{1}{3x}\right)$$

(see Problem **3.2.2**), *ie*, the straight line $x = 0$ is not a vertical asymptote.

As $x \to \frac{1}{3e} + 0$ we have

$$\lim_{x \to 1/(3e)+0} y = \frac{3}{2} \lim_{x \to 1/(3e)+0} x \ln\left(e - \frac{1}{3x}\right) + -\infty$$

ie, the line $x = 1/(3e)$ is a vertical asymptote.

Now let us find the inclined asymptotes:

$$k = \lim_{x \to \pm\infty} \frac{y}{x} = \frac{3}{2} \lim_{x \to \pm\infty} \ln\left(e - \frac{1}{3x}\right) = \frac{3}{2};$$

$$b = \lim_{x \to \pm\infty} [y - kx] = \frac{3}{2} \lim_{x \to \pm\infty} x\left[\ln\left(e - \frac{1}{3x}\right) - 1\right]$$

$$= \frac{3}{2} \lim_{x \to \pm\infty} \frac{\ln\left(1 - \frac{1}{3xe}\right)}{\frac{1}{x}} = \frac{3}{2}\left(-\frac{1}{3e}\right) = -\frac{1}{2e}.$$

Hence, the straight line $y = \frac{3x}{2} - \frac{1}{2e}$ is an inclined asymptote (see Fig. 48).

(g) The curve has no vertical asymptotes, since the function is continuous everywhere. Let us look for inclined asymptotes. The limits will be different as $x \to +\infty$ and $x \to -\infty$, therefore we have to consider two cases separately.

Find the right asymptote (as $x \to +\infty$) :

$$k_1 = \lim_{x \to +\infty} \frac{\sqrt{1+x^2} + 2x}{x} = \lim_{x \to +\infty} \frac{\sqrt{\frac{1}{x^2} + 1} + 2}{1} = 3;$$

$$b_1 = \lim_{x \to +\infty} (\sqrt{1+x^2} + 2x - 3x)$$

$$= \lim_{x\ +\infty} |\sqrt{1+x^2} - x| = \lim_{x\to+\infty} \frac{1+x^2-x^2}{\sqrt{1+x^2}+x} = 0\cdot$$

Thus, as $x \to +\infty$ the curve has an asymptote $y = 3x$.

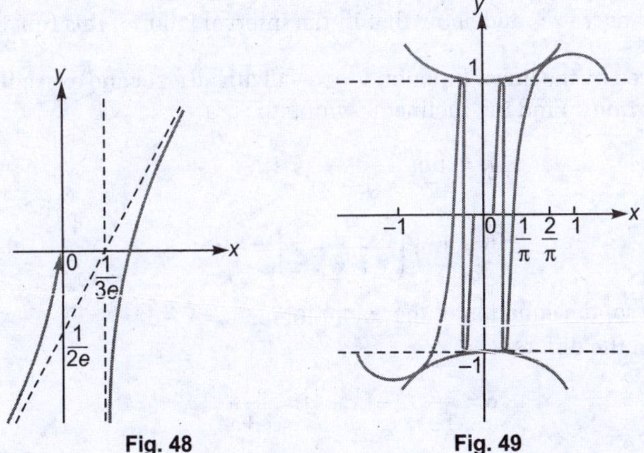

Fig. 48

Fig. 49

Find the left asymptote (as $x \to -\infty$).

$$k_2 = \lim_{x\to-\infty} \frac{\sqrt{1+x^2}+2x}{x} = \lim_{x\to-\infty} \frac{|x|\sqrt{\frac{1}{x^2}+1}+2x}{x} = 1,$$

$$b_2 = \lim_{x\to-\infty} |\sqrt{1+x^2}+2x-x| = \lim_{x\to-\infty} \frac{1}{\sqrt{1+x^2}-x} = 0.$$

Since both summands ($\sqrt{1+x^2}$ and $(-x)$) in the denominator are positive at $x < 0$.

And so , the curve has an asymptote $y = x$ as $x \to -\infty$.

(h) The curve has no vertical asymptotes, since it is continuous at $x \neq 0$, and in the neighbourhood of the point $x = 0$ the function is bounded.

Let us find the inclined asymptotes. We have

$$k = \lim_{x\to\pm\infty} \frac{y}{x} = \lim_{x\to\pm\infty} \frac{|x|\sqrt{1+\frac{1}{x^2}}\sin\frac{1}{x}}{x} = \pm 1\cdot 0 = 0$$

Then

$$b = \lim_{x\to\pm\infty} (y-kx) = \lim_{x\to\pm\infty} |x|\sqrt{1+\frac{1}{x^2}}\sin\frac{1}{x}$$

$$= \begin{cases} 1 & \text{as } x\to+\infty \\ -1 & \text{as } x\to-\infty \end{cases}$$

Thus, the curve has two horizontal asymptotes : $y = +1$ and $y = -1$. (see Fig. 49) The same result can be obtained proceeding from symmetry about the origin and keeping in mind that the function y is odd.

3.10.2. Find the inclined asymptote of the graph of the function $y = \frac{x^2}{1+x}$ as $x \to \infty$ and show that in the interval $(100, \infty)$ this function may be replaced by the linear function $y = x - 1$ with an error and exceeding 0.01.

Solution Find the inclined asymptote :

$$k = \lim_{x\to\infty} \frac{x^2}{x(1+x)} = 1;$$

$$b = \lim_{x\to\infty} \left(\frac{x^2}{1+x} - x\right) = -1.$$

And so, the equation of the asymptote is $y = x - 1$.

Form the difference :

$$\delta = \frac{x^2}{1+x} - (x-1) = \frac{1}{1+x}.$$

Hence, assuming

$$y = \frac{x^2}{1+x} \approx x - 1,$$

for all $x > 100$, we introduce an error of not more than 0.01.

3.10.3. Find the asymptotes of the following curves :

(a) $y = \frac{x^2 - 6x + 3}{x - 3}$; (b) $y = x \text{ arc tan } x$;

(c) $y = x + (\sin x)/x$; (d) $y = \text{In } (4 - x^2)$;

(e) $y = 2x - \text{arc cos } \frac{1}{x}$.

3.11. General Plan for Investigating Functions and Sketching Graphs

The analysis and graphing of functions by elementary methods were considered in Chapter I (1.3 and 1.5). Using the methods of differential calculus, we can now carry a out more profound and comprehensive study of various properties of a function, and explain the shape of its graph (rise, all, convexity, concavity, etc.).

It is convenient to investigate a function and construct its graph according to the following plan :

1. Find the domain of definition of the function.
2. Find out whether the function is even, odd or periodic.
3. Test the function for continuity, find out the discontinuities and their character.

4. Find the asymptotes of the graph of the function.

5. Find the points of extremum of the function and compute the values of the function at these points.

6. Find the points of inflection on the graph of the function, compute the values of the function and of its derivative at these points. Find the intervals of convexity of the graph of the function.

7. Graph the function using the results of this investigation. If it is necessary to specify certain regions of the curve, calculate the coordinates of several additional points (in particular, the x-and y-intercepts).

This is a very tentative plan, and various alternatives are possible. For instance, we recommend the student to begin sketching the graph as soon as he finds the asymptotes (if any), but in any case before the points of inflection are found. It should be remembered that in sketching the graph of a function the principal reference points are the points of the curve corresponding to the extremal values of the function, points of inflection, asymptotes.

3.11.1. Investigate and graph the following functions :

(a) $y = x^6 - 3x^4 + 3x^2 - 5$; (b) $y = \sqrt[3]{x} - \sqrt[3]{x+1}$;

(c) $y = \dfrac{2x^3}{x^2 - 4}$; (d) $y = \dfrac{1 - x^3}{x^2}$;

(e) $y = x + \ln (x^2 - 1)$; (f) $y = \dfrac{1}{2}\sin 2x + \cos x$;

(g) $y = x^2 e^{1/x}$; (h) $y = \text{arc sin}\dfrac{1 - x^2}{1 + x^2}$.

Solution (a) The function is defined and continuous throughout the number scale, therefore the curve has no vertical asymptote. The function is even, since $f(-x) = f(x)$. Consequently, its graph is symmetrical about the y-axis, and therefore it is sufficient to investigate the function only on the interval $[0, \infty)$.

There are no inclined asymptotes, since as $x \to \infty$ the quantity y turns out to be an infinitely large quantity of the sixth order with respect to x.

Investigate the first derivative :

$$y' = 6x^5 - 12x^3 + 6x = 6x(x^4 - 2x^2 + 1) = 6x(x^2 - 1)^2;$$

the critical points are :

$$x_1 = -1, x_2 = 0, x_3 = 1.$$

Since in the interval $[0, \infty)$ the derivative $y' \geq 0$, the function increases.

Investigate the second derivative :

$$y'' = 30x^4 - 36x^2 + 6 = 6(5x^4 - 6x^2 + 1).$$

The positive roots of the second derivative :

$$x_1 = 1/\sqrt{5}, x_2 = 1.$$

For convenience and pictorialness let us compile the following table, where all the points of interest are arranged in an ascending order :

x	0	$\left(0, \frac{1}{\sqrt{5}}\right)$	$\frac{1}{\sqrt{5}}$	$\left(\frac{1}{\sqrt{5}}, 1\right)$	1	$(1, \infty)$	2
y′	0	+	$\frac{96}{25\sqrt{5}} \approx 1.7$	+	0	+	
y″	6	+	0	−	0	+	
y	−5		−4.51		−4		23

On the right one more additional value of the function is computed to improve the graphs after the point of inflection.

Using the results of the investigation and the above table and taking into consideration the symmetry principle, we construct the graph of the function (see Fig. 50). As is seen from the graph, the function has roots $x = \pm\, a$, where $a \approx 1.6$.

(b) The function is defined and continuous over the entire number scale and is negative everywhere, since $\sqrt[3]{x} < \sqrt[3]{x+1}$.

The graph has neither vertical, nor inclined asymptotes, since the order of magnitude of y is less than unity as $x \to \infty$. Determine the horizontal asymptote :

$$\lim_{x\to\pm\infty} y = \lim_{x\to\pm\infty} (\sqrt[3]{x} - \sqrt[3]{x+1}) = \lim_{x\to\pm\infty} \frac{-1}{\sqrt[3]{x^2} + \sqrt[3]{x(x+1)} + \sqrt[3]{(x+1)^2}} = 0.$$

Hence, the straight line $y = 0$ is the horizontal asymptote of the graph.

The first derivative

$$y' = \frac{1}{3\sqrt[3]{x^2}} - \frac{1}{3\sqrt[3]{(x+1)^2}} = \frac{\sqrt[3]{(x+1)^2} - \sqrt[3]{x^2}}{3\sqrt[3]{x^2(x+1)^2}}$$

becomes zero at the point $x_2 = -\frac{1}{2}$ and infinity at the points

$$x_1 = -1,\ x_3 = 0.$$

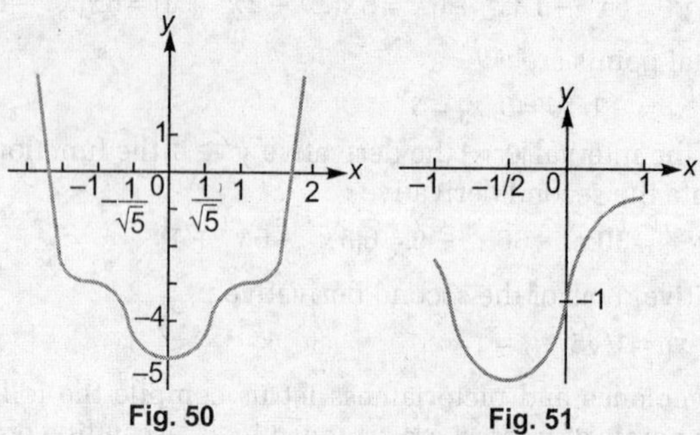

Fig. 50   Fig. 51

The second derivative

$$y'' = \frac{1}{3}\left(-\frac{2}{3}\right)\frac{1}{\sqrt[3]{x^5}} - \frac{1}{3}\left(-\frac{2}{3}\right)\frac{1}{\sqrt[3]{(x+1)^5}} = -\frac{2\left[\sqrt[3]{(x+1)^6} - \sqrt[3]{x^5}\right]}{9\sqrt[3]{[x(x+1)]^5}}$$

does not vanish and is infinite at the same points $x_1 = -1$, $x_2 = 0$. Compile a table :

x	-1	$\left(-1, -\frac{1}{2}\right)$	$-\frac{1}{2}$	$\left(-\frac{1}{2}, 0\right)$	0	$(0, \infty)$	1
y'	$-\infty$	$-$	0	$+$	∞	$+$	
y''	∞	$+$	$+\frac{16}{9\sqrt[3]{2}}$	$+$	∞	$-$	
y	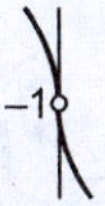 -1		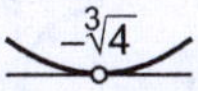 $-\sqrt[3]{4}$		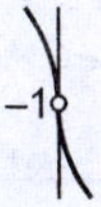 -1		-0.26

With the aid of this table, and of the asymptote $y = 0$ construct the graphs of the function (see Fig. 51).

(c) The function is defined and continuous over the entire axis except at the points $x = \pm 2$. The function is odd, its graph is symmetrical about the origin, therefore it is sufficient to investigate the function on the interval $[0, \infty)$.

The straight line $x = 2$ is a vertical asymptote :

$$\lim_{x\to 2-0} \frac{2x^3}{x^2-4} = -\infty; \quad \lim_{x\to 2+0} \frac{2x^3}{x^2-4} = +\infty.$$

Determine the inclined asymptote :

$$k = \lim_{x\to+\infty} \frac{y}{x} = \lim_{x\to+\infty} \frac{2x^2}{x^2-4} = 2,$$

$$b = \lim_{x\to+\infty} (y - 2x) = \lim_{x\to+\infty} \frac{8x}{x^2-4} = 0.$$

The curve has an inclined asymptote $y = 2x$, and

$$y - 2x = \frac{8x}{x^2-4}\begin{cases} > 0 \text{ at } x > 2, \\ < 0 \text{ at } x < 2 \end{cases}$$

The first derivative

$$y' = \frac{6x^2(x^2-4) - 4x^4}{(x^2-4)^2} = \frac{2x^2(x^2-12)}{(x^2-4)^2}$$

in the interval $[0, \infty)$ vanishes at the points

$$x = 0,\ x = 2\sqrt{3} \approx 3.46$$

and becomes infinite at the point $x = 2$.

The second derivative

$$y'' = \frac{16x(x^2+12)}{(x^2-4)^3}$$

becomes zero at the point $x = 0$ and infinite at $x = 2$.
Compile a table :

x	0	$(0, 2)$	2	$(2, 2\sqrt{3})$	$2\sqrt{3}$	$(2\sqrt{3}, \infty)$
y'	-0	$-$	∞	$-$	0	$+$
y''	$+0$	$-$	∞	$+$	$\frac{3\sqrt{3}}{2}$	$+$
y	0				$6\sqrt{3}$	

Using the results of the investigation, sketch the graph of the function. (see Fig. 52.)

(e) The function is defined and continuous at all values of x for which $x^2 - 1 > 0$ or $|x| > 1$, *ie*, on two intervals : $(-\infty, -1)$ and $(1, +\infty)$.

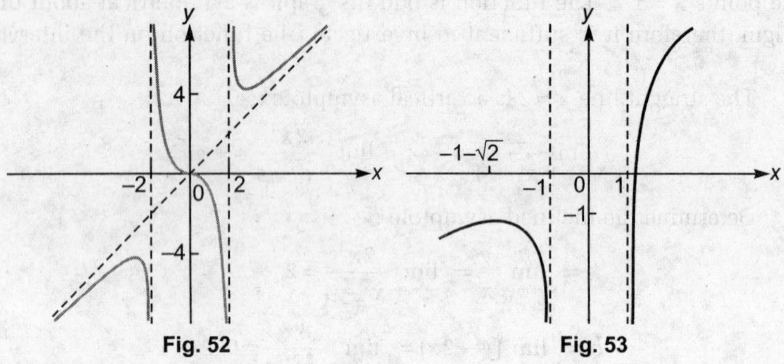

Fig. 52 Fig. 53

We seek the vertical asymptotes :

$$\lim_{x \to -1-0} y = \lim_{x \to -1-0} [x + \ln(x^2 - 1)] = -\infty;$$

$$\lim_{x \to 1+0} y = \lim_{x \to 1+0} [x + \ln(x^2 - 1)] = -\infty.$$

Thus, the curve has two vertical asymptotes :

$$x = -1 \quad \text{and} \quad x = +1.$$

Find inclined asymptotes :

$$k = \lim_{x \to \pm\infty} \frac{y}{x} = \lim_{x \to \pm\infty} \frac{x + \ln(x^2 - 1)}{x} = \lim_{x \to \pm\infty} \left[1 + \frac{\ln(x^2 - 1)}{x}\right] = 1,$$

$$b = \lim_{x \to \pm\infty} [y - x] = \lim_{x \to \pm\infty} \ln(x^2 - 1) = +\infty.$$

Hence, the curve has neither inclined, nor horizontal asymptotes. Since the derivative

$$y' = 1 + \frac{2x}{x^2 - 1}$$

exists and is finite at all points of the domain of definition of the function, only the zeros of the derivative

$$x_1 = -1 - \sqrt{2}; \quad x_2 = -1 + \sqrt{2}$$

can be critical points. At the point $x_2 = -1 + \sqrt{2}$ the function is not defined; hence, there is one critical point $x_1 = -1 - \sqrt{2}$ belonging to the interval $(-\infty, -1)$. In the interval $(1, \infty)$ both the derivative $y' > 0$ and the function increase.

The second derivative

$$y'' = -\frac{2(x^2 + 1)}{(x^3 - 1)^2} < 0,$$

hence, the curve is convex everywhere, and at the point $x_1 = -1 - \sqrt{2} \approx -2.41$ the function has a maximum

$$y(-1 - \sqrt{2}) \approx -1 - \sqrt{2} + \ln(2 + 2\sqrt{2}) \approx -0.84.$$

To plot the graph in the interval $(1, \infty)$, where there are no characteristic points, we choose the following additional points :

$$x = 2; y = 2 + \ln 3 \approx 3.10$$

and $\quad x = 1.2; y = 1.2 + \ln 0.44 \approx 0.38.$

The graph of the function is shown in Fig. 53.

(f) The function is defined and continuous throughout the number scale and has a period 2π. Therefore in investigating we may confine ourselves to the interval $[0, 2\pi]$. The graph of the function has no asymptote by virtue of continuity and periodicity. Find the first derivatives :

$$y' = \cos 2x - \sin x.$$

On the interval $[0, 2\pi]$ it has three roots :

$$x_1 = \frac{\pi}{6}, x_2 = \frac{5\pi}{6}, x_3 = \frac{3\pi}{2}.$$

Evaluate the second derivative :

$$y'' = -2\sin 2x - \cos x.$$

On the interval $[0, 2\pi]$ it has four roots :

$$x_1 = \frac{\pi}{2}, x_2 = \pi + \arcsin\left(\frac{1}{4}\right),$$

$$x_3 = \frac{3\pi}{2}, x_4 = 2\pi - \arcsin\left(\frac{1}{4}\right).$$

Let us draw up a table of the results of investigation of all critical points of the first and second derivatives (the table also includes the end-points of the interval $[0, 2\pi]$).

Since in the interval $\left(0, \dfrac{3\pi}{2}\right)$ the roots of the first and second derivatives alternate, the signs of the second derivative in the intervals between its critical points are indicated only for the last three intervals.

The results of the investigation enable us to construct the graph of the function. (see Fig. 54).

(g) The function is defined, positive and continuous on each of the intervals $(-\infty, 0)$ and $(0, \infty)$. The point $x = 0$ is a discontinuity. Since (see Problem **3.2.2**).

$$\lim_{x\to+0} y = \lim_{x\to+0} x^2 e^{1/x} = \lim_{x\to+\infty} \frac{e^t}{t^2} = \infty \left(t = \frac{1}{x}\right),$$

the straight line $x = 0$ is a vertical asymptote. But

$$\lim_{x\to-0} y = \lim_{x\to-0} x^2 e^{1/x} = 0.$$

x	0	$\frac{\pi}{6}$	$\frac{\pi}{2}$	$\frac{5\pi}{6}$	x_2	$\left(x_2, \frac{3\pi}{2}\right)$	$\frac{3\pi}{2}$	$\left(\frac{3\pi}{2}, x_4\right)$	x_4	$(x_4, 2\pi)$	2π
y'		0	-2	0	$1\frac{1}{8}$		0		$1\frac{1}{8}$		
y''		$-\frac{3\sqrt{3}}{2}$	0	$\frac{3\sqrt{3}}{2}$	0	$-$	0	$+$	0	$+$	
y	1	$\frac{3\sqrt{3}}{4}$	0	$-\frac{3\sqrt{3}}{4}$	$-\frac{3\sqrt{15}}{16}$		0		$\frac{3\sqrt{15}}{16}$		1

There are no inclined asymptotes, since the function $y = x^2 e^{1/x}$ has the second order of smallness with respect to x as $x \to \pm\infty$.

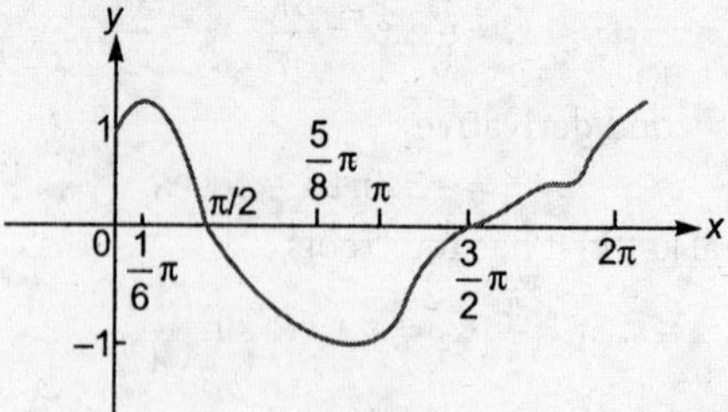

Fig. 54

Let us find the extrema of the function, for which purpose we evaluate the derivative :

$$y' = 2xe^{1/x} - e^{1/x} = 2e^{1/x}(x - 1/2),$$

whence we find the only critical point $x = \frac{1}{2}$.

Since for $x \neq 0$

$$y''(x) = 2e^{1/x} - \frac{2}{x}e^{1/x} + \frac{1}{x^2}e^{1/x}$$
$$= \frac{1}{x^2}e^{1/x}(2x^2 - 2x + 1) > 0,$$

on each of the intervals of the domain of definition the graph of the function is concave, and at the point $x = \frac{1}{2}$ the function has a minimum

$$y\left(\frac{1}{2}\right) = \frac{1}{4}e^2 \approx 1.87.$$

From the information obtained we can sketch the graph as in Fig. 55.

To specify the graphs in the intervals $(-\infty, 0)$ and $(1/2, \infty)$ the following additional points are used :

$$x = -1, y = e^{-1} \approx 0.37; x = 1, y = e \approx 2.72.$$

Fig. 55

(h) The function is defined and continuous throughout the number scale, since at any x

$$\left|\frac{1 - x^2}{1 + x^2}\right| \leq 1.$$

Since the function is even, we may confine ourselves to the investigation of the function at $x \geq 0$.

As the function is continuous, the graph has no vertical asymptotes, but it has a horizontal asymptote :

$$\lim_{x \to +\infty} y = \text{arc sin}(-1) = -\frac{\pi}{2}.$$

The first derivative

$$y' = \frac{1}{\sqrt{1 - \frac{(1 - x^2)^2}{(1 + x^2)^2}}} \times \frac{-2x(1 + x^2) - 2x(1 - x^2)}{(1 + x^2)^2}$$
$$= -\frac{1}{2|x|} \times \frac{4x}{(1 + x^2)^2}$$

is negative for $x > 0$, therefore the function decreases.

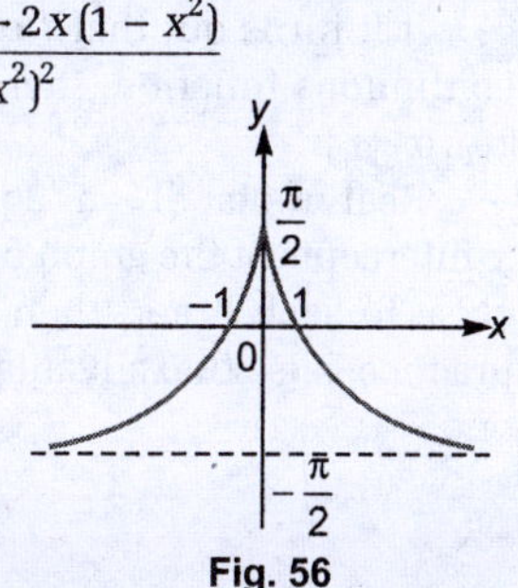

Fig. 56

The derivative is non-existent at the point $x = 0$. By virtue of the symmetry of the graph about the y-axis there will be a maximum at the point $y(0) = \frac{\pi}{2}$. Notice that at the point $x = 0$ the right derivative is equal to -1, and the left one to $+1$.

The second derivative is positive :

$$y''(x) = 2\frac{2(1+x^2)2x}{(1+x^2)^4} = \frac{8x}{(1+x^2)^3} > 0 \text{ for all } x > 0.$$

Hence, in the interval $(0, \infty)$ the graph of the function is concave. Also note that the curve intersects with the x-axis at the points $x = \pm 1$.

Taking into consideration the results of the investigation, construct the graph of the function (see Fig. 56).

3.11.2. Investigate and graph the following functions :

(a) $y = 1 + x^2 - \frac{x^4}{2}$; (b) $y = \frac{x^4}{(1+x)^3}$;

(c) $y = \frac{1}{x} + 4x^2$; (d) $y = \frac{x^3}{x^2 - 1}$;

(e) $y = \sqrt[3]{x^2} - \sqrt[3]{x^2 - 4}$; (f) $y = x^2 \ln(x+2)$; (g) $y = x^3 e^{-4x}$;

(h) $y = \begin{cases} x \arctan \frac{1}{x} & \text{at } x \neq 0, \\ 0 & \text{at } x = 0. \end{cases}$

3.12. Approximate Solution of Algebraic and Transcendental Equations

Approximate determination of isolated real roots of the equation $f(x) = 0$ is usually carried out in two stages :

1. Separating roots, *ie*, determining the intervals $[\alpha, \beta]$ which contain one and only one root of the equation.

2. Specifying the roots, *ie*, computing them with the required degree of accuracy.

The process of separation of roots beings with determining the signs of the function $f(x)$ at a number of points $x = \alpha_1, \alpha_2, \ldots$, whose choice takes into account the peculiarities of the function $f(x)$.

If it turns out that $f(\alpha_k) f(\alpha_{k+1}) < 0$, then, by virtue of the property of a continuous function, there is a root of the equation $f(x) = 0$ in the intervals (α_k, α_{k+1}).

Real roots of an equation can also be determined graphically as x-intercepts of the graph of the function $y = f(x)$. If the equation has no roots close to each other, then its roots are easily separated by this method. In practice, it is often advantageous to replace a given equation by an equivalent one

$$\psi_1(x) = \psi_2(x),$$

where the functions $\psi_1(x)$ and $\psi_2(x)$ are simpler than the function $f(x)$. Sketch the graph of the functions $y = \psi_1(x)$ and $y = \psi_2(x)$ and find the desired roots as the abscissas of the points of intersection of these graphs.

The Methods of Approximating a Root. 1. *Method of Chords.* If the interval $[a, b]$ contains the only real root ξ of the equation $f(x) = 0$ and $f(x)$ is continuous on the interval, then the first approximation x_1 is found by the formula

$$x_1 = a - \frac{f(a)}{f(b) - f(a)}(b - a).$$

To obtain the second approximation x_2 a similar formula is applied to that of the intervals $[a, x_1]$ or $[x_1, b]$, at the end-points of which the function $f(x)$ attains values having opposite signs. The process is continued until the required accuracy is obtained, which is judged of by the length of the obtained segment.

2. *Method of Tangents (Newton's method).* If $f(a)\,f(b) < 0$, and $f'(x)$ and $f''(x)$ are non-zero and retain definite signs for $a \le x \le b$, then, proceeding from the initial approximation $x_0 (x_0 \in [a, b])$ for which $f(x_0) f''(x_0) > 0$, we obtain all successive approximations of the root ξ by the formulas :

$$x_1 = x_0 - \frac{f(x_0)}{f'(x_0)},\ x_2 = x_1 - \frac{f(x_1)}{f'(x_1)}, \dots,\ x_n = x_{n-1} - \frac{f(x_{n-1})}{f'(x_{n-1})}.$$

To estimate the absolute error in the nth approximation we can apply the general formula

$$|\xi - x_n| \le \frac{|f(x_n)|}{m_1},$$

where $$m_1 = \min_{a \le x \le b} |f'(x)|.$$

Under the above conditions the method of chords and the method of tangents approximate the sought-for root from different sides. Therefore, it is usual practice to take advantage of their combination, *ie*, to apply both methods simultaneously. In this case one can obtain the most precise approximation of a root more rapidly and the calculations can be checked. Generally speaking, the calculation of the approximations $x_1, x_2, \dots, x_n$ should be continued until the decimal digits to be retained in the answer cease to change (in accordance with the predetermined degree or accuracy!). For intermediate transformations we have to take one or two spare digits.

3. *Iteration Method.* The equation $f(x) = 0$ is first reduced to the form $x = \varphi(x)$ where $|\varphi'(x)| \le q < 1$ $(q = \text{const})$ for $a \le x \le b$. Starting from any initial value $x_0 \in [a, b]$, successive approximations of the root ξ are computed by the formulas $x_1 = \varphi(x_0)$, $x_2 = \varphi(x_1), \dots, x_n = \varphi(x_{n-1})$. The absolute error in the nth approximation can be estimated by the following formulas :

$$|\xi - x_n| \le \frac{q}{1-q} |x_{n-1} - x_n|,$$

if the approximations x_{n-1} and x_m lie on the same side of the root, and

$$|\xi - x_n| \le \frac{q}{1+q} |x_{n-1} - x_n|,$$

if the approximations x_{n-1} and x_n lie on different sides of the root.

3.12.1. Locate the roots of the equation

$$f(x) \equiv x^3 - 6x + 2 = 0.$$

Solution Compile a table of signs of $f(x)$ at some chosen points

x	$f(x)$	x	$f(x)$
$-\infty$	$-$	1	$-$
-3	$-$	3	$+$
-1	$+$	$+\infty$	$+$
0	$+$		

From this table we draw the conclusion that the equation has three real roots lying in the intervals $(-3, -1)$, $(0, 1)$ and $(1, 3)$.

3.12.2. Determine the number of real roots of the equation

$$f(x) = x + e^x = 0$$

Solution Since $f'(x) = 1 + e^x > 0$; $f(-\infty) = -\infty$; $f(+\infty) = +\infty$, the given equation has only one real root.

3.12.3. An approximate value of the root of the equation $f(x) \equiv x^4 - x - 1 = 0$ is $\bar{x} = 1.22$. Estimate the absolute error in this root.

Solution We have $f(\bar{x}) = 2.2153 - 1.22 - 1 = -0.0047$. Since at $x = 1.23$

$$f(x) = 2.2888 - 1.23 - 1 = 0.0588,$$

the root ξ lies in the interval $(1.22, 1.23)$. The derivative $f'(x) = 4x^3 - 1$ increases monotonically, therefore its least value in the given interval is

$$m_1 = 4 \times 1.22^3 - 1 = 4 \times 1.816 - 1 = 6.264,$$

wherefrom we get an estimate of the error

$$|\bar{x} - \xi| \le \frac{|f(\bar{x})|}{m_1} = \frac{0.0047}{6.264} \approx 0.00075 < 0.001.$$

3.12.4. Solve graphically the equation

$$x \log x - 1 = 0.$$

Solution Let us rewrite the equation in the form

$$\log x = \frac{1}{x}.$$

Here $\psi_1(x) = \log x, \psi_2(x) = \frac{1}{x}$ (see Fig. 57). There are tables for the values of these functions, and this simplifies the construction of their graphs.

Constructing the graphs $y = \log x$ and $y = \frac{1}{x}$ (see Fig. 57), we find the approximate value of the only root $\xi \approx 2.5$.

3.12.5. Find the real root of the equation

$$f(x) \equiv x^3 - 2x^2 + 3x - 5 = 0$$

with an accuracy up to 10^{-4}:

(a) by applying the method of chords,

(b) by applying the method of tangents.

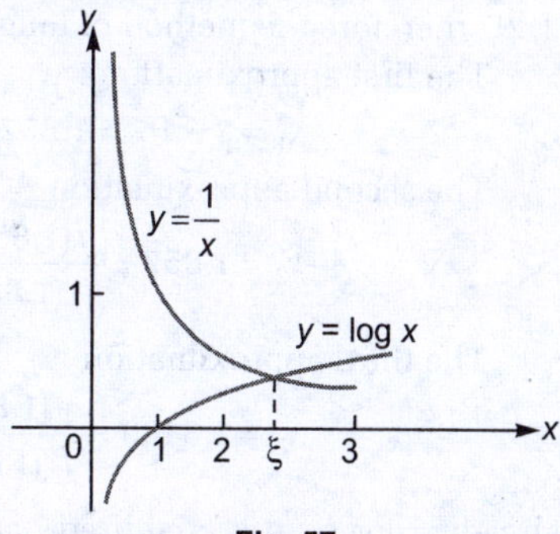

Fig. 57

Solution Let us first make sure that the given equation has only one real root. This follows from the fact that the derivative

$$f'(x) = 3x^2 - 4x + 3 > 0.$$

Then, from $f(1) = -3 < 0$, $f(2) = 1 > 0$ if follows that the given polynomial has a single positive root, which lies in the interval (1, 2).

(a) Using the method of chords, we obtain the first approximation :

$$x_1 = 1 - \frac{-3}{4} \cdot 1 = 1.75$$

Since $\quad f(1.75) = -0.5156 < 0,$

and $f(2) = 1 > 0$, then $1.75 < \xi < 2$.

The second approximation :

$$x_2 = 1.75 + \frac{0.5156}{1.5156} \cdot 0.25 = 1.75 + 0.0850 = 1.8350.$$

Since $f(1.835) = -0.05059 < 0$, then $1.835 < \xi < 2$.

The sequence of the approximations converges very slowly. Let us try to narrow down the interval, taking into account that the value of the function $f(x)$ at the point $x_2 = 1.835$ is considerably less in absolute value than $f(2)$. We have

$$f(1.9) = 0.339 > 0.$$

Hence, $\quad 1.835 < \xi < 1.9.$

Applying the method of chords to the interval (1.835, 1.9), we will get a new approximation :

$$x_3 = 1.835 - \frac{-0.05059}{0.339 + 0.05059} \cdot 0.065 = 1.8434$$

Further calculations by the method of chords yield

$$x_4 = 1.8437, \; x_5 = 1.8438,$$

and since $f(1.8437) < 0$, and $f(1.8438) > 0$, then $\xi \approx 1.8438$ with the required accuracy of 10^{-4}.

(b) For the method of tangents we choose $x_0 = 2$ as the initial approximation, since $f(2) = 1 > 0$ and $f''(x) = 6x - 4 > 0$ in the interval $(1, 2)$. The first derivative $f'(x) = 3x^2 - 4x + 3$ also retains its sign in the interval $(1, 2)$, therefore the method of tangents is applicable.

The first approximation :

$$x_1 = 2 - 1/7 = 1.857.$$

The second approximation :

$$x_2 = 1.857 - \frac{f(1.857)}{f'(1.857)} = 1.857 - \frac{0.0779}{5.9275} = 1.8439.$$

The third approximation :

$$x_3 = 1.8439 - \frac{f(1.8439)}{f'(1.8439)} = 1.8438,$$

already gives the required accuracy. Here the sequence of the approximations converges much more rapidly than in the method of chords, and in the third approximation we could obtain an accuracy up to 10^{-6}.

3.12.6. Find the least positive root of the equation $\tan x = x$ with an accuracy up to 0.0001 applying Newton's method.

3.12.7. Find the real root of the equation $2 - x - \log x = 0$ by combining the method of chords with the method of tangents.

Solution Rewrite the left member of the equation in the following way :

$$f(x) = (2 - x) + (-\log x),$$

whence it is seen that the function $f(x)$ is a sum of two monotonically decreasing functions, and therefore it decreases itself. Consequently, the given equation has a single root ξ.

Direct verification shows that this root lies in the interval $(1, 2)$. This interval can be narrowed still further :

$$1.6 < \xi < 1.8,$$

since $\quad f(1.6) = 0.1959 > 0;\ f(1.8) = -0.0553 < 0.$

Then $\quad f'(x) - 1 - \frac{1}{x}\log e;\ f''(x) = \frac{1}{x^2}\log e$

and $f'(x) < 0; f''(x) > 0$ over the whole interval $[1.6; 1.8]$.

Applying to this interval both the method of chords and the method of tangents with the initial point $x_0 = 1.6$ we obtain the first approximations :

$$x_1 = 1.6 - \frac{(1.8 - 1.6)\,f(1.6)}{f(1.8) - f(1.6)} = 1.6 + 0.1559 = 1.7559;$$

$$x'_1 = 1.6 - \frac{f(1.6)}{f'(1.6)} = 1.6 + 0.1540 = 1.7540.$$

Applying the same methods to the interval $[1.7540, 1.7559]$, we get the second approximations :

$$x_2 = 1.7559 - \frac{(1.7540 - 1.7559)\, f(1.7559)}{f(1.7540) - f(1.7559)} = 1.75558,$$

$$x'_2 = 1.7540 - \frac{f(1.7540)}{f'(1.7540)} = 1.75557.$$

Since $x_2 - x'_2 = 0.00001$, the root ξ is computed with an accuracy up to 0.00001.

3.12.8. Using the combined method find all roots of the equation $f(x) \equiv x^3 - 5x + 1 = 0$ accurate to three decimal places.

3.12.9. Applying the iteration method find the real roots of the equation $x - \sin x = 0.25$ accurate to three decimal places.

Solution Represent the given equation in the form $x - 0.25 = \sin x$. Using the graphical method, we find that the equation has one real root ξ, which is approximately equal to $x_0 = 1.2$ (see Fig. 58).

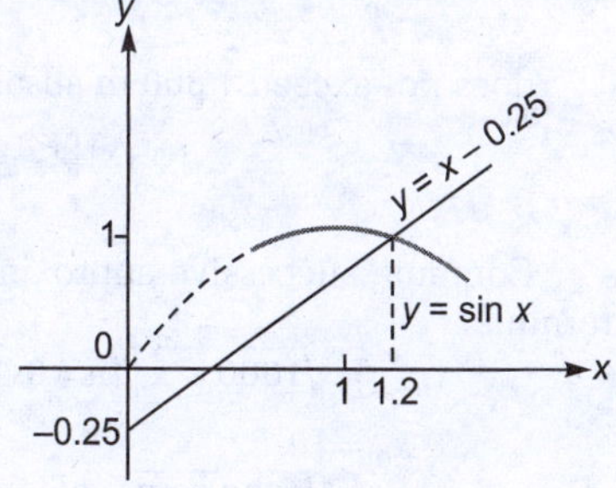

Fig. 58

Since
$\sin 1.1 = 0.8912 > 1.1 - 0.25$,
$\sin 1.3 = 0.9636 < 1.3 - 0.25$, the root ξ lies in the interval (1.1, 1.3). Let us rewrite the equation in the form $x = \varphi(x) = \sin x + 0.25$

Since the derivative $\varphi'(x) = \cos x$ in the interval (1.1, 1.3) does not exceed $\cos 1.1 < 0.46 < 1$ in absolute value, the iteration method is applicable. Let us write successive approximations

$x_n = \sin x_{n-1} + 0.25 \quad (n = 1, 2, \ldots)$, taking $x_0 = 1.2$ for the initial approximation:

$$x_1 = \sin 1.2 + 0.25 = 0.932 + 0.25 = 1.182;$$
$$x_2 = \sin 1.182 + 0.25 = 0.925 + 0.25 = 1.75;$$
$$x_3 = \sin 1.175 + 0.25 = 0.923 + 0.25 = 1.173;$$
$$x_4 = \sin 1.173 + 0.25 = 0.9219 + 0.25 = 1.1719;$$
$$x_6 = \sin 1.1719 + 0.25 = 0.9215 + 0.25 = 1.1715;$$
$$x_5 = \sin 1.1715 + 0.25 = 0.9211 + 0.25 = 1.1711.$$

Since $q = 0.46$ and hence, $\dfrac{q}{1-q} < 1$, we have $\xi = 1.171$ within the required accuracy.

3.12.10. Applying the iteration method, find the greatest positive root of the equation

$$x^3 + x = 1000$$

accurate to four decimal places.

Solution Rough estimation gives us the approximate value of the root $x_0 = 10$.

We can rewrite the given equation in the form

$$x = 1000 - x^3,$$

or in the form

$$x = \frac{1000}{x^2} - \frac{1}{x},$$

or in the form $x = \sqrt[3]{1000 - x}$ and so on.

The most advantageous of the indicated methods is the preceding one, since taking [9, 10] for the main interval and putting

$$\varphi(x) = \sqrt[3]{1000 - x},$$

we find that the derivative

$$\varphi'(x) = \frac{-1}{3\sqrt[3]{(1000 - x)^2}}$$

does not exceed 1/300 in absolute value :

$$|\varphi'(x)| \le \frac{1}{3\sqrt[3]{990^2}} \approx \frac{1}{300} = q.$$

Compute successive approximations of x_n with one spare digit by the formula

$$x_{n+1} = \sqrt[3]{1000 - x_n} \ (n = 0, 1, 2, \ldots),$$

$$x_0 = 10,$$

$$x_1 = \sqrt[3]{1000 - 10} = 9.96655,$$

$$x_2 = \sqrt[3]{1000 - 9.96655} = 9.96666,$$

$$x_3 = \sqrt[3]{1000 - 9.96666} = 9.96667.$$

We may put $\xi = 9.9667$ with an accuracy of 10^{-4}.

Note. Here, the relatively rapid convergence of the process of iteration is due to the smallness of the quantity q. In general, the smaller the q, the faster the process of iteration converges.

3.12.11. Applying the method of chords, find the positive root of the equation

$$f(x) = x^3 + 1.1x^2 + 0.9x - 1.4 = 0$$

with an accuracy of 0.0005.

3.12.12. Using the method of chords, find approximate values of the real roots of the following equations with an accuracy up to 0.01 :

(a) $(x - 1)^2 - 2\sin x = 0$; (b) $e^x - 2(1 - x)^2 = 0$.

3.12.13. Applying Newton's method, find with an accuracy up to 0.01 the positive roots of the following equations :

(a) $x^3 + 50x - 60 = 0$; (b) $x^3 + x - 32 = 0$.

3.12.14. Using the combined method find the values of the root of the equation

$$x^3 - x - 1 = 0$$

on the interval [1, 2] with an accuracy up to 0.005.

3.12.15. Applying the iteration method, find all roots of the equation $4x - 5\ln x = 5$ accurate to four decimal places.

3.13. Additional Problems

3.13.1. Does the function

$$f(x) = \begin{cases} x & \text{if } x < 1 \\ 1/x & \text{if } x \geq 1 \end{cases}$$

satisfy the conditions of the Lagrange theorem on the interval $[0, 2]$?

3.13.2. Prove that for the function $y = \alpha x^2 + \beta x + \gamma$ the number ξ in the Lagrange formula , used on an arbitrary interval $[a, b]$, is the arithmetic mean of the numbers a and b : $\xi = (a + b)/2$.

3.13.3. Prove that if the equation

$$a_0 x^n + a_1 x^{n-1} + \ldots + a_{n-1} x = 0$$

has a positive root x_0, then the equation

$$n a_0 x^{n-1} + (n-1) a_1 x^{n-2} + \ldots + a_{n-1} = 0$$

has a positive root less than x_0.

3.13.4. Prove that the equation $x^4 - 4x - 1 = 0$ has two different real roots.

3.13.5. Prove that the function $f(x) = x^n + px + q$ cannot have more than two real roots for n even and more than three for n odd.

3.13.6. Prove that all roots of the derivative of the given polynomial $f(x) = (x + 1)(x - 1)(x - 2)(x - 3)$ are real.

3.13.7. Find a mistake in the following reasoning.

The function $$f(x) = \begin{cases} x^2 \sin(1/x) & \text{for } x \neq 0, \\ 0 & \text{for } x = 0 \end{cases}$$

is differentiable for any x. By Lagrange's theorem

$$x^2 \sin\frac{1}{x} = x\left(2\xi \sin\frac{1}{\xi} - \cos\frac{1}{\xi}\right),$$

whence $$\cos\frac{1}{\xi} = 2\xi \sin\frac{1}{\xi} - x \sin\frac{1}{x} \qquad (0 < \xi < x).$$

As x tends to zero ξ will also tend to zero. Passing to the limit, we obtain $\lim\limits_{\xi \to 0} \cos(1/\xi) = 0$, whereas it is known that $\lim\limits_{x \to 0} \cos(1/x)$ is non-existent.

3.13.8. Find the mistake in the following deduction of Cauchy's formula. Let the functions $f(x)$ and $\varphi(x)$ satisfy all the conditions of the Cauchy theorem on the interval $[a, b]$. Then each of them will satisfy the conditions of Lagrange's theorem as well. Consequently, for each function we can write the Lagrange formula :

$$f(b) - f(a) = f'(\xi))(b - a), \quad a < \xi < b.$$
$$\varphi(b) - \varphi(a) = \varphi'(\xi)(b - a), \quad a < \xi < b.$$

Dividing the first expression by the second, we obtain :

$$\frac{f(b) - f(a)}{\varphi(b) - \varphi(a)} = \frac{f'(\xi)(b - a)}{\varphi'(\xi)(b - a)} = \frac{f'(\xi)}{\varphi'(\xi)}.$$

3.13.9. Prove the following inequalities :

(a) $\frac{a-b}{a} < \ln\frac{a}{b} < \frac{a-b}{b}$ if $0 < b < a$,

(b) $py^{p-1}(x - y) \le x^p - y^p \le px^{p-1}(x - y)$ if $0 < y < x$ and $p > 1$.

3.13.10. Prove that all roots of the Chebyshev-Laguerre polynomial $L_n(x) = e^x \frac{d^n}{dx^n}(x^n e^{-x})$ are positive.

3.13.11. Prove that if the function $f(x)$ satisfies the following conditions :

(1) it is defined and has a continuous derivative of the $(n-1)$ th order $f^{(n-1)}(x)$ on the interval $[x_0, x_n]$;

(2) it has a derivative of the nth order $f^{(n)}(x)$ in the interval (x_0, x_n);

(3) $f(x_0) = f(x_1) = \ldots = f(x_n)$ $(x_0 < x_1 < \ldots < x_n)$, then inside the interval $[x_0, x_n]$ there is at least one point ξ such that $f^{(n)}(\xi) = 0$.

3.13.12. The limit of the ratio of the functions

$$\lim_{x\to\infty} \frac{e^{-2x}(\cos x + 2\sin x)}{e^{-x}(\cos x + \sin x)} = \lim_{x\to\infty} e^{-x}\frac{1 + 2\tan x}{1 + \tan x}$$

is non-existent, since the expression $\frac{1 + 2\tan x}{1 + \tan x}$ is discontinuous at the points $x_n = n\pi + \pi/2$ $(n = 0, 1, \ldots)$, but at the same time the limit of the ratio of the derivatives does exist :

$$\lim_{x\to\infty} \frac{[e^{-2x}(\cos x + 2\sin x)]'}{[e^{-x}(\cos x + \sin x)]'} = \lim_{x\to\infty} \frac{-5e^{-2x}\sin x}{-2e^{-x}\sin x} = \frac{5}{2}\lim_{x\to\infty} e^{-x} = 0.$$

Explain this seeming contradiction.

3.13.13. Prove that the number θ in the remainder of the Taylor formula of the first order

$f(a + h = f(a) + hf'(a) + \frac{h^2}{2!}f''(a + \theta h)$ tends to 1/3 as $h \to 0$ if $f'''(x)$ is continuous at $x = a$ and $f'''(a) \ne 0$.

3.13.14. Prove that the number e is an irrational number.

3.13.15. Prove that for $0 < x \le \pi/2$ the function $f(x) = (\sin x)/x$ decreases. From this obtain the inequality $2x/\pi < \sin x < x$ for $0 < x < \pi/2$ and give its geometric meaning.

3.13.16. Show that the function $f(x) = x + \cos x - a$ increases; whence deduce that the equation $x + \cos x = a$ has no positive roots for $a < 1$ and has one positive root for $a > 1$.

3.13.17. Show that the equation $xe^x = 2$ has only one positive root found in the interval (0, 1).

3.13.18. Prove that the function

$$f(x) = \begin{cases} \frac{1}{2}x + x^2 \sin\frac{1}{x} & \text{for } x \neq 0, \\ 0 & \text{for } x = 0 \end{cases}$$

is not monotonic in any interval containing the origin. Sketch the graphs $f(x)$.

3.13.19. Prove the theorem if : (1) $f(x)$ and $\varphi(x)$ are continuous in the interval $[a, b]$ and differentiable inside it; (2) $f(a) = \varphi(a)$; and (3) $f'(x) > \varphi'(x)$ $(a < x < b)$, then $f(x) > \varphi(x)$ $(a < x < b)$.

3.13.20. Show that the function $f(x) = \dfrac{ax + b}{cx + d}$ has neither maxima, nor minima at $ad - bc \neq 0$.

3.13.21. In the trinomial $x^2 + px + q$ choose the coefficients p and q so that the trinomial has a minimum at $x = 3$ and that the minimum equals 5.

3.13.22. Test the function $f(x) = (x - x_0)^n \varphi(x)$ for extremum at the point $x = x_0$, where n is a natural number; the function $\varphi(x)$ is continuous at $x = x_0$ and $\varphi(x_0) \neq 0$.

3.13.23. Given a continuous function

$$f(x) = \begin{cases} \left(2 - \sin\frac{1}{x}\right)|x| & \text{at } x \neq 0, \\ 0 & \text{at } x = 0. \end{cases}$$

Show that $f(x)$ has a minimum at the point $x = 0$, but is not monotonic either on the left or on the right of $x = 0$.

3.13.24. Find the greatest and the least values of the following functions on the indicated intervals :

(a) $y = |x|$ for $-1 \leq x \leq 1$, (b) $y = E(x)$ for $-2 \leq x \leq 1$.

3.13.25. Do the following functions have the greatest and the least values on the indicated intervals ?

(a) $f(x) = \cos x$ for $-\pi/2 \leq x < \pi$

(b) $f(x) = \arcsin x$ for $-1 < x < 1$.

3.13.26. Prove that between two maxima (minima) of a continuous function there is a minimum (maximum) of this function.

3.13.27. Prove that the function

$$f(x) = \begin{cases} x^2 \sin^2(1/x) & \text{for } x \neq 0, \\ 0 & \text{for } x = 0 \end{cases}$$

has a minimum at the point $x_0 = 0$ (not a strict minimum).

3.13.28. Prove that if at the point of a minimum there exists a right-side derivative, then it is non-negative, and if there exists a left-side derivative, then it is non-positive.

3.13.29. Show that the function

$$y = \begin{cases} 1/x^2 & (x > 0), \\ 3x^2 & (x \le 0) \end{cases}$$

has a minimum at the point $x = 0$, though its first derivative does not change sign when passing through this point.

3.13.30. Let x_0 be the abscissa of the point of inflection on the curve $y = f(x)$. Will the point x_0 be a point of extremum for the function $y = f'(x)$?

3.13.31. Sketch the graph of the function $y = f(x)$ in the neighbourhood of the point $x = -1$ if

$$f(-1) = 2, f'(-1) = -1, f''(-1) = 0, f'''(x) > 0.$$

3.13.32. For what choice of the parameter h does the "curve of probabilities"

$$y = \frac{n}{\sqrt{\pi}} e^{-h^2 x^2} \quad (h > 0)$$

have points of inflection $x = \pm\,\sigma$?

3.13.33. Show that any twice continuously differentiable function has at least one abscissa of the point of inflection on the graph of the function between two points of extremum.

3.13.34. Taking the function $y = x^4 + 8x^3 + 18x^2 + 8$ as an example, ascertain that there any be no points of extremum between the abscissas of the points of inflection on the graph of a function.

3.13.35. Prove that any polynomial with positive coefficients, which is an even function, is concave everywhere and has only one point of minimum.

3.13.36. Prove that any polynomial of an odd degree $n \ge 3$ has at least one point of inflection.

3.13.37. Proceeding directly from the definition, ascertain that the straight line $y = 2x + 1$ is an asymptote of the curve $y = \dfrac{2x^4 + x^3 + 1}{x^3}$.

4

Indefinite Integrals, Basic Methods of Integration

4.1. Direct Integration and the Method of Expansion

Direct integration consists in using the following table of integrals :

(1) $\int u^n\,du = \dfrac{u^{n+1}}{n+1} + C \ (n \neq -1)$;

(2) $\int \dfrac{du}{u} = \ln|u| + C$;

(3) $\int a^u\,du = \dfrac{1}{\ln a}\,a^u + C$; $\quad \int e^u\,du = e^u + C$;

(4) $\int \cos u\,du = \sin u + C$; $\quad \int \sin u\,du = -\cos u + C$;

(5) $\int \cosh u\,du = \sinh u + C$; $\quad \int \sinh u\,du = \cosh u + C$;

(6) $\int \dfrac{du}{\cos^2 u} = \tan u + C$; $\quad \int -\dfrac{du}{\sin^2 u} = -\cot u + C$;

(7) $\int \dfrac{du}{u^2 + a^2} = \dfrac{1}{a}\,\text{arc tan}\,\dfrac{u}{a} + C = -\dfrac{1}{a}\,\text{arc cot}\,\dfrac{u}{a} + C_1 \ (a > 0)$;

(8) $\int \dfrac{du}{\sqrt{a^2 - u^2}} = \text{arc sin}\,\dfrac{u}{a} + C = -\text{arc cos}\,\dfrac{u}{a} + C_1 \ (a > 0)$;

(9) $\int \dfrac{du}{\sqrt{u^2 \pm a^2}} = \ln\left(u + \sqrt{u^2 \pm a^2}\right) + C$;

(10) $\int \dfrac{du}{u^2 - a^2} = \dfrac{1}{2a}\ln\left|\dfrac{u - a}{u + a}\right| + C.$

In all these formulas the variable u is either an independent variable or a differentiable function of some variable. If

$$\int f(u)\,du = F(u) + C,$$

then

$$\int f(ax + b)\,dx = \frac{1}{a}F(ax + b) + C.$$

The *method of expansion* consists in expanding the integrand into a linear combination of simpler functions and using the linearity property of the integral :

$$\int_{i=1}^{n} \Sigma a_i f_i(x)\, dx = \sum_{i=1}^{n} a_i \int f_i(x)\, dx \left(\sum_{i=1}^{n} |a_i| > 0 \right).$$

4.1.1. Find the integral $I = \int \frac{x^2 + 5x - 1}{\sqrt{x}}\, dx.$

Solution $I = \int \frac{x^2 + 5x - 1}{\sqrt{x}}\, dx = \int (x^{3/2} + 5x^{3/2} - x^{-1/2})\, dx$

$$= \int x^{3/2} dx + 5 \int x^{1/2} dx - \int x^{-1/2} dx$$

$$= \frac{2x^{3/2}}{5} + C_1 + \frac{5 \cdot 2}{3} x^{3/2} + C_2 - 2x^{1/2} + C_3$$

$$= 2\sqrt{x} \left(\frac{x^2}{5} + \frac{5x}{3} - 1 \right) + C.$$

Note. There is no need to introduce an arbitrary constant after calculating each integral (as is done in the above example). By combining all arbitrary constants we get a single arbitrary constant, denoted by letter C, which is added to the final answer.

4.1.2. $I = \int \frac{6x^3 + x^2 - 2x + 1}{2x - 1}\, dx.$

4.1.3. $I = \int \frac{dx}{\sin^2 x \cos^2 x}.$

Solution Transform the integrand in the following way :

$$\frac{1}{\sin^2 x \cos^2 x} = \frac{\sin^2 x + \cos^2 x}{\sin^2 x \cos^2 x}$$

$$= \frac{1}{\cos^2 x} + \frac{1}{\sin^2 x}.$$

Hence,

$$I = \int \frac{dx}{\cos^2 x} + \int \frac{dx}{\sin^2 x}$$

$$= \tan x - \cot x + C.$$

4.1.4. $I = \int \tan^2 x\, dx.$

Solution Since $\tan^2 x = \sec^2 x - 1$, then

$$I = \int \tan^2 x\, dx = \int \frac{dx}{\cos^2 x} - \int dx$$

$$= \tan x - x + C.$$

4.1.5. $I = \int (x^2 + 5)^3 dx.$

Solution Expanding the integrand by the binomial formula, we find

$$I = \int (x^6 + 15x^4 + 75x^2 + 125)\, dx$$

$$= \frac{x^7}{7} + \frac{15x^5}{5} + \frac{75x^3}{3} + 125x + C.$$

4.1.6. $I = \int (3x+5)^{17} dx.$

Solution Here it is not expedient to raise the binomial to the 17th power, since $u = 3x + 5$ is a linear function.

Proceeding from the tabular integral

$$\int u^{17} du = \frac{u^{18}}{18} + C,$$

we get

$$I = \frac{1}{3} \cdot \frac{(3x+5)^{18}}{18} + C.$$

4.1.7. $I = \int \frac{dx}{\sqrt{x+1} - \sqrt{x}}.$

4.1.8. $I = \int \cos(\pi x + 1)\, dx.$

Solution Proceeding from the tabular integral (4)

$$\int \cos u\, du = \sin u + C,$$

we obtain

$$I = \frac{1}{\pi} \sin(\pi x + 1) + C.$$

4.1.9. $I = \int \cos 4x \cos 7x\, dx.$

Solution When calculating such integrals it is advisable to use the trigonometric product formulas. Here

$$\cos 4x \cos 7x = \frac{1}{2}(\cos 3x + \cos 11x)$$

and therefore

$$I = \frac{1}{2}\int \cos 3x\, dx + \frac{1}{2}\int \cos 11x\, dx = \frac{1}{6}\sin 3x + \frac{1}{22}\sin 11x + C.$$

Note. When solving such problems it is expedient to use the following trigonometric identities :

$$\sin mx \cos nx = \frac{1}{2}[\sin(m-n)\, x + \sin(m+n)\, x];$$

$$\sin mx \sin nx = \frac{1}{2}[\cos(m-n)\, x - \cos(m+n)\, x];$$

$$\cos mx \cos nx = \frac{1}{2}[\cos(m-n)\, x + \cos(m+n) x].$$

4.1.10. $I = \int \cos x \cos 2x \cos 5x\, dx.$

Solution We have

$$(\cos x \cos 2x)\cos 5x = \frac{1}{2}(\cos x + \cos 3x)\cos 5x$$

$$= \frac{1}{4}[\cos 4x + \cos 6x] + \frac{1}{4}(\cos 2x + \cos 8x).$$

Thus, $I = \frac{1}{4}\left[\int \cos 2x\,dx + \int \cos 4x\,dx + \int \cos 6x\,dx + \int \cos 8x\,dx\right]$

$$= \frac{1}{8}\sin 2x + \frac{1}{16}\sin 4x + \frac{1}{24}\sin 6x + \frac{1}{32}\sin 8x + C.$$

4.1.11. $I = \int \sin^2 3x\,dx.$

Solution Since $\sin^2 3x = \frac{1 - \cos 6x}{2}$, then

$$I = \frac{1}{2}\int (1 - \cos 6x)\,dx$$

$$= \frac{1}{2}x - \frac{1}{12}\sin 6x + C.$$

4.1.12. $I = \int \cosh^2(8x + 5)\,dx.$

Solution Since $\cosh^2 u = \frac{\cosh 2u + 1}{2}$, then

$$I = \frac{1}{2}\int [1 + \cosh(16x + 10)]\,dx$$

$$= \frac{1}{2}x + \frac{1}{32}\sinh(16x + 10) + C.$$

4.1.13. $I = \int \frac{dx}{x^2 + 4x + 5}.$

Solution $I = \int \frac{dx}{x^2 + 4x + 5} = \int \frac{dx}{(x + 2)^2 + 1}.$

$$= \arctan(x + 2) + C.$$

4.1.14. $I = \int \frac{dx}{4x^2 + 25}.$

4.1.15. $I = \int \frac{dx}{x^2 + x + 1}.$

4.1.16. $I = \int \frac{dx}{\sqrt{4 - 9x^2}}.$

Solution $I = \int \frac{dx}{\sqrt{4 - 9x^2}} = \frac{1}{3}\int \frac{dx}{\sqrt{4/9 - x^2}} = \frac{1}{3}\arcsin\frac{3x}{2} + C.$

4.1.17. $I = \int \frac{dx}{\sqrt{5 - x^2 - 4x}}.$

Solution $I = \int \frac{dx}{\sqrt{5 - x^2 - 4x}} = \int \frac{dx}{\sqrt{9 - (x + 2)^2}}$

$$= \arcsin\frac{x + 2}{3} + C.$$

4.1.18. $I = \int \frac{dx}{\sqrt{x^2 + 6x + 1}}$.

4.1.19. $I = \int \frac{dx}{4 - x^2 - 4x}$.

Solution $I = \int \frac{dx}{4 - x^2 - 4x} = \int \frac{dx}{8 - (x+2)^2}$

$$= \frac{1}{4\sqrt{2}} \ln \left| \frac{2\sqrt{2} + x + 2}{2\sqrt{2} - (x+2)} \right| + C.$$

4.1.20. $I = \int \frac{dx}{10x^2 - 7}$.

4.1.21. Evaluate the following integrals :

(a) $\int \frac{dx}{x^2 - 6x + 13}$; (b) $\int \frac{x-1}{\sqrt[3]{x^2}} dx$;

(c) $\int \frac{3 - 2\cot^2 x}{\cos^2 x} dx$; (d) $\int \frac{2 + 3x^2}{x^2 (1 + x^2)} dx$.

4.1.22. Integrate :

(a) $\int \frac{\sqrt{1 - x^2} + \sqrt{1 + x^2}}{\sqrt{1 - x^4}} dx$; (b) $\int \frac{\cos 2x}{\cos x - \sin x} dx$;

(c) $\int \frac{2^{x+1} - 5^{x-1}}{10^x} dx$; (d) $\int (\sin 5x - \sin 5\alpha)\, dx$.

4.2. Integration by Substitution

The method of substitution (or change of variable) consists in substituting $\varphi(t)$ for x where $\phi(t)$ is a continuously differentiable function. On substituting we have :

$$\int f(x)\, dx = \int f[\varphi(t)]\, \varphi'(t)\, dt,$$

and after integration we return to the old variable by inverse substitution $t = \varphi^{-1}(x)$.

The indicated formula is also used in the reverse direction :

$$\int f[\varphi(t)]\, \varphi'(t)\, dt = \int f(x)\, dx, \text{ where } x = \varphi(t).$$

4.2.1. $I = \int x \sqrt{x - 5}\, dx$.

Solution Make the substitution

$$\sqrt{x - 5} = t.$$

Whence $x - 5 = t^2$, $x = t^2 + 5$, $dx = 2t\, dt$.

Substituting into the integral we get

$$I = \int (t^2 + 5)\, t \cdot 2t\, dt = 2 \int (t^4 + 5t^2)\, dt = 2\frac{t^5}{5} + \frac{10t^3}{3} + C.$$

Now return to the initial variable x:

$$I = \frac{2\,(x-5)^{5/2}}{5} + \frac{10\,(x-5)^{3/2}}{3} + C.$$

4.2.2. $I = \int \frac{dx}{1+e^x}$.

Solution Let us make the substitution $1 + e^x = t$. Whence

$$e^x = t - 1,\ x = \ln (t-1),\ dx = dt/(t-1).$$

Substituting into the integral, we get

$$I = \int \frac{dx}{1+e^x} = \int \frac{dt}{t\,(t-1)}.$$

But

$$\frac{1}{t(t-1)} = \frac{1}{t-1} - \frac{1}{t},$$

therefore

$$I = \int \frac{dt}{t-1} - \int \frac{dt}{t} = \ln|t-1| - \ln|t| + C.$$

Coming back to the variable x, we obtain

$$I = \ln \frac{e^x}{1+e^x} + C = x - \ln (1+e^x) + C.$$

Note. This integral can be calculated in a simpler way by multiplying both the numerator and denominator by e^{-x}:

$$\int \frac{e^{-x}}{e^{-x}+1}\,dx = -\int \frac{-e^{-x}}{e^{-x}+1}\,dx = -\ln (e^{-x}+1) + C$$

$$= -\ln \frac{e^x+1}{e^x} = x - \ln (e^x+1) + C.$$

4.2.3. $I = \int \frac{x^2+3}{\sqrt{(2x-5)^3}}\,dx.$

4.2.4. $I = \int \frac{(x^2-1)\,dx}{(x^4+3x^2+1)\arctan \frac{x^2+1}{x}}$.

Solution Transform the integrand

$$I = \int \frac{(1-1/x^2)\,dx}{[(x+1/x)^2+1]\arctan (x+1/x)}.$$

Make the substitution $x + \frac{1}{x} = t$; differentiating, we get

$$\left(1 - \frac{1}{x^2}\right) dx = dt.$$

Whence

$$I = \int \frac{dt}{(t^2+1)\,\text{arc tan}\, t}.$$

Make one more substitution : arc tan $t = u$. Then

$$\frac{dt}{t^2+1} = du$$

and

$$I = \int \frac{du}{u} = \ln|u| + C.$$

Returning first to t, and then to x, we have

$$I = \ln|\text{arc tan}\, t| + C = \ln\left|\text{arc tan}\left(x + \frac{1}{x}\right)\right| + C.$$

4.2.5. $I = \int \frac{\sqrt{a^2 - x^2}}{x^4}\, dx.$

Solution Make the substitution :

$$x = \frac{1}{t};\, dx = -\frac{dt}{t^2}.$$

Hence,

$$I = -\int \frac{\sqrt{a^2 - 1/t^2}}{(1/t^4)\,t^2}\, dt = -\int t\sqrt{a^2t^2 - 1}\, dt.$$

Now make one more substitution : $\sqrt{a^2t^2 - 1} = z$. Then $2a^2t\, dt = 2z\, dz$ and

$$I = -\frac{1}{a^2}\int z^2 dz = -\frac{1}{3a^2} z^3 + C.$$

Returning to t and then to x, we obtain

$$I = -\frac{(a^2 - x^2)^{3/2}}{3a^2x^3} + C.$$

4.2.6. $I = \int \frac{dx}{a^2 \sin^2 x + b^2 \cos^2 x}.$

Solution $I = \int \frac{dx}{a^2 \sin^2 x + b^2 \cos^2 x} = \frac{1}{b^2}\int \frac{1}{\frac{a^2}{b^2}\tan^2 x + 1} \cdot \frac{dx}{\cos^2 x}.$

Make the substitution $\frac{a}{b}\tan x = t;\, dt = \frac{a}{b}\frac{dx}{\cos^2 x}$. Then

$$I = \frac{1}{ab}\int \frac{dt}{1+t^2} = \frac{1}{ab}\,\text{arc tan}\, t + C.$$

Returning to x, we obtain

$$I = \frac{1}{ab}\,\text{arc tan}\left(\frac{a}{b}\tan x\right) + C.$$

4.2.7. $I = \int \sqrt[3]{1 + 3\sin x}\cos x\,dx.$

Solution Make the substitution $1 + 3\sin x = t \cdot 3\cos x\,dx = dt$. Then

$$I = \frac{1}{3}\int \sqrt[3]{t}\,dt = \frac{1}{3}\int t^{1/3}dt = \frac{1}{3}\cdot\frac{3}{4}t^{4/3} + C$$

$$= \frac{(1 + 3\sin x)^{4/3}}{4} + C.$$

4.2.8. $I = \int \frac{\sin x\,dx}{\sqrt{\cos x}}.$

4.2.9. $I = \int \frac{dx}{(\text{arc}\cos x)^5\sqrt{1 - x^2}}.$

Solution Make the substitution : $\text{arc}\cos x = t$; $-\frac{dx}{\sqrt{1 - x^2}} = dt$. Then

$$I = -\int \frac{dt}{t^5} = -\int t^{-5}dt = \frac{1}{4}t^{-4} + C = \frac{1}{4\,\text{arc}\cos^4 x} + C.$$

4.2.10. $I = \int \frac{x^2 + 1}{\sqrt[3]{x^3 + 3x + 1}}\,dx.$

4.2.11. $I = \int \frac{\sin 2x}{1 + \sin^2 x}\,dx.$

Solution Make the substitution :

$$1 + \sin^2 x = t;\ 2\sin x\cos x\,dx = \sin 2x\,dx = dt.$$

Then

$$I = \int \frac{dt}{t} = \ln t + C = \ln(1 + \sin^2 x) + C.$$

4.2.12. $I = \int \frac{1 + \ln x}{3 + x\ln x}\,dx.$

Solution Substitute

$$3 + x\ln x = t,\ (1 + \ln x)\,dx = dt$$

and get

$$I = \int \frac{dt}{t} = \ln|t| + C = \ln|3 + x\ln x| + C.$$

4.2.13. Evaluate the following integrals :

(a) $\int \frac{\sqrt[3]{1 + \ln x}}{x}\,dx$; (b) $\int \frac{dx}{x\ln x}$;

(c) $\int \frac{x\,dx}{\sqrt{3 - x^4}}$; (d) $\int \frac{x^{n-1}}{x^{2n} + a^2}\,dx$;

(e) $\int \frac{\sin\sqrt{x}}{\sqrt{x}}\,dx$; (f) $\int \left(\ln x + \frac{1}{\ln x}\right)\frac{dx}{x}.$

4.2.14. Find the following integrals :

(a) $\int x^2\sqrt[3]{1-x}\,dx$;   (b) $\int \frac{\ln x\,dx}{x\sqrt{1+\ln x}}$;

(c) $\int \cos^5 x\sqrt{\sin x}\,dx$;   (d) $\int \frac{x^5}{\sqrt{1-x^2}}\,dx$.

4.3. Integration by Parts

The formula

$$\int u\,dv = uv - \int v\,du$$

is known as the formula for *integration by parts,* where u and v are differentiable functions of x.

To use this formula the integrand should be reduced to the product of two factors : one function and the differential of another function. If the integrand is the product of a logarithmic or an inverse trigonometric function and a polynomial, then u is usually taken to be either the logarithmic or the inverse trigonometric function. But if the integrand is the product of a trigonometric or an exponential function and an algebraic one, then u usually denotes the algebraic function.

4.3.1. $I = \int \text{arc tan } x\,dx.$

Solution Let us put here

$$u = \text{arc tan } x,\ dv = dx$$

whence $$du = \frac{dx}{1+x^3};\ v = x;$$

$$I = \int \text{arc tan } x\,dx = x \text{ arc tan } x - \int \frac{x\,dx}{1+x^2}$$

$$= x \text{ arc tan } x - \frac{1}{2}\ln(1+x^2) + C.$$

4.3.2. $I = \int \text{arc sin } x\,dx.$

4.3.3. $I = \int x\cos x\,dx.$

Solution Let us put

$$u = x;\quad dv = \cos x\,dx,$$

whence

$$du = dx;\quad v = \sin x,$$

$$I = \int x\cos x\,dx = x\sin x - \int \sin x\,dx = x\sin x + \cos x + C.$$

We will show now that would result from an unsuitable choice of the multipliers u and dv.

In the integral $\int x\cos x\,dx$ let us put

$$u = \cos x;\quad dv = x\,dx,$$

whence

$$du = -\sin x\,dx; \quad v = \frac{1}{2}x^2.$$

In this case

$$I = \frac{1}{2}x^2 \cos x + \frac{1}{2}\int x^2 \sin x\,dx.$$

As is obvious, the integral has become more complicated.

4.3.4. $I = \int x^3 \ln x\,dx.$

Solution Let us put

$$u = \ln x; \quad dv = x^3 dx,$$

whence

$$du = \frac{dx}{x}; \quad v = \frac{1}{4}x^4,$$

$$I = \frac{1}{4}x^4 \ln x - \frac{1}{4}\int x^4 \frac{dx}{x} = \frac{1}{4}x^4 \ln x - \frac{1}{4}\int x^3 dx$$

$$= \frac{1}{4}x^4 \ln x - \frac{1}{16}x^4 + C.$$

4.3.5. $I = \int (x^2 - 2x + 5)\,e^{-x}\,dx.$

Solution Let us put

$$u = x^2 - 2x + 5; \quad dv = e^{-x}dx,$$

whence

$$du = (2x - 2)\,dx; \quad v = -e^{-x};$$

$$I = \int (x^2 - 2x + 5)\,e^{-x}\,dx$$

$$= -e^{-x}(x^2 - 2x + 5) + 2\int (x - 1)\,e^{-x}dx.$$

We again integrate the last integral by parts. Put

$$x - 1 = u; \quad dv = e^{-x}dx,$$

whence

$$du = dx; \quad v = -e^{-x}.$$

$$I_1 = 2\int (x - 1)\,e^{-x}dx = -2e^{-x}(x - 1) + 2\int e^{-x}dx = -2xe^{-x} + C.$$

Finally we get

$$I = -e^{-x}(x^2 - 2x + 5) - 2xe^{-x} + C = -e^{-x}(x^2 + 5) + C.$$

Note. As a result of calculation of integrals of the form $\int P(x)\,e^{\alpha x}dx$ we obtain a function of the form $Q(x)\,e^{\alpha x}$, where $Q(x)$ is a polynomial of the same degree as the polynomial $P(x)$.

This circumstance allows us to calculate the integrals of the indicated type using the method of indefinite coefficients, the essence of which is explained by the following example.

4.3.6. Applying the method of indefinite coefficients, evaluate

$$I = \int (3x^3 - 17)\, e^{2x} dx.$$

Solution $\int (3x^3 - 17)\, e^{2x} dx = (Ax^3 + Bx^2 + Dx + E)\, e^{2x} + C.$

Differentiating the right and the left sides, we obtain

$$(3x^3 - 17)\, e^{2x} = 2\,(Ax^3 + Bx^2 + Dx + E)\, e^{2x} + e^{2x}\,(3Ax^2 + 2Bx + D).$$

Cancelling e^{2x}, we have

$$3x^3 - 17 \equiv 2Ax^3 + (2B + 3A)\, x^2 + (2D + 2B)\, x + (2E + D).$$

Equating the coefficients at the equal powers of x in the left and right sides of this identity, we get

$$3 = 2A; \qquad 0 = 2B + 3A;$$
$$0 = 2D + 2B; \qquad -17 = 2E + D.$$

Solving the system, we obtain

$$A = \frac{3}{2}; \qquad B = -\frac{9}{4}; \qquad D = \frac{9}{4}; \qquad E = -\frac{77}{8}.$$

Hence,

$$\int (3x^3 - 17)\, e^{2x}\, dx = \left(\frac{3}{2}x^3 - \frac{9}{4}x^2 + \frac{9}{4}x - \frac{77}{8}\right) e^{2x} + C.$$

4.3.7. Integrate :

$$I = \int (x^3 + 1) \cos x\, dx.$$

Solution Let us put

$$u = x^3 + 1; \quad dv = \cos x\, dx,$$

whence

$$du = 3x^2\, dx; \quad v = \sin x.$$

$$I = (x^3 + 1) \sin x - 3 \int x^2 \sin x\, dx = (x^3 + 1) \sin x - 3I_1,$$

where $I_1 = \int x^2 \sin x\, dx$.

Integrating by parts again, we get

$$I_1 = -\,x^2 \cos x + 2I_2,$$

where $I_2 = \int x \cos x\, dx$.

Integrating by parts again, we obtain

$$I_2 = x \sin x + \cos x + C.$$

Finally, we have :

$$I = \int (x^3 + 1) \cos x\, dx$$
$$= (x^3 + 1) \sin x + 3x^2 \cos x - 6x \sin x - 6 \cos x + C$$
$$= (x^3 - 6x + 1) \sin x + (3x^2 - 6) \cos x + C.$$

Note. The method of indefinite coefficients may also be applied to integrals of the form

$$\int P(x)\sin ax\,dx,\ \int P(x)\cos ax\,dx.$$

4.3.8. $I = \int (x^2 + 3x + 5)\cos 2x\,dx.$

Solution Let us put

$$\int (x^2 + 3x + 5)\cos 2x\,dx$$
$$= (A_0x^2 + A_1\,x + A_2)\cos 2x + (B_0x^2 + B_1x + B_2)\sin 2x + C.$$

Differentiate both sides of the identity :

$$(x^2 + 3x + 5)\cos 2x = -2\,(A_0x^2 + A_1x + A_2)\sin 2x$$
$$+ (2\,A_0x + A_1)\cos 2x + 2\,(B_0x^2 + B_1x + B_2)\cos 2x$$
$$+ (2B_0x + B_1)\sin 2x$$
$$= [2B_0x^2 + (2B_1 + 2A_0)x + (A_1 + 2B_2)]\cos 2x$$
$$+ [-2\,A_0x^2 + (2B_0 - 2A_1)\,x + (B_1 - 2A_2)]\sin 2x.$$

Equating the coefficients at equal powers of x in the multipliers $\cos 2x$ and $\sin 2x$, we get a system of equations :

$$2B_0 = 1;\quad 2\,(B_1 + A_0) = 3;\quad A_1 + 2B_2 = 5;$$
$$-2A_0 = 0;\quad 2\,(B_0 - A_1) = 0;\quad B_1 - 2A_2 = 0.$$

Solving the system, we find

$$A_0 = 0;\quad B_0 = \frac{1}{2};\quad A_1 = \frac{1}{2};\quad B_1 = \frac{3}{2};\quad A_2 = \frac{3}{4};\quad B_2 = \frac{9}{4}.$$

Thus,

$$\int (x^2 + 3x + 5)\cos 2x dx = \left(\frac{x}{2} + \frac{3}{4}\right)\cos 2x + \left(\frac{1}{2}x^2 + \frac{3}{2}x + \frac{9}{4}\right)\sin^2 x + C.$$

4.3.9. $I = \int (3x^2 + 6x + 5)\,\text{arc tan}\,x\,dx.$

Solution Let us put

$$u = \text{arc tan}\,x;\quad dv = (3x^2 + 6x + 5)\,dx,$$

whence

$$du = \frac{dx}{1 + x^2};\quad v = x^3 + 3x^2 + 5x.$$

Hence,

$$I = (x^3 + 3x^2 + 5x)\,\text{arc tan}\,x - \int \frac{x^3 + 3x^2 + 5x}{1 + x^2}\,dx.$$

Single out the integral part under the last integral by dividing the numerator by the denominator :

$$I_1 = \int \frac{x^3 + 3x^2 + 5x}{1 + x^2}\,dx = \int (x + 3)\,dx + \int \frac{4x - 3}{x^2 + 1}\,dx$$

$$= \frac{x^2}{2} + 3x + 2\int \frac{2x\,dx}{x^2+1} - 3\int \frac{dx}{x^2+1}$$

$$= \frac{x^2}{2} + 3x + 2\ln(x^2+1) - 3\arctan x + C.$$

Substituting the value of I_1, we finally get

$$I = (x^3 + 3x^2 + 5x + 3)\arctan x - \frac{x^2}{2} - 3x - 2\ln(x^2+1) + C.$$

4.3.10. Find the integral

$$I = \int e^{5x} \cos 4x\,dx.$$

Solution Let us put

$$e^{5x} = u; \quad \cos 4x\,dx = dv,$$

whence

$$5e^{5x}\,dx = du; \quad v = \frac{1}{4}\sin 4x.$$

Hence,

$$I = \frac{1}{4}e^{5x}\sin 4x - \frac{5}{4}\int e^{5x}\sin 4x\,dx.$$

Integrating by parts again, we obtain

$$I_1 = \int e^{5x}\sin 4x\,dx = -\frac{1}{4}e^{5x}\cos 4x + \frac{5}{4}\int e^{5x}\cos 4x\,dx.$$

Thus,

$$I = \frac{1}{4}e^{5x}\sin 4x - \frac{5}{4}\left(-\frac{1}{4}e^{5x}\cos 4x + \frac{5}{4}\int e^{5x}\cos 4x\,dx\right),$$

ie,

$$I = \frac{1}{4}e^{5x}\left(\sin 4x + \frac{5}{4}\cos 4x\right) - \frac{25}{16}I.$$

Whence

$$I = \frac{4}{41}e^{5x}\left(\sin 4x + \frac{5}{4}\cos 4x\right) + C.$$

4.3.11. $I = \int \cos(\ln x)\,dx.$

Solution Let us put

$$u = \cos(\ln x); \qquad dv = dx,$$

whence $\quad du = -\sin(\ln x)\frac{dx}{x}; \qquad v = x.$

Hence, $\quad I = \int \cos(\ln x)\,dx = x\cos(\ln x) + \int \sin(\ln x)dx.$

Integrate by parts once again

$$u = \sin(\ln x); \qquad dv = dx,$$

whence $$du = \cos(\ln x)\frac{dx}{x}; \qquad v = x.$$

Hence, $$I_1 = \int \sin(\ln x)dx = x\sin(\ln x) - \int \cos(\ln x)\,dx.$$

Thus $$I = \int \cos(\ln x)dx = x\cos(\ln x) + x\sin(\ln x) - I.$$

Hence, $$I = \frac{x}{2}[\cos(\ln x) + \sin(\ln x)] + C.$$

4.3.12. $I = \int x \ln\left(1 + \frac{1}{x}\right)dx.$

Solution Let us transform the integrand

$$\ln\left(1 + \frac{1}{x}\right) = \ln\frac{x+1}{x} = \ln(x+1) - \ln x.$$

Hence $$I = \int x\ln(x+1)\,dx - \int x\ln x\,dx = I_1 - I_2.$$

Let us integrate I_1 and I_2 by parts. Put

$$u = \ln(x+1); \qquad dv = x\,dx,$$

whence $$du = \frac{dx}{1+x}; \qquad v = \frac{1}{2}(x^2 - 1).$$

Hence $$I_1 = \int x\ln(x+1)\,dx$$

$$= \frac{1}{2}(x^2 - 1)\ln(x+1) - \frac{1}{2}\int\frac{(x^2-1)\,dx}{1+x}$$

$$= \frac{x^2-1}{2}\ln(x+1) - \frac{1}{2}\int(x-1)\,dx$$

$$= \frac{x^2-1}{2}\ln(x+1) - \frac{1}{4}x^2 + \frac{1}{2}x + C.$$

Analogously,

$$I_2 = \int x\ln x\,dx = \frac{x^2}{2}\ln x - \frac{1}{4}x^2 + C.$$

Finally we have

$$I = \int x\ln\left(1 + \frac{1}{x}\right)dx = \frac{1}{2}(x^2 - 1)\ln(x+1) - \frac{x^2}{2}\ln x + \frac{x}{2} + C.$$

4.3.13. $I = \int \frac{\sqrt{x^2+1}\,[\ln(x^2+1) - 2\ln x]}{x^4}\,dx.$

Solution First apply the substitution

$$1 + \frac{1}{x^2} = t.$$

Then $$dt = -\frac{2dx}{x^3} \quad \text{or} \quad \frac{dx}{x^3} = -\frac{1}{2}dt.$$

Hence, $$I = \int \sqrt{1 + \frac{1}{x^2}} \ln \frac{x^2+1}{x^2} \cdot \frac{dx}{x^3} = -\frac{1}{2}\int \sqrt{t} \ln t \, dt.$$

The obtained integral is easily evaluated by parts. Let us put

$$u = \ln t; \qquad dv = \sqrt{t}\, dt.$$

Then $$du = \frac{dt}{t}; \qquad v = \frac{2}{3} t\sqrt{t}.$$

Whence

$$-\frac{1}{2}\int \sqrt{t} \ln t \, dt = -\frac{1}{2}\left[\frac{2}{3} t\sqrt{t} \ln t - \frac{2}{3}\int \sqrt{t}\, dt\right]$$

$$= -\frac{1}{2}\left[\frac{2}{3} t\sqrt{t} \ln t - \frac{4}{9} t\sqrt{t}\right] + C.$$

Returning to x, we obtain

$$I = -\frac{1}{2}\left[\frac{2}{3}\left(1 + \frac{1}{x^2}\right)^{3/2} \ln\left(1 + \frac{1}{x^2}\right) - \frac{4}{9}\left(1 + \frac{1}{x^2}\right)^{3/2}\right] + C$$

$$= \frac{(x^2+1)\sqrt{x^2+1}}{9x^3}\left[2 - 3\ln\left(1 + \frac{1}{x^2}\right)\right] + C.$$

4.3.14. $I = \int \sin x \ln \tan x \, dx.$

4.3.15. $I = \int \ln(\sqrt{1-x} + \sqrt{1+x})\, dx.$

Solution Let us put

$$u = \ln(\sqrt{1-x} + \sqrt{1+x}); \; dv = dx,$$

whence

$$du = \frac{1}{\sqrt{1-x} + \sqrt{1+x}}\left(-\frac{1}{2\sqrt{1-x}} + \frac{1}{2\sqrt{1+x}}\right) dx$$

$$= \frac{1}{2} \cdot \frac{\sqrt{1-x} - \sqrt{1+x}}{\sqrt{1-x} + \sqrt{1+x}} \cdot \frac{dx}{\sqrt{1-x^2}} = \frac{1}{2} \cdot \frac{\sqrt{1-x^2} - 1}{x\sqrt{1-x^2}} dx;$$

$$v = x$$

Hence, $$I = x \ln(\sqrt{1-x} + \sqrt{1+x}) - \frac{1}{2}\int x \frac{\sqrt{1-x^2} - 1}{x\sqrt{1-x^2}} dx$$

$$= x \ln(\sqrt{1-x} + \sqrt{1+x}) - \frac{1}{2}\int dx + \frac{1}{2}\int \frac{dx}{\sqrt{1-x^2}}$$

$$= x \ln(\sqrt{1-x} + \sqrt{1+x}) - \frac{1}{2} x + \frac{1}{2} \arcsin x + C.$$

Note. In calculating a number of integrals we had to use the method of integration by parts several times in succession. The result could be obtained more rapidly and in a more concise form by using the so-called *generalized formula for integration by parts (or the formula for multiple integration by parts):*

$$\int u(x)\,v\,(x)\,dx = u\,(x)\,v_1(x) - u'(x)\,v_2\,(x) + u''\,(x)\,v_3\,(x)$$

$$- \ldots + (-1)^{n-1}\,u^{(n-1)}\,(x)\,u_n\,(x) - (-1)^{n-1}\int u^{(n)}\,(x)\,u_n(x)\,dx,$$

where $v_1(x) = \int v(x)dx;\ v_2\,(x) = \int v_1(x)dx;\ldots;\ v_n(x) = \int v_{n-1}\,(x)\,dx.$

Here, of course, we assume that all derivatives and integrals appearing in this formula exist.

The use of the generalized formula for integration by parts is especially advantageous when calculating the integral $\int P_n(x)\,\varphi(x)\,dx$, where $P_n(x)$ is a polynomial of degree n, and the factor $\varphi\,(x)$ is such that it can be integrated successively $n+1$ times. For example,

$$\int P_n(x)\,e^{kx}\,dx = P_n(x)\frac{e^{kx}}{k} - P'_n\,(x)\frac{e^{kx}}{k^2} + \ldots + (-1)^n\,P_n^{(n)}\,(x)\frac{e^{kx}}{k^{n+1}} + C$$

$$= e^{kx}\left[\frac{P_n\,(x)}{k} - \frac{1}{k^2}\,P'_n\,(x) + \ldots + \frac{(-1)^n}{k^{n+1}}\,P_n^{(n)}\,(x)\right] + C.$$

4.3.16. Applying the generalized formula for integration by parts, find the following integrals :

(a) $\int (x^3 - 2x^2 + 3x - 1)\cos 2x\,dx,$

(b) $\int (2x^3 + 3x^2 - 8x + 1)\sqrt{2x+6}\,dx.$

Solution

(a) $\int (x^3 - 2x^2 + 3x - 1)\cos 2x\,dx = (x^3 - 2x^2 + 3x - 1)\dfrac{\sin 2x}{2}$

$$-(3x^2 - 4x + 3)\left(-\frac{\cos 2x}{4}\right) + (6x - 4)\left(-\frac{\sin 2x}{8}\right) - 6\,\frac{\cos 2x}{16} + C$$

$$= \frac{\sin 2x}{4}(2x^3 - 4x^2 + 3x) + \frac{\cos 2x}{8}(6x^2 - 8x + 3) + C;$$

(b) $\int (2x^3 + 3x^2 - 8x + 1)\sqrt{2x+6}\,dx$

$$= (2x^3 + 3x^2 - 8x + 1)\frac{(2x+6)^{3/2}}{3} - (6x^2 + 6x - 8)\frac{(2x+6)^{5/2}}{3\cdot 5}$$

$$+ (12x + 6)\frac{(2x+6)^{7/2}}{3\cdot 5\cdot 7} - 12\,\frac{(2x+6)^{9/2}}{3\cdot 5\cdot 7\cdot 9} + C$$

$$= \frac{\sqrt{2x+6}}{5\cdot 7\cdot 9}(2x+6)(70x^3 - 45x^2 - 396x + 897) + C.$$

Evaluate the following integrals :

4.3.17. $\int \ln(x + \sqrt{1 + x^4})\,dx.$

4.3.18. $\int \sqrt[3]{x}(\ln x)^2\,dx.$

4.3.19. $\int \dfrac{\arcsin x\,dx}{\sqrt{1+x}}.$

4.3.20. $\int \frac{x \cos x \, dx}{\sin^3 x}$.

4.3.21. $\int 3^x \cos x \, dx$.

4.3.22. $\int (x^3 - 2x^2 + 5) e^{3x} \, dx$.

4.3.23. $\int (1 + x^2)^2 \cos x \, dx$.

4.3.24. $\int (x^2 + 2x - 1) \sin 3x \, dx$.

4.3.25. $\int (x^2 - 2x + 3) \ln x \, dx$.

4.3.26. $\int x^3 \operatorname{arc\,tan} x \, dx$.

4.3.27. $\int x^2 \operatorname{arc\,cos} x \, dx$.

4.3.28. Applying the formula for multiple integration by parts, calculate the following integrals :

(a) $\int (3x^2 + x - 2) \sin^2 (3x + 1) \, dx$;

(b) $\int \frac{x^2 - 7x + 1}{\sqrt[3]{2x + 1}} \, dx$.

4.4. Reduction Formulas

Reduction formulas make it possible to reduce an integral depending on the index $n > 0$, called the order of the integral, to an integral of the same type with a smaller index.

4.4.1. Integrating by parts, derive reduction formulas for calculating the following integrals :

(a) $I_n = \int \frac{dx}{(x^2 + a^2)^n}$; (b) $I_{n,\,-m} = \int \frac{\sin^n x}{\cos^m x} \, dx$;

(c) $I_n = \int (a^2 - x^2)^n \, dx$.

Solution (a) We integrate by parts. Let us put

$$u = \frac{1}{(x^2 + a^2)^n}, \qquad dv = dx,$$

whence

$$du = -\frac{2n \, x \, dx}{(x^2 + a^2)^{n+1}}, \quad v = x.$$

Hence,

$$I_n = \frac{x}{(x^2 + a^2)^n} + 2n \int \frac{x^2}{(x^2 + a^2)^{n+1}} \, dx$$

$$= \frac{x}{(x^2 + a^2)^n} + 2n \int \frac{(x^2 + a^2) - a^2}{(x^2 + a^2)^{n+1}} \, dx$$

$$= \frac{x}{(x^2 + a^2)^n} + 2\,n I_n - 2\,n a^2 I_{n+1},$$

whence $$I_{n+1} = \frac{1}{2na^2} \cdot \frac{x}{(x^2 + a^2)^n} + \frac{2n-1}{2n} \cdot \frac{1}{a^2} I_n.$$

The obtained formula reduces the calculation of the integral I_{n+1} to the calculation of the integral I_n and, consequently, allows us to calculate completely and integral with a natural index, since

$$I_1 = \int \frac{dx}{x^2 + a^2} = \frac{1}{a} \text{arc tan} \frac{x}{a} + C.$$

For instance, putting $n = 1$, we obtain

$$I_2 = \int \frac{dx}{(x^2 + a^2)^2} = \frac{1}{2a^2} \cdot \frac{x}{x^2 + a^2} + \frac{1}{2a^2}$$

$$I_1 = \frac{1}{2a^2} \frac{x}{x^2 + a^2} + \frac{1}{2a^3} \text{arc tan} \frac{x}{a} + C;$$

putting $n = 2$, we get

$$I_3 = \int \frac{dx}{(x^2 + a^2)^3} = \frac{1}{4a^2} \cdot \frac{x}{(x^2 + a^2)^2} + \frac{3}{4a^2}$$

$$I_2 = \frac{1}{4a^2} \cdot \frac{x}{(x^2 + a^2)^2} + \frac{3}{8a^4} \cdot \frac{x}{x^2 + a^2} + \frac{3}{8a^5} \text{arc tan} \frac{x}{a} + C$$

(b) Let us apply the method of integration by parts, putting

$$u = \sin^{n-1} x; \qquad dv = \frac{\sin x}{\cos^m x} dx,$$

whence $$du = (n-1) \sin^{n-2} x \cos x \, dx;$$

$$v = \frac{1}{(m-1) \cos^{m-1} x} \quad (m \neq 1).$$

Hence, $$I_{n,-m} = \frac{\sin^{n-1} x}{(m-1) \cos^{m-1} x} - \frac{n-1}{m-1} \int \frac{\sin^{n-2} x \, dx}{\cos^{m-2} x}$$

$$= \frac{\sin^{n-1} x}{(m-1) \cos^{m-1} x} - \frac{n-1}{m-1} I_{n-2,\,2-m} \,(m \neq 1).$$

(c) Integrate by parts. putting

$$u = (a^2 - x^2)^n; \qquad dv = dx,$$

whence

$$du = -2nx\,(a^2 - x^2)^{n-1} dx; \qquad v = x.$$

Hence $$I_n = x\,(a^2 - x^2)^n + 2n \int x^2 (a^2 - x^2)^{n-1} dx$$

$$= x\,(a^2 - x^2)^n + 2n \int (x^2 - a^2 + a^2)(a^2 - x^2)^{n-1} dx$$

$$= x\,(a^2 - x^2)^n - 2nI_n + 2na^2 I_{n-1}.$$

Wherefrom, reducing the similar terms, we obtain

$$(1 + 2n)\, I_n = x\,(a^2 - x^2)^n + 2na^2 I_{n-1}.$$

Hence, $$I_n = \frac{x(a^2 - x^2)^n}{2n+1} + \frac{2na^2}{2n+1} I_{n-1}.$$

For instance, nothing that

$$I_{-1/2} = \int \frac{dx}{\sqrt{a^2 - x^2}} = \arcsin \frac{x}{a} + C,$$

we can find successively

$$I_{1/2} = \int \sqrt{a^2 - x^2}\, dx = \frac{x}{2}(a^2 - x^2)^{1/2} + \frac{a^2}{2} I_{-1/2}$$

$$= \frac{x}{2}\sqrt{a^2 - x^2} + \frac{a^2}{2} \arcsin \frac{x}{a} + C,$$

$$I_{\frac{3}{2}} = \int (a^2 - x^2)^{3/2} dx = \frac{x}{4}(a^2 - x^2)^{3/2} + \frac{3}{4} a^2 I_{1/2}, \text{ and so on.}$$

4.4.2. Applying integration by parts, derive the following reduction formulas :

(a) $I_n = \int (\ln x)^n dx = x(\ln x)^n - nI_{n-1}$;

(b) $I_n = \int x^\alpha (\ln x)^n dx = \dfrac{x^{\alpha+1}(\ln x)^n}{\alpha+1} - \dfrac{n}{\alpha+1} I_{n-1}$ $(\alpha \neq -1)$;

(c) $I_n = \int x^n e^x dx = x^n e^x - nI_{n-1}$;

(d) $I_n = \int e^{\alpha x} \sin^n x\, dx$

$$= \frac{e^{\alpha x}}{\alpha^2 + n^2} \sin^{n-1} x\,(\alpha \sin x - n \cos x) + \frac{n(n-1)}{\alpha^2 + n^2} I_{n-2}.$$

4.4.3. Derive the reduction formula for the integration of $I_n = \int \dfrac{dx}{\sin^n x}$ and use it for calculating the integral $I_3 = \int \dfrac{dx}{\sin^3 x}$.

4.4.4. Derive the reduction formulas for the following integrals :

(a) $I_n = \int \tan^n x\, dx$; (b) $I_n = \int \cot^n x\, dx$;

(c) $I_n = \int \dfrac{x^n dx}{\sqrt{x^2 + a}}$.

5 Basic Classes of Integrable Functions

5.1. Integration of Rational Functions

If the denominator $Q(x)$ of the proper rational fraction $\dfrac{P(x)}{Q(x)}$ can be represented in the following way :

$$Q(x) = (x-a)^k (x-b)^l \ldots (x^2+\alpha x+\beta)^r (x^2+\gamma x+\mu)^5 \ldots,$$

where the binomials and trinomials are different and, furthermore, the trinomials have no real roots, then

$$\frac{p(x)}{Q(x)} = \frac{A_1}{x-a} + \frac{A_2}{(x-a)^2} + \ldots + \frac{A_k}{(x-a)^k} +$$

$$+ \frac{B_1}{x-b} + \frac{B_2}{(x-b)^2} + \ldots + \frac{B_l}{(x-b)^l} + \ldots\ldots + \frac{M_1 x + N_1}{x^2+\alpha x+\beta}$$

$$+ \frac{M_2 x + N_2}{(x^2+\alpha x+\beta)^2} + \ldots + \frac{M_r x + N_r}{(x^2+\alpha x+\beta)^r} + \frac{R_1 x + L_1}{x^2+\gamma x+\mu}$$

$$+ \frac{R_2 x + L_2}{(x^2+\gamma x+\mu)^2} + \ldots + \frac{R_s x + L_s}{(x^2+\gamma x+\mu)^S} + \ldots,$$

where

$A_1, A_2, \ldots, B_1, B_2, \ldots, M_1, N_1, M_2, N_2, \ldots, R_1, L_1, R_2, L_2, \ldots,$

are some real constants to be determined. They are determined by reducing both sides of the above identity to integral form and then equating the coefficients at equal powers of x, which gives a system of linear equations with respect to the coefficients. (This method is called the *method of comparison of coefficients*). A system of equations for the coefficients can also be obtained by substituting suitably chosen numerical values of x into both sides of the identity. (This method is called the *method of particular values*). A successful combination of the indicated methods, prompted by experience, often allows us to simplify the process of finding the coefficients.

If the rational fraction $\dfrac{P(x)}{Q(x)}$ is *improper*, the integral part should first be singled out.

5.1.1. $I = \int \frac{15x^2 - 4x - 81}{(x-3)(x+4)(x-1)} dx$.

Solution The integrand is a proper rational fraction. Since all roots of the denominator are real and simple, the integral will appear in the form of the sum of three simple fractions of the form

$$\frac{15x^2 - 4x - 81}{(x-3)(x+4)(x-1)} = \frac{A}{(x-3)} + \frac{B}{x+4} + \frac{D}{x-1},$$

where A, B, D are the coefficients to be determined. Reducing the fractions to a common denominator and then rejecting it, we obtain the identity

$$15x^2 - 4x - 81 = A(x+4)(x-1) + B(x-3)(x-1) + \\ + D(x-3)(x+4). \quad (*)$$

Comparing the coefficients at equal powers of x in both sides of the identity, we get a system of equations for determining the coefficients

$$A + B + D = 15; \quad 3A - 4B + D = -4; \quad -4A + 3B - 12D = -81.$$

Solving the system of equations we find $A = 3, B = 5, D = 7$.

Hence, $$I = 3\int \frac{dx}{x-3} + 5\int \frac{dx}{x+4} + 7\int \frac{dx}{x-1}$$

$$= 3\ln|x-3| + 5\ln|x+4| + 7\ln|x-1| + C$$

$$= \ln|(x-3)^3 (x+4)^5 (x-1)^7| + C.$$

Note. Let us use the same example to demonstrate the application of the method of particular values.

The identity (*) is true for any value of x. Therefore, setting three arbitrary particular values, we obtain three equations for determining the three undetermined coefficients. It is most convenient to choose the roots of the denominator as the values of x, since they nullify some factors. Putting $x = 3$ in the identity (*), we get $A = 3$; putting $x = -4$, we obtain $B = 5$; and putting $x = 1$, we get $D = 7$.

5.1.2. $I = \int \frac{x^4\, dx}{(2+x)(x^2-1)}$.

5.1.3. $I = \int \frac{x^4 - 3x^2 - 3x - 2}{x^3 - x^2 - 2x} dx$.

Solution Since the power of the numerator is higher than that of the denominator, *ie*, the fraction is improper, we have to single out the integral part. Dividing the numerator by the denominator, we obtain

$$\frac{x^4 - 3x^2 - 3x - 2}{x^3 - x^2 - 2x} = x + 1 - \frac{x+2}{x(x^2 - x - 2)}.$$

Hence, $I = \int \frac{x^4 - 3x^2 - 3x - 2}{x^3 - x^2 - 2x} dx = \int (x+1)\, dx - \int \frac{(x+2)\, dx}{x(x-2)(x+1)}$.

Expand the remaining proper fraction into simple ones :

$$\frac{x+2}{x(x-2)(x+1)} = \frac{A}{x} + \frac{B}{x-2} + \frac{D}{x+1}.$$

Hence, $x + 2 = A(x-2)(x+1) + Bx(x+1) + Dx(x-2)$.

Substituting in turn the values $x_1 = 0$, $x_2 = 2$, $x^3 = -1$ (the roots of the denominator) into both sides of the equality, we obtain

$$A = -1; \quad B = \frac{2}{3}; \quad D = \frac{1}{3}.$$

And so

$$I = \int (x+1)\,dx + \int \frac{dx}{x} - \frac{2}{3}\int \frac{dx}{x-2} - \frac{1}{3}\int \frac{dx}{x+1}$$

$$= \frac{x^2}{2} + x + \ln|x| - \frac{2}{3}\ln|x-2|| - \frac{1}{3}\ln|x+1| + C.$$

5.1.4. $I = \int \frac{2x^2 - 3x + 3}{x^3 - 2x^2 + x}\,dx.$

Solution Here the integrand is a proper rational fraction, whose denominator roots are real but some of them are multiple:

$$x^3 - 2x^2 + x = x(x-1)^2.$$

Hence, the expansion into partial fractions has the form

$$\frac{2x^2 - 3x + 3}{x^3 - 2x^2 + x} = \frac{A}{x} + \frac{B}{(x-1)^2} + \frac{D}{x-1},$$

whence we get the identity:

$$2x^2 - 3x + 3 \equiv A(x-1)^2 + Bx + Dx(x-1)$$

$$= (A + D)x^2 + (-2A - D + B)x + A. \qquad (*)$$

Equating the coefficients at equal powers of x we get a system of equations for determining the coefficients A, B, D:

$$A + D = 2; \quad -2A - D + B = -3; \quad A = 3.$$

Whence $A = 3$; $B = 2$; $D = -1$

Thus, $$I = 3\int \frac{dx}{x} + 2\int \frac{dx}{(x-1)^2} - \int \frac{dx}{x-1}$$

$$= 3\ln|x| - \frac{2}{x-1} - \ln|x-1| + C.$$

Note. The coefficients can be determined in a somewhat simpler way if in the identity (*) we put $x_1 = 0$; $x_2 = 1$ (the denominator roots), and x_3 equal to any arbitrary value.

At $x = 0$ we get $3 = A$; at $x = 1$ we will have $2 = B$; at $x = 2$ we obtain

$$5 = A + 2B + 2D; \quad 5 = 3 + 4 + 2D;$$

whence $$D = -1.$$

5.1.5. $I = \int \frac{x^3 + 1}{x(x-1)^3}\,dx.$

5.1.6. $I = \int \frac{x\,dx}{x^3 + 1}.$

Solution Since $x^3 + 1 = (x + 1)(x^2 - x + 1)$ (the second factor is not expanded into real multipliers of the first power), the expansion of the given fraction will have the form

$$\frac{x}{x^3 + 1} = \frac{A}{x + 1} + \frac{Bx + D}{x^2 - x + 1}.$$

Hence,
$$x = A(x^2 - x + 1) + (Bx + D)(x + 1)$$
$$= (A + B)x^2 + (-A + B + D)x + (A + D).$$

Equating the coefficients at equal powers of x, we get

$$A = -\frac{1}{3};\ B = \frac{1}{3};\ D = \frac{1}{3}.$$

Thus,
$$I = -\frac{1}{3}\int \frac{dx}{x + 1} + \frac{1}{3}\int \frac{x + 1}{x^2 - x + 1}\,dx$$
$$= -\frac{1}{3}\ln|x + 1| + \frac{1}{3}I_1.$$

To calculate the integral

$$I_1 = \int \frac{x + 1}{x^2 - x + 1}\,dx$$

let us take the perfect square out of the denominator :

$$x^2 - x + 1 = \left(x - \frac{1}{2}\right)^2 + \frac{3}{4}\cdot$$

and make the substitution $x - \frac{1}{2} = t$. Then

$$I_1 = \int \frac{t + \frac{1}{2} + 1}{t^2 + \frac{3}{4}}\,dt = \int \frac{t\,dt}{t^2 + \frac{3}{4}} + \frac{3}{2}\int \frac{dt}{t^2 + \frac{3}{4}}$$
$$= \frac{1}{2}\ln\left(t^2 + \frac{3}{4}\right) + \sqrt{3}\arctan\frac{2t}{\sqrt{3}} + C.$$

Returning to x, we obtain

$$I_1 = \frac{1}{2}\ln(x^2 - x + 1) + \sqrt{3}\arctan\frac{2x - 1}{\sqrt{3}} + C.$$

Thus,

$$I = \int \frac{x}{x^3 + 1}\,dx = -\frac{1}{3}\ln|x + 1| + \frac{1}{6}\ln(x^2 - x + 1)$$
$$+ \frac{\sqrt{3}}{3}\arctan\frac{2x - 1}{\sqrt{3}} + C.$$

5.1.7. $I = \int \frac{dx}{(x^2+1)(x^2+4)}$.

Solution The denominator has two pairs of different conjugate complex roots, therefore

$$\frac{1}{(x^2+1)(x^2+4)} = \frac{Ax+B}{x^2+1} + \frac{Dx+E}{x^2+4},$$

hence

$$I = (Ax+B)(x^2+4) + (Dx+E)(x^2+1).$$

Here it is convenient to apply the method of particular values for determining the coefficients, since the complex roots of the denominator ($x = \pm i$ and $x = \pm 2i$) are sufficiently simple.

Putting $x = i$, we obtain

$$3B + 3Ai = 1,$$

whence $A = 0$, $B = \frac{1}{3}$. Putting $x = 2i$, we obtain $-3E - 6Di = 1$, whence $D = 0$, $E = -\frac{1}{3}$. Thus,

$$\int \frac{dx}{(x^2+1)(x^2+4)} = \frac{1}{3}\int \frac{dx}{x^2+1} - \frac{1}{3}\int \frac{dx}{x^2+4}$$

$$= \frac{1}{3}\text{ arc tan } x - \frac{1}{6}\text{ arc tan } \frac{x}{2} + C.$$

5.1.8. $I = \int \frac{(x+1)\,dx}{(x^2+x+2)(x^2+4x+5)}$.

5.1.9. $I = \int \frac{x^4+4x^3+11x^2+12x+8}{(x^2+2x+3)^2(x+1)}\,dx$.

Solution Here we already have multiple complex roots. Expand the fraction into partial fractions :

$$\frac{x^4+4x^3+11x^2+12x+8}{(x^2+2x+3)^2(x+1)} = \frac{Ax+B}{(x^2+2x+3)^2} + \frac{Dx+E}{x^2+2x+3} + \frac{F}{x+1}.$$

Find the coefficients :

$$A = 1;\quad B = -1;\quad D = 0;\quad E = 0;\quad F = 1.$$

Hence

$$I = \int \frac{x^4+4x^3+11x^2+12x+8}{(x^2+2x+3)^2(x+1)}\,dx$$

$$= \int \frac{x-1}{(x^2+2x+3)^2}\,dx + \int \frac{dx}{x+1}$$

$$= \ln|x+1| + I_1.$$

Calculate $I_1 = \int \frac{x-1}{(x^2+2x+3)^2}\,dx$.

Since $x^2 + 2x + 3 = (x+1)^2 + 2$, let us make the substitution $x + 1 = t$. Then we obtain

$$I_1 = \int \frac{t-2}{(t^2+2)^2}\,dt = \int \frac{t}{(t^2+2)^2}\,dt - 2\int \frac{dt}{(t^2+2)^2}$$
$$= -\frac{1}{2(t^2+2)} - 2I_2.$$

The integral

$$I_2 = \int \frac{dt}{(t^2+2)^2}$$

is calculated by the reduction formula (see Problem **4.4.1**) :

$$I_2 = \frac{1}{4}\frac{t}{t^2+2} + \frac{1}{4}\int \frac{dt}{t^2+2} = \frac{1}{4}\frac{t}{t^2+2}$$
$$+ \frac{1}{4\sqrt{2}} \text{arc tan} \frac{t}{\sqrt{2}} + C.$$

Thus

$$I_1 = -\frac{1}{2(t^2+2)} - \frac{t}{2(t^2+2)} - \frac{1}{2\sqrt{2}} \text{arc tan} \frac{t}{\sqrt{2}} + C.$$

Returning to x, we obtain

$$I_1 = -\frac{1}{2(x^2+2x+3)} - \frac{x+1}{2(x^2+2x+3)}$$
$$- \frac{1}{2\sqrt{2}} \text{arc tan} \frac{x+1}{\sqrt{2}}\ C.$$

We finally obtain

$$I = \int \frac{x^4 + 4x^3 + 11x^2 + 12x + 8}{(x^2+2x+3)^2 (x+1)}\,dx$$
$$= \ln|x+1| - \frac{x+2}{2(x^2+2x+3)}$$
$$- \frac{1}{2\sqrt{2}} \text{arc tan} \frac{x+1}{\sqrt{2}} + C.$$

Find the following integrals :

5.1.10. $\int \frac{5x^3 + 9x^2 - 22x - 8}{x^3 - 4x}\,dx.$

5.1.11. $\int \frac{dx}{(x+1)(x+2)^2(x+3)^3}.$

5.1.12. $\int \frac{dx}{(x^2-4x+4)(x^2-4x+5)}.$

5.1.13. $\int \frac{dx}{(1+x)(1+x^2)(1+x^3)}.$

5.1.14. $\int \frac{x^3+3}{(x+1)(x^2+1)}\,dx.$

5.2. Integration of Certain Irrational Expressions

Certain types of integrals of algebraic irrational expressions can be reduced to integrals of rational functions by an appropriate change of the variable. Such transformation of an integral is called its rationalization.

I. If the integrand is a rational function of fractional powers of an independent variable x, *ie*, the function $R(x, x^{\frac{p_1}{q_1}}, \ldots, x^{\frac{pk}{qk}})$, then the integral can be rationalized by the substitution $x = t^m$, where m is the least common multiple of the numbers $q_1, q_2, \ldots, q_k$.

II. If the integrand is a rational function of x and fractional powers of a linear fractional function of the form $\frac{ax+b}{cx+d}$, then rationalization of the integral is effected by the substitution) $\frac{ax+b}{cx+d} = t^m$, where m has the same sense as above.

5.2.1. $I = \int \frac{x + \sqrt[3]{x^2} + \sqrt[6]{x}}{x(1+\sqrt[3]{x})}\,dx.$

Solution The least common multiple of the numbers 3 and 6 is 6, therefore we made the substitution :

$$x = t^6, \qquad dx = 6t^5\,dt,$$

whence

$$I = 6\int \frac{(t^6 + t^4 + t)t^5}{t^6(1+t^2)}\,dt = 6\int \frac{t^5 + t^3 + 1}{1+t^2}\,dt$$

$$= 6\int t^3\,dt + 6\int \frac{dt}{t^2+1} = \frac{3}{2}t^4 + 6\arctan t + C.$$

Returning to x, we obtain

$$I = \frac{3}{2}x^{\frac{2}{3}} + 6\arctan\sqrt[6]{x} + C.$$

5.2.2. $I = \int \frac{\sqrt{x} + \sqrt[3]{x}}{\sqrt[4]{x^5} - \sqrt[6]{x^7}}\,dx.$

5.2.3. $I = \int \frac{(2x-3)^{\frac{1}{2}}\,dx}{(2x-3)^{\frac{1}{3}} + 1}.$

Solution The integrand is a rational function of $\sqrt[6]{2x-3}$, therefore we put $2x - 3 = t^6$, whence

$$dx = 3t^5\,dt;\quad (2x-3)^{\frac{1}{2}} = t^3;\quad (2x-3)^{\frac{1}{3}} = t^2.$$

Hence,

$$I = \int \frac{3t^8}{t^2+1}\,dt = 3\int (t^6 - t^4 + t^2 - 1)\,dt + 3\int \frac{dt}{1+t^2}$$

$$= 3\frac{t^7}{7} - 3\frac{t^5}{5} + 3\frac{t^3}{3} - 3t + 3\,\text{arc tan}\,t + C.$$

Returning to x, we get

$$I = 3\left[\frac{1}{7}(2x-3)^{\frac{7}{6}} - \frac{1}{5}(2x-3)^{\frac{5}{6}}\frac{1}{3}(2x-3)^{\frac{1}{2}}\right.$$

$$\left. -(2x-3)^{\frac{1}{6}} + \text{arc tan}\,(2x-3)^{\frac{1}{6}}\right] + C\cdot$$

5.2.4. $I = \int \dfrac{dx}{x\left(2+\sqrt[3]{\dfrac{x-1}{x}}\right)}.$

5.2.5. $I = \int \dfrac{2}{(2-x)^2}\sqrt[3]{\dfrac{2-x}{2+x}}dx.$

Solution The integrand is a rational function of x and the expression $\sqrt[3]{\dfrac{2-x}{2+x}}$, therefore let us introduce the substitution

$$\sqrt[3]{\frac{2-x}{2+x}} = t; \qquad \frac{2-x}{2+x} = t^3,$$

whence

$$x = \frac{2-2t^3}{1+t^3}; \quad 2-x = \frac{4t^3}{1+t^3}; \quad dx = \frac{-12t^2}{(1+t^3)^2}\,dt.$$

Hence

$$I = -\int \frac{2(1+t^3)^2\,t\cdot 12t^2}{16t^6(1+t^3)^2}\,dt = -\frac{3}{2}\int\frac{dt}{t^3} = \frac{3}{t^2} + C.$$

Returning to x, we get

$$I = \frac{3}{4}\sqrt[3]{\left(\frac{2+x}{2-x}\right)^2} + C.$$

5.2.6. $I = \int \dfrac{dx}{\sqrt[4]{(x-1)^3(x+2)^5}}.$

Solution Since

$$\sqrt[4]{(x-1)^3(x+2)^5} = (x-1)(x+2)\sqrt[5]{\frac{x+2}{x-1}},$$

the integrand is a rational function of x and $\sqrt[4]{\frac{x+2}{x-1}}$; therefore let us introduce the substitution $\sqrt[4]{\frac{x+2}{x-1}}=t; \frac{x+2}{x-1}=t^4$,

whence

$$x=\frac{t^4+2}{t^4-1}; \quad x-1=\frac{3}{t^4-1}; \quad x+2=\frac{3t^4}{t^4-1};$$

$$dx=\frac{-12t^3}{(t^4-1)^2}dt.$$

Hence $\qquad I=-\int\frac{(t^4-1)(t^4-1)\,12t^3\,dt}{3\cdot 3t^4t\,(t^4-1)^2}=-\frac{4}{3}\int\frac{dt}{t^2}=\frac{4}{3t}+C.$

Returning to x, we obtain

$$I=\frac{4}{3}\sqrt{\frac{x-1}{x+2}}+C.$$

5.2.7. $\int\frac{dx}{(1-x)\sqrt{1-x^2}}$.

5.2.8. $\int\frac{dx}{\sqrt[3]{(x+1)^2\,(x-1)^4}}$.

5.2.9. $\int(x-2)\sqrt{\frac{1+x}{1-x}}\,dx$.

5.3. Euler's Substitutions

Integrals of the form $\int R(x, \sqrt{ax^2+bx+c})\,dx$ are calculated with the aid of one of the three Euler substitutions :

(1) $\sqrt{ax^2+bx+c}=t\pm x\sqrt{a}$ if $a>0$;

(2) $\sqrt{ax^2+bx+c}=tx\pm\sqrt{c}$ if $c>0$;

(3) $\sqrt{ax^2+bx+c}=(x-\alpha)\,t$ if

$$ax^2+bx+c=a\,(x-\alpha)\,(x-\beta),$$

ie, if α is a real root of the trinomial ax^2+bx+c.

5.3.1. $I=\int\frac{dx}{1+\sqrt{x^2+2x+2}}$.

Solution Here $a=1>0$, therefore we make the substitution

$$\sqrt{x^2+2x+2}=t-x.$$

Squaring both sides of this equality and reducing the similar terms, we get

$$2x+2tx=t^2-2,$$

whence

$$x = \frac{t^2 - 2}{2(1+t)}; \qquad dx = \frac{t^2 + 2t + 2}{2(1+t)^2}\,dt;$$

$$1 + \sqrt{x^2 + 2x + 2} = 1 + t - \frac{t^2 - 2}{2(1+t)} = \frac{t^2 + 4t + 4}{2(1+t)}.$$

Substituting into the integral, we obtain

$$I = \int \frac{2(1+t)(t^2 + 2t + 2)}{(t^2 + 4t + 4)\,2(1+t)^2}\,dt = \int \frac{(t^2 + 2t + 2)\,dt}{(1+t)(t+2)^2}.$$

Now let us expand the obtained proper rational fraction into partial fractions :

$$\frac{t^2 + 2t + 2}{(t+1)(t+2)^2} = \frac{A}{t+1} + \frac{B}{t+2} + \frac{D}{(t+2)^2}.$$

Applying the method of undetermined coefficients we find : $A = 1$, $B = 0, D = -2$.

Hence,

$$\int \frac{t^2 + 2t + 2}{(t+1)(t+2)^2}\,dt = \int \frac{dt}{t+1} - 2\int \frac{dt}{(t+2)^2} = \ln|t+1| + \frac{2}{t+2} + C.$$

Returning to x, we get

$$I = \ln\left(x + 1 + \sqrt{x^2 + 2x + 2}\right) + \frac{2}{x + 2 + \sqrt{x^2 + 2x + 2}} + C.$$

5.3.2. $I = \int \dfrac{dx}{x + \sqrt{x^2 - x + 1}}$.

Solution Since here $c = 1 > 0$, we can apply the second Euler substitution

$$\sqrt{x^2 - x + 1} = tx - 1,$$

whence

$$(2t - 1)\,x = (t^2 - 1)\,x^2; \; x = \frac{2t - 1}{t^2 - 1};$$

$$dx = -2\,\frac{t^2 - t + 1}{(t^2 - 1)^2}\,dt; \quad x + \sqrt{x^2 - x + 1} = \frac{t}{t-1}.$$

Substituting into I, we obtain an integral of a rational fraction :

$$\int \frac{dx}{x + \sqrt{x^2 - x + 1}} = \int \frac{-2t^2 + 2t - 2}{t(t-1)(t+1)^2}\,dt,$$

$$\frac{-2t^2 + 2t - 2}{t(t-1)(t+1)^2} = \frac{A}{t} + \frac{B}{t-1} + \frac{D}{(t+1)^2} + \frac{E}{t+1}.$$

By the method of undetermined coefficients we find

$$A = 2;\ \ B = -\frac{1}{2};\ \ D = -3;\ \ E = -\frac{3}{2}.$$

Hence

$$I = 2\int\frac{dt}{t} - \frac{1}{2}\int\frac{dt}{t-1} - 3\int\frac{dt}{(t+1)^2} - \frac{3}{2}\int\frac{dt}{t+1}$$

$$= 2\ln|t| - \frac{1}{2}\ln|t-1| + \frac{3}{t+1} - \frac{3}{2}\ln|t+1| + C,$$

where $t = \dfrac{\sqrt{x^2 - x + 1} + 1}{x}$.

5.3.3. $I = \displaystyle\int\frac{dx}{(1+x)\sqrt{1+x-x^2}}$.

5.3.4. $I = \displaystyle\int\frac{x\,dx}{(\sqrt{7x-10-x^2})^3}$.

Solution In this case $a < 0$ and $c < 0$ therefore neither the first, nor the second Euler substitution is applicable. But the quadratic trinomial $7x - 10 - x^2$ has real roots $\alpha = 2, \beta = 5$, therefore we use the third Euler substitution :

$$\sqrt{7x - 10 - x^2} = \sqrt{(x-2)(5-x)} = (x-2)\,t.$$

Whence

$$5 - x = (x-2)\,t^2;$$

$$x = \frac{5 + 2t^2}{1 + t^2};$$

$$dx = -\frac{6t\,dt}{(1+t^2)^2};$$

$$(x-2)\,t = \left(\frac{5+2t^2}{1+t^2} - 2\right)t = \frac{3t}{1+t^2}.$$

Hence

$$I = -\frac{6}{27}\int\frac{5+2t^2}{t^2}\,dt = -\frac{2}{9}\int\left(\frac{5}{t^2} + 2\right)dt$$

$$= -\frac{2}{9}\left(-\frac{5}{t} + 2t\right) + C,$$

where

$$t = \frac{\sqrt{7x - 10 - x^2}}{x - 2}$$

Calculate the following integrals with the aid of one of the Euler substitutions :

5.3.5. $\int \frac{dx}{x - \sqrt{x^2 + 2x + 4}}$.

5.3.6. $\int \frac{dx}{\sqrt{1 - x^2} - 1}$.

5.3.7. $\int \frac{dx}{\sqrt{(2x - x^2)^3}}$.

5.3.8. $\int \frac{\left(x + \sqrt{1 + x^2}\right)^{15}}{\sqrt{1 + x^2}} dx$.

5.4. Other Methods of Integrating Irrational Expressions

The Euler substitutions often lead to rather cumbersome calculations, therefore they should be applied only when it is difficult to find another method for calculating a given integral. For calculating many integrals of the form

$$\int R(x, \sqrt{ax^2 + bx + c})\, dx,$$

simpler methods are used.

I. Integrals of the form

$$I = \int \frac{Mx + N}{\sqrt{ax^2 + bx + c}} dx$$

are reduced by the substitution $x + \frac{b}{2a} = t$ to the form

$$I = M_1 \int \frac{t\, dt}{\sqrt{at^2 + K}} + N_1 \int \frac{dt}{\sqrt{at^2 + K}},$$

where M_1 , N_1 , K are new coefficients.

The first integral is reduced to the integral of a power function, while the second, being a tabular one, is reduced to a logarithm (for $a > 0$) or to an arc sine (for $a < 0$, $K > 0$).

II. Integrals of the form

$$\int \frac{P_m(x)}{\sqrt{ax^2 + bx + c}} dx,$$

where $P_m(x)$ is a polynomial of degree m, are calculated by the reduction formula :

$$\int \frac{P_m(x)\, dx}{\sqrt{ax^2 + bx + c}} = P_{m-1}(x) \sqrt{ax^2 + bx + c} + K \int \frac{dx}{\sqrt{ax^2 + bx + c}}, \quad (1)$$

where $P_{m-1}(x)$ is a polynomial of degree $m-1$, and K is some constant number.

The coefficients of the polynomial $P_{m-1}(x)$ and the constant number K are determined by the method of undetermined coefficients.

III. Integrals of the form

$$\int \frac{dx}{(x-a)^m \sqrt{ax^2+bx+c}}$$

are reduced to the preceding type by the substitution

$$x - a_1 = \frac{1}{t}.$$

IV. For trigonometric and hyperbolic substitutions see ■▌5.7.

5.4.1. $I = \int \frac{(x+3)\,dx}{\sqrt{4x^2+4x-3}}.$

Solution Make the substitution $2x+1=t$, whence

$$x = \frac{t-1}{2}, \quad dx = \frac{1}{2}\,dt.$$

Hence

$$I = \frac{1}{4}\int \frac{(t+5)\,dt}{\sqrt{t^2-4}} = \frac{1}{4}\sqrt{t^2-4} + \frac{5}{4}\ln|t+\sqrt{t^2-4}| + C.$$

Returning to x, we get

$$I = \frac{1}{4}\sqrt{4x^2+4x-3} + \frac{5}{4}\ln|2x+1 + \sqrt{4x^2+4x-3}| + C.$$

5.4.2. $I = \int \frac{5x+4}{\sqrt{x^2+2x+5}}\,dx.$

5.4.3. $I = \int \frac{x^3-x-1}{\sqrt{x^2+2x+2}}\,dx.$

Solution Here, $P_m(x) = x^3 - x - 1$. Hence,

$$P_{m-1}(x) = Ax^2 + Bx + D.$$

We seek the integral in the form

$$I = (Ax^2+Bx+D)\sqrt{x^2+2x+2} + K\int \frac{dx}{\sqrt{x^2+2x+2}}.$$

Differentiating this equality, we obtain

$$I' = \frac{x^3-x-1}{\sqrt{x^2+2x+2}}$$

$$= (2Ax+B)\sqrt{x^2+2x+2} + (Ax^2+Bx+D)\frac{x+1}{\sqrt{x^2+2x+2}} + \frac{k}{\sqrt{x^2+2x+2}}.$$

Reduce to a common denominator and equate the numerators

$$x^3 - x - 1 = (2Ax + B)(x^2 + 2x + 2) + (Ax^2 + Bx + D)(x + 1) + K.$$

Equating the coefficients at equal powers of x, we get the following system of equations :

$$2A + A = 1, \ B + 4A + B + A = 0;$$

$$2B + 4A + D + B = -1; \ 2B + D + K = -1.$$

Solving the system, we obtain

$$A = \frac{1}{3}; \ B = -\frac{5}{6}; \ D = \frac{1}{6}; \ K = \frac{1}{2}.$$

Thus,

$$I = \left(\frac{1}{3}x^2 - \frac{5}{6}x + \frac{1}{6}\right)\sqrt{x^2 + 2x + 2} + \frac{1}{2}\int \frac{dx}{\sqrt{x^2 + 2x + 2}},$$

where

$$I_1 = \int \frac{dx}{\sqrt{x^2 + 2x + 2}} = \int \frac{dx}{\sqrt{(x + 1)^2 + 1}}$$

$$= \ln(x + 1 + \sqrt{x^2 + 2x + 2}) + C.$$

5.4.4. $I = \int \sqrt{4x^2 - 4x + 3}\, dx$

Solution Transform the integral to the form

$$I = \int \frac{4x^2 - 4x + 3}{\sqrt{4x^2 - 4x + 3}} dx$$

$$= (AX + B)\sqrt{4x^3 - 4x + 3} + K\int \frac{dx}{\sqrt{4x^2 - 4x + 3}}.$$

Applying the method of undetermined coefficient, we get

$$I = \left(\frac{1}{2}x - \frac{1}{4}\right)\sqrt{4x^2 - 4x + 3} + \int \frac{dx}{\sqrt{(2x - 1)^2 + 2}}$$

$$= \left(\frac{1}{2}x - \frac{1}{4}\right)\sqrt{4x^2 - 4x + 3} + \frac{1}{2}\ln(2x - 1$$

$$+ \sqrt{4x^2 - 4x + 3}) + C.$$

5.4.5. $\int \frac{9x^3 - 3x^2 + 2}{\sqrt{3x^2 - 2x + 1}} dx \cdot$

5.4.6. $\int \sqrt{x^2 + x + 1}\, dx \cdot$

5.4.7. $I = \int \frac{(x + 4)\, dx}{(x - 1)(x + 2)^2 \sqrt{x^2 + x + 1}}.$

Solution Represent the given integral as follows :

$$\int \frac{(x+4)\,dx}{(x-1)(x+2)^2\sqrt{x^2+x+1}} = \int \frac{x+4}{(x-1)(x+2)^2} \cdot \frac{dx}{\sqrt{x^2+x+1}}.$$

Expand the fraction $\frac{x+4}{(x-1)(x+2)^2}$ into partial fractions

$$\frac{x+4}{(x-1)(x+2)^2} = \frac{A}{x-1} + \frac{B}{(x+2)^2} + \frac{D}{x+2}.$$

Find the coefficients

$$A = \frac{5}{9};\quad B = -\frac{2}{3};\quad D = -\frac{5}{9}.$$

Hence

$$I = \int \left[\frac{5}{9(x-1)} - \frac{2}{3(x+2)^2} - \frac{5}{9(x+2}\right] \cdot \frac{dx}{\sqrt{x^2+x+1}}$$

$$= \frac{5}{9}\int \frac{dx}{(x-1)\sqrt{x^2+x+1}} - \frac{2}{3}\int \frac{dx}{(x+2)^2\sqrt{x^2+x+1}}$$

$$- \frac{5}{9}\int \frac{dx}{(x+2)\sqrt{x^2+x+1}}.$$

The first integral is calculated by the substitution $x - 1 = \frac{1}{t}$, the second and the third by the substitution $x + 2 = \frac{1}{t}$.

We leave the **Solution** to the reader.

5.4.8. $\int \frac{x^3 - 6x^2 + 11x - 6}{\sqrt{x^2 + 4x + 3}}\,dx.$

5.4.9. $\int \frac{3x^3 + 5x^2 - 7x + 9}{\sqrt{2x^2 + 5x + 7}}\,dx.$

5.4.10. $\int \frac{dx}{(x+1)^5\sqrt{x^2+2x}}.$

5.4.11. $\int \frac{x\,dx}{(x^2 - 3x + 2)\sqrt{x^2 - 4x + 3}}.$

5.4.12. $\int \frac{dx}{(x+1)^3\sqrt{x^2+3x+2}}.$

5.4.13. $\int \frac{(x^3 - 1)\,dx}{x\sqrt{1 + 3x^2 + x^4}}.$

5.5. Integration of a Binomial Differential

The integral $\int x^m(a+bx^n)^P\,dx$, where m, n, p are rational numbers, is expressed through elementary functions only in the following three cases :

Case I. p is an integer. Then, if $p>0$, the integrand is expands by the formula of the Newton binomial; but if $p<0$, then we put $x=t^k$, where k is the common denominator of the fractions m and n.

Case II. $\dfrac{m+1}{n}$ is an integer. We put $a+bx^n=t^\alpha$, where α is the denominator of the fraction p.

Case III. $\dfrac{m+1}{n}+p$ is an integer. We put $a+bx^n=t^\alpha x^n$, where α is the denominator of the fraction p.

5.5.1. $I=\int \sqrt[3]{x}(2+\sqrt{x})^2dx.$

Solution $I=\int x^{\frac{1}{3}}\left(2+x^{\frac{1}{2}}\right)^2 dx.$ Here $p=2$, *ie*, an integer, hence, we have Case I.

$$I=\int x^{\frac{1}{3}}\left(x+4x^{\frac{1}{2}}+4\right)dx=\int\left(x^{\frac{4}{3}}+4x^{\frac{5}{6}}+4x^{\frac{1}{3}}\right)dx$$

$$=\frac{3}{7}x^{\frac{7}{3}}+\frac{24}{11}x^{\frac{11}{6}}+3x^{\frac{4}{3}}+C.$$

5.5.2. $I=\int x^{-\frac{2}{3}}\left(1+x^{\frac{2}{3}}\right)^{-1}dx.$

5.5.3. $I=\int \frac{\sqrt{1+\sqrt[3]{x}}}{\sqrt[3]{x^2}}dx.$

Solution $I=\int x^{-\frac{2}{3}}\left(1+x^{\frac{1}{3}}\right)^{\frac{1}{2}}dx.$

Here $m=-\dfrac{2}{3}; n=\dfrac{1}{3}; p=\dfrac{1}{2}$; $\dfrac{m+1}{n}=\dfrac{\left(-\frac{2}{3}+1\right)}{\frac{1}{3}}=1$, *ie*, an integer.

We have Case II. Let us make the substitution

$$1+x^{\frac{1}{3}}=t^2;\ \frac{1}{3}x^{-\frac{2}{3}}dx=2t\,dt.$$

Hence,

$$I=6\int t^2dt=2t^3+C=2\left(1+x^{\frac{1}{3}}\right)^{\frac{3}{2}}+C.$$

5.5.4. $I = \int x^{\frac{1}{3}}\left(2 + x^{\frac{2}{3}}\right)^{\frac{1}{4}} dx.$

5.5.5. $I = \int x^5(1 + x^3)^{\frac{2}{3}} dx.$

5.5.6. $I = \int x^{-11}(1 + x^4)^{-\frac{1}{2}} dx.$

Solution Here $p = -\frac{1}{2}$ is a fraction, $\frac{m+1}{n} = \frac{-11+1}{4} = -\frac{5}{2}$ also a fraction, but $\frac{m+1}{n} + p = -\frac{5}{2} - \frac{1}{2} = -3$ is an integers, *ie*, we have

Case III. We put $1 + x^4 = x^4t^2$. Hence

$$x = \frac{1}{(t^2-1)^{\frac{1}{4}}}; \qquad dx = -\frac{t\,dt}{2\,(t^2-1)^{\frac{5}{4}}}.$$

Substituting these expressions into the integral, we obtain

$$I = -\frac{1}{2}\int (t^2-1)^{\frac{11}{4}}\left(\frac{t^2}{t^2-1}\right)^{-\frac{1}{2}} \frac{t\,dt}{(t^2-1)^{\frac{5}{4}}}$$

$$= -\frac{1}{2}\int (t^2-1)^2 dt = -\frac{t^5}{10} + \frac{t^3}{3} - \frac{t}{2} + C.$$

Returning to x, we get

$$I = -\frac{1}{10x^{10}}\sqrt{(1+x^4)^5} + \frac{1}{3x^6}\sqrt{(1+x^4)^3} - \frac{1}{2x^2}\sqrt{1+x^4} + C\cdot$$

5.5.7. $\int \frac{\sqrt[3]{1+\sqrt[4]{x}}}{\sqrt{x}} dx.$

5.5.8. $\int \frac{dx}{x\,(1+\sqrt[3]{x})^2}.$

5.5.9. $\int x^3(1 + x^2)^{\frac{1}{2}} dx.$

5.5.10. $\int \frac{dx}{x^4\sqrt{1+x^2}}.$

5.5.11. $\int \sqrt[3]{x}\,\sqrt[7]{1+\sqrt[3]{x^4}}\,dx.$

5.5.12. $\int \frac{dx}{x^3\sqrt[5]{1+\frac{1}{x}}}.$

5.6. Integration of Trigonometric and Hyperbolic Functions

I. Integrals of the form

$$I = \int \sin^m x \cos^n x\,dx,$$

where m and n are rational numbers, are reduced to the integral of the binomial different

$$I = \int t^m (1 - t^2)^{\frac{n-1}{2}}\,dt, t = \sin x$$

and are therefore, integrated in elementary functions only in the following three cases :

(1) n is odd $\left(\frac{n-1}{2}\text{ an integer}\right)$,

(2) m is odd $\left(\frac{m+1}{2}\text{ an integer}\right)$,

(3) $m + n$ is even $\left(\frac{m+1}{2} + \frac{n-1}{2}\text{ an integer}\right)$,

If n is an odd number, the substitution $\sin x = t$ is applied.

If m is an odd number, the substitution $\cos x = t$ is applied.

If the sum $m + n$ is an even number, use the substitution $\tan x = t$ (or $\cot x = t$).

In particular, this kind of substitution is convenient for integrals of the form

$$\int \tan^n x\,dx \text{ (or } \int \cot^n x\,dx),$$

where n is a positive integer. But the last substitution is inconvenient if both m and n are positive numbers. If m and n are non-negative even numbers, then it appears more convenient to use the method of reducing the power with the aid of trigonometric transformations :

$$\cos^2 x = \frac{1}{2}(1 + \cos 2x), \sin^2 x = \frac{1}{2}(1 - \cos 2x)$$

or $$\sin x \cos x = \frac{1}{2}\sin 2x.$$

5.6.1. $I = \int \frac{\sin^3 x}{\sqrt[3]{\cos^2 x}}\,dx.$

Solution Here $m = 3$ is an odd number. We put $\cos x = t$, $\sin x\,dx = -dt$, which gives

$$I = -\int (1 - t^2) t^{-\frac{2}{3}}\,dt = -3t^{\frac{1}{3}} + \frac{3}{7}t^{\frac{7}{3}} + C$$

$$= 3\sqrt[3]{\cos x}\left(\frac{1}{7}\cos^2 x - 1\right) + C.$$

5.6.2. $I = \int \frac{\cos^3 x}{\sin^6 x}\, dx.$

5.6.3. $I = \int \sin^4 x \cos^6 x\, dx.$

Solution Here both m and n are positive even numbers. Let us use the method of reducing the power :

$$I = \frac{1}{16}\int (2\sin x\cos x)^4 \cos^2 x\, dx$$
$$= \frac{1}{32}\int \sin^4 2x\,(1+\cos 2x)\, dx = I_1 + I_2.$$

The second of the obtained integrals is calculated by the substitution :

$$\sin 2x = t, \cos 2x\, dx = \frac{1}{2}\, dt,$$

$$I_2 = \frac{1}{32}\int \sin^4 2x \cos 2x\, dx = \frac{1}{64}\int t^4 dt$$
$$= \frac{t^5}{320} + C = \frac{1}{320}\sin^5 2x + C.$$

We again apply to the first integral the method of reducing the power :

$$I_1 = \frac{1}{32}\int \sin^4 2x\, dx = \frac{1}{128}\int (1-\cos 4x)^2\, dx$$
$$= \frac{1}{128}\left(x - \frac{1}{2}\sin 4x\right) + \frac{1}{256}\int (1+\cos 8x)\, dx$$
$$= \frac{3}{256}x - \frac{1}{256}\sin 4x + \frac{1}{2043}\sin 8x + C.$$

And so, finally,

$$I = \frac{3}{256}x - \frac{1}{256}\sin 4x + \frac{1}{2048}\sin 8x + \frac{1}{320}\sin^5 2x + C.$$

5.6.4. $I = \int \frac{\sin^2 x}{\cos^6 x}\, dx.$

Solution Here both m and n are even numbers, but one of them is negative. Therefore, we put

$$\tan x = t\,;\ \frac{1}{\cos^2 x} = 1 + t^2\,;\ \frac{dx}{\cos^2 x} = dt.$$

Hence

$$I = \int t^2(1+t^2)\, dt = \frac{t^3}{5} + \frac{t^5}{5} + C = \frac{\tan^3 x}{3} + \frac{\tan^5 x}{5} + C.$$

5.6.5. $I = \int \frac{\cos^4 x}{\sin^2 x}\, dx.$

Solution Here we can put $\cot x = t$, but it is simpler to integrate by expansion ;

$$I = \int \frac{(1-\sin^2 x)^2}{\sin^2 x}\,dx = \int \left(\frac{1}{\sin^2 x} - 2 + \sin^2 x\right) dx$$

$$= -\cot x - 2x + \frac{1}{2}\int (1-\cos 2x)\,dx$$

$$= -\left(\cot x + \frac{\sin 2x}{4} + \frac{3x}{2}\right) + C.$$

5.6.6. $I = \int \frac{dx}{\cos^4 x}$.

5.6.7. $I = \int \frac{dx}{\sqrt[3]{\sin^{11} x \cos x}}$.

Solution Here both exponents $\left(-\frac{11}{3} \text{ and } -\frac{1}{3}\right)$ are negative numbers and their sum $-\frac{11}{3} - \frac{1}{3} = -4$ is an even number, therefore we put

$$\tan x = t\,; \frac{dx}{\cos^2 x} = dt.$$

$$I = \int \frac{dx}{\cos^4 x \sqrt[3]{\tan^{11} x}} = \int \frac{1+t^2}{\sqrt[3]{t^{11}}}\,dt$$

$$= \int \left(t^{-\frac{11}{3}} + t^{-\frac{5}{3}}\right) dt = -\frac{3}{8} t^{-\frac{8}{3}} - \frac{3}{2} t^{-\frac{2}{3}} + C$$

$$= -\frac{3\,(1+4\tan^2 x)}{8\tan^2 x \sqrt[3]{\tan^2 x}} + C.$$

5.6.8. Find the integrals of tan x and cot x.

Solution $\int \tan x\,dx = \int \frac{\sin x}{\cos x}\,dx = -\ln|\cos x| + C\,;$

$$\int \cot x\,dx = \int \frac{\cos x}{\sin x}\,dx = \ln|\sin x| + C;$$

5.6.9. $I = \int \tan^7 x\,dx.$

Solution We put $\tan x = t$, $x = \arctan t; dx = \frac{dt}{1+t^2}$. We get

$$I = \int t^7 \frac{dt}{1+t^2} = \int \left(t^5 - t^3 + t - \frac{t}{1+t^2}\right) dt$$

$$= \frac{t^6}{6} - \frac{t^4}{4} + \frac{t^2}{2} - \frac{1}{2}\ln(1+t^2) + C$$

$$= \frac{1}{6}\tan^6 x - \frac{1}{4}\tan^4 x + \frac{1}{2}\tan^2 x + \ln|\cos x| + C.$$

5.6.10. (a) $I = \int \cot^6 x\, dx$; (b) $I = \int \tan^3 x\, dx$.

5.6.11. $I = \int \frac{\cos^4 x}{\sin^3 x} dx.$

Solution Here sin x is raised to an odd power. Let us put

$$\cos x = t, -\sin x\, dx = dt.$$

We obtain an integral of a rational function.

$$I = \int \frac{\cos^4 x \sin x}{\sin^4 x} dx = -\int \frac{t^4}{(1-t^2)^2} dt.$$

Here, it is simpler to integrate by parts than to use the general methods of integration of rational functions (cf. Problem **4.4.1** (b)).

Let us put

$$u = t^3; \qquad dv = \frac{t\, dt}{(1-t^2)^2}.$$

Then
$$du = 3t^2\, dt; \qquad v = \frac{1}{2(1-t^2)}.$$

Hence
$$I = -\frac{t^3}{2(1-t^2)} + \frac{3}{2}\int \frac{t^2\, dt}{1-t^2}$$

$$= -\frac{t^3}{2(1-t^2)} + \frac{3}{2}\int \frac{t^2-1+1}{1-t^2} dt$$

$$= -\frac{t^3}{2(1-t^2)} - \frac{3}{2}t + \frac{3}{4}\ln\left|\frac{1+t}{1-t}\right| + C$$

$$= -\frac{\cos^3 x}{2\sin^2 x} - \frac{3}{2}\cos x + \frac{3}{4}\ln\left|\frac{1+\cos x}{1-\cos x}\right| + C.$$

5.6.12. $I = \int \frac{\sin^4 x}{\cos x} dx.$

II. Integrals of the form $\int R(\sin x, \cos x)\, dx$ where R is a rational function of sin x and cos x are transformed into integrals of a rational function by the substitution :

$$\tan\left(\frac{x}{2}\right) = t\ (-\pi < x < \pi).$$

This is so-called universal substitution. In this case

$$\sin x = \frac{2t}{1+t^2};\ \cos x = \frac{1-t^2}{1+t^2};$$

$$x = 2\,\text{arc}\tan t\ ; dx = \frac{2dt}{1+t^2}.$$

Sometimes instead of the substitution $\tan \frac{x}{2} = t$ it is more advantageous to make the substitution $\cot \frac{x}{2} = t$ $(0 < x < 2\pi)$.

Universal substitution often leads to very cumbersome calculations. Indicated below are the cases when the aim can be achieved with the aid of simpler substitutions :

(a) if the equality

$$R(-\sin x, \cos x) \equiv -R(\sin x, \cos x)$$

or

$$R(\sin x, -\cos x) \equiv -R(\sin x, \cos x)$$

is satisfied, then it is more advantageous to apply the substitution $\cos x = t$ to the former equality, and $\sin x = t$ to the latter;

(b) if the equality

$$R(-\sin x, -\cos x) \equiv R(\sin x, \cos x)$$

is fulfilled, then a better effect is gained by substituting $\tan x = t$ or $\cot x = t$.

The latter case is encountered, for example, in integrals of the form $\int R(\tan x)\, dx$.

5.6.13. $I = \int \frac{dx}{\sin x\,(2 + \cos x - 2\sin x)}$.

Solution Let us put $\tan \frac{x}{2} = t$; then we have

$$I = \int \frac{\frac{2dt}{1+t^2}}{\frac{2t}{1+t^2}\left(2 + \frac{1-t^2}{1+t^2} - \frac{4t}{1+t^2}\right)} = \int \frac{(1+t^2)\,dt}{t\,(t^2 - 4t + 3)}.$$

Expand into simple fractions

$$\frac{1+t^2}{t\,(t-3)\,(t-1)} = \frac{A}{t} + \frac{B}{t-3} + \frac{D}{t-1}.$$

Find the coefficients

$$A = \frac{1}{3};\quad B = \frac{5}{3};\quad D = -1.$$

Hence

$$I = \frac{1}{3}\int \frac{dt}{t} + \frac{5}{3}\int \frac{dt}{t-3} - \int \frac{dt}{t-1}$$

$$= \frac{1}{3}\ln|t| + \frac{5}{3}\ln|t-3| - \ln|t-1| + C$$

$$= \frac{1}{3}\ln\left|\tan\frac{x}{2}\right| + \frac{5}{3}\ln\left|\tan\frac{x}{2} - 3\right| - \ln\left|\tan\frac{x}{2} - 1\right| + C.$$

5.6.14. $I = \int \frac{dx}{5 + \sin x + 3\cos x}.$

5.6.15. $I = \int \frac{dx}{\sin x\,(2\cos^2 x - 1)}.$

Solution If in the expression $\frac{1}{\sin x\,(2\cos^2 x - 1)}$ we substitute $-\sin x$ for $\sin x$, then fraction will change its sign. Hence, we take advantage of the substitution $t = \cos x; dt = -\sin x\,dx$. This gives

$$I = -\int \frac{dt}{(1 - t^2)(2t^2 - 1)}$$

Since $$\frac{1}{(1 - t^2)(1 - 2t^2)} = \frac{(2 - 2t^2) - (1 - 2t^2)}{(1 - t^2)(1 - 2t^2)} = \frac{2}{1 - 2t^2} - \frac{1}{1 - t^2},$$

then

$$I = 2\int \frac{dt}{1 - 2t^2} - \int \frac{dt}{1 - t^2} = \frac{1}{\sqrt{2}} \ln\left|\frac{1 + t\sqrt{2}}{1 - t\sqrt{2}}\right| - \frac{1}{2}\ln\left|\frac{1 + t}{1 - t}\right| + C$$

$$= \frac{1}{\sqrt{2}} \ln\left|\frac{1 + \sqrt{2}\cos x}{1 - \sqrt{2}\cos x}\right| + \frac{1}{2}\ln\left|\frac{1 - \cos x}{1 + \cos x}\right| + C$$

$$= \frac{1}{\sqrt{2}} \ln\left|\frac{1 + \sqrt{2}\cos x}{1 - \sqrt{2}\cos x}\right| + \ln\left|\tan\frac{x}{2}\right| + C.$$

5.6.16. $I = \int \frac{\sin^2 x \cos x}{\sin x + \cos x}\,dx.$

Solution Since the integrand does not change sign when $\sin x$ and $\cos x$ do change their signs, we take advantage of the substitution

$$t = \tan x;\quad dt = \frac{dx}{\cos^2 x}.$$

Hence $$I = \int \frac{\tan^2 x \cdot \cos^4 x}{(\tan x + 1)} \frac{dx}{\cos^2 x}$$

$$= \int \frac{t^2\,dt}{(t + 1)(t^2 + 1)^2}.$$

Expand into partial fractions

$$\frac{t^2}{(t + 1)(t^2 + 1)^2} = \frac{A}{t + 1} + \frac{Bt + D}{t^2 + 1} + \frac{Et + F}{(t^2 + 1)^2}.$$

Find the coefficients

$$A = \frac{1}{4};\quad B = -\frac{1}{4};\quad D = -\frac{1}{4};\quad E = \frac{1}{2};\quad F = -\frac{1}{2}.$$

Hence

$$I = \frac{1}{4}\int \frac{dt}{t + 1} - \frac{1}{4}\int \frac{t - 1}{t^2 + 1}\,dt + \frac{1}{2}\int \frac{t - 1}{(t^2 + 1)^2}\,dt;$$

$$I = \frac{1}{4} \ln \frac{1+t}{\sqrt{1+t^2}} - \frac{1}{4} \cdot \frac{1+t}{1+t^2} + C$$

$$= \frac{1}{4} \ln |\sin x + \cos x| - \frac{1}{4} \cos x (\sin x + \cos x) + C.$$

5.6.17. $I = \int \frac{2 \tan x + 3}{\sin^2 x + 2 \cos^2 x} dx.$

Solution Dividing the numerator and denominator by $\cos^2 x$ and substituting $\tan x = t; \frac{dx}{\cos^2 x} = dt$, we obtain

$$I = \int \frac{2 \tan x + 3}{\sin^2 x + 2 \cos^2 x} dx = \int \frac{(2 \tan x + 3) \frac{dx}{\cos^2 x}}{\tan^2 x + 2}$$

$$= \int \frac{2t + 3}{t^2 + 2} dt = \ln (t^2 + 2) + \frac{3}{\sqrt{2}} \text{arc tan} \frac{t}{\sqrt{2}} + C$$

$$= \ln (\tan^2 x + 2) + \frac{3}{\sqrt{2}} \text{arc tan} \frac{\tan x}{\sqrt{2}} + C \cdot$$

5.6.18. $I = \int \frac{\sin x}{1 + \sin x} dx.$

Solution This integral, of course, can be evaluated with the aid of the universal substitution $\tan \frac{x}{2} = t$, but it is easier to get the desired result by resorting to the following transformation of the integrand :

$$\frac{\sin x}{1 + \sin x} = \frac{\sin x (1 - \sin x)}{(1 + \sin x)(1 - \sin x)} = \frac{\sin x (1 - \sin x)}{\cos^2 x}$$

$$= \frac{\sin x}{\cos^2 x} - \frac{\sin^2 x}{\cos^2 x} = \frac{\sin x}{\cos^2 x} - \tan^2 x.$$

Whence

$$I = \int \frac{\sin x}{\cos^2 x} dx - \int \sec^2 x \, dx + \int dx$$

$$= \frac{1}{\cos x} - \tan x + x + C.$$

5.6.19. $I = \int \frac{1}{\cos^4 x \sin^2 x} dx.$

Solution Here the substitution $\tan x = t$ can be applied, but it is simpler to transform the integrand. Replacing, in the numerator, unity by the trigonometric identity raised to the second power, we get

$$I = \int \frac{(\sin^2 x + \cos^2 x)^2}{\cos^4 x \sin^2 x} dx$$

$$= \int \frac{\sin^4 x + 2 \sin^2 x \cos^2 x + \cos^4 x}{\cos^4 x \sin^2 x} dx$$

$$= \int \frac{\sin^2 x}{\cos^4 x} dx + 2 \int \frac{dx}{\cos^2 x} + \int \frac{dx}{\sin^2 x}$$

$$= \int \tan^2 x \frac{dx}{\cos^2 x} + 2 \tan x - \cot x$$

$$= \frac{1}{3} \tan^3 x + 2 \tan x - \cot x + C.$$

III. **Integration of hyperbolic functions.** Functions rationally depending on hyperbolic functions are integrated in the same way as trigonometric functions.

Keep in mind the following basic formulas :

$$\cosh^2 x - \sinh^2 x = 1 ; \qquad \sinh^2 x = \frac{1}{2} (\cosh 2x - 1) ;$$

$$\cosh^2 x = \frac{1}{2} (\cosh 2x + 1) ; \qquad \sinh x \cosh x = \frac{1}{2} \sinh 2x.$$

If $\tanh \frac{x}{2} = t$, then $\sinh x = \frac{2t}{1-t^2}$; $\cosh x = \frac{1+t^2}{1-t^2}$;

$$x = 2 \operatorname{Artanh} t = \ln \left(\frac{1+t}{1-t} \right) (-1 < t < 1) ; dx = \frac{2dt}{1-t^2}.$$

5.6.20. $I = \int \cosh^2 x \, dx.$

Solution

$$I = \int \frac{1}{2} (\cosh 2x + 1) \, dx = \frac{1}{4} \sinh 2x + \frac{1}{2} x + C.$$

5.6.21. $I = \int \cosh^3 x \, dx.$

Solution Since $\cosh x$ is raised to an odd power, we put $\sinh x = t$; $\cosh x \, dx = dt$. We obtain

$$I = \int \cosh^2 x \cosh x \, dx = \int (1 + t^2) \, dt = t + \frac{t^2}{3} + C$$

$$= \sinh x + \frac{1}{3} \sinh^3 x + C.$$

5.6.22. Find the integrals :

(a) $\int \sinh^2 x \cosh^2 x \, dx$; (b) $\int \frac{dx}{\sinh x + 2 \cosh x}$.

5.7. Integration of Certain Irrational Functions with the Aid of Trigonometric or Hyperbolic Substitutions

Integration of functions rationally depending on x and $\sqrt{ax^2 + bx + c}$ can be reduced to finding integrals of one of the following forms :

I. $\int R(t, \sqrt{p^2t^2 + q^2})\, dt$;

II. $\int R(t, \sqrt{p^2t^2 - q^2})\, dt$;

III. $\int R(t, \sqrt{q^2 - p^2t^2})\, dt$,

where $t = x + \frac{b}{2a}$; $ax^2 + bx + c = \pm\, p^2t^2 \pm q^2$ (singling out a perfect square).

Integrals of the forms I to III can be reduced to integrals of expressions rational with respect to sine or cosine (ordinary or hyperbolic) by means of the following substitutions :

I. $t = \frac{q}{p} \tan z$ or $t = \frac{q}{p} \sinh z$.

II. $t = \frac{q}{p} \sec z$ or $t = \frac{q}{p} \cosh z$.

III. $t = \frac{q}{p} \sin z$ or $t = \frac{q}{p} \tanh z$.

5.7.1. $I = \int \frac{dx}{\sqrt{(5 + 2x + x^2)^3}}$.

Solution $5 + 2x + x^2 = 4 + (x + 1)^2$. Let us put $x + 1 = t$. Then

$$I = \int \frac{dx}{\sqrt{(5 + 2x + x^2)^3}} = \int \frac{dt}{\sqrt{(4 + t^2)^3}}.$$

We have obtained an integral of the form I. Let us introduce the substitution :

$$t = 2 \tan z; \quad dt = \frac{2dz}{\cos^2 z};$$

$$\sqrt{4 + t^2} = 2\sqrt{1 + \tan^2 z} = \frac{2}{\cos z}.$$

We get

$$I = \frac{1}{4}\int \cos z\, dz$$

$$= \frac{1}{4} \sin z + C = \frac{1}{4} \frac{\tan z}{\sqrt{1 + \tan^2 z}} + C = \frac{1}{4} \frac{t^2}{\sqrt{1 + \frac{t^2}{4}}} + C$$

$$= \frac{x + 1}{4\sqrt{5 + 2x + x^2}} + C.$$

5.7.2. $I = \int \frac{dx}{(x+1)^2 \sqrt{x^2 + 2x + 2}}$.

Solution $x^2 + 2x + 2 = (x+1)^2 + 1$.

Let us put $x + 1 = t$; then

$$I = \int \frac{dt}{t^2 \sqrt{t^2 + 1}}.$$

Again we have an integral of the form I. Make the substitution $t = \sinh z$. Then

$$dt = \cosh z\, dz; \qquad \sqrt{t^2 + 1} = \sqrt{1 + \sinh^2 z} = \cosh z.$$

Hence,
$$I = \int \frac{\cosh z\, dz}{\sinh^2 z \cosh z} = \int \frac{dz}{\sinh^2 z} = -\coth z + C$$

$$= -\frac{\sqrt{1 + \sinh^2 z}}{\sinh z} + C = -\frac{\sqrt{1 + t^2}}{t} + C$$

$$= -\frac{\sqrt{x^2 + 2x + 2}}{x + 1} + C.$$

5.7.3. $I = \int x^2 \sqrt{x^2 - 1}\, dx$.

5.7.4. $I = \int \frac{\sqrt{x^2 + 1}}{x^2}\, dx$.

5.7.5. $I = \int \sqrt{(x^2 - 1)^3}\, dx$.

Solution Perform the substitution :

$$x = \cosh t; \quad dx = \sinh t\, dt.$$

Hence
$$I = \int \sqrt{(\cosh^2 t - 1)^3} \sinh t\, dt = \int \sinh^4 t\, dt$$

$$= \int \left(\frac{\cosh 2t - 1}{2} \right)^2 dt$$

$$= \frac{1}{4} \int \cosh^2 2t\, dt - \frac{1}{2} \int \cosh 2t\, dt + \frac{1}{4} \int dt$$

$$= \frac{1}{8} \int (\cosh 4t + 1)\, dt - \frac{1}{4} \sinh 2t + \frac{1}{4} t$$

$$= \frac{1}{32} \sinh 4t - \frac{1}{4} \sinh 2t + \frac{3}{8} t + C.$$

Let us return to x :

$$t = \text{Arcosh } x = \ln (x + \sqrt{x^2 - 1});$$

$$\sinh 2t = 2 \sinh 2t \cosh 2t = 2x \sqrt{x^2 - 1};$$

$$\sinh 4t = 2 \sinh 2t \cosh 2t = 4x \sqrt{x^2 - 1}\, (2x^2 - 1)$$

Hence $I = \frac{1}{8} x (2x^2 - 1) \sqrt{x^2 - 1} - \frac{1}{2} x \sqrt{x^2 - 1} + \frac{3}{8} \ln (x + \sqrt{x^2 - 1}) + C$.

5.7.6. $I = \int \frac{dt}{(1+\sqrt{x})\sqrt{x - x^2}}$.

Solution We make the substitution

$$x = \sin^2 t; \quad dx = 2 \sin t \cos t \, dt$$

and get

$$I = \int \frac{2 \sin t \cos t \, dt}{(1+\sin t)\sqrt{\sin^2 t - \sin^4 t}} = \int \frac{2\, dt}{1+\sin t}$$

$$= 2\int \frac{1-\sin t}{\cos^2 t} dt = 2 \tan t - \frac{2}{\cos t} + C$$

$$= \frac{2\sqrt{x}}{\sqrt{1-x}} - \frac{2}{\sqrt{1-x}} + C = \frac{2(\sqrt{x}-1)}{\sqrt{1-x}} + C.$$

5.7.7. $I = \int \sqrt{3 - 2x - x^2}\, dx$.

5.7.8. $I = \int \frac{dx}{(x^2 - 2x + 5)^{\frac{3}{2}}}$.

5.8. Integration of Other Transcendental Functions

5.8.1. $I = \int \frac{\ln x}{x^2} dx$.

Solution We integrate by parts, putting

$$u = \ln x; \qquad dv = \frac{dx}{x^2};$$

$$du = \frac{dx}{x}; \qquad v = -\frac{1}{x};$$

$$I = -\frac{\ln x}{x} + \int \frac{dx}{x^2} = -\frac{\ln x}{x} - \frac{1}{x} + C.$$

5.8.2. $I = \int \frac{\ln x \, dx}{\sqrt{1-x}}$.

5.8.3. $I = \int \frac{e^x \, dx}{(1+e^{2x})^2}$.

Solution Let us put : $e^x = t; e^x \, dx = dt$. We get :

$$I = \int \frac{dt}{(1+t^2)^2}.$$

Apply the reduction formula (see problem **4.4.1**) :

$$I = I_2 = \frac{t}{2(t^2+1)} + \frac{1}{2}\int \frac{dt}{1+t^2};$$

$$I = \frac{t}{2(t^2+1)} + \frac{1}{2} \text{arc} \tan t + C$$

$$= \frac{e^x}{2(1+e^{2x})} + \frac{1}{2} \text{arc} \tan e^x + C.$$

5.8.4. $I = \int e^{-x} \ln(e^x + 1)\, dx.$

Solution We integrate by parts :

$$u = \ln(e^x + 1); \qquad dv = e^{-x}\, dx;$$

$$du = \frac{e^x}{1 + e^x}\, dx; \qquad v = -e^{-x};$$

$$I = -e^{-x} \ln(1 + e^x) + \int \frac{dx}{1 + e^x}$$

$$= -e^{-x} \ln(1 + e^x) + \int \frac{e^x + 1 - e^x}{1 + e^x}\, dx$$

$$= -e^{-x} \ln(1 + e^x) + x - \ln(1 + e^x) + C.$$

5.8.5. $I = \int \frac{e^{\alpha \arctan x}}{(1 + x^2)^{\frac{3}{2}}}\, dx.$

5.8.6. $I = \int \frac{x \arctan x\, dx}{\sqrt{1 + x^2}}.$

Solution Integrating by parts, we get

$$u = \arctan x; \quad dv = \frac{x\, dx}{\sqrt{1 + x^2}}; \qquad du = \frac{dx}{1 + x^2}; \quad v = \sqrt{1 + x^2};$$

$$I = \sqrt{1 + x^2} \arctan x - \int \sqrt{1 + x^2}\, \frac{dx}{1 + x^2}$$

$$= \sqrt{1 + x^2} \arctan x - \ln\left(x + \sqrt{x^2 + 1}\right) + C.$$

5.9. Methods of Integration

(List of Basic Forms of Integrals)

No.	Integral	Method of Integration
1.	$\int F[\varphi(x)]\varphi'(x)\, dx$	Substitution $\varphi(x) = t$
2.	$\int (x)\, \varphi'(x)\, dx$	Integration by parts $\int f(x)\, \varphi'(x)\, dx = f(x)\, \varphi(x) - \int \phi(x) f'(x)\, dx.$ This method is applied, for example, to integrals of the form $\int p(x)\, f(x)\, dx$, where $p(x)$ is polynomial, and $f(x)$ is one of the following function : $e^{\alpha x}$; $\cos \alpha x$; $\sin \alpha x$; $\ln x$; $\arctan x$; $\arcsin x$, etc. and also to integrals of products of an exponential function by cosine or sine.

No.	Integral	Method of Integration
3.	$\int f(x)\,\varphi^{(n)}(x)\,dx$	Reduced to integration of the product $f^{(n)}(x)\,\varphi(x)$ by the formula for multiple integration by parts $\int f(x)\,\varphi^{(n)}(x)\,dx = f(x)\,\varphi^{(n-1)}(x) - f'(x)\,\varphi^{(n-2)}(x) + f''(x)\,\varphi^{(n-3)}(x) - \ldots + (-1)^{n-1} f^{(n-1)}(x)\,\varphi(x) + (-1)^n \int f^{(n)}(x)\,\varphi(x)\,dx$
4.	$\int e^{\alpha x}\, p_n(x)\,dx$, where $p_n(x)$ is a polynomial of degree n.	Applying the formula for multiple integration by parts (see above), we get $\int e^{\alpha x} p_n(x)\,dx = e^{\alpha x}\left[\frac{p_n(x)}{\alpha} - \frac{p_n{}'(x)}{\alpha^2} + \frac{p_n{}''(x)}{\alpha^3} - \ldots + (-1)^n \frac{p_n^{(n)}(x)}{\alpha^{n+1}}\right] + C$
5.	$\int \frac{Mx+N}{x^2+px+q}\,dx$, $p^2 - 4q < 0$	Substitution $x + \frac{p}{2} = t$
6.	$I_n = \int \frac{dx}{(x^2+1)^n}$	Reduction formula is used $I_n = \frac{x}{(2n-2)(x^2+1)^{n-1}} + \frac{2n-3}{2n-2} I_{n-1}$
7.	$\int \frac{P(x)}{Q(x)}\,dx$, where $\frac{P(x)}{Q(x)}$ is a proper rational fraction $Q(x) = (x-x_1)^l (x-x_2)^m \ldots (x^2+px+q)^k \ldots$	Integrand is expressed in the form of a sum of partial fractions $\frac{P(x)}{Q(x)} = \frac{A_1}{(x-x_1)} + \frac{A_2}{(x-x_1)^2} + \ldots + \frac{A_l}{(x-x_1)^l} + \frac{B_1}{(x-x_2)} + \frac{B_2}{(x-x_2)^2} + \ldots + \frac{B_m}{(x-x_2)^m} + \ldots + \frac{M_1 x + N_1}{x^2+px+q} + \frac{M_2 x + N_2}{(x^2+px+q)^2} + \ldots + \frac{M_k x + N_k}{(x^2+px+q)^k} + \ldots$
8.	$\int R\left(x, x^{\frac{m}{n}}, \ldots, x^{\frac{r}{s}}\right) dx$, where R is a rational functions of its arguments.	Reduced to the integral of a rational fraction by the substitution $x = t^k$, where k is a common denominator of the fractions $\frac{m}{n}, \ldots, \frac{r}{s}$
9.	$\int R\left[x, \left(\frac{ax+b}{cx+d}\right)^{\frac{1}{n}}\right] dx$, where R is a rational function of its arguments.	Reduced of the integral of a rational fraction by the substitution $\frac{ax+b}{cx+d} = t^n$

No.	Integral	Method of Integration
10.	$\int \frac{Mx+N}{\sqrt{ax^2+bx+c}}\,dx$	By the substitution $x+\frac{b}{2a}=t$ the integral is reduced to a sum of two integrals : $\int \frac{Mx+N}{\sqrt{ax^2+bx+c}}\,dx$ $= M_1 \int \frac{tdt}{\sqrt{at^2+m}} + N_1 \int \frac{dt}{\sqrt{at^2+m}}$ The first integrals is reduced to the integral of a power function and the second one is a tabular integral.
11.	$\int R(x, \sqrt{ax^2+bx+c})\,dx$, where R is a rational function of x and $\sqrt{ax^2+bx+c}$	Reduced to an integral of rational fraction by the Euler substitutions : $\sqrt{ax^2+bx+c} = t \pm \sqrt{a}\ (a>0)$, $\sqrt{ax^2+bx+c} = tx \pm \sqrt{c}\ (c>0)$, $\sqrt{ax^2+bx+c} = t\,(x-x_1)\,(4ac-b^2<0)$. where x_1 is the root of the trinomial ax^2+bx+c. The indicated integral can also be evaluated by the trigonometric substitutions : $x+\frac{b}{2a} = \begin{cases} \frac{\sqrt{b^2-4ac}}{2a}\sin t \\ \frac{\sqrt{b^2-4ac}}{2a}\cos t\ (a<0,\ 4ac-b^2<0) \end{cases}$ $x+\frac{b}{2a} = \begin{cases} \frac{\sqrt{b^2-4ac}}{2a}\sec t \\ \frac{\sqrt{b^2-4ac}}{2a}\operatorname{cosec} t\ (a>0,\ 4ac-b^2>0) \end{cases}$ $x+\frac{b}{2a} = \begin{cases} \frac{\sqrt{4ac-b^2}}{2a}\tan t \\ \frac{\sqrt{4ac-b^2}}{2a}\cot t\ (a>0,\ 4ac-b^2>0) \end{cases}$
12.	$\int \frac{P_n(x)}{\sqrt{ax^2+bx+c}}\,dx$, where $P_n(x)$ is a polynomial of degree n	Write the equality $\int \frac{P_n(x)\,dx}{\sqrt{ax^2+bx+c}} = Q_{n-1}(x)\sqrt{ax^2+bx+c} + k\int \frac{dx}{\sqrt{ax^2+bx+c}}$, where $Q_{n-1}(x)$ is a polynomial of degree $n-1$. Differentiating both parts of this equality and multiplying by $\sqrt{ax^2+bx+c}$, we get the identity

No.	Integral	Method of Integration
		$P_n(x) = Q'_{n-1}(x)(ax^2 + bx + c) + \frac{1}{2} Q_{n-1}(x)(2ax + b) + k,$ which gives a system of $n + 1$ linear equations for determining the coefficients of the polynomial $Q_{n-1}(x)$ and factor k. And the integral $\int \frac{dx}{\sqrt{ax^2 + bx + c}}$ is taken by the method considered in No. 10 $(M = 0 ; N = 1)$.
13.	$\int \frac{dx}{(x - x_1)^m \sqrt{ax^2 + bx + c}}$	This integral is reduced to the above-considered integral by the substitution $x - x_1 = \frac{1}{t}$
14.	$\int x^m (a + bx^n)^p dx,$ where m, n, p are rational numbers (an integral of a binomial differential).	This integral is expressed through elementary functions only if one of the following conditions is fulfilled : (1) if p is an integer (2) if $\frac{m+1}{n}$ is an integer, (3) if $\frac{m+1}{n} + p$ is an integer. *1st case* (a) if p is a positive integer, remove the brackets $(a + bx^n)^p$ according to the Newton binomial and calculate the integrals of powers ; (b) if p is a negative integer, then the substitution $x = t^k$, where k is the common denominator of the fractions m and n, leads to the integral of a rational fraction ; *2nd case* if $\frac{m+1}{n}$ is an integer, then the substitution $a + bx^n = t^k$ is applied, where k is the denominator off the fraction p ; *3rd case* if $\frac{m+1}{n} + p$ is an integer, then the substitution $a + bx^n = x^n t^k$ is applied, where k is the denominator of the fraction p.
15.	$\int R(\sin x, \cos x)\, dx$	Universal substitution $\tan \frac{x}{2} = t$.

No.	Integral	Method of Integration
		If $R(-\sin x, \cos x) = -R(\sin x, \cos x)$, then the substitution $\cos x = t$ is applied. If $R(\sin x, -\cos x) = -R(\sin x, \cos x)$, then the substitution $\sin x = t$ is applied. If $R(-\sin x, -\cos x) = R(\sin x, \cos x)$ then the substitution $\tan x = t$ is applied.
16.	$\int R(\sinh x, \cosh x)\, dx$	The substitution $\tanh \frac{x}{2} = t$ is used. In this case $\sinh x = \frac{2t}{1-t^2}$; $\cosh x = \frac{1+t^2}{1-t^2}$; $dx = \frac{2dt}{1-t^2}$.
17.	$\int \sin ax \sin bx\, dx$ $\int \sin ax \cos bx dx$ $\int \cos ax \cos bx\, dx$	Transform the product of trigonometric functions into a sum of difference, using one of the following formulas : $\sin ax \sin bx = \frac{1}{2}[\cos(a-b)x - \cos(a+b)x]$ $\cos ax \cos bx = \frac{1}{2}[\cos(a-b)x + \cos(a+b)x]$ $\sin ax \cos bx = \frac{1}{2}[\sin(a-b)x + \sin(a+b)x]$
18.	$\int \sin^m x \cos^n x\, dx$, where m and n are integers.	If m is an odd positive number, then apply the substitution $\cos x = t$. If n is an odd positive number, apply the substitution $\sin x = t$. If $m + n$ is an even negative number, apply the substitution $\tan x = t$. If m and n are even non-negative numbers, use the formulas $\sin^2 x = \frac{1-\cos 2x}{2}$; $\cos^2 x = \frac{1+\cos 2x}{2}$
19.	$\sin^p x \cos^q x\, dx$ $(0 < x < \pi/2)$, p and q rational numbers.	Reduce to the integral of the binomial differential by the substitution $\sin x = t$ $\int \sin^p x \cos^q x\, dx = \int t^p (1-t^2)^{q-1} dt$ (see No. 14).
20.	$\int R(e^{ax})\, dx$	Transform into an integral of a rational function by the substitution $e^{ax} = t$

6 The Definite Integral

6.1. Statement of the Problem. The Lower and Upper Integral Sums

Let a function $f(x)$ be defined in the closed interval $[a, b]$. The following is called the *integral sum* :

$$I_n = \sum_{i=0}^{n-1} f(\xi_1)\Delta x_i,$$

where $a = x_0 < x_1 < x_2 < \ldots < x_{n-1} < x_n = b$,

$$\Delta x_i = x_{i+1} - x_i;\ \xi_1 \in [x_i, x_{i+1}]\ (i = 0, 1, \ldots, n-1).$$

The sum $S_n = \sum_{i=0}^{n-1} M_i \Delta x_i$ is called the *upper* (integral) *sum,* and $s_n = \sum_{i=0}^{n-1} m_i \Delta x_i$where $M_i =$ is called the *lower* (integral) *sum,* sup $f(x)$ $[m_i = \inf f(x)]$ for $x \in [x_i, x_{i+1}]$.

The *definite integral* of the function $f(x)$ on the interval $[a, b]$ is the limit of the integral sums

$$\int_a^b f(x)\,dx = \lim \sum_{i=0}^{n-1} f(\xi_i)\Delta x_i \text{ when } \max |\Delta x_i| \to 0.$$

If this limit exists, the function is called *integrable* on the interval $[a, b]$. Any continuous function is integrable.

6.1.1. For the integral

$$\int_0^{\pi} \sin x\,dx$$

find the upper and lower integral sums corresponding to the division of the closed interval $[0, \pi]$ into 3 and 6 equal subintervals.

Solution Divide the closed interval $[0. \pi]$ into 3 equal parts by the points :

$$x_0 = 0,\ x_1 = \frac{\pi}{3},\ x_2 = \frac{2\pi}{3},\ x_3 = \pi.$$

The function $\sin x$ increases monotonically on the interval $\left[0, \frac{\pi}{3}\right]$, and therefore for this interval we have $m_0 = \sin 0 = 0$, $M_0 = \sin\frac{\pi}{3} = \frac{\sqrt{3}}{2}$. The least value of the function on the interval $\left[\frac{\pi}{3}, \frac{2\pi}{3}\right]$ is $m_1 = \sin\frac{\pi}{3} = \frac{\sqrt{3}}{2}$, and the greatest value is $M_1 = \sin\frac{\pi}{2} = 1$. On the interval $\left[\frac{2\pi}{3}, \pi\right]$ the function $\sin x$ decreases monotonically and therefore

$$m_2 = \sin\pi = 0, \qquad M_2 = \sin\frac{2\pi}{3} = \frac{\sqrt{3}}{2}.$$

Since all Δx_k are equal to $\frac{\pi}{3}$,

$$s_3 = \sum_{k=0}^{2} m_k\,\Delta x_k = \frac{\pi}{3}\left(0 + \frac{\sqrt{3}}{2} + 0\right) = \frac{\pi\sqrt{3}}{6} \approx 0.907,$$

$$S_3 = \sum_{k=0}^{2} M_k\,\Delta x_k = \frac{\pi}{3}\left(\frac{\sqrt{3}}{2} + 1 + \frac{\sqrt{3}}{2}\right) = \frac{\pi\,(\sqrt{3}+1)}{3} \approx 2.86.$$

When subdividing the closed interval $[0, \pi]$ into 6 equal intervals by the points $x_0 = 0, x_1 = \frac{\pi}{6}, x_2 = \frac{\pi}{3}, x_3 = \frac{\pi}{2}, x_4 = \frac{2\pi}{3}, x_5 = \frac{5\pi}{6}, x_6 = \pi$, we find by analogy :

$$m_0 = 0, \qquad M_0 = \sin\frac{\pi}{6} = \frac{1}{2},$$

$$m_1 = \sin\frac{\pi}{6} = \frac{1}{2}, \qquad M_1 = \sin\frac{\pi}{3} = \frac{\sqrt{3}}{2},$$

$$m_2 = \sin\frac{\pi}{3} = \frac{\sqrt{3}}{2}, \qquad M_2 = \sin\frac{\pi}{2} = 1,$$

$$m_3 = \sin\frac{2\pi}{3} = \frac{\sqrt{3}}{2}, \qquad M_3 = \sin\frac{\pi}{2} = 1,$$

$$m_4 = \sin\frac{5\pi}{6} = \frac{1}{2}, \qquad M_4 = \sin\frac{2\pi}{3} = \frac{\sqrt{3}}{2},$$

$$m_5 = \sin\pi = 0, \qquad M_5 = \sin\frac{5\pi}{6} = \frac{1}{2}.$$

For this division we obtain

$$s_6 = \frac{\pi}{6}(m_0 + m_1 + \ldots + m_5) = \frac{\pi}{6}(1 + \sqrt{3}) \approx 1.43,$$

$$S_6 = \frac{\pi}{6}(M_0 + M_1 + \ldots + M_5) = \frac{\pi}{6}(3 + \sqrt{3}) \approx 2.48.$$

As would be expected, the inequalities

$$s_3 \le s_6 \le \int_0^{\pi} \sin x\,dx \le S_6 \le S_3$$

hold true (the exact value of the integral is equal to 2).

6.1.2. At what $\delta > 0$ does the relation

$$\left| \int_0^{\pi} \sin x\,dx - \sum_{i=0}^{n-1} \sin\xi_k\,\Delta x_k \right| < 0.001$$

follow from the inequality $\max \Delta x_i < \delta$.

Solution Since $s_n < I_n < S_n$, then for the required inequality to hold true it is sufficient that the upper and the lower integral sums differ by less than 0.001:

$$0 < S_n - s_n < 0.001.$$

But $$S_n - s_n = \sum_{i=0}^{n-1} (M_i - m_i)\Delta x_i < \delta \sum_{i=0}^{n-1} (M_i - m_i),$$

where M_i and m_i are the greatest and the least values of the function sin x on the interval $[x_i, x_{i+1}]$ $(i = 0, 1, \dots, n-1)$. Assuming for simplicity that the point $\frac{\pi}{2}$ is chosen as one of the points of division and taking advantage of monotonicity of the function sin x on the intervals $\left[0, \frac{\pi}{2}\right]$ and $\left[\frac{\pi}{2}, \pi\right]$, we obtain

$$\sum_{i=0}^{n-1} (M_i - m_i) = 2\left(\sin\frac{\pi}{2} - \sin 0\right) = 2.$$

Consequently, the required inequality is satisfied if $2\delta < 0.001$, *ie*, $\delta < 0.0005$.

6.1.3. Show that the Dirichlet function [see Problem 1.14.4 (b)] is not integrable in the interval [0, 1].

Solution In dividing the closed interval [0, 1] into a fixed number of parts we must take into consideration, in particular, two possible cases: (1) all points ξ_i are rational; (2) all points ξ_i are irrational. In the first case the integral sum is equal to unity, in the second to zero. Hence, no matter how we reduce the maximum length of subintervals, we always get integral sums equal to unity and integral sums equal to zero. Therefore, the limit of integral sums is non-existent, which means that the Dirichlet function is not integrable on the interval [0, 1].

6.1.4. Find the distance covered by a body in a free fall within the time interval from $t = a$ sec to $t = b$ sec.

Solution A body moves in a free fall with constant acceleration g and initial velocity $v_0 = 0$. Consequently, the velocity at the instant t is equal to the velocity increment within the time interval from 0 to t, *ie*, $v(t) = \Delta v$. For a short time period Δt the velocity increment is approximately equal to the acceleration at the instant t multiplied by Δt. But in our case acceleration is constant, therefore $\Delta v = g\Delta t$, and hence, $v(t) = gt$, since $\Delta t = t - 0 = t$.

Let us subdivide the time interval from $t = a$ to $t = b$ into n equal parts; then the duration Δt of each subinterval will be equal to $\Delta t = \frac{b-a}{n}$. We assume that during each subinterval of time the body moves uniformly with a velocity equal to its velocity at the beginning of this interval, *ie*,

$$v_0 = ga,$$
$$v_1 = g\left(a + 1\frac{b-a}{n}\right),$$
$$v_2 = g\left(a + 2\frac{b-a}{n}\right),$$
$$\ldots\ldots\ldots\ldots\ldots\ldots$$
$$v_{n-1} = g\left[a + (n-1)\frac{b-a}{n}\right].$$

Whence we find the distance covered by the body during the ith subinterval: $\frac{v_i(b-a)}{n}$. The entire distance covered by the body is approximately equal to

$$s \approx s_n = \frac{b-a}{n}(v_0 + v_1 + \ldots + v_{n-1})$$
$$= \frac{b-a}{n} g\left[na + 1\frac{b-a}{n} + 2\frac{b-a}{n} + \ldots + (n-1)\frac{b-a}{n}\right]$$
$$= (b-a)g\left[a + \frac{b-a}{n^2}\frac{n(n-1)}{2}\right]$$

With n increasing the distance covered can be evaluated more accurately. The exact value of s is found as the limit s_n as $n \to \infty$:

$$s = \lim_{n\to\infty} s_n = \lim_{n\to\infty} g(n-a)\left[a + \frac{1}{2}(b-a)\left(1 - \frac{1}{n}\right)\right]$$
$$= g(b-a)\left[a + \frac{1}{2}(b-a)\right] = \frac{g}{2}(b^2 - a^2).$$

Since s_n is an integral sum

$$s_n = \sum_{i=0}^{n-1} v_i \Delta t_i \left(\Delta t_i = \Delta t = \frac{b-a}{n}\right),$$

the distance s is an integral :

$$s = \int_a^b v\,dt = \int_a^b gt\,dt = \frac{g}{2}(b^2 - a^2).$$

6.1.5. Proceeding from the definition, compute the integral $\int_0^1 x\,dx$.

Solution By definition

$$\int_0^1 x\,dx = \lim \sum_{i=0}^{n-1} \xi_i \Delta x_i \text{ as } \max \Delta x_i \to 0,$$

where $0 = x_0 < x_1 < \ldots < x_n = 1, \xi_i \in [x_i, x_{i+1}]$,

$$\Delta x_i = x_{i+1} - x_i.$$

1. Subdivide the closed interval [0, 1] into n equal parts by the points $x_i = \frac{i}{n}$ $(i = 0, 1, 2, \ldots, n)$.

The length of each subinterval is equal to $\Delta x_i = \frac{1}{n}$, and $\frac{1}{n} \to 0$ as $n \to \infty$.

Let us take the right-hand end-points of the subintervals as the points $\xi_i : \xi_i = x_{i+1} = \frac{i+1}{n}$ $(i = 0, 1, \ldots, n-1)$.

Form an integral sum :

$$I_n = S_n = \sum_{i=0}^{n-1} \frac{i+1}{n} \cdot \frac{1}{n} = \frac{1}{n^2}(1 + 2 + \ldots + n) = \frac{n(n+1)}{2n^2}.$$

As $n \to \infty$ the limit of this sum is equal to

$$\lim_{n \to \infty} \frac{n+1}{2n} = \frac{1}{2}.$$

Hence,

$$\int_0^1 x\,dx = \frac{1}{2}.$$

2. Using this example, we will show that for any other choice of points ξ_i the limit of the integral sum will be the same.

Take, for instance, the mid-points of the subintervals as $\xi_i : \xi_i$

$$= \frac{i + \frac{1}{2}}{n} \; (i = 0, 1, .., n-1).$$

Form an integral sum

$$I_n = \sum_{i=0}^{n-1} \frac{2i+1}{2n} \cdot \frac{1}{n} = \frac{1}{2n^2}[1 + 3 + 5 + \ldots + (2n-1)] = \frac{2n^2}{4n^2} = \frac{1}{2}.$$

Hence $$\lim_{n \to \infty} I_n = \frac{1}{2}.$$

6.1.6. Proceeding from the definition, compute the integral :

$$\int_a^b x^m\,dx \; (m \neq -1, 0 < a < b).$$

Solution In this example the following points can be conveniently chosen as points of division :

$$x_0 = a;\; x_1 = a\left(\frac{b}{a}\right)^{\frac{1}{n}}, \ldots, x_i = a\left(\frac{b}{a}\right)^{\frac{i}{n}}, \ldots, x_n = a\left(\frac{b}{a}\right)^{\frac{n}{n}} = b.$$

They form a geometric progression with the common ratio

$$q = \left(\frac{b}{a}\right)^{\frac{1}{n}} > 1.$$

The length of the ith subinterval is equal to

$$\Delta x_i = aq^{i+1} - aq^i = aq^i(q-1).$$

Therefore the maximum length of the subintervals equals $\max \Delta x_i$

$= aq^{n-1}(q-1) = a\left(\frac{b}{a}\right)^{\frac{n-1}{n}}\left[\left(\frac{b}{a}\right)^{\frac{1}{n}} - 1\right]$ and tends to zero with increasing n,

since $\lim\limits_{n\to\infty} q = 1$.

Now let us choose the right-hand end-points of the subintervals as $\xi_i : \xi_i = x_{i+1} = aq^{i+1} (i = 0, 1, 2, \ldots, n-1)$.

Form an integral sum :

$$I_n = \sum_{i=0}^{n-1} \xi_i^m \Delta x_i = \sum_{i=0}^{n-1} a^m q^{(i+1)m} aq^i(q-1)$$

$$= a^{m+1}(q-1)q^m[1 + q^{m+1} + \ldots + q^{(n-1)(m+1)}]$$

$$= a^{m+1}(q-1)q^m \frac{q^{(m+1)n} - 1}{q^{m+1} - 1} = (b^{m+1} - a^{m+1})q^m \frac{q-1}{q^{m+1} - 1}.$$

Let us calculate the limit of the integral sum as $\max \Delta x_i \to 0$, *ie*, as $q \to 1$:

$$\lim I_n = (b^{m+1} - a^{m+1}) \lim_{q\to 1} q^m \frac{q-1}{q^{m+1} - 1}$$

$$= (b^{m+1} - a^{m+1}) \frac{1}{m+1}.$$

Thus,

$$\int_a^b x^m \, dx = \frac{1}{m+1}(b^{m+1} - a^{m+1}).$$

6.1.7. Proceeding from the definition, compute the integral :

$$\int_1^2 \frac{dx}{x}.$$

Solution Subdivide the interval [1, 2] into n parts so that the points of division x_i $(i = 0, 1, 2, \ldots, n)$ form the geometric progression :

$$x_0 = 1; \quad x_1 = q; \quad x_2 = q^2; \quad x_3 = q^3; \ldots; x_n = q^n = 2,$$

whence $q = \sqrt[n]{2}$.

The length of the ith subinterval is equal to

$$\Delta x_i = q^{i+1} - q^i = q^i(q-1),$$

and so $\max \Delta x_i = q^{n-1}(q-1) \to 0$ as $n \to \infty$, *ie*, as $q \to 1$.

Now let us choose the right-hand end-points of the subintervals as the points ξ_i, *ie*, $\xi_i = x_{i+1} = q^{i+1}$.

Form an integral sum :

$$I_n = \sum_{i=0}^{n-1} \frac{1}{\xi_i} \Delta x_i = \sum_{i=0}^{n-1} \frac{1}{q^{i+1}} q^i (q-1) = \frac{n}{q}(q-1) = \frac{1}{2^{\frac{1}{n}}} n\left(2^{\frac{1}{n}} - 1\right).$$

$$\lim_{n\to\infty} I_n = \lim_{n\to\infty} \frac{n\left(2^{\frac{1}{n}} - 1\right)}{2^{\frac{1}{n}}} = \ln 2,$$

since $2^{\frac{1}{n}} - 1 \sim \frac{1}{n} \ln 2$ as $n \to \infty$.

And so, $\int_1^2 \frac{dx}{x} = \ln 2.$

6.1.8. Evaluate the integral

$$I = \int_0^5 \sqrt{25 - x^2}\, dx,$$

proceeding from its geometric meaning.

Solution The curve $y = \sqrt{25 - x^2}$ is the upper half of the circle $x^2 + y^2 = 25$. The portion of the curve corresponding to the variation of x from 0 to 5 lies in the first quadrant. Hence, we conclude that the curvilinear trapezoid bounded by the lines $x = 0$; $x = 5$; $y = 0$, and $y = \sqrt{25 - x^2}$ is a quarter of the circle $x^2 + y^2 = 25$; and its area is equal to $\frac{25\pi}{4}$.

Hence

$$I = \int_0^5 \sqrt{25 - x^2}\, dx = \frac{25\pi}{4}.$$

6.1.9. Evaluate the integral, proceeding from its geometric meaning :

$$I = \int_1^5 (4x - 1)\, dx.$$

6.1.10. Prove that

$$I = \int_0^x \sqrt{a^2 - x^2}\, dx$$

$$= \frac{1}{2} x\sqrt{a^2 - x^2} + \frac{a^2}{2} \arcsin \frac{x}{a} \; (0 < x \le a)..$$

Solution The integral

$$I = \int_0^x \sqrt{a^2 - x^2}\, dx$$

expresses the area S_{OAMx} of the portion of a circle of radius a lying in the first quadrant (see Fig. 59). This area equals the sum of the areas of the triangle OMx and the sector OAM.

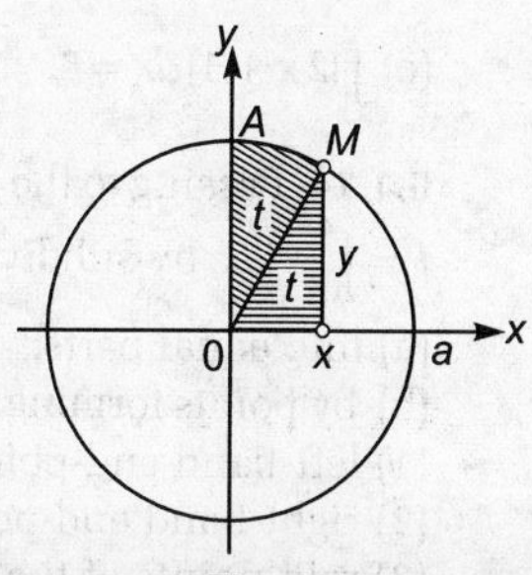

Fig. 59

$$S_{Omx} = \frac{xy}{2} = \frac{x}{2}\sqrt{a^2 - x^2}.$$

The area of the sector

$$S_{OAM} = \frac{1}{2}a^2 t,$$

where $\sin t = \frac{x}{a}$.

Hence, $$S_{OAM} = \frac{a^2}{2} \arcsin \frac{x}{a},$$

and consequently,

$$I = \frac{x}{2}\sqrt{a^2 - x^2} + \frac{a^2}{2} \arcsin \frac{x}{a}.$$

6.1.11. Proceeding from the geometric meaning of the integral, show that

(a) $\int_0^{2\pi} \sin^3 x\, dx = 0$; (b) $\int_{-1}^{1} e^{-x^2} dx = 2\int_0^1 e^{-x^2} dx$.

Solution (a) The graph of the function $y = \sin^3 x$ is shown in Fig. 60. Let us show that the area situated above the x-axis is equal to that lying below this axis. Indeed, let $\pi \le x \le 2\pi$, then $x = \pi + x_1$ where $0 \le x_1 \le \pi$ and $\sin^3 x = \sin^3(\pi + x_1) = -\sin^3 x_1$. Therefore, the second half of the graph is obtained from the first one by shifting it to the right by π and using the symmetry about the x-axis.

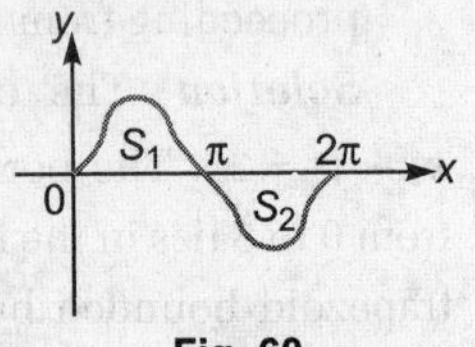

Fig. 60

Hence, $$\int_0^{2\pi} \sin^3 x\, dx = 0.$$

6.1.12. Given the function $f(x) = x^3$ on the interval $[-2, 3]$, find the lower (s_n) and the upper (S_n) integral sums for the given interval by subdividing it into n equal parts.

6.1.13. Proceeding from the geometric meaning of the definite integral, prove that :

(a) $\int_0^{\pi} \sin 2x\, dx = 0$; (b) $\int_0^{2\pi} \cos^3 x\, dx = 0$;

(c) $\int_1^2 (2x + 1)\, dx = 6$; (d) $\int_{-3}^{3} \sqrt{9 - x^2}\, dx = \frac{9\pi}{2}$.

6.1.14. Passing to the limit from the integral sums, compute the integral $I = \int_1^4 x^3 dx$, by subdividing the interval $[1, 4]$:

(a) into equal parts;

(b) by points forming a geometric progression. In both cases choose ξ_i as :

(1) left-hand end-points of the subintervals;

(2) right-hand end-points of the subintervals;

(3) mid-points of the subintervals $[x_i, x_{i+1}]$.

6.2. Evaluating Definite Integrals by the Newton-Leibnitz Formula

The following is known as the Newton-Leibnitz formula :

$$\int_a^b f(x)\,dx = F(x)\Big|_a^b = F(b) - F(a),$$

where $F(x)$ is one of the antiderivatives of the function $f(x)$, *ie*,

$$F'(x) \equiv f(x) \quad (a < x \le b).$$

6.2.1. Evaluate the integral

$$I = \int_1^{\sqrt{3}} \frac{dx}{1+x^2}.$$

Solution Since the function $F(x) = \text{arc tan } x$ is one of the antiderivatives of the function $f(x) = \dfrac{1}{1+x^2}$, using the Newton-Leibnitz formula we get

$$I = \int_1^{\sqrt{3}} \frac{dx}{1+x^2} = \text{arc tan } x \Big|_1^{\sqrt{3}}$$

$$= \text{arc tan } \sqrt{3} - \text{arc tan } 1 = \frac{\pi}{3} - \frac{\pi}{4} = \frac{\pi}{12}.$$

6.2.2. Compute the integrals :

(a) $\int_0^{\pi/2} \sin 2x\,dx$; (b) $\int_{\pi/6}^{\pi/2} \frac{\cos x}{\sin^3 x}\,dx$; (c) $\int_0^2 \frac{dx}{\sqrt{16-x^2}}$.

6.2.3. Given the function

$$f(x) = \begin{cases} x^2 & \text{for } 0 \le x \le 1, \\ \sqrt{x} & \text{for } 1 \le x \le 2. \end{cases}$$

Evaluate $\int_0^2 f(x)\,dx.$

Solution By the additivity property of the integral

$$\int_0^2 f(x)\,dx = \int_0^1 f(x)\,dx + \int_1^2 f(x)\,dx = \int_0^1 x^2\,dx + \int_1^2 \sqrt{x}\,dx$$

$$= \frac{x^3}{3}\Big|_0^1 + \frac{2}{3}x^{\frac{3}{2}}\Big|_1^2 = \frac{1}{3} + \frac{4\sqrt{2}}{3} - \frac{2}{3} = \frac{1}{3}(4\sqrt{2} - 1).$$

6.2.4. Evaluate the integral

$$I = \int_0^2 |1-x|\,dx.$$

Solution Since

$$|1-x| = \begin{cases} 1-x & \text{for } 0 \le x \le 1, \\ x-1 & \text{for } 1 \le x \le 2, \end{cases}$$

we obtain, taking advantage of the additivity property of the integral,

$$\int_0^2 |1-x|\,dx = \int_0^1 (1-x)\,dx + \int_1^2 (x-1)\,dx$$

$$= -\frac{(1-x)^2}{2}\Big|_0^1 + \frac{(x-1)^2}{2}\Big|_1^2 = \frac{1}{2} + \frac{1}{2} = 1.$$

6.2.5. Evaluate the integral

$$I = \int_a^b \frac{|x|}{x}\,dx,$$

where $a < b$.

Solution If $0 \le a < b$, then $f(x) = \frac{|x|}{x} = 1$, therefore $\int_a^b f(x)\,dx$

$= b - a$. If $a < b \le 0$, then $f(x) = -1$ and $\int_a^b f(x)\,dx = -b - (-a)$

$= a - b$. Finally, if $a < 0 < b$, then divide the integral $\int_a^b f(x)\,dx$

into two integrals :

$$\int_a^b f(x)\,dx = \int_a^0 f(x)\,dx + \int_0^b f(x)\,dx = b - (-a).$$

The above three cases may be represented by a single formula :

$$\int_a^b \frac{|x|}{x}\,dx = |b| - |a|.$$

Note. When evaluating integrals with the aid of the Newton-Leibnitz formula attention should be paid to the conditions of its legitimate use. This formula may be applied to compute the definite integral of a function *continuous* on the interval $[a, b]$ only when the equality $F'(x) = f(x)$ is fulfilled *in the whole interval* $[a, b]$ [$F(x)$ is an antiderivative of the function $f(x)$]. In particular, the antiderivative must be a function continuous on the whole interval $[a, b]$. A discontinuous function used as an antiderivative will lead to the wrong result.

6.2.6. Find a mistake in the following evaluation :

$$\int_0^{\sqrt{3}} \frac{dx}{1+x^2} = \frac{1}{2}\arctan\frac{2x}{1-x^2}\Big|_0^{\sqrt{3}} = \frac{1}{2}[\arctan(-\sqrt{3}) - \arctan 0] = -\frac{\pi}{6},$$

where $\left(\frac{1}{2}\arctan\frac{2x}{1-x^2}\right)' = \frac{1}{1+x^2}\ (x \ne 1)$.

Solution The result is a *priori* wrong: the integral of a function positive everywhere turns out to be negative. The mistake is due to the fact that the function $\frac{1}{2}\arctan\frac{2x}{1-x^2}$ has a discontinuity of the first kind at the point $x = 1$:

$$\lim_{x\to 1-0}\frac{1}{2}\arctan\frac{2x}{1-x^2} = \frac{\pi}{4}; \qquad \lim_{x\to 1+0}\frac{1}{2}\arctan\frac{2x}{1-x^2} = -\frac{\pi}{4}.$$

The correct value of the integral under consideration is equal to

$$\int_0^{\sqrt{3}} \frac{dx}{1+x^2} = \arc\tan x \Big|_0^{\sqrt{3}} = \arc\tan \sqrt{3} - \arc\tan 0 = \frac{\pi}{3}.$$

Here the Newton-Leibnitz formula is applicable, since the function $F(x) = \text{arc tan } x$ is continuous on the interval $\left[0, \frac{\pi}{3}\right]$ and the equality $F'(x) = f(x)$ is fulfilled on the whole interval.

6.2.7. Find a mistake in the following evaluation of the integral :

$$\int_0^{\pi} \frac{dx}{1+2\sin^2 x} = \int_0^{\pi} \frac{dx}{\cos^2 x + 3\sin^2 x}$$

$$= \int_0^{\pi} \frac{\frac{dx}{\cos^2 x}}{1+3\tan^2 x} = \frac{1}{\sqrt{3}} \text{arc tan}(\sqrt{3}\tan x)\Big|_0^{\pi} = 0.$$

(The integral of a function positive everywhere turns out to be zero!)

Solution The Newton-Leibnitz formula is not applicable here, since the antiderivative $F(x) = \frac{1}{\sqrt{3}} \text{arc tan}(\sqrt{3} \tan x)$ has a discontinuity at the point $x = \frac{\pi}{2}$. Indeed,

$$\lim_{x \to \frac{\pi}{2} - 0} F(x) = \lim_{x \to \frac{\pi}{2} - 0} \frac{1}{\sqrt{3}} \text{arc tan}(\sqrt{3}\tan x)$$

$$= \frac{1}{\sqrt{3}} \text{arc tan}(+\infty) = \frac{\pi}{2\sqrt{3}},$$

$$\lim_{x \to \frac{\pi}{2} + 0} F(x) = \lim_{x \to \frac{\pi}{2} + 0} \frac{1}{\sqrt{3}} \text{arc tan}(\sqrt{3}\tan x)$$

$$= \frac{1}{\sqrt{3}} \text{arc tan}(-\infty) = -\frac{\pi}{2\sqrt{3}}.$$

The correct result can be obtained in the following way :

$$\int_0^{\pi} \frac{dx}{\cos^2 x + 3\sin^2 x} = \int_0^{\pi} \frac{1}{\cot^2 x + 3} \frac{dx}{\sin^2 x}$$

$$= -\frac{1}{\sqrt{3}} \text{arc tan}(\sqrt{3}\cot x)\Big|_0^{\pi} = \frac{\pi}{\sqrt{3}}.$$

It can also be found with the aid of the function $F(x) = \frac{1}{\sqrt{3}} \text{arc tan}(\sqrt{3}\tan x)$. For this purpose divide the interval of integration $[0, \pi]$ into two subintervals, $\left[0, \frac{\pi}{2}\right]$ and $\left[\frac{\pi}{2}, \pi\right]$, and take into consideration the above-indicated limit values of the function $F(x)$ as $x \to \frac{\pi}{2} \mp 0$. Then the antiderivative becomes a continuous function on each of the subintervals, and the Newton-Leibnitz formula becomes applicable :

$$\int_0^{\pi} \frac{dx}{\cos^2 x + 3\sin^2 x} = \int_0^{\pi/2} + \int_{\pi/2}^{\pi}$$

$$= \frac{1}{\sqrt{3}} \operatorname{arc\,tan}(\sqrt{3}\tan x)\Big|_0^{\frac{\pi}{2}} + \frac{1}{\sqrt{3}} \operatorname{arc\,tan}(\sqrt{3}\tan x)\Big|_{\frac{\pi}{2}}^{\pi}$$

$$= \frac{1}{\sqrt{3}}\left[\left(\frac{\pi}{2} - 0\right) + \left(0 - \left(-\frac{\pi}{2}\right)\right)\right] = \frac{\pi}{\sqrt{3}}.$$

6.2.8. Compute the integral

$$\int_0^{\pi} \sqrt{\frac{1+\cos 2x}{2}}\, dx.$$

Solution $\sqrt{\dfrac{1+\cos 2x}{2}} = \sqrt{\dfrac{2\cos^2 x}{2}} = |\cos x|$

$$= \begin{cases} \cos x, & 0 \le x \le \dfrac{\pi}{2}, \\ -\cos x, & \dfrac{\pi}{2} \le x \le \pi. \end{cases}$$

Therefore

$$\int_0^{\pi} \sqrt{\frac{1+\cos 2x}{2}}\, dx = \int_0^{\pi/2} \cos x\, dx + \int_{\pi/2}^{\pi} (-\cos x)\, dx$$

$$= \sin x \Big|_0^{\frac{\pi}{2}} + (-\sin x)\Big|_{\frac{\pi}{2}}^{\pi} = (1 - 0) + (0 - (-1)) = 2.$$

Note. If we ignore the fact that $\cos x$ is negative in $\left[\dfrac{\pi}{2}, \pi\right]$ and put

$$\sqrt{\frac{1+\cos 2x}{2}} = \cos x,$$

we get the wrong result :

$$\int_0^{\pi} \cos x dx = \sin x \Big|_0^{\pi} = 0.$$

6.2.9. Evaluate the integral

$$I = \int_0^{100\pi} \sqrt{1 - \cos 2x}\, dx.$$

Solution We have $\sqrt{1-\cos 2x} = \sqrt{2}\,|\sin x|$.

Since $|\sin x|$ has a period π, then

$$\int_0^{100\pi} \sqrt{1-\cos 2x}\, dx = \sqrt{2}\int_0^{100\pi} |\sin x|\, dx$$

$$= 100\sqrt{2}\int_0^{\pi} \sin x\, dx = 200\sqrt{2}.$$

6.2.10. Evaluate the integrals :

(a) $I = \int_{-2}^{-1} \frac{dx}{(11+5x)^3}$; (b) $I = \int_{-3}^{-2} \frac{dx}{x^2-1}$;

(c) $I = \int_{-\pi}^{\pi} \sin^2 \frac{x}{2}\, dx$; (d) $I = \int_{0}^{\pi/4} \frac{x^2}{x^2+1}\, dx$;

(e) $I = \int_{e}^{e^2} \frac{dx}{x \ln x}$; (f) $I = \int_{1/\pi}^{2/\pi} \frac{\sin \frac{1}{x}}{x^2}\, dx$;

(g) $I = \int_{0}^{1} \frac{e^x}{1+e^{2x}}\, dx$; (h) $I = \int_{0}^{1} \frac{x^3 dx}{1+x^3}$;

(i) $I = \int_{0}^{3} \frac{x\, dx}{\sqrt{x+1}+\sqrt{5x+1}}$; (j) $I = \int_{-\pi/2}^{\pi/2} \sqrt{\cos x - \cos^3 x}\, dx$;

(k) $I = \int_{1}^{\sqrt{3}} \frac{dx}{(1+x^2)^{\frac{3}{2}}}$.

6.3. Estimating an Integral.

The Definite Integral as a Function of Its Limits

1. If $f(x) \le \varphi(x)$ for $a \le x \le b$, then

$$\int_a^b f(x)\,dx \le \int_a^b \varphi(x)\,dx.$$

In particular,

$$\left|\int_a^b f(x)\,dx\right| \le \int_a^b |f(x)|\,dx.$$

2. $$m(b-a) \le \int_a^b f(x)\,dx \le M(b-a),$$

where m is the least value, and M the greatest value of the function $f(x)$ on the interval $[a, b]$ *(estimation of an integral)*.

3. If the function $f(x)$ is continuous on the interval $[a, b]$, then

$$\int_a^b f(x)\,dx = f(\xi)\,(b-a),\ a < \xi < b$$

(mean-value theorem).

4. If the functions $f(x)$ and $\varphi(x)$ are continuous on $[a, b]$, and $\varphi(x)$, in addition, retains its sign on the interval, then

$$\int_a^b f(x)\varphi(x)\,dx = f(\xi)\int_a^b \varphi(x)\,dx,\ \ a < \xi < b$$

(generalized mean-value theorem).

5. $\frac{d}{dx}\int_a^x f(t)\,dt = f(x)$; $\frac{d}{dx}\int_x^a f(t)\,dt = -f(x)$ at each point x of continuity of the function $f(x)$.

6.3.1. Estimate the following integrals :

(a) $I = \int_1^3 \sqrt{3 + x^3}\, dx$; (b) $I = \int_{\pi/4}^{\pi/3} \frac{\sin x}{x} dx$;

(c) $I = \int_0^2 \frac{x^2 + 5}{x^2 + 2} dx$.

Solution (a) Since the function $f(x) = \sqrt{3 + x^3}$ increases monotonically on the interval $[1, 3]$, then $m = 2$, $M = \sqrt{30}, b - a = 2$.

Hence, the estimation of the integral has the form

$$2 \cdot 2 \le \int_1^3 \sqrt{3 + x^3}\, dx \le \sqrt{30} \cdot 2,$$

ie,

$$4 \le \int_1^3 \sqrt{3 + x^3}\, dx \le 2\sqrt{30} \approx 10.95.$$

(b) The integrand $f(x) = \frac{\sin x}{x}$ decreases on the interval $\left[\frac{\pi}{4}, \frac{\pi}{3}\right]$, since its derivative

$$f'(x) = \frac{x \cos x - \sin x}{x^2} = \frac{(x - \tan x)\cos x}{x^2} < 0.$$

Hence, the least value of the function :

$$m = f\left(\frac{\pi}{3}\right) = \frac{3\sqrt{3}}{2\pi},$$

its greatest value being $M = f\left(\frac{\pi}{4}\right) = \frac{2\sqrt{2}}{\pi}$.

Therefore,

$$\frac{3\sqrt{3}}{2\pi}\left(\frac{\pi}{3} - \frac{\pi}{4}\right) \le \int_{\pi/4}^{\pi/3} \frac{\sin x}{x} dx \le \frac{2\sqrt{2}}{\pi}\left(\frac{\pi}{3} - \frac{\pi}{4}\right),$$

ie,

$$0.22 \approx \frac{\sqrt{3}}{8} \le \int_{\pi/4}^{\pi/3} \frac{\sin x}{x} dx \le \frac{\sqrt{2}}{6} \approx 0.24$$

6.3.2. Estimate the absolute value of the integral

$$\int_{10}^{19} \frac{\sin x}{1 + x^8} dx.$$

Solution Since $|\sin x| \le 1$, for $x \ge 10$ the inequality

$$\left|\frac{\sin x}{1 + x^8}\right| < 10^{-8} \text{ is fulfilled.}$$

Therefore

$$\left|\int_{10}^{19} \frac{\sin x}{1 + x^8} dx\right| < (19 - 10)\, 10^{-8} < 10^{-7}$$

(The true value of the integral $\approx -10^{-8}$).

6.3.3. Which of the two integrals

$$\int_0^1 \sqrt{x}\, dx, \int_0^1 x^3 dx$$

is the greater ?

Solution As is known, $\sqrt{x} > x^3$ for $0 < x < 1$.

Therefore $$\int_0^1 \sqrt{x}\,dx > \int_0^1 x^3 dx.$$

6.3.4. Prove the inequalities :

(a) $0 < \int_0^1 \frac{x^7 dx}{\sqrt[3]{1+x^8}} < \frac{1}{8}$; (b) $1 < \int_0^1 e^{x^2} dx < e$.

Solution (a) Since $0 < \frac{x^7}{\sqrt[3]{1+x^8}} < x^7$ for $0 < x \le 1$, then

$$0 < \int_0^1 \frac{x^7 dx}{\sqrt[3]{1+x^8}} < \int_0^1 x^7 dx = \left.\frac{x^8}{8}\right|_0^1 = \frac{1}{8}.$$

(b) Since for $0 < x < 1$ there exists the inequality $1 < e^{x^2} < e$, then

$$\int_0^1 dx < \int_0^1 e^{x^2} dx < \int_0^1 e\,dx.$$

Hence the inequality under consideration holds true.

6.3.5. Prove the inequality

$$\int_0^{\pi/2} e^{-R\sin x} dx < \frac{\pi}{2R}(1 - e^{-R})\ (R > 0).$$

Solution Since the function $f(x) = \frac{\sin x}{x}$ decreases on $\left(0, \frac{\pi}{2}\right)$

[sec Problem 6.3.1 (b)], then for $0 < x < \frac{\pi}{2}$

$$f(x) = \frac{\sin x}{x} > f\left(\frac{\pi}{2}\right) = \frac{2}{\pi}.$$

Hence, on this interval $\sin x > \frac{2}{\pi} x$, therefore

$$e^{-R\sin x} < e^{-\frac{2R}{\pi}x}$$

and $$\int_0^{\pi/2} e^{-R\sin x} dx < \int_0^{\pi/2} e^{-\frac{2R}{\pi}x} dx = -\frac{\pi}{2R}\left[e^{-\frac{2R}{\pi}x}\right]_0^{\frac{\pi}{2}} = \frac{\pi}{2R}(1 - e^{-R}).$$

6.3.6. Prove that for any function $f(x)$ and $g(x)$, integrable on the interval (a, b), the Schwarz-Bunyakovsky inequality takes place :

$$\left|\int_a^b f(x)\,g(x)\,dx\right| \le \sqrt{\int_a^b f^2(x)\,dx \int_a^b g^2(x)\,dx}.$$

Solution Consider the function

$$F(x) = [f(x) - \lambda g(x)]^2,$$

where λ is any real number. Since $F(x) \ge 0$, then

$$\int_a^b [f(x) - \lambda g(x)]^2 dx \geq 0,$$

or
$$\lambda^2 \int_a^b g^2(x)dx - 2\lambda \int_a^b f(x)\, g(x)\, dx + \int_a^b f^2(x)\, dx \geq 0.$$

The expression in the left side of the latter inequality is a quadratic trinomial with respect to λ. If follows from the inequality that at any λ this trinomial is non-negative. Hence, its discriminant is non-positive, *ie*,

$$\left\{\int_a^b f(x)\, g(x)\, dx\right\}^2 - \int_a^b f^2(x)\, dx \int_a^b g^2(x)\, dx \leq 0.$$

Hence

$$\left|\int_a^b f(x)\, g(x)\, dx\right| \leq \sqrt{\int_a^b f^2(x)\, dx \int_a^b g^2(x)\, dx},$$

which completes the proof.

6.3.7. Estimate the integral from above

$$I = \int_0^1 \frac{\sin x}{1 + x^3} dx$$

Solution By the generalized mean-value theorem we have

$$\int_0^1 \frac{\sin x}{1 + x^2} dx = \sin\xi \int_0^1 \frac{dx}{1 + x^2} = \sin \xi \arctan x \Big|_0^1 = \frac{\pi}{4} \sin \xi \; (0 < \xi < 1).$$

Since the function $\sin x$ increases on the interval $[0, 1]$ then $\sin \xi < \sin 1$. Whence we get an upper estimate of the integral :

$$\int_0^1 \frac{\sin x}{1 + x^2} dx < \frac{\pi}{4} \sin 1 \approx 0.64.$$

It is possible to get a better estimation if we apply the same theorem in the form

$$\int_0^1 \frac{\sin x}{1 + x^2} dx = \frac{1}{1 + \xi^2} \int_0^1 \sin x\, dx = \frac{1}{1 + \xi^2}(1 - \cos 1) < 1 - \cos 1 \approx 0.46.$$

6.3.8. Proceeding from geometric reasoning, prove that :

(a) if the function $f(x)$ increases and has a concave graph in the interval $[a, b]$, then

$$(b - a)\, f(a) < \int_a^b f(x)\, dx < (b - a)\frac{f(a) + f(b)}{2};$$

(b) if the function $f(x)$ increases and has a convex graph in the interval $[a, b]$, then

$$(b - a)\frac{f(a) + f(b)}{2} < \int_a^b f(x)\, dx < (b - a)\, f(b).$$

Solution (a) Without limitation of generality we may assume $f(x) > 0$. Concavity of the graph of a function means, in particular, that the curve lies below the chord through the points $A(a, f(a))$ and $B(b, f(b))$ (see Fig. 61).

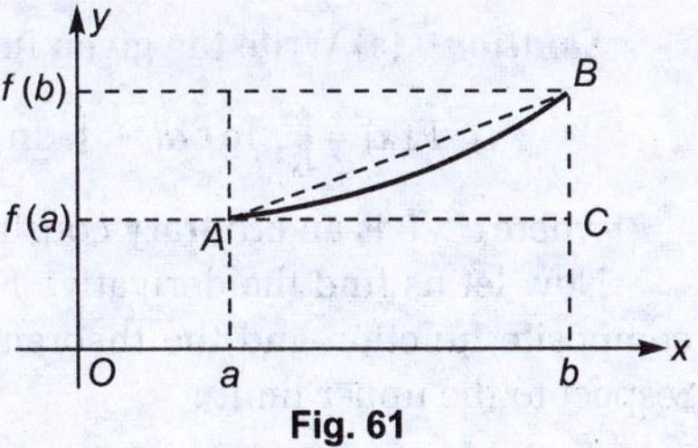

Fig. 61

Therefore the area of trapezoid $aABb$ is greater than that of the curvilinear trapezoid bounded above by the graph of the function, *ie*,

$$\int_a^b f(x)\,dx < S_{aABb} = (b-a)\cdot\frac{f(a)+f(b)}{2}.$$

The inequality

$$(b-a)f(a) < \int_a^b f(x)\,dx \quad \text{is}$$

obvious.

6.3.9. Estimate the integral $\int_0^1 \sqrt{1+x^4}\,dx$ using

(a) the mean-value theorem for a definite integral,
(b) the result of the preceding problem,
(c) the inequality $\sqrt{1+x^4} < 1 + \frac{x^4}{2}$,
(d) the Schwarz-Bunyakovsky inequality (see Problem 6.3.6).

Solution (a) By the mean-value theorem

$$I = \int_0^1 \sqrt{1+x^4}\,dx = \sqrt{1+\xi^4}, \text{ where } 0 \le \xi \le 1.$$

But $$1 < \sqrt{1+\xi^4} < \sqrt{2},$$

whence $$1 < I < \sqrt{2} \approx 1.414.$$

(b) The function $f(x) = \sqrt{1+x^4}$ is concave on the interval [0, 1], since

$$f''(x) = \frac{2x^2(x^4+3)}{(1+x^4)^{3/2}} > 0, 0 \le x \le 1.$$

On the basis of the preceding problem we get

$$1 < \int_0^1 \sqrt{1+x^4}\,dx < \frac{1+\sqrt{2}}{2} \approx 1.207.$$

(c) $$1 < I = \int_0^1 \sqrt{1+x^4}\,dx < \int_0^1 \left(1+\frac{x^4}{2}\right)dx = 1 + \frac{1}{10} = 1.1.$$

(d) Put $f(x) = \sqrt{1+x^4}, g(x) = 1$ and take advantage of the Schwarz-Bunyakovsky inequality

$$\left|\int_0^1 \sqrt{1+x^4}\,dx\right| = \int_0^1 \sqrt{1+x^4}\,dx = I < \sqrt{\int_0^1 (1+x^4)\,dx \cdot \int_0^1 1^2 dx}$$
$$= \sqrt{1.2} \approx 1.095.$$

6.3.10. Find the derivative with respect to x of the following functions :

(a) $F(x) = \int_{x^2}^{x^3} \ln t\,dt \ (x > 0)$,

(b) $f(x) = \int_{1/x}^{\sqrt{x}} \cos(t^2)\,dt \ (x > 0)$.

Solution (a) Write the given integral in the following way :

$$F(x) = \int_{x^2}^{c} \ln t\, dt + \int_{c}^{x^2} \ln t\, dt = \int_{c}^{x^2} \ln t\, dt - \int_{c}^{x^2} \ln t dt.$$

where $c > 0$ is an arbitrary constant.

Now let us find the derivative $F'(x)$ using the rule for differentiating a composite function and the theorem on the derivative of an integral with respect to the upper limit :

$$F'_x(x) = \left[\int_{c}^{x^3} \ln t\, dt\right]'_{x^2} (x^3)'_x - \left[\int_{c}^{x^2} \ln t\, dt\right]'_{x^2} (x^2)'_x = \ln x^3 3x^2 - \ln x^2\, 2x$$

$$= (9x^2 - 4x) \ln x.$$

(b) $F(x) = \int_{1/x}^{c} \cos(t^2)\, dt + \int_{c}^{\sqrt{x}} \cos(t^2)\, dt$

$$= -\int_{c}^{1/x} \cos(t^2)\, dt + \int_{c}^{\sqrt{x}} \cos(t^2)\, dt;$$

$$F'(x) = -\left[\int_{c}^{1/x} \cos(t^2)\, dt\right]'_{1/x} \left(\frac{1}{x}\right)'_x + \left[\int_{c}^{\sqrt{x}} \cos(t^2)\, dt\right]'_{\sqrt{x}} (\sqrt{x})'_x$$

$$= -\cos\frac{1}{x^2}\left(-\frac{1}{x^2}\right) + \cos x \cdot \frac{1}{2\sqrt{x}} = \frac{1}{x^2}\cos\frac{1}{x^2} + \frac{1}{2\sqrt{x}}\cos x.$$

6.3.11. Find the derivative with respect to x of the following functions :

(a) $F(x) = \int_{0}^{2x} \frac{\sin t}{t}\, dt;$ (b) $f(x) = \int_{x}^{0} \sqrt{1 + t^4}\, dt.$

6.3.12. Find the points of extremum of the function $F(x) = \int_{0}^{x} \frac{\sin t}{t}\, dt$ in the domain $x > 0$.

Solution Find the derivative

$$F'(x) = \left[\int_{0}^{x} \frac{\sin t}{t}\, dt\right]'_x = \frac{\sin x}{x}.$$

The critical points are :

$$x = n\pi \qquad (n = 1, 2, \ldots), \text{where } \sin x = 0.$$

Find the second derivative at these points :

$$F''(x) = \frac{x\cos x - \sin x}{x^2};$$

$$F''(n\pi) = \frac{1}{n\pi}\cos(n\pi) = \frac{1}{n\pi}(-1)^n \neq 0.$$

Since the second derivative is non-zero at the points $x = n\pi$ $(n = 1, 2, \ldots)$, these points are points of extremum of the function, namely: maxima if n is odd, and minima if n is even.

6.3.13. Find the derivative of y, with respect to x, of the function represented parametrically :

$$x = \int_1^{t^3} \sqrt[3]{z} \ln z dz; \; y = \int_{\sqrt{t}}^{3} z^2 \ln z dz.$$

Solution As is known, $y_x' = \dfrac{y_t'}{x_t'}$.

Find x_t' and y_t':

$$x_t' = \left(\int_1^{t^3} \sqrt[3]{z} \ln z dz\right)_{t^3} (t^3)_t' = t \ln t^3 \cdot 3t^2 = 9t^3 \ln t;$$

$$y_t' = \left(\int_{\sqrt{t}}^{3} z^2 \ln z dz\right)_{\sqrt{t}} (\sqrt{t})_t' = -t \ln \sqrt{t} \frac{1}{2\sqrt{t}} = -\frac{1}{4} \sqrt{t} \ln t;$$

whence

$$y_x' = \frac{9t^3 \ln t}{-\frac{1}{4}\sqrt{t} \ln t} = -36t^2\sqrt{t} \; (t > 0).$$

6.3.14. Find the limits :

(a) $\lim\limits_{x\to 0} \dfrac{\int_0^{x^3} \sin\sqrt{x}\, dx}{x^3}$; (b) $\lim\limits_{x\to +\infty} \dfrac{\int_0^{\pi} (\text{arc tan } x)^2 dx}{\sqrt{x^2+1}}$;

(c) $\lim\limits_{x\to +\infty} \dfrac{\left(\int_0^{x} e^{x^2} dx\right)^2}{\int_0^{\pi} e^{2x^2} dx}$.

Solution (a) At $x = 0$ the integral $\int_0^{x^2} \sin\sqrt{x}\, dx$ equals zero; it is easy to check the fulfilment of the remaining conditions that that ensure the legitimacy of using the L'Hospital rule. Therefore

$$\lim_{x\to 0} \frac{\int_0^{x^3} \sin\sqrt{x}\, dx}{x^3} = \lim_{x\to 0} \frac{\left[\int_0^{x^3} \sin\sqrt{x}\, dx\right]_{x^3} (x^2)_x'}{3x^2} = \lim_{x\to 0} \frac{2x \sin x}{3x^2} = \frac{2}{3}.$$

(c) We have an indeterminate form of the type $\frac{\infty}{\infty}$. Use the L'Hospital rule :

$$\lim_{x\to +\infty} \frac{\left(\int_0^{x} e^{x^2} dx\right)^2}{\int_0^{x} e^{2x^2} dx} = \lim_{x\to +\infty} \frac{2\int_0^{x} e^{x^2} dx \cdot e^{x^2}}{e^{2x^2}}$$

$$= \lim_{x\to +\infty} \frac{2\int_0^{x} e^{x^2} dx}{e^{x^2}} = \lim_{x\to +\infty} 2 \frac{e^{x^3}}{e^{x^2} \cdot 2x} = 0.$$

6.3.15. Find the derivative $\dfrac{dy}{dx}$ of the following implicit functions :

(a) $\int_0^{y} e^{-t^2} dt + \int_0^{x^3} \sin^2 t\, dt = 0$; (b) $\int_0^{y} e^t dt + \int_0^{x} \sin t\, dt = 0$;

(c) $\int_{\pi/2}^{x} \sqrt{3 - 2\sin^2 z}\, dz + \int_0^{y} \cos t\, dt = 0$.

Solution (a) Differentiate the left side of the equation with respect to x, putting $y = y(x)$:

$$\left[\int_0^y e^{-t^2} dt\right]'_y \cdot \frac{dy}{dx} + \left[\int_0^{x^3} \sin^2 t\, dt\right]'_{x^3} (x^2)'_x = 0;$$

$$e^{-y^2} \frac{dy}{dx} + \sin^2 x^2 \cdot 2x = 0.$$

Hence, solving the equation with respect to $\frac{dy}{dx}$, we get

$$\frac{dy}{dx} = -2xe^{+y^2} \sin^2 x^2.$$

(c) Differentiate the left side of the equation with respect to x, putting $y = y(x)$:

$$\left[\int_{\pi/2}^x \sqrt{3 - 2\sin^2 z}\, dx\right]'_x + \left[\int_0^y \cos t\, dt\right]_y \frac{dy}{dx} = 0.$$

Whence

$$\sqrt{3 - 2\sin^2 x} + \cos y \frac{dy}{dx} = 0; \quad \frac{dy}{dx} = -\frac{\sqrt{3 - 2\sin^2 x}}{\cos y}.$$

6.3.16. Find : (a) the points of extremum and the points of inflection on the graph of the function

$$I = \int_0^x (t-1)(t-2)^2 dt;$$

(b) curvature of the line defined by the parametric equations :

$$\begin{cases} x = a\sqrt{x} \int_0^t \cos \frac{\pi t^2}{2} dt, \\ y = a\sqrt{\pi} \int_0^t \sin \frac{\pi t^2}{2} dt \end{cases}$$

(the Cornu spiral).

Solution (a) The function is defined and continuously differentiable throughout the entire number scale. Its derivative

$$I'_x = (x-1)(x-2)^2$$

equals zero at the points $x_1 = 1$, $x_2 = 2$, and when passing through the point x_1 it changes sign from minus to plus, whereas in the neighbourhood of the point x_2 the sign remains unchanged. Consequently, there is a minimum at the point $x_1 = 1$, and there is no extremum at the point $x_2 = 2$.

The second derivative

$$I''_x = 3x^2 - 10x + 8$$

vanishes at the points $x_1 = \frac{4}{3}$, $x_2 = 2$ and changes sign when passing through these points. Hence, these points are the abscissas of the points of inflection.

(b) We have

$$x'_t = a\sqrt{\pi}\cos\frac{\pi t^2}{2},\ y'_t = a\sqrt{\pi}\sin\frac{\pi t^2}{2},$$

hence

$$y'_x = \frac{y_t}{x'_t} = \tan\frac{\pi t^2}{2},\ y''_{xx} = \frac{(y'_x)'_t}{x'_t} = \frac{\sqrt{\pi}\,t}{a\cos^3\frac{\pi t^2}{2}};$$

whence the curvature

$$K = \frac{|y''|}{[1+(y')^2]^{\frac{3}{2}}} = \frac{\sqrt{\pi}\,t}{a}.$$

6.3.17. Prove that the function $L(x)$, defined in the interval $(0, \infty)$ by the integral

$$L(x) = \int_1^x \frac{dt}{t},$$

is an inverse of the function e^x.

Solution Let us take the derivative

$$L'(x) = \frac{1}{x}\ (x > 0).$$

Since the derivative is positive, the function $y = L(x)$ increases and, hence, has an inverse function

$$x = L^{-1}(y).$$

The derivative of this inverse function is equal to

$$\frac{dx}{dy} = \frac{1}{L'(x)} = x,$$

whence it follows (see Problem 3.1.10) that

$$x = Ce^y.$$

To find C, substitute $x = 1$. Since

$$L(1) = 0, ie, y|_{x=1} = 0,$$

then $1 = Ce^0 = C$, which proves our assertion :

$$x = L^{-1}(y) = e^y.$$

6.3.18. Given the graph of the function $y = f(x)$ (Fig. 62), find the shape of the graph of the antiderivative $I = \int_0^x f(t)\,dt$.

Solution On the interval $[0, a]$ the given function is positive consequently, the antiderivative increases. On the interval $\left[0, \frac{a}{2}\right]$ the derivative of the given function is positive; hence, the curve $I = I(x)$ is concave. On the interval $\left[\frac{a}{2}, a\right]$ the derivative of the given function is negative; consequently, the curve $I = I(x)$ is convex, the point $x = \frac{a}{2}$ being a point of inflection. The interval $[a, 2a]$ is considered in a similar way. The point $x_1 = 0$ is a point of minimum, since the derivative $I'(x) = f(x)$ changes its sign from minus to plus; the point $x_2 = a$ is a point of maximum, since the sign of the derivative changes from plus to minus.

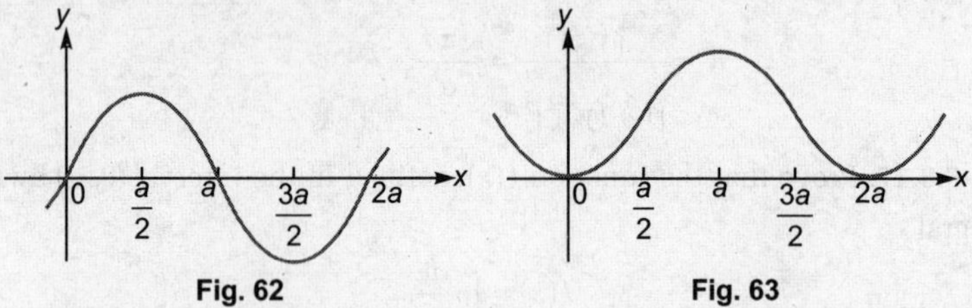

Fig. 62 Fig. 63

The antiderivative $I(x)$ is a periodic function with period $2a$, since the areas lying above and below the x-axis are mutually cancelled over intervals of length $2a$. Taking all this into account, we can sketch the graph of the antiderivative (see Fig. 63).

6.3.19. Find the polynomial $P(x)$ of the least degree that has a maximum equal to 6 at $x = 1$, and a minimum equal to 2 at $x = 3$.

Solution The polynomial is an everywhere-differentiable function. Therefore, the points of extremum can only be roots of the derivative. Furthermore, the derivative of a polynomial is a polynomial. The polynomial of the least degree with roots $x_1 = 1$ and $x_2 = 3$ has the form $a(x-1)(x-3)$. Hence

$$P'(x) = a(x-1)(x-3) = a(x^2 - 4x + 3).$$

Since at the point $x = 1$ there must be $P(1) = 6$, we have

$$P(x) = \int_1^x P'(x)\,dx + 6 = a\int_1^x (x^2 - 4x + 3)\,dx + 6$$

$$= a\left(\frac{x^3}{3} - 2x^2 + 3x - 1\frac{1}{3}\right) + 6.$$

The coefficient a is determined from the condition $P(3) = 2$, whence $a = 3$.

Hence $$P(x) = x^3 - 6x^2 + 9x + 2.$$

6.3.20. Find the polynomial $P(x)$ of the least degree whose graph has three points of inflection : $(-1, -1), (1, 1)$ and a point with abscissa 0 at which the curve is inclined to the axis of abscissas at an angle of 60°.

Solution Since the required function is a polynomial, the abscissas of the points of inflection can only be among the roots of the second derivative.

The polynomial of the least degree with roots −1, 0, 1 has the form $ax(x^2 - 1)$. Consequently,

$$P''(x) = a(x^3 - x).$$

Since at the point $x = 0$ the derivative $P'(0) = \tan 60° = \sqrt{3}$, we have

$$P'(x) = \int_0^x P''(x)\,dx + \sqrt{3} = a\left(\frac{x^4}{4} - \frac{x^2}{2}\right) + \sqrt{3}.$$

Then, since $P(1) = 1$, we get

$$P(x) = \int_1^x P'(x)\,dx + 1 = a\left(\frac{x^5}{20} - \frac{x^3}{6} + \frac{7}{60}\right) + \sqrt{3}(x-1) + 1.$$

The coefficient a is determined from the last remaining condition $P(-1) = -1$, whence $a = \frac{60(\sqrt{3} - 1)}{7}$. Hence,

$$P(x) = \frac{\sqrt{3} - 1}{7}(3x^5 - 10x^3) + x\sqrt{3}.$$

6.3.21. Taking advantage of the mean-value theorem for the definite integral, prove that

(a) $3 < \int_0^1 \sqrt{q + x^2}\,dx < 10$,

(b) $\frac{\pi}{2} < \int_0^{\pi/2} \sqrt{1 + \frac{1}{2}\sin^2 x}\,dx < \frac{\pi}{2}\sqrt{\frac{3}{2}}$,

(c) $\frac{2\pi}{13} < \int_0^{2\pi} \frac{dx}{10 + 3\cos x} < \frac{2\pi}{7}$.

6.3.22. Using the Schwarz-Bunyakovsky inequality, prove that $\int_0^1 \sqrt{1 + x^3}\,dx < \frac{\sqrt{5}}{2}$. Make sure that the application of the mean-value theorem yields a rougher estimate.

6.3.23. Find the derivatives of the following functions :

(a) $F(x) = \int_1^x \ln t\,dt \ (x > 0)$; (b) $F(x) = \int_{2/x}^{x^2} \frac{dt}{t}$.

6.3.24. Find the derivative $\frac{dy}{dx}$ of functions represented parametrically :

(a) $x = \int_2^1 \frac{\ln z}{z}\,dz,\ y = \int_5^{\ln t} e^z\,dz$;

(b) $x = \int_{c^2}^{\sin t} \arcsin z\,dz,\ y = \int_n^{\sqrt{t}} \frac{\sin z^2}{z}\,dz$.

6.3.25. Find the points of extremum of the following functions :

(a) $F(x) = \int_1^x e^{-\frac{t^2}{2}}(1 - t^2)\,dt$;

(b) $F(x) = \int_0^{x^2} \frac{t^2 - 5t + 4}{2 + e^t}\,dt$.

6.4. Changing the Variable in a Definite Integral

If a function $x=\varphi(t)$ satisfies the following conditions :

(1) $\varphi(t)$ is a continuous single-valued function defined in $[\alpha,\beta]$ and has in this interval a continuous derivative $\varphi'(t)$;

(2) with t varying on $[\alpha,\beta]$ the values of the function $x=\varphi(t)$ do not leave the limits of $[a,b]$;

(3) $\varphi(\alpha)=a$ and $\varphi(\beta)=b$,

then the formula for *changing the variable* (or *substitution*) *in the definite integral* is valid for any function $f(x)$ which is continuous on the interval $[a,b]$:

$$\int_a^b f(x)\,dx=\int_\alpha^\beta f[\varphi(t)]\,\varphi'(t)\,dt.$$

Instead of the substitution $x=\varphi(t)$ the inverse substitution $t=\psi(x)$ is frequently used. In this case the limits of integration α and β are determined directly from the equalities $\alpha=\psi(a)$ and $\beta=\psi(b)$. In practice, the substitution is usually performed with the aid of monotonic, continuously differentiable functions. The change in the limits of integration is conveniently expressed in the tabular form :

x	t
a	α
b	β

6.4.1. Compute in integral $\int_{-\sqrt{3}}^{\sqrt{2}}\sqrt{4-x^2}\,dx$.

Solution Make the substitution $x=2\sin t$, assuming that $-\frac{\pi}{3}\le t\le\frac{\pi}{3}$.

The function $x=\varphi(t)=2\sin t$ on the interval $\left[-\frac{\pi}{3},\frac{\pi}{3}\right]$ satisfies all the conditions of the theorem on changing the variable in a definite integral, since it is continuously differentiable, monotonic and

$$\varphi\left(-\frac{\pi}{3}\right)=-\sqrt{3},\varphi\left(\frac{\pi}{3}\right)=\sqrt{3}\cdot$$

And so,

$$x=2\sin t;\quad dx=2\cos t\,dt;\quad \sqrt{4-x^2}=2|\cos t|=2\cos t,$$

since $\cos t>0$ on the interval $\left[-\frac{\pi}{3},\frac{\pi}{3}\right]$.

Thus, $\int_{-\sqrt{3}}^{\sqrt{3}}\sqrt{4-x^2}dx=4\int_{-\pi/3}^{\pi/3}\cos^2 t\,dt=2\int_{-\pi/3}^{\pi/3}(1+\cos 2t)\,dt$

$$=2\left[t+\frac{1}{2}\sin 2t\right]_{-\frac{\pi}{3}}^{\frac{\pi}{3}}=\frac{4\pi}{3}+\sqrt{3}.$$

6.4.2. Compute the integral $\int_2^4 \frac{\sqrt{x^2-4}}{x^4}\,dx$.

Solution Make the substitution

$$x = 2\sec t; \qquad dx = 2\frac{\sin t}{\cos^2 t}\,dt;$$

x	t
2	0
4	$\pi/3$

On the interval $\left[0, \frac{\pi}{3}\right]$ the function $2\sec t$ is monotonic, therefore the substitution is valid.

Hence

$$\int_2^4 \frac{\sqrt{x^2-4}}{x^4}\,dx = \int_0^{\pi/2} \frac{\sqrt{4\sec^2 t-4}}{16\sec^4 t}\cdot 2\frac{\sin t}{\cos^2 t}\,dt$$

$$= \frac{1}{4}\int_0^{\pi/2} \sin^2 t\cos t\,dt = \frac{1}{12}\sin^3 t\Big|_0^{\frac{\pi}{3}} = \frac{\sqrt{3}}{32}.$$

6.4.3. Compute the integrals :

(a) $\int_0^a x^2\sqrt{a^2-x^2}\,dx$; (b) $\int_1^{\sqrt{x}} \frac{dx}{\sqrt{(1+x^2)^3}}$

6.4.4. Compute the integrals :

(a) $\int_0^{\pi/2} \frac{\cos x\,dx}{6-5\sin x+\sin^2 x}$; (b) $\int_0^{\pi/2} \frac{dx}{2+\cos x}$.

Solution (a) Apply the substitution

$$\sin x = t; \qquad \cos x\,dx = dt;$$

x	t
0	0
$\pi/2$	1

The inverse function $x = \arcsin t\left(0 \le x \le \frac{\pi}{2} \text{ for } 0 \le t \le 1\right)$ satisfies all conditions of the theorem on changing the variable. Hence,

$$I = \int_0^{-\pi/2} \frac{\cos x\,dx}{6-5\sin x+\sin^2 x} = \int_0^1 \frac{dt}{6-5t+t^2} = \ln\frac{t-3}{t-2}\Big|_0^1 = \ln\frac{4}{3}.$$

(b) Make the substitution $t = \tan\frac{x}{2}$

$$x = 2\arctan t, \qquad dx = \frac{2dt}{1+t^2},$$

x	t
0	0
$\pi/2$	1

which is valid due to monotonicity of the function $\tan\frac{x}{2}$ on the interval $\left[0, \frac{\pi}{2}\right]$.

$$\int_0^{\pi/2} \frac{2dx}{2+\cos x} = \int_0^1 \frac{1}{2+\dfrac{1-t^2}{1+t^2}} \cdot \frac{2dt}{1+t}$$

$$= 2\int_0^1 \frac{dt}{3+t^2}$$

$$= \frac{2}{\sqrt{3}} \operatorname{arc\,tan} \frac{1}{\sqrt{3}} \Big|_0^1$$

$$= \frac{2}{\sqrt{3}} \left(\operatorname{arc\,tan} \frac{1}{\sqrt{3}} - \operatorname{arc\,tan} 0 \right) = \frac{\pi}{3\sqrt{3}}.$$

6.4.5. Compute the integral

$$\int_0^{\pi/4} \frac{dx}{a^2\cos^2 x + b^2 \sin^2 x} \quad (a > 0, b > 0).$$

Solution Make the substitution

$$\tan x = t, \qquad \frac{dx}{\cos^2 x} = dt,$$

x	t
0	0
$\pi/4$	1

Hence, $$\int_0^{\pi/4} \frac{dx}{a^2\cos^2 x + b^2\sin^2 x} = \int_0^1 \frac{dt}{a^2 + b^2 t^2} = \frac{1}{b^2}\int_0^1 \frac{dt}{\dfrac{a^2}{b^2} + t^2}$$

$$= \frac{1}{b^2} \cdot \frac{b}{a} \operatorname{arc\,tan} \frac{bt}{a}\Big|_0^1 = \frac{1}{ab} \operatorname{arc\,tan} \frac{b}{a}.$$

If $a = b = 1$, then $\frac{1}{ab} \operatorname{arc\,tan} \frac{b}{a} = \operatorname{arc\,tan} 1 = \frac{\pi}{4}$, which exactly coincides with the result of the substitution $a = b = 1$ into the initial integral

$$\int_0^{\pi/4} \frac{dx}{a^2\cos^2 x + b^2\sin^2 x} = \int_0^{\pi/4} dx = \frac{\pi}{4}.$$

6.4.6. Compute the integrals :

(a) $\int_1^{\sqrt{3}} \frac{\sqrt{1+x^2}}{x^2} dx$;

(b) $\int_1^{e^2} \frac{dx}{x\sqrt{1+\ln x}}$;

(c) $\int_3^2 \frac{\sqrt[3]{(x-2)^2}}{3+\sqrt[3]{(x-2)^2}} dx$.

6.4.7. Compute the integral

$$I = \int_0^{\pi} \frac{x \sin x}{1+\cos^2 x} dx.$$

Solution Reduce this integral to the sum of two integrals :

$$I = \int_0^{\pi/2} \frac{x \sin x}{1 + \cos^2 x} dx + \int_{\pi/2}^{\pi} \frac{x \sin x}{1 + \cos^2 x} dx = I_1 + I_2.$$

To the integral

$$I_2 = \int_{\pi/2}^{\pi} \frac{x \sin x}{1 + \cos^2 x} dx$$

apply the substitution

$$x = \pi - t,$$
$$dx = -dt,$$

x	t
$\pi/2$	$\pi/2$
π	0

Then

$$I_2 = -\int_{\pi/2}^{0} \frac{(\pi - t)\sin(\pi - t)}{1 + \cos^2(\pi - t)} dt = \int_0^{\pi/2} \frac{(\pi - t)\sin t}{1 + \cos^2 t} dt$$

$$= \pi \int_0^{\pi/2} \frac{\sin t}{1 + \cos^2 t} dt - \int_0^{\pi/2} \frac{t \sin t}{1 + \cos^2 t} dt.$$

Hence

$$I = I_1 + I_2 = \int_0^{\pi/2} \frac{x \sin x \, dx}{1 + \cos^2 x} + \pi \int_0^{\pi/2} \frac{\sin t \, dt}{1 + \cos^2 t} - \int_0^{\pi/2} \frac{t \sin t \, dt}{1 + \cos^2 t}.$$

Since the first and the third integrals differ only in the notation of the variable of integration, we have

$$I = \pi \int_0^{\pi/2} \frac{\sin t \, dt}{1 + \cos^2 t}.$$

To this integral apply the substitution

$$u = \cos t,$$
$$du = -\sin t \, dt,$$

t	u
0	1
$\pi/2$	0

$$I = -\pi \int_1^0 \frac{du}{1 + u^2} = \pi \int_0^1 \frac{du}{1 + u^2} = \frac{\pi^2}{4}.$$

Note. The indefinite integral $\int \frac{x \sin x}{1 + \cos^2 x} dx$ is not expressed in elementary functions. But the given definite integral, as we have shown, can be computed with the aid of an artificial method.

6.4.8. Evaluate the integral

$$I = \int_0^1 \frac{\ln(1 + x)}{1 + x^2} dx.$$

Solution Make the substitution

$$x = \tan t,$$
$$dx = \frac{dt}{\cos^2 t},$$

x	t
0	0
1	$\pi/4$

Hence $$I = \int_0^{\pi/4} \frac{\ln(1+\tan t)\sec^2 t}{\sec^2 t}\,dt = \int_0^{\pi/4} \ln(1+\tan t)\,dt.$$

Transform the sum $1 + \tan t$:

$$1 + \tan t = \tan\frac{\pi}{4} + \tan t = \frac{\sqrt{2}\sin\left(t + \dfrac{\pi}{4}\right)}{\cos t}.$$

Substituting into the integral, we obtain

$$\begin{aligned} I &= \int_0^{\pi/4} \frac{1}{2}\ln 2\,dt + \int_0^{\pi/4} \ln\sin\left(t + \frac{\pi}{4}\right)dt - \int_0^{\pi/4} \ln\cos t\,dt \\ &= \frac{1}{2}t\ln 2\Big|_0^{\frac{\pi}{4}} + \int_0^{\pi/4} \ln\sin\left(t + \frac{\pi}{4}\right)dt - \int_0^{\pi/4} \ln\cos t\,dt \\ &= \frac{\pi}{8}\ln 2 + \int_0^{\pi/4} \ln\sin\left(t + \frac{\pi}{4}\right)dt - \int_0^{\pi/4} \ln\cos t\,dt. \\ &= \frac{\pi}{8}\ln 2 + I_1 - I_2. \end{aligned}$$

Now let us show that $I_1 = I_2$. To this end apply the substitution

$$t = \frac{\pi}{4} - z,$$

$$dt = -dz,$$

t	z
0	$\pi/4$
$\pi/4$	0

to the integral $I_2 = \int_0^{\pi/4} \ln\cos t\,dt$.

Then $$I_2 = -\int_{\pi/4}^{0} \ln\cos\left(\frac{\pi}{4} - z\right)dz = \int_0^{\pi/4} \ln\sin\left[\frac{\pi}{2} - \left(\frac{\pi}{4} - z\right)\right]dz$$

$$= \int_0^{\pi/4} \ln\sin\left(\frac{\pi}{4} + z\right)dz = I_1,$$

Therefore, $$I = \frac{\pi}{8}\ln 2.$$

Note. That in this problem, as well as in the preceding one, the indefinite integral $\int \frac{\ln(1+x)}{1+x^2}dx$ is not expressed in elementary functions.

6.4.9. Prove that for any given integral with finite limits a and b one can always choose the linear substitution $x = pt + q$ (p, q constants) so as to transform this integral into a new one with limits 0 and 1.

Solution We notice that the substitution $x = pt + q$ satisfies explicitly the conditions of the theorem on changing the variable. Since t must equal zero at $x = a$ and t must equal unity at $x = b$ we have for p and q the following system of equations

$$a = p \cdot 0 + q,$$
$$b = p \cdot 1 + q;$$

whence $p = b - a, q = a$. Hence,

$$\int_a^b f(x)\,dx = (b-a)\int_0^1 f[(b-a)t + a]\,dt.$$

6.4.10. Compute the sum of two integrals

$$\int_{-4}^{-5} e^{(x+5)^2}\,dx + 3\int_{1/3}^{2/3} e^{9\left(x-\frac{2}{3}\right)^2}\,dx.$$

Solution Let us transform each of the given integrals into an integral with limits 0 and 1 (see the preceding problem).

To this end apply the substitution $x = -t - 4$ to the first integral. Then $dx = -dt$ and

$$I_1 = \int_{-4}^{-5} e^{(x+5)^2}\,dx = -\int_0^1 e^{(-t+1)^2}\,dt = -\int_0^1 e^{(t-1)^2}\,dt.$$

Apply the substitution $x = \frac{t}{3} + \frac{1}{3}$ to the second integral. Then $dx = \frac{dt}{3}$ and

$$I_2 = 3\int_{1/3}^{2/3} e^{9\left(x-\frac{2}{3}\right)^2}\,dx = \int_0^1 e^{(t-1)^2}\,dt.$$

Hence, $$I_1 + I_2 = -\int_0^1 e^{(t-1)^2}\,dt + \int_0^1 e^{(t-1)^2}\,dt = 0.$$

Note. The neither of the integrals $\int e^{(x+5)^2}\,dx$ and $\int e^{9\left(x-\frac{2}{3}\right)^2}\,dx$ is evaluated separately in elementary functions.

6.4.11. Prove that the integral

$$\int_0^{\pi} \frac{\sin 2kx}{\sin x}\,dx$$

equals zero if k an integer.

Solution Make the substitution

$$x = \pi - t,\qquad dx = -dt,$$

x	t
0	π
π	0

Then at k an integral number we get :

$$\int_0^{\pi} \frac{\sin 2kx}{\sin x}\,dx = -\int_{\pi}^{0} \frac{\sin 2k(\pi - t)}{\sin(\pi - t)}\,dt = -\int_0^{\pi} \frac{\sin 2kt}{\sin t}\,dt.$$

Since the definite integral does not depend on notation of the variable of integration, we have

$$I = -I, \quad \text{whence} \quad I = 0.$$

6.4.12. Compute the integral

$$\int_{1/2}^{\sqrt{3}/2} \frac{dx}{x\sqrt{1-x^2}}.$$

Solution Apply the substitution $x = \sin t$ (the given function is not monotonic), $dx = \cos t\,dt$. The new limits of integration t_1 and t_2 are found from the equations $\frac{1}{2} = \sin t$; $\frac{\sqrt{3}}{2} = \sin t$. We may put $t_1 = \frac{\pi}{6}$ and $t_2 = \frac{\pi}{3}$, but other values may also be chosen, for instance, $t_1 = \frac{5\pi}{6}$ and $t_2 = \frac{2\pi}{3}$.

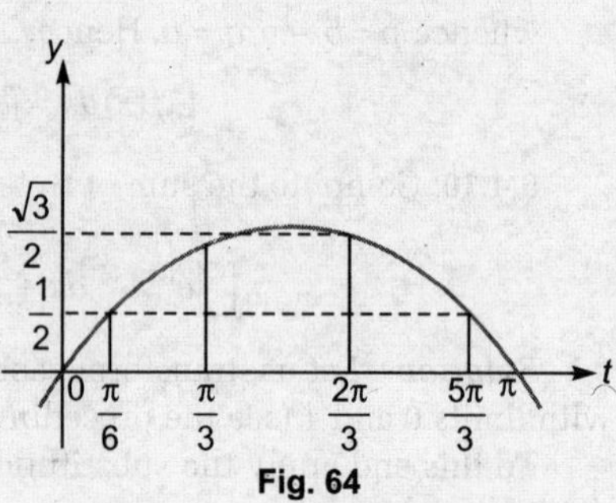

Fig. 64

In both cases the variable $x = \sin t$ runs throughout the entire interval $\left[\frac{1}{2}, \frac{\sqrt{3}}{2}\right]$ (see Fig. 64), the function $\sin t$ being monotonic both on $\left[\frac{\pi}{6}, \frac{\pi}{3}\right]$ and $\left[\frac{2\pi}{3}, \frac{5\pi}{6}\right]$.

Let us show that the result to the integrations will coincide. Indeed,

$$\int_{1/2}^{\sqrt{3}/2} \frac{dx}{x\sqrt{1-x^2}} = \int_{\pi/6}^{\pi/3} \frac{\cos t\,dt}{\sin t \cos t} = \int_{\pi/6}^{\pi/3} \frac{dt}{\sin t} = \ln\left|\tan\frac{t}{2}\right|_{\frac{\pi}{6}}^{\frac{\pi}{3}}$$

$$= \ln\tan\frac{\pi}{6} - \ln\tan\frac{\pi}{12} = \ln\frac{2+\sqrt{3}}{\sqrt{3}}.$$

On the other hand, taking into consideration that $\cos t$ is negative on the interval $\left[\frac{2\pi}{3}; \frac{5\pi}{6}\right]$, we obtain

$$\int_{1/2}^{\sqrt{3}/2} \frac{dx}{x\sqrt{1-x^2}} = \int_{5\pi/6}^{2\pi/3} \frac{\cos t\,dt}{\sin t\,(-\cos t)} = \int_{2\pi/3}^{5\pi/6} \frac{dt}{\sin t}$$

$$= \ln\left|\tan\frac{t}{2}\right|_{\frac{2\pi}{3}}^{\frac{5\pi}{6}} = \ln\frac{\tan\frac{5\pi}{12}}{\tan\frac{\pi}{3}} = \ln\frac{2+\sqrt{3}}{\sqrt{3}}.$$

Note. Do not take $t_1 = \frac{5\pi}{6}$, $t_2 = \frac{\pi}{3}$, since, with t varying on the interval $\left[\frac{\pi}{3}, \frac{5\pi}{6}\right]$, the values of the function $x = \sin t$ lie beyond the limits of the interval $\left[\frac{1}{2}, \frac{\sqrt{3}}{2}\right]$.

6.4.13. Prove that the function $L(x)$ defined on the interval $(0, \infty)$ by the integral $L(x) = \int_1^x \frac{dt}{t}$ possesses the following properties :

$$L(x_1 x_2) = L(x_1) + L(x_2),$$
$$L\left(\frac{x_1}{x_2}\right) = L(x_1) - L(x_2).$$

Solution By the additivity property

$$L(x_1 x_2) = \int_1^{x_1 x_2} \frac{dt}{t} = \int_1^{x_1} \frac{dt}{t} + \int_{x_1}^{x_1 x_2} \frac{dt}{t}.$$

Let us change the variable in the second integral

$$t = x_1 z, \qquad dt = x_1 dz,$$

t	z
x_1	1
$x_1 x_2$	x_2

Then $$L(x_1 x_2) = \int_1^{x_1} \frac{dt}{t} + \int_1^{x_2} \frac{dz}{z} = L(x_1) + L(x_2).$$

Putting here $x_1 x_2 = x_3; x_2 = \frac{x_3}{x_1}$, we obtain

$$L(x_3) = L(x_1) + L\left(\frac{x_3}{x_1}\right), ie, L\left(\frac{x_3}{x_1}\right) = L(x_3) - L(x_1).$$

It is also easy to obtain the other corollary $L\left(x^{\frac{m}{n}}\right) = \frac{m}{n} L(x)$ for any integral m and n.

Indeed, for positive m and n this follows from the relations

$$L\left(x^{\frac{m}{n}}\right) = mL\left(x^{\frac{1}{n}}\right), L(x) = nL\left(x^{\frac{1}{n}}\right),$$

and for a negative exponent, from

$$L(1) = 0, L(x^{-1}) = L\left(\frac{1}{x}\right) - L(1) - L(x) = -L(x).$$

Now, taking advantage of the continuity of the integral as a function of the upper limit, we get the general property $L(x^a) = aL(x)$.

Note. As is known, $L(x) = \ln x$. Here we have obtained the principal properties of the logarithm proceeding only from its determination with the aid of the integral.

6.4.14. Transform the integral $\int_0^3 (x-2)^2 dx$ by the substitution $(x-2)^2 = t$.

Solution A formal application of the substitution throughout the interval $[0, 3]$ would lead to the wrong result, since the inverse function $x = \varphi(t)$ is double-valued; $x = 2 \pm \sqrt{t}$, *ie*, the function x has two branches : $x_1 = 2 - \sqrt{t}$; $x_2 = 2 + \sqrt{t}$. The former branch cannot attain values $x > 2$, the latter values $x < 2$. To obtain a correct result we have to break up the given integral in the following way :

$$\int_0^3 (x-2)^2 dx = \int_0^2 (x-2)^2 dx + \int_2^3 (x-2)^3 dx,$$

and to put $x = 2 - \sqrt{t}$ in the first integral, and $x = 2 + \sqrt{t}$ in the second. Then we get

$$I_1 = \int_0^2 (x-2)^2 dx = -\int_4^0 t\,\frac{dt}{2\sqrt{t}} = \frac{1}{2}\int_0^4 \sqrt{t}\,dt = \frac{8}{3},$$

$$I_2 = \int_2^3 (x-2)^2 dx = \int_0^1 t\,\frac{dt}{2\sqrt{t}} = \frac{1}{2}\int_0^1 \sqrt{t}\,dt = \frac{1}{3}.$$

Hence, $I = \frac{8}{3} + \frac{1}{3} = 3$, which is a correct result. It can be was easily verified by directly computing the initial integral :

$$\int_0^3 (x-2)^2 dx = \left.\frac{(x-2)^3}{3}\right|_0^3 = \frac{1}{3} + \frac{8}{3} = 3.$$

6.4.15. Compute the integrals :

(a) $I = \int_0^1 \frac{dx}{1+\sqrt{x}}$; (b) $I = \int_0^5 \frac{dx}{2x + \sqrt{3x+1}}$;

(c) $I = \int_{\pi/4}^{\pi/3} \frac{dx}{1 - \sin x}$; (d) $I = \int_0^1 \sqrt{2x - x^2}\,dx$;

(e) $I = \int_0^{\pi/4} \frac{\sin x + \cos x}{3 + \sin 2x}\,dx$; (f) $I = \int_0^a x^2 \sqrt{\frac{a-x}{a+x}}\,dx, a > 0$;

(g) $I = \int_0^{2a} \sqrt{2ax - x^2}\,dx$; (h) $I = \int_{-1}^1 \frac{dx}{(1+x^2)^2}$.

6.4.16. Applying a suitable change of the variable, find the following definite integrals :

(a) $\int_0^2 \frac{dx}{\sqrt{x+1} + \sqrt{(x+1)^3}}$; (b) $\int_0^a \frac{dx}{x + \sqrt{a^2 - x^2}}$.

(c) $\int_1^2 \frac{dx}{x(1+x^4)}$; (d) $\int_{\sqrt{(3a^2+b^2)/2}}^{\sqrt{(a^2+b^2)/2}} \frac{x\,dx}{\sqrt{(x^2-a^2)(b^2-x^2)}}$.

6.4.17. Consider the integral $\int_{-2}^2 \frac{dx}{4+x^2}$. It is easy to conclude that it is equal to $\frac{\pi}{4}$. Indeed,

$$\int_{-2}^2 \frac{dx}{4+x^2} = \frac{1}{2}\,\text{arc tan}\left.\frac{x}{2}\right|_{-2}^2 = \frac{1}{2}\left[\frac{\pi}{4} - \left(-\frac{\pi}{4}\right)\right] = \frac{\pi}{4}.$$

On the other hand, making the substitution $x = \frac{1}{t}$, we have

$$dx = -\frac{dt}{t^2}, \quad \begin{array}{c|c} x & t \\ \hline -2 & -1/2 \\ 2 & 1/2 \end{array}$$

$$\int_{-2}^{2} \frac{dx}{4+x^2} = -\int_{-1/2}^{1/2} \frac{dt}{t^2\left(4+\frac{1}{t^2}\right)} = -\int_{-1/2}^{+1/2} \frac{dt}{4t^2+1}$$

$$= \frac{1}{2}\text{arc tan } 2t \Big|_{-\frac{1}{2}}^{\frac{1}{2}} = -\frac{\pi}{4}.$$

This result is obviously wrong, since the integrand $\frac{1}{4+x^2} > 0$, and, consequently, the definite integral of this function cannot be equal to a negative number $-\frac{\pi}{4}$. Find the mistake.

6.4.18. Consider the integral $I = \int_0^{2\pi} \frac{dx}{5-2\cos x}$. Making the substitution $\tan\frac{x}{2} = t$ we have

$$\int_0^{2\pi} \frac{dx}{5-2\cos x} = \int_0^0 \frac{2\,dt}{(1+t^2)\left(5-2\frac{1-t^2}{1`+t^2}\right)} = 0.$$

The result is obviously wrong, since the integrand is positive, and, consequently, the integral of this function cannot be equal to zero. Find the mistake.

6.4.19. Make sure that a formal change of the variable $t = x^{\frac{2}{5}}$ leads to the wrong result in the integral $\int_{-2}^{2} \sqrt[5]{x^2}\,dx$. F ind the mistake and explain it.

6.4.20. Is it possible to make the substitution $x = \sec t$ in the integral $I = \int_0^1 \sqrt{x^2+1}\,dx$?

6.4.21. Given the integral $\int_0^1 \sqrt{1-x^2}\,dx$. Made the substitution $x = \sin t$. It is possible to take the numbers π and $\pi/2$ as the limits for t ?

6.4.22. Prove the equality

$$\int_{-a}^{a} f(x)\,dx = \int_0^a [f(x) + f(-x)]\,dx$$

for any continuous function $f(x)$.

6.4.23. Transform the definite integral $\int_0^{2\pi} f(x)\cos x\,dx$ by the substitution $\sin x = t$.

6.5. Simplification of Integrals Based on the Properties of Symmetry of Integrands

1. If the function $f(x)$ is even on $[-a, a]$, then

$$\int_{-a}^{a} f(x)\,dx = 2\int_{0}^{a} f(x)\,dx.$$

2. If the function $f(x)$ is odd on $[-a, a]$, then

$$\int_{-a}^{a} f(x)\,dx = 0.$$

3. If the function $f(x)$ is periodic with period T, then

$$\int_{a}^{b} f(x)\,dx = \int_{a+nT}^{b+nT} f(x)\,dx,$$

when n is an integer.

6.5.1. Compute the integral $\int_{-1}^{1} |x|\,dx$.

Solution Since, the integrand $f(x) = |x|$ is an even function, we have

$$\int_{-1}^{1} |x|\,dx = 2\int_{0}^{1} |x|\,dx = 2\int_{0}^{1} x\,dx = x^2\,\Big|_0^1 = 1.$$

6.5.2. Compute the integral

$$\int_{-7}^{7} \frac{x^4 \sin x}{x^6 + 2}\,dx.$$

Solution Since, the integrand is odd, we conclude at once that the integral equals zero.

6.5.3. Evaluate the integral

(a) $\int_{-\pi}^{\pi} f(x)\cos nx\,dx$;

(b) $\int_{-\pi}^{\pi} f(x)\sin nx\,dx$,

if : (1) $f(x)$ is an even function; (2) $f(x)$ is an odd function.

6.5.4. Calculate the integral $\int_{-5}^{5} \frac{x^5 \sin^2 x}{x^4 + 2x^2 + 1}\,dx$.

6.5.5. Compute the integral $\int_{\pi}^{\frac{5}{4}\pi} \frac{\sin 2x}{\cos^4 x + \sin^4 x}\,dx$.

Solution The integrand is a periodic function with period π, since,

$$f(x+\pi) = \frac{\sin 2(x+\pi)}{\cos^4(x+\pi) + \sin^4(x+\pi)} = \frac{\sin 2x}{\cos^4 x + \sin^4 x} = f(x).$$

Therefore it is possible to subtract the number π from the upper and lower limits :

$$\int_{\pi}^{\frac{5}{4}\pi} \frac{\sin 2x\,dx}{\cos^4 x + \sin^4 x} = \int_{0}^{\frac{\pi}{4}} \frac{\sin 2x\,dx}{\cos^4 x + \sin^4 x} = 2\int_{0}^{\frac{\pi}{4}} \frac{\tan x\,dx}{\cos^2 x\,(1 + \tan^4 x)}.$$

Make the substitution

$$t = \tan x, \qquad dt = \frac{dx}{\cos^2 x},$$

x	t
0	0
$\pi/4$	1

$$2\int_0^{\pi/4} \frac{\tan x\, dx}{\cos^2 x\,(1+\tan^4 x)} = \int_0^1 \frac{2t\, dt}{1+t^4} = \text{arc}\tan t^2 \Big|_0^1 = \frac{\pi}{4}.$$

6.5.6. Prove the equality

$$\int_{-0}^{a} \cos x f(x^2)\, dx = 2\int_0^a \cos x f(x^2)\, dx.$$

Solution It is sufficient to show that the integrand is even :

$$\cos(-x)\, f[(-x)^2] = \cos x f(x^2).$$

6.5.7. Compute the integral

$$\int_{-\sqrt{2}}^{\sqrt{2}} \frac{2x^7+3x^6-10x^5-7x^3-12x^2+x+1}{x^2+2}\, dx.$$

Solution $\displaystyle\int_{-\sqrt{2}}^{\sqrt{2}} \frac{2x^7+3x^6-10x^5-7x^3-12x^2+x+1}{x^2+2}\, dx.$

$$= \int_{-\sqrt{2}}^{\sqrt{2}} \frac{2x^7-10x^5-7x^3+x}{x^2+2}\, dx + \int_{-\sqrt{2}}^{\sqrt{2}} \frac{3x^2(x^4-4)+1}{x^2+2}\, dx$$

$$= 0 + 2\int_0^{\sqrt{2}} \left[3(x^4-2x^2) + \frac{1}{x^2+1}\right] dx$$

$$= \frac{6}{5}x^5 - 4x^3 + \frac{2}{\sqrt{2}} + \text{arc}\tan\frac{x}{\sqrt{2}}\Bigg|_0^{\sqrt{2}} = -\frac{16}{5}\sqrt{2} + \frac{\pi}{2\sqrt{2}}.$$

In calculating we expanded the given integral into the sum of two integrals so as to obtain an odd integrand in the first integral and an even integrand in the second.

6.5.8. Compute the integral

$$\int_{-1/2}^{1/2} \cos x \ln\frac{1+x}{1-x}\, dx.$$

Solution The function $f(x) = \cos x$ is even. Let us prove that the function $\phi(x) = \ln\dfrac{1+x}{1-x}$ is odd :

$$\phi(-x) = \ln\frac{1-x}{1+x} = \ln\left(\frac{1+x}{1-x}\right)^{-1} = -\ln\frac{1+x}{1-x} = -\phi(x).$$

Thus, the integrand is the product of an even function by an odd one, *ie*, an odd function, therefore

$$\int_{-1/2}^{1/2} \cos x \ln\frac{1+x}{1-x}\, dx = 0.$$

6.5.9. Prove that validity of the following equalities :

(a) $\int_{-\frac{\pi}{8}}^{\frac{\pi}{8}} x^8 \sin^9 x\, dx = 0;$ (b) $\int_{-\frac{1}{2}}^{\frac{1}{2}} e^{\cos x}\, dx = 2\int_0^{1/2} e^{\cos x}\, dx;$

(c) $\int_{-\pi}^{\pi} \sin mx \cos nx\, dx = 0$ (m and n natural numbers);

(d) $\int_{-a}^{a} \sin x f(\cos x)\, dx = 0.$

6.5.10. Prove that the equality

$$\int_a^h f(x)dx = \int_a^b f(a+b-x)\, dx.$$

Solution In the right-hand integral make the substitution

$$x = a + b - t, \qquad dx = -dt,$$

x	t
a	b
b	a

Then we obtain

$$\int_a^b f(a+b-x)\, dx = -\int_b^a f(t)\, dt = \int_a^b f(t)\, dt = \int_a^b f(x)\, dx.$$

Note. The relation established between the integrals can be explained geometrically.

The graph of the function $f(x)$, considered on the interval $[a, b]$, is symmetrical to that of the function $f(a+b-x)$, considered on the same interval, about the straight line $x = \frac{a+b}{2}$. Indeed, if the point A lies on the x-axis and has the abscissa x, then the point A', which is symmetrical to it about the indicated straight line, has the abscissa $x' = a + b - x$. Therefore, $f(a+b-x') = f[a+b-(a+b-x)] = f(x)$. But symmetrical figures have equal areas which are expressed by definite integrals. And so, the proved equality is an equality of areas of two symmetrical curvilinear trapezoids.

6.5.11. Prove that the equality

$$\int_0^t f(x)\, g(t-x)\, dx = \int_0^t g(x)\, f(t-x)\, dx.$$

Solution Apply the substitution $t - x = z$ in the right-hand integral; then we have

$$-\int_t^0 g(t-z)\, f(z)\, dz = \int_0^t f(z)\, g(t-z)\, dz.$$

6.5.12. Prove that the equality $\int_0^{\pi/2} \sin^m x\, dx = \int_0^{\pi/2} \cos^m x\, dx$ and apply the obtained result in computing the following integrals :

$$\int_0^{\pi/2} \cos^2 x\, dx \quad \text{and} \quad \int_0^{\pi/2} \sin^2 x\, dx.$$

Solution On the basis of Problem 6.5.10 we have

$$\int_0^{\pi/2} \sin^m x\,dx = \int_0^{\pi/2} \sin^m\left(\frac{\pi}{2} - x\right) dx = \int_0^{\pi/2} \cos^m x\,dx.$$

Hence, in particular,

$$I = \int_0^{\pi/2} \sin^2 x\,dx = \int_0^{\pi/2} \cos^2 x\,dx;$$

add these integrals :

$$2I = \int_0^{\pi/2} (\sin^2 x + \cos^2 x)\,dx = \int_0^{\pi/2} dx = \frac{\pi}{2};$$

hence $\quad I = \frac{\pi}{4}.$

6.5.13. Prove the equality

$$\int_0^{\pi} f(\sin x)\,dx = 2\int_0^{\pi/2} f(\sin x)\,dx.$$

Solution Since,

$$\int_0^{\pi} f(\sin x)\,dx = \int_0^{\pi/2} f(\sin x)\,dx + \int_{\pi/2}^{\pi} f(\sin x)\,dx,$$

it is sufficient to prove that

$$\int_{\pi/2}^{\pi} f(\sin x)\,dx = \int_0^{\pi 2} f(\sin x)\,dx.$$

In the left integral make the substitution

$$x = \pi - t, \quad dx = -dt,$$

x	t
$\pi/2$	$\pi/2$
π	0

Then

$$\int_{\pi/2}^{\pi} f(\sin x)\,dx = -\int_{\pi/2}^{0} f[\sin(\pi - t)]\,dt$$

$$= \int_0^{\pi/2} f(\sin t)\,dt = \int_0^{\pi/2} f(\sin x)\,dx.$$

6.5.14. Prove that equality

$$\int_0^{\pi} xf(\sin x)\,dx = \frac{\pi}{2}\int_0^{\pi} f(\sin x)\,dx.$$

Solution In the left integral make the substitution

$$x = \pi - t, \quad dx = -dt,$$

x	t
0	π
π	0

Then we obtain

$$\int_0^{\pi} xf(\sin x)\,dx = -\int_{\pi}^{0} (\pi - t)\,f[\sin(\pi - t)]\,dt$$

$$= \int_0^{\pi} \pi f(\sin t)\,dt - \int_0^{\pi} t\,f(\sin t)\,dt.$$

Whence

$$2\int_0^{\pi} xf(\sin x)\,dx = \pi\int_0^{\pi} f(\sin x)\,dx,$$

which is equivalent to the given equality.

6.5.15. Using the equality

$$\frac{\sin\left(n+\frac{1}{2}\right)x}{2\sin\frac{\pi}{2}} = \frac{1}{2} + \cos x + \cos 2x + \ldots + \cos nx,$$

prove that

$$\int_0^{\pi} \frac{\sin\left(n+\frac{1}{2}\right)x}{\sin\frac{x}{2}}\,dx = \pi.$$

6.5.16. Prove that if $\phi(x) = \frac{1}{2}a_0 + a_1 \cos x + b_1 \sin x + a_2 \cos 2x + b_2 \sin 2x + \ldots + a_n \cos nx + b_n \sin nx$, then

(a) $\int_0^{2\pi} \phi(x)\,dx = \pi a_0$;

(b) $\int_0^{2\pi} \phi(x) \cos kx\,dx = \pi a_k$,

(c) $\int_0^{2\pi} \phi(x) \sin kx\,dx = \pi b_k$ $(k = 1, 2, \ldots, n)$.

6.6. Integration by Parts. Reduction Formulas

It u and v are functions of x have continuous derivatives, then

$$\int_a^b u(x)\,v'(x)\,dx = u(x)\,v(x)\big|_a^b - \int_a^b v(x)\,u'(x)\,dx$$

or more briefly,

$$\int_a^b u\,dv = uv\big|_a^b - \int_a^b v\,du.$$

6.6.1. Compute the integral $\int_0^1 xe^x\,dx$.

Solution Let us put

$$x = u, \qquad e^x\,dx = dv;$$
$$du = dx; \qquad v = e^x,$$

which is quite legitimate, since the functions $u = x$ and $v = e^x$ are continuous and have continuous derivatives on the interval $[0, 1]$.

Using the formula for integration by parts we obtain.

$$\int_0^1 xe^x\,dx = xe^x\Big|_0^1 - \int_0^1 e^x dx = e - e^x\big|_0^1 = 1.$$

6.6.2. Compute the integral $I = \int_0^{\pi/b} e^{ax} \sin bx\,dx$.

Solution Let us put

$$u = \sin bx, \qquad dv = e^{ax}\,dx;$$
$$du = b\cos bx\,dx, \quad v = \frac{1}{a}e^{ax}.$$

Since the functions $u = \sin bx$, $v = \frac{1}{a} e^{ax}$ together with their derivatives are continuous on the interval $[0, \pi]$, the formula for integration by parts is applicable :

$$I = \frac{1}{a} e^{ax} \sin bx \Big|_0^{\pi/b} - \frac{b}{a} \int_0^{\pi/b} e^{ax} \cos bx \, dx$$

$$= -\frac{b}{a} \int_0^{\pi/b} e^{ax} \cos bx \, dx = -\frac{b}{a} I_1.$$

Now let us integrate by parts the integral I_1. Put

$$u = \cos bx, \qquad dv = e^{ax} \, dx,$$

$$du = -b \sin bx \, dx, \qquad v = \frac{1}{a} e^{ax}.$$

Then

$$I = -\frac{b}{a} \left(\frac{1}{a} e^{ax} \cos bx \Big|_0^{\pi/b} + \frac{b}{a} \int_0^{\pi/b} e^{ax} \sin bx \, dx \right)$$

$$= -\frac{b}{a} \left(-\frac{e^{\frac{a\pi}{b}}}{a} - \frac{1}{a} \right) - \frac{b^2}{a^2} I = \frac{b\left(e^{\frac{a\pi}{b}} + 1\right)}{a^2} - \frac{b^2}{a^2} I.$$

Hence $\frac{a^2 + b^2}{a^2} I = \frac{b\,(e^{\frac{a\pi}{b}} + 1)}{a^2}$, $I = \frac{b(e^{\frac{a\pi}{b}} + 1)}{a^2 + b^2}$.

In particular, at $a = b = 1$ we get

$$\int_0^{\pi} e^x \sin x \, dx = \frac{1}{2} (e^{\pi} + 1).$$

6.6.3. Compute the integral $\int_1^e \ln^3 x \, dx$.

6.6.4. Compute the integral $\int_0^{\pi^2/4} \sin \sqrt{x} \, dx$.

Solution First make the substitution

$$\sqrt{x} = t, \quad x = t^2, \quad dx = 2t \, dt,$$

x	t
0	0
$\pi^2/4$	$\pi/2$

Whence

$$\int_0^{\pi^2/4} \sin \sqrt{x} \, dx = 2 \int_0^{\pi/2} t \sin t \, dt.$$

Integrate by parts the latter integral.
Put

$$t = u; \qquad \sin t \, dt = dv;$$

$$du = dt; \qquad v = -\cos t.$$

Then $2\int_0^{\pi/2} t \sin t \, dt = 2\left[-t \cos t \,|_2^{\pi/2} + \int_0^{\pi/2} \cos t \, dt\right] = 2 \sin t \,|_0^{\pi/2} = 2.$

6.6.5. Compute the integral $I = \int_0^1 \frac{\text{arc sin } x}{\sqrt{1+x}} dx.$

6.6.6. Compute the integral $\int_0^{\pi/2} x^2 \sin x \, dx.$

6.6.7. Compute the integral $I_n = \int_0^a (a^2 - x^2)^n \, dx$, where n is a natural number.

Solution The integral can be computed by expanding the integrand $(a^2 - x^2)^n$ according to the formula of the Newton binomial, but it involves cumbersome calculations. It is simpler to deduce a formula for reducing the integral I_n to the integral I_{n-1}. To this end let us expand the integral I_n in the following way :

$$I_n = \int_0^a (a^2 - x^2)^{n-1} (a^2 - x^2) \, dx = a^2 I_{n-1} - \int_0^a x(a^2 - x^2)^{n-1} \, x \, dx$$

and integrate the latter integral by parts :

$$u = x; \qquad (a^2 - x^2)^{n-1} \, x \, dx = dv,$$

$$du = dx; \qquad v = -\frac{1}{2n}(a^2 - x^2)^n \; (n \neq 0).$$

We obtain

$$I_n = a^2 I_{n-1} + \frac{1}{2n} x \, (a^2 - x^2)^n \Big|_0^a - \frac{1}{2n}\int_0^a (a^2 - x^2)^n \, dx$$

$$= a^2 \, I_{n-1} - \frac{1}{2n} I_n.$$

Whence $\qquad I_n = a^2 \dfrac{2n}{2n+1} I_{n-1}.$

This formula is valid at any real n other than 0 and $-\frac{1}{2}$.

In particular, at natural n, taking into account that

$$I_0 = \int_0^a dx = a,$$

we get

$$I_n = a^{2n+1} \frac{2n\,(2n-2)\,(2n-4)\ldots 6 \cdot 4 \cdot 2}{(2n+1)\,(2n-1)\,(2n-3)\ldots 5 \cdot 3}$$

$$= a^{2n+1} \frac{(2n)!!}{(2n+1)!!},$$

where

$$(2n)!! = 2 \cdot 4 \cdot 4 \ldots (2n),$$

$$(2n+1)!! = 1 \cdot 3 \cdot 5 \ldots (2n+1).$$

6.6.8. Using the result of the preceding problem obtain the following formula :

$$1-\frac{C_n^1}{3}+\frac{C_n^2}{5}-\frac{C_n^3}{7}+\ldots+(-1)^n\frac{C_n^n}{2n+1}=\frac{(2n)!!}{(2n+1)!!},$$

where C_n^k are binomial coefficients.

Solution Consider the integral

$$I_n=\int_0^1(1-x^2)^n dx=\frac{(2n)!!}{(2n+1)!!}.$$

Expanding the integrand by the formula of the Newton binormial and integrating within the limits from 0 to 1, we get :

$$I_n=\int_0^1(1-x^2)^n\,dx$$

$$=\int_0^1(1-C_n^1x^2+C_n^2x^4-C_n^3x^6+\ldots+(-1)^n\,C_n^x\,x^{2n})\,dx$$

$$=\left[x-\frac{C_n^1x^3}{3}+\frac{C_n^2x^5}{5}-\frac{C_n^2x^7}{7}+\ldots+\frac{(-1)^n\,x^{2n+1}}{2n+1}\right]_0^1$$

$$=1-\frac{C_n^1}{3}+\frac{C_n^2}{5}-\frac{C_n^2}{7}+\ldots+\frac{(-1)^n}{2n+1},$$

which completes the proof.

6.6.9. Compute the integral

$H_m=\int_0^{\pi/2}\sin^m x\,dx=\int_0^{\pi/2}\cos^m x\,dx$ (m a natural number).

Solution The substitution

$$\sin x=t,\quad \cos x\,dx=dt,$$

x	t
0	0
π/2	1

reduces the second intergral to the integral

$$H_m=\int_0^{\pi/2}(1-\sin^2 x)^{\frac{m-1}{2}}\cos x\,dx\int_0^1(1-t^2)^{\frac{m-1}{2}}\,dt,$$

considered in Problem **6.6.7** with $a=1$ and $n=\frac{m-1}{2}$. Therefore, the reduction formula

$$H_m=\frac{m-1}{m}H_{m-2}\ (m\neq 0, m\neq 1)$$

is valid here, since

$$H_m=I_{\frac{m-1}{2}}=\frac{2\cdot\frac{m-1}{2}}{2\cdot\frac{m-1}{2}+1}I_{\frac{m-1}{2}-1}=\frac{m-1}{m}I_{\frac{m-3}{2}}=\frac{m-1}{m}H_{m-2}$$

If m is an odd number, the obtained reduction formula reduces. H_m to

$$H_1=\int_0^{\pi/2}\cos x\,dx=1,$$

therefore, $$H_m = \frac{(m-1)!!}{m!!}.$$

If m is an even number then the reduction formula transforms H_m into

$$H_0 = \int_0^{\pi/2} dx = \frac{\pi}{2},$$

therefore $$H_m = \frac{(m-1)!!}{m!!}\frac{\pi}{2}.$$

6.6.10. Compute the integral

$$I = \int_0^{\pi} x \sin^m x\, dx$$

(m is natural number).

Solution Taking advantage of the results of Problems **6.5.14** and **6.5.13**, we gt

$$I = \int_0^{\pi} x \sin^m x\, dx = \frac{\pi}{2}\int_0^{\pi} \sin^m dx = \pi \int_0^{\pi/2} \sin^m x\, dx,$$

which, taking into consideration the result of Problem **6.6.9**, gives

$$I = \int_0^{\pi} x \sin^m x\, dx = \begin{cases} \dfrac{\pi^2}{2}\cdot\dfrac{(m-1)!!}{m!!} & \text{if } m \text{ is even,} \\ \pi\,\dfrac{(m-1)!!}{m!!} & \text{if } m \text{ is odd,} \end{cases}$$

6.6.11. Compute the integral $I_n = \int_0^1 x^m (\ln x)^n\, dx;\ m > 0, n$ is a natural number.

Solution First of all note that, though the integrand $f(x) = x^m(\ln x)^n$ has no meaning at $x = 0$ it can be made continuous on the interval $[0, 1]$ for any $m > 0$ and $n > 0$, by putting $f(0) = 0$. Indeed,

$$\lim_{x\to+0} x^m (\ln x)^n = \lim_{x\to+0}\left(x^{\frac{m}{n}} \ln x\right)^n = 0$$

by virtue of Problem 3.2.4.

Hence, in particular, it follows that the integral I_n exists at $m > 0, n > 0$. To compute it we integrate by parts, putting.

$$u = (\ln x)^n, \qquad dv = x^m\, dx,$$

$$du = \frac{n(\ln x)^{n-1}}{x}dx, \qquad v = \frac{x^{m+1}}{m+1}.$$

Hence,

$$I_n = \int_0^1 x^m (\ln x)^n\, dx = \left.\frac{x^{m+1}(\ln x)^n}{m+1}\right|_0^1 - \frac{n}{m+1}\int_0^1 x^m (\ln x)^{n-1}\, dx$$

$$= -\frac{n}{m+1} I_{n-1}.$$

The formula obtained reduces I_n to I_{n-1}. In particular, with a natrual n, taking into account that

$$I_0 = \int_0^1 x^m\, dx = \frac{1}{m+1},$$

we get $$I_n = (-1)^n \frac{n!}{(m+1)^{n+1}}.$$

6.6.12. Compute the integral $I_{m,\,n} = \int_0^1 x^m (1-x)^n\, dx$, where m and n are non-negative integers.

Solution Let us put

$$(1-x)^n = u; \qquad x^m\, dx = dv;$$

$$du = -n(1-x)^{n-1}\, dx; \qquad v = \frac{x^{m+1}}{m+1}.$$

Then

$$I_{m,\,n} = \left[\frac{x^{m+1}}{m+1}(1-x)^n\right]_0^1 + \frac{n}{m+1}\int_0^1 x^{m+1}(1-x)^{n-1}\, dx$$

$$= \frac{n}{m+1} I_{m+1,\, n-1}.$$

The obtained formula is valid for all $n > 0$, and $m > -1$. If n is a positive integer, then, applying this formula successively n times, we get

$$I_{m,\,n} = \frac{n}{m+1} I_{m+1,\, n-1} = \frac{n(n-1)}{(m+1)(m+2)} I_{m+2,\, n-2} = \ldots$$

$$= \frac{n(n-1)\ldots[n-(n-1)]}{(m+1)(m+2)\ldots(m+n)} I_{m+n,\, 0}.$$

But $$I_{m+n,\,0} = \int_0^1 x^{m+n}\, dx = \left.\frac{x^{m+n+1}}{m+n+1}\right|_0^1 = \frac{1}{m+n+1}.$$

Hence, $$I_{m,\,n} = \frac{n(n-1)(n-2)\ldots 3\cdot 2\cdot 1}{(m+1)(m+2)\ldots(m+n)(m+n+1)}.$$

The obtained result, with m a non-negative integer, can be written in the form

$$I_{m,\,n} = \frac{m!\,n!}{(m+n+1)!}.$$

6.6.13. Compute the integrals :

(a) $\int_0^1 \text{arc tan}\sqrt{x}\, dx$; (b) $\int_0^1 (x-1)e^{-x}\, dx$;

(c) $\int_{\pi/4}^{\pi/3} \frac{x\, dx}{\sin^2 x}$; (d) $\int_0^1 x\, \text{arc tan}\, x\, dx$;

(e) $\int_0^1 x \ln(1 + x^2)\, dx$;

(f) $\int_0^{\pi/4} \ln(1 + \tan x)\, dx$;

(g) $\int_0^{\pi/2} \sin 2x \arctan(\sin x\, dx$;

(h) $\int_1^{16} \arctan \sqrt{\sqrt{x} - 1}\, dx$.

6.6.14. Prove that

$$\int_0^1 (\arccos x)^n\, dx = n\left(\frac{\pi}{2}\right)^{n-1} - n(n-1)\int_0^1 (\arccos x)^{n-2}\, dx \ (n > 1).$$

6.6.15. Prove that if $f''(x)$ is continuous on $[a, b]$, then the following formula is valid.

$$\int_a^b x f''(x)\, dx = [bf'(b) - f(b)] - [af'(a) - f(a)].$$

6.7. Approximating Definite Integrals

1. Trapezoidal formula. Divide the interval $[a, b]$ into n equal parts by points $x_k = a + kh$, where $h = \frac{b-a}{n}$, $k = 0, 1, \ldots, n$ and apply the formula

$$\int_a^b (x)\, dx \approx \frac{b-a}{n}\left[\frac{1}{2} f(x_0) + f(x_1) + \ldots + f(x_{n-1}) + \frac{1}{2} f(x_n)\right].$$

The error R in this formula is estimated as follows :

$$|R| \le \frac{M_2(b-a)^3}{12n^2}, \text{where } M_2 = \sup_{a \le x \le b} |f''(x)|$$

(assuming that the second derivative is bounded).

2. Simpson's formula. Divide the interval $[a, b]$ into $2n$ equal parts by points $x_k = a + kh$, where $h = \frac{b-a}{2n}$, and apply the formula

$$\int_a^b f(x)\, dx \approx \frac{b-a}{6n}\{f(x_0) + f(x_{2n}) + 4[f(x_1) + f(x_3) + \ldots + f(x_{2n-1})] + 2[f(x_2) + f(x_4) + \ldots + f(x_{2n-2})]\}.$$

Assuming that $f^{iv}(x)$ exists and is bounded, the error in this formula is estimated in the following way :

$$|R| \le \frac{M_4 (b-a)^5}{180\,(2n)^4}, \text{where } M_4 = \sup_{a \le x \le b} |f^{iv}(x)|.$$

6.7.1. Approximate the integral $I = \int_0^1 \frac{dx}{1+x}$ using the trapezoidal formula at $n = 10$.

Solution Let us tabulate the values of the integral, the ordinates $y_i = f(x_i)$ $(i = 0, 1, \ldots, 10)$ being calculated within four decimal places.

x_i	$1 + x_i$	$y_i = \frac{1}{1 + x_i}$	x_i	$1 + x_i$	$y_i = \frac{1}{n + x_i}$
0.0000	1.0000	1.0000	0.6000	1.6000	0.6250
0.1000	1.1000	0.9091	0.7000	1.7000	0.5882
0.2000	1.2000	0.8333	0.8000	1.8000	0.5556
0.3000	1.3000	0.7692	0.9000	1.9000	0.5263
0.4000	1.4000	0.7143	1.0000	2.0000	0.5000
0.5000	1.5000	0.6667			

Using the trapezoidal formula, we obtain

$$I = \int_0^1 \frac{dx}{1+x} \approx \frac{1}{10}\left(\frac{1.0000 + 0.5000}{2} + 0.9091 + 0.8333 + 0.7692 + 0.7143 + 0.6667 + 0.6250 + 0.5882 + 0.5556 + 0.5263\right) = \frac{1}{10} \cdot 6.9377 = 0.69377 \approx 0.6938.$$

Estimate the error in the result obtained. We have $f''(x) = \frac{2}{(1+x)^3} \cdot$ Since $0 \le x \le 1$, then $|f''(x)| \le 2$. Consequently, we take the number 2 as M_2 and estimate the error :

$$|R| \le \frac{2}{12 \times 10^2} = \frac{1}{600} < 0.0017.$$

We calculated the ordinates accurate to four decimal places, and the round-off error does not exceed $\frac{0.00005}{10}(1 + 9 \times 1) = 0.00005$ (more precisely, $\frac{0.00005}{10} \cdot 9 = 0.000045$, since the ordinates y_0 and y_{10} are exact numbers). Thus, the total error due to using the trapezoidal formula and rounding off the ordinates does not exceed 0.0018.

Note that when computing the given integral by the Newton Leibnitz formula we obtain

$$I = \int_0^1 \frac{dx}{1+x} = \ln(1+x)\Big|_0^1 = \ln 2 \approx 0.69315.$$

Thus, the error in the result obtained does not exceed 0.0007, *ie*, we have obtained a result accurate to three decimal places.

6.7.2. Evaluate by Simpson's formula the integral $\int_{0.5}^{1.5} \frac{e^{0.1x}}{x} dx$ accurate to four decimal places.

Solution To give a value of $2n$ which ensures the required accuracy, we find $f^{iv}(x)$. Successively differentiating $f(x) = \dfrac{e^{0.1x}}{x}$, we get $f^{iv}(x) = \dfrac{e^{0.1x}}{x^5}(0.0001x^4 - 0.004x^3 + 0.12x^2 - 2.4x + 24) = \dfrac{P(x)}{x^5}e^{0.1x}$, where $P(x)$ is the polynomial in parentheses. On the interval [0.5, 1.5] the function $\phi(x) = e^{0.1x}$ increases and therefore reaches its greatest value at $x = 1.5$: $\varphi(1.5) = e^{0.15} < 1.2$. The upper estimate of the absolute value of the polynomial $P(x)$ divided by x^5 can be obtained as the sum of moduli of its separate terms. The greatest value of each summand is attained at $x = 0.5$, therefore

$$\left|\frac{P(x)}{x^5}\right| < \frac{0.0001}{x} + \frac{0.004}{x^2} + \frac{0.12}{x^3} + \frac{2.4}{x^4} + \frac{24}{x^5} \le$$

$$\le 0.0002 + 0.016 + 0.96 + 38.4 + 768 < 808.$$

And so, $|f^{iv}(x)| < 1.2 \times 808 < 1000$. Hence, the number 1000 may be taken as M_4.

We have to compute the integral accurate to four decimal places. To ensure such accuracy it is necessary that the sum of errors of the method, operations and final rounding off should not exceed 0.0001. For this purpose we choose a value of $2n$ (which will determine the step of integration h) so that the inequality

$$|R| < \frac{1}{2} \cdot 0.0001 = 5.10^{-5}$$

is satisfied.

Solving the inequality

$$\frac{1^5 \times 1000}{180\,(2n)^4} < 5 \times 10^{-5},$$

we obtain

$$2n > 19.$$

Let us take $2n = 20$; then the step of integration h will be equal to

$$h = \frac{b-a}{2n} = \frac{1}{20} = 0.05.$$

A more accurate calculation shows that at $2n = 20$

$$|R| < 3.5 \times 10^{-5}.$$

If we calculate y_i within five decimal places, *ie*, with an error not exceeding 10^{-5}, then the error of the final rounding off will also be not greater than 10^{-5}. Thus, the total error will be less than $4.5 \times 10^{-5} < 0.0001$.

Now compile a table of values of the function $y = \frac{e^{0.1x}}{x}$ for the values of x from 0.5 to 1.5 with the step $h = 0.05$. The calculations are carried out within five decimal places.

t	x_i	$0.1\,x_i$	$e^{0.1x}$	y_i
0	0.50	0.050	1.05127	2.10254
1	0.55	0.055	1.05654	1.92098
2	0.60	0.060	1.06184	1.76973
3	0.65	0.065	1.06716	1.64178
4	0.70	0.070	1.7251	1.53216
5	0.75	0.075	1.7788	1.43717
6	0.80	0.080	1.08329	1.35411
7	0.85	0.085	1.08872	1.28085
8	0.90	0.090	1.09417	1.21574
9	0.95	0.095	1.09966	1.15754
10	1.00	0.100	1.10517	1.10517
11	1.50	0.105	1.11071	1.05782
12	1.10	0.110	1.11628	1.01480
13	1.15	0.115	1.12187	0.97554
14	1.20	0.120	1.12750	0.93958
15	1.25	0.125	1.13315	0.90652
16	1.30	0.130	1.13883	0.87602
17	1.35	0.135	1.14454	0.84781
18	1.40	0.140	1.15027	0.82162
19	1.45	0.145	1.15604	0.79727
20	1.50	0.150	1.16183	0.77455

For pictorialness sake we use the tabular data to compile the following calculation chart :

i	x_i	y_i		
		at $i = 0$ and $i = 20$	at an odd i	at an even i
0	0.50	2.10254		
1	0.55		1.92098	
2	0.60			1.76973
3	0.65		1.64178	
4	0.70			1.53216
5	0.75		1.43717	

i	x_i	y_i		
		at $i = 0$ and $i = 20$	at an odd i	at an even i
6	0.80			1.35411
7	0.85		1.28085	
8	0.90			1.21574
9	0.95		1.15754	
10	1.00			1.10517
11	1.05		1.05782	
12	1.10			1.01480
13	1.15		0.97554	
14	1.20			0.93958
15	1.25		0.90652	
16	1.30			0.87602
17	1.35		0.84781	
18	1.40			0.82162
19	1.45		0.79727	
20	1.50	0.77455		
	Sums	2.87709	12.02328	10.62893

Using Simpson's formula, we get

$$\int_{0.5}^{1.5} \frac{e^{0.1x}}{x}\, dx \approx \frac{1}{60}(2.87709 + 4 \times 12.02328$$

$$+ 2 \times 10.62893 = \frac{1}{60} \cdot 72.22807 = 1.2038.$$

6.7.3. The river is 26 m wide. The table below shows the successive depths of the river measured across its section at steps of 2 m :

x	0	2	4	6	8	10	12	14	16	18	20	22	24	26
y	0.3	0.9	1.7	2.1	2.8	3.4	3.3	3.0	3.5	2.9	1.7	1.2	0.8	0.6

Here x denotes the distance from one bank and y, the corresponding depth (in metres). Knowing that the mean rate of flow is 1.3 m/sec, determine the flowrate per second Q of the water in the river.

Solution By the trapezoidal formula the area S of the cross-section.

$$S = \int_0^{26} y\, dx \approx 2\left[\frac{1}{2}(0.3 + 0.6) + 0.9 + 1.7 + 2.1 + 2.8 + 3.4\right.$$

$$\left. + 3.3 + 3.0 + 3.5 + 2.9 + 1.7 + 1.2 + 0.8 \right] = 55.5\ (\text{m}^2).$$

Hence, $Q = 55.5 \times 1.3 \approx 72\ (\text{m}^2/\text{sec})$.

It is impossible to estimate the error accurately in this case. Some indirect methods of estimation enable us to indicate approximately the order of the error. The error in S is about 3`m^2, hence, the error in Q is about 4 m^3/sec.

6.7.4. Compute the following integrals :

(a) $\int_{\pi/4}^{\pi/2} \frac{\sin x}{x}\,dx$ accurate to three decimal places, using Simpson's formula;

(b) $\int_0^1 e^{-x^2}\,dx$ accurate to three decimal places, by the trapezoidal formula.

6.7.5. By Simpson's formula, approximate the integral

$$I = \int_{1.05}^{1.36} f(x)\,dx,$$

If the integrand is defined by the following table :

x	1.05	1.10	1.15	1.20	1.25	1.30	1.35
***f*(x)**	2.36	2.50	2.74	3.04	3.46	3.98	4.6

6.8. Additional Problems

6.8.1. Given the function

$$f(x) = \begin{cases} 1 - x & \text{at } 0 \le x \le 1, \\ 0 & \text{at } 1 < x \le 2, \\ (2 - x)^2 & \text{at } 2 < x \le 3. \end{cases}$$

Check directly that the function

$$F(x) = \int_0^x f(t)\,dt$$

is continuous on the interval [0,. 3] and that its derivative at each interior point of this interval exists and is equal to $f(x)$.

6.8.2. Show that the function

$$f(x) = \begin{cases} \dfrac{x \ln x}{1 - x} & \text{at } 0 < x < 1, \\ 0 & \text{at } x = 0 \\ -1 & \text{at } x = 1 \end{cases}$$

is integrable on the interval [0, 1].

6.8.3. Can one assert that if a function is absolutely integrable on the interval $[a, b]$, then it is integrable on this interval ?

6.8.4. A line tangent to the graph of the function $y = f(x)$ at the point $x = a$ forms an angle $\frac{\pi}{3}$ with the axis of abscissas and an angle $\frac{\pi}{4}$ at the point $x = b$.

Evaluate $\int_a^b f''(x)\,dx$, if $f''(x)$ is a continuous function.

6.8.5. Prove that

$$\int_0^x E(x)\,dx = \frac{E(x)\,(E(x)-1)}{2} + E(x)\,[x - E(x)].$$

6.8.6. Given that integral $\int_0^{\pi} \frac{dx}{1+\cos^2 x}\cdot$ Make sure that the functions

$$F_1(x) = \frac{1}{\sqrt{2}} \text{ arc cos } \frac{\sqrt{2}\cos x}{\sqrt{1+\cos^2 x}} \text{ and } F_2(x) = \frac{1}{\sqrt{2}} \text{ arc tan } \frac{\tan x}{\sqrt{2}}$$

are antiderivatives for the itnegrand. Is it possible to use both antiderivatives for computing the definite integral by the Newton Leibnitz formula ? If not, which of the antiderivatives can be used ?

6.8.7. For $f(x)$ find such an antiderivative which attains the given magnitude $y = y_0$ at $x = x_0$ (Cauchy's problem).

6.8.8. At what value of ξ is the equality $\int_a^b e^{2x}\,dx = e^{2\,\xi}\,(b-a)$ fulfilled ? Show aht

$$\xi > \frac{a+b}{2}.$$

6.8.9. Investigate the function defined by the definite integral $F(x) = \int_0^x \sqrt{1-t^4}\,dt$.

6.8.10. Show that the inequalities

$$0.692 \le \int_0^1 x^x\,dx \le 1$$

are valid.

6.8.11. With the aid of the inequality $x \ge \sin x \ge \frac{2}{\pi}x \left(0 \le x \le \frac{\pi}{2}\right)$ show that $1 < \int_0^{\pi/2} \frac{\sin x}{x}\,dx < \frac{\pi}{2}$.

6.8.11. Using the inequality $\sin x \ge x - \frac{x^3}{6}$ $(x \ge 0)$ and the Schwarz Bunyakovsky inequality, show that

$$1.096 < \int_0^{\pi/2} \sqrt{x \sin x}\,dx < 1.111.$$

6.8.13. Assume that integrable functions $p_1(x), p_2(x), p_3(x), p_4(x)$ are given on the interval $[a, b]$, the function $p_1(x)$ is non-negative,and the functions $p_2(x), p_3(x), p_4(x)$ satisfy the inequality

$$p_3(x) \le p_2(x) \le p_4(x).$$

Prove that

$$\int_a^b p_3(x)\, p_1(x)\, dx \le \int_a^b p_2(x)\, p_1(x)\, dx \le \int_a^b p_4(x)\, p_1(x)\, dx.$$

6.8.14. Let the function $f(x)$ be positive on the interval $[a, b]$. Prove that the expression

$$\int_a^b f(x)\, dx \cdot \int_a^b \frac{dx}{f(x)}$$

reaches the least value only if $f(x)$ is constant on this interval.

6.8.15. Prove that

$$\int_0^1 \frac{\arctan x}{x}\, dx = \frac{1}{2}\int_0^{\pi/2} \frac{t}{\sin t}\, dt$$

6.8.16. Prove that one of the antiderivatives of an even function is an odd function, and any antiderivative of an odd function is an even function.

6.8.17. Prove that if $f(x)$ is a continuous periodic function with period T, then the integral $I = \int_a^{a+T} f(x)\, dx$ does not depend on a.

6.8.18. Prove that if $u = u(x)$, $v = v(x)$ and their derivatives through order n are continuous on the interval $[a, b]$, then

$$\int_a^b uv^{(n)} dx = [uv^{(n-1)} - u' v^{(n-2)} + \ldots + (-1)^{n-1} u^{(n-1)} v] \Big|_a^b + (-1)^n \int_a^b u^{(n)} v\, dx.$$

7

Applications of the Definite Integral

7.1. Computing the Limits of Sums with the Aid of Definite Integrals

It is often necessary to compute the limit of a sum when the number of summands increases unlimitedly. In some cases such limits can be found with the aid of the definite integral if it is possible to transform the given sum into an integral sum.

For instance, considering the points $\frac{1}{n}, \frac{2}{n}, \ldots, \frac{\pi}{n}$ as points of division of the interval $[0, 1]$ into n equal parts of length $\Delta x = \frac{1}{n}$, for each continuous function $f(x)$, we have

$$\lim_{n \to \infty} \frac{1}{n}\left[f\left(\frac{1}{n}\right) + f\left(\frac{2}{n}\right) + \ldots + f\left(\frac{n}{n}\right)\right] = \int_0^1 f(x)\, dx.$$

7.1.1. Compute

$$\lim_{n \to \infty} \frac{\pi}{n}\left|\sin\frac{\pi}{n} + \sin\frac{2\pi}{n} + \ldots + \sin\frac{(n-1)\pi}{n}\right|.$$

Solution The numbers in brackets represent the values of the function $f(x) = \sin x$ at the points

$$x_1 = \frac{\pi}{n};\ x_2 = \frac{2\pi}{n};\ \ldots;\ x_{n-1} = \frac{(n-1)\,\pi}{n},$$

subdividing the interval $[0, \pi]$ into n equal parts of length $\Delta x = \frac{\pi}{n}\cdot$

Therefore, if we add the summand $\sin\frac{n\pi}{n} = 0$ to our sum, the later will be the intergral sum for the function $f(x) = \sin x$ on the interval $[0, \pi]$.

By definition, the limit of such an integral sum as $n \to \infty$ is the definite integral of the function $f(x) = \sin x$ from 0 to π :

$$\lim_{n \to \infty} \frac{\pi}{n}\left(\sin\frac{\pi}{n} + \sin\frac{2\pi}{n} + \ldots + \sin\frac{(n-1)\pi}{n} + \sin\frac{n\pi}{n}\right)$$

$$= \int_0^{\pi} \sin x\, dx = -\cos x\,\Big|_0^{\pi} = 2.$$

7.1.2. Compute the limit

$$\lim_{n\to\infty}\left(\frac{1}{\sqrt{4n^2-1}}+\frac{1}{\sqrt{4n^2-2^2}}+\ldots+\frac{1}{\sqrt{4n^2-n^2}}\right).$$

Solution Transform the sum in parentheses in the following way :

$$\frac{1}{\sqrt{4n^2-1}}+\frac{1}{\sqrt{4n^2-2^2}}+\ldots+\frac{1}{\sqrt{4n^2-n^2}}$$

$$=\frac{1}{n}\left(\frac{1}{\sqrt{4-\dfrac{1}{n^2}}}+\frac{1}{\sqrt{4-\left(\dfrac{2}{n}\right)^2}}+\ldots+\frac{1}{\sqrt{4-\left(\dfrac{n}{n}\right)^2}}\right).$$

The obtained sum is the integral sum for the function $f(x)=\dfrac{1}{\sqrt{4-x^2}}$ on the interval [0, 1] subdivided into n equal parts. The limit of this sum as $n\to\infty$ is equal to the definite integral of this function from 0. to 1 :

$$\lim_{n\to\infty}\left(\frac{1}{\sqrt{4n^2-1}}+\frac{1}{\sqrt{4n^2-2^2}}+\ldots+\frac{1}{\sqrt{4n^2-n^2}}\right)$$

$$=\int_0^1\frac{dx}{\sqrt{4-x^2}}=\text{arc sin}\left.\frac{x}{2}\right|_0^1=\frac{\pi}{6}.$$

7.1.3. Compute

$$\lim_{n\to\infty}\frac{3}{n}\left[1+\sqrt{\frac{n}{n+3}}+\sqrt{\frac{n}{n+6}}+\sqrt{\frac{n}{n+9}}+\ldots+\sqrt{\frac{n}{n+3\,(n-1)}}\right].$$

Solution Transform the given expression ib the following way

$$\frac{3}{n}\left[1+\sqrt{\frac{n}{n\;+3}}+\sqrt{\frac{n}{n+6}}+\ldots.+\sqrt{\frac{n}{n+3\,(n-1)}}\right]$$

$$=\frac{3}{n}\left[\sqrt{\frac{1}{1+0}}+\sqrt{\frac{1}{1+\dfrac{3}{n}}}+\sqrt{\frac{1}{1+\dfrac{6}{n}}}+\ldots+\sqrt{\frac{1}{1+\dfrac{3\,(n-1)}{n}}}\right].$$

The obtained sum is the integral sum for the function $f(x)=\sqrt{\dfrac{1}{1+x}}$ on the interval [0, 3] ; therefore, by definition,

$$\lim_{n\to\infty}\frac{3}{n}\left(1+\sqrt{\frac{n}{n+3}}+\sqrt{\frac{n}{n+6}}+\ldots+\sqrt{\frac{n}{n+3\,(n-1)}}\right)$$

$$=\int_0^3\sqrt{\frac{1}{1+x}}\,dx=\int_0^3(1+x)^{-\frac{1}{2}}\,dx=2\left.\sqrt{1+x}\,\right|_0^3=4-2=2.$$

7.1.4. Using the definite integral, compute the following limits :

(a) $\lim_{n\to\infty}\left(\frac{1}{n+1}+\frac{1}{n+2}+\ldots+\frac{1}{n+n}\right)$;

(b) $\lim_{n\to\infty}\frac{1}{n}\left(\sqrt{1+\frac{1}{n}}+\sqrt{1+\frac{2}{n}}+\ldots+\sqrt{1+\frac{n}{n}}\right)$;

(c) $\lim_{n\to\infty}\frac{1+\sqrt[3]{2}+\sqrt[3]{3}+\ldots+\sqrt[3]{n}}{\sqrt[3]{n^4}}$;

(d) $\lim_{n\to\infty}\frac{\pi}{2n}\left(1+\cos\frac{\pi}{2\pi}+\cos\frac{2\pi}{2n}+\ldots+\cos\frac{(n-1)\pi}{2n}\right)$;

(e) $\lim_{n\to\infty} n\left[\frac{1}{(n+1)^2}+\frac{1}{(n+2)^2}+\ldots+\frac{1}{(2n)^2}\right]$;

7.1.5. Compute the limit $A=\lim_{n\to\infty}\frac{\sqrt[n]{n!}}{n}$.

Solution Let us take lograithms

$$\ln A=\lim_{n\to\infty}\frac{\sqrt[n]{n!}}{n}$$

$$=\lim_{n\to\infty}\frac{1}{n}\left[\ln\frac{1}{n}+\ln\frac{2}{n}+\ldots+\ln\frac{n}{n}\right].$$

The expression is brackets is the integral sum for the integral

$$\int_0^1 \ln x\,dx=(x\ln x-x)\Big|_0^1=-1.$$

Consequently, $\ln A=-1$ and $\lim_{n\to\infty}\frac{\sqrt[n]{n!}}{n}=e^{-1}$.

7.2. Finding Average Values of a Function

The average value of $f(x)$ over the interval $[a,b]$ is the number

$$\mu=\frac{1}{b-a}\int_a^b f(x)\,dx.$$

The square root $\left\{\frac{1}{b-a}\int_a^b [f(x)]^2dx\right\}^{\frac{1}{2}}$ of the average value of the square of the function is called the *root mean square* (rms) of the function $f(x)$ over $[a,b]$.

7.2.1. Find the average value μ of the function $f(x)=\sqrt[3]{x}$ over the interval $[0,1]$.

Solution In this case

$$\mu=\frac{1}{b-a}\int_0^1\sqrt[3]{x}\,dx=\left.\frac{3x^{\frac{4}{3}}}{4}\right|_0^1=\frac{3}{4}.$$

7.2.2. Find the average values of this functions :

(a) $f(x) = \sin^2 x$ over $[0, 2\pi]$ (b) $f(x) = \dfrac{1}{e^x + 1}$ over $[0, 2]$.

7.2.3. Determine the average length of all vertical chords of the hyperbola $\dfrac{x^2}{a^2} - \dfrac{y^2}{b^2} = 1$ over the interval $a \le x \le 2a$.

Solution The problem consists in finding the average value of the function $f(x) = 2y = 2\dfrac{b}{a}\sqrt{x^2 - a^2}$ over the interval $[a, 2a]$:

$$\mu = 2\frac{1}{a}\int_a^{2a} \frac{b}{a}\sqrt{x^2 - a^2}\,dx$$

$$= \frac{2b}{a^2}\left[\frac{x}{2}\sqrt{x^2 - a^2} - \frac{a^2}{2}\ln\left(x + \sqrt{x^2 - a^2}\right)\right]_a^{2a} = b\,[2\sqrt{3} - \ln(2 + \sqrt{3})].$$

7.2.4. Find the average ordinate of the sinusoid $y = \sin x$ over the interval $[0, \pi]$.

Solution $\mu = \dfrac{1}{\pi}\displaystyle\int_0^{\pi} \sin x\,dx = -\frac{1}{\pi}\cos x\Big|_0^{\pi} = \frac{2}{\pi} \approx 0.637.$

Rewrite the obtained result in the following way :

$$\mu \cdot \pi = \frac{2}{\pi}\pi = \int_0^{\pi} \sin x\,dx.$$

Using the geometric meaning of the definite integral, we can say that the area of the rectangle with the altitude $\mu = \dfrac{2}{\pi}$ and the base π equals that area of a figure bounded by a half-wave of the sinusoid $y = \sin x, 0 \le x \le \pi$, and by the x-axis.

7.2.5. Find the average length of all positive ordinates of the circle $x^2 + y^2 = 1$.

7.2.6. Show that the average value of the function $f(x)$, continuous on the interval $[a, b]$, is the limit of the arithmetic mean of the values of this function taken over equal intervals of the argument x.

Solution Subdivide the interval $[a, b]$ into n equal parts by the points $x_i = a + i\dfrac{b - a}{n}$ $(i = 0, 1, 2, \ldots, n)$.

From the arithmetic mean of the values of the function $f(x)$ at n points of division $x_0, x_1, \ldots, x_{n-1}$:

$$\mu_n = \frac{f(x_0) + f(x_1) + \ldots + f(x_{n-1})}{n} = \frac{1}{n}\sum_{i=0}^{n-1} f(x_i).$$

This mean may be represented in the following form :

$$\mu_n = \frac{1}{b - a}\sum_{i=0}^{n-1} f(x_i)\,\Delta x_i\,;$$

where

$$\Delta x_i = \frac{b-a}{n}.$$

The latter sum is the integral sum for the function $f(x)$, therefore

$$\lim_{n\to\infty} \mu_n = \frac{1}{b-a} \lim_{n\to\infty} \sum_{i=0}^{n-1} f(x_i)\,\Delta x_i = \frac{1}{b-a}\int_a^b f(x)\,dx = \mu,$$

which completes the solution.

7.2.7. Find the average value of pressure (p_m) varying from 2 to 10 atm if the pressure p and the volume v are related as follows :

$$pv^{\frac{3}{2}} = 160.$$

Solution As p varies from 2. to 10. atm, v traverses the interval $[4\sqrt[3]{4}, 4\sqrt[3]{100}]$; hence,

$$p_m = \frac{1}{4(\sqrt[3]{100}-\sqrt[3]{4})}\int_{4\sqrt[3]{4}}^{4\sqrt[3]{100}} 160^{-\frac{3}{2}}\,dv =$$

$$= \frac{320}{4(\sqrt[3]{100}-\sqrt[3]{4})}\, v^{-\frac{1}{2}}\Bigg|_{4\sqrt[3]{4}}^{4\sqrt[3]{100}} = \frac{40}{\sqrt[3]{20}\,(\sqrt[3]{10}+\sqrt[3]{2})} \approx 4.32 \text{ atm.}$$

7.2.8. In hydraulics there is Bazrin's formula expressing the velocity v of water flowing in a wide rectangular channel as a function of the depth h at which the point under consideration is situated below the open surface,

$$v = v_0 - 20\sqrt{HL}\left(\frac{h}{H}\right)^2,$$

where v_0 is the velocity on the open surface, H is the depth of the channel, L its slope.

Find the average velocity v_m of flow in the cross-section of the channel.

Solution We have

$$v_m = \frac{1}{H}\int_0^H \left[v_0 - 20\sqrt{HL}\left(\frac{h}{H}\right)^2\right] dh = v_0 - \frac{20}{3}\sqrt{HL}.$$

7.2.9. Determine the average value of the electromotive force E_m over one period, *ie*, over the time from $t = 0$ to $t = T$, if electromotive force is computed by the formula

$$E = E_0 \sin\frac{2\pi t}{T}.$$

where T is the duration of the period in seconds, E_0 the amplitude (the maximum value) of the electromotive force corresponding to the value $t = 0.25\,T$. The fraction $\frac{2\pi t}{T}$ is called the *phase*.

Solution $E_m = \frac{E_0}{T}\int_0^T \sin\frac{2\pi t}{T}\,dt = \frac{E_0 T}{T\cdot 2\pi}\left[-\cos\frac{2\pi t}{T}\right]_0^T = 0.$

Thus, the average value of the electromotive force over one period equals zero.

7.2.10. Each of the two vertical poles *OA* and *CD* is equipped with an electric lamp of luminous intensity i fixed at a height h. The distance between the poles is d. Find the average illumination of the straight line *OC* connecting the bases of the poles.

7.2.11. Find the average value of the square of the electromotive force $(E^2)_m$ over the interval from $t = 0$ to $t = \frac{T}{2}$ (see Problem **7.2.9**).

Solution Since

$$E = E_0 \sin\frac{2\pi t}{T},$$

we have

$$(E^2)_m = \frac{2}{T}E_0^2\int_0^{T/2}\sin^2\frac{2\pi t}{T}\,dt = \frac{2}{T}E_0^2\int_0^{T/2}\frac{1-\cos\frac{4\pi t}{T}}{2}\,dt$$

$$= \frac{E_0^2}{T}\left[t - \frac{T}{4\pi}\sin\frac{4\pi t}{T}\right]_0^{\frac{T}{2}} = \frac{E_0^2}{2}$$

7.2.12. If a function $f(x)$ is defined on a infinite interval $[0, \infty)$, then its average value will be

$$\mu = \lim_{b\to\infty}\frac{1}{b}\int_0^b f(x)\,dx,$$

if this limit exists. Find the average power consumption of an alternating current circuit if the current intensity I and voltage u are expressed by the following formulas, respectively :

$$I = I_0\cos(\omega t + \alpha);$$

$$u = \mu_0\cos(\omega t + \alpha + \varphi),$$

where φ is the constant phase shift of the voltage as compared with the current intensity (the parameters ω and α will not enter into the expression for the average power).

Solution The average power consumption

$$\omega_m = \lim_{T\to\infty}\frac{1}{T}\int_0^t I_0\cos(\omega t + \alpha)\,\mu_0\cos(\omega t + \alpha + \varphi)\,dt.$$

Taking into consideration that

$$\cos\alpha\cos\beta = \frac{1}{2}[\cos(\alpha+\beta) + \cos(\alpha-\beta)],$$

we will get

$$\omega_m = \lim_{T\to\infty f}\frac{I_0\mu_0}{2T}\int_0^T[\cos(2\omega t + 2\alpha + \varphi) + \cos\varphi]\,dt$$

$$= \lim_{T\to\infty}\left\{\frac{I_0\mu_0}{4\omega}\cdot\frac{\sin(2\omega T + 2\alpha + \varphi) - \sin(2\alpha + \varphi)}{T} + \frac{I_0\mu_0}{2}\cos\varphi\right\}$$

$$= \frac{I_0\mu_0}{2}\cos\varphi.$$

Hence, it is clear why so much importance is attached to the quantity $\cos\varphi$ in electrical engineering.

7.2.13. Find the average value of μ of the function $f(x)$ over the indicated intervals :

(a) $f(x) = 2x^2 + 1$ over $[0, 1]$;

(b) $f(x) = \frac{1}{x}$ over $[1, 2]$;

(c) $f(x) = 3^x - 2x + 3$ over $[0, 2]$.

7.2.14. A body falling to the ground from a state of rest acquires a velocity $v_1 = \sqrt{2gs_1}$ on covering a vertical path $s = s_1$. Show that the average velocity v_m over this path is equal to $\frac{2v_1}{3}$.

7.2.15. The cross-section of the trough has the form of a parabolic segment with a base a and depth h. Find the average depth of the trough.

7.2.16. Find the average value I_m of alternating current intensity over time interval from 0 to $\frac{\pi}{\omega}$ (see Problem **7.2.12**)

7.2.17. Prove that the average value of the focal radius of an ellipse $\rho = \frac{a}{1 - b\cos\varphi}$, where $\rho = \frac{b^2}{a}$; a, b are the semi-axis and ε is eccentricity, is equal to b.

7.2.18. On the segment AB of length a a point P is taken at a distance x from the end-point A. Show that the average value of the areas of the rectangles constructed on the segments AP and PB is equal to $\frac{a^2}{6}$.

7.2.19. Find the average value of the function

$$f(x) = \frac{\cos^2 x}{\sin^2 x + 4\cos^2 x}$$

over the interval $\left[0, \frac{\pi}{2}\right]$. Check directly that this average, equal to $\frac{1}{6}$, is the value of the function $f(x)$ for a certain $x = \xi$ lying within the indicated interval.

7.3. Computing Areas in Rectangular Coordinates

If a plane figure is bounded by the straight lines $x = a$, $x = b$ $(a < b)$ and the curves $y = y_1(x)$, $y = y_2(x)$, provided $y_1(x) \le y_2(x)$ $(a \le x \le b)$, then its area is computed by the formula

$$S = \int_a^b [y_2(x) - y_1(x)]\, dx.$$

In certain cases the left boundary $x = a$ (or the right boundary $x = b$) can degenerate into a point of intersection of the curves $y = y_1(x)$ and $y = y_2(x)$.

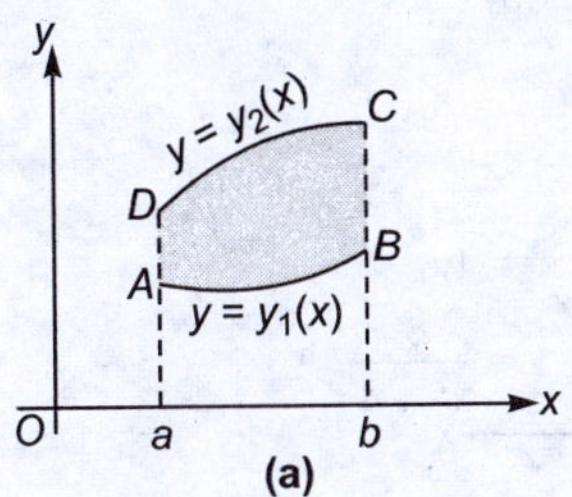

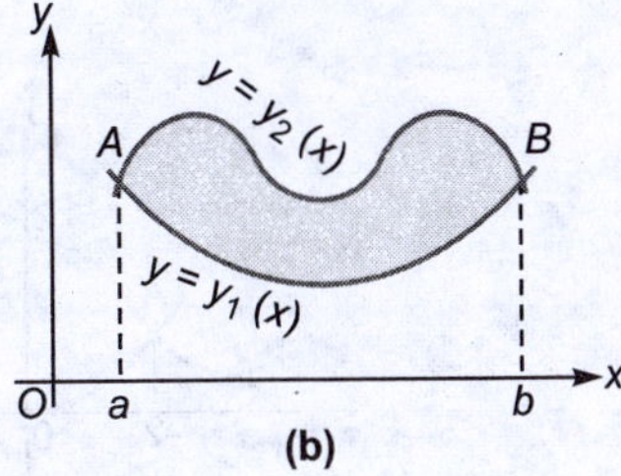

Fig. 65

Then a and b are found as the abscissas of the points of intersection of the indicated curves (Fig. 65, (a), (b)).

7.3.1. Compute the area of the figure bounded by the straight lines $x = 0$, $x = 2$ and the curves $y = 2^x$, $y = 2x - x^2$ (Fig. 66).

Solution Since the maximum of the function $y = 2x - x^2$ is attained at the point $x = 1$ and is equal to 1, and the function $y = 2^x \geq 1$ on the interval [0, 2], we have

$$S = \int_0^2 [2^x - (2x - x^2)]\, dx = \left.\frac{2^x}{\ln 2}\right|_0^2 - \left.\left(x^2 - \frac{x^3}{3}\right)\right|_0^2 = \frac{3}{\ln 2} - \frac{4}{3}$$

7.3.2. Compute the area of the figure bounded by the parabolas $x = -2y^2$, $x = 1 - 3y^2$ (Fig. 67)

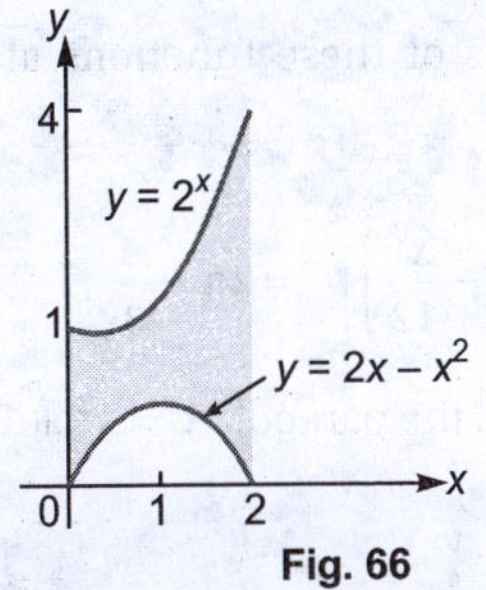

Fig. 66

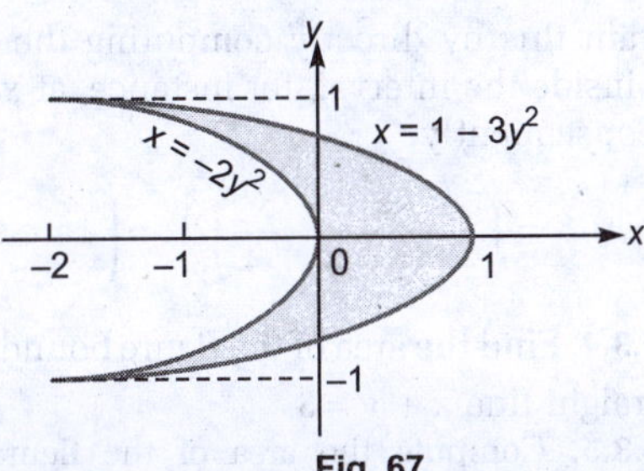

Fig. 67

Solution Solving the system of equations

$$\begin{cases} x = 2y^2 \; ; \\ x = 1 - 3y^2, \end{cases}$$

find the ordinates of the points of intersection of the curves $y_1 = -1$, $y_2 = 1$. Since $1 - 3y^2 \geq -2y^2$ for $-1 \leq y \leq 1$, then we have

$$S = \int_{-1}^{1} [(1 - 3y^2) - (-2y^2)]\, dy = 2\left.\left(y - \frac{y^3}{3}\right)\right|_0^1 = \frac{4}{3}.$$

7.3.3. Find the area of the figure contained between the parabola $x^2 = 4y$ and the witch of Agnesi $y = \dfrac{8}{x^2 + 4}$ (see Fig. 68)

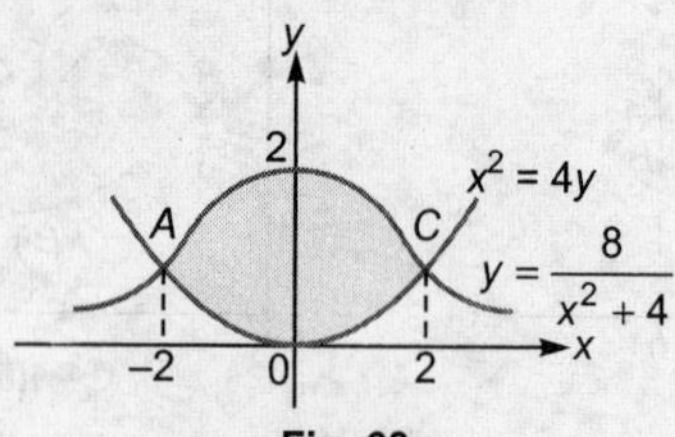

Fig. 68

Solution Find the abscissas of the points A and C of intersection of the curves. For this purpose eliminate y from the system of equations

$$\begin{cases} y = \dfrac{8}{x^2 + 4} \\ y = \dfrac{x^2}{4}, \end{cases}$$

whence

$$\frac{8}{x^2 + 4} = \frac{x^2}{4}, \quad x^4 + 4x^2 - 32 = 0.$$

The real roots of this equation are the points $x_1 = -2$ and $x_2 = 2$. As is seen from the figure, $\dfrac{8}{x^2 + 4} \geq \dfrac{x^2}{4}$ on the interval $[-2, 2]$. (It is also possible to ascertain this by directly computing the values of these functions at any point inside the interval, for instance, at $x = 0$).

Consequently,

$$S = \int_{-2}^{2} \left(\frac{8}{x^2 + 4} - \frac{x^2}{4} \right) dx = \left(4 \arctan \frac{x}{2} - \frac{x^3}{12} \right) \Bigg|_{-2}^{2} = 2\pi - \frac{4}{3}.$$

7.3.4. Find the area of the figure bounded the the parabola $y = x^2 + 1$ and the straight line $x + y = 3$.

7.3.5. Compute the area of the figure which lies in the first quadrant inside the circle $x^2 + y^2 = 3a^2$ and is bounded by the parabolas $x^2 = 2ay$ and $y^2 = 2ax$ $(a > 0)$ (Fig. 69).

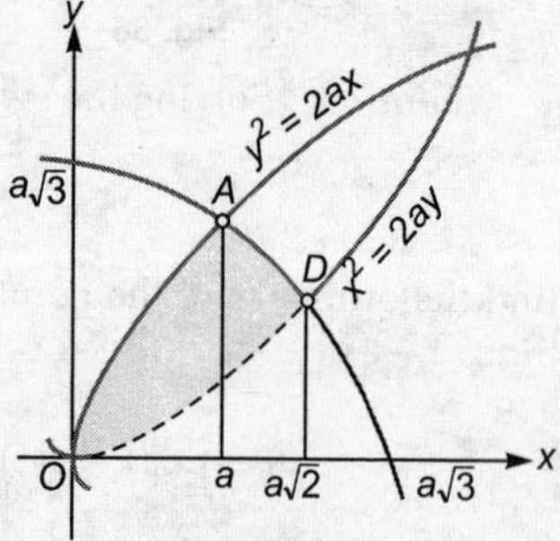

Fig. 69

Solution Find the abscissa of the point A of intersection of the parabola $y^2 = 2ax$ and the circle $x^2 + y^2 = 3a^2$. Eliminating y from the system of equations

$$\begin{cases} x^2 + y^2 = 3a^2, \\ y^2 = 2ax, \end{cases}$$

we obtain $x^2 + 2ax - 3a^2 = 0$, whence we get the only positive root $x_A = a$. Analogously, we find the abscissa of the point D of intersection of the circle $x^2 + y^2 = 3a^2$ and the parabola $x^2 = 2ay$; $x_D = a\sqrt{2}$.

Thus, the sought-for area is equal to

$$S = \int_0^{a\sqrt{2}} [y_2(x) = y_1(x)]\, dx,$$

where $y_1(x) = \dfrac{x^2}{2a}$, $y_2(x) = \begin{cases} \sqrt{2ax} & \text{for} \quad 0 \le x \le a, \\ \sqrt{3a^2 - x^2} & \text{for} \quad a < x \le a\sqrt{2}. \end{cases}$

By the additivity property of the integral

$$S = \int_0^{a} \left(\sqrt{2ax} - \frac{x^2}{2a} \right) dx + \int_0^{a\sqrt{2}} \left(\sqrt{3a^2 - x^2} - \frac{x^2}{2a} \right) dx$$

$$= \left[\sqrt{2a} \cdot \frac{2}{3}\, x^{\frac{3}{2}} - \frac{x^3}{6a} \right]_0^a + \left[\frac{x}{2}\sqrt{3a^2 - x^2} + \frac{3a^2}{2} \text{arc sin} \frac{x}{a\sqrt{3}} - \frac{x^3}{6a} \right]_a^{a\sqrt{2}}$$

$$= \frac{2\sqrt{2}}{3} a^2 - \frac{a^2}{6} + \frac{3a^2}{2} \left(\text{arc sin} \frac{\sqrt{2}}{\sqrt{3}} - \text{arc sin} \frac{1}{\sqrt{3}} \right) - \frac{\sqrt{2}}{3} a^2 + \frac{1}{6} a^2$$

$$= \left(\frac{\sqrt{2}}{3} + \frac{3}{2} \text{arc sin} \frac{1}{3} \right) a^2.$$

Here we make use of the trigonometric formula :

$\text{arc sin}\, \alpha - \text{arc sin}\, \beta = \text{arc sin}\, (\alpha \sqrt{1 - \beta^2} - \beta \sqrt{1 - \alpha^2})\ (\alpha\beta > 0)$ for transforming

$$\text{arc sin} \sqrt{\frac{2}{3}} - \text{arc sin} \frac{1}{\sqrt{3}} = \text{arc sin} \left(\sqrt{\frac{2}{3}} \sqrt{\frac{2}{3}} - \frac{1}{\sqrt{3}} \frac{1}{\sqrt{3}} \right)$$

$$= \text{arc sin} \frac{1}{3}.$$

7.3.6. Compute the area of the figure lying in the first quadrant and bounded by the curves $y^2 = 4x$, $x^2 = 4y$ and $x^2 + y^2 = 5$.

7.3.7. Compute the area of the figure bounded by the lines $y = x + 1$, $y = \cos x$ and the x-axis (Fig. 70).

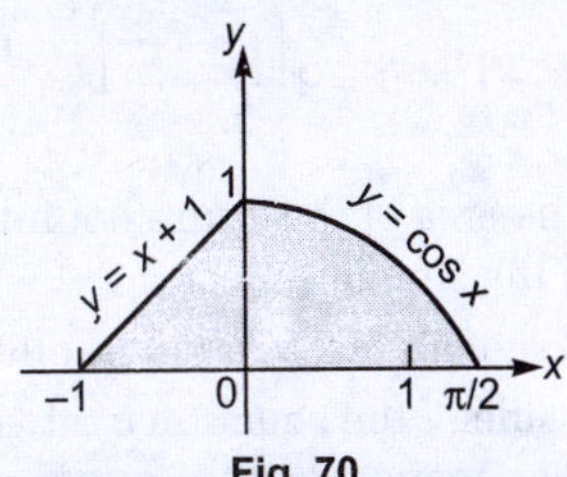

Fig. 70

Solution The function

$$y = f(x) = \begin{cases} x+1 & \text{if } -1 \le x \le 0, \\ \cos x & \text{if } 0 \le x \le \frac{\pi}{2} \end{cases}$$

is continuous on the interval $\left[-1, \frac{\pi}{2}\right]$. The area of the curvilinear trapezoid is equal to

$$= \int_{-1}^{\pi/2} f(x)\,dx = \int_{-1}^{0} (x+1)\,dx + \int_{0}^{\pi/2} \cos x\,dx = \left.\frac{(x+1)^2}{2}\right|_{-1}^{0} + \sin x\Big|_{0}^{\frac{3}{2}} = \frac{3}{2}.$$

7.3.8. Find the area of the segment of the curve $y^2 = x^3 - x^2$ if the line $x = 2$ is the chord determining the segment.

Solution From the equality $y^2 = x^2(x-1)$ it follows that $x^2(x-1) \ge 0$, therefore either $x = 0$ or $x \ge 1$. In other words, the domain of definition of the implicit function $y^2 = x^3 - x^2$ consists of the point $x = 0$ and the interval $[1, \infty)$. In computing the area the isolated point $(0, 0)$ does not play any role, therefore, the interval of integration is $[1, 2]$ (see Fig. 71).

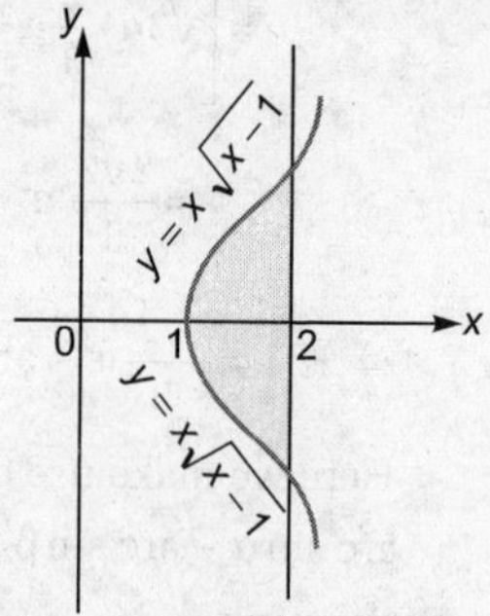

Fig. 71

Passing over to explicit representation $y = \pm\, x\sqrt{x-1}$, we see that the segment is bounded above by the curve $y = x\sqrt{x-1}$ and below by the curve $y = -\sqrt{x-1}$. Hence,

$$S = \int_1^2 [x\sqrt{x-1} - (-x\sqrt{x-1})]\,dx = 2\int_1^2 x\sqrt{x-1}\,dx.$$

Make the substitution

$$x - 1 = t^2, \qquad dx = 2t\,dt,$$

x	t
1	0
2	1

Then

$$S = 4\int_0^1 (t^2+1)\,t^2 dt = 4\left[\frac{t^5}{5} + \frac{t^2}{3}\right]_0^1 = \frac{32}{15}.$$

7.3.9. Determine the area of the figure bounded by two branches of the curve $(y - x)^2 = x^3$ and the straight line $x = 1$.

Solution Note first of all that y, as an implicit function of x, is defined only for $x \ge 0$; the left side of the equation of always non-negative. Now we find the equations of two branches of the curve $y = x - x\sqrt{x}$, $y = x + x\sqrt{x}$. Since $x \ge 0$, we have $x + x\sqrt{x} \ge x - x\sqrt{x}$, and therefore

$$S = \int_0^1 (x + x\sqrt{x} - x + x\sqrt{x})\,dx = 2\int_0^1 x\sqrt{x}\,dx = \frac{4}{5}x^{\frac{5}{2}}\Big|_0^1 = \frac{4}{5}.$$

7.3.10. Compute the area enclosed by the loop of the curve $y^2 = x(x-1)^2$.

Solution The domain of definition of the implicit function y is the interval $0 \le x < +\infty$. Since the equation of the curve contains y to the second power, the curve is symmetrical about the x-axis. The positive branch $y_1(x)$ is given by the equation

$$y = y_1(x) = \sqrt{x}\,|x-1| = \begin{cases} \sqrt{x}\,(1-x), & 0 \le x \le 1, \\ \sqrt{x}\,(x-1), & x > 1. \end{cases}$$

The common points of the symmetrical branches $y_1(x)$ and $y_2(x) = -y_1(x)$ must lie on the x-axis. But $y_1(x) = \sqrt{x}\,|x-1| = 0$ only at $x_1 = 0$ and $x_2 = 1$.

Consequently, the loop is formed by the curves $y = \sqrt{x}\,(1-x)$ and $y = -\sqrt{x}\,(1-x), 0 \le x \le 1$ (see Fig. 72) the area enclosed being

$$S = 2\int_0^1 \sqrt{x}\,(1-x)\,dx = 2\int_0^1 \left(x^{\frac{1}{2}} - x^{\frac{3}{2}}\right)dx = \frac{8}{15}.$$

7.3.11. Find the area enclosed by the loop of the curve $y^2 = (x-1)(x-2)^2$.

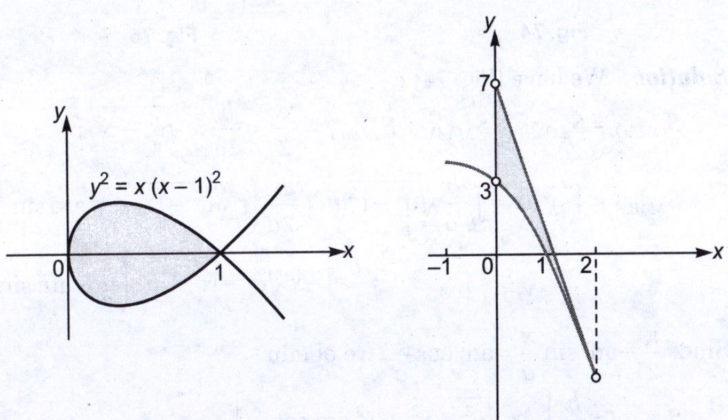

Fig. 72

Fig. 73

7.3.12. Find the area of the figure bounded by the parabola $y = -x^2 + 2x + 3$, the line tangent to it at the point $M(2, -5)$ and the y-axis.

Solution The equation of the tangent at the point $M(2, -5)$ has the form $y + 5 = -6(x-2)$ or $y = 7 - 6x$. Since the branches of the parabola are directed downward, the parabola lies below the tangent *ie*, $7 - 6x \ge -x^2 - 2x + 3$ on the interval $[0, 2]$ (see Fig. 73).

Hence, $S = \int_0^1 [7 - 6x - (-x^2 - 2x + 3)]\,dx = \int_0^3 (x^2 - 4x + 4)\,dx = \frac{8}{3}.$

7.3.13. Find the area bounded by the parabola $y = x^2 - 2x + 2$, the line tangent to it at the point $M(3, 5)$ and the axis of ordinates.

7.3.14. We take on the ellipse

$$\frac{x^2}{a^2} + \frac{y^2}{b^2} = 1 \ (a > b)$$

a point $M(x, y)$ lying in the first quadrant.

Show that the sector of the ellipse bonded by its semi-major axis and the focal radius drawn to the point M has an area.

$$S = \frac{ab}{2} \text{ arc cos } \frac{x}{a}.$$

With the aid of this result deduce a formula for computing the area of the entire ellipse.

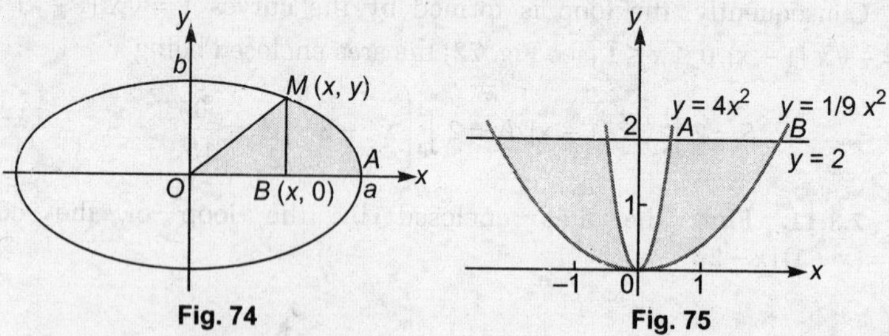

Fig. 74 Fig. 75

Solution We have (Fig. 74) :

$$S_{OMAO} = S_{\Delta OMB} + S_{MABM}\ ;\ S_{\Delta OMB} = \frac{xy}{2} = \frac{b}{2a} x\sqrt{a^2 - x^2}\,;$$

$$S_{MABM} = \int_x^a y\,dx = \int_x^a \frac{b}{a}\sqrt{a^2 - t^2}\,dt = \frac{b}{2a}\left(t\sqrt{a^2 - t^2} + a^2 \text{ arc sin } \frac{t}{a}\right)\Bigg|_x^a$$

$$= \frac{b}{2a}\left[-x\sqrt{a^2 - x^2} + a^2\left(\frac{\pi}{2} - \text{arc sin } \frac{x}{a}\right)\right].$$

Since $\frac{\pi}{2} - \text{arc sin } \frac{x}{a} = \text{arc cos } \frac{x}{a}$, we obtain

$$S_{MABM} = \frac{b}{2a}\left[-x\sqrt{a^2 - x^2} + a^2 \text{ arc cos } \frac{x}{a}\right].$$

Hence $\quad S_{OMAO} = S_{\Delta OMB} + S_{MABM} + \frac{ab}{2} \text{ arc cos } \frac{x}{a}.$

At $x = 0$, the sector becomes a quarter of the ellipse *ie*,

$$\frac{1}{4} S_{\text{ellipse}} = \frac{ab}{2} \text{ arc cos } 0 = \frac{ab}{2} \cdot \frac{\pi}{2} = \frac{ab}{4}\pi,$$

and consequently, $S_{\text{ellipse}} = \pi ab$. At $a = b$ we get the area of a circle $S_{\text{circle}} = \pi a^2$.

7.3.15. Find the area bounded by the parabolas $y = 4x^2$, $y = \frac{x^2}{9}$ and the straight line $y = 2$.

Solution In this case it is advisable to integrate with respect to y and take advantage of the symmetry of the figures (see Fig. 75). Therefore, solving the equations of the parabolas for x, we have

$$x = \pm \frac{\sqrt{y}}{2}, \; x = \pm 3\sqrt{y}.$$

By symmetry of the figure about the y-axis the area sought is equal to the doubled area S_{OABO} :

$$S = 2S_{OABO} = 2\int_0^3 \left(3\sqrt{y} - \frac{1}{2}\sqrt{y}\right) dy = 5\int_0^2 \sqrt{y}\, dy = \frac{20\sqrt{2}}{3}.$$

7.3.16. From an arbitrary point $M(x, y)$ of the curve $y = x^m (m > 0)$ perpendiculars MN and ML $(x > 0)$ are dropped onto the coordinate axes. What part of the area of the rectangle $ONML$ does the area $ONMO$ (Fig. 76) constitute ?

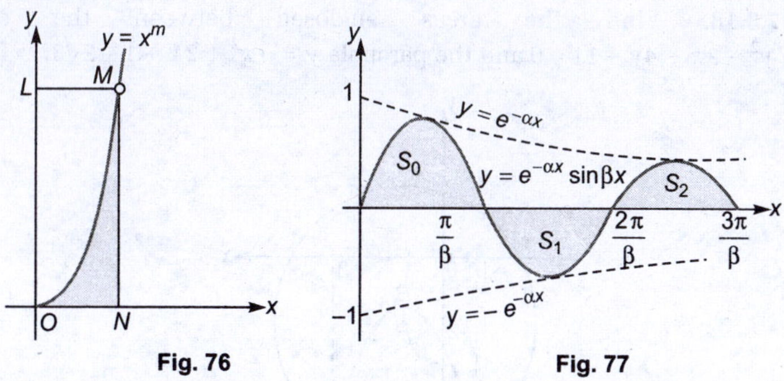

Fig. 76 **Fig. 77**

7.3.17. Prove that the areas $S_0, S_1, S_2, . S_3, \ldots$, bounded by the x-axis and half-waves o the curve $y = e^{-\alpha x} \sin \beta x$, $x \geq 0$, from a geometric progression with the common ratio $q = e^{-\frac{\alpha x}{\beta}}$.

Solution The curve of Fig. 77 intersects the positive semi-axis Ox at the points where $\sin \beta x = 0$, whence

$$x_n = \frac{n\pi}{\beta}, \; n = 0, , 2, \ldots$$

The function $y = e^{-\alpha x} \sin \beta x$ is positive in the intervals (x_{2k}, x_{2k+1}) and negative in (x_{2k+1}, x_{2k+2}), *ie*, the sign of the function in the interval (x_n, x_{n+1}) coincides with that of the number $(-1)^n$. Therefore

$$S_n = \int_{n\pi/\beta}^{(n+1)\pi/\beta} |y|\, dx = (-1)^n \int_{n\pi/\beta}^{(n+1)\pi/\beta} e^{-\alpha x} \sin \beta x\, dx.$$

But the indefinite integral is equal to

$$\int e^{-\alpha x} \sin \beta x \, dx = -\frac{e^{-\alpha x}}{\alpha^2 + \beta^2} (\alpha \sin \beta x + \beta \cos \beta x) + C.$$

Consequently,

$$S_n = (-1)^{n+1} \left[\frac{e^{-\alpha x}}{\alpha^2 + \beta^2} (\alpha \sin \beta x + \beta \cos \beta x) \right] \Bigg|_{\frac{n\pi}{\beta}}^{\frac{(n+1)\pi}{\beta}}$$

$$= \frac{(-1)^{n+1}}{\alpha^2 + \beta^2} [(e^{-\alpha(n+1)\pi/\beta} \beta (-1)^{n+1} - e^{\alpha n\pi/\beta} \beta (-1)^n]$$

$$= \frac{\beta}{\alpha^2 + \beta^2} e^{-\alpha n\pi/\beta} (1 + e^{-\alpha\pi/\beta}).$$

Hence, $q = \dfrac{S_{n+1}}{S_n} = \dfrac{e^{-\alpha(n+1)\pi/\beta}}{e^{-\alpha n\pi/\beta}} = e^{-\alpha\pi/\beta}$,

which completes the proof.

7.3.18. Find the areas enclosed between the circle $x^2 + y^2 - 2x + 4y - 11 = 0$ and the parabola $y = -x^2 + 2x + 1 - 2\sqrt{3}$.

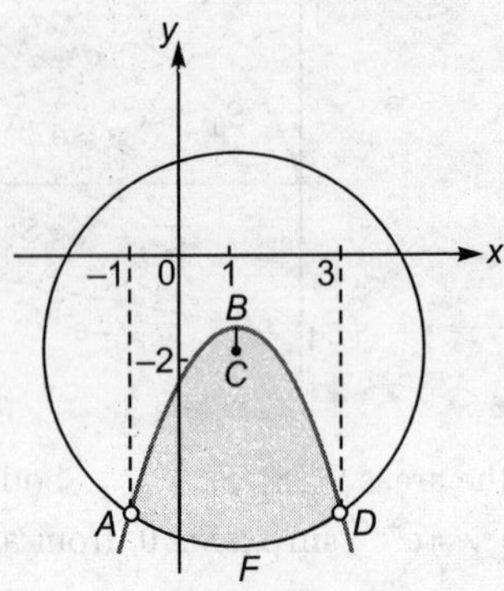

Fig. 78

Solution Rewriting the equation of the curves, we have :

$$(x-1)^2 + (y+2)^2 = 16,$$

$$y = -(x-1)^2 - 2\sqrt{3} + 2.$$

Consequently, the centre of the circle lies at the point $C(1, -2)$ and the radius of the circle equals 4. The axis of the parabola coincides with the straight line $x = 1$ and its vertex lies at the point $B(1, 2, -2\sqrt{3})$ (Fig. 78).

The area S_{ABDFA} of the smaller figure is found by the formula

$$S_{ABDFA} = \int_{x_A}^{x_D} (y_{\text{par}} - y_{\text{circle}}) \, dx,$$

where x_A and x_D are determined from the system of equations

$$\begin{cases} (x-1)^2 + (y+2)^2 = 16, \\ y + 2 = -(x-1)^2 - 2\sqrt{3} + 4, \end{cases}$$

whence $x_A = -1$, $x_D = 3$.

Hence

$$S_{ABDFA} = \int_{-1}^{3} [(-x^2 + 2x + 1 - 2\sqrt{3}) + (2 + \sqrt{16 - (x-1)^2})]\, dx$$

$$= \left[-\frac{x^3}{3} + x^2 + (3 - 2\sqrt{3})\, x + \frac{x-1}{2}\sqrt{16 - (x-1)^2} + \frac{16}{2} \arcsin \frac{x-1}{4} \right]_{-1}^{3}$$

$$= \frac{32}{3} - 8\sqrt{3} + 2\sqrt{12} + 16 \arcsin \frac{1}{2} = \frac{32}{3} - 4\sqrt{3} + \frac{8}{3}\pi.$$

The area of the second figure is easy to determine.

Note. The computation of the integral can be simplified by using the shift $x - 1 = z$ and taking advantage of the evenness of the integrand.

7.3.19. Compute the area bounded by the curves $y = (x-4)^2$, $y = 16 - x^2$ and the x-axis.

7.3.20. Compute the area enclosed between the parabolas

$$x = y^2 \; ; \; x = \frac{3}{4} y^2 + 1.$$

7.3.21. Compute the area of the portions cut off by the hyperbola $x^2 - 3y^2 = 1$ from the ellipse $x^2 + 4y^2 = 8$.

7.3.22. Compute the area enclosed by the curve $y^2 = (1 - x^2)^3$.

7.3.23. Compute the area enclosed by the loop of the curve $4(y^2 - x^2) + x^3 = 0$.

7.3.24. Compute the area of the figure bounded by the curve $\sqrt{x} + \sqrt{y} = 1$ and the straight line $x + y = 1$.

7.3.25. Compute the area of the figure enclosed by the curve $y^2 = x^2(1 - x^2)$.

7.3.26. Compute the area enclosed by the loop of the curve $x^3 + x^2 - y^2 = 0$.

7.3.27. Compute the area bounded by the axis of ordinates and the curve $x = y^2(1 - y)$.

7.3.28. Compute the area bounded by the curve $y = x^4 - 2x^3 + x^2 + 3$, the axis of abscissas and two ordinates corresponding to the points of minimum of the function $y(x)$.

7.4. Computing Areas with Parametrically Represented Boundaries

If the boundary of a figure is represented by parametric equations

$$x = x(t), \quad y = y(t),$$

then the area of the figure is evaluated by one of the three for formulas :

$$S = -\int_{\alpha}^{\beta} y(t)\, x'(t)\, dt \; ; S = \int_{\alpha}^{\beta} x(t)\, y'(t)\, dt \; ; S = \frac{1}{2}\int_{\alpha}^{\beta} (xy' - yx')\, dt,$$

where α and β are the values of the parameter t corresponding respectively to the beginning and the end of the traversal of the contour in the positive direction (the figure remains on the left).

7.4.1. Compute the area enclosed by the ellipse

$$x = a\cos t, \quad y = b\sin t \; (0 \le t \le 2\pi).$$

Solution Here, it is convenient first to compute

$$xy' - yx' = a\cos t \times b\cos t + b\sin t \times a\sin t = ab.$$

Hence

$$S = \frac{1}{2}\int_{0}^{2\pi} (xy' - yx')\, dt = \frac{1}{2}\int_{0}^{2\pi} ab\, dt = \pi ab.$$

7.4.2. Find the area enclosed by the astroid $\left(\frac{x}{a}\right)^{\frac{2}{3}} + \left(\frac{y}{a}\right)^{\frac{2}{3}} = 1.$

Solution Let us write the equation of the astroid in parametric from : $x = a\cos^3 t,\ y = a\sin^3 t, 0 \le t \le 2\pi$. Here it is also convenient to evaluate first

$$xy' - yx' = a^2 (\cos^3 t \cdot 3\sin^2 t\cos t + \sin^3 t \cdot 3\cos^2 t\sin t)$$
$$= 3a^2\cos^2 t\sin^2 t.$$

Hence,

$$S = \frac{1}{2}\int_{0}^{2\pi} (xy' - yx')\, dt = \frac{3}{8}a^2\int_{0}^{2\pi} \sin^2 2t\, dt = \frac{3}{8}a^2\pi.$$

7.4.3. Find the area of the region bounded by an arc of the cycloid $x = a(t - \sin t),\ y = a(1 - \cos t)$ and the x-axis.

Solution Here the contour consists of an arc of the cycloid $(0 \le t \le 2\pi)$ and a segment of the x-axis $(0 \le x \le 2\pi a)$. Let us apply the formula $S = -\int_{\alpha}^{\beta} yx'\, dt.$

Since, on the segment of the x-axis we have $y = 0$, it only remains to compute the integral (taking into account the direction of a boundary traversal) :

$$S = -\int_{2\pi}^{0} a(1 - \cos t)\, a(1 - \cos t)\, dt = a^2\int_{0}^{2\pi} (1 - \cos t)^2 dt$$
$$= a^2\int_{0}^{2\pi} \left[1 - 2\cos t + \frac{1}{2}(1 + \cos 2t)\right] dt = 3\pi a^2$$

7.4.4. Compute the area of the region enclosed by the curve $x = a\sin t,\ y = b\sin 2t$.

Solution When constructing the curve one should bear in mind that it is symmetrical about the axis of coordinates. Indeed, if we substitute $\pi - t$ for t, the variable x remains unchanged, while y only changes its sign; consequently, the curve is symmetrical about the x-axis. When substituting $\pi + t$ for t the variable y remains unchanged, and x only changes its sign, which means that the curve is symmetrical about the y-axis.

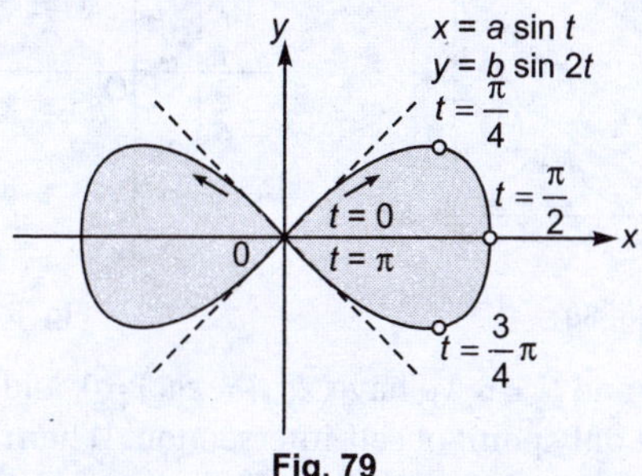

Fig. 79

Furthermore, since the functions $x = a\sin t$; $y = b\sin 2t$ have a common period 2π, it is sufficient to confine ourselves to the following interval of variation of the parameter : $0 \le t \le 2\pi$.

From the equations of the curves it readily follows that the variables x and y simultaneously retain non-negative values only when the parameter t varies on the interval $\left[0, \frac{\pi}{2}\right]$, therefore at $0 \le t \le \frac{\pi}{2}$ we obtain the portion of the curve situated in the first quadrant. The curve is shown in Fig. 79.

As is seen from the figure, it is sufficient to evaluate the area enclosed by one loop of the curve corresponding to the variation of the parameter t from 0 to π and then to double the result

$$S = 2\int_0^{\pi} yx'\,dt = 2\int_0^{\pi} b\sin 2t \times a\cos t\,dt = 4ab\int_0^{\pi}\cos^2 t\sin t\,dt$$

$$= -4ab\left(\frac{\cos^3 t}{3}\right)\Bigg|_0^{\pi} = \frac{8}{3}ab.$$

7.4.5. Find the area of the region enclosed by the loop of the curve

$$x = \frac{t}{3}(6-t); \qquad y = \frac{t^2}{8}(6-t).$$

Solution Locate the points of self-intersection of the curve. Both functions $x(t)$ and $y(t)$ are defined throughout the entire number scale $-\infty < t < \infty$.

At the point of self-intersection the values of the abscissa (and ordinate) coincide at different values of the parameter. Since $x = 3 - \frac{1}{3}(t-3)^2$, the abscissas coincide at $t = 3 \pm \lambda$. For the function $y(t)$ to take on one and the same value at the same values of the parameter t, the equality $\frac{(3+\lambda)^2}{8}(3-\lambda) = \frac{(3-\lambda)^2}{8}(3+\lambda)$ must be fulfilled for $\lambda \neq 0$, whence $\lambda = \pm 3$.

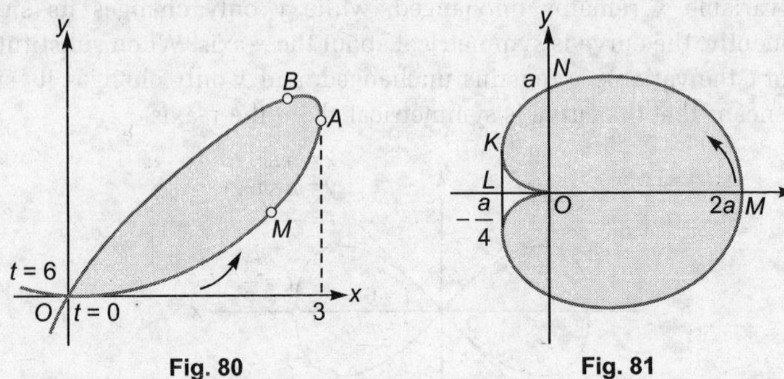

Fig. 80

Fig. 81

Thus, at $t_1 = 0$ and $t_2 = 6$ we have $x(t_1) = x(t_2) = 0$, and $y(t_1) = y(t_2) = 0$, *ie*, the point (0, 0) is the only point of self-intersection. When t changes from 0 to 6, the points of the curve are found in the first quadrant. As t varies from 0 to 3, the point $M(x, y)$ describes the lower part of the loop, since in the indicated interval $x(t)$ and $y(t) = \frac{3tx}{8}$ increases, and then the function $x(t)$ begins to decreases, while $y(t)$ still keeps increasing. Figure 80 shows the traversal of the curve corresponding to increasing t (the figure remains on the left).

In computing the area enclosed by the loop sought it is convenient to use the formula

$$S = \frac{1}{2}\int_0^6 (xy' - yx')\,dt = \frac{1}{2}\int_0^6 \frac{t^2(6-t)^2}{24}\,dt = \frac{27}{5}$$

7.4.6. Find the area enclosed by the loop of the curve : $x = t^2$; $y = t - \frac{t^3}{3}$.

7.4.7. Compute the area enclosed by the cardioid : $x = a\cos t\,(1 + \cos t)$; $y = a\sin t\,(1 + \cos t)$.

Solution Since $x(t)$ and $y(t)$ are periodic functions, it is sufficient to consider the interval $[-\pi, \pi]$. The curve is symmetrical about the x-axis, since on substituting $-t$ for t the values of the variable x remains unchanged, while y only changes its sign, and $y \geq 0$ as t varies from 0 to π.

As t changes from 0 to π the function $u = \cos t$ decreases from 1 to -1, and the abscissa $x = au(1 + u) = a\left[-\frac{1}{4} + \left(u + \frac{1}{2}\right)^2\right]$ first decreases from $x|_{u=1} = 2a$ to $x|_{u=-\frac{1}{2}} = -\frac{a}{4}$ and then increases to $x|_{u=-1} = 0$. We can show that the ordinate y increases on the interval $\left(0 \le t \le \frac{\pi}{3}\right)$ and decreases on the interval $\left(\frac{\pi}{3} \le t \le \pi\right)$.

The curve is shown in Fig. 81, the arrow indicating the direction of its traversal as t increases.

Consequently,

$$S = \frac{1}{2}\int_{-\pi}^{\pi}(xy' - yx')\,dt = a^2\int_0^{\pi}(1+\cos t)^2 dt = \frac{3}{2}\pi a^2.$$

7.4.8. Compute the area of the region enclosed by the curve $x = \cos t,\ y = b\sin^3 t$.

7.4.9. Compute the areas enclosed by the loops of the curves :

(a) $x = t^2 - 1,\ y = t^3 - t$;

(b) $x = 2t - t^2$; $y = 2t^2 - t^3$;

(c) $x = t^2$; $y = \frac{t}{3}(3 - t^2)$.

7.4.10. Compute the area of the region enclosed by the curve $x = a\cos t$; $y = b\sin t\cos^2 t$.

7.4.11. Compute the area enclosed by the evolute of the ellipse

$$x = \frac{c^2}{a}\cos^3 t; \quad y = -\frac{c^2}{b}\sin^3 t; \quad c^2 = a^2 - b^2.$$

7.5. The Area of a Curvilinear Sector in Polar Coordinates

In polar coordinates the area of a sector bounded by the curve $\rho = \rho(\varphi)$ and the rays $\varphi_1 = \alpha$ and $\varphi_2 = \beta$ is expressed by the integral

$$S = \frac{1}{2}\int_{\alpha}^{\beta}\rho^2(\varphi)\,d\varphi.$$

7.5.1. Find the area of the region situated in the first quadrant and bounded by the parabola $y^2 = 4ax$ and the straight lines $y = x - a$ and $x = a$.

Solution Let us introduce a polar system of coordinates by placing the pole at the focus F of the parabola and directing the polar axis in the positive direction along the x-axis. Then the equation of the parabola will be $\rho = \frac{p}{1-\cos\varphi}$, where p is the parameter of the parabola. In this case $p = 2a$, and the focus F has the coordinates $(a, 0)$. Hence, the equation of the parabola will acquire the form

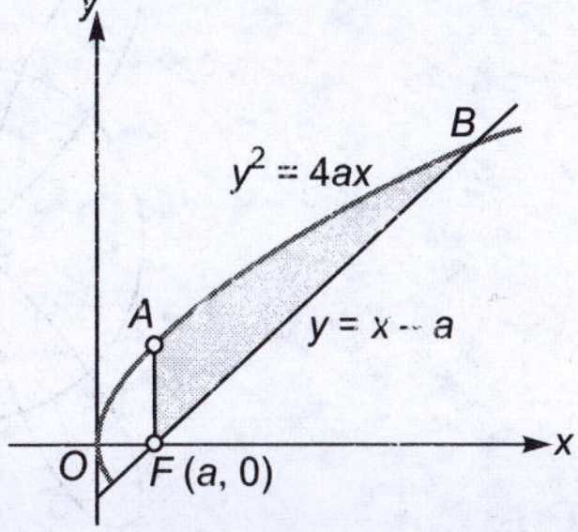

Fig. 82

$\rho = \dfrac{2a}{1-\cos\varphi}$, and those of the straight lines will become $\varphi = \dfrac{\pi}{4}$ and $\varphi = \dfrac{\pi}{2}$ (Fig. 82). Therefore,

$$S_{FABF} = \frac{1}{2}\int_{\pi/4}^{\pi/2} \frac{4a^2}{(1-\cos\varphi)^2}\,d\varphi = 2a^2 \int_{\pi/4}^{\pi/2} \frac{d\varphi}{4\sin^4\dfrac{\varphi}{2}}.$$

Changing the variable :

$$\cot\frac{\varphi}{2} = z, \qquad -\frac{d\varphi}{2\sin^2(\varphi/2)} = dz,$$

φ	z
$\pi/4$	$\cot(\pi/8)$
$\pi/2$	1

we obtain

$$S_{FABF} = a^2 \int_1^{\cot(\pi/8)} (1+z^2)\,dz = a^2\left(\cot\frac{\pi}{8} + \frac{1}{3}\cot^3\frac{\pi}{8} - 1 - \frac{1}{3}\right)$$

or, taking into account that $\cot\dfrac{\pi}{8} = \dfrac{1+\cos(\pi/4)}{\sin(\pi/4)} = 1+\sqrt{2}$,

$$S_{FABF} = 2a^2\left(1 + \frac{4}{3}\sqrt{2}\right).$$

7.5.2. Compute the area of the region enclosed by
(a) the cardioid $\rho = 1 + \cos\varphi$;
(b) the curve $\rho = a\cos\varphi$.

7.5.3. Find the area of the regions bounded by the curve $\rho = 2a\cos 3\varphi$ and the arcs of the circle $\rho = a$ and situated outside the circle.

Solution Since the function $\rho = 3a\cos 3\varphi$ has a period $T = \dfrac{2\pi}{3}$, the radius vector describes three equal loops of the curve as φ varies between $-\pi$ and π. Permissible values for φ are those at which $\cos 3\varphi \ge 0$, whence

$$-\frac{\pi}{6} + \frac{2k\pi}{3} \le \varphi \le \frac{\pi}{6} + \frac{2k\pi}{3} \quad (k = 0, \pm 1, \pm 2, \ldots).$$

Consequently, one of the loops is described as φ varies between $-\dfrac{\pi}{6}$ and $\dfrac{\pi}{6}$, and the other two loops as φ varies between $\dfrac{\pi}{2}$ and $\dfrac{5\pi}{6}$, and between $\dfrac{7\pi}{6}$ and

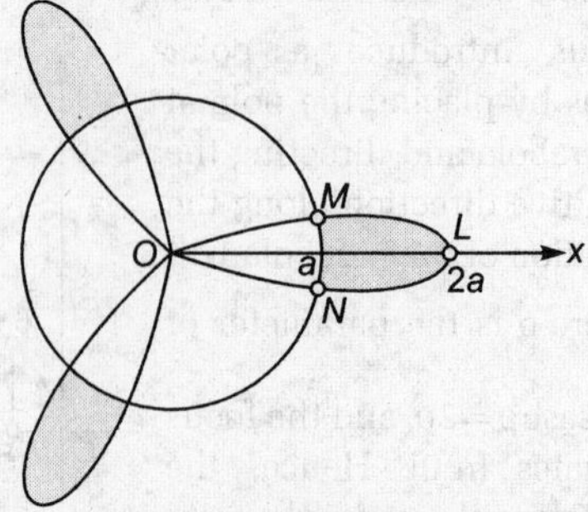

Fig. 83

$\frac{3\pi}{2}$, respectively (Fig. 83), Cutting out the parts, belonging to the circle $\rho = a$, we get the figure whose area is sought. Clearly, it is equal to the triple area S_{MLNM}.

Let us find the polar coordinates of the points of intersection M and N. For this purpose solve the equation $2a\cos 3\varphi = a$, *ie*, $\cos 3\varphi = \frac{1}{2}$. Between $-\frac{\pi}{6}$ and $\frac{\pi}{6}$ only the roots $-\frac{\pi}{9}$ and $\frac{\pi}{9}$ $(k = 0)$ are found. Thus, the point N is specified by the polar angle $\varphi_1 = -\frac{\pi}{9}$, the point M by $\varphi_2 = \frac{\pi}{9}$. As is seen from the figure,

$$S_{MLNM} = S_{OMLNO} - S_{OMNO}$$
$$= \frac{1}{2}\int_{-\pi/9}^{\pi/9} 4a^2\cos^2 3\varphi\, d\varphi - \frac{1}{2}\int_{-\pi/9}^{\pi/9} a^2 d\varphi = a^2\left(\frac{\pi}{9} + \frac{\sqrt{3}}{6}\right).$$

7.5.4. Compute the area of the figure bounded by the circle $\rho = 3\sqrt{2}\, a\cos\varphi$ and $\rho = 3a\sin\varphi$.

Solution The first circle lies in the right half-plane and passes through the pole $\rho = 0$, touching the vertical line. The second circle is situated in the upper half-plane and passes through the pole $\rho = 0$, touching the horizontal line. Consequently, the pole is a point of intersection of the circles. The other point of intersection of the circles B is found from the equation $3\sqrt{2}\, a\cos\varphi = 3a\sin\varphi$, whence $B\,(\arctan\sqrt{2}, a\sqrt{6})$. As is seen from Fig. 84, the sought-for area S is equal to the sum of the areas of the circular segments $OABO$ and $OCBO$ adjoining each other the ray $\varphi = \arctan\sqrt{2}$.

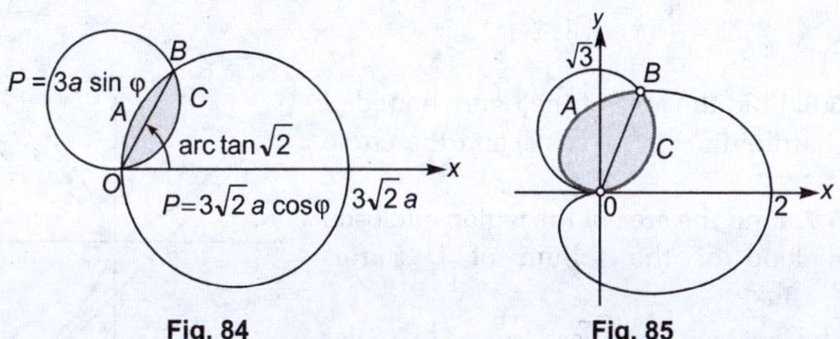

Fig. 84

Fig. 85

The arc BAO is described by the end-point of the polar radius ρ of the first circle for $\arctan\sqrt{2} \le \varphi \le \frac{\pi}{2}$, and the arc OCB by the end- point of the polar radius ρ of the second circle for $0 \le \varphi \le \arctan\sqrt{2}$. Therefore

$$S_{OABO} = 9a^2\int_{\arctan\sqrt{2}}^{\pi/2} \cos^2\varphi\, d\varphi = \frac{9}{2}a^2\left(\frac{\pi}{2} - \arctan\sqrt{2} - \frac{\sqrt{2}}{3}\right),$$

$$S_{OCBO} = \frac{9}{2}a^2 \int_0^{\arctan\sqrt{2}} \sin^2\varphi\, d\varphi = \frac{9}{4}a^2\left(\arctan\sqrt{2} - \frac{\sqrt{2}}{3}\right).$$

Hence, $S_{OABO} + S_{OCBO} = 2.25a^2(\pi - \arctan\sqrt{2} - \sqrt{2})$.

7.5.5. Find the area of the figure cut only by the circle $\rho = \sqrt{3}\sin\varphi$ from the cardioid $\rho = 1 + \cos\varphi$ (Fig. 85).

Solution Let us first find the points of intersection of these curves. To this end solve the system

$$\begin{cases} \rho = \sqrt{3}\sin\varphi, 0 \le \varphi \le \pi, \\ \rho = 1 + \cos\varphi, \end{cases}$$

whence $\qquad \varphi_1 = \dfrac{\pi}{3}, \varphi_2 = \pi.$

The sought-for area is the sum of two areas : one is a circular segment, the other a segment of the cardioid; the segments adjoin each other along the ray $\varphi = \frac{\pi}{3}$. The arc BAO is described by the end-point of the polar radius ρ of the cardioid as the polar angle φ changes from $\frac{\pi}{3}$ to π, and the arc OCB by the end-point of the polar radius ρ of the circle for $0 \le \varphi \le \frac{\pi}{3}$.

Therefore

$$S = \frac{1}{2}\int_0^{\pi/3} 3\sin^2\varphi\, d\varphi + \frac{1}{2}\int_{\pi/3}^{\pi} (1 + \cos\varphi)^2 d\varphi$$

$$= \frac{3}{4}\left(\varphi - \frac{\sin 2\varphi}{2}\right)\Bigg|_0^{\frac{\pi}{3}} + \frac{1}{2}\left(\varphi + 2\sin\varphi + \frac{\varphi}{2} + \frac{\sin 2\varphi}{4}\right)\Bigg|_{\frac{\pi}{2}}^{\pi}$$

$$= \frac{3}{4}(\pi - \sqrt{3}).$$

7.5.6. Find the area of the figure bounded by the cardioid $\rho = a(1 - \cos\varphi)$ and the circle $\rho = a$.

7.5.7. Find the area of the region enclosed by the loop of the folium of Descartes $x^3 + y^3 = 3axy$.

Solution Let us pass over to polar coordinates using the usual formulas $x = \rho\cos\varphi$, $y = \rho\sin\varphi$. Then the equation of the curve is :

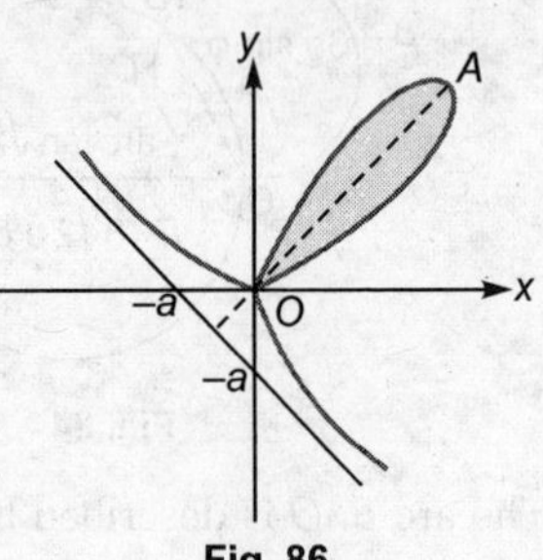

Fig. 86

$$\rho^3(\cos^3\varphi + \sin^3\varphi) = 3a\rho^2\sin\varphi\cos\varphi$$

or

$$\rho = \frac{3a\sin\varphi\cos\varphi}{\cos^3\varphi + \sin^3\varphi} = \frac{3a\sin 2\varphi}{(\sin\varphi + \cos\varphi)(2 - \sin 2\varphi)}.$$

It follows from this equation that, firstly, $\rho = 0$ at $\varphi = 0$ and at $\varphi = \frac{\pi}{2}$ and secondly, $\rho \to \infty$ as $\varphi \to \frac{3\pi}{4}$ and $\varphi \to -\frac{\pi}{4}$. The latter means that the folium of Descartes has an asymptote, whose equation $y = -x - a$ can be found in the usual way in rectangular coordinates. Consequently, the loop of the folium of Descartes is described as φ changes from 0 to $\frac{\pi}{2}$ and is situated in the first quadrant (see Fig. 86).

Thus, the sought-for area is equal to

$$S_{OAO} = \frac{1}{2}\int_0^{\pi/2} \frac{9a^2 \cos^2\varphi \sin^2\varphi}{(\cos^3\varphi + \sin^3\varphi)^2}\, d\varphi.$$

Taking advantage of the curve's symmetry about the bisector $y = x$, *ie*, about the ray $\varphi = \frac{\pi}{4}$, we can compute the area of half of the loop $\left(\text{from } \varphi = 0 \text{ to } \varphi = \frac{\pi}{4}\right)$ and then double it. This enables us to apply the substitution

$$\tan\varphi = z, \quad \frac{d\varphi}{\cos^2\varphi} = dz,$$

φ	z
0	0
$\pi/4$	1

which gives

$$S_{OAO} = 9a^2 \int_0^{\pi/4} \frac{\cos^2\varphi \sin^2\varphi}{(\cos^3\varphi + \sin^3\varphi)^2}\, d\varphi = 9a^2 \int_0^1 \frac{z^2 dz}{(1 + z^3)^3}.$$

Still new substitution

$$1 + z^3 = v, \quad 3z^3 dz = dv,$$

z	v
0	1
1	2

leads to the integral

$$S_{OAD} = 3a^2 \int_1^2 \frac{dv}{v^2} = \frac{3}{2}a^2.$$

7.5.8. Compute the area of the region enclosed by one loop of the curves

(a) $\rho = a\cos 2\varphi$; (b) $\rho = a\sin 2\varphi$.

7.5.9. Compute the area enclosed by the portion of the cardioid $\rho = a(1 - \cos\varphi)$ lying inside the circle $\rho = a\cos\varphi$.

7.5.10. Compute the area of the region enclosed by the curve $\rho = a\sin\varphi\cos^2\varphi$, $a > 0$.

7.5.11. Compute the area of the region enclosed by the curve $\rho = a\cos^3 a$ $(a > 0)$.

7.5.12. Compute the area of the portion $\left(\text{lying inside the circle } \rho = \frac{a}{\sqrt{2}}\right)$ of the figure bounded by the Bernouli's lemniscate $\rho = a\sqrt{\cos 2\varphi}$.

7.5.13. Passing over to polar coordinates, compute the area of the region enclosed by the curve $(x^2 + y^2)^3 = 4a^2x^2y^2$.

7.5.14. Passing over to polar coordinates, evaluate the area of the region enclosed by the curve $x^4 + y^4 = a^2(x^2 + y^2)$.

7.6. Computing the Volume of Solid

The volume of a solid is expressed by the integral

$$V = \int_a^b S(x)\,dx$$

where $S(x)$ is the area of the section of the solid by a plane perpendicular to the x-axis at the point with abscissa x ; a and b are the left and right boundaries of variation of x. The function $S(x)$ is supposed to be known and continuously changing as x varies between a and b.

The volume V_x of a solid generated by revolution about the x-axis of the curvilinear trapezoid bounded by the curve $y = f(x)$ ($f(x) \geq 0$), the x-axis and the straight lines $x = a$ and $x = b$ $(a < b)$ is expressed by the integral

$$V_x = \pi \int_a^b y^2 dx.$$

The volume V_x of a solid obtained by revolving about the x-axis the figure bounded by the curves $y = y_1(x)$ and $y = y_2(x)$ $[0 \leq y_1(x) \leq y_2(x)]$ and the straight lines $x = a$, $x = b$ is expressed by the integral

$$V_x = \pi \int_a^b (y_2^2 - y_1^2)\,dx.$$

If the curve is represented parametrically or in polar coordinates, the appropriate change of the variable should be made in the above formulas.

7.6.1. Find the volume of the ellipsoid

$$\frac{x^2}{a^2} + \frac{y^2}{b^2} + \frac{z^2}{c^2} = 1.$$

Solution The section of the ellipsoid by the plane $x = \text{const}$ is an ellipse (Fig. 87)

$$\frac{y^2}{b^2\left(1 - \frac{x^2}{a^2}\right)} + \frac{z^2}{c^2\left(1 - \frac{x^2}{a^2}\right)} = 1$$

with semi-axis $b\sqrt{1 - \frac{x^2}{a^2}}$; $c\sqrt{1 - \frac{x^2}{a^2}}$. Hence the area of the section (see Problem **7.4.1**)

$$S(x) = \pi b\sqrt{1 - \frac{x^2}{a^2}} \times c\sqrt{1 - \frac{x^2}{a^2}} = \pi bc\left(1 - \frac{x^2}{a^2}\right) \quad (-a \leq x \leq a).$$

Therefore the volume V of the ellipsoid is

$$V = \int_{-a}^{a} \pi bc\left(1 - \frac{x^2}{a^2}\right) dx = \pi\, bc\left[x - \frac{x^3}{3a^2}\right]_{-a}^{a} = \frac{4}{3}\pi\, abc.$$

In the particular case $a = b = c$ the ellipsoid turns into a sphere, and we have $V_{\text{sphere}} = \frac{4}{3}\pi a^3$.

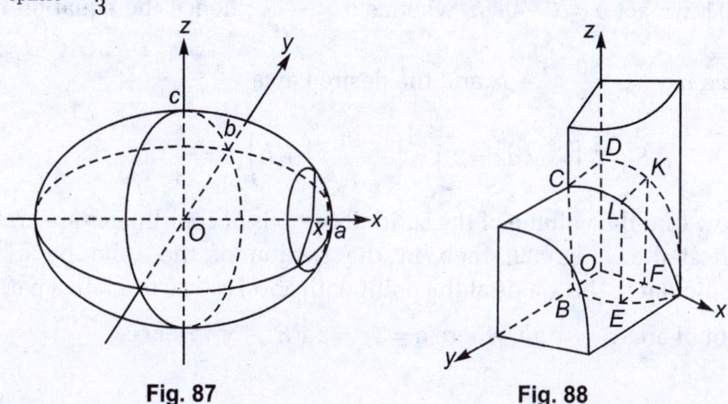

Fig. 87

Fig. 88

7.6.2. Compute the volume of the solid spherical segment of two bases cut out by the planes $x = 2$ and $x = 3$ from the sphere $x^2 + y^2 + z^2 = 16$.

7.6.3. The axes of two identical cylinders with bases of radius a intersect at right angles. Find the volume of the solid constituting the common portion of the two cylinders.

Solution Take the axes of the cylinders to be the y and z-axis (Fig. 88). The solid $OABCD$ constitutes one-eighth of the soughtior solid.

Let its cut this solid by a plane perpendicular to the x-axis at a distance x from 0. In the section we get a square $EFKL$ with side $EF = \sqrt{a^2 - x^2}$, therefore $S(x) = a^2 - x^2$ and $V = 8\int_0^a (a^2 - x^2)\, dx = \frac{16}{3}a^3$.

7.6.4. On all chords (parallel to one and the same direction) a circle of radius R symmetrical parabolic segments of the same altitude h are constructed. The planes of the segments are perpendicular to the plane of the circle.

Find the volume of the solid thus obtained (Fig. 89).

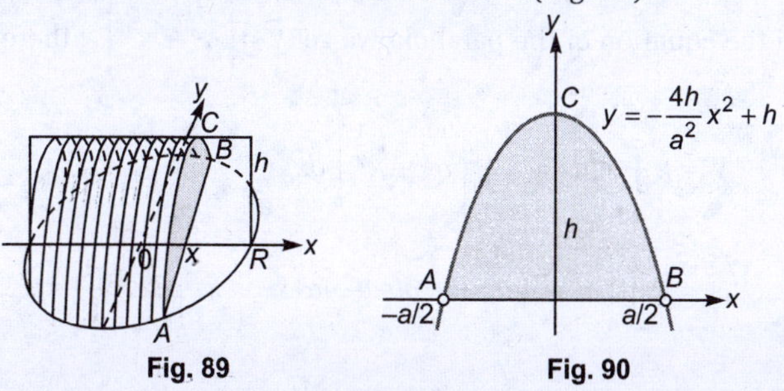

Fig. 89

Fig. 90

Solution First compute the area of the parabolic segment with base a and altitude h. If we arrange the axes of coordinates as indicated in Fig. 90, then the equation of the parabola will be $y = \alpha x^2 + h$.

Determine the parameter α. Substituting the coordinates of the point $B\left(\frac{a}{2}, 0\right)$, we get $0 = \alpha \frac{a^2}{4} + h$, whence $\alpha = -\frac{4h}{a^2}$; hence the equation of the parabola is $y = -\frac{4h}{a^2} x^2 + h$, and the desired area

$$S = 2\int_0^{a/2} y\,dx = 2\int_0^{a/2}\left(-\frac{4h}{a^2}x^2 + h\right)dx = \frac{2}{3}ah.$$

Now find the volume of the solid. If the axis of coordinates are arranged as indicated in Fig. 89, then in the section of the solid by a plane perpendicular to the x-axis at the point with abscissa x we obtain a parabolic segment of area $S = \frac{2}{3}ah$, where $a = 2y = 2\sqrt{R^2 - x^2}$. Hence,

$$S(x) = \frac{4}{3}\sqrt{R^2 - x^2}\,h$$

and

$$V = \int_{-R}^{R} S\,dx = \frac{8}{3}h\int_0^R S\sqrt{R^2 - x^2}\,dx = \frac{2}{3}\pi h R^2.$$

7.6.5. The plane of a moving triangle remains perpendicular to the fixed diameter of a circle of radius a ; the base of the triangle is a chord o the circle, and its vertex lies on a straight line parallel to the fixed diameter at a distance h from the plane of the circle. Find the volume of the solid generated by the movement of this triangle from one end of the diameter to the other.

7.6.6. Compute the volume of the solid generated by revolving about the x-axis the area bounded by the axes of coordinates and the parabola $x^{\frac{1}{2}} + y^{\frac{1}{2}} = a^{\frac{1}{2}}$.

Solution Let us find the points of intersection of the curve and the axes of coordinates : at $x = 0$ $y = a$, at $y = 0$ $x = a$. Thus we have the interval of integration of $[0, a]$.

From the equation of the parabola we get $y = \left(a^{\frac{1}{2}} - x^{\frac{1}{2}}\right)^2$; therefore

$$V = \pi\int_0^a y^2 dx = \pi\int_0^a \left(a^{\frac{1}{2}} - x^{\frac{1}{2}}\right)^4 dx$$

$$= \pi\int_0^a \left(a^2 - 4a^{\frac{3}{2}}x^{\frac{1}{2}} + 6ax - 4a^{\frac{1}{2}}x^{\frac{3}{2}} + x^2\right)dx = \frac{1}{15}\pi a^3.$$

7.6.7. The figure bounded by an arc of the sinusoid $y = \sin x$, the axis of ordinates and the straight line $y = 1$ resolves about the y-axis (Fig. 91).

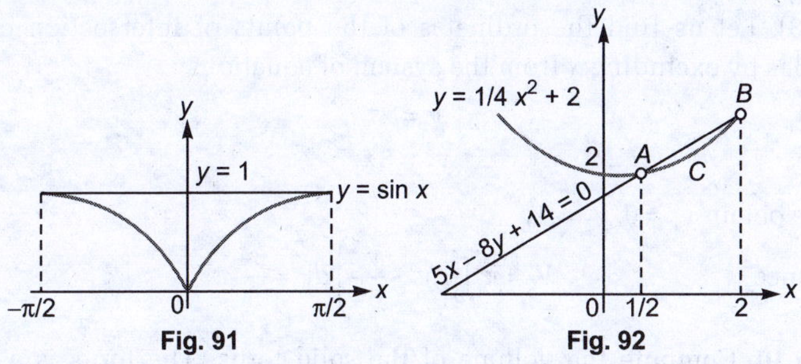

Fig. 91 **Fig. 92**

Compute the volume V of the solid of revolution thus generated.

Solution The inverse function $x = \arcsin y$ is considered on the interval [0, 1]. Therefore

$$V = \pi \int_{y_1}^{y_2} x^2 dy = \pi \int_0^1 (\arcsin y)^2 dy.$$

Apply the substitution $\arcsin y = t$. Hence,

$$y = \sin t, \quad dy = \cos t\, dt, \quad \begin{array}{c|c} y & t \\ \hline 0 & 0 \\ 1 & \pi/2 \end{array}.$$

And so, $V = \pi \int_0^{\pi/2} t^2 \cos t\, dt$. Integrating by parts, we get $V = \dfrac{\pi(\pi^2 - 8)}{4}$.

7.6.8. Compute the volume of the solid generated by revolving about the x-axis the figure bounded by the parabola $y = 0.25\, x^2 + 2$ and the straight line $5x - 8y + 14 = 0$.

Solution The solid is obtained by resolving the area $ABCA$ (Fig. 92) about the x-axis. To find the abscissas of the points A and B solve the system of equations.

$$\begin{cases} y = \dfrac{1}{4} x^2 + 2, \\ 5x - 8y + 14 = 0. \end{cases}$$

whence $x_A = \dfrac{1}{2}$; $x_B = 2$. In our case $y_1(x) = \dfrac{1}{4} x^2 + 2$ and $y_2(x) = (5/8)\, x + 7/4$. Hence,

$$V = \pi \int_{1/2}^{2} \left[\frac{1}{16} \left(\frac{5}{2} x + 7 \right)^2 - \left(\frac{1}{4} x^2 + 2 \right)^2 \right] dx = \frac{891}{1180} \pi.$$

7.6.9. Compute the volume of the solid generated by revolving about the y-axis the figure bounded by the parabolas $y = x^2$ and $8x = y^2$

Solution It is obvious that $x_2(y) = \sqrt{y} \geq x_1(y) = \dfrac{y^2}{8}$ on the interval from the origin of the coordinates to the point of intersection of the parabolas (Fig. 93). Let us find the ordinates of the points of intersection of the parabolas by excluding x from the system of equations :

$$\begin{cases} y = x^2, \\ y^2 = 8x. \end{cases}$$

We obtain $y_1 = 0, y_2 = 4$.

Hence $$V = \pi \int_0^4 \left(y - \frac{y^4}{64} \right) dy = \frac{24}{5}\pi.$$

7.6.10. Compute the volume of the solid torus. The torus is a solid generated by revolving a circle of radius a about an axis lying in its plane at a distance b from the centre ($b \geq a$). (A tire, for example, has the form of the torus).

7.6.11. Compute the volume of the solid obtained by revolving about the x-axis the figure bounded by two branches of the curve $(y - x)^2 = x^3$ and the straight line $x = 1$.

7.6.12. Find the volume of the solid generated by revolving about the line $y = -2a$ the figure bounded by the parabola $y^2 = 4ax$ and the straight line $x = a$ (Fig. 94).

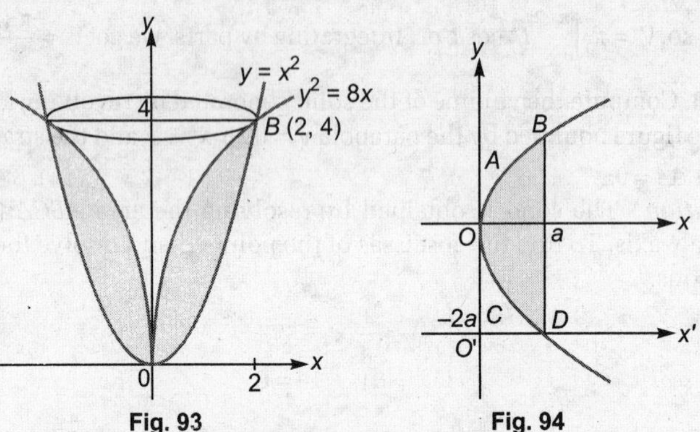

Fig. 93

Fig. 94

Solution If we transfer the origin of coordinates into the point $O'(0, -2a)$ retaining the direction of the axes, then in the new system of coordinates the equation of the parabola will be

$$(y' - 2a)^2 = 4ax.$$

Hence $y_2 = 2a + \sqrt{4ax}$ (for the curve OAB), and $y_1 = 2a - \sqrt{4ax}$ (for the curve OCD). The sought for volume is equal to

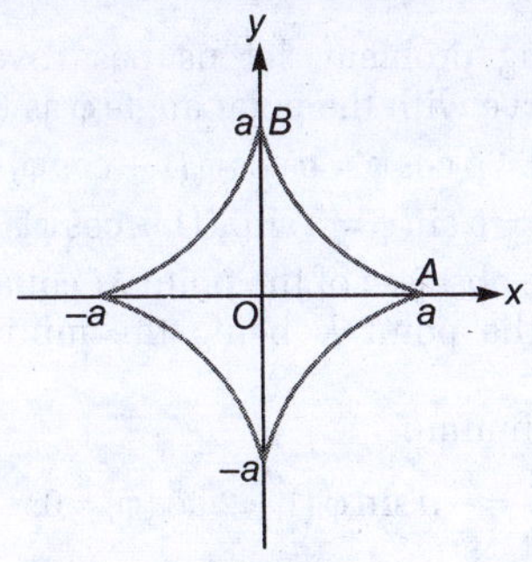

Fig. 95

$$V = \pi \int_0^a (y_2^2 - y_1^2)\, dx = \pi \int_0^a [(2a + 2\sqrt{ax})^2$$

$$- (2a - \sqrt{2}\,\sqrt{ax})^2]\, dx = \frac{32}{3}\pi c^3.$$

7.6.13. Find the volume of the solid generated by revolving about the x-axis the figure enclosed by the astroid : $x = a\cos^3 t$; $y = a\sin^3 t$.

Solution The sought-for volume V is equal to double the volume obtained by revolving the figure OAB (Fig. 95). Therefore,

$$V = 2\pi \int_0^a y_2\, dx.$$

Change the variable

$$x = a\cos^2 t,$$

$$dx = -3a\cos^2 t \sin t\, dt,$$

$$y = a\sin^3 t,$$

x	t
0	$\pi/2$
a	0

Hence $$V = 2\pi \int_{\pi/2}^0 a^2 \sin^6 t\,(-3a\cos^2 t \sin t)\, dt$$

$$= 6\pi a^3 \left[\int_0^{\pi/2} \sin^7 t\, dt - \int_0^{\pi/2} \sin^9 t\, dt\right].$$

Using the formula from Problem **6.6.9.** for computing the above integrals, we get

$$V = 6\pi a^3 \left(\frac{6}{7}\times\frac{4}{5}\times\frac{2}{3} - \frac{8}{9}\times\frac{6}{7}\times\frac{4}{5}\times\frac{2}{3}\right) = \frac{32}{105}\pi a^2$$

7.6.14. Compute the volume of the solid generated by revolving one arc of the cycloid $x = a(t - \sin t)$, $y = a(1 - \cos t)$ about the x-axis.

7.6.15. Compute the volume of the solid obtained by revolving about the polar axis the cardioid $\rho = a(1 + \cos\varphi)$ shown in Fig. 81.

Solution The sought-for volume represents the difference between the volumes generated by revolving the figures $MNKLO$ and $OKLO$ about the x-axis (which is the polar axis at the same time).

As in the preceding problem, let us pass over to the parametric representation of the curve with the polar angle φ as the parameter :

$$x = \rho \cos\varphi = a \cos\varphi\,(1 + \cos\varphi),$$
$$y = \rho \sin\varphi = a \sin\varphi\,(1 + \cos\varphi).$$

It is obvious that the abscissa of the point M equals $2a$ (the value of x at $\varphi = 0$), the abscissa of the point K being the minimum of the function $x = a(1 + \cos\varphi)\cos\varphi$.

Let us find this minimum :

$$\frac{dx}{d\varphi} = -a \sin\varphi\,(1 + 2\cos\varphi) = 0,$$

$$\varphi_1 = 0\,;\ \varphi_2 = \frac{2}{3}\pi.$$

At $\varphi_1 = 0$ we obtain $x_M = 2a$, at $\varphi_2 = \frac{2}{3}\pi$, $x_K = -\frac{a}{4}$.

Hence, the sought-for volume is equal to

$$V = \pi \int_{-a/4}^{2a} y_2^2\,dx - \pi \int_{-a/4}^{0} y_1^2\,dx$$

Changing the variable $x = a\cos\varphi\,(1 + \cos\varphi)$, we get

$$y^2 = a^2(1 + \cos\varphi)^2 \sin^2\varphi$$
$$dx = -a \sin\varphi\,(1 + 2\cos\varphi)\,d\varphi,$$

x	φ
$-a/4$	$2\pi/3$
$2a$	0

x	φ
$-a/4$	$2\pi/3$
0	π

Thus,

$$V = \pi \int_{2/3\,\pi}^{0} a^2\,(1 + \cos\varphi)^2 \sin^2\varphi\,[-a\sin\varphi\,(1 + 2\cos\varphi)]\,d\varphi$$
$$- \pi \int_{2/3\,\pi}^{\pi} a^2(1 + \cos\varphi)^2 \sin^2\varphi\,[-a\sin\varphi\,(1 + 2\cos\varphi)]\,d\varphi$$
$$= \pi a^3 \int_0^{\pi} \sin^3\varphi\,(1 + \cos\varphi)^2\,(1 + 2\cos\varphi)\,d\varphi$$
$$= \pi a^3 \int_{-1}^{1} (1 - u^2)\,(1 + u)^2\,(1 + 2u)\,du = \frac{8}{3}\pi a^3\ (u = \cos\varphi).$$

7.6.16. Compute the volume of the solid bounded by :

(a) the hyperboloid of one sheet $\frac{x^2}{a^2} + \frac{y^2}{b^2} - \frac{z^2}{c^2} = 1$ and the planes $z = -1$ and $z = 1$;

(b) the parabolic cylinder $z = 4 - y^2$, the planes of coordinates and the plane $x = a$;

(c) the elliptic paraboloid $z = \frac{x^2}{a^2} + \frac{y^2}{b^2}$ and the plane $z = k$ $(k > 0)$.

7.6.17. A wedge is cut off from a right circular cylinder of radius a by a plane passing through the diameter of the cylinder base and inclined at an angle α to the base. Find the volume of the wedge.

7.6.18. Compute the volume of the solid generated by revolving the figure bounded by the following lines :

(a) $xy = 4$, $x = 1$, $x = 4$, $y = 0$ about the x-axis;
(b) $y = 2x - x^2$, $y = 0$ about the x-axis;
(c) $y = x^3$, $y = 0$, $x = 2$ about the y-axis;
(d) $y = \sin x$ (one wave), $y = 0$ about the x-axis;
(e) $x^2 - y^2 = 4$, $y = \pm 2$ about the y-axis.
(f) $(y - a)^2 = ax$, $x = 0$, $y = 2a$ about the x-axis

7.6.19. Find the volume of the solid obtained by revolving the curve $y^2 = \dfrac{ax^3 - x^4}{a^2}$ about the x-axis.

7.6.20. Compute the volume of the solid generated by revolving about the x-axis the figure bounded by the lines $y = \sin x$ and $y = \dfrac{2}{\pi} x$.

7.6.21. Compute the volume of the solid generated by revolving about the x-axis the curvilinear trapezoid bounded by the catenary $y = \dfrac{a}{2}\left(e^{\frac{x}{a}} + e^{-\frac{x}{a}}\right) = a\cosh\dfrac{x}{a}$ and the straight lines $x_1 = -c$, $x_2 = c$ $(c > 0)$.

7.6.22. Compute the volume of the solid generated by revolving about the x-axis the figure bounded by the cosine line $y = \cos x$ and the parabola $y = \dfrac{9}{2\pi^2} x^2$.

7.6.23. Compute the volume of the solid generated by revolving about the x-axis the figure bounded by the circle $x^2 + y^2 = 1$ and parabola $y^2 = \dfrac{3}{2} x$.

7.6.24. On the curve $y = x^3$ take two points A and B, whose abscissas are $a = 1$ and $b = 2$, respectively.

Find the volume of the solid generated by revolving the curvilinear trapezoid $aABb$ about the x-axis.

7.6.25. An arc of the evolute of the ellipse $x = a\cos t$; $y = b\sin t$ situated in the first quadrant revolves about the x-axis

Find the volume of the solid thus generated.

7.6.26. Compute the volume of the solid generated by revolving the region enclosed by the loop of the curve $x = at^2$, $y = a\left(t - \dfrac{t^3}{3}\right)$ about the x-axis.

7.6.27. Compute the volumes of the solids generated by revolving the region enclosed by the lemniscate $(x^2 + y^2) = a^2 (x^2 - y^2)$ about the x and y-axes.

7.6.28. Compute the volume of the solid generated by revolving the region enclosed by the curve $\rho = a\cos^2\varphi$ about the polar axis.

7.7. The Arc Length of a Plane Curve in Rectangular Coordinates

If a plane curve is given by the equation $y = y(x)$ and the derivative $y'(x)$ is continuous, then the length of an arc of this curve is expressed by the integral

$$I = \int_a^b \sqrt{1 + y'^2}\, dx$$

where a and b are the abscissas of the end-points of the given arc.

7.7.1. Compute the length of the arc of the semicubical parabola $y^2 = x^3$ between the points (0, 0) and (4, 8) (Fig. 96)

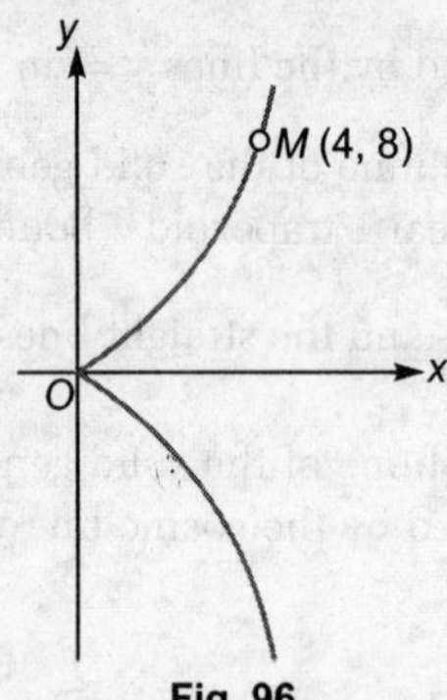

Fig. 96

Solution The function $y(x)$ is defined for $x \geq 0$. Since the given points lie in the first quadrant, $y = x^{\frac{3}{2}}$. Hence, $y' = \frac{3}{2}\sqrt{x}$ and $\sqrt{1 + y'^2} = \sqrt{1 + \frac{9}{4}x}$.

Consequently,

$$I = \int_0^4 \sqrt{1 + \frac{9}{4}x}\, dx = \frac{4}{9}\cdot\frac{2}{3}\left(1 + \frac{9}{4}x\right)^{\frac{3}{2}}\Bigg|_0^4$$

$$= \frac{8}{27}(10\sqrt{10} - 1).$$

7.7.2. Compute the length of the arc cut off from the curve $y^2 = x^3$ by the straight line $x = \frac{4}{3}$.

7.7.3. Compute the arc length of the curve $y = \ln \cos x$ between the points with the abscissas $x = 0$, $x = \frac{\pi}{4}$.

Solution Since, $y' = -\tan x$, then $\sqrt{1 + y'^2} = \sqrt{1 + \tan^2 x} = \sec x$.

Hence, $I = \int_0^{\pi/4} \sec x\, dx = \ln \tan\left(\frac{\pi}{4} + \frac{x}{2}\right)\Big|_0^{\frac{\pi}{4}} = \ln \tan \frac{3\pi}{8}$

7.7.4. Compute the arc length of the curve $y = \ln \frac{e^x + 1}{e^x - 1}$ from $x_1 = a$ to $x_2 = b$ $(b > a)$.

7.7.5. Find the arc length of the curve $x = \frac{1}{4}y^2 - \frac{1}{2}\ln y$ between the points with the ordinates $y = 1$ and $y = 2$.

Solution Here it is convenient to adopt y as the independent variable; then

$$x' = \frac{1}{2}y - \frac{1}{2y} \quad \text{and} \quad \sqrt{1 + x'^2} = \sqrt{\left(\frac{1}{2}y + \frac{1}{2y}\right)^2} = \frac{1}{2}y + \frac{1}{2y}.$$

Hence $I = \int_1^2 \sqrt{1 + x'^2}\, dy = \int_1^2 \left(\frac{1}{2}y + \frac{1}{2y}\right) dy = \frac{3}{4} + \frac{1}{2}\ln 2.$

7.7.6. Find the length of the astroid $x^{\frac{2}{3}} + y^{\frac{2}{3}} = a^{\frac{2}{3}}$.

Solution As is known, the astroid is symmetrical about the axis of coordinates and the bisectors of the coordinate angles. Therefore, it is sufficient to compute the arc length of the astroid between the bisector $y = x$ and the x-axis and multiply the result by 8.

In the first quadrant $y = \left(a^{\frac{2}{3}} - x^{\frac{2}{3}}\right)^{\frac{2}{3}}$ and $y = 0$ at $x = a$, $y = x$ at $x = \frac{a}{2^{3/2}}$.

Further,
$$y' = \frac{3}{2}\left(a^{\frac{2}{3}} - x^{\frac{2}{3}}\right)^{\frac{1}{2}}\left(-\frac{2}{3}\right)x^{-\frac{1}{3}}$$

$$= -x^{-\frac{1}{3}}\left(a^{\frac{2}{3}} - x^{\frac{2}{3}}\right)^{\frac{1}{2}}$$

and
$$\sqrt{1 + y'^2} = \sqrt{1 + x^{-\frac{2}{3}}\left(a^{\frac{2}{3}} - x^{\frac{2}{3}}\right)} = \left(\frac{a}{x}\right)^{\frac{1}{3}}.$$

Consequently,
$$I = 8\int_{\frac{a}{2^{3/2}}}^{a} a^{\frac{1}{3}} x^{-\frac{1}{3}}\, dx = 6a.$$

Note. If we compute the arc length of an astroid situated in the first quadrant, we get the integral

$$\int_0^a a^{\frac{1}{3}} x^{-\frac{1}{3}}\, dx,$$

whose integrand increases infinitely as $x \to 0$.

7.7.7. Compute the length of the path $OABCO$ consisting of portions of the curves $y^2 = 2x^3$ and $x^2 + y^2 = 20$ (Fig. 97).

Solution It is sufficient to compute the arc length l_{OA} and l_{AB} since by symmetry of the figure about the x-axis

$$l = 2\,(l_{OA} + l_{AB}).$$

Solving the system of equations

$$\begin{cases} x^2 + y^2 = 20, \\ y^2 = 2x^3, \end{cases}$$

we find the point A (2, 4). Find l_{OA}. Here

$$y = \sqrt{2}\, x^{\frac{3}{2}},\ y' = \frac{3}{2}\sqrt{2x},\ \sqrt{1 + y'^2} = \sqrt{1 + \frac{9}{2}x}.$$

Hence,

$$l_{OA} = \int_0^2 \sqrt{1 + \frac{9}{2}x}\, dx = \frac{4}{27}(10\sqrt{10} - 1).$$

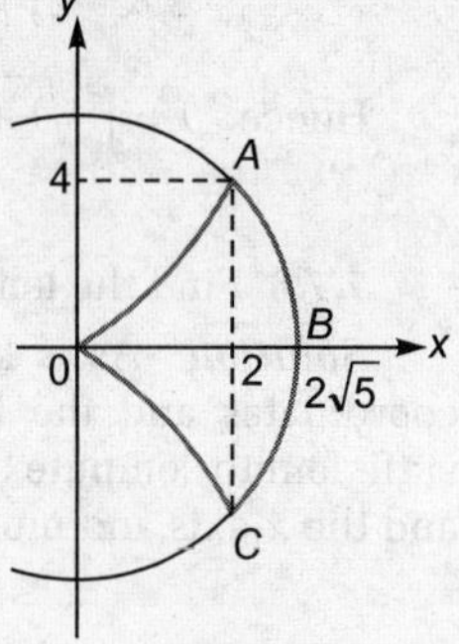

Fig. 97

Since, on the circle of radius $\sqrt{20}$ l_{AB} is the length of an arc corresponding to the central angle arc tan 2,

$$l_{AB} = \sqrt{20} \text{ arc tan } 2.$$

Finally we have

$$l = \frac{8}{27}(10\sqrt{10} - 1) + 4\sqrt{5} \text{ arc tan } 2.$$

7.7.8. Compute the arc length of the curve :

(a) $y = \dfrac{x^2}{2} - 1$ cut off by the x-axis;

(b) $y = \ln(2\cos x)$ between the adjacent points of intersection with the x-axis.

(c) $3y^2 = x(x-1)^2$ between the adjacent points of intersection with the x-axis (half the loop length)

7.7.9. Compute the arc length of the curve

$$y = \frac{1}{2}\left[x\sqrt{x^2 - 1} - \ln\left(x + \sqrt{x^2 - 1}\right)\right]$$

between $x = 1$ and $x = a + 1$.

7.7.10. Find the arc length of the path consisting of portions the curves $x^2 = (y+1)^3$ and $y = 4$.

7.8. The Arc Length of a Curve Represented Parametrically

If a curve is given by the equations in the parametric from $x = x(t)$, $y = y(t)$ and the derivatives $x'(t)$, $y'(t)$ are continuous on the interval $[t_1, t_2]$, then the arc length of the curve is expressed by the integral

$$I = \int_{t_1}^{t_2} \sqrt{x'^2(t) + y'^2(t)}\, dt,$$

where t_1 and t_2 are the values of the parameter t corresponding to the end-point of the arc $(t_1 < t_2)$.

7.8.1. Compute the arc length of the involute of a circle $x = a(\cos t + t\sin t)$, $y = a(\sin t - t\cos t)$ from $t = 0$ to $t = 2\pi$.

Solution Differentiating with respect to t, we obtain

$$x'_t = at\cos t,\ y'_t = at\sin t$$

whence $\sqrt{x'^2_t + y'^2_t} = at$. Hence

$$I = \int_0^{2\pi} at\, dt = \frac{at^2}{2}\Bigg|_0^{2\pi} = 2a\pi^2 .$$

7.8.2. Find the length of one arc of the cycloid :

$$x = a(t - \sin t),\ y = a(1 - \cos t).$$

7.8.3. Compute the length of the astroid : $x = a\cos^3 t$, $y = a\sin^3 t$.

Solution Differentiating with respect to t, we obtain

$$x'_t = -3a\cos^2 t\sin t$$

$$y'_t = 3a\sin^2 t\cos t$$

Hence,

$$\sqrt{x'^2 + y'^2} = \sqrt{9a^2\sin^2 t\cos^2 t} = 3a|\sin t\cos t| = \frac{3a}{2}|\sin 2t|.$$

Since the function $|\sin 2t|$ has as period $\frac{\pi}{2}$,

$$I = 4 \times \frac{3a}{2}\int_0^{\pi/2} \sin 2t\, dt = 6a.$$

Note. If we forget that we have to take the arithmetic value of the root and put $\sqrt{x'^2_t + y'^2_t} = 3a\sin t\cos t$, we shall obtain the wrong result since,

$$3a\int_0^{2\pi} \sin t\cos t\, dt = \frac{3a}{2}\sin^2 t\Bigg|_0^{2\pi} = 0\cdot$$

7.8.4. Compute the length of the loop of the curve $x = \sqrt{3}\,t^2$, $y = t - t^3$.

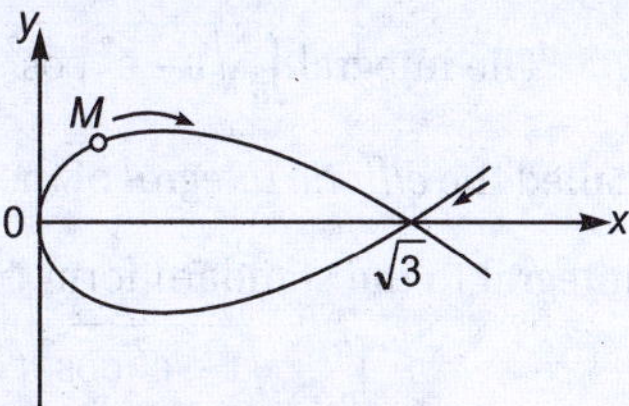

Fig. 98

Solution Let us find the limits of integration. Both functions $x(t)$ and $y(t)$ are defined for all values of t. Since the function $x = \sqrt{3}t^2 \geq 0$, the curve lies in the right half-plane. Since with a change in sign of the parameter t, $x(t)$ remains unchanged, while $y(t)$ changes sign, the curve is symmetrical about the x-axis. Furthermore, the function $x(t)$ takes on one and the same value not more than twice. Hence. it follows that the point of self-intersection of the curve lie on the x-axis *ie*, at $y = 0$ (Fig. 98).

The direction in which the moving point $M(x, y)$ runs along the curves as t changes from $-\infty$ to ∞ is indicated by the arrows.

But $y = 0$ at $t_1 = 0$, $t_{2,3} = \pm 1$. Since $x(t_2) = x(t_3) = \sqrt{3}$, the point $(\sqrt{3}, 0)$ is the only point of self-intersection of the curve. Consequently, we must integrate within the limits $t_2 = -1$ and $t_3 = 1$. Differentiating the parametric equations of the curve with respect to t, we get $x'_t = 2\sqrt{3}t$, $y'_t = 1 - 3t^2$, whence

$$\sqrt{x'^2_t + y'^2_t} = 1 + 3t^2.$$

Consequently,

$$I = \int_{-1}^{1} (1 + 3t^2)\, dt = 4.$$

7.8.5. Compute the arc length of the curve $x = \frac{t^6}{6}$, $y = 2 - \frac{t^4}{4}$ between the points of intersection with the axes of coordinates.

7.8.6. Compute the arc length of the ellipse $\frac{x^2}{a^2} + \frac{y^2}{b^2} = 1$.

Solution Let us pass over to parametric representation of the ellipse

$$x = \cos t, \quad y = b \sin t, \quad 0 \le t \le 2\pi.$$

Differentiating with respect to t, we obtain

$$x'_t = -a \sin t; \quad y'_t = b \cos t,$$

whence,

$$\sqrt{x'^2_t + y'^2_t} = \sqrt{a^2 \sin^2 t + b^2 \cos^2 t} = a\sqrt{1 - \varepsilon^2 \cos^2 t}$$

where ε is the eccentricity of the ellipse,

$$\varepsilon = \frac{c}{a} = \frac{\sqrt{a^2 - b^2}}{a}.$$

Thus,

$$I = a\int_0^{2\pi} \sqrt{1 - \varepsilon^2 \cos^2 t}\, dt = 4a\int_0^{\pi/2} \sqrt{1 - \varepsilon^2 \cos^2 t}\, dt.$$

The integral $\int_0^t \sqrt{1 - \varepsilon^2 \cos^2 t}\, dt$ is not taken in elementary functions; it is called the *elliptic integral* of the *second kind*. Putting $t = \frac{\pi}{2} - \tau$, we reduce the integral to the standard form :

$$\int_0^{\pi/2} \sqrt{1 - \varepsilon^2 \cos^2 t}\, dt = \int_0^{\pi/2} \sqrt{1 - \varepsilon^2 \sin^2 \tau}\, d\tau = E(\varepsilon),$$

where $E(\varepsilon)$ is the notation for the so-called *complete elliptic integral of the second kind*. Consequently, for the arc length of an ellipse the formula $l = 4aE(\varepsilon)$ holds good.

It is usual practice to put $\varepsilon = \sin\alpha$ and to use the tables of values the function

$$E_1(\alpha) = E_1(\arcsin\varepsilon) = E(\varepsilon).$$

For instance, if $a = 10$ and $b = 6$, then

$$\varepsilon = \frac{\sqrt{10^2 - 6^2}}{10} = 0.8 = \sin 53°.$$

Using the table of values of elliptic integrals of the second kind, we find

$$I = 40E_1(53°) = 40 \times 1.2776 \approx 51.1.$$

7.8.7. Compute the arc length of the curve

$$x = t^2, \qquad y = \frac{t}{3}(t^2 - 3)$$

between the points of intersection with the x-axis.

7.8.8. Find the arc length of the cardioid

$$x = a(2\cos t - \cos 2t)$$
$$y = a(2\sin t - \sin 2t).$$

7.8.9. Find the length of the closed curve

$$x = 4\sqrt{2}\, a\sin t\,;\, y = a\sin 2t.$$

7.8.10. Find the arc length of the evolute of the ellipse

$$x = \frac{c^2}{a}\cos^3 t, y = -\frac{c^2}{b}\sin^3 t, c^2 = a^2 - b^2.$$

7.8.11. Compute the arc length of the curve

$$x = (t^2 - 2)\sin t + 2t\cos t,$$
$$y = (2 - t^2)\cos t + 2t\sin t.$$

between $t_1 = 0$ and $t_2 = \pi$

7.8.12. On the cycloid $x = a(t - \sin t)$; $y = a(1 - \cos t)$ find the point which divides the length of the first arc of the cycloid in the ratio 1 : 3.

7.9. The Arc Length of a Curve in Polar Coordinates

If a smooth curve is given by the equation $\rho = \rho(\varphi)$ in polar coordinates, then the arc length of the curve is expressed by the integral :

$$I = \int_{\varphi_1}^{\varphi_2} \sqrt{\rho^2 + \rho'^2_\varphi}\, d\varphi,$$

where φ_1 and φ_2 are the values of the polar angle φ at the end points of the arc $(\varphi_1 < \varphi_2)$.

7.9.1. Find the length of the first turn of the spiral of the Archimedes $\rho = a\varphi$.

Solution The first turn of the spiral is formed as the polar angle φ changes from 0 to 2π. Therefore.

$$I = \int_0^{2\pi} \sqrt{a^2\varphi^2 + a^2}\, d\varphi = a\int_0^{2\pi} \sqrt{\varphi^2 + 1}\, d\varphi$$

$$= a\left[\pi\sqrt{4\pi^2+1}+\frac{1}{2}\ln\left(2\pi+\sqrt{4\pi^2+1}\right)\right].$$

7.9.2. Find the length of the logarithmic spiral $\rho = ae^{m\phi}$ between a certain point (ρ_0, φ_0) and a moving point (ρ, φ).

Solution In this case (no matter which of the magnitudes, ρ or ρ_0, is greater)

$$I = \left|\int_{\varphi_0}^{\varphi}\sqrt{a^2e^{2m\varphi}+a^2m^2e^{2m\varphi}}\,d\varphi\right|$$

$$= a\sqrt{1+m^2}\left|\int_{\varphi_0}^{\varphi}e^{m\varphi}d\varphi\right| = a\frac{\sqrt{1+m^2}}{m}\left|e^{m\varphi}-e^{m\varphi_0}\right|$$

$$= \frac{\sqrt{1+m^2}}{m}\left|\rho-\rho_0\right| = \frac{\sqrt{1+m^2}}{m}\left|\Delta\rho\right|.$$

ie, the length of the logarithmic spiral is proportional to the increment of the polar radius of the arc.

7.9.3. Find the arc length of the cardioid $\rho = a(1+\cos\varphi)$ $(a > 0, 0 \le \varphi \le 2\pi)$.

Solution Here $\rho_\varphi{}' = -a\sin\varphi$,

$$\sqrt{\rho'^2_\varphi+\rho^2} = \sqrt{2a^2(1+\cos\varphi)} = \sqrt{4a^2\cos^2(\varphi/2)}$$

$$= 2a\left|\cos(\varphi/2)\right| = \begin{cases} 2a\cos(\varphi/2), & 0\le\varphi\le\pi \\ -2a\cos(\varphi/2), & \pi\le\varphi\le 2\pi \end{cases}.$$

Hence, by virtue of symmetry

$$I = 2a\int_0^{2\pi}\left|\cos\frac{\varphi}{2}\right|d\varphi = 4a\int_0^{\pi}\cos\frac{\varphi}{2}\,d\varphi = 8a.$$

7.9.4. Find the length of the lemniscate $\rho^2 = 2a^2\cos 2\varphi$ between the right-hand vertex corresponding to $\varphi = 0$ and any point with a polar angle $\varphi < \dfrac{\pi}{4}$.

Solution If $0 \le \varphi < \dfrac{\pi}{4}$, then $\cos 2\varphi > 0$. Therefore

$$\rho = a\sqrt{2\cos 2\varphi}\,;\ \rho_\varphi = -\frac{a\sqrt{2}\sin 2\varphi}{\sqrt{\cos 2\varphi}};$$

$$\sqrt{\rho^2+\rho'^2_\varphi} = \sqrt{2a^2\left(\cos 2\varphi+\frac{\sin^2 2\varphi}{\cos 2\varphi}\right)} = \frac{a\sqrt{2}}{\sqrt{\cos 2\varphi}}.$$

Hence,

$$I = a\sqrt{2}\int_0^{\varphi}\frac{d\varphi}{\sqrt{\cos 2\varphi}} = a\sqrt{2}\int_0^{\varphi}\frac{d\varphi}{\sqrt{1-2\sin^2\varphi}}.$$

The latter integral is called the *elliptic integral of the first kind*. It can be reduced to a form convenient for computing with the aid of special tables.

7.9.5. Find the arc length of the curve $\rho = a\sin^3\dfrac{\varphi}{3}$.

7.9.6. Compute the length of the segment of the straight line $\rho = a\sec\left(\varphi - \dfrac{\pi}{3}\right)$ between $\varphi = 0$ and $\varphi = \dfrac{\pi}{2}$.

Solution $\rho'_\varphi = a\sec\left(\varphi - \dfrac{\pi}{3}\right)\tan\left(\varphi - \dfrac{\pi}{3}\right)$;

$$\sqrt{\rho^2 + \rho'^2_\varphi} = a\sec\left(\varphi - \frac{\pi}{3}\right)\sqrt{1 + \tan^2\left(\varphi - \frac{\pi}{3}\right)} = a\sec^2\left(\varphi - \frac{\pi}{3}\right).$$

(The sign of modulus in the function $\sec\left(\varphi - \dfrac{\pi}{3}\right)$ is omitted, since on the interval $\left[0, \dfrac{\pi}{2}\right]$ this function is positive).

$$I = a\int_0^{\pi/2} \sec^2\left(\varphi - \frac{\pi}{3}\right) d\varphi = \frac{4\sqrt{3}}{3}\, a.$$

7.9.7. Find the length of the closed curve $\rho = a\sin^4\dfrac{\varphi}{4}$.

Solution Since the function $\rho = a\sin^4\dfrac{\varphi}{4}$ is even, the given curve is symmetrical about the polar axis. Since the function $\sin^4\dfrac{\varphi}{4}$ has a period 4π, during half the period from 0 to 2π the polar radius increases from 0 to a, and will describe half the curve by virtue of its symmetry (Fig. 99).

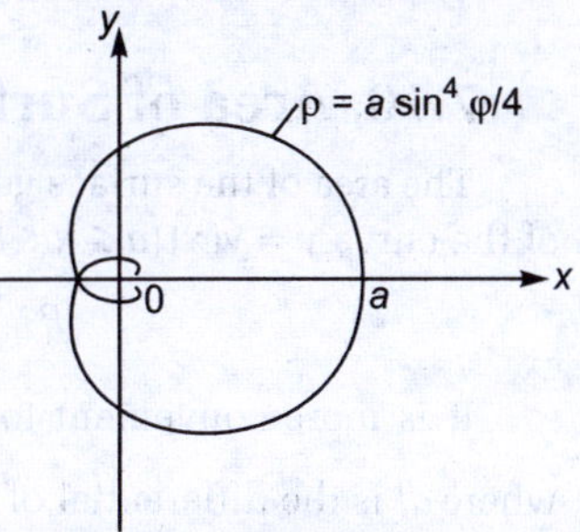

Fig. 99

Further, $\rho'_\varphi = a\sin^3(\varphi/4)\cos(\varphi/4)$ and

$$\sqrt{\rho^2 + \rho'^2_\varphi} = \sqrt{a^2\sin^8(\varphi/4) + a^2\sin^6(\varphi/4)\cos^2(\varphi/4)} = a\sin^3(\varphi/4),$$

if $0 \le \varphi \le 2\pi$.

Hence,

$$I = 2a\int_0^{2\pi} \sin^3\left(\frac{\varphi}{4}\right) d\varphi = 8a\int_0^{\pi/2} \sin^3 t\, dt = \frac{16}{3}\, a\ (\varphi = 4t)$$

7.9.8. Find the length of the curve $\varphi = \dfrac{1}{2}(\rho + 1/\rho)$ between $\rho = 2$ and $\rho = 4$

Solution. The differential of the arc dl is equal to

$$dl = \sqrt{\rho^2 + \rho'^2_{\varphi}}\, d\varphi = \sqrt{\rho^2 d\varphi^2 + d\rho^2} = \sqrt{\rho^2\left(\frac{d\varphi}{d\rho}\right)^2 + 1}\, d\rho \cdot$$

From the equation of the curve we find $\frac{d\varphi}{d\rho} = \frac{1}{2}\left(1 - \frac{1}{\rho^2}\right)$.

Hence

$$I = \int_2^4 \sqrt{\rho^2 \cdot \frac{1}{4}\left(1 - \frac{1}{\rho^2}\right)^2 + 1}\, d\rho = \int_2^4 \sqrt{\frac{1}{4}\left(\rho^2 - 2 + \frac{1}{\rho^2} + 4\right)}\, d\rho$$

$$= \frac{1}{2}\int_2^4 \sqrt{\left(\rho + \frac{1}{\rho}\right)^2}\, d\rho = \frac{1}{2}\left(\frac{\rho^2}{2} + \ln\rho\right)\Big|_2^4 = 3 + \frac{\ln 2}{2} \cdot$$

7.9.9. Find the length of the hyperbolic spiral $\rho\varphi = 1$ between $\varphi_1 = \frac{3}{4}$ and $\varphi_2 = \frac{4}{3}$.

7.9.10. Compute the length of the closed curve $\rho = 2a(\sin\varphi + \cos\varphi)$.

7.9.11. Compute the arc length of the curve $\rho = \frac{\rho}{1 + \cos\varphi}$ from $\varphi_1 = -\frac{\pi}{2}$ to $\varphi_2 = \frac{\pi}{2}$.

7.10. Area of Surface of Revolution

The area of the surface generated by revolving about the x-axis the arc L of the curve $y = y(x)$ $(a \le x \le b)$ is expressed by the integral

$$P = 2\pi \int_a^b y\sqrt{1 + y'^2}\, dx \cdot$$

It is more convenient to write this integral in the form $P = 2\pi\int_L y\, dl$, where dl is the differential of the arc length.

If a curve is represented parametrically or in polar coordinates, then it is sufficient to change the variable in the above formula, expressing appropriately the differential of the arc length (see **7.8.** and **7.9**)

7.10.1. Find the area of the surface formed by revolving the astroid $x^{2/3} + y^{2/3} = a^{2/3}$ about the x-axis.

Solution Differentiating the equation of the astroid we get

$$\frac{2}{3}x^{-1/3} + \frac{2}{3}y^{-1/3}y' = 0,$$

whence

$$y' = -\frac{y^{1/3}}{x^{1/3}} \cdot$$

Then, $\sqrt{1+y'^2}=\sqrt{1+\dfrac{y^{2/3}}{x^{2/3}}}=\dfrac{a^{1/3}}{|x|^{1/3}}$. Since the astroid is symmetrical about the y-axis, in computing the area of the surface we may first assume $x \ge 0$, and then double the result. In other words, the desired area P is equal to

$$P = 2\times 2\pi\int_0^a y\sqrt{1+y'^2}\,dx = 4\pi\int_0^a (a^{3/2}-x^{2/3})^{3/2}a^{1/3}x^{-1/3}\,dx.$$

Make the substitution

$$a^{2/3}-x^{2/3}=t^2,$$

$$-\frac{2}{3}x^{-1/3}\,dx = 2t\,dt,$$

x	t
0	$a^{\frac{1}{3}}$
a	0

Then, $P = 12\pi a^{1/3}\displaystyle\int_0^{a^{1/3}} t^4\,dt = \frac{12}{5}\pi a^2.$

7.10.2. Find the area of the surface generated by revolving about the x-axis a closed contour $OABCO$ formed by the curves $y=x^2$ and $x=y^2$ (Fig. 100).

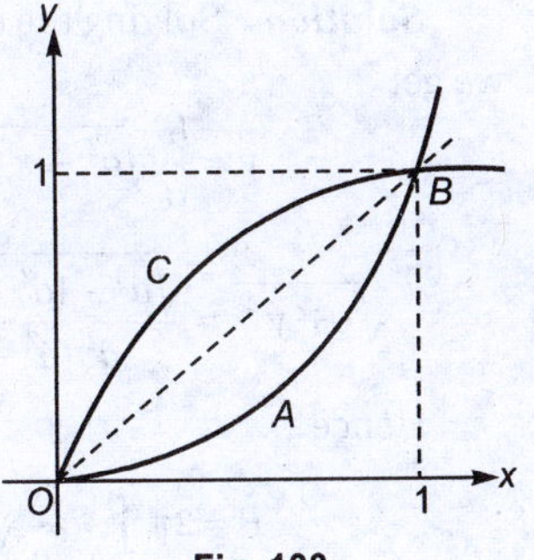

Fig. 100

Solution It is easy to check that the given parabolas intersect at the points $O(0,0)$ and $B(1,1)$. The sought-for area $P=P_1+P_2$, where the area P_1 is formed by revolving the arc OCB, and P_2 by revolving the arc OAB.

Compute the area P_1. From the equation $x=y^2$ we get $y=\sqrt{x}$ and $y'=\dfrac{1}{2\sqrt{x}}$.

Hence,

$$P_1 = 2\pi\int_0^1\sqrt{x}\sqrt{1+\frac{1}{4x}}\,dx = 2\pi\int_0^1\frac{\sqrt{4x+1}}{2}\,dx$$

$$=\frac{\pi}{6}(4x+1)^{3/2}\Big|_0^1 = \frac{\pi}{6}(5\sqrt{5}-1).$$

Now compute the area P_2. We have $y=x^2$, $y'=2x$ and

$$P_2 = 2\pi\int_0^1 x^2\sqrt{[1+4x^2}\,dx.$$

The substitution $x=\dfrac{1}{2}\sinh t,\ dx=\dfrac{1}{2}\cosh t\,dt$ gives

$$P_2 = \frac{\pi}{4}\int_0^{\text{Arsinh } 2}\sinh^2 t\cosh^2 t\,dt = \frac{\pi}{32}\left(\frac{1}{4}\sinh 4t - t\right)\Big|_0^{\text{Arsinh } 2}$$

$$=\frac{9\sqrt{5}\pi}{16}-\frac{1}{32}\pi\ln(2+\sqrt{5}).$$

Thus,

$$P = P_1 + P_2 = \frac{(5\sqrt{5}-1)\pi}{6} + \frac{9\sqrt{5}\pi}{16} - \frac{1}{32}\pi \ln(2+\sqrt{5})$$
$$= \frac{67\sqrt{5}\pi}{48} - \frac{\pi}{32}\ln(2+\sqrt{5}) - \frac{\pi}{6}.$$

7.10.3. Compute the area of the surface generated by revolving :

(a) the portion of the curve $y = \frac{x^2}{2}$, cut off by the straight line $y = \frac{3}{2}$, about the y-axis;

(b) the portion of the curve $y^2 = 4 + x$, cut off by the straight line $x = 2$, about the x-axis.

7.10.4. Find the surface area of the ellipsoid formed by revolving the ellipse $\frac{x^2}{a^2} + \frac{y^2}{b^2} = 1$ about the x-axis $(a > b)$.

Solution Solving the equation of the ellipse with respect to y for $y \geq 0$, we get

$$y = \frac{b}{a}\sqrt{a^2 - x^2}\ ;\ y' = -\frac{b}{a}\cdot\frac{x}{\sqrt{a^2 - x^2}};$$

$$\sqrt{1 + y'^2} = \frac{\sqrt{a^4 - (a^2 - b^2)\,x^2}}{a^2\,(a^2 - x^2)}.$$

Hence

$$P = 2\pi \int_{-a}^{a} \frac{b}{a}\sqrt{a^2 - x^2}\sqrt{\frac{a^4 - (a^2 - b^2)\,x^2}{a^2\,(a^2 - x^2)}}\,dx$$
$$= \frac{4\pi b}{a}\int_0^a \sqrt{a^2 - \varepsilon^2 x^2}\,dx = 2\pi ab\left(\sqrt{1-\varepsilon^2} + \frac{\text{arc sin}\,\varepsilon}{\varepsilon}\right),$$

where the quantity $\varepsilon = \sqrt{\frac{a^2 - b^2}{a^2}} = \frac{c}{a}$ is the eccentricity of the ellipse.

When $b \to a$ the eccentricity ε tends to zero and

$$\lim_{\varepsilon \to 0} \frac{\text{arc sin}\,\varepsilon}{\varepsilon} = 1,$$

since the ellipse turns into a circle, in the limit we get the surface area of the sphere :

$$P = 4\pi a^2.$$

7.10.5. Compute the area of the surface obtained by revolving the ellipse $4x^2 + y^2 = 4$ about the y-axis.

7.10.6. An arc of the catenary

$$y = \frac{a}{2}\left(e^{\frac{x}{a}} + e^{-\frac{x}{a}}\right) = a\cosh\frac{x}{a},$$

whose end-points have abscissas 0 and x, respectively, revolves about the x-axis.

Show that the surface area P and the volume V of the solid thus generated are related by the formula $P = \frac{2V}{a}\cdot$

Solution Since $y' = \sinh\frac{x}{a}$, we have $\sqrt{1+y'^2} = \cosh\frac{x}{a}$. Therefore

$$P = 2\pi\int_0^x y\sqrt{1+y'^2}dx = 2a\pi\int_0^x \cosh^2\frac{x}{a}dx = \frac{2}{a}\pi\int_0^x a^2\cosh^2\frac{x}{a}dx,$$

but

$$\pi\int_0^x a^2\cosh^2\frac{x}{a}dx = \pi\int_0^x y^2\,dx = V,$$

hence, $P = \frac{2V}{a}\cdot$

7.10.7. Find the area of the surface obtained by revolving a loop of the curve $9ax^2 = y(3a-y)^2$ about the y-axis.

Solution The loop is described by a moving point as y changes from 0 to $3a$. Differentiate with respect to y both sides of the equation of the curve :

$$18axx' = (3a-y)^2 - 2y(3a-y) = 3(3a-y)(a-y),$$

whence $xx' = \frac{(3a-y)(a-y)}{6a}$. Using the formula for computing the area of the surface of a solid of revolution about the y-axis, we have

$$P = 2\pi\int_{y_1}^{y_2} x\sqrt{1+x'^2}\,dy = 2\pi\int_{y_1}^{y_2}\sqrt{x^2+(xx')^2}dy$$

$$= 2\pi\int_0^{3a}\sqrt{\frac{y(3a-y)^2}{9a} + \frac{(3a-y)^2(a-y)^2}{36a^2}}\,dy$$

$$= \frac{\pi}{3a}\int_0^{3a}(3a^2+2ay-y^2)\,dy = 3\pi a^2.$$

7.10.8. Compute the area of the surface generated by revolving the curve $8y^2 = x^2 - x^4$ about the x-axis.

7.10.9. Compute the area of a surface generated by revolving about the x-axis an arc of the curve $x = t^2;\ y = \frac{t}{3}(t^2-3)$ between the points of intersection of the curve and the x-axis.

Solution Putting $y = 0$, find $t_1 = 0$ and $t_{2,3} = \pm\sqrt{3}$, and, hence, $x_1 = 0$ and $x_{2,3} = 3$. Whence it follows that the curve intersects with the x-axis at two points: (0, 0) and (3, 0). When the parameter t changes sign, the sign of the function $(x)t$ remains unchanged, and the

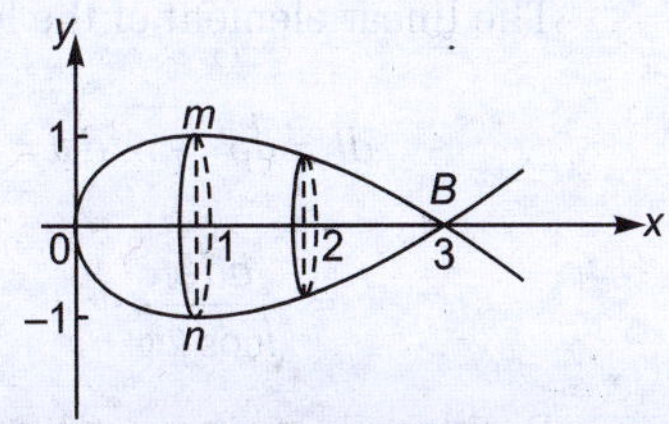

Fig. 101

function $y(t)$ changes its sign, which means that the curve is symmetrical about the x- axis (Fig. 101).

To find the area of the surface is sufficient to confine ourselves to the lower portion of the curve OnB that corresponds to the variation of the parameter between 0 and $\pm\sqrt{3}$. Differentiating with respect to t, we find

$$x'_t = 2t;\ y'_t = t^2 - 1$$

and the linear element

$$dt = \sqrt{x'^2_t + y'^2_t}dt = (1 + t^2)\,dt.$$

Hence,

$$P = 2\pi \int_{t_1}^{t_2} |y(t)| \sqrt{x'^2_t + y'^2_t}\,dt$$

$$= 2\pi \int_0^{\sqrt{3}} -\frac{t}{3}(t^2 - 3)(1 + t^2)\,dt$$

$$= -\frac{2}{3}\pi \int_0^{\sqrt{3}} (t^5 - 2t^3 - 3t)\,dt = 3\pi.$$

7.10.10. Compute the surface area of the torus generated by revolving the circle $x^2 + (y - b)^2 = r^2$ $(0 < r < b)$ about the x-axis.

Solution Let us represent the equation of the circle in parametric form $x = r\cos t;\ y = b + r\sin t$:

Hence

$$x'_t = -r\sin t;\ y'_t = r\cos t$$

The desired area is

$$P = 2\pi \int_0^{2\pi} (b + r\ \sin t)\sqrt{(-r\sin t)^2 + (r\cos t)^2}dt$$

$$= 2\pi r \int_0^{2\pi} (b + r\sin t)\,dt = 4\pi^2 br.$$

7.10.11. Compute the area of the surface formed by revolving the lemniscate $\rho = a\sqrt{\cos 2\varphi}$ about the polar axis.

Solution Real values for ρ are obtained for $\cos 2\varphi \geq 0$, *ie*, for $-\frac{\pi}{4} \leq \varphi \leq \frac{\pi}{4}$ (the right-hand branch of the lemniscate), or for $\frac{3}{4}\pi \leq \varphi \leq \frac{5}{4}\pi$

(the left-hand branch of the lemniscate).

The linear element of the lemniscate is equal to

$$dl = \sqrt{\rho^2 + \rho'^2}d\varphi = \sqrt{a^2\cos 2\varphi + \left(\frac{a\sin 2\varphi}{\sqrt{\cos 2\varphi}}\right)^2}\,d\varphi$$

$$= \frac{a\,d\varphi}{\sqrt{\cos 2\varphi}}.$$

Besides, $y = \rho\sin\varphi = a\sin\varphi\sqrt{\cos 2\varphi}$.

The sought-for surface area P is equal to double the area of the surface generated by revolving the right-hand branch. Therefore

$$P = 2 \times 2\pi \int_L y\, dl = 4\pi a^2 \int_0^{\frac{\pi}{4}} \frac{\sqrt{\cos 2\varphi}\, \sin \varphi\, d\varphi}{\sqrt{\cos 2\varphi}} = 2\pi a^2 (2 - \sqrt{2}).$$

7.10.12. Compute the area of the surface formed by revolving about the straight line $x + y = a$ the quarter of the circle $x^2 + y^2 = a^2$ between $A(a, 0)$ and $B(0, a)$.

Solution Find the distance MN from the moving point $M(x, y)$, lying on the circle $x^2 + y^2 = a^2$, to the straight line $x + y = a$,

$$MN = \frac{|x + \sqrt{a^2 - x^2} - a|}{\sqrt{2}} = \frac{x + \sqrt{a^2 - x^2} - a}{\sqrt{2}}$$

since for the points of the circle that lie in the first quadrant $x + y \geq a$. Further,

$$dl = \sqrt{1 + y'^2}\, dx = \sqrt{1 + \left(\frac{x}{\sqrt{a^2 - x^2}}\right)^2}\, dx = \frac{a\, dx}{\sqrt{a^2 - x^2}}.$$

Hence,

$$P = 2\pi \int_0^a \frac{x + \sqrt{a^2 - x^2} - a}{\sqrt{2}} \cdot \frac{a dx}{\sqrt{a^2 - x^2}}$$

$$= \sqrt{2}\, \pi a \left[-\sqrt{a^2 - x^2} + x - a \arcsin \frac{x}{a} \right]_0^a = \frac{\pi a^2}{\sqrt{2}} (4 - \pi).$$

7.10.13. Computes the area of the surface formed by revolving one branch of the lemniscate $\rho = a\sqrt{\cos 2\varphi}$ about the straight line $\varphi = \frac{\pi}{4}$.

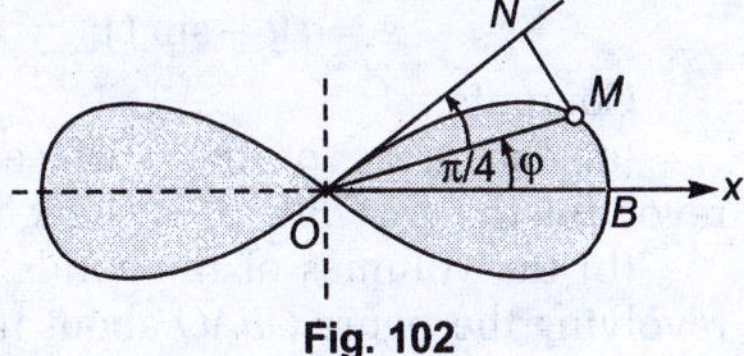

Fig. 102

Solution From the triangle OMN(Fig.102.) we find the distance MN of an arbitrary point M of the right-hand branch from the axis of revolution $\varphi = \frac{\pi}{4}$.

$$MN = \rho \sin\left(\frac{\pi}{4} - \varphi\right) = a\sqrt{\cos 2\varphi}\, \sin\left(\frac{\pi}{4} - \varphi\right);$$

then

$$dl = \frac{a\, d\varphi}{\sqrt{\cos 2\varphi}}.$$

Therefore

$$P = 2\pi \int_{-\pi/4}^{\pi/4} a\sqrt{\cos 2\varphi}\, \sin\left(\frac{\pi}{4} - \varphi\right) \frac{a\, d\varphi}{\sqrt{\cos 2\varphi}} = 2\pi a^2.$$

7.10.14. Compute the area of the surface formed by revolving about the x-axis the arc of the curve $y=\frac{x^2}{3}$ between $x=-2$ and $x=2$.

7.10.15. Compute the area of the surface generated by revolving one half-wave of the curve $y=\sin x$ about the x-axis.

7.10.16. Compute the area of the surface generated by revolving about the y-axis the arc of the parabola $x^2=4ay$ between the points of intersection of the curve and the straight line $y=3a$.

7.10.17. Find the area of the surface formed by revolving about the x-axis the arc of the curve $x=e^t\sin t$; $y=e^t\cos t$ between $t=0$ and $t=\frac{\pi}{2}$.

7.10.18. Compute the area of the surface obtained by revolving about the x-axis the arc of the curve $x=\frac{t^3}{3}$; $y=4-\frac{t^2}{2}$ between the points of its intersection with the axes of coordinates.

7.10.19. Compute the area of the surface generated by revolving the curve $\rho=2a\sin\varphi$ about the polar axis.

7.10.20. Compute the area of the surface formed by revolving about the x-axis the cardioid

$$x=a(2\cos t-\cos 2t),\ y=a(2\sin t-\sin 2t).$$

7.11. Geometrical Applications of the Definite Integral

7.11.1. Given : the cycloid (Fig. 103)

$$x=a(t-\sin t);\quad y=a(1-\cos t);\quad 0\le t\le 2\pi.$$

Compute :

(a) the areas of the surfaces formed by revolving the arc OBA about the x and y- axis;

(b) the volumes of the solids generated by revolving the figure $OBAO$ about the y-axis and the axis BC;

(c) the area of the surface generated by revolving the arc BA about the axis BC;

(d) the volume of the solid generated by revolving the figure $ODBEABO$ about the tangent line DE touching the figure at the vertex B;

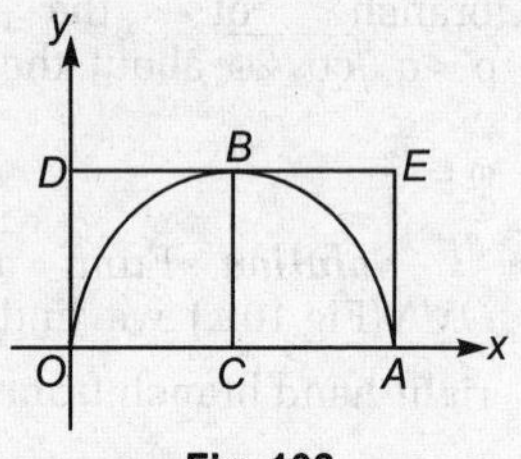

Fig. 103

(e) the area of the surface formed by revolving the arc of the cycloid [see item (d)]

Solution (a) When revolving about the x-axis the arc OBA generates a surface of area

$$P_x=2\pi\int_L y\,dl=2\pi\int_0^{2\pi}a(1-\cos t)\,2a\sin\frac{t}{2}\,dt$$

$$=8a^2\pi\int_0^{2\pi}\sin^3\frac{t}{2}\,dt=\frac{64\pi a^2}{3}.$$

When revolving about the y-axis the arc are OBA generates a surface of area

$$P_y = 2\pi \int_L x\,dl = 4\pi a^2 \int_0^{\pi} (t - \sin t) \sin \frac{t}{2}\, dt$$

$$+ 4\pi a^2 \int_{\pi}^{2\pi} (t - \sin t) \sin \frac{t}{2}\, dt = 4\pi a^2 \int_0^{2\pi} (t - \sin t) \sin \frac{t}{2}\, dt = 16\pi^2 a^2.$$

(b) When revolving about the y-axis the figure $OBAO$ generates a solid of volume

$$V_y = \pi \int_0^{2a} (x_2^2 - x_1^2)\, dy = \pi \int_0^{2a} x_2^2\, dy - \pi \int_0^{2a} x_1^2\, dy,$$

where $x = x_1(y)$ is the equation of the curve BA, and $x = x_2(y)$ is the equation of the curve OB.

Making the substitution $y = a(1 - \cos t)$, take into consideration that for the first integral t varies between 2π and π, and for the second integral between 0 and π. Consequently,

$$V_y = \pi \int_{2\pi}^{\pi} a^2 (t - \sin t)^2\, a \sin t\, dt - \pi \int_0^{\pi} a^2 (t - \sin t)^2\, a \sin t\, dt$$

$$= \pi a^3 \int_{2\pi}^{0} (t - \sin t)^2 \sin t\, dt$$

$$= \pi a^3 \left[\int_{2\pi}^{0} t^2 \sin t\, dt - \int_{2\pi}^{0} t\,(1 - \cos 2t)\, dt + \int_{2\pi}^{0} \sin^3 t\, dt \right]$$

$$= 6\pi^3 a^3.$$

For computing the volume of the solid obtained by revolving the figure $OBAO$ about the axis BC it is convenient first to transfer the origin into the point C, which yields the following equations in the new system of coordinates

$$x' = a(t - \pi - \sin t);\ y' = a(1 - \cos t).$$

Taking into account only the arc BA, we get

$$V = \pi \int_0^{2a} x'^2\, dy' = \pi a^3 \int_{2\pi}^{\pi} (t - \pi - \sin t)^2 \sin t\, dt.$$

Putting $t - \pi = z$, we obtain

$$V = -\pi a^3 \int_{\pi}^{0} (z + \sin z)^2 \sin z\, dz = \pi a^3 \int_0^{\pi} (z + \sin z)^2 \sin z\, dz$$

$$= \frac{\pi a^3}{6} (9\pi^2 - 16).$$

(c) Making the above-indicated shift of the origin, we get

$$dl = 2a \sin \frac{t}{2} |\, dt\, | = -2a \sin \frac{t}{2}\, dt.$$

Therefore

$$P = \int_0^{2a} 2\pi x\, dl = -4\pi a^2 \int_{2\pi}^{\pi} (t - \pi - \sin t) \sin \frac{t}{2}\, dt$$

$$= 4\pi a^2 \int_0^{\pi} (z + \sin z) \cos x \frac{z}{2}\, dz = 4\left(2\pi - \frac{8}{3}\right) \pi a^2.$$

(d) Transferring the origin into the point B and changing the direction of the y-axis, we get

$$x' = a(t - \pi - \sin t),\ y' = a(1 + \cos t).$$

Putting $t - \pi = z$, we have

$$x' = a(z + \sin z),\ y' = a(1 - \cos z),$$

z changing from $-\pi$ to π for the arc OBA. Hence

$$V = \pi \int_{-\pi}^{\pi} a^3 (1 - \cos z)^2 (1 + \cos z)\, dz = \pi^2 a^3 .$$

(e) $P = 2\pi \int_{-\pi}^{\pi} y\, dt = 4\pi a^2 \int_{-\pi}^{\pi} (1 - \cos z) \cos \frac{z}{2}\, dz = \frac{32}{3} \pi a^2.$

7.11.2. Find the volume of the solid bounded by the surfaces $z^2 = 8(2 - x)$ and $x^2 + y^2 = 2x$

Solution The first surface is a parabolic cylinder with generatrices parallel to the y-axis and the directrix $z^2 = 8(2 - x)$ in the plane xOz, and the second is a circular cylinder with generatrices parallel to the z-axis and the directrix $x^2 + y^2 = 2x$ in the plane xOy.

The volume V is computed by the formula $V = \int_0^2 S(x)\, dx.\ S(x)$ represents the area of a triangle whose base is equal to $2y$ and altitude to $2z$:

$$S(x) = 2y \times 2z = 4\sqrt{2x - x^2}\ \sqrt{8(2 - x)}.$$

Hence,

$$V = \int_0^2 4\sqrt{x(2 - x)\, 8(2 - x)}\, dx = 4\sqrt{8} \int_0^2 (2 - x)\sqrt{x}\, dx$$

$$= 4\sqrt{8}\left(\frac{2}{3}\, 2\sqrt{x^3} - \frac{2}{5}\sqrt{x^5}\right)\Bigg|_0^2 = \frac{256}{15}$$

7.11.3. Prove that if the figure S is bounded by a simple convex contour and is situated between the ordinates y_1 and y_2(Fig. 104), then the volume of the solid generated by revolving this figure about the x-axis can be expressed by the formula

$$V = 2\pi \int_{y_1}^{y_2} yh\, dy,$$

where

$$h = x_2(y) - x_1(y),$$

$x = x_1(y)$ being the equation of the left portion of the contour and $x = x_2(y)$ that of the right portion.

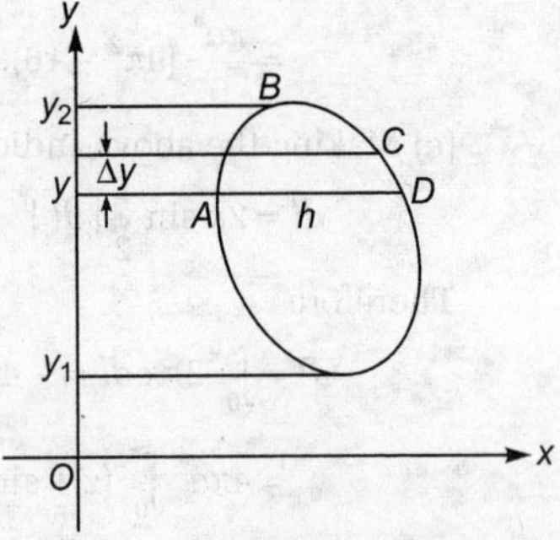

Fig. 104

Solution Let the generating figure S be bounded by a simple convex contour and contained between the ordinates $y_1$and y_2. Subdivide the interval $[y_1, y_2]$ into parts and pass through the points of division straight lines parallel to the axis of revolution, thus cutting the figure S into horizontal strips. Single out one strip and replace it by the rectangle $ABCD$, whose lower base is equal to chord $AD = h$ specified by the ordinate y, its altitude AB being equal to Δy. The solid generated by revolving the rectangle $ABCD$ about the x-axis is a hollow cylinder whose volume may be approximately taken for the element of volume

$$\Delta V \approx \pi (y + \Delta y)^2 h - \pi y^2 h = 2\pi y \Delta y h + \pi h (\Delta y)^2.$$

Rejecting the infinitesimal of the second order with respect to Δy, we get the principal part or the differential of volume

$$dV = 2\pi\, yh\, dy.$$

Knowing the differential of the volume, we get the volume proper through intergration :

$$V = 2\pi \int_{y_1}^{y_2} yh\, dy.$$

Thus, we obtain one more formula for computing the volume of the solid of revolution.

7.11.4. The planer region bounded by the parabola $y = 2x^2 + 3$, the x-axis and the verticals $x = 0$ and $x = 1$ revolves about the y-axis. Compute the volume of the solid of revolution thus generated.

Solution Divide the area of the figure into elementary strips by straight lines parallel to the y-axis. The volume ΔV of the elementary cylinder generated by revolving one strip is

$$\Delta V = \pi (x + \Delta x)^2\, y - \pi x^2 y - 2\pi xy\, \Delta x + \pi y\, (\Delta x)^2,$$

where Δx is the width of the strip.

Neglecting the infintesimal of the second order with respect to Δx, we get the differential of the desired volume

$$dV = 2\pi\, xy\, dx.$$

Hence

$$V = \int_0^1 2\pi\, xy\, dx = 2\pi \int_0^1 x\,(2x^2 + 3)\, dx = 4\pi.$$

7.11.5. Compute the area of the portion of the cylinder surface $x^2 + y^2 = ax$ situated inside the sphere

$$x^2 + y^2 + z^2 = a^2.$$

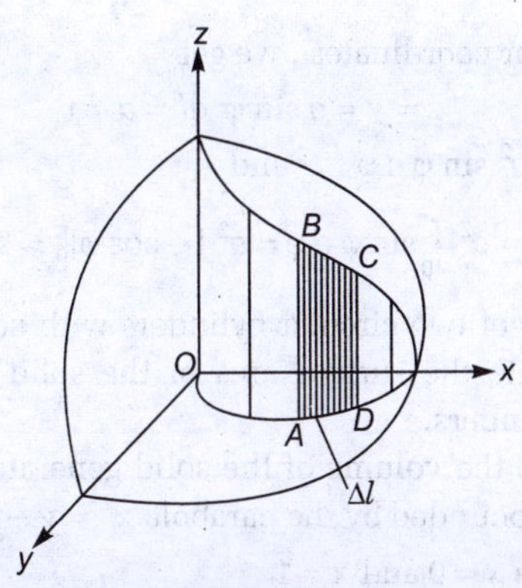

Fig. 105

Solution The generatrices of the cylinder are parallel to the *z*-axis the circle $\left(x-\frac{a}{2}\right)^2+y^2=\frac{a^2}{4}$ serving as directrix (Fig. 105. shows a quarter of the sought for surface).

Subdivide the portion of the circle shown in Fig. 105 into small arcs Δl. The generatrices passing through the points of division cut the cylinder surface into strips. If infinitesimals of higher order are neglected, the area of the strip *ABCD* is equal to $CD \cdot \Delta l$.

If ρ and φ are the polar coordinates of the point *D*, then $\rho = a\cos\varphi$ and $CD=\sqrt{a^2-\rho^2}=a\sin\varphi$ and $\Delta l = a\cdot\Delta\varphi$, whence we find the element of area :

$$dP = a^2\sin\varphi\, d\varphi.$$

Hence,

$$P = 4\int_0^{\pi/2} a^2\sin\varphi\, d\varphi = 4a^2.$$

7.11.6. Find the area of the surface cut off from a right circular cylinder by a plane passing through the diameter of the base and inclined at an angle of 45° to the base.

Solution Let the cylinder axis be the *z*-axis and the given diameter the *x*-axis. Then the equation of the cylindrical surface will be $x^2+y^2=a^2$, and that of the plane forming an angle of 45° with the coordinate plane *xOy* will be $y = z$.

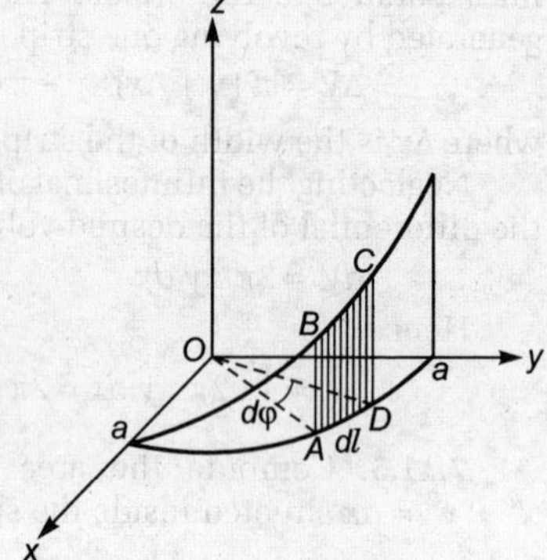

Fig. 106

The area of the infinitely narrow strip *ABCD* (see Fig. 106) will be $dP = z\,dl$ (accurate to infinitesimals of a higher order), where dl is the length of the elementary arc of the circumference of the base.

Introducing polar coordinates , we get

$$z = y = a\sin\varphi;\ dl = a\, d\varphi.$$

Hence $\quad dP = a^2\sin\varphi\, d\varphi \quad$ and

$$P = a^2\int_0^{\pi}\sin\varphi\, d\varphi = a^2\,[-\cos\varphi]_0^{\pi} = 2a^2.$$

7.11.7. The axes of two circular cylinders with equal bases intersect at right angles. Compute the surface area of the solid constituting the part common to both cylinders.

7.11.8. Compute the volume of the solid generated by revolving about the *y*-axis the figure bounded by the parabola $x^2 = y-1$, the axis of abscissas and the straight lines $x = 0$ and $x = 1$.

7.11.9. Find the area S of the ellipse given by the equation $Ax^2 + 2Bxy + Cy^2 = 1$ $(\Delta = AC - B^2 > 0; C > 0)$.

Solution Solving the equation with respect to y, we get

$$y_1 = \frac{-Bx - \sqrt{C - \Delta x^2}}{C}; \; y_2 = \frac{-Bx + \sqrt{c - \Delta x^2}}{C},$$

where the values of x must satisfy the inequality

$$C - \Delta x^2 \geq 0.$$

Solving this inequality, we obtain the limits of integration :

$$-\sqrt{\frac{C}{\Delta}} \leq x \leq \sqrt{\frac{C}{\Delta}}.$$

Consequently, the sought for area is equal to

$$S = \int_{-\sqrt{\frac{C}{\Delta}}}^{\sqrt{\frac{C}{\Delta}}} (y_2 - y_1)\, dx = \frac{4}{C}\int_0^{\sqrt{\frac{C}{\Delta}}} \sqrt{C - \Delta x^2}\, dx = \frac{\pi}{\sqrt{\Delta}}.$$

7.11.10. Find the areas of the figures bounded by the curves represented parametrically :

(a) $x = 2t - t^2; y = 2t^2 - t^3$;

(b) $x = \dfrac{t^2}{1+t^2}; \; y = \dfrac{t\,(1-t^2)}{1+t^2}.$

7.11.11. Find the areas of the figures bounded by the curves given in polar coordinates :

(a) $\rho = a \sin 3\varphi$ (a three-leaved rose);

(b) $\rho = \dfrac{p}{1 - \cos\varphi}\left[\dfrac{\pi}{4} \leq \varphi \leq \dfrac{\pi}{2}\right];$

(c) $\rho = 3 \sin \varphi$ and $\rho = \sqrt{3} \cos \varphi$.

7.11.12. Find the arc length of the curve $y^2 = \dfrac{4}{9}(2 - x)^2$ cut off by the straight line $x = -1$.

7.11.13. Find the length of the arc OA of the curve

$$y = a \ln \frac{a^2}{a^2 - x^2},$$

where $O\,(0, 0)$; $A\left(\dfrac{a}{2}, a \ln \dfrac{4}{3}\right)$.

7.11.14. Compute the arc length of the curve $y^2 = \dfrac{2}{3}(x - 1)^3$ contained inside the parabola $y^2 = \dfrac{x}{3}$.

7.11.15. Prove that the length of the ellipse

$$x = \sqrt{2}\sin t;\ y = \cos t$$

is equal to the wavelength of the sinusoid $y = \sin x$.

7.11.16. Prove that the arc of the parabola $y = \frac{1}{2p}x^2$ corresponding to the interval $0 \le x \le a$ has the same length as the arc of the spiral $\rho = P\varphi$ corresponding to the interval $0 \le \rho \le a$.

7.11.17. Find the ratio of the area enclosed by the loop of the curve $y = \pm\left(\frac{1}{3} - x\right)\sqrt{x}$ to the area of a circle the circumference of which is equal to length of the contour of this curve.

7.11.18. Find the volume of the segment cut off from the elliptical paraboloid $\frac{y^2}{2p} + \frac{z^3}{2q} = x$ by the plane $x = a$.

7.11.19. Compute the volume of the solid bounded by the hyperboloid $\frac{x^2}{a^2} + \frac{y^2}{b^2} - \frac{z^2}{c^2} = -1$ and the planes $z = c$ and $z = l > c$.

7.11.20. Find the volume of the right elliptical cone whose base is an ellipse with semi-axes a and b, its altitude being equal to h.

7.11.21. Find the volume of the solid generated by revolving about the x-axis the figure bounded by the straight lines $y = x + 1$; $y = 2x + 1$ and $x = 2$.

7.11.22. Find the volume of the solid generated by revolving about the x-axis the figure bounded by the hyperbola $\frac{x^2}{a^2} - \frac{y^2}{b^2} = 1$, the straight line $2ay - bx = 0$ and the axis of abscissas.

7.11.23. Find the volume of the solid generated by revolving the curve $\rho = a\cos^2\varphi$ about the polar axis.

7.11.24. Find the areas of the surfaces generated by revolving the following curves :

(a) $y = \tan x \left(0 \le x \le \frac{\pi}{4}\right)$ about the x-axis;

(b) $y = x\sqrt{\frac{x}{a}}$ $(0 \le x \le a)$ about the x-axis;

(c) $x^2 + y^2 - 2rx = 0$ about the x-axis between 0 and h.

7.12. Computing Pressure, Work and Other Physical Quantities by the Definite Integrals

I. To compute the force of liquid pressure we use Pascal's law, which states that the force of pressure of a liquid P on an area S at a depth of immersion h is $P = \gamma hS$, where γ is the specific weight of the liquid.

II. If a variable force $X = f(x)$ acts in the direction of the x-axis, then the work of this force over an interval $[x_1, x_2]$ is expressed by the integral

$$A = \int_{x_1}^{x^2} f(x)\,dx.$$

III. The kinetic energy of a material point of mass m and velocity v is defined as

$$K = \frac{mv^2}{2}.$$

IV. Electric charges repulse each other with a force $F = \frac{e_1 e_2}{r^2}$, where e_1 and e_2 are the values of the charges, and r is the distance between them.

Note. When solving practical problems we assume that all the data are expressed in one and the same system of units and omit the dimensions of the corresponding quantities.

7.12.1. Compute the force of pressure experienced by a vertical triangle with base b and altitude h submerged base downwards in water so that is vertex touches the surface of the water.

Solution Introduce a system of coordinates as indicated in Fig. 107 and consider a horizontal strip of thickness dx located at an arbitrary depth x.

Assuming this strip to be a rectangle, find the differential of area $dS = MN\,dx$. From the similarity of the triangles BMN and ABC we have $\frac{MN}{b} = \frac{x}{h}$, whence $MN = \frac{bx}{h}$ and $dS = \frac{bx}{h}\,dx$.

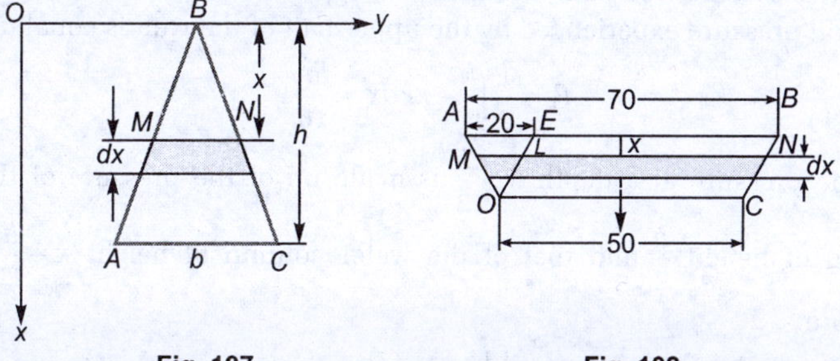

Fig. 107

Fig. 108

The force of pressure experienced by this strip is equal to $dP = x\,dS$ accurate to infinitesimals of higher order (taking into consideration that the specific weight of water is unity). Consequently, the entire force of water pressure experienced by the triangle is equal to

$$P = \int_0^h x\,dS = \frac{b}{h}\int_0^h x^2\,dx = \frac{1}{3}bh^2.$$

7.12.2. Find the force of pressure experienced by a semicircle of radius R submerged vertically in a liquid so that its diameter is flush with the liquid surface (the specific weight of the liquid is γ).

7.12.3. A vertical dam has the form of a trapezoid whose upper base is 70 m long, the lower one 50 m, and the altitude 20 m. Find the force of water pressure experienced by the dam (Fig. 108).

Solution The differential (dS) of area of the hatched figure is approximately equal to $dS = MN\,dx$. Taking into consideration the similarity of the triangles OML and OAE, we find $\frac{ML}{20} = \frac{20 - x}{20}$; whence $ML = 20 - x$, $MN = 20 - x + 50 = 70 - x$. Thus, $dS = MN \times dx = (70 - x)\,dx$ and the differential of the force of water pressure is equal to

$dP = x\,dS = x\,(70 - x)\,dx.$

Integrating with respect to x from 0 to 20, we get

$$P = \int_0^{20} (70x - x^2)\,dx = 11333\frac{1}{3}.$$

7.12.4. Calculate the work performed in pumping the water out of a semispherical boiler of radius R.

7.12.5. A rectangular vessel is filled with equal volumes of water and oil; water is twice as heavy as oil. Show that the force of pressure of the mixture on the wall will reduce by one fifth if the water is replaced by oil.

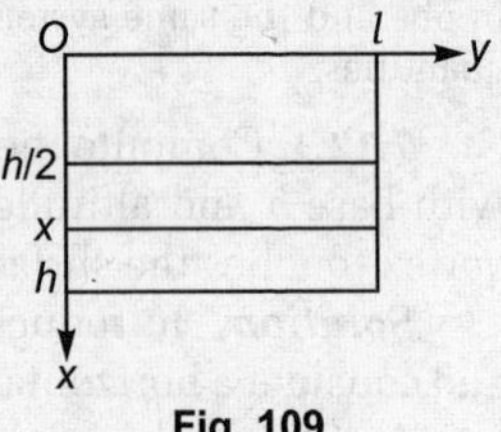

Fig. 109

Solution Let h be the depth of the vessel and l the length of the wall. Let us introduce a system of coordinates as shown in Fig. 109. Since the oil is situated above the water and occupies the upper half of the vessel, the force of the oil pressure experienced by the upper half of the wall is equal to

$$P_1 = \frac{1}{2}\int_0^{h/2} xl\,dx = \frac{lh^2}{16}.$$

The pressure at a depth $x > \frac{h}{2}$ is made up of the pressure of the oil column of height $\frac{h}{2}$ and that of the water column of height $x - \frac{h}{2}$, and therefore

$$dP_2 = \left[\frac{h}{2} \times \frac{1}{2} + \left(x - \frac{h}{2}\right)\right] l\,dx = \left(x - \frac{h}{4}\right) l\,dx.$$

Consequently, the force of pressure of the mixture on the lower half of the wall is

$$P_2 = \int_{h/2}^{h} l\left(x - \frac{h}{2}\right) dx = \frac{lh^2}{4}.$$

The entire pressure of the mixture on the wall is equal to

$$P = P_1 + P_2 = \frac{lh^2}{4} + \frac{lh^2}{16} = \frac{5}{16} lh^2.$$

If the vessel were filled only with oil, the force of pressure $\overline{P}$ on the same wall would be

$$\overline{P} = \frac{1}{2}\int_0^h xl\,dx = \frac{lh^2}{4}.$$

Hence

$$P - \overline{P} = \frac{1}{16}\,lh^2 = \frac{1}{5}\,P.$$

7.12.6. The electric charge E concentrated at the origin of coordinates repulses the charge e from the point $(a, 0)$ to the point $(b, 0)$. Find the work A of the repulsive force F.

Solution The differential of the work of the force over displacement dx is $dA = F\,dx = \dfrac{eE}{x^2}\,dx.$

Hence, $$A = eE\int_a^b \frac{dx}{x^2} = eE\left(\frac{1}{a} - \frac{1}{b}\right).$$

As $b \to \infty$ the work A tends to $\dfrac{eE}{a}$.

7.12.7. Calculate the work performed in launching a rocket of weight P from the ground vertically upwards to a height h.

Solution Let us denote the force of attraction of the rocket by the Earth by F, the mass of the rocket by m_R, and the mass of the Earth by m_E. According to Newton's law

$$F = k\,\frac{m_R m_E}{x^2},$$

where x is the distance between the rocket and the centre of the Earth. Putting $km_R m_E = K$, we get $F(x) = \dfrac{K}{x^2}$, $R \le x \le h + R$, R being the radius of the Earth. At $x = R$ the force $F(R)$ will be the weight of the rocket P, *ie*, $F(R) = P = \dfrac{K}{R^2}$, whence $K = PR^2$ and $F(x) = \dfrac{PR^2}{x^2}$.

Thus, the differential of the work is

$$dA = f(x)\,dx = \frac{PR^2}{x^2}\,dx.$$

Integrating, we obtain

$$A = \int_R^{R+h} F(x)\,dx = PR^2\int_R^{R+h}\frac{dx}{x^2} = \frac{PRh}{R+h}.$$

The limit $\lim\limits_{h\to\infty} A(h) = \lim\limits_{h\to\infty}\dfrac{PRh}{R+h} = PR$ is equal to work performed by the rocket engine to achieve complete escape of the rocket from the Earth's gravity field (the Earth's motion is neglected).

7.12.8. Calculate the work that has to be done to stop an iron sphere of radius R rotating about its diameter with an angular velocity ω.

Solution The amount of required work is equal to the kinetic energy of the sphere. To calculate this energy divide the sphere into concentric hollow cylinders of thickness dx; the velocity of the points of such a cylinder of radius x is ωx.

The element of volume of such a cylinder is $dV = 4\pi x\sqrt{R^2 - x^2}\,dx$, the element of mass $dM = \gamma dV$, where γ is the density of iron, and the differential of kinetic energy $dK = 2\pi\gamma\omega^2 x^3\sqrt{R^2 - x^2}\,dx$.

Hence,

$$K = 2\pi\gamma\omega^2 \int_0^R x^3\sqrt{R^2 - x^2}\,dx = \frac{4\pi\gamma R^3}{3}\cdot\frac{\omega^2 R^2}{5} = \frac{M\omega^2 R^2}{5}.$$

7.12.9. Calculate the kinetic energy of a disk of mass M and radius R rotating with an angular velocity ω about an axis passing through its centre perpendicular to its plane.

7.12.10. Find the amount of heat released by an alternating sinusoidal current

$$I = I_0 \sin\left(\frac{2\pi}{T}t - \varphi\right)$$

during a cycle T in a conductor with resistance R.

Solution For direct current the amount of heat released during a unit time is determined by the Joule-Lenz law

$$Q = 0.24\, I^2 R.$$

For alternating current the differential of amount of heat is $dQ = 0.24\, I^2\,(t)\,R\,dt$, whence

$$Q = 0.24 R \int_{t_1}^{t_2} I^2\,dt.$$

In this case

$$Q = 0.24\, R I_0^2 \int_0^T \sin^2\left(\frac{2\pi}{T}t - \varphi\right)dt$$

$$= 0.12\, R I_0^2 \left[t - \frac{T}{2\pi}\,\frac{\sin^2\left(\frac{2\pi}{T}t - \varphi\right)}{2}\right]_0^T = 0.12 R T\, I_0^2.$$

7.12.11. Find the pressure of a liquid of specific weight d on a vertical ellipse with axes $2a$ and $2b$ whose centre is submerged in the liquid to a level h $(h \geq b)$.

7.12.12. Find the pressure of a liquid of specific weight d on the wall of a circular cylinder of base radius r and altitude h if the cylinder is full of liquid.

7.12.13. Calculate the work performed to overcome the force of gravity in pumping the water out of a conical vessel with the vertex downwards; the radius of the cone base is R and its altitude is H.

7.12.14. Compute the work required to stretch a spring by 6 cm, if a force of one kilogram is required to stretch it by 1 cm.

7.13. Computing Static Moments and Moments of Inertia. Determining Coordinates of the Centre of Gravity

In all problems of this paragraph we will assume that the mass is distributed uniformly in a body (linear, two and three-dimensional) and that its density is equal to unity.

1. For a plane curve L the static moments M_x and M_y about the x- and y-axis are expressed by the formulas

$$M_x = \int_L y\,dl, Ml = \int_L x\,dl.$$

The moment of inertia about the origin of coordinates

$$I_0 = \int_L (x^2 + y^2)\,dl.$$

If the curve L is given by the explicit equation $y = y(x)$ $(a \le x \le b)$, then dl has to be replaced by $\sqrt{1 + y'^2}\,dx$ in the above formulas.

If the curve L is given by the parametric equations $x = x(t)$, $y = y(t)$ $(t_1 \le t \le t_2)$, then dl should be replaced by $\sqrt{x'^2 + y'^2}\,dt$ in these formulas.

2. For the plane figure bounded by the curves $y = y_1(x)$, $y = y_2(x)$, $y_1(x) \le y_2(x)$ and the straight lines $x = a$, $x = b$ $(a \le x \le b)$ the static moments are expressed by the formulas

$$M_x = \frac{1}{2}\int_a^b (y_2^2 - y_1^2)dx;\ M_y$$
$$= \int_a^b x\,(y_2 - y_1)\,dx.$$

3. The centre of gravity of a plane curve has the following coordinates: $x_c = \dfrac{M_y}{l}$, $y_c = \dfrac{M_x}{l}$, where l is the length of the curve L.

The centre of gravity of a plane figure has the coordinates: $x_c = \dfrac{M_y}{S}$.

$Y_c = \dfrac{M_x}{S}$, where S is the area of the figure.

7.13.1. Find the static moment of the upper portion of the ellipse

$$\frac{x^2}{a^2} + \frac{y^2}{b^2} = 1$$

about the x-axis.

Solution For the ellipse

$$y\,dl = y\sqrt{1 + y'^2}\,dx = \sqrt{y^2 + (yy')^2}\,dx;$$

since $y^2 = b^2 - \dfrac{b^2}{a^2}x^2$ and $yy' = -\dfrac{b^2}{a^2}x$, we have

$$y\,dl = \sqrt{b^2 - \frac{b^2}{a^2}x^2 + \frac{b^4}{a^4}x^2}\,dx = \frac{b}{a}\sqrt{a^2 - \varepsilon^2 x^2}\,dx,$$

where ε is the eccentricity of the ellipse, $\varepsilon = \dfrac{\sqrt{a^2 - b^2}}{a}$.

Integrating from $-a$ to a, we find

$$M_x = \frac{b}{a}\int_{-a}^{a}\sqrt{a^2 - \varepsilon^2 x^2}\,dx = \frac{2b}{a}\int_0^a \sqrt{a^2 - \varepsilon^2 x^2}\,dx$$

$$= \frac{b}{a}\left(a\sqrt{a^2 - \varepsilon^2 a^2} + \frac{a^2}{\varepsilon}\text{arc sin }\varepsilon\right)$$

$$= b\left(b + \frac{a}{\varepsilon}\text{arc sin }\varepsilon\right).$$

In the case of a circle, *ie*, at $a = b$, we shall have $M_x = 2a^2$, since $\varepsilon = 0$ and $\lim\limits_{e \to 0}\dfrac{\text{arc sin }\varepsilon}{\varepsilon} = 1$.

7.13.2. Find the moment of inertia of a rectangle with base b and altitude h about its base.

Solution Let us consider an elementary strip of width dy cut out from the rectangle and parallel to the base and situated at a distance y from it. The mass of the strip is equal to its area $dS = b\,dy$, the distances from all its points to the base being equal to y accurate to dy. Therefore, $dI_x = by^2\,dy$ and

$$I_x = \int_0^h by^2\,dy = \frac{bh^3}{3}.$$

7.13.3. Find the moment of inertia of an arc of the circle $x^2 + y^2 = R^2$ lying in the first quadrant about the y-axis.

7.13.4. Calculate the moment of inertia about the y-axis of the figure bounded by the parabola $y^2 = 4ax$ and the straight line $x = a$.

Solution We have $dI_x = x^2\,dS$, where dS is the area of a vertical strip situated at a distance x from the y-axis. (Fig. 110)

$$dS = 2\,|\,y\,|\,dx = 2\sqrt{4ax}\,dx.$$

Hence,

$$I_x = \int_0^a 4x^2\sqrt{ax}\,dx = 4\sqrt{a}\int_0^a x^{5/2}\,dx = \frac{8}{7}a^4.$$

7.13.5. In designing wooden girder bridges we often have to deal with logs flattened on two opposite sides. Figure 111. shows the cross-section of such a log. Determine the moment of inertia of this cross-section about the horizontal centre line.

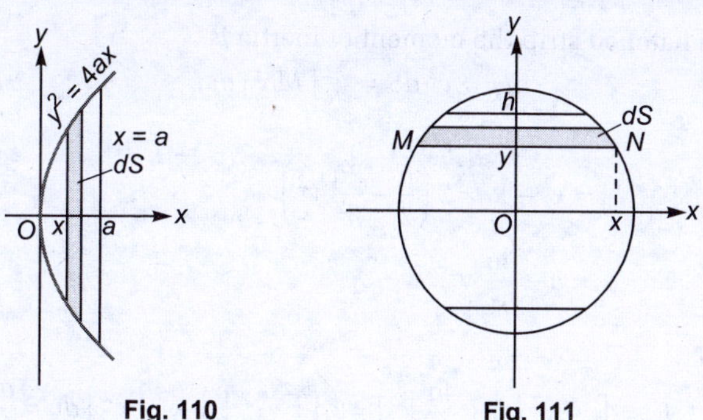

Fig. 110

Fig. 111

Solution Arrange the system of coordinates as is shown in the accompanying drawing. Then

$$dI_x = y^2 dS, \text{ where } dS = MN\,dy = 2x dy = 2x dy = 2\sqrt{R^2 - y^2}\,dy.$$

Whence

$$I_x = 2\int_{-h}^{h} y^2\sqrt{R^2 - y^2}\,dy = 4\int_0^h y^2\sqrt{R^2 - y^2}\,dy.$$

Substituting $y = R\sin t; dy = R\cos t\,dt; t_1 = 0; t_2 = \arcsin(h/R)$, we get

$$I_x = 4\int_0^h y^2\sqrt{R^2 - y^2}\,dy$$

$$= 4\int_0^{\arcsin(h/R)} R^2\sin^2 t \cdot R\cos t\, R\cos t\,dt$$

$$= 4R^4\int_0^{\arcsin(h/R)} \sin^2 t\cos^2 t\,dt = \frac{R^4}{2}$$

$$= \int_0^{\arcsin(h/R)} (1 - \cos 4t)\,dt$$

$$= \frac{R^4}{2}\arcsin\frac{h}{R} + \frac{h}{R}(2h^2 - R^2)\sqrt{R^2 - h^2}.$$

When $h = R$, we obtain the moment of inertia of the circle about one of its diameters: $I_x = \dfrac{\pi R^4}{4}$

7.13.6. Find the moment of inertia about the x-axis of the figure bounded by two parabolas with dimensions indicated in. (Fig. 112)

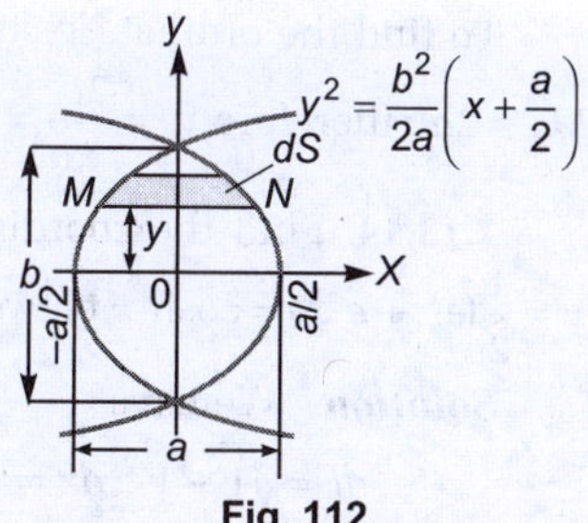

Fig. 112

Solution Arrange the system of coordinates as shown in Fig. 112 and write the equations of the parabolas.

The equation of the left parabola is:

$y^2 = \dfrac{b^2}{2a}\left(x + \dfrac{a}{2}\right)$, the equation of the right parabola, $y^2 = \dfrac{b^2}{2a}\left(\dfrac{a}{2} - x\right)$.

For the hatched strip the moment of inertia is

$$dI_x = y^2\, dS = y^2 \,|\, MN \,|\, dy,$$

where

$$|\, MN \,| = x_2 - x_1 = 2\left(\frac{a}{2} - \frac{2a}{b^2}\, y^2\right)$$

$$= a - \frac{4a}{b^2}\, y^2.$$

Hence,

$$I_x = \int_{-b/2}^{b/2} y^2 \left(a - \frac{4a}{b^2}\, y^2\right) = 2\int_0^{b/2} y^2 \left(a - \frac{4a}{b^2}\, y^2\right) dy = \frac{ab^3}{30}.$$

7.13.7. Find the static moments about the x-axis and y-axis of the arc of the parabola $y^2 = 2x$ between $x = 0$ and $x = 2\ (y > 0)$.

7.13.8. Find the static moments about the axes of coordinates of the line segment $\frac{x}{a} + \frac{y}{b} = 1$ whose end-points lie on the coordinate axes.

7.13.9. Find the static moment about the x-axis of the arc of the curve $y = \cos\, x$ between $x_1 = -\frac{\pi}{2}$ and $x_2 = \frac{\pi}{2}$.

7.13.10. Find the static moment about the x-axis of the figure bounded by the lines $y = x^2$; $y = \sqrt{x}$.

7.13.11. Find the moments of inertia about the x-and y-axis of the triangle bounded by the lines $x = 0$, $y = 0$ and $\frac{x}{a} + \frac{y}{b} = 1\ (a > 0, b > 0)$

7.13.12. Find the moment of inertia of the trapezoid $ABCD$ about its base AD if $AD = a$, $BC = b$ and the altitude of the trapezoid is equal to h.

7.13.13. Find the centre of gravity of the semicircle $x^2 + y^2 = a^2$ situated above the x-axis.

Solution Since the arc of the semicircle is symmetrical about the y-axis, the centre of gravity of the lies on the y-axis, *ie*, $x_c = 0$.

To find the ordinate y_c, take advantage of the result of Problem 7.13.1: $M_x = 2a^2$; therefore $y_c = \frac{2a^2}{\pi a} = \frac{2a}{\pi}$. Thus, $x_c = 0$, $y_c = \frac{2a}{\pi}$.

7.13.14. Find the coordinates of the centre of gravity of the catenary $y = \frac{1}{2}(e^x + e^{-x}) = \cosh\, x$ between $A(0, 1)$ and $B(a, \cosh\, a)$.

Solution We have

$$dl = \sqrt{1 + y'^2}\, dx = \sqrt{1 + \sinh^2\, x}\, dx = \cosh\, x\, dx$$

whence we find

$$= \int_L dl = \int_0^a \cosh\, x\, dx = \sinh\, a.$$

Then

$$M_y = \int_L x\,dl = \int_0^a x\cosh x\,dx = x\sinh x\Big|_0^a - \int_0^a \sinh x\,dx$$

$$= a\sinh a - \cosh a + 1.$$

Hence

$$x_c = \frac{a\sinh a - (\cosh a - 1)}{\sinh a} = a - \frac{\cosh a - 1}{\sinh a} = a - \tanh\frac{a}{2}.$$

Analogously,

$$M_x = \int_L y\,dl = \int_0^a \cosh^2 x\,dx = \frac{1}{2}\int_0^a (1+\cosh 2x)\,dx$$

$$= \frac{1}{2}\left(x + \frac{\sinh 2x}{2}\right)\Big|_0^a = \frac{a}{2} + \frac{\sinh 2a}{4};$$

$$y_c = \frac{\frac{a}{2} + \frac{\sinh 2a}{4}}{\sinh a} = \frac{a}{2\sinh a} + \frac{\cosh a}{2}.$$

7.13.15. Find the centre of gravity of the first arc of the cycloid:

$$x = a(t - \sin t),\ y = a(1 - \cos t)\ (0 \le t \le 2\pi).$$

Solution The first arc of the cycloid is symmetrical about the straight line $x = \pi a$, therefore the centere of gravity of the arc of the cycloid lies on this straight line and $x_c = \pi a$. Since the length of the first arc of the cycloid $l = 8a$, we have

$$y_c = \frac{1}{l}\int_L y\,dl = \frac{1}{8a}2a^2\int_0^{2\pi}(1-\cos t)\sin\frac{t}{2}\,dt = \frac{a}{2}\int_0^{2\pi}\sin^3\frac{t}{2}\,dt = \frac{4}{3}a.$$

7.13.16. Determine the coordinates of the centere of gravity of the portion of the arc of the astroid $x^{2/3} + y^{2/3} = a^{2/3}$ situated in the first quadrant.

7.13.17. Find the Cartesian coordinates of the center of gravity of the arc of the cardioid $\rho = a(1 + \cos\varphi)$ between $\varphi = 0$ and $\varphi = \pi$.

Solution Let us represent the equation of the cardioid in parametric form:

$$x = \rho\cos\varphi = a(1+\cos\varphi)\cos\varphi;$$

$$y = \rho\sin\varphi = a(1+\cos\varphi)\sin\varphi.$$

As the parameter φ varies between 0. and π the running point describes the upper portion of the curve. Since the length of the entire cardioid equals $8a$ and $dl = \sqrt{(x'_\varphi)^2 + (y'_\varphi)^2}\,d\varphi = 2a\cos\frac{\varphi}{2}\,d\varphi$. (see Problem **7.9.3**), we have

$$x_c = \frac{1}{l}\int_L y\,dl = \frac{1}{4a}\int_0^\pi a\sin\varphi(1+\cos\varphi)\,2a\cos\frac{\varphi}{2}\,d\varphi$$

$$= 2a\int_0^\pi \cos^4\frac{\varphi}{2}\sin\frac{\varphi}{2}\,d\varphi = -\frac{4}{5}a\cos^5\frac{\varphi}{2}\Big|_0^\pi = \frac{4}{5}a.$$

Analogously,

$$y_c = \frac{1}{4a}\int_L x\,dl = \frac{1}{4a}\int_0^{\pi} a\cos\varphi\,(1+\cos\varphi)\,2a\cos\frac{\varphi}{2}\,d\varphi$$

$$= a\int_0^{\pi}\cos\varphi\cos^3\frac{\varphi}{2}\,d\varphi = a\int_0^{\pi}\left(2\cos^5\frac{\varphi}{2}-\cos^3\frac{\varphi}{2}\right)d\varphi.$$

Putting $\frac{\varphi}{2} = t$ we get (see Problem **6.6.9**)

$$y_c = 2a\int_0^{\pi/2}(2\cos^5 t - \cos^3 t)\,dt = 4a\frac{4\cdot 2}{5\cdot 3} - 2a\frac{2}{3} = \frac{4}{5}a.$$

And so, $x_c = y_c = \frac{4a}{5}$.

It is interesting to note that the centre of gravity of the above considered half of the arc of the cardioid lies on the bisector of the first coordinate angle, though the arc itself is not symmetrical about this bisector.

7.13.18. Find the centre of gravity of the figure bounded by the ellipse $4x^2 + 9y^2 = 36$ and the circle $x^2 + y^2 = 9$ and situated in the first quadrant (Fig. 113).

Solution Let us First calculate the static moments:

$$M_y = \int_0^3 x(y_2 - y_1)\,dx = \int_0^3 x\left[\sqrt{9-x^2} - \frac{2}{3}\sqrt{9-x^2}\right]dx$$

$$= \frac{1}{3}\int_0^3 x\sqrt{9-x^2}\,dx = 3;$$

$$M_x = \frac{1}{2}\int_0^3 (y_2^2 - y_1^2)\,dx = \frac{1}{2}\int_0^3\left[(9-x^2) - \frac{4}{9}(9-x^2)\right]dx$$

$$= \frac{1}{2}\int_0^3\left(5 - \frac{5}{9}x^2\right)dx = 5.$$

The area of a quarter of a circle of radius 3 is equal to $\frac{9\pi}{4}$, and the area of a quarter of an ellipse with semi-axes $a = 3$ and $b = 2$ equals $\frac{3\pi}{2}$, therefore the area of the figure under consideration is $S = \frac{9\pi}{4} - \frac{3\pi}{2} = \frac{3\pi}{4}$.

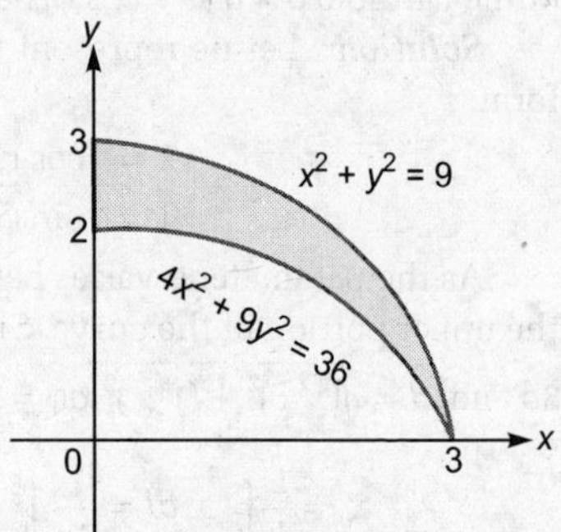

Fig. 113

Thus,

$$x_c = \frac{M_y}{S} = \frac{4}{\pi};\ y_c = \frac{M_x}{S} = \frac{10}{3\pi}.$$

7.13.19. Find the centre of gravity of the figure bounded by the parabola $x^{1/2} + y^{1/2} = a^{1/2}$ and the axes of coordinates.

7.13.20. Find the Cartesian coordinates of the centre of gravity of the figure enclosed by the curve = $a \cos^3 \varphi$ $(a > 0)$.

Solution Since $\rho \geq 0$ in all cases, the given curve is traced when φ changes from $-\frac{\pi}{2}$ to $\frac{\pi}{2}$. By virtue of evenness of the function $\cos \varphi$ it is symmetrical about the polar axis and passes through the origin of coordinates at $\varphi = \pm \frac{\pi}{2}$.

Compute the area S of the figure obtained:

$$S = 2 \times \frac{1}{2} \int_0^{\pi/2} \rho^2 d\varphi = a^2 \int_0^{\pi/2} \cos^6 \varphi \, d\varphi$$

$$= a^2 \frac{1 \times 3 \times 5}{2 \times 4 \times 6} \times \frac{\pi}{2} = \frac{5}{32} \pi a^2.$$

Now arrange the axes of coordinates as shown in Fig. 114. Then the parametric equations of the curve are

$$x = \rho \cos \varphi = a \cos^4 \varphi;$$

$$y = \rho \sin \varphi = a \sin \varphi \cos^2 \varphi.$$

The centre of gravity of the figure lies on the x-axis, *ie*, $y_c = 0$ by virtue of symmetry about the x-axis. Finally, determine x_c:

$$x_c = \frac{2\int_0^a xy\, dx}{S} = \frac{8a^2}{S} \int_0^{\pi/2} \cos^{10} \varphi \sin^2 \varphi \, d\varphi$$

$$= \frac{8a^2}{S} \int_0^{\pi/2} (\cos^{10} \varphi - \cos^{12} \varphi) \, d\varphi$$

$$= \frac{8a^2}{(5/32)\pi a^2} \left(\frac{1 \times 3 \times 5 \times 7 \times 9}{2 \times 4 \times 6 \times 8 \times 10} - \frac{1 \times 3 \times 5 \times 7 \times 9 \times 11}{2 \times 4 \times 6 \times 8 \times 10 \times 12} \right) \frac{\pi}{2}$$

$$= \frac{21}{40} a$$

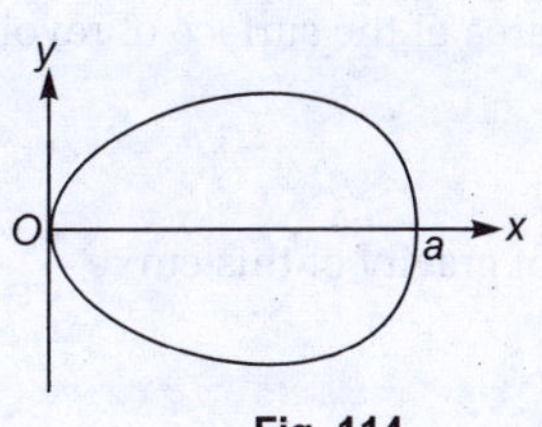

Fig. 114

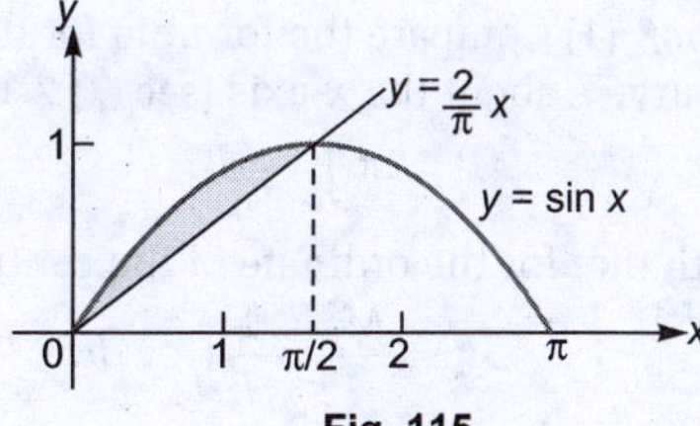

Fig. 115

7.13.21. Find the coordinates of the centre of gravity of the figure bounded by the straight line $y = \frac{2}{\pi} x$ and the sinusoid $y = \sin x$ $(x \geq 0)$ (Fig. 115).

Solution The straight line $y = \frac{2}{\pi} x$ and the sine line $y = \sin x$ intersect at the points (0, 0) and $\left(\frac{\pi}{2}, 1\right)$. The area of the figure bounded by these lines is

$$S = \int_0^{\pi/2} \left(\sin x - \frac{2}{\pi} x\right) dx = \frac{4 - \pi}{4}.$$

Hence,

$$x_c = \frac{\frac{1}{2}\int_0^{\pi/2} \left(\sin^2 x - \frac{4}{\pi^2} x^2\right) dx}{\frac{4-\pi}{4}} = \frac{2}{4-\pi} \int_0^{\pi/2} \left(\sin^2 x - \frac{4}{\pi^2} x^2\right) dx$$

$$= \frac{2}{4-\pi}\left[\frac{1}{2} x - \frac{\sin 2x}{4} - \frac{4}{3\pi^2} x^3\right]\Big|_0^{\pi/2} = \frac{\pi}{6\,(4-\pi)};$$

$$y_c = \frac{\int_0^{\pi/2} x\left(\sin x - \frac{2}{\pi} x\right) dx}{\frac{4-\pi}{4}}$$

$$= \frac{4}{4-\pi}\int_0^{\pi/2} x \sin x \, dx - \frac{8}{\pi\,(4-\pi)} \int_0^{\pi/2} x^2 \, dx$$

$$= \frac{4}{4-\pi} - \frac{\pi^3}{3\,(4-\pi)} = \frac{12-\pi^2}{12-3\pi}.$$

7.13.22. Prove the following theorems (Guldin's theorems).

Theorem 1. The area of a surface obtained by revolving an arc of a plane curve about some axis lying in the plane of the curve and not intersecting it is equal to the product of the length of the curve by the circumference of the circle described by the centre of gravity of the arc of the curve.

Theorem 2. The volume of a solid obtained by revolving a plane figure about some axis lying in the plane of the figure and not intersecting it is equal to the product of the area of this figure by the circumference of the circle described by the centre of gravity of the figure.

Proof. (1) Compare the formula for the area of the surface of revolution of the curve L about the x-axis (see ■ 7.10)

$$P = 2\pi \int_L y \, dl.$$

with that for the ordinate of the centre of gravity of this curve

$$y_c = \frac{M_x}{l} - \frac{1}{l}\int_L y \, dl.$$

Hence we conclude that $P = 2\pi\, l y_c = l \cdot 2\pi y_c$,
where l is the length of the revolving arc, and $2\pi y_c$ is the length of a circle of radius y_c, *ie*, the length of the circle described by the centre of gravity when revolving about the x-axis.

Proof (2) Compare the formula for the volume of a solid generated by revolving a plane figure about the x-axis (see ■ ❙ 7.6)

$$V = \pi \int_a^b (y_2^2 - y_1^2)\, dx$$

with that for the ordinate of the centre of gravity of this figure

$$y_C = \frac{M_x}{S} = \frac{1}{2S} \int_a^b (y_2^2 - y_1^2)\, dx.$$

Hence we conclude that

$$V = \pi \cdot 2S\ y_c = S \cdot 2\pi y_c$$

where S is the area of the revolving figure, and $2\pi y_c$ is the length of the circumference described by the centre of gravity when revolving about the x-axis.

7.13.23. Using the first Guldin theorem, find the centre of gravity of a semicircle of radius a.

Solution Arrange the coordinate axes as shown in Fig. 116. By virtue of symmetry $x_c = 0$. Now it remains to find y_c. If the semicircle revolves about the x-axis, then the surface P of the solid of revolution is equal to $4\pi r^2$, and the arc length $l = \pi a$. Therefore, according to the first Goldin theorem,

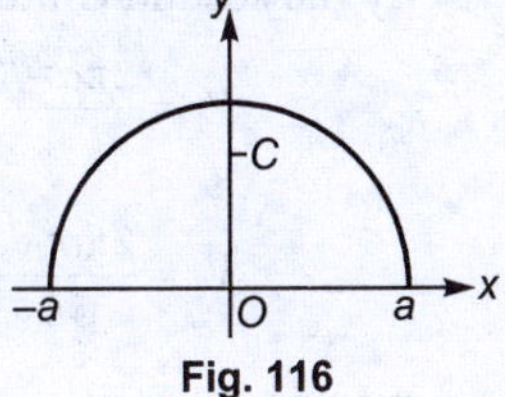

Fig. 116

$$4\pi a^2 = \pi a \cdot 2\pi y_C;\ y_c = 2\frac{a}{\pi}.$$

7.13.24. Using the second Guldin theorem, find the coordinates of the centre of gravity of the figure bounded by the x-axis and one arc of the cycloid: $x = a\,(t - \sin t)$; $y = a\,(1 - \cos t)$.

Solution By virtue of the symmetry of the figure about the straight line $x = \pi a$. its centre of gravity lies on this straight line; hence, $x_c = \pi a$.

The volume V obtained by revolving this figure about the x-axis is equal to $5\pi^2 a^2$ (see Problem 7.6.14), the area S of the figure being equal to $3\pi a^2$ (see Problem 7.4.3). Using the second Guldin theorem, we get

$$y_C = \frac{V}{2\pi S} = \frac{5\pi^2 a^3}{2\pi \cdot 3\pi a^3} = \frac{5a}{6}.$$

7.13.25. An equilateral triangle with side a revolves about an axis parallel to the base and situated at a distance $b > a$ from the base.

Find the volume of the solid of revolution.

Solution There are two possible ways of arranging the triangle with respect to the axis of revolution which are shown in Fig. 117, a and b.

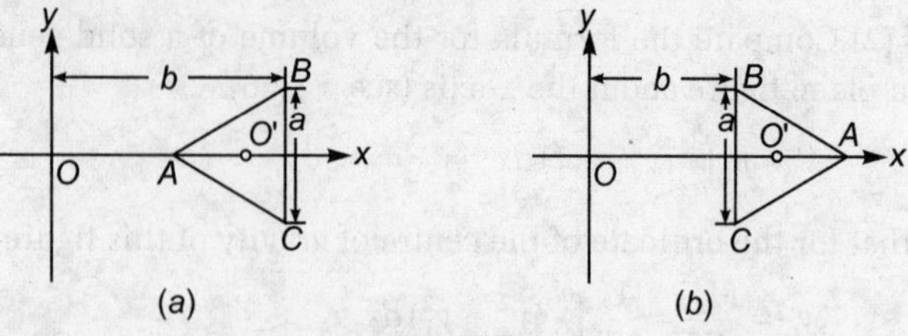

Fig. 117

The altitude of the equilateral triangle is $h = \dfrac{a\sqrt{3}}{2}$, the area $S = \dfrac{a^2\sqrt{3}}{4}$. The centre of gravity O' is situated at the point of intersection of the medians and at a distance of $b - \dfrac{a\sqrt{3}}{6}$ from the axis of revolution in the first case, and $b + \dfrac{a\sqrt{3}}{6}$ in the second.

By the second Guldin theorem

$$V_1 = \frac{2\pi a^2\sqrt{3}}{4}\left(b - \frac{a\sqrt{3}}{6}\right) = \pi\left(\frac{a^2 b\sqrt{3}}{2} - \frac{a^3}{4}\right),$$

$$V_2 = \frac{2\pi a^2\sqrt{3}}{4}\left(b + \frac{a\sqrt{3}}{6}\right) = \pi\left(\frac{a^2 b\sqrt{3}}{2} + \frac{a^3}{4}\right).$$

7.13.26. Find the centre of gravity of the arc of a circle of radius R subtending a central angle 2α.

7.13.27. Find the centre of gravity of the figure bounded by the arc of the cosine line $y = \cos x$ between $x = -\dfrac{\pi}{3}$ and $x = \dfrac{\pi}{3}$ and the straight line $y = \dfrac{1}{2}$.

7.13.28. Find the coordinates of the centre of gravity of the figure enclosed by line $y^2 = ax^3 - x^4$.

7.13.29. Find the eartesian coordinates of the centre of gravity of the arc of the logarithmic spiral $\rho = ae^{\varphi}$ from $\varphi_1 = \dfrac{\pi}{2}$ to $\varphi_2 = \pi$.

7.13.30. A regular hexagon with side a revolves about one of its sides. Find the volume of the solid of revolution thus generated.

7.13.31. Using Guldin's theorem, find the centre of gravity of a semicircle of radius R.

7.14. Additional Problems

7.14.1. Find the area of the portion of the figure bounded by the curves $y^m = x^n$ and $y^n = x^m$ (m and n positive integers) situated in the first quadrant. Consider the area of the entire figure depending on whether the numbers m and n are even or odd.

7.14.2. (a) Prove that the area of the curvilinear trapezoid bounded by the x-axis, straight lines $x = a, x = b$ and parabola $y = Ax^3 + Bx^2 + Cx + D$ can be computed using Chebyshev's formula

$$S = \frac{b-a}{3}\left[y\left(\frac{a+b}{2} - \frac{1}{\sqrt{2}}\frac{b-a}{2}\right) + y\left(\frac{a+b}{2}\right) + y\left(\frac{a+b}{2} + \frac{1}{\sqrt{2}}\frac{b-a}{2}\right)\right].$$

(b) Prove that an analogous area for a parabola of the fifth order $y = f(x) = Ax^5 + Bx^4 + Cx^3 + Dx^2 + Ex + F$

can be computed using the Gauss formula

$$S = \frac{b-a}{9}\left[5f\left(\frac{a+b}{2} - \sqrt{\frac{3}{5}}\frac{b-a}{2}\right) + 8f\left(\frac{a+b}{2}\right) + 5f\left(\frac{a+b}{2} + \sqrt{\frac{3}{5}}\frac{b-a}{2}\right)\right].$$

7.14.3. Show that the area of a figure bounded by any two radius vectors of the logarithmic spiral $\rho = ae^{m\varphi}$ and its arc is proportional to the difference of the squares of these radii.

7.14.4. Prove that if two solids contained between parallel planes P and Q possess the property that on being cut by any plane R parallel to these planes equivalent figures are obtained in their section, then the volumes of these solids are equal (Cavalieri's principle).

7.14.5. Prove that if the function $S(x)$ $(0 \le x \le h)$ expressing the area of the section of a solid by a plane perpendicular to the x-axis is a polynomial of a degree not higher than three, then the volume of this solid is equal to $V = \frac{h}{6}\left[S(0) + 4S\left(\frac{h}{2}\right) + S(h)\right]$. Using this formula, deduce formulas for computing the volume of a sphere, spherical segments of two and one bases, cone, first trum of a cone, ellipsoid, and paraboloid of revolution.

7.14.6. Prove that the volume of a solid generated by revolving about the y-axis the figure $a \le x \le b$, $0 \le y \le y(x)$, where $y(x)$ is a single valued continuous function, is equal to

$$V = 2\pi \int_a^b xy(x)\,dx.$$

7.14.7. Prove that the volume of the solid formed by revolving about the polar axis, a figure $0 \le \alpha \le \varphi \le \beta \le \pi, 0 \le \rho \le \rho(\varphi)$ is equal to

$$V = \frac{2\pi}{3}\int_\alpha^\beta \rho^3(\varphi)\sin\varphi\,d\varphi.$$

7.14.8. Prove that the arc length of the curve given by the parametric equations.

$$x = f''(t)\cos t + f'(t)\sin t \qquad (t_1 \le t \le t_2)$$

$$y = -f''(t)\sin t + f'(t)\cos t$$

is equal to $[f(t) + f''(t)]_{t_1}^{t_2}$.

7.14.9. Find the arc length of the curve represented parametrically

$$x = \int_1^t \frac{\cos z}{z}\,dz, \quad y = \int_1^t \frac{\sin z}{z}\,dz$$

between the origin and the nearest point from the vertical tangent line.

7.14.10. Deduce the formula for the arc length in polar coordinates proceeding from the definition without passing over from Cartesian coordinates to polar ones.

7.14.11. Prove that the arc length $l(x)$ of the catenary $y = \cosh x$ measured from the point $(0, 1)$ is expressed by the formula $l(x) = \sinh x$ and find parametric equations of this line, using the arc length as the parameter.

7.14.12. A flexible thread is suspended at the points A and B located at one and the same height. The distance between the points is $AB = 2b$, the deflection of the thread is f. Assuming the suspended thread to be a parabola, show that the length of the thread

$$l = 2b\left(1 + \frac{2}{3}\frac{f^2}{b^2}\right)$$

at a sufficiently small $\frac{f}{b}$.

7.14.13. Find the ratio of the area enclosed by the loop of the curve $y = \pm\left(\frac{1}{3} - x\right)\sqrt{x}$ to the area of the circle, whose circumference is equal in length of the contour of the curve.

7.14.14. Compute the length of the arc formed by the intersection of the parabolic cylinder

$$(y + z)^2 = 4ax$$

and the elliptic cone

$$\frac{4}{3}x^2 + y^2 - z^2 = 0,$$

between the origin and the point $M\,(x, y, z)$.

7.14.15. Prove that the area of the ellipse

$$Ax^2 + 2Bxy + Cy^2 + 2Dx + 2Ey + F = 0\;(AC - B^2 > 0)$$

is equal to

$$S = -\frac{\pi\,\Delta}{(AC - B^2)^{3/2}} \text{ where } \Delta = \begin{vmatrix} A & B & D \\ B & C & E \\ D & E & F \end{vmatrix}$$

7.14.16. Find : (a) the area S of the figure bounded by the hyperbola $x^2 - y^2 = 1$, the positive part of the x-axis and the radius vector connecting the origin of coordinates and the point $M\,(x, y)$ lying on this hyperbola.

(b) The area of the circular sector Q bounded by the x-axis and the radius drawn from the centre to the point $N\,(x, y)$ lying on the circle $x^2 + y^2 = 1$.

Prove that the coordinates of the points M and N are expressed respectively through the areas S and Q by the formulas

$$x_M = \cosh 2S, \quad y_M = \sinh 2S, \quad x_N = \cos 2Q, \quad y_N = \sin 2Q$$

7.14.17. Using Guldin's theorem, prove that the centre of gravity of a triangle is one third of the altitude distant from its base.

7.14.18. Let ξ be the abscissa of the centre of gravity of a curvilinear trapezoid bounded by the continuous curve $y = f(x)$, the x-axis and the straight lines $x = a$ and $x = b$. Prove the validity of the following equality

$$\int_a^b (ax + b)\, f(x)\, dx = (a\xi + b) \int_a^b f(x)\, dx$$

(Vereschagin's rule)

7.14.19. Let a curvilinear sector be bounded by two radius vectors and a continuous curve $\rho = f(\varphi)$. Prove that the coordinates of the centre of gravity of this sector are expressed by the following formulas

$$x_c = \frac{2}{3} \frac{\int_{\varphi_1}^{\varphi_2} \rho^3 \cos\varphi\, d\varphi}{\int_{\varphi_1}^{\varphi_2} \rho^2 d\varphi}; \quad y_c = \frac{2}{3} \frac{\int_{\varphi_1}^{\varphi^2} \rho^3 \sin\varphi\, d\varphi}{\int_{\varphi_1}^{\varphi^2} \rho^2 d\varphi}$$

7.14.20. Prove that the Cartesian coordinates of the centre of gravity of an arc of the curve $\rho = f(\varphi)$ are expressed by the following formulas

$$x_c = \frac{\int_{\varphi_1}^{\varphi_2} \rho \cos\varphi \sqrt{\rho^2 + \rho'^2}\, d\varphi}{\int_{\varphi_1}^{\varphi_2} \sqrt{\rho^2 + \rho'^2}\, d\varphi}; \quad y_c = \frac{\int_{\varphi_1}^{\varphi_2} \rho \sin\varphi \sqrt{\rho^2 + \rho'^2}\, d\varphi}{\int_{\varphi_1}^{\varphi_2} \sqrt{\rho^2 + \rho'^2}\, d\varphi}.$$

8

Improper Integrals

8.1. Improper Integrals with Infinite Limits

Let the function $f(x)$ be defined for all $x \geq a$ and integrable on any interval $[a, A]$. Then $\lim\limits_{A \to +\infty} \int_a^A f(x)\,dx$ is called the *improper integral* of the function $f(x)$ in the interval $[a, +\infty]$ and is denoted by the symbol $\int_a^{+\infty} f(x)\,dx$.

We similarly define the integrals $\int_{-\infty}^{B} f(x)\,dx$ and $\int_{-\infty}^{+\infty} f(x)\,dx$.

Thus,
$$\int_a^{+\infty} f(x)\,dx = \lim_{A \to +\infty} \int_a^A f(x)\,dx;$$
$$\int_{-\infty}^{B} f(x)\,dx = \lim_{A \to -\infty} \int_A^B f(x)\,dx;$$
$$\int_{-\infty}^{+\infty} f(x)\,dx = \lim_{A \to -\infty} \int_A^C f(x)\,dx + \lim_{B \to +\infty} \int_C^B f(x)\,dx.$$

If the above limits exist and are finite, the appropriate integrals are called *convergent;* otherwise, they are called *divergent.*

Comparison test. Let $f(x)$ and $g(x)$ be defined for all $x \geq a$ and integrable on each interval $[a, A]$, $A \geq a$. If $0 \leq f(x) \leq g(x)$ for all $x \geq a$, then from convergence of the integral $\int_a^{\infty} g(x)\,dx$ it follows that the integral $\int_a^{\infty} f(x)\,dx$ is also convergent, and $\int_a^{\infty} f(x)\,dx \leq \int_a^{\infty} g(x)\,dx$; from divergence of the integral $\int_a^{\infty} f(x)\,dx$ it follows that the integral $\int_a^{\infty} g(x)\,dx$ is also divergent.

Special comparison test. If as $x \to \infty$ the function $f(x) \geq 0$ is an infinitesimal of order $\lambda > 0$ is compared with $\frac{1}{x}$, then the integral $\int_a^{+\infty} f(x)\,dx$ converges for $\lambda > 1$ and diverges for $\lambda \leq 1$.

Absolute and conditional convergence. Let the function $f(x)$ be defined for all $x \geq a$. If the integral $\int_a^{\infty} |f(x)|\,dx$ converges, then the integral $\int_a^{\infty} f(x)\,dx$ also converges and is called *absolutely convergent.* In this case
$$\left| \int_a^{\infty} f(x)\,dx \right| \leq \int_a^{\infty} |f(x)|\,dx.$$

If the integral $\int_a^{\infty} f(x)\,dx$ converges, and $\int_a^{\infty} |f(x)|\,dx$ diverges, then the integral $\int_a^{\infty} f(x)\,dx$ is called conditionally convergent.

The change of the variable in an improper integral is based on the following theorem.

Theorem. *Let the function f(x) be defined and continuous for $x \geq a$. If the function $x = \varphi(t)$, defined on the interval $\alpha < t < \beta$ (α and β may also be improper numbers $-\infty$ and ∞), is monotonic, has a continuous derivative $\varphi'(t) \neq 0$ and $\lim_{t\to\alpha+0} \varphi(t) = a$, $\lim_{t\to\beta-0} \varphi(t) = +\infty$, then*

$$\int_a^{\infty} f(x)\,dx = \int_{\alpha}^{\beta} f(\varphi(t))\varphi'(t)\,dt.$$

Integration by parts involves no difficulties.

8.1.1. Evaluate the following improper integrals with infinite limits or prove their divergence taking advantage of their definition

(a) $\int_{e^2}^{\infty} \frac{dx}{x \ln^3 x}$; (b) $\int_{-\infty}^{\infty} \frac{dx}{x^2 + 2x + 5}$;

(c) $\int_0^{\infty} x \sin x\,dx$.

Solution (a) By definition,

$$\int_{e^2}^{\infty} \frac{dx}{x \ln^3 x} = \lim_{A\to+\infty} \int_{e^2}^{A} \frac{dx}{x \ln^3 x} = \lim_{A\to+\infty} \left(-\frac{1}{2 \ln^2 x}\bigg|_{e^2}^{A} \right)$$

$$= \lim_{A\to+\infty} \left(\frac{1}{8} - \frac{1}{2 \ln^2 A} \right) = \frac{1}{8}$$

(b) By definition,

$$\int_{-\infty}^{\infty} \frac{dx}{x^2 + 2x + 5} = \lim_{B\to-\infty} \int_B^0 \frac{dx}{x^2 + 2x + 5} + \lim_{A\to+\infty} \int_0^A \frac{dx}{x^2 + 2x + 5}$$

(instead of the point $x = 0$ any other finite point of the x-axis may be taken as an intermediate limit of integration).

Compute each of the limits standing in the right side of the above equality :

$$\lim_{B\to-\infty} \int_B^0 \frac{dx}{x^2 + 2x + 5} = \lim_{B\to-\infty} \frac{1}{2} \text{arc tan} \frac{x+1}{2}\bigg|_B^0$$

$$= \frac{1}{2} \text{arc tan} \frac{1}{2} + \frac{\pi}{4}, \quad \lim_{A\to+\infty} \int_0^A \frac{dx}{x^2 + 2x + 5} = \lim_{A\to+\infty} \frac{1}{2} \text{arc tan} \frac{x+1}{2}\bigg|_0^A$$

$$= \frac{\pi}{4} - \frac{1}{2} \text{arc tan} \frac{1}{2}.$$

Hence,

$$\int_{-\infty}^{\infty} \frac{dx}{x^2 + 2x + 5} = \frac{\pi}{2}.$$

(c) By definition,

$$\int_0^{\infty} x \sin x\,dx = \lim_{A\to+\infty} \int_0^A x \sin x\,dx.$$

Putting $u = x, dv = \sin x\,dx$ and integrating by parts, we get

$$\lim_{A\to+\infty}\int_0^A x\sin x\,dx = \lim_{A\to+\infty}\left(-x\cos x\,\Big|_0^A + \int_0^A \cos x\,dx\right)$$
$$= \lim_{A\to+\infty}(-A\cos A + \sin A).$$

But the last limit does not exit, Consequently, the integral $\int_0^\infty x\sin x\,dx$ diverges.

8.1.2. Evaluate the following improper integrals with infinite limits on the basis of their definition :

(a) $\int_2^\infty \frac{x\,dx}{\sqrt{(x^2-3)^3}}$; (b) $\int_1^\infty \frac{dx}{x+x^3}$;

(c) $\int_0^\infty \frac{x\,dx}{\sqrt{(4x^2+1)^3}}$; (d) $\int_1^\infty \frac{dx}{x^2(1+x)}$;

(e) $\int_{-\infty}^\infty \frac{dx}{x^2-6x+10}$; (f) $\int_0^\infty e^{-x}\sin x\,dx$.

Solution (a) By definition

$$\int_2^\infty \frac{x\,dx}{\sqrt{(x^2-3)^3}} = \lim_{A\to+\infty}\int_2^A \frac{x\,dx}{\sqrt{(x^2-3)^3}} = \lim_{A\to+\infty}\left[\frac{1}{2}\frac{(x^2-3)^{-1/2}}{-1/2}\Bigg|_2^A\right]$$
$$= -\lim_{A\to+\infty}\left[\frac{1}{\sqrt{A^2-3}} - 1\right] = 1.$$

8.1.3. Prove that the integrals of the form

$$\int_a^{+\infty} e^{-px}\,dx \text{ and } \int_{-\infty}^b e^{px}\,dx$$

converge for any constant $p > 0$ and diverge for $p < 0$.

8.1.4. Test the integral $\int_0^\infty \frac{dx}{1+2x^2+3x^4}$ for convergence.

Solution The integrand

$$f(x) = \frac{1}{1+2x^2+3x^4}$$

is positive and is an infinitesimal of order $\lambda = 4$ as compared with $\frac{1}{x}$ as $x \to \infty$. Since $4 > 1$, the integral converges according to the special comparison test.

8.1.5. Test the integral

$$\int_1^\infty \frac{dx}{x+\sin^2 x}$$

for convergence.

Solution The integrand $f(x) = \dfrac{1}{x + \sin^2 x}$ is continuous and positive for $x \geq 1$.

As $x \to \infty$ the function $f(x)$ is an infinitesimal of order $\lambda = 1$ as compared with $\dfrac{1}{x}$; according to the special comparison test the integral diverges.

8.1.6. Test the following integrals for convergence :

(a) $\displaystyle\int_1^{\infty} \frac{\ln(x^2+1)}{x}\,dx$; (b) $\displaystyle\int_1^{\infty} \frac{\tan\frac{1}{x}}{1 + x\sqrt{x}}\,dx$;

(c) $\displaystyle\int_1^{\infty} \frac{2+\cos x}{\sqrt{x}}\,dx$; (d) $\displaystyle\int_2^{\infty} \frac{3 + \arcsin\frac{1}{x}}{1 + x\sqrt{x}}\,dx$;

(e) $\displaystyle\int_1^{\infty} \frac{\arctan x}{x}\,dx$.

8.1.7. Test the integral $\displaystyle\int_1^{\infty} \frac{(x + \sqrt{x+1})\,dx}{x^2 + 2\sqrt[5]{x^4} + 1}$ for convergence.

Solution The integrand is continuous and positive for $x \geq 1$. Determine its order of smallness λ with respect to $\dfrac{1}{x}$ as $x \to \infty$; since

$$\frac{x + \sqrt{x+1}}{x^2 + 2\sqrt[5]{x^4} + 1} = \frac{1}{x} \times \frac{1 + \sqrt{\frac{1}{x} + \frac{1}{x^2}}}{1 + 2\sqrt[5]{\frac{1}{x^5} + \frac{1}{x^{10}}}},$$

the order of smallness $\lambda = 1$. According to the special comparison test the integral $\displaystyle\int_1^{\infty} \frac{x + \sqrt{x+1}}{x^2 + 2\sqrt[5]{x^4} + 1}\,dx$ diverges.

8.1.8. Test the integral

$$\int_3^{\infty} \frac{dx}{\sqrt{x(x-1)(x-2)}}$$

for convergence.

Solution Since the function

$$f(x) = \frac{1}{\sqrt{x^3\left(1 - \frac{1}{x}\right)\left(1 - \frac{2}{x}\right)}} = \frac{1}{x^{\frac{3}{2}}} \times \frac{1}{\sqrt{\left(1 - \frac{1}{x}\right)\left(1 - \frac{2}{x}\right)}}$$

is an infinitesimal of order $\lambda = \dfrac{3}{2}$ with respect to $\dfrac{1}{x}$ as $x \to +\infty$, according to the special comparison test the integral converges.

8.1.9. Test the integral

$$\int_2^{\infty} \frac{\sqrt[7]{3+2x^2}}{\sqrt[5]{x^3-1}}\,dx$$

for convergence.

Solution The integrand is continuous and positive for $x \ge 2$. Determine its order of smallness with respect to $\frac{1}{x}$ as $x \to +\infty$:

$$\frac{\sqrt[7]{3+2x^2}}{\sqrt[5]{x^3-1}} = \frac{1}{x^{\frac{11}{35}}} \times \frac{\sqrt[7]{2+\frac{3}{x^2}}}{\sqrt[5]{1-\frac{1}{x^3}}}.$$

Since the second multiplier has the limit $\sqrt[7]{2}$ as $x \to +\infty$, we have $\lambda = \frac{11}{35} < 1$. Consequently, the given integral diverges.

8.1.10. Test the integral

$$\int_1^{\infty} \left(1 - \cos\frac{2}{x}\right) dx$$

for convergence.

Solution The integrand $f(x) = 1 - \cos\frac{2}{x} = 2\sin^2\frac{1}{x}$ is positive and continuous for $x \ge 1$. Since $2\sin^2\frac{1}{x} \sim 2\left(\frac{1}{x}\right)^2 = \frac{2}{x^2}$, the given integral converges (by the special comparison test).

8.1.11. Test the integral

$$\int_1^{\infty} \ln\frac{e^{\frac{1}{x}} + (n-1)}{n}\,dx,\ n > 0$$

for convergence.

Solution Transform the integrand :

$$f(x) = \ln\frac{e^{\frac{1}{x}} + (n-1)}{n} = \ln\left[1 + \frac{e^{\frac{1}{x}} - 1}{n}\right].$$

Since the function $\frac{e^{\frac{1}{x}} - 1}{n}$ is an infinitesimal as $x \to \infty$, then $f(x) \sim \frac{e^{\frac{1}{x}} - 1}{n} \sim \frac{1}{nx}$. In other words, $\lim\limits_{x \to \infty} \frac{f(x)}{1/x} = \frac{1}{n}$. According to the special comparison test the given integral diverges.

8.1.12. Test the integral

$$\int_1^{\infty} \frac{1-4\sin 2x}{x^3+\sqrt[3]{x}}\,dx$$

for convergence.

Solution The function $f(x)=\dfrac{1-4\sin 2x}{x^3+\sqrt[3]{x}}$ changes its sign together with the change in sign of the numerator . Test the integral

$$\int_1^{\infty} \frac{|1-4\sin 2x|}{x^3+\sqrt[3]{x}}\,dx$$

for convergence. Since $\dfrac{|1-4\sin 2x|}{x^3+\sqrt[3]{x}}<\dfrac{5}{x^3}$, and the integral $\int_1^{\infty}\dfrac{5dx}{x^3}$ converges, the integral $\int_1^{\infty} \dfrac{|1-4\sin 2x|}{x^3+\sqrt[3]{x}}\,dx$ converges as well (according to the comparison test). Thus, the given integral converges absolutely.

8.1.13. Prove that the Dirichlet integral converges conditionally.

$$I=\int_0^{\infty}\frac{\sin x}{x}\,dx$$

Solution Let us represent the given integral as the sum of two integrals :

$$I=\int_0^{\infty}\frac{\sin x}{x}\,dx=\int_0^{\pi/2}\frac{\sin x}{x}\,dx+\int_{\pi/2}^{\infty}\frac{\sin x}{x}\,dx.$$

The first is a proper integral $\left(\text{since } \lim\limits_{x\to 0}\dfrac{\sin x}{x}=1\right)$. Applying the method of integration by parts to the second integral, we have

$$\int_{\pi/2}^{\infty}\frac{\sin x}{x}\,dx=\lim_{A\to\infty}\int_{\pi/2}^{A}\frac{\sin x}{x}\,dx$$

$$=\lim_{A\to\infty}\left[-\frac{\cos x}{x}\Bigg|_{\frac{\pi}{2}}^{A}-\int_{\pi/2}^{A}\frac{\cos x\,dx}{x^2}\right]=-\int_{\pi/2}^{\infty}\frac{\cos x}{x^2}\,dx.$$

But the improper integral $\int_{\pi/2}^{\infty}\dfrac{\cos x}{x^2}\,dx$ converges absolutely, since $\dfrac{|\cos x|}{x^2}\le\dfrac{1}{x^2}$, and the integral $\int_{\pi/2}^{\infty}\dfrac{dx}{x^2}$ converges.

Therefore, the integral $\int_0^{\infty}\dfrac{\sin x}{x}\,dx$ converges.

Reasoning in a similar way it is easy to prove that the integral $\int_{\pi/2}^{\infty}\dfrac{\cos x}{x}\,dx$ also converges. Now let us prove that the integral $\int_{\pi/2}^{\infty}\dfrac{|\sin x|}{x}\,dx$ diverges.

Indeed,

$$\frac{|\sin x|}{x}\ge\frac{\sin^2 x}{x}=\frac{1-\cos 2x}{2x},$$

but the integral

$$\int_{\pi/2}^{\infty} \frac{1-\cos 2x}{2x} dx = \lim_{A\to\infty} \frac{1}{2}\int_{\pi/2}^{A} \frac{dx}{x} - \frac{1}{2}\int_{\pi/2}^{\infty} \frac{\cos 2x}{x} dx$$

$$= \frac{1}{2}\lim_{A\to\infty} \ln A - \frac{1}{2}\ln\frac{\pi}{2} - \frac{1}{2}\int_{\pi/2}^{\infty} \frac{\cos 2x}{x} dx$$

diverges, since $\lim_{A\to\infty} \ln A = \infty$, and the integral $\int_{\pi/2}^{\infty} \frac{\cos 2x}{x} \cdot dx$ converges.

8.1.14. Prove that the following integrals converge

(a) $\int_0^{\infty} \sin(x^2)\,dx$; $\int_0^{\infty} \cos(x^2)\,dx$; (b) $\int_0^{\infty} 2x\cos(x^4)\,dx$.

Solution (a) Putting $x = \sqrt{t}$, we find

$$\int_0^{\infty} \sin(x^2)\,dx = \frac{1}{2}\int_0^{\infty} \frac{\sin t}{\sqrt{t}} dt.$$

Let us represent the integral on the right side as the sum of two integrals :

$$\int_0^{\infty} \frac{\sin t}{\sqrt{t}} dt = \int_0^{\pi/2} \frac{\sin t}{\sqrt{t}} dt + \int_{\pi/2}^{\infty} \frac{\sin t}{\sqrt{t}} dt.$$

The first summand is a proper integral, since $\lim_{x\to 0} \frac{\sin t}{\sqrt{t}} = 0$. Let us apply to the second summand the method of integration by parts, putting

$$u = 1/\sqrt{t}, \quad \sin t\,dt = dv,$$

$$\int_{\pi/2}^{\infty} \frac{\sin t}{\sqrt{t}} dt = -\frac{\cos t}{\sqrt{t}}\Bigg|_{\pi/2}^{\infty} - \frac{1}{2}\int_{\pi/2}^{\infty} \frac{\cos t\,dt}{t^{3/2}} = -\frac{1}{2}\int_{\pi/2}^{\infty} \frac{\cos t}{t^{3/2}} dt.$$

The last integral converges absolutely, since $\frac{|\cos t|}{t^{3/2}} \le \frac{1}{t^{3/2}}$, and the integral $\int_{\pi/2}^{\infty} \frac{dt}{t^{3/2}}$ converges. We can prove analogously that the integral $\int_0^{\infty} \cos(x^2)\,dx$ is convergent. The integrals considered are called *Fresnel's integrals*. They are used in explaining the phenomenon of light diffraction.

(b) By the substitution $x^2 = t$ this integral is reduced to the integral $\int_0^{\infty} \cos(t^2)\,dt$. The latter integral converges as has just been proved.

Note. Fresnel's integrals show that an improper integral can converge even when the integrand does not vanish as $x \to \infty$. The last convergent integral considered in item (b) shows that an improper integral can converge even if the integrand is not bounded. Indeed, at $x = \sqrt[4]{n\pi}$ $(n = 0, 1, 2, \ldots)$ the integrand attains the values $\pm\sqrt[4]{n\pi}$, *ie*, it is unbounded.

8.1.15. Evaluate the improper integral

$$\int_0^{\infty} \frac{dx}{(1+x^2)^n}, n \text{ natural number}.$$

Solution Make the substitution $x = \tan t$, where $0 \le t < \frac{\pi}{2}$. Then $x = 0$ at $t = 0, x \to +\infty$ as $t \to \frac{\pi}{2} - 0$ and $x'_t = \frac{1}{\cos^2 t} \ne 0$. Consequently, by the theorem on changing a variable in an improper integral

$$\int_0^\infty \frac{dx}{(1+x^2)^n} \int_0^{\pi/2} \frac{1}{\sec^{2n} t} \times \sec^2 t\, dt = \int_0^{\pi/2} \cos^{2n-2} t\, dt.$$

On changing the variable we obtain the proper integral which was computed in Problem **6.6.9.**

Therefore,

$$\int_0^\infty \frac{dx}{(1+x^2)^n} = \begin{cases} \pi/2, n = 1, \\ \dfrac{1 \cdot 3 \cdot 5 \ldots (2n-3)}{2 \cdot 4 \cdot 6 \ldots (2n-2)} \cdot \dfrac{\pi}{2}, n > 1. \end{cases}$$

8.1.16. Compute the integral $I = \int_0^\infty \frac{x^2}{1+x^4} dx$.

Solution Apply the substitution

$$x = 1/t; \qquad dx = -(1/t^2)dt; \qquad t_1 = \infty, t_2 = 0;$$

$$I = \int_0^\infty \frac{x^2}{1+x^4} dx = \int_0^\infty \frac{(1/t^4)dt}{1+1/t^4} = \int_0^\infty \frac{dt}{t^4+1}.$$

If another integral I is added to the right and left sides then we get

$$2I = \int_0^\infty \frac{1+t^2}{1+t^4} dt = \int_0^\infty \frac{1/t^2+1}{t^2+1/t^2} dt.$$

Make the substitution $z = t - 1/t$, $(1 + 1/t^2)dt = dz$. Then, as $t \to +0, z \to -\infty$ and as $t \to +\infty, z \to +\infty$. Hence,

$$I = \frac{1}{2}\int_{-\infty}^\infty \frac{dz}{z^2+2} = \frac{1}{2}\left[\lim_{B \to -\infty} \int_B^0 \frac{dz}{z^2+2} + \lim_{A \to +\infty} \int_0^A \frac{dz}{z^2+2}\right]$$

$$= -\frac{1}{2\sqrt{2}} \lim_{B \to -\infty} \arctan \frac{B}{\sqrt{2}} + \frac{1}{2\sqrt{2}} \lim_{A \to +\infty} \arctan \frac{A}{\sqrt{2}}$$

$$= \frac{1}{2\sqrt{2}}\left(\frac{\pi}{2} + \frac{\pi}{2}\right) = \frac{\pi}{2\sqrt{2}}.$$

8.1.17. Evaluate the following improper integrals :

(a) $\int_0^\infty \frac{\ln x}{1+x^2} dx$; (b) $\int_0^\infty e^{-x^2} x^{2m+1} dx$.

8.1.18. Compute the integral

$$I = \int_1^\infty \frac{\sqrt{x^3 - x^2 + 1}}{x^5 + x^2 + 1} dx$$

accurate to two decimal places.

Solution Represent the given integral in the form of a sum of two integrals

$$I_1 = \int_1^N \frac{\sqrt{x^3 - x^2 + 1}}{x^5 + x^2 + 1}\,dx,$$

$$I_2 = \int_N^\infty \frac{\sqrt{x^3 - x^2 + 1}}{x^5 + x^2 + 1}\,dx.$$

Compute the former with the required accuracy, using Simpson's formula, and estimate the latter. Since for $x \ge 1$ we have

$$0 < \frac{\sqrt{x^3 - x^2 + 1}}{x^5 + x^2 + 1} < \frac{x^{3/2}}{x^5} = x^{-7/2},$$

then

$$0 < I_2 = \int_N^\infty x^{-7/2}\,dx = \frac{2}{5} N^{-5/2}.$$

At $N = 7$ we get the estimate $I_2 < \frac{2}{5} \times \frac{1}{49\sqrt{7}} < 0.0031.$

Computation of the integral

$$I_1 = \int_1^7 \frac{\sqrt{x^3 - x^2 + 1}}{x^5 + x^2 + 1}\,dx$$

by Simpson's formula for a step $h = 1$ gives

$$S_1 = 0.2155,$$

and for a step $\frac{h}{2} = 0.5$

$$S_{0.5} = 0.2079.$$

Since the difference between the values is 0.0076, the integral I_1 gives a more accurate value $S_{0.5} = 0.2079$ with an error of the order $\frac{0.0076}{15} \cong 0.0005.$

Consequently, the sought-for integral is approximately equal to

$$I \approx 0.208$$

with an error not exceeding 0.004, or $I = 0.21$ with all true decimal places.

8.2. Improper Integrals of Unbounded Functions

If the function $f(x)$ is defined for $a \le x < b$, integrable on any interval $[a, b - \varepsilon], 0 < \varepsilon < b - a$ and unbounded to the left of the point b, then, by definition, we put

$$\int_a^b f(x)\,dx = \lim_{\varepsilon \to +0} \int_a^{b-\varepsilon} f(x)\,dx.$$

If this limit is existent and finite, then the improper integral is said to be *convergent*. Otherwise it is called *divergent*.

Analogously, if the function $f(x)$ is unbounded to the right from the point a, then

$$\int_a^b f(x)\,dx = \lim_{\varepsilon\to+0}\int_{a+\varepsilon}^b f(x)\,dx.$$

Finally, if the function is unbounded in the neighbourhood of an interior point c of the interval $[a,b]$, then, by definition,

$$\int_a^b f(x)\,dx = \int_a^c f(x)\,dx + \int_c^b f(x)\,dx.$$

Let the function $f(x)$ be continuous on the interval $[a,b]$ except at a finite number of points. If there exists a function $F(x)$ continuous on $[a,b]$ for which $F'(x) = f(x)$ except at a finite number of points, then the Newton-Leibnitz formula

$$\int_a^b f(x)\,dx = F(b) - F(a)$$

holds good.

Sometimes the function $F(x)$ is called a *generalized antiderivative* for the function $f(x)$ on the interval $[a,b]$.

For the functions defined and positive on the interval $a \le x < b$ convergence tests (comparison tests) analogous to the comparison tests for improper integrals with infinite limits are valid.

Comparison test. Let the function $f(x)$ and $g(x)$ be defined on the interval $a \le x < b$ and integrable on each interval $[a, b-\varepsilon]$, $0 < \varepsilon < b-a$. If $0 \le f(x) \le g(x)$, then from the convergence of the integral $\int_a^b g(x)\,dx$ follows the convergence of the integral $\int_a^b f(x)\,dx$, and $\int_a^b f(x)\,dx \le \int_a^b g(x)\,dx$; from the divergence of the integral $\int_a^b f(x)\,dx$ follows the divergence of the integral $\int_a^b g(x)\,dx$.

Special comparison test. If the function $f(x) \ge 0$ is defined and continuous on the interval $a \le x < b$ and is an infinitely large quantity of the order λ as compared with $\dfrac{1}{b-x}$ as $x \to b-0$, then the integral $\int_a^b f(x)\,dx$ converges for $\lambda < 1$ and diverges for $\lambda \ge 1$.

In particular, the integral

$$\int_a^b \frac{dx}{(b-x)^\lambda}$$

converges for $\lambda < 1$ and diverges for $\lambda \ge 1$.

Absolute and conditional convergence. Let the function $f(x)$ be defined on the interval $a \le x < b$ and integrable on each interval $[a, b-\varepsilon]$; then from the convergence of the integral $\int_a^b |f(x)|\,dx$ follows the convergence of the integral $\int_a^b f(x)\,dx$.

In this case the integral $\int_a^b f(x)\,dx$ is called *absolutely convergent.* But if the integral $\int_a^b f(x)\,dx$ converges, and the integral $\int_a^b |f(x)|\,dx$ diverges, then the integral $\int_a^b f(x)\,dx$ is called *conditionally convergent.*

Analogous tests are also valid for improper integrals $\int_a^b f(x)\,dx$, where $f(x)$ is unbounded to the right from the point a.

8.2.1. Proceeding from the definition, evaluate the following improper integrals (or prove their divergence) :

(a) $\int_1^e \frac{dx}{x\sqrt[3]{\ln x}}$; (b) $\int_0^{\pi/2} \frac{dx}{\cos x}$;

(c) $\int_1^3 \frac{dx}{\sqrt{4x - x^2 - 3}}$; (d) $\int_0^2 \frac{dx}{\sqrt{|1 - x^2|}}$;

(e) $\int_0^1 \frac{x^2 + \sqrt[3]{x} - 2}{\sqrt[5]{x^3}}\,dx$; (f) $\int_0^1 \frac{dx}{1 - x^3}$.

Solution (a) The integrand $f(x) = \frac{1}{x\sqrt[3]{\ln x}}$ is unbounded in the neighbourhood of the point $x = 1$. It is integrable on any interval $(1 + \varepsilon, e]$, since it is a continuous function.

Therefore

$$\int_1^e \frac{dx}{x\sqrt[3]{\ln x}} = \lim_{\varepsilon \to +0} \int_{1+\varepsilon}^e \frac{dx}{x\sqrt[3]{\ln x}} = \lim_{\varepsilon \to +0} \left[\frac{3}{2}\sqrt[3]{\ln^2 x}\right]_{1+\varepsilon}^e$$

$$= \lim_{\varepsilon \to +0} \left[\frac{3}{2} - \frac{3}{2}\sqrt[3]{\ln^2(1+\varepsilon)}\right] = \frac{3}{2}.$$

(b) The integrand $f(x) = \frac{1}{\cos x}$ is unbounded in the neighbourhood of the point $x = \frac{\pi}{2}$ and integrable on any interval $\left[0, \frac{\pi}{2} - \varepsilon\right]$ as a continuous function. Therefore

$$\int_0^{\pi/2} \frac{dx}{\cos x} = \lim_{\varepsilon \to +0} \int_0^{\frac{\pi}{2} - \varepsilon} \frac{dx}{\cos x}$$

$$= \lim_{\varepsilon \to +0} \ln\tan\left(\frac{x}{2} + \frac{\pi}{4}\right)\Bigg|_0^{\frac{\pi}{2} - \varepsilon} = \lim_{\varepsilon \to +0} \ln\tan\left(\frac{\pi}{2} - \frac{\varepsilon}{2}\right) = \infty.$$

Hence, the given integral diverges.

(c) The integrand is unbounded in the neighbourhood of the points $x = 1$ and $x = 3$. Therefore, by definition,

$$\int_1^3 \frac{dx}{\sqrt{4x - x^2 - 3}} = \int_1^2 \frac{dx}{\sqrt{4x - x^2 - 3}} + \int_2^3 \frac{dx}{\sqrt{4x - x^2 - 3}}$$

(instead of the point $x = 2$ we can take any other interior point of the interval [1, 3]). Let us now compute each summand separately :

$$\int_1^2 \frac{dx}{\sqrt{4x - x^2 - 3}} = \lim_{\varepsilon \to +0} \int_{1+\varepsilon}^2 \frac{dx}{\sqrt{1 - (x-2)^2}} = \lim_{\varepsilon \to +0} \arcsin(x-2)\Big|_{1+\varepsilon}^{2}$$

$$= \lim_{\varepsilon \to +0} [0 - \arcsin(\varepsilon - 1)] = \frac{\pi}{2};$$

$$\int_2^3 \frac{dx}{\sqrt{4x - x^2 - 3}} = \lim_{\varepsilon \to +0} \int_2^{3-\varepsilon} \frac{dx}{\sqrt{1 - (x-2)^2}} = \lim_{\varepsilon \to +0} \arcsin(x-2)\Big|_{2}^{3-\varepsilon}$$

$$= \lim_{\varepsilon \to +0} [\arcsin(1 - \varepsilon) - 0] = \frac{\pi}{2}.$$

Hence,

$$\int_1^3 \frac{dx}{\sqrt{4x - x^2 - 3}} = \frac{\pi}{2} + \frac{\pi}{2} = \pi.$$

(d) The integrand $f(x) = \dfrac{1}{\sqrt{|1 - x^2|}}$ is unbounded in the neighbourhood of the point $x = 1$, which is an interior point of the interval of integration. Therefore, by definition,

$$\int_0^2 \frac{dx}{\sqrt{|1 - x^2|}} = \int_0^1 \frac{dx}{\sqrt{|1 - x^2|}} + \int_1^2 \frac{dx}{\sqrt{|1 - x^2|}}.$$

Evaluate each summand separately. If $0 \le x < 1$, then

$$\int_0^1 \frac{dx}{\sqrt{|1 - x^2|}} = \int_0^1 \frac{dx}{\sqrt{1 - x^2}} = \lim_{\varepsilon \to +0} \int_0^{1-\varepsilon} \frac{dx}{\sqrt{1 - x^2}}$$

$$= \lim_{\varepsilon \to +0} \arcsin x\Big|_0^{1-\varepsilon} = \lim_{\varepsilon \to +0} [\arcsin(1 - \varepsilon) - 0] = \frac{\pi}{2}.$$

If $1 < x \le 2$, then

$$\int_1^2 \frac{dx}{\sqrt{|1 - x^2|}} = \int_1^2 \frac{dx}{\sqrt{x^2 - 1}} = \lim_{\varepsilon \to +0} \int_{1+\varepsilon}^2 \frac{dx}{\sqrt{x^2 - 1}}$$

$$= \lim_{\varepsilon \to +0} \ln(x + \sqrt{x^2 - 1})\Big|_{1+\varepsilon}^{2}$$

$$= \lim_{\varepsilon \to +0} [\ln(2 + \sqrt{3}) - \ln(1 + \varepsilon + \sqrt{(1+\varepsilon)^2 - 1})]$$

$$= \ln(2 + \sqrt{3}).$$

Hence,

$$\int_0^2 \frac{dx}{\sqrt{|1 - x^2|}} = \frac{\pi}{2} + \ln(2 + \sqrt{3}).$$

(e) Represent the given integral as a sum of three items, dividing each term of the numerator by $\sqrt[5]{x^3}$,

$$\int_0^1 \frac{x^3 + \sqrt[3]{x} - 2}{\sqrt[5]{x^3}}\,dx = \int_0^1 x^{12/5}\,dx + \int_0^1 \frac{dx}{x^{4/15}} - 2\int_0^1 \frac{dx}{x^{3/5}}.$$

The first summand is a proper integral evaluated by the Newton-Leibnitz formula :

$$\int_0^1 x^{12/5} dx = \frac{5}{17}\,x^{17/5}\Big|_0^1 = \frac{5}{17}.$$

The second and third summands are unbounded to the right of the point $x = 0$. Therefore,

$$\int_0^1 \frac{dx}{x^{4/15}} = \lim_{\varepsilon\to+0} \int_\varepsilon^1 \frac{dx}{x^{4/15}} = \lim_{\varepsilon\to+0} \frac{15}{11}\,x^{11/15}\Big|_\varepsilon^1 = \frac{15}{11};$$

analogously,

$$\int_0^1 \frac{dx}{x^{3/5}} = \lim_{\varepsilon\to+0} \int_\varepsilon^1 \frac{dx}{x^{3/5}} = \lim_{\varepsilon\to+0} \frac{5}{2}\,x^{2/5}\Big|_\varepsilon^1 = \frac{5}{2}.$$

Hence,

$$\int_0^1 \frac{x^3 + \sqrt[3]{x} - 2}{\sqrt[5]{x^3}}\,dx = \frac{5}{17} + \frac{15}{11} - 2\cdot\frac{5}{2} = -\frac{625}{187}.$$

(f) Represent the integrand $f(x) = \dfrac{1}{1 - x^3}$ in the form of a sum of partial fractions :

$$f(x) = \frac{1}{1 - x^3} = \frac{1}{(1 - x)(1 + x + x^2)} = \frac{1}{3}\left[\frac{1}{1 - x} + \frac{x + 2}{1 + x + x^2}\right].$$

Then $\displaystyle\int_0^1 \frac{dx}{1 - x^3} = \frac{1}{3}\int_0^1 \frac{dx}{1 - x} + \frac{1}{3}\int_0^1 \frac{x + 2}{1 + x + x^2}\,dx$. Since

$$\int_0^1 \frac{dx}{1 - x} = \lim_{\varepsilon\to+0} \int_0^{1-\varepsilon} \frac{dx}{1 - x} = -\lim_{\varepsilon\to+0} \ln(1 - x)\Big|_0^{1-\varepsilon} = \infty,$$

the given integral diverges. There is no need to compute the second summand representing a proper integral.

Note. Evaluation of the improper integrals from Problem **8.2.1.** (a to f) can be considerably simplified by using a generalized antiderivative and applying the Newton-Leibniz formula. For instance, in Problem **8.2.1.** (a) the function $F(x) = \frac{3}{2}\sqrt[3]{\ln^2 x}$ is continuous on the interval $[1, e]$ and differentiable at each point of the interval $1, x \le e$, and $F'(x) = f(x)$ on this interval. Therefore

$$\int_1^e \frac{dx}{x\sqrt[3]{\ln x}} = \frac{3}{2}\sqrt[3]{\ln^2 x}\,\Big|_1^e = \frac{3}{2}.$$

8.2.2. Proceeding from the definition, compute the following improper integrals (or prove their divergence) :

(a) $\int_0^{3a} \frac{2x\,dx}{(x^2 - a^2)^{2/3}}$; (b) $\int_0^{2/\pi} \sin\frac{1}{x} \cdot \frac{dx}{x^2}$;

(c) $\int_0^1 \cos\frac{\pi}{1-x} \cdot \frac{dx}{(1-x)^2}$; (d) $\int_2^6 \frac{dx}{\sqrt[3]{(4-x)^2}}$;

(e) $\int_{-1}^{-2} \frac{dx}{x\sqrt{x^2 - 1}}$; (f) $\int_1^2 \frac{dx}{x \ln^p x}$.

8.2.3. Evaluate the following improper integrals :

(a) $\int_{-3}^{3} \frac{x^2\,dx}{\sqrt{9 - x^2}}$; (b) $\int_0^2 \sqrt{\frac{2+x}{2-x}}\,dx$.

Solution (a) Find the indefinite integral

$$\int \frac{x^2 dx}{\sqrt{9 - x^2}} = \frac{1}{2}\left(9 \text{ arc sin}\frac{x}{3} - x\sqrt{9 - x^2}\right) + C.$$

The function $F(x) = \frac{1}{2}\left(9 \text{ arc sin}\frac{x}{3} - x\sqrt{9 - x^2}\right)$ is a generalized antiderivative for $f(x) = \frac{x^2}{\sqrt{9 - x^2}}$ on the interval $[-3, 3]$, since it is continuous on this interval and $F'(x) = f(x)$ at each point of the interval $(-3, 3)$. Therefore, applying the Newton-Leibnitz formula, we get

$$\int_{-3}^{3} \frac{x^2 dx}{\sqrt{9 - x^2}} = \frac{1}{2}\left(9 \text{ arc sin}\frac{x}{3} - x\sqrt{9 - x^2}\right)\Bigg|_{-3}^{3} = \frac{9}{2}\pi.$$

(b) Transform the integrand

$$f(x) = \sqrt{\frac{2+x}{2-x}} = \frac{2+x}{\sqrt{4 - x^2}} = \frac{2}{\sqrt{4 - x^2}} + \frac{x}{\sqrt{4 - x^2}}.$$

The indefinite integral is equal to

$$\int \sqrt{\frac{2+x}{2-x}}\,dx = 2 \text{ arc sin}\frac{x}{2} - \sqrt{4 - x^2} + C.$$

The function $F(x) = 2 \text{ arc sin}\frac{x}{2} - \sqrt{4 - x^2}$ is a generalized antiderivative for $f(x)$ on the interval $[0, 2]$, since it is continuous on this interval and $F'(x) = f(x)$ on the interval $[0, 2)$.

Therefore, applying the Newton-Leibniz formula, we get

$$\int_0^2 \sqrt{\frac{2+x}{2-x}}\,dx = \left(2 \text{ arc sin}\frac{x}{2} - \sqrt{4 - x^2}\right)\Bigg|_0^2 = \pi + 2.$$

8.2.4. Test the integral

$$\int_{-1}^{1} \frac{dx}{x\sqrt[3]{x}}$$

for convergence.

Solution At the point $x = 0$ the integrand goes to infinity. Both integrals $\int_{-1}^{0} \frac{dx}{x\sqrt[3]{x}}$ and $\int_{0}^{1} \frac{dx}{x\sqrt[3]{x}}$ diverge, since $\lambda = \frac{4}{3} > 1$. Consequently, the given integral diverges. If this were ignored, and the Newton-Leibniz formula applied to this integral, we would obtain the wrong result :

$$\int_{-1}^{1} \frac{dx}{x\sqrt[3]{x}} = \left(-\frac{3}{\sqrt[3]{x}}\right)\Big|_{-1}^{1} = -6.$$

And this is because the integrand is positive.

8.2.5. Test the following improper integrals for convergence :

(a) $\int_{0}^{1} \frac{e^x}{\sqrt{1-\cos x}}\,dx$; (b) $\int_{0}^{1} \frac{\sin x + \cos x}{\sqrt[5]{1-x^3}}\,dx$.

Solution (a) The integrand is infinitely large as $x \to +0$. Since

$$\sqrt{1-\cos x} = \sqrt{2}\sin\frac{x}{2} \sim \frac{\sqrt{2}}{2}x \text{ as } x \to +0,$$

the integrand has the order $\lambda = 1$ as compared with $\frac{1}{x}$. According to the special comparison test the given integral diverges.

(b) Rewrite the integrand in the following way :

$$f(x) = \frac{\sin x + \cos x}{\sqrt[5]{1 + x + x^2}} \cdot \frac{1}{\sqrt[5]{1-x}}.$$

This function is infinitely large as $x \to 1$, its order is equal to $\lambda = \frac{1}{5}$ as compared with $\frac{1}{1-x}$, since the first multiplier tends to 1 as $x \to 0$. Therefore, by the special comparison test, the given integral converges.

8.2.6. Test the following improper integrals for convergence :

(a) $\int_{0}^{2} \frac{\ln(1+\sqrt[5]{x^3})}{e^{\sin x} - 1}\,dx$; (b) $\int_{1}^{2} \frac{\sqrt{x^2+1}}{\sqrt[3]{16-x^4}}\,dx$;

(c) $\int_{0}^{1} \frac{\cos x\,dx}{\sqrt[4]{x} - \sin x}$.

Solution (a) The integrand $f(x) = \frac{\ln(1+\sqrt[5]{x^3})}{e^{\sin x} - 1}$ is positive in the interval (0, 2) and is not defined at $x = 0$. Let us show that $\lim_{x \to +0} f(x) = \infty$. Indeed, since

$e^{\sin x} - 1 \sim \sin x \sim x$, $\ln(1+\sqrt[5]{x^3}) \sim \sqrt[5]{x^3}$ as $x \to 0$,

we have

$$\lim_{x \to 0} \frac{\ln(1+\sqrt[5]{x^3})}{e^{\sin x} - 1} = \lim_{x \to 0} \frac{\sqrt[5]{x^3}}{x} = \lim_{x \to 0} \frac{1}{\sqrt[5]{x^2}} = \infty.$$

At the same time we have shown that $f(x) \sim \frac{1}{\sqrt[5]{x^3}}$ as $x \to 0$, *ie*, that $f(x)$ is an infinitely large quantity of order $\lambda = \frac{2}{5} < 1$ as compared with $\frac{1}{x}$. Consequently, by the special comparison test, the given integral converges.

(b) Determine the order of the infinitely large function $f(x) = \frac{\sqrt{x^2+1}}{\sqrt[3]{16-x^4}}$ in the neighbourhood of the point $x = 2$ with respect to $\frac{1}{2-x}$. To this end transform the expression for $f(x)$:

$$f(x) = \frac{\sqrt{x^2+1}}{\sqrt[3]{16-x^4}} = \frac{\sqrt{x^2+1}}{\sqrt[3]{4+x^2}\,\sqrt[3]{2+x}} \cdot \frac{1}{\sqrt[3]{2-x}}.$$

Hence it is obvious that the function $f(x)$ is an infinitely large quantity of order $\lambda = \frac{1}{3} < 1$ as $x \to 2$. According to the special comparison test the given integral converges.

(c) The integrand $f(x) = \frac{\cos x}{\sqrt[4]{x} - \sin x}$ is unbounded in the neighbourhood of the point $x = 0$. Since

$$f(x) = \frac{\cos x}{\sqrt[4]{x} - \sin x} = \frac{\cos x}{\sqrt[4]{x}\left(1 - \frac{\sin x}{\sqrt[4]{x}}\right)} \sim \frac{1}{\sqrt[4]{x}} \ (x \to +0),$$

as $x \to +0$ the function $f(x)$ is an infinitely large quantity of order $\lambda = 1/4 < 1$ as compared with $1/x$ and, by the special comparison test, the integral converges.

8.2.7. Investigate the following improper integrals for convergence :

(a) $\int_0^1 \frac{e^x dx}{\sqrt{1-x^3}}$; (b) $\int_0^1 \frac{x^2 dx}{\sqrt[3]{(1-x^2)^5}}$;

(c) $\int_0^1 \sqrt{\frac{x}{1-x^4}}\, dx$; (d) $\int_0^1 \frac{dx}{1-x^3+x^5}$;

(e) $\int_0^1 \frac{dx}{x-\sin x}$; (f) $\int_0^2 \frac{\ln(\sqrt[4]{x}+1)}{e^{\tan x}-1}\, dx$.

8.2.8. Prove that the integral

$$\int_0^1 \frac{\sin 1/x}{\sqrt{x}}\, dx$$

converges.

Solution For $0 < x \le 1$

$$0 \le \left| \frac{\sin \frac{1}{x}}{\sqrt{x}} \right| \le \frac{1}{\sqrt{x}}.$$

But the integral $\int_0^1 \frac{dx}{\sqrt{x}}$ converges, therefore, by the comparison test, the integral $\int_0^1 \left|\frac{\sin(1/x)}{\sqrt{x}}\right| dx$ also converges, and consequently the given integral converges absolutely.

8.2.9. Prove the convergence of the integral

$$I = \int_0^{\pi/2} \ln \sin x \, dx$$

and evaluate it.

Solution Integrate by parts, putting $u = \ln(\sin x), dx = dv$:

$$\int_0^{\pi/2} \ln \sin x \, dx = x \ln \sin x \Big|_0^{\frac{\pi}{2}} - \int_0^{\pi/2} x \frac{\cos x}{\sin x} dx = -\int_0^{\pi/2} \frac{x}{\tan x} dx.$$

Since $\lim\limits_{x \to +0} \frac{x}{\tan x} = 1$, $\lim\limits_{x \to \frac{\pi}{2} - 0} \frac{x}{\tan x} = 0$, the last integral is a proper one.

Consequently, the initial integral converges.

Now make the substitution $x = 2t$ in integral I. Then $dx = 2dt$; $x = 0$ at $t_1 = 0$; $x = \frac{\pi}{2}$ at $t_2 = \frac{\pi}{4}$. On substituting we get :

$$\int_0^{\pi/2} \ln \sin x \, dx = 2\int_0^{\pi/4} \ln \sin 2t \, dt = 2\int_0^{\pi/4} (\ln 2 + \ln \sin t + \ln \cos t) dt$$

$$= 2t \ln 2 \Big|_0^{\pi/4} + 2\int_0^{\pi/4} \ln \sin t \, dt + 2\int_0^{\pi/4} \ln \cos t \, dt$$

$$= \frac{\pi}{2} \ln 2 + 2\int_0^{\pi/4} \ln \sin t \, dt + 2\int_0^{\pi/4} \ln \cos t \, dt.$$

In the last integral make the substitution $t = \pi/2 - z$. Then $dt = -dz; t = 0$ at $z_1 = \pi/2; t = \pi/4$ at $z_2 = \pi/4$. Hence,

$$2\int_0^{\pi/4} \ln \cos t \, dt = -2\int_{\pi/2}^{\pi/4} \ln \cos\left(\frac{\pi}{2} - z\right) dz = 2\int_{\pi/4}^{\pi/2} \ln \sin z \, dz.$$

Thus,

$$I = \int_0^{\pi/2} \ln \sin x \, dx$$

$$= \frac{\pi}{2} \ln 2 + 2\int_0^{\pi/4} \ln \sin t \, dt + 2\int_{\pi/4}^{\pi/2} \ln \sin z \, dz$$

$$= \frac{\pi}{2} \ln 2 + 2\int_0^{\pi/4} \ln \sin t \, dt = \frac{\pi}{2} \ln 2 + 2I.$$

Whence $\quad I = \int_0^{\pi/2} \ln \sin x \, dx = -\frac{\pi}{2} \ln 2.$

8.2.10. Compute the integral

$$\int_0^1 \frac{x^n dx}{\sqrt{1 - x^2}} \text{ (}n\text{ a natural number).}$$

Solution The integrand is an infinitely large quantity of order $\lambda = \frac{1}{2}$ with respect to $\frac{1}{1-x}$ as $x \to 1-0$. Therefore, the integral converges.

Make the substitution $x = \sin t$ in the integral. Then $dx = \cos t\, dt$, $x = 0$ at $t = 0$, $x = 1$ at $t = \pi/2$. On substituting we get

$$\int_0^1 \frac{x^n dx}{\sqrt{1-x^2}} = \int_0^{\pi/2} \frac{\sin^n t \cdot \cos t\, dt}{\cos t} = \int_0^{\pi/2} \sin^n t\, dt.$$

The last integral is evaluated in Problem 6.6.9. :

$$\int_0^{\pi/2} \sin^n t\, dt = \begin{cases} \frac{n-1}{n} \cdot \frac{n-3}{n-2} \ldots \frac{1}{2}\frac{\pi}{2}, & n \text{ even}, \\ \frac{n-1}{n} \cdot \frac{n-3}{n-2} \ldots \frac{2}{3} \cdot & n \text{ odd}. \end{cases}$$

Consequently, the given integral is also computed by the same formula.

8.2.11. Evaluate the following improper integrals (or prove their divergence) :

(a) $\int_0^{1/2} \frac{dx}{x \ln x}$; (b) $\int_1^2 \frac{dx}{x\sqrt{\ln x}}$; (c) $\int_0^1 \frac{3x^2+2}{\sqrt[3]{x^2}} dx.$

8.2.12. Compute the improper integral

$$I_n = \int_0^1 x^m \ln^n x\, dx \; (n \text{ natural}, \; m > -1).$$

Solution At $n = 0$ the integral is evaluated directly :

$$I_0 = \int_0^1 x^m dx = \frac{x^{m+1}}{m+1}\bigg|_0^1 = \frac{1}{m+1}.$$

For $n > 0$ integrate I_n by parts, putting

$$u = \ln^n x; \qquad dv = x^m dx;$$

$$du = n \ln^{n-1} x \frac{dx}{x}; \quad v = \frac{x^{m+1}}{m+1}.$$

We get

$$I_n = \frac{x^{m+1}}{m+1} \ln^n x \bigg|_0^1 - \frac{n}{m+1} \int_0^1 x^m \ln^{n-1} x\, dx = -\frac{n}{m+1} I_{n-1}.$$

This gives a formula by means of which one can reduce I_n to I_0 for any natural n :

$$I_n = -\frac{n}{m+1} I_{n-1} = +\frac{n(n-1)}{(m+1)^2} I_{n-2} = \ldots = \frac{(-1)^n n!}{(m+1)^n} I_0$$

And finally,

$$I_n = \frac{(-1)^n n!}{(m+1)^{n+1}}.$$

8.2.13. Compute the integral

$$I = \int_{0.3}^{2.0} \frac{e^{-x}dx}{\sqrt[4]{2 + x - x^2}}$$

accurate to 0.03.

Solution The integral has a singularity at the point $x = 2$, since $2 + x - x^2 = (2 - x)(1 + x)$. Let us represent it as the sum of two integrals :

$$I_1 = \int_{0.3}^{2-\varepsilon} \frac{e^{-x}dx}{\sqrt[4]{2 + x - x^2}}, I_2 = \int_{2-\varepsilon}^{2} \frac{e^{-x}\,dx}{\sqrt[4]{2 + x - x^2}}.$$

Now compute the first integral to the required accuracy, and estimate the second one. For $\varepsilon \le 0.1$ we have

$$0 < I_2 < \frac{e^{-1.9}}{\sqrt[4]{2.9}} \int_{2-\varepsilon}^{2} \frac{dx}{\sqrt[4]{2 - x}} = 0.115 \times \frac{4}{3}\varepsilon^{\frac{3}{4}} = 0.153\,\varepsilon^{\frac{3}{4}}.$$

Putting $\varepsilon = 0.1$ we get the estimate $I_2 < 0.028$. Evaluation of the integral

$$I_1 = \int_{0.3}^{1.9} \frac{e^{-x}dx}{\sqrt[4]{2 + x - x^2}}$$

by Simpson's formula with a step $h = 0.8$ gives

$$S_{0.8} = 0.519,$$

and with a step $h/2 = 0.4$,

$$S_{0.4} = 0.513.$$

And so, integral I_1 gives the more accurate value, 0.513, with an error not exceeding 0.001. Taking into consideration that integral I_2 is positive, we round off the obtained value to

$$I \approx 0.52$$

with an error not exceeding 0.03.

Note. By putting $\varepsilon = 0.01$, we get the estimate $I_2 < 0.005$, but the computation of the integral

$$I_1 = \int_{0.3}^{1.99} \frac{e^{-x}\,dx}{\sqrt[4]{2 + x - x^2}}$$

would involve much more cumbersome calculations.

8.2.14. Investigate the following integrals for convergence :

(a) $\int_0^1 \frac{dx}{\sqrt{\sin x}}$;

(b) $\int_0^1 \frac{dx}{e^x - \cos x}$;

(c) $\int_0^1 \frac{\cos^2 x\,dx}{(1 - x)^2}$;

(d) $\int_0^1 \frac{\tan x\,dx}{\sqrt{1 - x^2}}$;

(e) $\int_{1/2}^{6/5} \frac{\sin x\,dx}{\sqrt{|1 - x^2|}}$.

8.3. Geometric and Physical Applications of Improper Integrals

8.3.1. Find the area of the figure bounded by the curve $y=\frac{1}{1+x^2}$ (the witch of Agnesi) and its asymptote.

Solution The function $y=\frac{1}{1+x^2}$ is continuous throughout the entire number scale, and $\lim\limits_{x\to\infty} y=0$. Consequently, the x-axis is the asymptote of the given curve which is shown in Fig. 118. It is required to find the area S of the figure that extends without bound along the x-axis. In other words, it is required to evaluate the improper integral $S=\int_{-\infty}^{\infty}\frac{dx}{1+x^2}$. By virtue of the symmetry of the figure about the y-axis we have

$$S=\int_{-\infty}^{\infty}\frac{dx}{1+x^2}=2\int_0^{\infty}\frac{dx}{1+x^2}=2\lim_{A\to\infty}\arctan x\Big|_0^A=2\cdot\frac{\pi}{2}=\pi.$$

8.3.2. Find the surface area generated by revolving about the x-axis the arc of the curve $y=e^{-x}$ between $x=0$ and $x=+\infty$.

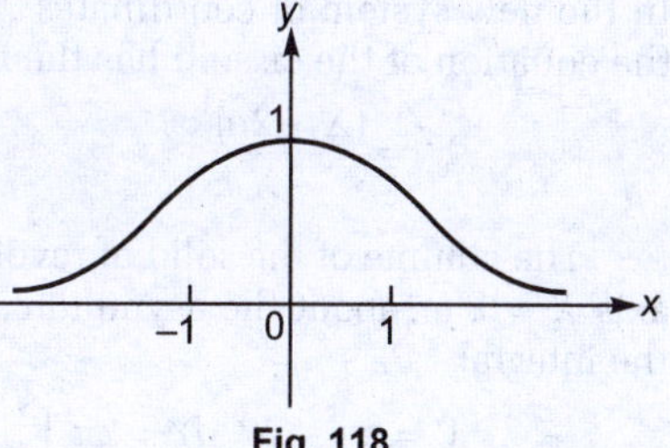

Fig. 118

Solution The area of the surfaces is equal to the improper integral

$$S=2\pi\int_0^{+\infty}e^{-x}\sqrt{1+e^{-2x}}\,dx.$$

Making the substitution $e^{-x}=t, dt=-e^{-x}dx$, we get $x=0$ at $t=1$, $x=\infty$ at $t=0$; hence

$$S=2\pi\int_0^1\sqrt{1+t^2}dt=2\pi\cdot\frac{1}{2}[t\sqrt{1+t^2}+\ln(t+\sqrt{1+t^2})]_0^1$$
$$=\pi[(\sqrt{2}+\ln(1+\sqrt{2})].$$

8.3.3. Compute the area enclosed by the loop of the folium of Descartes

$$x^3+y^3-3axy=0.$$

Solution The folium of Descartes is shown in Fig. 86. Let us represent the curve in polar coordinates :

$$x=\rho\cos\varphi; \qquad y=\rho\sin\varphi.$$

Then $\rho^3\cos^3\varphi+\rho^3\sin^3\varphi-3a\rho^2\cos\varphi\sin\varphi=0$, whence, cancelling ρ^2, we get

$$\rho=\frac{3a\cos\varphi\sin\varphi}{\cos^3\varphi+\sin^3\varphi}.$$

Since the loop of the curve corresponds to the variation of φ between 0. and $\frac{\pi}{2}$ the sought-for area is equal to

$$S = \frac{1}{2}\int_0^{\pi/2} \rho^2 d\varphi = \frac{9a^2}{2}\int_0^{\pi/2} \frac{\sin^2\varphi\cos^2\varphi}{(\sin^3\varphi + \cos^3\varphi)^2} d\varphi.$$

To evaluate the obtained proper integral make the substitution $\tan\varphi = t; \frac{d\varphi}{\cos^2\varphi} = dt; \varphi = 0$ at $t = 0, \varphi = \frac{\pi}{2}$ at $t = \infty$. Thus we get

$$S = \frac{9a^2}{2}\int_0^{\infty} \frac{t^2\, dt}{(1+t^3)^2} = \frac{9a^2}{2}\lim_{A\to\infty}\int_0^A \frac{t^2 dt}{(1+t^3)^2}$$

$$= -\frac{3a^2}{2}\lim_{A\to\infty}\left[\frac{1}{1+t^3}\right]_0^4 = \frac{3}{2}a^2$$

8.3.4. Find the volume of the solid generated b revolving the cis soid $y^2 = \frac{x^3}{2a - x}$ about its asymptote $x = 2a$.

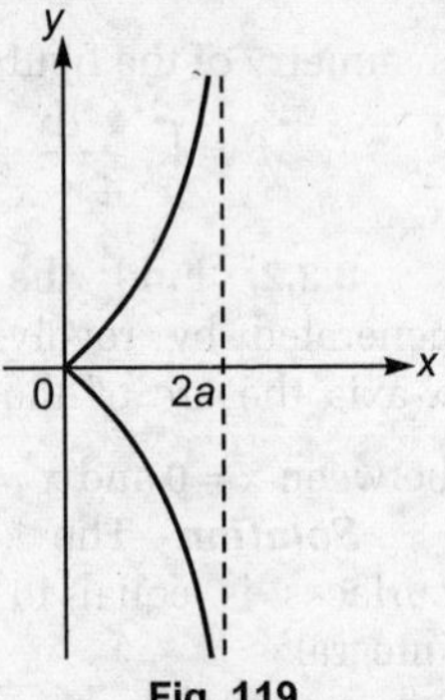

Fig. 119

Solution The cissoid is shown in the Fig. 119. Transfer the origin of coordinates to the point $O'(2a, 0)$ without changing the direction of the axes. In the new system of coordinates $X = x - 2a, Y = y$ the equation of the cissoid has the following form ;

$$Y^2 = \frac{(X - 2a)^3}{-X}.$$

The volume of the solid of revolution about the axis $X = 0$, *ie*, about the asymptote, is expressed by the integral

$$V = \pi\int_{-\infty}^{\infty} X^2\, dY = 2\pi\int_0^{\infty} X^2\, dY.$$

Let us pass over to the variable X. For this purpose we find $dY = Y'\, dX$. Differentiating the equation of the cissoid in the new coordinates as an identity with respect to X, we get

$$2YY' = -\frac{3(X+2a)^2 X - (X+2a)^3}{X^2} = -\frac{2(X+2a)^2(X-a)}{X^2}$$

whence for $Y > 0$ we have

$$Y' = -\frac{(X+2a)^2(X-a)}{X^2 Y} = -\frac{(X+2a)(X-a)}{X^2\sqrt{-(X+2a)/X}}.$$

Hence, $$V = -2\pi\int_{-2a}^{0} \frac{(X+2a)(X-a)}{\sqrt{-(X+2a)/X}} dX.$$

Make the substitution $(X + 2a)/X = -t^2$; $X = -2a$ at $t = 0$, $X = 0$ at ; $t = \infty$. Then :

$$X = -\frac{2a}{1+t^2}; dX = \frac{4at}{(1+t^2)^2}dt; X + 2a = \frac{2at^2}{1+t^2};$$

$$X - a = -\frac{3a + at^2}{1+t^2};$$

whence, $V = 2\pi \int_0^{\infty} \frac{2at^2\,(3a + at^2)\,4at\,dt}{t(1+t^2)(1+t^2)(l+t^2)^2}$

$$= 48\pi a^3 \int_0^{\infty} \frac{t^2}{(1+t^2)^4}\,dt + 16\pi a^3 \int_0^{\infty} \frac{t^4}{(1+t^2)^4}\,dt.$$

Putting $t = \tan z$, $dt = \sec^2 z\,dz$, we get $t = 0$ at $z = 0$, $t = \infty$ at $z = \frac{\pi}{2}$. Hence,

$$V = 48\pi a^2 \int_0^{\pi/2} \sin^2 z \cos^4 z\,dz + 16\pi a^3 \int_0^{\pi/2} \cos^2 z \sin^4 z\,dz$$

$$= 48\,\pi a^3 \int_0^{\pi/2} \cos^4 z\,dz - 48\pi a^3 \int_0^{\pi/2} \cos^6 z\,dz$$

$$+ 16\pi a^3 \int_0^{\pi/2} \sin^4 z\,dz - 16\pi a^3 \int_0^{\pi/2} \sin^6 z\,dz.$$

Using the known formulas for the integrals $\int_0^{\pi/2} \sin^n x\,dx, \int_0^{\pi/2} \cos^n x\,dx$ (see Problem **6.6.9**), we get

$$= 64\pi a^3\,\frac{\pi}{2}\cdot\frac{1\times 3}{2\times 4} - 64\pi a^3\,\frac{\pi}{2}\cdot\frac{1\times 3\times 5}{2\times 4\times 6} = 2\pi^2 a^3.$$

8.3.5. Prove that the area of the region bounded by the curve $y = \frac{1}{\sqrt{1-x^2}}$, the axis of abscissas, the axis of ordinates and the asymptote $x = 1$ is finite and equals $\frac{\pi}{2}$.

8.3.6. Prove that the area of the region bounded by the curve $y = \frac{1}{\sqrt[3]{x^2}}$, the axis of abscissas and the straight lines $x = \pm 1$ is finite and equals 6, and the area of the region contained between the curve $y = \frac{1}{x^2}$, the axis of abscissas and the straight lines $x = \pm 1$ is infinite.

8.3.7. Find the volumes of the solids enclosed by the surfaces generated by revolving the lines $y = e^{-x}$, $x = 0$, $y = 0$ $(0 \le x < +\infty)$;

(a) about the x-axis, (b) about the y-axis.

8.3.8. Compute the area contained between the cissoid $y^2 = \frac{x^3}{2a - x}$ and its asymptote.

8.3.9. Compute the area bounded by the curve $y = e^{-2x}$ (at $x > 0$) and the axes of coordinates.

8.3.10. Find the volume of the solid generated by revolving, about the x-axis, the infinite branch of the curve $y = 2\left(\frac{1}{x} - \frac{1}{x^2}\right)$ for $x \ge 1$.

8.3.11. Let a mass m be located at the origin O and attract a material point M found on the x-axis at a distance x from O and having a mass of 1, with a force $F = \frac{m}{x^2}$ (according to Newton's law). Find the work performed by the force F as the point M moves along the x-axis from $x = r$ to infinity.

Solution The work will be negative, since, the direction of the force is opposite to the direction of motion, hence,

$$A = \int_r^{\infty} -\frac{m}{x^2}\,dx = \lim_{N\to\infty}\int_t^{N} -\frac{m}{x^2}\,dx = -\frac{m}{r}.$$

During the reverse displacement of the point M from infinity to the point $x = r$ the force of Newtonian attraction will perform positive work $\frac{m}{r}$. This quantity is called the *potential* of the force under consideration at the point $x = r$ and serves as the measure of potential energy accumulated at a point.

8.3.12. In studying a decaying current resulting from a discharge "'ballistic" instruments are sometimes used whose readings are proportional to the "integral current intensity" $g = \int_0^{\infty} I\,dt$ of the "integral square of current intensity" $S = \int_0^{\infty} I^2 dt$ and not to the instantaneous value of the current intensity I or to its square I^2. Here t is time measured from the beginning of the discharge; I is alternating-current intesity depending on time. Theoretically, the process continues indefinitely, though, practically, the current intensity becomes imperceptible already after a finite time interval. To simplify the formulae we usually assume the time interval to be infinite in all calculations involved.

Compute g and S for the following processes :

(a) $I = I_0\, e^{-kt}$ (a simple a periodic process); k is a constant coefficient, which is greater than zero.

(b) $I = I_0 e^{-kt} \sin \omega t$ (simple oscillating process); coefficients k and ω are constants.

Solution (a) $g = \int_0^{\infty} I_0 e^{-kt}\,dt = \lim_{A\to\infty}\int_0^{A} I_0 e^{-kt}\,dt = I_0 \lim_{A\to 0}\left[\frac{-e^{-kt}}{k}\right]_0^A = \frac{I_0}{K};$

$$S = \int_0^{\infty} I_0^2\, e^{-2kt} dt = \frac{I_0^2}{2k};$$

(b) $g = \int_0^{\infty} I_0 e^{-kt} \sin \omega t\, dt = \lim_{A\to\infty}\int_0^{A} I_0\, e^{-kt} \sin \omega t\, dt$

$$= \frac{I_0}{\omega^2 + k^2} \lim_{A\to 0} [(\omega \cos \omega t + k \sin \omega t) e^{-kt}]_0^A = \frac{I_0 \omega}{\omega^2 + k^2};$$

$$S = \int_0^{\infty} I_a^2\, e^{-2kt} \sin^2 \omega t\, dt = \lim_{A\to\infty}\int_0^{A} I_0^2 e^{-2kt}\, \frac{1 - \cos 2\,\omega t}{2}\, dt$$

$$= -\frac{I_0^2}{4k} \lim_{A\to\infty}\left[1 - \frac{1}{\omega^2 + k^2}(k^2 \cos 2\omega t + \omega k \sin 2\omega t)\right] e^{-2kt}\Bigg|_0^A$$

$$= \frac{I_0^2\, \omega^2}{4k\,(k^2 + \omega^2)}.$$

8.3.13. Let an infinitely extended (in both directions) beam lying on an elastic foundation be bent by a concentrated force P, If the x-axis is brought to coincidence with the initial position of the axis of the beam (before the latter is bent) and the y-axis is drawn through the point O (at which the force is applied) and directed downwards, then, on bending, the beam axis will have the following equation

$$y = \frac{P\alpha}{2k} e^{-\alpha|x|} (\cos \alpha x + \sin \alpha | x |),$$

where α and k are certain constants. Compute the potential energy of elastic deformation by the formula

$$W = Ee \int_0^\infty (y'')^2 \, dx \qquad (E, e \text{ const}).$$

Solution Find y'';

$$y'' = \frac{P\alpha^3}{k} e^{-\alpha x} [(\cos \alpha x + \sin \alpha x) - 2(-\sin \alpha x + \cos \alpha x)$$

$$+ (-\sin \alpha x - \cos \alpha x)] = \frac{P\alpha^3}{k} e^{-\alpha x} (\sin \alpha x - \cos \alpha x).$$

Hence,

$$W = \frac{P^2\alpha^6 Ee}{k^2} \int_0^\infty e^{-2\alpha x} (1 - 2 \sin \alpha x \cos \alpha x) \, dx$$

$$= \frac{P^2\alpha^6 Ee}{k^2} \left[\frac{1}{2\alpha} - \frac{2\alpha}{4\alpha^2 + 4\alpha^2} \right] = \frac{P^2\alpha^5 Ee}{4k^2}.$$

8.3.14. What work has to be performed to move a body of mass m from the Earth's surface to infinitely ?

8.3.15. Determine the work which has to be done to bring an electric charge $e_2 = 1$ from infinity to a unit distance from a charge e_1.

8.4. Additional Problems

8.4.1. Prove that the integral

$$\int_1^\infty \frac{dx}{x^p \ln^q x}$$

converges for $p > 1$ and $q < 1$.

8.4.2. Prove that the integral

$$\int_0^\infty x^p \sin x^q \, dx, \; q \neq 0$$

converges absolutely for $-1 < (p + 1)/q < 0$ and converges conditionally for $0 \leq (p + 1)/q < 1$.

8.4.3. Prove that the Euler integral of the first kind (beta function)

$$B(p, q) = \int_0^1 x^{p-1} (1 - x)^{q-1} dx$$

converges for $p > 0$ and $q > 0$.

8.4.4. Prove that

$$\lim_{T \to \infty} \frac{1}{T} \int_0^T \sin \alpha x \cdot \sin \beta x \, dx = 0,$$

if $|\alpha| \neq |\beta|$.

8.4.5. Prove that

$$I = \int_0^{\infty} e^{-x^2} \cdot x^{2n+1}\, dx = \frac{n!}{2} \text{ (} n \text{ natural).}$$

8.4.6. Prove that if the integral $\int_a^{\infty} \frac{f(x)}{x}\, dx$ converges for any positive a and if $f(x)$ tends to A as $x \to 0$, then the integral

$$\int_0^{\infty} \frac{f(\alpha x) - f(\beta x)}{x}\, dx \ (\alpha > 0, \beta > 0)$$

converges and equals $A \ln\left(\frac{\beta}{\alpha}\right)$.

8.4.7. Prove that

$$\int_0^{\infty} \frac{e^{-\alpha x} - e^{-\beta x}}{x}\, dx = \int_0^{\infty} \frac{\cos \alpha x - \cos \beta x}{x}\, dx = \ln \frac{\beta}{\alpha}.$$

8.4.8. At what values of m does the integral $\int_0^{2} \frac{1 - \cos x}{x^m}\, dx$ converge ?

8.4.9. Prove that the integral $\int_0^{\pi} \frac{dx}{(\sin x)^k}$ converges if $k < 1$, and diverges if $k \geq 1$.

8.4.10. Prove that the integral $\int_0^{\infty} \frac{\sin x\,(1 - \cos x)}{x^s}\, dx$ converges if $0 < s < 4$, and converges absolutely if $1 < s < 4$.

8.4.11. Suppose the integral

$$\int_a^{+\infty} f(x)\, dx \quad \text{...(1)}$$

converges and the function $\varphi(x)$ is bounded.

Does the integral

$$\int_a^{+\infty} f(x)\, \varphi(x)\, dx \quad \text{...(2)}$$

necessarily converge ?

What can be said about the convergence of integral (2), if integral (1) converges absolutely ?

8.4.12. Prove the validity of the relation

$$f(x) = 2f\left(\frac{\pi}{4} + \frac{x}{2}\right) - 2f\left(\frac{\pi}{4} - \frac{x}{2}\right) - x \ln 2,$$

where $f(x) = -\int_0^{x} \ln \cos y\, dy$.

Compute the aid of the relation obtained

$$f\left(\frac{\pi}{2}\right) = -\int_0^{\pi/2} \ln \cos y\, dy.$$

8.4.13. Deduce the reduction formula for the integral

$$I_n = \int_0^{\pi/2} \ln \cos x \cdot \cos 2n\, x\, dx \ (n \text{ natural})$$

and evaluate this integral.

Answers and Hints

Chapter 1

1.1.5. (b) ***Hint.*** Prove by the rule of contraries, putting $2 = \frac{p^2}{q^2}$, where p and q are positive integers without common multipliers.

1.1.8. ***Hint.*** You may take $k = \frac{s^2 - 2}{2s}$.

1.1.9. (b) $x \geq 4, x \leq 0$; (c) $-4 \leq x \leq 2$.

1.1.11. (a) $x < -1$ or $x \geq 1$. ***Hint.*** The equality is valid for those values of x for which $\frac{x-1}{x+1} \geq 0$; (b) $2 \leq x \leq 3$. ***Hint.*** The equality holds true for those values of x for which $x^2 - 5x + 6 \leq 0$.

1.1.13. (a) $x < \frac{2}{5}$ or $x > 8$; (b) $x < 0$ or $0 < x < 5$. ***Hint.*** The inequality $|a - b| > |a| - |b|$ holds good when a and b are opposite in sign or when $|a| < |b|$.

1.2.3. $0; \frac{a+2}{[a(a^2 + 3a + 3)]}; (a^3 + a)(a^3 - 1)$.

1.2.4. $b^2 + ab + a^2; \frac{(a+b)^3}{8} - 1$. **1.2.6.** $4\sqrt{2} + 1; \frac{\sqrt{2}+1}{2}; 2\sqrt{10} - 5$.

1.2.11. $f(x) = 10 + 5 \times 2^x$.

1.2.13. $f(3x) = \frac{45x^2 + 1}{2 - 3x}; f(x^3) = \frac{5x^6 + 1}{2 - x^3}; 3f(x) = \frac{15x^2 + 3}{2 - x}$;

$[f(x)]^3 = \frac{125x^6 + 75x^4 + 15x^2 + 1}{8 - 12x + 6x^2 - x^3}$.

1.2.14. $f(2) = 5; f(0) = 4; f(0.5) = 4; f(-0.5) = \frac{\sqrt{3}}{3}; f(3) = 8$.

1.2.15. ***Hint.*** From $x_{n+1} = x_n + d$ it follows that $y_{n+1} = a^{x_n + 1} = a^{x_n + d} = a^{x_n} a^d$.

1.2.16. $x = \pm 2; \pm 3$. **1.2.17.** $f(x) = x^2 - 5x + 6$.

1.2.18. $f(x) = 23; \varphi(x) = 527$.

1.2.19. $x \leq -1$ or $x \geq 2$.

1.2.20. $P = 2b + 2\left(1 - \frac{b}{h}\right)x; S = b\left(1 - \frac{x}{h}\right)x$.

1.2.21. (b) (2, 3); (c) $(-\infty, -1)$ and ((2, ∞); (d) $x = \frac{\pi}{2} + 2k\pi$ $(k = 0, \pm 1, \pm 2, \ldots)$.

Hint. Since $\sin x \le 1$, the function is defined only when $\sin x = 1$; (g) $(-\infty, 2)$ and $(3, \infty)$; (h) [1, 4); (i) $(-2, 0)$ and (0, 1); (j) $-\frac{\pi}{2} + 2k\pi < x < \frac{\pi}{2} + 2k\pi$ $(k = 0, \pm 1, \pm 2, \ldots)$.

1.2.22. (d) The function is defined over the entire number scale, except the points $x = \pm 2$.

1.2.24. (a) $(-\infty, \infty)$; (b) $(3 - 2\pi, 3 - \pi)$ and (3, 4); (c) $[-1, 3]$; (d) $(-1, 0)$ and $(0, \infty)$.

1.2.25. (b) $5 \le x \le 6$.

1.2.26. (a) $2k\pi \le x \le (2k + 1)\pi$ $(k = 0, \pm 1, \pm 2, \ldots)$; (b) $\left[-\frac{3}{2}, -1\right]$.

1.3.3. (b) ***Hint.*** Consider the difference $\frac{x_2}{1 + x_2^2} - \frac{x_1}{1 + x_1^2}$.

1.3.4. (b) It increases for $-\frac{5\pi}{6} + k\pi < x < \frac{\pi}{6} + k\pi$ $(k = 0, \pm 1, \pm 2, \ldots)$ and decreases on the other intervals.

1.3.7. The function decreases on the interval $0 < x \le \frac{\pi}{4}$ from $+\infty$ to 2 and increases on the interval $\frac{\pi}{4} \le x < \frac{\pi}{2}$ from 2 to $+\infty$.

1.3.9. (c) The function is neither even, nor odd, (d) even.

1.3.10. (a) Even; (b) odd; (c) odd; (d) neither even, nor odd; (e) even.

1.3.12. (a) $|A| = 5, \omega = 4, \varphi = 0, T = \frac{\pi}{2}$; (b) $|A| = 4, \omega = 3, \varphi = \frac{\pi}{4}, T = \frac{2\pi}{3}$; (c) $|A| = 5, \omega = \frac{1}{2}, \varphi = \arctan\frac{4}{3}$, $T = 4\pi$.

Hint. $3\sin\frac{x}{2} + 4\cos\frac{x}{2} = 5\sin\left(\frac{x}{2} + \varphi\right)$, where $\cos\varphi = \frac{3}{5}, \sin\varphi = \frac{4}{5}$.

1.3.13. (b) $T = 2\pi$; (c) $T = 1$.

1.3.16. The greatest value $f(1) = 2$. ***Hint.*** The function reaches the greatest value at the point where the quadratic trinomial $2x^2 - 4x + 3$ reaches the least value.

1.3.17. (a) Even; (b) even; (c) odd; (d) even.

1.3.18. (a) $T = \pi$; (b) $T = 6\pi$.

1.3.19. ***Hint.*** (a) Assume the contrary. Then

$$x + T + \sin(x + T) = x + \sin x,$$

whence $\cos\left(x + \frac{T}{2}\right) = -\frac{T}{2\sin\frac{T}{2}}$, which is impossible for any constant T, since the left side is not constant; (b) suppose the contrary. Then $\cos\sqrt{x + T} = \cos\sqrt{x}$, whence either $\sqrt{x + T} + \sqrt{x} = 2\pi k$, or $\frac{T}{\sqrt{x+T}+\sqrt{x}} = 2\pi k$ $(k = 0, \pm 1, \pm 2, \dots)$, which is impossible, since the left-hand members of these equalities are functions of a continuous argument x.

1.4.6. (a) $x = \frac{1 + \arc\sin y}{3}$; (b) $x = 3\sin y$; (c) $x = y^{\frac{1}{\log 5}} (y > 0)$;

(d) $x = \frac{\log_2 y}{\log_2 y - 1} = \frac{\log y}{\log \frac{y}{2}}$ $(0 < y < 2 \text{ or } 2 < y < \infty)$.

1.6.3. (a) $\frac{\sqrt{3}}{2}, \frac{\sqrt{3}}{2}, 0, -\frac{\sqrt{3}}{2}, \dots$; (b) $-\frac{1}{2}, \frac{1}{4}, -\frac{1}{8}, \frac{1}{16}, \dots$;

(c) $2; 2.25; 2\frac{10}{27}; 2\frac{113}{256}, \dots$.

1.6.9. ***Hint.*** The inequality $\left|\frac{2n+3}{n+1} - 2\right| < \varepsilon$ is satisfied for $n > N$ $= E\left(\frac{1}{\varepsilon} - 1\right)$. At $\varepsilon = 0.1$ the inequality is fulfilled beginning with $n = 10$, at $\varepsilon = 0.01$ beginning with $n = 100$, at $\varepsilon = 0.001$ beginning with $n = 1000$.

1.6.10. ***Hint.*** Verify that the sequence $\{x_{2n-1}\}$ tends to 1 as $n \to \infty$, and the sequence $\{x_{2n}\}$ tends to 0 as $n \to \infty$.

1.6.12. (a) It has; (b) it does not have; (c) it has; (d) it does not have.

1.6.14. ***Hint.*** (a) $|x_n| \le \frac{2}{n}$; (b) $|x_n| \le \frac{1}{n}$.

1.6.19. ***Hint.*** For $a > 1$ put $\sqrt[n]{a} = 1 + \alpha_n (\alpha_n > 0)$ and, with the aid of the inequality $a = (1 + \alpha_n)^n > n\alpha_n$, prove that α_n is an infinitesimal. For $a < 1$ put $\sqrt[n]{a} = \frac{1}{1+\alpha_n} (\alpha_n > 0)$ and make use of the inequality $\frac{1}{a} = (1 + \alpha_n)^n > n\alpha_n$.

1.7.1. (b) $\frac{5}{4}$; (c) 0; (e) $\frac{1}{2}$. **1.7.2.** (b) $\frac{1}{16}$; (e) 1; (f) 1.

1.7.4. (b) 1; (f) 0. ***Hint.*** Multiply and divide by imperfect of a sum, square and then divide by $n^{\frac{4}{3}}$; (g) $-\frac{1}{3}$; (h) 1. ***Hint.*** Represent each summand of x_n in the form of the difference

$$\frac{1}{1 \times 2} = 1 - \frac{1}{2}, \frac{1}{2 \times 3} = \frac{1}{2} - \frac{1}{3}; \dots; \frac{1}{n(n+1)} = \frac{1}{n} - \frac{1}{n+1}.$$

which will bring x_n to the form $x_n = 1 - \frac{1}{n+1}$.

1.7.5. (a) $\frac{1}{2}$; (b) 1; (c) 0; (d) $-\frac{1}{2}$. ***Hint.*** The quantity $\frac{1}{2n}$ is an infinitesimal, and $\cos n^3$ is a bounded quantity; (e) 0; (f) $\frac{4}{3}$.

1.8.6. (b) ***Hint.*** The sequence is bounded due to the fact that $n! = 1 \times 2 \times 3 \times \ldots \times n \geq 2^{n-1}$ and therefore

$$x_n \leq 2 + \frac{1}{2} + \left(\frac{1}{2}\right)^2 + \ldots + \left(\frac{1}{2}\right)^{n-1} = 3 - \left(\frac{1}{2}\right)^{n-1} < 3.$$

1.8.7. (b) 0. ***Hint.*** Take advantage of the fact that $\frac{x_{n+1}}{x_n} = \frac{2}{n+3} < 1.$

1.8.9. ***Hint.*** For all n, beginning with a certain value, the inequalities $\frac{1}{n} < a < n$ are fulfilled; therefore $\frac{1}{\sqrt[n]{n}} < \sqrt[n]{a} < \sqrt[n]{n}$, and $\lim \sqrt[n]{n} = \lim \frac{1}{\sqrt[n]{n}} = 1.$

1.8.10. ***Hint.*** The sequence $\{y_n\}$ decreases, since $y_{n+1} = a^{\frac{1}{2^n+1}}$ $= a^{\frac{1}{2^n \times 2}} = \sqrt{y_n} (y_n > 1).$

The boundedness of the sequence from below follows from $a > 1$. Denote $\lim\limits_{n\to\infty} y_n$ by b and from the relation $y_{n+1} = \sqrt{y_n}$ find $b = 1$.

1.8.11. ***Hint.*** Ascertain that the sequence increases. Establish the boundedness from the inequalities.

$$\frac{1}{n^2} < \frac{1}{n(n-1)} = \frac{1}{n-1} - \frac{1}{n} \, (n \geq 2);$$

$$x_n < 1 + \left(1 - \frac{1}{2}\right) + \left(\frac{1}{2} - \frac{1}{3}\right) + \ldots + \left(\frac{1}{n-1} - \frac{1}{n}\right) = 2 - \frac{1}{n}.$$

1.8.12. ***Hint.*** Transform x_n into the form $x_n = \frac{2n}{\sqrt{n^2+1}+n}$ and take advantage of the inequalities

$$\frac{2n}{2n+1} < \frac{2n}{\sqrt{n^2+1}+n} < 1.$$

1.8.13. ***Hint.*** See Problem 1.8.7 (a).

1.8.14. ***Hint.*** Establish the boundedness of the sequence by comparing x_n with the sum of some geometric progression.

1.9.2. (b) ***Hint.*** Choose the sequences

$$x_n = \frac{1}{n} \quad \text{and} \quad x_n = -\frac{1}{n} \; (n = 1, 2, \ldots)$$

and ascertain that the sequences of appropriate values of the function have different limits :

$$\lim 2^{\frac{1}{x_n}} = +\infty, \qquad \lim 2^{\frac{1}{x'_n}} = 0.$$

19.3. (e) ***Hint.*** Take advantage of the inequality

$$\frac{\pi}{2} - \text{arc tan } x < \tan\left(\frac{\pi}{2} - \text{arc tan } x\right) = \frac{1}{x} \, (x > 0).$$

(f) ***Hint.*** Transform the difference

$$\sin x - \frac{1}{2} = \sin x - \sin\frac{\pi}{6}$$

into a product and apply the inequality $|\sin\alpha| \le |\alpha|$.

1.10.1. (d) $\frac{p}{q}$; (e) $\frac{5}{6}$; (f) $-\frac{1}{12}$. ***Hint.*** Multiply the numerator and denominator by imperfect trinomial square $(\sqrt[3]{10-x}+2)$; (g) $\frac{34}{23}$; (h) $\log_a 6$.

Hint. $\lim\limits_{x\to 3}\left[\log_a \frac{x-3}{\sqrt{x+6}-3}\right] = \log_a\left[\lim\limits_{x\to 3}\frac{(x-3)\sqrt{x+6}+3}{x-3}\right] = \log_a 6$;

(i) $\frac{2}{3}$; (h) $\frac{7}{12}$.

1.10.2. (e) $\frac{1}{2}$. ***Hint.*** On removing the irrationality to the denominator divide the numerator and denominator by x.

1.10.3. (b) 32. (c) $\frac{5}{3}$. ***Hint.*** Put $x = z^{15}$; (f) ∞. ***Hint.*** Put $\frac{\pi}{2} - x = z; x = \frac{\pi}{2} - z$; $z \to 0$ as $x \to \frac{\pi}{2}$; (g) -3. ***Hint.*** Put $\sin x = y$.

1.10.5. (b) $e^{\frac{1}{3}}$; (c) e^{-1}; (d) e^{mk}; (f) 4; (g) $\frac{1}{a}$; (h) 2.

1.10.7. (b) $\frac{1}{4}$. **1.10.8.** (b) 1; (c) $\frac{1}{e}$; (d) $e^{\cot a}$.

1.10.11. (a) $\frac{1}{2}$; (b) $-\frac{3}{4}$; (c) $\frac{1}{2}$; (d) $\frac{2}{5}$; (e) 0; (f) -1.

1.10.12. (a) $\frac{1}{20}$; (b) -2; (c) $\frac{\pi}{2}$; (d) $\frac{1}{2}$; (e) -24.

1.10.13. (a) e^4; (b) -1; (c) $2\ln a$; (d) e^3; (e) $e^{-\frac{1}{2}}$; (f) e^{-1}; (g) 1; (h) 1; (i) 9; (j) 1; (k) $\alpha-\beta$. ***Hint.*** $\lim\limits_{x\to 0}\frac{e^{\alpha x}-e^{\beta x}}{x} = \lim\limits_{x\to 0} e^{\beta x}\frac{e^{(\alpha-\beta)x}-1}{x} = \alpha-\beta$.

1.10.14. (a) $\sqrt{2}$. ***Hint.*** Replace $\arccos(1-x)$ by $\arcsin\sqrt{2x-x^2}$; (b) 1; (c) a.

1.11.5. (b) It is of the third order of smallness.

Hint. $\lim\limits_{\alpha\to 0}\frac{\tan\alpha - \sin\alpha}{\alpha^3} = \frac{1}{2}$.

1.11.6. (b) They are of the same order; (c) they are equivalent.

1.11.8. (a) $100x$ is an infinitesimal of the same order as x; (b) x^2 is an infinitesimal of an order higher than x; (c) $6\sin x$ is an infinitesimal of the same order as x; (d) $\sin^3 x$ is an infiniltesimal of an order higher than x; (e) $\sqrt[3]{\tan^2 x}$ is an infinitesimal of an order of smallness lower than x.

1.11.9. (a) It is of the fourth order of smallness; (b) of the first order of smallness; (c) of the third order of smallness; (d) of the third order of smallness; (e) of the first order of smallness; (f) of the order of smallness $\frac{1}{2}$; (g) of the first order of smallness; (h) of the first order of smallness; (i) of the second order of smallness. ***Hint.*** Multiply and divide the difference $\cos x - \sqrt[3]{\cos x}$ by imperfect trinomial square; (j) of the first order of smallness.

1.11.10. The diagonal d is of the first order of smallness; the area S is of the second order of smallness; the volume V is of the third order of smallness.

1.12.3. (b) 4; (f) 3; (g) $\frac{1}{2}$; (i) 2. **1.12.6.** (a) 1; (b) 2.

1.12.7. (a) 1; (b) $\frac{1}{3}$. **1.12.8.** (a) $\frac{3}{5}$; (b) $\frac{4}{5}$; (c) $\frac{3}{2}$; (d) $\frac{3}{2}$; (e) $\frac{2}{9}$; (f) $\frac{3}{4}$; (g) -2; (h) 1.

1.12.9. 10.14. ***Hint.*** $1042 = 10^3 \times (1 + 0.042)$.

1.13.1. (b) $f(1-0) = -2$. $f(1+0) = 2$; (f) $f(2-0) = -\infty$; $f(2+0) = +\infty$.

1.13.3. (a) $f(-0) = \frac{1}{2}$, $f(+0) = 0$; (b) $f(-0) = 0$, $f(+0) = +\infty$; (c) $f(-0) = -1$, $f(+0) = 1$.

1.14.2. (b) The function has a discontinuity of the first kind at the point $x = 3$. The jump is equal to 27.

1.14.3. (c) The function is continuous everywhere; (e) the function has a discontinuity of the first kind at the point $x = 0$; the jump equals π.

Hint. $\operatorname{arc\,tan}(-\infty) = -\frac{\pi}{2}$, $\operatorname{arc\,tan}(+\infty) = +\frac{\pi}{2}$.

1.14.6. (b) At the point $x_0 = 5$ there is a discontinuity of the first kind: $f(5-0) = -\frac{\pi}{2}$, $f(5+0) = \frac{\pi}{2}$; (c) at the point $x_0 = 0$, a discontinuity of the first kind; $f(-0) = 1$, $f(+0) = 0$; (d) at the point $x_0 = \frac{\pi}{2}$, an infinite discontinuity of the second kind :

$$f\left(\frac{\pi}{2} - 0\right) = +\infty, f\left(\frac{\pi}{2} + 0\right) = -\infty.$$

1.14.7. (a) At the point $x = 0$ there is a removable disconinuity. To remove the discontinuity it is sufficient to redefine the function, putting $f(0) = 1$; (b) at the point $x = 0$ there is a removable discontinuity. To remove the discontinuity it is sufficient to extend the function putting $f(0) = 1$; (c) at the point $x = 0$ there is a discontinuity of the second kind: $f(-0) = 0$, $f(+0) = +\infty$; (d) at the points $x = (2k+1)\frac{\pi}{2}$ $(k = 0, \pm 1, \pm 2, \ldots)$, removable discontinuities, since

$$f(x) = \lim_{n\to\infty} (\sin x)^{2n} = \begin{cases} 0 \text{ if } |\sin x| < 1, \\ 1 \text{ if } |\sin x| = 1; \end{cases}$$

(e) at the points $x = k\pi$ $(k = 0, \pm 1, \pm 2, \ldots)$, discontinuities of the 1st kind, since

$$f(x) = \frac{|\sin x|}{\sin x} \begin{cases} 1 \text{ if } \sin x > 0, \\ -1 \text{ if } \sin x < 0; \end{cases}$$

(f) at the points $x = n = 0, \pm 1, \pm 2, \ldots$ removable discontinuities, since

$$f(x) = \begin{cases} -1 \text{ if } x = n, \\ 0 \text{ if } x \neq n. \end{cases}$$

1.14.8. (a) At the point $x = 1$ there is an infinite discontinuity of the second kind; (b) at the point $x = -2$, a discontinuity of the first kind (the jump being equal to 2); (c) at the point $x = 0$, an infinite discontinuity of the second kind, at the point $x = 1$, a discontinuity of the first kind (the jump being equal to -4); (d) at the point $x = 1$, an infinite discontinuity of the second kind.

1.14.9. (a) $f(0) = 1$; (b) $f(0) = -\frac{3}{2}$; (c) $f(0) = \frac{1}{2}$; (d) $f(0) = 2$.

1.15.2. (b) The function is continuous on the interval $(0, +\infty)$.

1.15.3. (b) The function is continuous everywhere. At the only possible point of discontinuity $x = 0$ we have

$$\lim_{x\to -0} y = \lim_{u\to 1} u^2 = 1; \lim_{x\to +0} y = \lim_{u\to -1} u^2 = 1; y|_{x=0} = y|_{u=-1} = 1;$$

(c) at the points $x = \frac{\pi}{2} + n\pi$ $(n = 0, \pm 1, \pm 2, \ldots)$ there are removable discontinuities, since $\lim\limits_{x\to\frac{\pi}{2}} y = \lim\limits_{u\to\pm\infty} y = -1$.

1.16.2. Yes. **1.16.12.** 1.53

1.16.13. No. For instance, the function $y = x^2$ on the interval $[-1, 1]$.

1.17.1. (a) ***Hint.*** Multiply the obvious inequalities:

$$\sqrt{1\cdot n} < \frac{n+1}{2};$$

$$\sqrt{2(n-1)} < \frac{n+1}{2};$$

....

$$\sqrt{(n-1)\cdot 2} < \frac{n+1}{2};$$

$$\sqrt{n\cdot 1} < \frac{n+1}{2}.$$

(b) ***Hint.*** Let $A = \frac{1}{2} \times \frac{3}{4} \times \frac{5}{6} \times \ldots \times \frac{2n-1}{2n}$, $B = \frac{2}{3} \times \frac{4}{5} \times \frac{6}{7} \times \ldots . \times \frac{2n}{2n+1}$.

Then $A < B$ since $\frac{2n-1}{2n} < \frac{2n}{2n+1}$ and $A^2 < AB = \frac{1}{2n+1}$.

1.17.2. (a) ***Hint.*** Extract the 101st root from both sides of the inequality and reduce both sides by 101^2.

(b) Multiply the obvious inequalities :

$$99 \times 101 < 100^2,$$
$$98 \times 102 < 100^2,$$
$$\ldots\ldots\ldots\ldots\ldots\ldots$$
$$2 \times 198 < 100^2,$$
$$1 \times 100 \times 199 \times 200 < 100^4.$$

1.17.3. (a) $-3 < x < -1$ or $1 < x < 3$; (b) $x < -\frac{1}{3}$ or $x > \frac{5}{3}$; (c) the inequality has no solutions, since it is equivalent to the contradictory system $x - 2 > 0$, $x(4x^2 - x + 4) < 0$. **1.17.4.** Yes. **1.17.5.** (a) No; (b) Yes.

1.17.7. ***Hint.*** Apply the method of mathematical induction. At $n = 1$ the relation is obvious. Supposing that the inequality $(1 + x_1)(1 + x_2) \ldots (1 + x_{n-1}) \geq 1 + x_1 + x_2 + \ldots + x_{n-1}$ holds true, multiply both its sides by $1 + x_n$ and take into consideration the conditions $1 + x_n > 0$, $x_i \cdot x_n > 0$ $(i = 1, 2, \ldots, n-1)$.

1.17.8. (a) $[1, +\infty)$; (b) $(2n\pi)^2 \leq x \leq (2n+1)^2 \pi^2$ $(n = 0, 1, 2, \ldots)$;

(c) $x = 0, \pm 1, \pm 2, \ldots$; (d) $(-\infty, 0)$ for $f(x)$; $g(x)$ is nowhere defined;

(e) $[-4, -2]$ or $[2, 4]$; (f) $x = (2n+1)\frac{\pi}{2}$ $(n = 0, \pm 1, \pm 2, \ldots)$.

1.17.9. (a) No : $\varphi(0) = 1$, and $f(0)$ is not defined; (b) No: $f(x)$ is defined for all x, and $\varphi(x)$ only for $x \geq 0$; (c) Yes; (d) No: $f(x)$ is defined only for $x > 2$, and $\varphi(x)$ for $x > 2$ and for $x < 1$.

1.17.10. (a) $(0, \infty)$; (b) $[1, \infty)$. **1.17.11.** $V = 8\pi(x-3)(6-x)$, $3 < x < 6$.

1.17.12. (a) $x = 5$. ***Hint.*** The domain of definition is specified by the inequalities $x + 2 \geq 0$, $x - 5 \geq 0$, $5 - x \geq 0$, which are fulfilled only at the point $x = 5$. Verify that the number $x = 5$ satisfies the given inequality.

(b) ***Hint.*** The domain of definition is specified by the contradictory inequalities $x - 3 > 0; 2 - x > 0$.

1.17.17. (a) $f(x) = \frac{2}{1+x^2} + \frac{x}{1+x^2}$; (b) $a^x = \frac{a^x + a^{-x}}{2} + \frac{a^x - a^{-x}}{2}$

(see Problem **1.17.16**).

1.17.18. An even extension defines the function

$$\varphi(x) = \begin{cases} f(x) = x^2 + x \text{ for } & 0 \leq x \leq 3, \\ f(-x) = x^2 - x \text{ for } & -3 \leq x < 0. \end{cases}$$

An odd extension defines the function

$$\psi(x)=\begin{cases} f(x)=x^2+x \text{ for } & 0\le x\le 3,\\ -f(-x)=-x^2+x \text{ for } & -3\le x<0.\end{cases}$$

1.17.21. ***Hint.*** If the function $f(x)$ has a period T_1, and the function $\varphi(x)$ has a period T_2, and $T_1 = n_1 d$, $T_2 = n_2 d$ (n_1, n_2 positive integers), then the period of the sum and the product of these functions will be $T = nd$, where n is the least common multiple of the numbers n_1 and n_2.

1.17.22. ***Hint.*** For any rational number r

$$\lambda(x+r)=\lambda(x)=\begin{cases}1 \text{ for rational } x,\\ 0 \text{ for irrational } x.\end{cases}$$

But there is no least number in the set of positive rational numbers.

1.17.23. ***Hint.*** It we denote the period of the function $f(x)$ by T, then from $f(T) = f(0) = f(-T)$ we get

$$\sin T + \cos aT = 1 = \sin(-T) + \cos(-aT),$$

whence $\sin T = 0, \cos aT = 1$, and hence $T = k\pi, aT = 2n\pi, a = \dfrac{2n}{k}$ is rational.

1.17.25. The difference of two increasing functions is not necessarily a monotonic function. For example, the functions $f(x) = x$ and $g(x) = x^2$ increase for $x \ge 0$, but their difference $f(x) - g(x) = x - x^2$ is not monotonic for $x \ge 0$; it increases on $\left[0, \frac{1}{2}\right]$ and decreases on $\left[\frac{1}{2}, \infty\right)$.

1.17.26. Example :

$$y=\begin{cases} x \text{ if } x \text{ is rational},\\ -x \text{ if } x \text{ is irrational}.\end{cases}$$

1.17.27. (a) $x = \dfrac{1}{2}\ln\dfrac{1+y}{1-y}\ (-1 < y < 1)$;

(b) $$x=\begin{cases} y & \text{for } -\infty < y < 1,\\ \sqrt{y} & \text{for } 1\le y\le 16,\\ \log_2 y & \text{for } 16 < y < \infty.\end{cases}$$

1.17.28. ***Hint.*** The functions $y = x^2 + 2x + 1\ (x \ge -1)$ and $y = -1 + \sqrt{x}$ $(x \ge 0)$ are mutually inverse, but the equation $y = x$, *ie*, $x^2 + 2x + 1 = x$ has no real roots (see. Problem **1.4.4.**).

1.17.30. (c) ***Hint.*** If E is the domain of definition of the function $f(x)$, then the function $y = f[f(x)]$ is defined only for those $x \in E$ for which $f(x) \in E$. How the points of the desired graph are plotted is shown in Fig. 120.

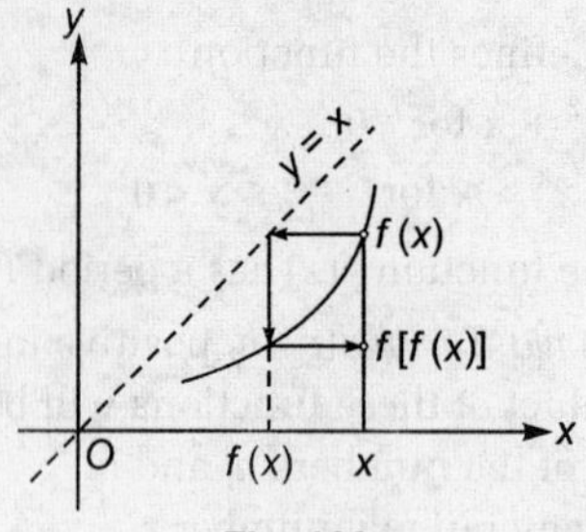

Fig. 120

1.17.32. ***Hint.*** The quantity $T = 2(b - a)$ is a period: from the conditions of symmetry $f(a + x) = f(a - x)$ and $f(b + x) = f(b - x)$ it follows that

$$f[x + 2(b - a)] = f[b + (b + x - 2a)] = f(2a - x) = f[a + (a - x)] = f(x).$$

1.17.33. (a) It diverges; (b) it may either converge or diverge. Examples:

$$x_n = \frac{1}{n}; \qquad y_n = \frac{[1 + (-1)^n]}{2}; \quad \lim_{n\to\infty}(x_n y_n) = 0,$$

$$x_n = \frac{1}{n}; \qquad y_n = n^2; \qquad \lim_{n\to\infty}(x_n y_n) = \infty.$$

1.17.34. (a) No. Example : $x_n = n$; $y_n = -n + 1$; (b) No.

1.17.35. $\alpha_n = \dfrac{\pi(n-2)}{n}$ $(n = 3, 4 \ldots)$.

1.17.36. ***Hint.*** Take into account that $||x_n| - |a|| \le |x_n - a|$. The converse is incorrect. Example: $x_n = (-1)^{n+1}$.

1.17.38. ***Hint.*** The sequence α_n may attain only the following values: $0, 1, \ldots, 9$. If this sequence turned out to be monotonic, then the irrational number would be represented by a periodic decimal fraction.

1.17.39. ***Hint.*** If the sequence $\dfrac{a_n}{b_n}$ increases, then

$$\frac{a_i}{b_i} < \frac{a_{n+1}}{a_{n+1}}, \ ie, \ b_{n+1}a_i < a_{n+1}b_i \ (i = 1, 2, \ldots, n),$$

whence it follows that

$$b_{n+1}(a_1 + a_2 + \ldots + a_n) < a_{n+1}(b_1 + b_2 + \ldots + b_n),$$

and hence

$$\frac{a_1 + a_2 + \ldots + a_{n+1}}{b_1 + b_2 + \ldots + b_{n+1}} - \frac{a_1 + a_2 + \ldots + a_n}{b_1 + b_2 + \ldots + b_n}$$

$$= \frac{a_{n+1}(b_1 + b_2 + \ldots + b_n) - b_{n+1}(a_1 + a_2 + \ldots + a_n)}{(b_1 + b_2 + \ldots + b_{n+1})(b_1 + b_2 + \ldots + b_n)} > 0.$$

1.17.40. (a) 2; (b) 0; (c) 0.

1.17.41. ***Hint.*** From the inequalities $nx - 1 < E(nx) \le nx$ it follows that $x - 1 < x - \frac{1}{n} < \frac{E(nx)}{n} \le x.$

1.17.42. ***Hint.*** From the inequalities

$$\sum_{k=1}^{n} (kx - 1) \le \sum_{k=1}^{n} E(kx) \le \sum_{k=1}^{n} kx,$$

it follows that

$$x\frac{n+1}{2n} - \frac{1}{n} \le \frac{1}{n^2}\sum_{k=1}^{n} E(kx) \le x\frac{n+1}{2n}.$$

1.17.43. ***Hint.*** Take advantage of the fact that $\lim_{n\to\infty} a^{\frac{1}{n}} = \lim_{n\to\infty} \sqrt[n]{a} = 1$ (see Problem **1.6.19**), $\lim_{n\to\infty} a^{-\frac{1}{n}} = \frac{1}{\lim_{n\to\infty}\sqrt[n]{a}} = 1$, and for $a > 1, |h| < \frac{1}{n}$ the inequalities $a^{-\frac{1}{n}} - 1 < a^{n} - 1 < a^{\frac{1}{n}} - 1$ take place.

1.17.45. ***Hint.*** Divide the numerator and denominator by x^m.

1.17.46. (a) $a = 1; b = -1$; (b) $a = 1; b = \frac{1}{2}$. ***Hint.*** To find the coefficient a divide the expression by x and pass over to the limit.

1.17.47. (a) $f(x) = \begin{cases} 1 \text{ for } 0 \le x \le 1, \\ x \text{ for } x > 1. \end{cases}$

(b) $f(x) = \begin{cases} 0 \text{ for } x \ne \frac{\pi}{2} + n\pi, \\ 1 \text{ for } x = \frac{\pi}{2} + n\pi \end{cases} \quad (n = 0, \pm 1, \pm 2, \ldots).$

1.17.48. ***Hint.*** Take advantage of the identity

$$(1 - x)(1 + x)(1 + x^2)\ldots(1 + x^{2^n}) = 1 - x^{2^n}.$$

1.17.49. Generally speaking, one can't. For example,

$$\lim_{x\to 0} \frac{\ln(1 + x) + \ln(1 - x)}{x^2} = \lim_{x\to 0} \frac{\ln(1 - x^2)}{x^2} = -1,$$

and if the replace $\ln(1 + x)$ by x and $\ln(1 - x)$ by $-x$ we will get the wrong result : $\lim_{x\to 0} \frac{x - x}{x^2} = 0.$

1.17.50. $\frac{1}{2}$. ***Hint.*** If α is a central angle subtended by the arc under consideration, then the chord is equal to $2R\sin\frac{\alpha}{2} \sim R\alpha$, and the sagitta to $R(1 - \cos\alpha) \sim R\frac{\alpha^2}{2}$.

1.17.51. 2. ***Hint.*** The difference of the perimeters of a circumscribed and inscribed regular n-gons is equal to

$$2Rn\left(\tan\frac{\pi}{n} - \sin\frac{\pi}{n}\right) = 2\pi R\frac{\tan\alpha - \sin\alpha}{\alpha} \sim \pi R\alpha^2,$$

where $\alpha = \frac{\pi}{n}$, and the side of an inscribed n-gon is

$$2R\sin\frac{\pi}{n} = 2R\sin\alpha \sim 2R\alpha.$$

1.17.52. On the equivalence of $(1+\alpha)^3 - 1$ and 3α as $\alpha \to 0$.

1.17.53. No, $\log(1+x) = \frac{\ln(1+x)}{\ln 10} \sim \frac{x}{\ln 10}$ as $x \to 0$.

1.17.54. (a) Yes. ***Hint.*** If the function $\varphi(x) = f(x) + g(x)$ is continuous at this point; $x = x_0$, then the function $g(x) = \phi(x) - f(x)$ is also continuous at this point; (b) No. Example: $f(x) = -g(x) = \operatorname{sign} x$ (see Problem **1.5.11** (p)); both functions are discontinuous at the point $x = 0$, and their sum is identically equal to zero, and is, hence, continuous.

1.17.55. (a) No. Example : $f(x) = x$ is continuous everywhere, and $g(x) = \sin\frac{\pi}{x}$ for $x \neq 0$ $g(0) = 0$ being discontinuous at the pont $x = 0$. The product of these functions is a function continuous at $x = 0$ since $\lim\limits_{x\to 0} x\sin\frac{\pi}{x} = 0$; (b) No. Example : $f(x) = -g(x) = \begin{cases} 1 \text{ for } x \geq 0, \\ -1 \text{ for } x < 0; \end{cases}$ both functions are discontinuous at the point $x = 0$, their product $f(x)g(x) = -1$ being continuous everywhere.

1.17.56. No. Example : $f(x) = \begin{cases} 1 \text{ if } x \text{ is rational,} \\ -1 \text{ if } x \text{ is irrational.} \end{cases}$ We may write $f(x) = 2\lambda(x) - 1$, where $\lambda(x)$ is the Dirichlet function (see Problem **1.14.4** (b)).

1.17.57. (a) $x = 0$ is a discontinuity of the second kind, $x = 1$ is a discontinuity of the first kind; (b) $x = 1$ is a discontinuity of the first kind: $f(1-0) = 0, f(1+0) = 1$; (c) $\varphi(x)$ is discontinuous at all points except $x = 0$.

1.17.58. (a) $x = n = 0, \pm 1, \pm 2, \ldots$ are discontinuities of the first kind: $\lim\limits_{x\to n-0} y = 1$, $\lim\limits_{x\to n+0} y = y|_{x=n} = 0$. The function has a period of 1; (b) $x = \pm\sqrt{n}$ $(n = \pm 1, \pm 2, \ldots)$ are points of discontinuity of the first kind:

$$\lim_{x\to\sqrt{n}-0} y = 2n - 1;\quad \lim_{x\to\sqrt{n}+0} y = y|_{x=\sqrt{n}} = 2n.$$

The function is even; (c) $x = \pm\sqrt{n}\,(n = \pm 1, \pm 2, \ldots)$ are the points of discontinuity of the first kind; at these points the function passes over from the value 1 to -1 and returns to 1. the function is even;

$$\text{(d) } y = \begin{cases} x \text{ if } |\sin x| < \frac{1}{2}, ie, -\frac{\pi}{6} + \pi n < x < \frac{\pi}{6} + \pi n, \\ \frac{x}{2} \text{ if } |\sin x| = \frac{1}{2}, ie, x = \pm\frac{\pi}{6} + \pi n, \\ 0 \text{ if } |\sin x| > \frac{1}{2}, ie, \frac{\pi}{6} + \pi n < x < \frac{5\pi}{6} + \pi n. \end{cases}$$

$x = \pm\frac{\pi}{6} + \pi n$ are discontinuities of the first kind.

1.17.59. The function $f[g(x)]$ has discontinuities of the first kind at the points $x = -1; 0; +1$. The function $g[f(x)]$ is continuous everywhere. ***Hint.*** The function $f(u)$ is discontinuous at $u = 0$, and the function $g(x)$ changes sign at the points $x = 0, \pm 1$. The function $g[f(x)] = 0$, since $f(x)$ attains only the values $0, \pm 1$.

1.17.61. ***Hint.*** Write the function in the form

$$f(x) = \begin{cases} x+1 \text{ for } -2 \le x < 0, \\ 0 \text{ for } x = 0, \\ (x+1)2^{-\frac{2}{x}} \text{ for } 0 < x \le 2. \end{cases}$$

Make sure that the function increases from -1 to 1 on the interval $[-2, 0)$ and from 0 to $\frac{3}{2}$ on the interval $[0, 2]$. Apply the intermediate value theorem to the intervals $[-2, -1]$ and $[0, 2]$. The function is discontinuous at the point $x = 0 : f(-0) = 1, f(+0) = 0$.

1.17.62. ***Hint.*** Suppose $\varepsilon > 0$ is given and the point $x_0 \in |a, b|$ is chosen. We may consider that

$$\varepsilon \le \min[f(x_0) - f(a), f(b) - f(x_0)].$$

Choose the points x_1 and x_2, $x_1 < x_0 < x_2$ so that

$$f(x_1) = f(x_0) - \varepsilon, f(x_2) = f(x_0) + \varepsilon,$$

and put $\delta = \min(x_0 - x_1, x_2 - x_0)$.

1.17.63. ***Hint.*** Apply the intermediate value theorem to the function $g(x) = f(x) - x$.

1.17.64. ***Hint.*** Apply the intermediate value theorem to the function $f(x)$ on the interval $[x_1, x_n]$, noting that

$$\min[f(x_1), \ldots, f(x_n)] \le \frac{1}{n}[f(x_1) + f(x_2) + \ldots + f(x_n)] \le \max[f(x_1), \ldots, f(x_n)].$$

1.17.65. ***Hint.*** Apply the intermediate value theorem to the function $g(x) = 2^x - \frac{1}{x}$ on the interval $\left[\frac{1}{4}, 1\right]$.

1.17.66. ***Hint.*** At sufficiently large values of the independent variable the values of the polynomial of an even degree have the same sign as the coefficient at the superior power of x; therefore the polynomial changes sign at least twice.

1.17.67. ***Hint.*** The inverse function

$$x = \begin{cases} -\sqrt{-y-1} & \text{for } \; y < -1, \\ 0 & \text{for } \; y = 0, \\ \sqrt{y-1} & \text{for } \; y > 1, \end{cases}$$

is continuous in the intervals $(-\infty, -1)$ and $(1, \infty)$ and has one isolated point $y = 0$.

Chap

2.1.1. ($-\frac{20}{21}$. .2. (b) $y' = 10x - 2$. **2.1.5.** $v_{av} = 25$ m/sec.

2.1.6. (a) $y' = 3x^2$; (b) $y' = -\frac{2}{x^3}$.

2.1.7. The function is non-differentiable at the indicated points.

2.2.1. (b) $y' = -\frac{2}{3}ax^{-\frac{5}{3}} + \frac{4}{3}bx^{-\frac{7}{3}}$. **2.2.2.** (c) $y' = 2x \text{ arc tan } x + 1$.

2.2.3. (b) -9000. **2.2.4.** (a) $y' = 6x^2 + 3$; (b) $y' = \frac{1}{2\sqrt{x}} - \frac{1}{2x\sqrt{x}} + x^9$;

(c) $y' = \frac{-3x^2 + 2x + 2}{(x^2 - x + 1)^2}$; (d) $y' = -\frac{3\sqrt{x} + 8\sqrt{x} + 2\sqrt{1/x}}{6(x - 2\sqrt[3]{x})}$;

(e) $y' = \frac{\cos\varphi - \sin\varphi - 1}{(1 - \cos\varphi)^2}$; (f) $y' = 2e^x + \frac{1}{x}$; (g) $y' = 2e^x \cos x$;

(h) $y' = \frac{x(\cos x - \sin x) - \sin x - e^x}{x^2 e^x}$.

2.2.5. (f) $30 \ln^4(\tan^3 x)\frac{1}{\sin 6x}$; (g) $\sin\frac{2}{\sqrt{1-x}} \cdot \frac{1}{2(1-x)^{\frac{3}{2}}}$.

2.2.6. (b) $y' = -3(3 - \sin x)^2 \cos x$;

(c) $y' = \frac{2\cos x}{3\sin x\sqrt[3]{\sin^2 x}} + \frac{2\sin x}{\cos^3 x}$;

(d) $y' = \frac{2e^x + 2^x \ln 2}{3\sqrt[3]{(2e^x - 2^x + 1)^2}} + \frac{5\ln^4 x}{x}$;

(e) $y' = 3\cos 3x - \frac{1}{5}\sin\frac{x}{5} + \frac{1}{2\sqrt{x}}\sec^2\sqrt{x}$;

(f) $y' = (2x - 5)\cos(x^2 - 5x + 1) - \frac{a}{x^2}\sec^2\frac{a}{x}$;

(h) $y' = \frac{1}{x\sqrt{1 + \ln^2 x}} + \frac{1}{\text{arc tan } x} + \frac{1}{1 + x^2}$;

(i) $y' = 2\ln \text{arc tan}\frac{x}{3} \cdot \frac{1}{\text{arc tan}\frac{x}{3}} \cdot \frac{3}{9 + x^2}$.

2.2.8. (b) $y' = -\frac{1}{\sinh^2(\tan x)}\sec^2 x + \frac{1}{\cosh^2(\cot x)}\text{cosec}^2 x$;

(d) $y' = 3x \times (x\sinh 2x^3 + \cosh x^2 \cdot \sinh 2x^2)$;

(e) $y' = e^{\sinh ax} e^{bx(a\cosh ax + b)}$.

2.2.9. (c) $y' = \sqrt[3]{x^2}\,\dfrac{1-x}{1+x^2}\sin^3 x\cos^2 x$

$$\left(\frac{2}{3x} - \frac{1}{1-x} - \frac{2x}{1+x^2} + 3\cot x - 2\tan x\right);$$

(d) $y' = (\tan x)^{\frac{(x+1)}{2}}\left(\dfrac{1}{2}\ln\tan x + \dfrac{x+1}{\sin 2x}\right).$

2.2.13. (a) $f'(x) = \dfrac{1}{2}\left(\cosh\dfrac{x}{2} + \sinh\dfrac{x}{2}\right);$

(b) $f'(x) = \tanh x$; (c) $f'(x) = \sqrt{\cosh x + 1}$; (d) $f'(x) = \dfrac{1}{\cosh x}$;

(e) $f'(x) = 4\sinh 4x$;

(f) $f'(x) = (a+b)e^{ax} \times (\cosh bx + \sinh bx) = (a+b)e^{(a+b)x}$.

2.2.14. (a) $y' = (\cos x)^{\sin x}(\cos x \ln\cos x - \tan x\sin x)$;

(b) $y' = \dfrac{\cos 3x}{\sqrt[3]{\sin^2 3x(1-\sin 3x)^4}}$;

(c) $y' = \dfrac{5x^2 + x - 24}{3(x-1)^{\frac{1}{2}}(x+2)^{\frac{5}{3}}(x+3)^{\frac{5}{2}}}$.

2.2.17. (a) $y' = \dfrac{\ln 3}{\sqrt{81^x - 1}} \cdot \dfrac{\tan\sqrt{\arcsin 3^{-2x}}}{\sqrt{\arcsin 3^{-2x}}}$;

(b) $y' = -\dfrac{\sin\ln^3 x\cdot\ln^2 x}{5x\sqrt[5]{\cos^4\ln^3 x}\,(1+\sqrt[5]{\cos^2\ln^3 x})\sqrt[3]{(\arctan\sqrt[5]{\cos\ln^3 x})^2}}$

2.3.1. (b) $k^n e^{kx}$; (e) $2^{n-1}\sin\left(2x + n\dfrac{\pi}{2}\right)$;

(f) $\dfrac{1}{4}\sin\left(x + n\dfrac{\pi}{2}\right) + \dfrac{3^n}{2}\sin\left(3x + n\dfrac{\pi}{2}\right) + \dfrac{5^n}{4}\sin\left(5x + n\dfrac{\pi}{2}\right)$.

2.3.4. (b) $e^x(x^2 + 48x + 551)$;

(c) $e^{ax}\left\{\sin\beta x\left[\alpha^n - \dfrac{n(n-1)}{1.2}\alpha^{n-2}\beta^2 + \ldots\right]\right.$

$$\left. + \cos\beta x\left[n\alpha^{n-1}\beta - \frac{n(n-1)(n-2)}{1\times 2\times 3}a^{n-3}\beta^3 + \ldots\right]\right\}.$$

2.3.6. (a) $\dfrac{2x^2 + 3x}{(1+x^2)\sqrt{1+x^2}}$; (b) $\dfrac{(1+2x^2)\arcsin x}{(1-x^2)^{\frac{3}{2}}} + \dfrac{3x}{(1-x^2)^2}$;

(c) $2e^{-x^2} \times (2x^2 - 1)$

2.3.8. (a) $x^3\sin x - 60x^2\cos x - 1140x\sin x + 8640\cos x$;

(b) $2e^{-x} \times (\sin x + \cos x)$; (c) $e^x\,[3x^2 + 6nx + 3n(n-1) - 4]$;

(d) $(-1)^n\,[(4n^2 + 2n + 1 - x^2)\cos x - 4nx\sin x]$.

2.3.9. (a) $100!\left[\frac{1}{(x-2)^{101}}-\frac{1}{(x-1)^{101}}\right]$;

(b) $\frac{1\times 3\times 5\times\ldots\times 197\times(399-x)}{2^{100}(1-x)^{\frac{201}{2}}}$. ***Hint.*** $y=2(1-x)^{-\frac{1}{2}}-(1-x)^{\frac{1}{2}}$.

2.4.1. (b) $x''_{yy}=-\frac{4\cos x}{(6+\sin x)^3}$.

2.4.3. (b) $y'_x=-\cot\frac{k-1}{2}t$; (d) $y'_x=-2e^{-2ct}$.

2.4.4. (b) $y''_{xx}=\frac{4t}{3(t^2+1)^3}$; (c) $y''_{xx}=\frac{1}{at\cos^3 t}$.

2.4.5. (b) $y'''_{xxx}=-3\sin t\sec^2 t$.

2.4.6. (b) $y'_x=\frac{y}{x}+e^{-\frac{y}{x}}$; (c) $y'_x=\frac{2-x}{y-5}$; (d) $y'_x=-\sqrt[3]{\frac{y}{x}}$.

2.4.7. (b) $y''_{xx}=\frac{(e^x-e^y)(1-e^{x+y})}{(1+e^y)^3}$;

(c) $y''_{xx}=\frac{4e^{x-y}}{(e^{x-y}+1)^3}=\frac{4(x+y)}{(x+y+1)^3}$.

2.4.9. (a) $\frac{2a-2x-y}{x+2y-2a}$; (b) $\frac{x+y}{x-y}$; (c) $-\frac{e^x\sin y+e^{-y}\sin x}{e^x\cos y+e^{-y}\cos x}$; (d) $-\frac{1}{e}$.

2.4.10. (a) $-\frac{2y^2+2}{y^5}$; (b) $\frac{111}{256}$.

2.4.11. (a) $-\frac{c\sin t}{a(b+\cos t)}$; (b) $\frac{t}{2}$; (c) $\frac{t^2+1}{4t^3}$; (d) $\frac{e^{t^2}}{2t(2t^2+2t+1)}$;

(e) $\frac{(a\cos t-b\sin t)\cos^3\frac{t}{2}}{4\sin\frac{t}{2}}$;

(f) $-\sqrt{\frac{1-4t^2}{2-t^2}}$; (g) $-\sqrt{1-t^2}$.

2.5.1. (b) $6x+2y-9=0; 2x-6y+37=0$.

2.5.2. (c) $M_1\left(-\frac{2}{\sqrt{3}},5+\frac{10}{3\sqrt{3}}\right), M_2\left(\frac{2}{\sqrt{3}},5-\frac{10}{3\sqrt{3}}\right)$.

2.5.3. (b) $\varphi=\arctan 2\sqrt{2}$. **2.5.8.** (b) $x+y-2=0; y=x$.

2.5.15. (a) $\frac{\pi}{4}$; (b) $y=1$, $x+2y-2=0$; (c) $y+\frac{39}{16}=-\frac{2}{3}\left(x+\frac{5}{4}\right)$; (d) $\frac{\pi}{4}$.

2.5.16. 11.

2.5.17. 26,450. **2.5.19.** $s = at - \frac{gt^2}{2}$; $v = a - gt$; $s_{\max} = s\big|_{t=\frac{a}{g}} = \frac{a^2}{2g}$.

2.5.20. $v = r'_t = \frac{2\pi a\varepsilon}{P}\sin M(1 + 2\varepsilon\cos M)$. **2.6.3.** $\Delta y \approx dy = 0.05$.

2.6.5. (b) $\log 10.21 \approx 1.009$; (d) $\cot 45°10' \approx 0.9942$.

2.6.7. (c) $\Delta_y = |\cos x|\Delta_x$; (d) $\Delta_y = (1 + \tan^2 x)\Delta_x$.

2.6.9. (a) $d^2y = 4^{-x^2}2\ln 4(2x^2\ln 4 - 1)dx^2$;

(b) $d^2y = \frac{4\ln x - 4 - \ln^3 x}{x^2\sqrt{(\ln^2 x - 4)^3}}dx^2$;

(c) $d^3y = -4\sin 2x\,dx^3$.

2.6.10. (a) $d^2y = -\frac{4(1+3x^4)}{(1-x^4)^2}dx^2$; (b) $d^2y = -\frac{4(1+3x^4)}{(1-x^4)^2}dx^2 - \frac{4x}{1-x^4}dx^2$;

in particular at $x = \tan t$, $d^2y = -\frac{4}{\cos^2 2t}dt^2$.

2.6.11. $\Delta V = 4\pi r^2\Delta r + 4\pi r\,\Delta r^2 + \frac{4}{3}\pi\Delta r^3$ is the volume contained between two spheres of radii r and $r + \Delta r$; $dV = 4\pi r^2\Delta r$ is the volume of a thin layer with a base area equal to the sphere's surface area $4\pi r^2$ and a height Δr.

2.6.12. $\Delta s = gt\,\Delta t + \frac{1}{2}g\,\Delta t^2$ is the distance covered by a body within the time Δt; $ds = gt\,\Delta t = v\,dt$ is the distance covered by a body which would move at a velocity $v = gt$ during the entire interval of time.

2.7.1. (a) It does not exist; (b) it exists and equals zero.

2.7.2. 90°. ***Hint.*.** Since

$$y = \begin{cases} e^x, & x \geq 0 \\ e^{-x}, & x < 0. \end{cases}$$

$$f'_-(0) = -1,\ f'_+(0) = 1.$$

2.7.3. $f'_-(a) = -\varphi(a)$; $f'_+(a) = \varphi(a)$.

2.7.4. ***Hint*..** For $x \neq 0$ the derivative

$$f'(x) = -\cos\left(\frac{1}{x}\right) + 2x\sin\left(\frac{1}{x}\right).$$

At $x = 0$ the derivative equals zero:

$$f'(0) = \lim_{\Delta x \to 0}\frac{\Delta x^2\sin\frac{1}{\Delta x}}{\Delta x} = 0.$$

Thus, the derivative $f'(x)$ exists for all x, but has a discontinuity of the second kind at the point $x = 0$.

2.7.5. $a = 2x_0, b = -x_0^2$. **2.7.7. *Hint.*.** The formula for the sum of a geometric progression represents an identity with respect to x. Equating the derivatives of both sides of the identity, we get

$$1 + 2x + 3x^2 + \ldots + nx^{n-1} = \frac{nx^{n+1} - (n+1)x^n + 1}{(1-x)^2};$$

multiplying both sides of this equality by x and differentiating again, we get

$$1^2 + 2^2 x + \ldots + n^2 x^{n-1} = \frac{1 + x - (n+1)^2 x^n + (2n^2 + 2n - 1)x^{n+1} - nx^{n+2}}{(1-x)^3}.$$

2.7.8. $\sin x + 3\sin 3x + \ldots + (2n-1)\sin(2n-1)x$

$$= \frac{(2n+1)\sin(2n-1)x - (2n-1)\sin(2n+1)x}{4\sin^2 x}.$$

Hint. To prove the identity multiply its left side by $2\sin x$ and apply the formula $2\sin\alpha\sin\beta = \cos(\alpha-\beta) - \cos(\alpha+\beta)$. to deduce the desired formula differentiate both sides of the identity and equate the derivatives.

2.7.9. (a) $\sin 2x\,[f'(\sin^2 x) - f'(\cos^2 x)]$;

(b) $e^{f(x)}[e^x f'(e^x) + f'(x)f(e^x)]$;

(c) $\dfrac{\psi'(x)}{\psi(x)} \cdot \dfrac{1}{\ln\varphi(x)} - \dfrac{\varphi'(x)}{\varphi(x)} \cdot \dfrac{\ln\psi(x)}{\ln^2\varphi(x)}$.

2.7.10. (a) No; (b) No; (c) Yes; (d) No.

2.7.11. *Hint.* Differentiate the identity $f(-x) = f(x)$ or $f(-x) = -f(x)$.

This fact is easily illustrated geometrically if we take into consideration that the graph of the even function is symmetrical about the y-axis, and the graph of the odd function about the origin.

2.7.12. *Hint.* Differentiate the identity $f(x+T) = f(x)$.

2.7.13. $F'(x) = 6x^2$. **2.7.14.** $y' = 2|x|$.

2.7.15. The composite function $f[\varphi(x)]$ may be non-differentiable only at points where $\varphi'(x)$ does not exist and where $\varphi(x)$ attains such values of $\varphi(x) = u$ at which $f'(u)$ does not exist. But the function $y = u^2 = |x|^2$ has a derivative $y' = 0$ at the point $x = 0$, though at this point the function $u = |x|$ has no derivative.

2.7.16. (a) $y'' = 6|x|$; (b) $y'' = 2|\sin|\frac{1}{x} - \frac{2}{x}\cos\frac{1}{x} - \frac{1}{x^2}\sin\frac{1}{x}$ at $x \neq 0$, $y''(0)$ does not exist, since $y'(x)$ is discontinuous at $x = 0$.

2.7.17. *Hint.* (a) Verify that $f^{(k)}\frac{1}{k!} = C_n^k\,(k = 0, 1, \ldots, n)$ and take advantage of the property of the binomial coefficients. (b) Designate: $f(x) = u_n$; show that $u_n' = (n-1)u_{n-1} - u_{n-2}$ and use the method of mathematical induction.

2.7.18. *Hint.* Apply the Leibnitz formula for the n th derivative of the product of the functions $u = e^{-\frac{x}{a}}$ and $v = x^2$.

2.7.19. $y^{(n)}(0) = \begin{cases} 0 & \text{at } n = 2k \\ [1 \times 3 \times \ldots \times (2k-1)]^2 & \text{at } n = 2k+1\ (k = 1, 2, \ldots). \end{cases}$

Hint. Differentiate the identity $n-2$ times and, putting $x = 0$, obtain $y^{(n)}(0) = (n-2)^2 y^{(n-2)}(0) \quad (n \geq 2)$.

2.7.21. ***Hint.*** Take advantage of the definition

$$e^{-x^2} H_{n+1}(x) = (e^{-x^2})^{(n+1)} = (-2xe^{-x^2})^{(n)}$$

and the Leibnitz formula for the nth derivative of the product $u = e^{-x^2}$ and $v = -2x$.

2.7.22. $y'_x = \dfrac{1}{3(y^2+1)}$.

2.7.23. $x_{1.2} = \pm\sqrt{1+\sqrt{1-y}}\ (-\infty < y \leq 1)$,

$$x_{3.4} = \pm\sqrt{1-\sqrt{1-y}}\ (0 \leq y \leq 1),$$

$$x'_i = \frac{1}{4x_i(1-x_i^2)}\ (i = 1, 2, 3, 4) \text{for } x_i \neq 0, \pm 1.$$

Hint. Solve the biquadratic equation $x^4 - 2x^2 + y = 0$ and find the domains of definition of the obtained functions $x_i(y)$.

2.7.25. (a) $x_1 = -3$; $x_2 = 1$; (b) $x = \pm 1$.

2.7.26. ***Hint.*** Note that the function $x = 2t - |t| = \begin{cases} t, t \geq 0, \\ 3t, t < 0 \end{cases}$ has no derivative at $t - 0$. But $t = \begin{cases} x, & x \geq 0, \\ \dfrac{x}{3}, & x < 0, \end{cases}$ therefore we can express $y = t^2 + t|t| = \begin{cases} 2t^2, & t \geq 0, \\ 0, & t < 0 \end{cases}$ through $x : y = \begin{cases} 2x^2, & x \geq 0, \\ 0, & x < 0. \end{cases}$ This function is differentiable everywhere.

2.7.27. $a = c = \dfrac{1}{4}; b = \dfrac{1}{2}$.

2.7.28. ***Hint.*** The curves intersect at the points where $\sin ax = 1$. Since at these points $\cos ax = 0$,

$$y'_2 = f'(x)\sin ax + f(x)a\cos ax = f'(x) = y'_1,$$

ie, the curve are tangent.

2.7.30. ***Hint.*** For $t \neq \pi n$ the equations of the tangent and the normal are reduced to the form :

$$y = \cot\frac{t}{2}(x - at) + 2a;\ y = -\tan\frac{t}{2}(x - at),$$

respectively. For $t = \pi(2k-1)\ (k = 1, 2, \ldots)$ the tangent line $(y = 2a)$ touches the circle at the highest point, and the normal $(x = at)$ passes through the highest and lowest points; for $t = 2k\pi$ $(k = 0, 1, \ldots)$ the tangent line $(x = at)$ passes through both points, and the normal $(y = 0)$ touches the circle at the lowest point. **2.7.34.** $\frac{d^2y}{dt^2} + y$.

2.7.35. The relative error $\delta = \frac{\Delta l}{l} \approx \frac{2d\varphi}{\sin 2\varphi}$. The most reliable result, *ie*, the result with the least relative error, corresponds to the value $\varphi = 45°$.

Chapter 3

3.1.2. (b) Yes; (c) No, since the derivative is non-existent at the point 0. **3.1.5.** $\xi = e - 1$. **3.1.7.** No, since $g(-3) = g(3)$. **3.1.9.** (d) ***Hint.*** Consider the functions

$$f(x) = \arcsin \frac{2x}{1 + x^2} + 2 \arctan x \text{ for } |x| > 1,$$

$$g(x) = \arcsin \frac{2x}{1 + x^2} - 2 \arctan x \text{ for } |x| < 1.$$

3.1.15. (a) $\xi = \frac{7}{2}$; (b) $\xi = \frac{2}{\ln 3}$; (c) $\xi = \frac{10 \pm \sqrt{52}}{24}$; (d) it is not applicable, since the function has no derivative at the point $x = 0$.

3.1.16. $1.26 < \ln(1 + e) < 1.37$. ***Hint.*** Write the Lagrange formula for the function $f(x) = \ln x$ on the interval $[e, e + 1]$ and estimate the right-hand side in the obtained relation: $\ln(1 + e) = 1 + \frac{1}{\xi}$ $(e < \xi < e + 1)$.

3.1.17. ***Hint.*** Apply the Lagrange formula to the function $f(x) = \ln x$ on the interval $[1, 1 + x]$, $x > 0$, and estimate the right-hand side in the obtained relation $\ln(1 + x) = \frac{x}{\xi}$ $(1 < \xi < 1 + x)$. **3.2.1.** (c) 2; (d) 0; (f) $-\frac{1}{2}$.

3.2.3. (b) 0. ***Hint.*** Represent $\cot x - \frac{1}{x} = \frac{x - \tan x}{x \tan x}$; (c) $\frac{1}{2}$.

3.2.5. (b) $e^1 = e$.

3.2.6. (a) 1; (b) 1. **3.2.9.** (a) $\frac{4}{7}$; (b) $\ln a - 1$; (c) 2; (d) $\frac{\pi\sqrt{3}}{6}$; (e) $\frac{1}{a}$; (f) 0; (g) 1; (h) $\ln a$; (i) $e^{-m^2\frac{n}{2}}$; (j) $\frac{2}{\pi}$; (k) -1; (l) e; (m) $\frac{2}{3}$; (n) $\frac{1}{2}$; (o) $\frac{a^2}{2}$; (p) $e^{-\frac{1}{30}}$; (q) 1; (r) $-\frac{1}{2}$.

3.3.5. (b) 0.34201.

3.3.6. $\sqrt[4]{83} \approx 3.018350$. ***Hint.*** $\sqrt[4]{83} = \sqrt[4]{81 + 2} = 3\left(1 + \frac{2}{81}\right)^{\frac{1}{4}}$. Apply the binomial formula and retain four terms.

3.3.7. ***Hints.*** (b) Write the Maclaurin formula for the function $f(x) = \tan x$ with the remainder $R_4(x)$; (c) write the Maclaurin formula for the function $f(x) = (1+x)^{\frac{1}{2}}$ with remainders $R_2(x)$ and $R_3(x)$.

3.4.2. (a) $f(x) = \frac{1}{2}x^2 - \frac{1}{3}x^3 - \frac{1}{5}x^5 + o(x^5)$;

(b) $f(x) = x - \frac{x^2}{2} + \frac{x^3}{6} - \frac{x^4}{12} + \frac{x^5}{24} + o(x^5)$

3.4.3. (b) $-\frac{1}{2}$; (c) $-\frac{1}{12}$; (d) $\frac{1}{3}$; (e) 1.

3.4.4. (a) $1 + 2x + x^2 - \frac{2}{3}x^3 - \frac{5}{6}x^4 - \frac{1}{15}x^5$;

(b) $-\frac{x^2}{2} - \frac{x^4}{12} + \frac{x^6}{45}$; (c) $1 - \frac{x}{2} + \frac{x}{12} - \frac{x^4}{720}$.

3.5.1. (d) The function decreases on the interval $(-\infty, 0)$ and increases on $(0, \infty)$; (e) the function increases on the intervals $\left(-\infty, \frac{1}{2}\right)$ and $(3, +\infty)$ and decreases on $\left(\frac{1}{2}, 3\right)$; (f) the function increases over the entire number scale.

3.5.2. (b) The function increases on the intervals $\left(0, \frac{\pi}{4}\right)$ and $\left(\frac{5\pi}{4}, 2\pi\right)$ and decreases on $\left(\frac{\pi}{4}, \frac{5\pi}{4}\right)$.

3.5.8. (a) The function increases throughout the number scale; (b) the function increases on the interval $(-1, 0)$ and decreases on $(0, 1)$, (c) the function decreases throughout the number scale; (d) the function increases on both intervals $(-\infty, 0)$ and $(0, \infty)$ where it is defined; (e) the function decreases on the intervals $(0, 1)$ and $(1, e)$ and increases on $(e, +\infty)$; (f) the function decreases on the intervals $(-\infty, 1)$ and $(1, \infty)$, increases on $(-1, 1)$.

3.5.10. $a \le 0$. **3.5.11.** $b \ge 1$. **3.6.1.** (b) The minimum is $f(1) = f(3) = 3$, the maximum $f(2) = 4$; (d) the minimum $f\left(\frac{7}{5}\right) = -\frac{1}{24}$.

3.6.2. (b) The minima are $f(\pm 1) = \sqrt{3}$; the maximum $f(0) = 2$.

3.6.3. (b) The maximum is $f(-2) = 160$; the minimum $f(0) = 2$.

3.6.7. (b) The minimum is $f(0) = 0$.

3.6.8. (b) On the interval $[0, 2\pi]$: the minimum is $f\left(\frac{\pi}{2}\right) = -4$; the maximum $f\left(\frac{3\pi}{2}\right) = 4$. **3.6.10.** (a) The minimum is $f(0) = 0$, the maximum $f(2) = 4e^{-2}$; (b) the minimum is $f(-2) = -1$, the maximum $f(2) = 1$; (c) the maximum is $f(0) = 0$, the minimum $f\left(\frac{5}{3}\right) = -\frac{25}{9}\sqrt[5]{\frac{1}{9}}$; (d) the maximum is

$f(\pm 2) = -1$, the minimum $f(0) = 7$; (e) the maximum is $f(-3) = 3\sqrt[3]{3}$, the minimum $f(2) = -\sqrt[3]{44}$.

3.6.11. (a) There is no extremum; (b) there is no extremum; (c) the maximum is $f(0) = 0$; (d) the minimum is $f(0) = 0$.

3.7.1. (c) The greatest value is $f(1) = \frac{1}{e}$, the least value $f(0) = 0$; (d) the greatest value is $f\left(\pm\frac{1}{2}\right) = \frac{3}{\sqrt{8}}$, the least value $f(\pm 1) = 0$.

3.7.2. (b) The greatest value is $y(0) = \frac{\pi}{2}$, the least value $y\left(\pm\frac{\sqrt{2}}{2}\right) = \frac{\pi}{3}$; (c) the greatest value is $y(4) = 6$, the least value $y(0) = 0$.

3.7.6. (a) The greatest value is $f(-2) = \frac{16}{3}$, the least value $f(3) = -\frac{37}{4}$; (b) the greatest value is $f(0) = 2$, the least value $f(\pm 2) = 0$; (c) the greatest value is $f\left(\frac{1}{\sqrt{3}}\right) = \frac{\pi}{6} + 0.25 \ln 3$, the least value $f(\sqrt{3}) = \frac{\pi}{3} - 0.25 \ln 3$; (d) the greatest value is $f\left(\frac{\pi}{3}\right) = \frac{3\sqrt{3}}{2}$, the least value $f\left(\frac{3\pi}{2}\right) = -2$; (e) the greatest value is $f(1) = 1$, the least value $f(2) = 2(1 - \ln 2)$; (f) there is no greatest value, the least value is $f(0) = 1$.

3.8.3. $H = R\sqrt{2}$, where H is the height of the cylinder, R is the radius of the sphere. **3.8.7.** $x = a\sin\alpha$, $y = a\cos\alpha$, where $\alpha = 0.5$ arc tan 2.

Hint. The problem is reduced to finding the greatest value of the function

$$S = 4xy + 4x(y - x) = 4a^2(\sin 2\alpha - \sin^2\alpha)$$

in the interval $0 < \alpha < \frac{\pi}{4}$. **3.8.8.** $P_{max} = \frac{E^2}{4W_i}$ at $W = W_i$.

3.8.9 $h = 2R = 2\sqrt[3]{\frac{3v}{2\pi}}$. **3.8.10.** The radius of the cylinder base is $r = \frac{R}{2}$, where R is the radius of the cone base. **3.8.11.** The equation of the desired straight line is $\frac{x}{2} + \frac{y}{4} = 1$.

3.8.12. $x = a - p$ for $a > p$ and $x = 0$ for $a \le p$.

3.8.13. $v = \sqrt[3]{\frac{a}{2b}}$. ***Hint.*** It will take $\frac{1}{v}$ hours to cover one knot. The appropriate expenses are expressed by the formula $T = \frac{a + bv^3}{v} = \frac{a}{v} + bv^2$.

3.8.14. $\varphi = \frac{\pi}{3}$ ***Hint.*** At the board width a the cross-sectional area of the trough is equal to $a^2(1 + \cos\varphi)\sin\varphi$, where φ is the angle of inclination of the walls to the bottom.

3.8.15. $\frac{h}{2}$. ***Hint.*** The point of fall of the jet is at a distance of $\frac{v\sqrt{2H}}{g}$ from the tank base, where $H = h - x$ is the height at which the orifice should be located, v is the rate flow; therefore the length of the jet is determined by the expression $\sqrt{2gx}\sqrt{\frac{2(h-x)}{g}} = 2\sqrt{x(h-x)}$.

3.8.16. After $\frac{a}{2v}$ hours the least distance will be equal to $\frac{a}{2}$ km.

3.9.1. (b) The intervals of concavity are $\left(-\infty, \frac{1}{3}\right)$ and $(1, \infty)$, of convexity $\left(\frac{1}{3}, 1\right)$; the points of inflection are $\left(\frac{1}{3}, 12\frac{11}{27}\right)$, $(1, 13)$; (c) the intervals of concavity are $(-\sqrt{3}, 0)$ and $(\sqrt{3}, \infty)$ of convexity $(-\infty, -\sqrt{3})$ and $(0, \sqrt{3})$; the points of inflection are $\left(-\sqrt{3}, -\frac{\sqrt{3}}{10}\right)$, $(0, 0)$, $\left(\sqrt{3}, \frac{\sqrt{3}}{10}\right)$; (e) the curve is concave everywhere; (f) the intervals of concavity are $(0, x_1)$ and (x_2, ∞), of convexity (x_1, x_2), where $x_1 = e^{\frac{3-\sqrt{5}}{2}}$, $x_2 = e^{\frac{3+\sqrt{5}}{2}}$; the points of inflection are (x_1, y_1), (x_2, y_2), where

$$y_1 = \left(\frac{3-\sqrt{5}}{2}\right)^2 e^{\frac{\sqrt{5}-3}{2}} \quad y_2 = \left(\frac{3+\sqrt{5}}{2}\right)^2 e^{-\frac{3+\sqrt{5}}{2}}$$

3.9.5. (a) The point of inflection is $(3, 3)$; the curve is convex for $x < 3$ and concave for $x > 3$; (b) the abscissa of the point of inflection $x = \arcsin\frac{\sqrt{5}-1}{2}$; the curve is concave in $\left(-\frac{\pi}{2}, \arcsin\frac{\sqrt{5}-1}{2}\right)$, and convex in $\left(\arcsin\frac{\sqrt{5}-1}{2}, \frac{\pi}{2}\right)$.

3.10.1. (c) $y = 0$; (d) $x = 0$; (i) $y = 2x$ as $x \to +\infty$ and $y = -2x$ as $x \to -\infty$.

3.10.3. (a) $x = 3$, $y = x - 3$; (b) $y = \pm\frac{\pi x}{2} - 1$; (c) $y = x$; (d) $x = \pm 2$; (e) $y = 2x - \frac{\pi}{2}$.

3.11.2. (a) The function is defined everywhere, it is even. The graph is symmetrical about the y-axis and has no asymptotes. The minimum is $y(0) = 1$, maxima $y(1) = y(-1) = \frac{3}{2}$. The points of inflection are $\left(\pm\frac{\sqrt{3}}{3}, \frac{23}{18}\right)$; (b) the function is defined in $(-\infty, -1)$ and $(-1, +\infty)$. The graph has a vertical asymptote $x = -1$ and an inclined asymptote $y = x - 3$. The minimum is $y(0) = 0$, maximum $y(-4) = -\frac{256}{27}$. The points of inflection are $\left(-6, -\frac{3296}{125}\right)$ and $\left(2, \frac{16}{27}\right)$; (c) the function is defined in $(-\infty, 0)$ and $(0, +\infty)$. The graph has a vertical asymptote $x = 0$. The minimum is $y\left(\frac{1}{2}\right) = 3$. The point of inflection is $\left(-\frac{\sqrt[3]{2}}{2}, 0\right)$; (d) the function is defined in the intervals $(-\infty, -1)$, $(-1, 1)$ and $(1, \infty)$; it is odd. The graph is symmetrical about the origin, has two vertical asymptotes $x = \pm 1$ and an inclined asymptote $y = x$. The minimum is $y(\sqrt{3}) = +3\frac{\sqrt{3}}{2}$, the maximum $y(-\sqrt{3}) = -\frac{3\sqrt{3}}{2}$. The point of inflection is $(0, 0)$; (e) the function is defined everywhere, it is even. The graph is symmetrical about the y-axis and has a horizontal asymptote $y = 0$. The minimum is $y(0) = \sqrt[3]{4}$, the maxima $y(\pm\sqrt{2}) = 2\sqrt[3]{2}$. The points of inflection are $(\pm 2, \sqrt[3]{4})$; (f) the function is defined in $(-2, +\infty)$. The vertical asymptote is $x = -2$. The minimum is $y(0) = 0$, the maximum $y(-0.73) \approx 0.12$. The point of inflection is $(-0.37; 0.075)$; (g) the function is defined everywhere. The horizontal asymptote is $y = 0$ as $x \to +\infty$. The maximum is $y\left(\frac{3}{4}\right) = \left(\frac{3}{4e}\right)^3$. The points of inflection are $(0, 0)$,

$$\left(\frac{3-\sqrt{3}}{4}, \left(\frac{3-\sqrt{3}}{4}\right)^3 e^{\sqrt{3}-3}\right), \left(\frac{3+\sqrt{3}}{4}, \left(\frac{3+\sqrt{3}}{4}\right)^3 e^{-3-\sqrt{3}}\right);$$

(h) the function is defined and continuous everywhere. The horizontal asymptote is $y = 1$. The minimum is $y(0) = 0$, the point $(0, 0)$ being a corner point on the graph: $y'_-(0) = -\frac{\pi}{2}, y'_+(0) = +\frac{\pi}{2}$.

3.12.6. 4.4934. **3.12.8.** $x_1 = -2.330$; $x_2 = 0.202$; $x_3 = 2.128$.

3.12.11. 0.6705. **3.12.12.** (a) 0.27; 2.25; (b) 0.21.

3.12.13. (a) 1.17; (b) 3.07. **3.12.14.** 1.325.

3.12.15. 0.5896 and 2.2895. ***Hint.*** To approximate the smaller root more precisely write the equation in the form $x = e^{0.8x-1}$, to find a more accurate value of the larger root represent it in the form $x = 1.25(1 + \ln x)$.

3.13.1. No. ***Hint.*** Show that at the point $x = 1$ the derivative is non-existent : $f'_-(1) = 1; f'_+(1) = -1$.

3.13.2. ***Hint.*** Check the equality $f(b) - f(a) = (b-a)f'\left(\frac{a+b}{2}\right)$.

3.13.3. ***Hint.*** Apply the Rolle theorem to the function $f(x) = a_0x^n + \ldots + a_{n-1}(x)$ on the interval $[0, x_0]$.

3.13.4. ***Hint.*** Make sure that the derivative $f'(x) = 4(x^3 - 1)$ has only one real root, $x = 1$, and apply the Rolle theorem.

3.13.5. ***Hint.*** The derivative $f'(x) = nx^{n-1} + p$ has only one real root at an even n and not more than two real roots at an odd n.

3.13.6. ***Hint.*** The derivative is a polynomial of the third degree and has three roots. Take advantage of the fact that between the roots of the polynomial lies the root of its derivative.

3.13.7. ***Hint.*** From the correct equality $\lim_{x\to 0} \cos\frac{1}{\xi} = 0\ (0 < \xi < x)$, where ξ is determined from the mean value theorem, it does not follow that $\lim_{x\to 0} \cos\frac{1}{x} = 0$, since it cannot be asserted that the variable ξ attains all intermediate values in the neighbourhood of zero as $x \to 0$. Moreover, ξ takes on only such a sequence of values E for which $\lim \cos\frac{1}{\xi} = 0\ (\xi \in E)$.

3.13.8. ***Hint.*** The mistake is that in the Lagrange formula one and the same point ξ is taken for $f(x)$ and $\varphi(x)$.

3.13.9. ***Hint.*** Apply the Lagrange formula to the function $\ln x$ on the interval $[b, a]$; (b) apply the Lagrange formula to the function z^p on the interval $[y, x]$.

3.13.10. ***Hint.*** With the aid of the Leibniz formula ascertain that the coefficients of the chebyshev-Laguerre polynomial alternate in sign, the odd powers of x having negative coefficients. Whence deduce that $L_n(x) > 0$ for $x < 0$.

3.13.11. ***Hint.*** Using the Rolle theorem, show that inside the interval $[x_0, x_n]$ there are at least n roots of the first derivative, $n - 1$ roots of the second derivative, and so on.

3.13.12. ***Hint.*** The L'Hospital rule is not applicable here, since the derivatives of both the numerator and denominator vanish at all points where the factor $\sin x$ (which we cancelled in computing the limit of the ratio of derivatives) vanishes.

3.13.13. ***Hint.*** Write the Taylor formula with the remainder R_2:

$$f(a + h) = f(a) = hf'(a) = \frac{h^2}{2!} f''(a) + \frac{h^3}{3!} f'''(a + \theta_1 h).$$

Comparing it with the expansion given in the problem, get the equality $\frac{f''(a+\theta h) - f''(a)}{h} = \frac{1}{3} f'''(a + \theta_1 h))$ and pass over to the limit as $h \to 0$.

3.13.14. ***Hint.*** Prove by using the rule of contraries. Suppose that $e = \frac{p}{q}$, where p and q are natural numbers, $p > q > 1$, and, using the Taylor formula, get for $n > p$

$$\frac{p}{q}=1+\frac{1}{1!}+\frac{1}{2!}+\ldots+\frac{1}{n!}+\frac{1}{(n+1)!}\left(\frac{p}{q}\right)^{\theta}\quad(0<\theta<1).$$

Multiply both sides of this equality by $n!$, and noting, that $\frac{p}{q}n!$ and $\left(1+\frac{1}{1!}+\ldots+\frac{1}{n!}\right)n!$ are positive integers and $\frac{1}{n+1}\left(\frac{p}{q}\right)^{\theta}<\frac{1}{n+1}\cdot\frac{p}{q}<1$, obtain a contradictory result.

3.13.15. *Hint.* Verify that the function

$$f(x)=\begin{cases}\dfrac{\sin x}{x}, & 0<x\le\dfrac{\pi}{2}\\ 1, & x=0\end{cases}$$, is continuous on the interval $\left[0,\frac{\pi}{2}\right]$.

Ascertain that the derivative $f'(x)<0$ is inside the interval.

3.13.16. *Hint.* Show that $f'(x)\ge 0$. Ascertain that

$$f(0)=1-a\begin{cases}>0 \text{ for } a<1,\\ <0 \text{ for } a>1,\end{cases}$$

and take advantage of the fact that the function increases.

3.13.17. *Hint.* Show that the function $f(x)=xe^{x}-2$ increases and has opposite signs at the end-points of the interval (0, 1).

3.13.18. *Hint.* Show that the derivative

$$f'(x)=\frac{1}{2}+2x\sin\frac{1}{x}-\cos\frac{1}{x}\;(x\ne 0)$$

is equal to $\frac{3}{2}$ at the points $x=\frac{1}{(2n+1)\pi}$ $(n=0,\pm 1,\pm 2,\ldots)$, and to $-\frac{1}{2}$ at the points $x=\frac{1}{2n\pi}$, *ie*, the derivative changes sign in any vicinity of the origin.

3.13.19. *Hint.* Ascertain that the auxiliary function $\psi(x)=f(x)-\varphi(x)$ increases.

3.13.20. *Hint.* Make sure that at all points of the domain of definition of the function the derivative retains its sign if $ad-bc\ne 0$. But if $ad-bc=0$, *ie*, $\frac{a}{c}=\frac{b}{d}$, then the function is constant. **3.13.21.** $p=-6, q=14$.

3.13.22. A minimum $f(x_0)=0$ if $\varphi(x_0)>0$ and n is even; a maximum $f(x_0)=0$ if $\varphi(x_0)<0$ and n is even; the point x_0 is not an extremum if n is odd. ***Hint.*** At an even n, in a certain neighbourhood of the point x_0 the function retains its sign and is either rigorously greater than zero or rigorously less than zero, depending on the sign of $\varphi(x_0)$. At an odd n the function changes sign in a certain neighbourhood of the point x_0.

3.13.23. *Hint.* For $x\ne 0$ $f(x)>0$, hence $f(0)$ is a minimum. For $x>0$ the derivative $f'(x)=2-\sin\frac{1}{x}+\frac{1}{x}\cos\frac{1}{x}$ is positive at the points $x=\frac{1}{2\pi n}$ and negative at the points $x = \frac{1}{(2n+1)\pi}$. The case $x < 0$ is investigated analogously.

3.13.24. (a) 1 and 0; (b) 1 and −2.

3.13.25. (a) The least value is non-existent, the greatest value equals 1; (b) the function has neither the greatest, nor the least value.

3.13.30. Yes. ***Hint.*** Since $f''(x)$ changes sign when passing through the point x_0, the latter is a point of extremum for the function $f'(x)$.

3.13.31. The graph passes through the pont $M(-1, 2)$ and has a tangent line $y - 2 = -(x + 1)$; M is a point of inflection, the curve being concave downward to the left of the point M, and upward to the right of it. ***Hint.*** The function $f''(x)$ increases and changes sign when passing through $x = -1$.

3.13.32. $h = \frac{1}{\sigma\sqrt{2}}$. **3.13.33.** ***Hint.*** According to the Rolle theorem, between the roots of the first derivative there is at least one root of the second derivative. when passing through one of these roots the second derivative. must change sign.

3.13.35. ***Hint.*** The polynomial has the form $a_0x^{2n} + a_1x^{2n-2} + \ldots + a_{n-1}x^2 + a_n$. Polynomials of this form with positive coefficients have no real roots.

3.13.36. ***Hint.*** Take advantage of the fact that a polynomial of an odd degree (and, hence also its second derivative) has at least one real root and changes sign at least once.

3.13.37. ***Hint.*** Find $\lim\limits_{x\to\infty}\left(\frac{2x^4 + x^3 + 1}{x^3 - 2x - 1}\right)$.

Chapter 4

4.1.2. $I = x^3 + x^2 + 0.5 \ln|2x - 1| + C$.

4.1.7. $I = \frac{2}{3}(x+1)^{\frac{3}{2}} + \frac{2}{3}x^{\frac{3}{2}} + C$. ***Hint.*** Eliminate the irrationality from the denominator.

4.1.14. $I = \frac{1}{10}\,\text{arc tan}\,\frac{2x}{5} + C$.

4.1.15. $I = \frac{2}{\sqrt{3}}\,\text{arc tan}\,\frac{2x+1}{\sqrt{3}} + C$.

4.1.18. $I = \ln|x + 3 + \sqrt{x^2 + 6x + 1}| + C$.

4.1.20. $I = \frac{1}{2\sqrt{70}}\ln\left|\frac{\sqrt{10}x - \sqrt{7}}{\sqrt{10}x + \sqrt{7}}\right| + C$.

4.1.21. (a) $\frac{1}{2}\,\text{arc tan}\,\frac{x-3}{2} + C$; (b) $\frac{3}{4}(x-4)\sqrt[3]{x} + C$;

(c) $3\tan x + 2\cot x + C$; (d) $-\dfrac{2}{x} + \text{arc tan}\, x + C$.

4.1.22. (a) $\ln(x + \sqrt{1 + x^2}) + \text{arc sin}\, x + C$; (b) $\sin x - \cos x + C$;

(c) $-\dfrac{2}{\ln 5} 5^{-x} + \dfrac{1}{5\ln 2} 2^{-x} + C$; (d) $-0.2\cos 5x - x\sin 5\alpha + C$.

4.2.3. $I = \dfrac{1}{12}\sqrt{(2x-5)^3} + \dfrac{5}{2}\sqrt{2x-5} - \dfrac{37}{4\sqrt{2x-5}} + C$.

4.2.8. $I = -2\sqrt{\cos x} + C$. **4.2.10.** $I = \dfrac{1}{2}(x^3 + 3x + 1)^{\frac{2}{3}} + C$.

4.2.13. (a) $0.75\sqrt[3]{(1 + \ln x)^4} + C$; (b) $\ln|\ln x| + C$; (c) $\dfrac{1}{2}\text{arc sin}\dfrac{x^2}{\sqrt{3}} + C$;

(d) $\dfrac{1}{na}\text{arc tan}\dfrac{x^n}{a} + C$; (e) $-2\cos\sqrt{x} + C$; (f) $\dfrac{1}{2}\ln^2 x + \ln|\ln x| + C$.

4.2.14. (a) $-\dfrac{3}{140}(35 - 40x + 14x^2)(1 - x)^{\frac{4}{3}} + C$;

(b) $\dfrac{2}{3}(\ln x - 5)\sqrt{1 + \ln x} + C$;

(c) $\left(\dfrac{2}{3} - \dfrac{2}{7}\sin^2 x + \dfrac{2}{11}\sin^4 x\right)\sqrt{\sin^3 x} + C$;

(d) $-\dfrac{1}{15}(8 + 4x^2 + 3x^4)\sqrt{1 - x^2} + C$.

4.3.2. $x\,\text{arc sin}\, x + \sqrt{1 - x^2} + C$.

4.3.14. $-\cos x \ln\tan x + \ln\left|\tan\left(\dfrac{x}{2}\right)\right| + C$.

4.3.17. $x\ln(x + \sqrt{1 + x^2}) - \sqrt{1 + x^2} + C$.

4.3.18. $\dfrac{3}{4}x\sqrt[3]{x}\left[(\ln x)^2 - \dfrac{3}{2}\ln x + \dfrac{9}{8}\right] + C$.

4.3.19. $2\sqrt{1 + x}\,\text{arc sin}\, x + 4\sqrt{1 - x} + C$.

4.3.20. $-0.5\left(\dfrac{x}{\sin^2 x} + \cot x\right) + C$.

4.3.21. $\dfrac{3^x(\sin x + \cos x \ln 3)}{1 + (\ln 3)^2} + C$.

4.3.22. $\left(\dfrac{1}{3}x^3 - x^2 + \dfrac{2}{3}x + \dfrac{13}{9}\right)e^{3x} + C$.

4.3.23. $(x^4 - 10x^2 + 21)\sin x + x(4x^2 - 20)\cos x + C$.

4.3.24. $\dfrac{9x^2 + 18x - 11}{27}\cos 3x + \dfrac{2x + 2}{9}\sin 3x + C$.

4.3.25. $\left(\dfrac{x^3}{3} - x^2 + 3x\right)\ln x - \dfrac{x^3}{9} + \dfrac{x^2}{2} - 3x + C$.

4.3.26. $\frac{x^4-1}{4}\text{arc tan } x - \frac{x^3}{12} + \frac{x^2}{4} + C.$

4.3.27. $\frac{x^3}{3}\text{arc cos } x - \frac{2+x^2}{9}\sqrt{1-x^2} + C.$

4.3.28. (a) $-\frac{18x^2+6x-13}{72}\sin(6x+2) - \frac{6x+1}{72}\cos(6x+2) + \frac{1}{2}x^3$

$+\frac{1}{4}x^2 - x + C;$ (b) $\frac{3}{4}(x^2-7x+1)(2x+1)^{\frac{2}{3}}$

$-\frac{9}{40}(2x-7)(2x+1)^{\frac{5}{3}} + \frac{27}{320}(2x+1)^{\frac{8}{3}} + C.$

4.4.2. (d) ***Hint.*** Apply the generalized formula for integration by parts and express I_n from the relation thus obtained

$$I_n = \frac{e^{\alpha x}}{\alpha^2}\sin^{n-1} x(\alpha\sin x - n\cos x) + \frac{n(n-1)}{\alpha^2}I_{n-2} - \frac{n^2}{\alpha^2}I_n.$$

4.4.3. $I_n = -\frac{\cos x}{(n-1)\sin^{n-1} x} + \frac{n-2}{n-1}I_{n-2}\ (n \geq 2);$

$$I_3 = -\frac{\cos x}{2\sin^2 x} + \frac{1}{2}I_1 = -\frac{\cos x}{2\sin^2 x} + \frac{1}{2}\ln\left|\tan\frac{x}{2}\right| + C.$$

4.4.4. (a) $I_n = \frac{1}{n-1}\tan^{n-1} x - I_{n-2}; I_1 = -\ln|\cos x| + C; I_0 = x + C;$

(b) $I_n = \frac{1}{n-1}\cot^{n-1} x - I_{n-2}; I_1 = \ln|\sin x| + C; I_0 = x + C;$

(c) $I_n = \frac{1}{n}x^{n-1}\sqrt{x^2+a} - \frac{n-1}{n}\alpha I_{n-2}; I_1 = \sqrt{x^2+a} + C;$

$I_0 = \ln|x + \sqrt{x^2+a}| + C.$

Chapter 5

5.1.2. $\frac{x^2}{2} - 2x + \frac{1}{6}\ln\left|\frac{x-1}{(x+1)^3}\right| + \frac{16}{3}\ln|x+2| + C.$

5.1.5. $2\ln|x-1| - \ln|x| - \frac{x}{(x-1)^2} + C.$

5.1.8. $\frac{2}{3\sqrt{7}}\text{arc tan}\frac{2x+1}{\sqrt{7}} - \frac{1}{3}\text{arc tan}(x+2) + C.$

5.1.10. $5x + \ln x^2(x+2)^4|x-2|^3 + C.$

5.1.11. $\frac{9x^2+50x+68}{4(x+2)(x+3)^2} + \frac{1}{8}\ln\left|\frac{(x+1)(x+2)^{16}}{(x+3)^{17}}\right| + C.$

5.1.12. $-\frac{1}{x-2} - \text{arc tan}(x-2) + C.$

5.1.13. $-\dfrac{1}{6(1+x)}+\dfrac{1}{6}\ln\dfrac{(1+x)^2}{1-x+x^2}+\dfrac{1}{2}\text{arc tan }x$

$-\dfrac{1}{3\sqrt{3}}\text{arc tan}\dfrac{2x-1}{\sqrt{3}}+C.$

5.1.14. $\dfrac{x+2}{2(x^2+1)}+2\,\text{arc tan }x+\ln\dfrac{\sqrt{x+1}}{\sqrt[4]{x^2+1}}+C.$

5.2.2. $4\sqrt[4]{x}+6\sqrt[6]{x}+24\sqrt[12]{x}+24\ln|\sqrt[12]{x}-1|+C.$

5.2.4. $-\dfrac{1}{\sqrt{3}}\text{arc tan}\dfrac{2t+1}{\sqrt{3}}+\ln\left|\dfrac{\sqrt[3]{(t+2)^4}}{\sqrt[3]{t-1}\cdot\sqrt{t^2+t+1}}\right|+C$, where $t=\sqrt[3]{\dfrac{x-1}{x}}$.

5.2.7. $\sqrt{\dfrac{x+1}{1-x}}+C.$ **5.2.8.** $\dfrac{3}{2}\sqrt[3]{\dfrac{1+x}{1-x}}+C.$

5.2.9. $\left(1-\dfrac{1}{2}x\right)\sqrt{1-x^2}-\dfrac{3}{2}\text{arc sin }x+C.$

5.3.3. $-2\,\text{arc tan}\left(\dfrac{\sqrt{1+x-x^2}+1}{x}+1\right)+C.$

5.3.5. $2\ln|\sqrt{x^2+2x+4}-x|-\dfrac{3}{2(\sqrt{x^2+2x+4}-x-1)}$

$-\dfrac{3}{2}\ln|\sqrt{x^2+2x+4}-x-1|+C.$

5.3.6. $\dfrac{1+\sqrt{1-x^2}}{x}+2\,\text{arc tan}\sqrt{\dfrac{1+x}{1-x}}+C.$

5.3.7. $\dfrac{x-1}{\sqrt{2x-x^2}}+C.$ **5.3.8.** $\dfrac{(x+\sqrt{1+x^2})^{15}}{15}+C.$

5.4.2. $\sqrt[5]{x^2+2x+5}-\ln(x+1+\sqrt{x^2+2x+5})+C.$

5.4.5. $\dfrac{3x^2+x-1}{3}\sqrt{3x^2-2x+1}+C.$

5.4.6. $\dfrac{2x+1}{4}\sqrt{x^2+x+1}+\dfrac{3}{8}\ln|2x+1+2\sqrt{x^2+x+1}|+C.$

5.4.8. $\dfrac{1}{3}(x^2-14x+111)\sqrt{x^2+4x+3}-66\ln|x+2+\sqrt{x^2+4x+3}|+C.$

5.4.9. $\dfrac{1}{64}(32x^2-20x-373)\sqrt{2x^2+5x+7}+\dfrac{3297}{128\sqrt{2}}\ln|4x+5$

$+2\sqrt{4x^2+10x+14}|+C.$

5.4.10. $\dfrac{3x+5}{8(x+1)^2}\sqrt{x^2+2x}-\dfrac{3}{8}\text{arc sin}\dfrac{1}{(x+1)}+C.$

5.4.11. $-\dfrac{\sqrt{x^2-4x+3}}{x-1}-2\,\text{arc sin}\dfrac{1}{x-2}+C.$

5.4.12. $-\frac{2}{15}\sqrt{\frac{x+2}{x+1}}\frac{8x^2+12x+7}{(x+1)^2}+C.$

5.4.13. $\ln\left|\frac{x^2+1+\sqrt{x^4+3x^2+1}}{x}\right|+C.$

Hint. First make the substitution $x^2=t$.

5.5.2. $3\arctan\sqrt[3]{x}+C.$ **5.5.4.** $\frac{2}{3}\left(2+x^{\frac{2}{3}}\right)^{\frac{9}{4}}-\frac{12}{5}\left(2+x^{\frac{2}{3}}\right)^{\frac{5}{4}}+C.$

5.5.5. $\frac{3}{22}(1+x^2)^{11/3}-\frac{3}{8}(1+x^2)^{8/3}+\frac{3}{10}(1+x^2)^{5/3}+C.$

5.5.7. $\frac{12}{7}\sqrt[3]{(1+\sqrt[4]{x})^7}-3\sqrt[3]{(1+\sqrt[4]{x})^4}+C.$

5.5.8. $3\ln\frac{\sqrt[3]{x}}{1+\sqrt[3]{x}}+\frac{3}{1+\sqrt[3]{x}}+C.$ **5.5.9.** $\frac{(1+x^2)^{3/2}(3x^2-2)}{15}+C.$

5.5.10. $\frac{\sqrt{1+x^2}\,(2x^2-1)}{3x^3}+C.$ **5.5.11.** $\frac{21}{32}\sqrt[7]{(1+\sqrt[3]{x^4})^8}+C.$

5.5.12. $\frac{5}{4}\left(1+\frac{1}{x}\right)^{4/5}-\frac{5}{9}\left(1+\frac{1}{x}\right)^{9/5}+C.$ **5.6.2.** $\frac{1}{3\sin^3 x}-\frac{1}{5\sin^5 x}+C.$

5.6.6. $\tan x+\frac{1}{3}\tan^3 x+C$.

5.6.10. (a) $-\cot x+\frac{1}{3}\cot^3 x-\frac{1}{5}\cot^5 x-x+C;$

(b) $\frac{1}{2}\tan^2 x-\frac{1}{2}\ln(1+\tan^2 x)+C=\frac{1}{2}\tan^2 x+\ln|\cos x|+C.$

5.6.12. $-\sin x-\frac{1}{3}\sin^3 x+\frac{1}{2}\ln\left|\frac{1+\sin x}{1-\sin x}\right|+C$.

5.6.14. $\frac{2}{\sqrt{15}}\arctan\left(\frac{1+2\tan\frac{x}{2}}{\sqrt{15}}\right)+C$.

5.6.22. (a) $-\frac{x}{8}+\frac{\sinh 4x}{32}+C;$ (b) $\frac{2}{\sqrt{3}}\arctan\left(\frac{2\tanh\frac{x}{2}+1}{\sqrt{3}}\right)+C.$

5.7.3. $\frac{-1}{8}\ln(x+\sqrt{x^2-1})+\frac{1}{8}x(2x^2-1)\sqrt{x^2-1}+C.$

5.7.4. $\ln(x+\sqrt{x^2+1})-\frac{\sqrt{x^2+1}}{x}+C$.

5.7.7. $I=\arcsin\frac{x+1}{2}+C$.

5.7.8. $I=\frac{x-1}{4\sqrt{x^2-2x+5}}+C.$

5.8.2. $I = 4\sqrt{1-x} + 2\ln(2 - x - 2\sqrt{1-x}) - 2(1 + \sqrt{1-x})\ln x + C.$

5.8.5. $I = e^{\alpha t}\dfrac{\alpha\cos t + \sin t}{\alpha^2 + 1} + C$, where $t = \text{arc tan } x$.

Chapter 6

6.1.9. $I = 4\cdot\dfrac{3+19}{2} = 44$ as the area of a trapezoid whose height is $5 - 1 = 4$ and bases $4 \times 1 - 1 = 3$ and $4 \times 5 - 1 = 19$.

6.1.12. $s_n = 16\frac{1}{4} - \dfrac{175}{2n} + \dfrac{125}{4n^2}; S_n = 16\frac{1}{4} + \dfrac{175}{2n} + \dfrac{125}{4n^2}.$

6.2.2. (a) 1; (b) $\frac{3}{2}$; (c) $\frac{\pi}{6}$.

6.2.10. (a) $\frac{7}{72}$; (b) $\frac{1}{2}\ln\frac{3}{2}$; (c) π; (d) $\frac{\pi}{4} - \text{arc tan}\frac{\pi}{4}$; (e) ln 2; (f) 1; (g) $\text{arc tan } e - \frac{\pi}{4}$; (h) $\frac{\pi}{16}$; (i) $\frac{14}{15}$; (j) $\frac{4}{3}$; (k) $\dfrac{\sqrt{3}-\sqrt{2}}{2}$.

6.3.1. (c) $3 < I < 5$. ***Hint.*** $M = f(0) = \frac{5}{2}$, $m = f(2) = \frac{3}{2}$.

6.3.11. (a) $\dfrac{\sin 2x}{x}$; (b) $-\sqrt{1 + x^4}$. **6.3.14.** (b) $\dfrac{\pi^2}{4}$.

6.3.15. (b) $\dfrac{dy}{dx} = -e^{-y}\sin x$. **6.3.23.** (a) ln x; (b) $\dfrac{3}{x}$.

6.3.24. (a) $y'_x = \dfrac{t}{\ln t}$; (b) $y'_x = \dfrac{\tan t}{t^2}$.

6.3.25. (a) The maximum is at $x = 1$, the minimum at $x = -1$; (b) the minima are at $x = -2; 0; 2$, the maxima at $x = \pm 1$.

6.4.3. (a) $\dfrac{\pi a^4}{16}$ (substitution $x = a\sin t$); (b) $\dfrac{\sqrt{3}-\sqrt{2}}{2}$ (substitution $x = \tan t$).

6.4.6. (a) $\sqrt{2} - \dfrac{2}{\sqrt{3}} + \ln\dfrac{2+\sqrt{3}}{1+\sqrt{2}}$; (b) $2(\sqrt{3} - 1)$; (c) $8 + \dfrac{3\sqrt{3}}{2}\pi$.

6.4.15. (a) $2 - 2\ln 2$; (b) $0.2 \ln 112$; (c) $\dfrac{\sin\frac{\pi}{24}}{\sin\frac{\pi}{8}\sin\frac{\pi}{12}}$; (d) $\sqrt{3} - 0.5\ln(2 + \sqrt{3})$; (e) 0.25 ln 3 (substitution $\sin x - \cos x = t$); (f) $a^3\left(\dfrac{\pi}{4} - \dfrac{2}{3}\right)$ (substitution $x = a\cos t$); (g) $\dfrac{\pi a^2}{2}$ (substitution $x = 2a\sin^2 t$); (h) $\frac{\pi}{4} + \frac{1}{2}$.

6.4.16. (a) $\frac{\pi}{6}$; (b) $\frac{\pi}{4}$; (c) $\frac{1}{4}\ln\frac{32}{17}$ (substitution $x^4 = t$); (d) $\dfrac{\pi}{12}$ (substitution $x^2 = a^2\cos^2 t + b^2\sin^2 t$).

6.4.17. The substitution $x = \frac{1}{t}$ will not do, since this function is discontinuous at $t = 0$.

6.4.18. The substitution $t = \tan \frac{x}{2}$ will not do, since this function is discontinuous at $x = \pi$.

6.4.19. ***Hint.*** The inverse function $x = \pm \sqrt{t^5}$ is double-valued. To obtain the correct result it is necessary to divide the initial interval of integration into two parts :

$$\int_{-2}^{2} \sqrt[5]{x^2}\,dx = \int_{-2}^{0} \sqrt[5]{x^2}\,dx + \int_{0}^{2} \sqrt[5]{x^2}\,dx$$

and apply the substitutions $x = -\sqrt{t^5}$ in $-2 < x < 0$ and $x = +\sqrt{t^5}$ in $0 < x < 2$.

6.4.20. It is impossible, since $\sec t \geq 1$ and the interval of integration is [0, 1].

6.4.21. It is possible; see Problem **6.4.12.**

6.4.22. ***Hint.*** On writing $\int_{-a}^{a} f(x)\,dx = \int_{-a}^{0} f(x)dx + \int_{-0}^{a} f(x)dx$, make the substitution $x = -t$ in the first integral.

6.4.23. $\int_0^1 f(\text{arc sin}\, t)\,dt + \int_1^{-1} f(\pi - \text{arc sin}\, t)\,dt + \int_{-1}^{0} f(2\pi + \text{arc sin}\, t)\,dt$.

Hint. Represent the given integral as the sum of three integrals for the intervals : $\left(0, \frac{\pi}{2}\right), \left(\frac{\pi}{2}, \frac{3\pi}{2}\right), \left(\frac{3\pi}{2}, 2\pi\right)$ and substitute the variable: $x = \text{arc sin}\, t$, $x = \pi - \text{arc sin}\, t$, $x = 2\pi + \text{arc sin}\, t$ respectively.

6.5.3. (1) If $f(x)$ is an even function, then

$$\int_{-\pi}^{\pi} f(x) \cos nx\,dx = 2\int_0^{\pi} f(x) \cos nx\,dx, \text{ and } \int_{-\pi}^{\pi} f(x) \sin x\,dx = 0.$$

(2) If $f(x)$ is an odd function, then $\int_{-\pi}^{\pi} f(x) \cos nx\,dx = 0$, and $\int_{-\pi}^{\pi} f(x) \sin nx\,dx = 2\int_0^{\pi} f(x) \sin n\,dx$.

6.5.4. 0. **6.6.3.** $-2e$. **6.6.5.** $\pi\sqrt{2} - 4$. **6.6.6.** $\pi - 2$.

6.6.13. (a) $\frac{\pi}{2} - 1$; (b) $-\frac{1}{e}$; (c) $\frac{\pi}{4} - \frac{\sqrt{3}}{9}\pi + \frac{1}{2}\ln\frac{3}{2}$; (d) $\frac{\pi}{4} - \frac{1}{2}$; (e) $\ln 2 - \frac{1}{2}$; (f) $\ln\frac{2}{8}$; (g) $\frac{\pi}{2} - 1$; (h) $\frac{16\pi}{3} - 2\sqrt{3}$.

6.6.14. ***Hint.*** Integrate by parts twice, putting $u = (\text{arc cos}\, x)^n$ the first time and $u = (\text{arc cos}\, x)^{n-1}$ the second time.

6.6.15. ***Hint.*** Integrate by parts, putting $u = x$.

6.7.4. (a) 0.601. ***Hint.*** Estimate $|f^{\text{IV}}(x)|$ on the interval $\left[\frac{\pi}{4}, \frac{\pi}{2}\right]$ and put $2n = 6$; (b) 0.7462. **6.7.5.** 0.96

6.8.1. $F(x) = \begin{cases} \dfrac{x - x^2}{2} & \text{for } 0 \leq x \leq 1, \\ \dfrac{1}{2} & \text{for } 1 < x \leq 2, \\ \dfrac{(x-2)^3}{3} + \dfrac{1}{2} & \text{for } 2 < x \leq 3. \end{cases}$

Continuity is checked directly. The assertion concerning the derivative requires checking only at the points $x = 1$, $x = 2$.

6.8.2. ***Hint.*** Make sure that the function $f(x)$ is continuous both inside the interval $(0, 1)$ and at the end-points ($\lim\limits_{x\to+0} f(x) = f(0)$ and $\lim\limits_{x\to1-0} f(x) = f(1)$).

6.8.3. No. ***Hint.*** Consider the function

$$\varphi(x) = \begin{cases} 1 \text{ if } x \text{ is rational,} \\ -1 \text{ if } x \text{ is irrational on the interval } [0, 1]. \end{cases}$$

6.8.4. $1 - \sqrt{3}$. ***Hint.*** $\int_a^b f''(x)\,dx = f'(b) - f'(a)$.

6.8.5. ***Hint.*** Putting for definiteness $x > 0$ and $E(x) = n \le x < n + 1$, take advantage of the additivity of the integral

$$\int_0^x E(x)\,dx = \int_0^1 E(x)\,dx + \int_1^2 E(x)\,dx + \ldots + \int_{n-1}^n E(x)\,dx + \int_n^x E(x)\,dx.$$

6.8.6. The antiderivative $F_1(x)$ will lead to the correct result and $F_2(x)$ to the wrong one, since this function is discontinuous in the interval $[0, \pi]$.

6.8.7. $F(x) = y_0 + \int_{x_0}^x f(t)\,dt$. ***Hint.*** Any antiderivative $F(x)$ can be represented in the form $F(x) = \int_{x_0}^x f(t)\,dt + C$. Putting $x = x_0$, find $C = y_0$.

6.8.8. $\xi = \frac{1}{2} \ln \frac{e^{2b} - e^{2a}}{2b - 2a}$.

6.8.9. The function is defined on the interval $[-1, 1]$, it is odd, and increasing; convex on the interval $[-1, 0]$ and concave on the interval $[0, 1]$; the point $[0, 0]$ is a point of inflection.

6.8.10. ***Hint.*** The function

$$f(x) = \begin{cases} x^x \text{ at } 0 < x \le 1 \\ 1 \text{ at } x = 0 \end{cases}$$

is continuous on the interval, it reaches the least value $m = e^{-\frac{1}{e}} \approx 0.692$ at $x = \frac{1}{e}$ and the greatest value $M = 1$ at $x = 0$ and at $x = 1$.

6.8.11. ***Hint.*** Integrate the inequality $\frac{2}{\pi} \le \frac{\sin x}{x} \le 1$.

6.8.12. ***Hint.*** Integrate the inequality

$$\sqrt{x \sin x} > \sqrt{x^2 - \frac{x^4}{6}} = x\sqrt{1 - \frac{x^2}{6}} \text{ at } 0 \le x \le \frac{\pi}{6}$$

and write Schwarz-Bunyakovsky inequality

$$\int_0^{\frac{\pi}{2}} \sqrt{x \sin x}\,dx \le \sqrt{\int_0^{\frac{\pi}{2}} x\,dx \int_0^{\frac{\pi}{2}} \sin x\,dx} = \sqrt{\frac{\pi^2}{8}} = \frac{\pi}{2\sqrt{2}}$$

6.8.14. ***Hint.*** Apply the Schwarz-Bunyakovsky inequality in the form

$$\left[\int_a^b \sqrt{f(x)\cdot\frac{1}{f(x)}}\,dx\right]^2 \le \int_a^b f(x)\,dx \int_a^b \frac{1}{f(x)}\,dx.$$

6.8.15. ***Hint.*** Make the substitution $\arctan x = \frac{t}{2}$.

6.8.16. ***Hint.*** If $f(x)$ is an even function, then $F(x) = \int_0^x f(t)\,dt$ is an odd function, since

$$F(-x) = \int_0^{-x} f(t)\,dt = -\int_0^x f(-z)\,dz = -F(x)\ (t = -z).$$

And if $f(x)$ is an odd function, then $F(x) = \int_0^x f(t)\,dt$ is an even function, since

$$F(-x) = \int_0^{-x} f(t)\,dt = -\int_0^x f(-z)\,dz = F(x)\ (t = -z);$$

all the remaining antiderivatives have the form $F(x) + C$ and, therefore, are also even functions.

6.8.17. ***Hint.*** The derivative of the integral I with respect to a equals zero: $\frac{dI}{da} = f(a+T) - f(a) = 0$.

Chapter 7

7.1.4. (a) ln 2; (b) $\frac{2}{3}(2\sqrt{2}-1)$; (c) $\frac{3}{4}$; (d) 1; (e) $\frac{1}{2}$.

7.2.2. (a) $\frac{1}{2}$; (b) $\frac{1}{2} + \frac{1}{2}\ln\frac{2}{e+1} \approx 0.283$. **7.2.5.** $\frac{\pi}{4}$. **7.2.10.** $\frac{2i}{h\sqrt{d^2+h^2}}$.

7.2.13. (a) $\mu = \frac{5}{3}$; (b) $\mu = \ln 2$; (c) $\mu = \frac{8}{\ln 3} + 2$. **7.2.15.** $\frac{2h}{3}$.

7.2.16. $\frac{2I_0}{\pi}$. **7.3.4.** $\frac{35}{6}$. **7.3.6.** $\frac{2}{3} + \frac{5}{2}\arcsin\frac{3}{5}$. **7.3.11.** $\frac{8}{15}$.

7.3.13. 9. **7.3.16.** $\frac{1}{m+1}$.

7.3.19. $\frac{64}{3}$. **7.3.20.** $\frac{8}{3}$. **7.3.21.** $2\pi - (2\sqrt{3})\ln(2+\sqrt{3})$.

7.3.22. 0.75π. **7.3.23.** $\frac{128}{15}$. **7.3.24.** $\frac{1}{3}$. **7.3.25.** $\frac{4}{3}$. **7.3.26.** $\frac{8}{15}$.

7.3.27. $\frac{1}{12}$. **7.3.28.** $\frac{91}{30}$. **7.4.6.** $\frac{8}{5}$.

7.4.8. $0.75\pi ab$. ***Hint.*** The curve is symmetrical about the coordinate axes and intersects them at the points $x = \pm a$, $y = \pm b$.

7.4.9. (a) $\frac{8}{15}$. ***Hint.*** The curve is symmetrical about the x-axis, intersection it twice at the origin at $t = \pm 1$. The loop is situated in the second and third quadrants; (b) $\frac{8}{15}$. ***Hint.*** The points of self-intersection of the curve are found in the following way : $y = tx(t)$, therefore $y(t_1) = t_1 x(t_1) = t_2 x(t_2)$ at $t_1 \neq t_2$ and $x(t_1) = x(t_2)$, only if $x(t_1) = x(t_2) = 0$, *ie*, $t_1 = 0$; $t_2 = 2$; (c) $\frac{8\sqrt{3}}{5}$.

7.4. 10. $0.25\,\pi ab$. ***Hint.*** The curve is symmetrical with respect to both axes of coordinates and passes twice through the origin forming two loops. Therefore, it is sufficient to compute a quarter of the desired area corresponding to the variation of t from 0 to $\frac{\pi}{2}$ and multiply the obtained result by 4.

7.4.11. $\frac{3c^4\pi}{8ab}$. ***Hint.*** The curve resembles an astroid extended in the vertical direction.

7.5.2. (a) $\frac{3\pi}{2}$; (b) $\frac{\pi a^2}{4}$. ***Hint.*** The curve is a circle of radius $\frac{a}{2}$ passing through the pole and symmetrical about the polar axis, $-\frac{\pi}{2} \le \varphi \le \frac{\pi}{2}$.

7.5.6. $2a^2\left(\frac{5\pi}{8} - 1\right)$. **7.5.8.** (a) $\frac{\pi a^2}{8}$; (b) $\frac{\pi a^2}{8}$. **7.5.9.** $a^2\left(\frac{7\pi}{12} - \sqrt{3}\right)$.

7.5.10. $\frac{\pi a^2}{32}$. ***Hint.*** The curve passes through the pole forming two loops located symmetrically about the y-axis in the first and fourth quadrants. It is sufficient to calculate the area enclosed by one loop corresponding to variation of φ from 0 to $\frac{\pi}{2}$ and double the result thus obtained.

7.5.11. $\frac{5}{32}\pi a^2$. ***Hint.*** The curve passes through the pole, it is symmetrical about the polar axis and situated in the first and fourth quadrants. It is sufficient to calculate the area of the upper portion of the figure which corresponds to variation of φ from 0 to $\frac{\pi}{2}$ and double the result thus obtained.

7.5.12. $a^2\left(1 + \frac{\pi}{6} - \frac{\sqrt{3}}{2}\right)$.

7.5.13. $\frac{\pi a^2}{2}$. ***Hint.*** The curve is symmetrical about the coordinate axes and intersects them only at the origin, forming four loops-one in each quadrant (*a four-leaved rose*). Therefore, it is sufficient to find the area of one loop corresponding to the variation of φ from 0 to $\frac{\pi}{2}$ and multiply the result by 4.

7.5.14. $\sqrt{2}\,\pi a^2$. ***Hint.*** The curve is symmetrical about the axes of coordinates and the bisectors of the coordinate angles; it cuts off equal intercepts on the axes. The origin is an isolated point. It is sufficient to compute the area of one-eighth of the figure corresponding to variation of φ from 0 to $\frac{\pi}{4}$ and multiply the result by 8.

7.6.2. $9\frac{2}{3}\pi$. ***Hint.*** A plane perpendicular to the x-axis at the point x will cut the sphere along a circle of radius $r=\sqrt{16-x^2}$, therefore the cross-sectional area $S(x)=\pi(16-x^2)$.

7.6.5. $0.5\,\pi a^2 h$. ***Hint.*** The area of a triangle situated at a distance x from the centre of the circle is equal to $h\sqrt{a^2-x^2}$.

7.6.10. $2\pi^2 a^2 b$. **7.6.11.** $\frac{8}{7}$ (see Problem **7.3.9**). **7.6.14.** $5\pi^2 a^3$.

7.6.16. (a) $2\pi ab\left(1+\frac{1}{3c^2}\right)$; (b) $\frac{16}{3}a$; (c) $\frac{1}{2}abk^2\pi$.

7.6.17. $\frac{2}{3}a^3\tan\alpha$.

7.6.18. (a) 12π; (b) $\frac{16}{15}\pi$; (c) $\frac{64}{5}\pi$; (d) π^2; (e) $\frac{64}{3}\pi$; (f) $\frac{4}{3}\pi a^3$.

7.6.19. $\frac{\pi a^3}{20}$. **7.6.20.** $\frac{\pi^2}{12}$.

7.6.21. $\frac{1}{4}\pi a^3(e^{2c/a}-e^{-2c/a})+\pi a^2 c=\frac{\pi a^3}{2}\sinh\frac{2c}{a}+\pi a^2 c$.

7.6.22. $\frac{\pi}{20}(6\pi+5\sqrt{3})$. ***Hint.*** The abscissas of the points of intersection are: $x_1=-\frac{\pi}{3}$; $x_2=\frac{\pi}{3}$. **7.6.23.** $\frac{19}{48}\pi$. **7.6.24.** $\frac{127}{7}\pi$. **7.6.25.** $\frac{26\pi c^6}{105ab^2}$.

Hint. Represent the evoluate of the ellipse parametrically as follows: $x=\frac{c^2}{a}\cos^3 t$; $y=\frac{c^2}{b}\sin^3 t$, where $c=\sqrt{a^2-b^2}$.

7.6.26. $\frac{4}{3}\pi a^3$.

7.6.27. $\frac{\pi^2 a^3}{4\sqrt{2}}$; $\frac{\pi a^3}{4}\left[\sqrt{2}\ln(1+\sqrt{2})-\frac{2}{3}\right]$. ***Hint.*** Pass over to polar coordinates.

7.6.28. $\frac{4}{21}\pi a^3$. **7.7.2.** $\frac{112}{27}$. **7.7.4.** $\ln\frac{e^b-e^{-b}}{e^a-e^{-a}}$.

7.7.8. (a) $\sqrt{6}+\ln(\sqrt{2}+\sqrt{3})$; (b) $2\ln(2-\sqrt{3})$. ***Hint.*** $x_1=-\frac{\pi}{2}$; $x_2=\frac{\pi}{3}$; (c) $\frac{2\sqrt{3}}{3}$. **7.7.9.** $\frac{a(a+2)}{2}$.

7.7.10. $10\left(\frac{67}{27}+\sqrt{5}\right)$. **7.8.2.** $8a$. **7.8.5.** $\frac{13}{3}$.

Hint. The curve intersects the axes at $t_1=0$ and $t_2=\sqrt[4]{8}$.

7.8.7. $4\sqrt{3}$. **7.8.8.** $16a$. **7.8.9.** $8\pi a$. ***Hint.*** See Fig. 79.

7.8.10. $\frac{4(a^3-b^3)}{ab}$. **7.8.11.** $\frac{\pi^3}{3}$.

7.8.12. At $t = \frac{2\pi}{3}$ the point $M\left[a\left(\frac{2\pi}{3} - \frac{\sqrt{3}}{2}\right), \frac{3a}{2}\right]$. **7.9.5.** $1.5\pi a$.

7.9.9. $\frac{5}{12} + \ln\frac{3}{2}$. **7.9.10.** $2\sqrt{2}\,\pi a$.

Hint. The curve $\rho = 2\sqrt{2}\,a\cos\left(\varphi - \frac{\pi}{4}\right)$ is a circle.

7.9.11. $p[\sqrt{2} + \ln(1 + \sqrt{2})]$. **7.10.3.** (a) $\frac{14\pi}{3}$; (b) $\frac{62\pi}{3}$.

7.10.5. $2\pi\left(1 + \frac{4\pi}{3\sqrt{3}}\right)$. **7.10.8.** $\frac{\pi}{2}$. **7.10.14.** $(34\sqrt{17} - 2)\frac{\pi}{9}$.

7.10.15. $2\pi[\sqrt{2} + \ln(1 + \sqrt{2})]$. **7.10.16.** $\frac{56}{3}\pi a^2$.

7.10.17. $\frac{2\sqrt{2}}{5}\pi(e^{\pi} - 2)$. **7.10.18.** 29.6π. **7.10.19.** $4\pi^2 a^2$.

7.10.20. $\frac{128}{5}\pi a^2$.

7.11.7. $16a^2$ where a is the radius of the cylinders base.

7.11.8. 1.5π. **7.11.10.** (a) $\frac{8}{15}$; (b) $\frac{7}{50} - \frac{1}{4}\arctan\frac{1}{2}$.

7.11.11. (a) $\frac{\pi a^2}{4}$; (b) $\frac{p^2}{6}(3 + 4\sqrt{2})$; (c) $\frac{1}{8}(5\pi + 6\sqrt{3})$.

7.11.13. $\frac{a}{2}(2\ln 3 - 1)$. **7.11.14.** $\frac{\sqrt{2}}{3}(5\sqrt{5} - 2\sqrt{2})$.

7.11.17. $2\pi\frac{\sqrt{3}}{15}$. **7.11.18.** $\pi a^2\sqrt{pq}$. **7.11.19.** $\pi ab\left(\frac{l^3}{3c^2} - l + \frac{2c}{3}\right)$.

7.11.20. $\frac{\pi abh}{3}$. **7.11.21.** 12π. **7.11.22.** $\left(\frac{4\sqrt{3} - 6}{9}\right)\pi b^2 a$.

7.11.23. $\frac{4}{21}\pi a^3$.

7.11.24. (a) $\pi\left[(\sqrt{5} - \sqrt{2}) + (\sqrt{2} + 1)\frac{\sqrt{5} - 1}{2}\right]$;

(b) $\frac{4\pi a^2}{243}\left(21\sqrt{13} + 2\ln\frac{3 + \sqrt{13}}{2}\right)$; (c) $2\pi rh$. **7.12.2.** $\frac{2}{3}\gamma R^3$.

7.12.4. $\frac{\pi R^4}{4}$. **7.12.9.** $\frac{MR^2\omega^2}{4}$. **7.12.11.** $\pi abhd$. **7.12.12.** πrdh^2.

7.12.13. $\frac{1}{12}\pi R^2 H$. **7.13.3.** $0.25\pi R^3$.

7.13.7. $M_x = \frac{1}{3}(5\sqrt{5} - 1)$; $M_y = \frac{9}{8}\sqrt{5} + \frac{1}{16}\ln(2 + \sqrt{5})$.

7.13.8. $M_x = \frac{b}{2}\sqrt{a^2 + b^2}$; $M_y = \frac{a}{2}\sqrt{a^2 + b^2}$.

7.13.9. $\sqrt{2} + \ln(1+\sqrt{2})$. **7.13.10.** 0.15.

7.13.11. $I_x = \frac{ab^3}{12}$; $I_y = \frac{a^3b}{12}$. **7.13.12.** $\frac{(a+3b)h^3}{12}$.

7.13.16. $x_c = y_c = 0.4a$.

7.13.19. $x_c = y_c = \frac{a}{5}$. **7.13.26.** $x_c = R\frac{\sin\alpha}{\alpha}$; $y_c = 0$.

7.13.28. $x_c = \frac{5a}{8}$; $y_c = 0$.

7.13.29. $x_c = -\frac{0.2(2e^{2\pi} - e^{\pi})}{e^{\pi} - e^{\pi/2}}$; $y_c = \frac{0.2a(e^{2\pi} - 2e^{\pi})}{e^{\pi} - e^{\pi/2}}$. **7.13.30.** $4.5\pi a^3$.

7.13.31. $x_c = 0$; $y_c = \frac{4R}{3\pi}$.

7.14.1. $\left|\frac{m-n}{m+n}\right|$; $4\left|\frac{m-n}{m+n}\right|$ if both m and n are even; $2\left|\frac{m-n}{m+n}\right|$ if both m and n are odd; $\left|\frac{m-n}{m+n}\right|$ if m and n are of different evenness. ***Hint.*** The curves $y^m = x^n$ and $y^n = x^m$ have two common points (0, 0) and (1, 1) in the first quadrant. The area of the figure situated in the first quadrant is equal to $\left|\int_0^1 (x^{n/m} - x^{m/n})\,dx\right|$. Depending on evenness and oddness of m and n this figure is mapped symmetrically either about the coordinate axes (m, n even) or about the origin (m, n odd). If m and n are of different evenness, then the curves enclose only the area lying in the first quadrant.

7.14.3. ***Hint.*** Take advantage of the formula for computing the area in polar coordinates.

7.14.4. ***Hint.*** Since the figure are of equal area, the function $S(x)$ appearing in the formula for the volume $V = \int_a^b S(x)\,dx$ is the same and, consequently, the values of the integrals are also equal.

7.14.5. ***Hint.*** The formula follows directly from Simpson's formula

$$\int_0^h f(x)\,dx = \frac{h}{6}\left[f(0) + 4f\left(\frac{h}{2}\right) + f(h)\right],$$

for a sphere $S(x) = \pi(r^2 - x^2)$; for a cone $S(x) = \frac{\pi r^2 x^2}{h^2}$; for a paraboloid of revolution $S(x) = 2\pi px$ and so on.

7.14.6. ***Hint.*** Divide the curvilinear trapezoid into strips Δx wide and write an expression for the element of volume $\Delta V = 2\pi\, xy\,\Delta x$.

7.14.8. ***Hint.*** Use the formula for calculating the length of a curve represented parametrically.

7.14.9. $\ln\frac{\pi}{2}$. ***Hint.*** The point ($t = 1$) nearest to the origin with a vertical tangent corresponds to $t = \frac{\pi}{2}$.

7.14.13. $2\pi\frac{\sqrt{3}}{15}$. **7.14.14.** $\sqrt{2}\cdot z$.

7.14.16. (a) $0.5\ln(x+y)$; (b) $\frac{\pi}{4}-0.5\arcsin x$

Chapter 8

8.1.2. (b) $\frac{1}{2}\ln 2$; (c) 1; (d) $1-\ln 2$; (e) π; (f) $\frac{1}{2}$.

8.1.6. (a) It diverges. ***Hint.*** $\frac{\ln(x^2+1)}{x}>\frac{1}{x}$ for $x>\sqrt{e-1}$; (b) converges; (c) diverges. ***Hint.*** $\frac{2+\cos x}{\sqrt{x}}>\frac{1}{\sqrt{x}}$; (d) converges; (e) diverges.

8.1.17. (a) 0. ***Hint.*** Represent the integral as the sum of two items : $\int_0^{\infty}\frac{\ln x}{1+x^2}dx=\int_0^1\frac{\ln x}{1+x^2}dx+\int_1^{\infty}\frac{\ln x}{1+x^2}dx$. Make the substitution $x=\frac{1}{t}$ in the second summand and show that $\int_1^{\infty}\frac{\ln x}{1+x^2}dx=-\int_0^1\frac{\ln x}{1+x^2}dx$; (b) $\frac{m!}{2}$.

8.2.2. (a) $9a^{2/3}$; (b) it diverges; (c) diverges; (d) $6\sqrt[3]{2}$; (e) $\frac{\pi}{3}$; (f) converges for $p<1$ and diverges for $p\geq 1$.

8.2.7. (a) It converges; (b) diverges; (c) converges; (d) converges; (e) diverges; (f) converges. **8.2.11.** (a) It diverges; (b) $2\sqrt{\ln 2}$; (c) $\frac{51}{7}$.

8.2.14. (a) It converges; (b) diverges; (c) diverges; (d) converges; (e) converges. **8.3.7.** (a) $\frac{\pi}{2}$; (a) 2π. **8.3.8.** $3\pi a^2$. **8.3.9.** $\frac{1}{2}$.

8.3.10. $\frac{4\pi}{3}$.

8.3.14. mgR. ***Hint.*** The law of attraction of a body by the Earth is determined by the formula $f=\frac{mgR^2}{r^2}$, where m is the mass of the body, r is the distance between the body and the centre of the Earth, R is the radius of the Earth.

8.3.15. e_1 . ***Hint.*** Electric charges interact with a force $\frac{e_1e_2}{r^2}$, where e_1 and e_2 are the magnitudes of the charges and r is the distance between them.

8.4.1. ***Hint.*** Represent the integral in the form of the sum

$$\int_1^{+\infty}\frac{dx}{x^p\ln^q x}=\int_1^{a}\frac{dx}{x^p\ln^q x}+\int_a^{+\infty}\frac{dx}{x^p\ln^q x}\ (a>1)$$

and apply special tests for convergence, taking into consideration that in the first integral $\ln x=\ln[1+(x-1)]\sim x-1$ as $x\to 1$, and in the second integral the logarithmic function increases slower for $q<0$ than any power function.

8.4.2. *Hint.* Making the substitution $x^q = t$, reduce the given integral to the form $\pm\frac{1}{q}\int_0^{+\infty}\frac{p+1}{t^{q-1}}\sin t\,dt$. Represent the integral $\int_0^{+\infty}\frac{p+1}{t^{q-1}}\sin t\,dt$ as the sum $\int_0^1\frac{\sin t}{t^\alpha}dt + \int_1^{+\infty}\frac{\sin t}{t^\alpha}$ where $\alpha = 1 - \frac{p+1}{q}$, and show that the integral converges absolutely for $1 < \alpha < 2$ and conditionally for $0 < \alpha \le 1$. Note that at $\frac{p+1}{q} = 0$ the integral is reduced to the conditionally converging integral $\int_0^{+\infty}\frac{\sin t}{t}dt$, and at $\frac{p+1}{q} = -1$ to the diverging integral $\int_0^{+\infty}\frac{\sin t}{t^2}dt$.

8.4.3 *Hint.* Represent the given integral as the sum $\int_0^{1/2} x^{p-1}(1-x)^{q-1}dx + \int_{1/2}^1 x^{p-1}(1-x)^{q-1}dx$ and apply the special comparison test.

8.4.4. *Hint.* if $|\alpha| \neq |\beta|$, then $\int_0^T \sin\alpha x \cdot \sin\beta x\,dx$ is bounded.

8.4.5. *Hint.* By substituting $t = x^2$ the integral is reduced to the Euler gamma-function.

8.4.6. *Hint.* $\int_a^\infty \frac{f(\alpha x) - f(\beta x)}{x}dx = \int_{a\alpha}^\infty \frac{f(x)}{x}dx - \int_{a\beta}^\infty \frac{f(x)}{x}dx$

$$= \int_{a\alpha}^{a\beta}\frac{f(x)}{x}dx = A\ln\frac{\beta}{\alpha} + \int_{\alpha a}^{\beta a}\frac{f(x)-A}{x}dx.$$

Applying the generalized mean value theorem, show that the last integral tends to zero as $a \to 0$.

8.4.7. *Hint.* Take the function $f(x) = e^{-x}$ for the first integral, the function $f(x) = \cos x$ for the second and take advantage of the results of Problem 8.4.6.

8.4.8. It converges for $m < 3$ and diverges for $m \ge 3$. ***Hint.*** Take advantage of the equivalence of $1 - \cos x$ and $\frac{x^2}{2}$ as $x \to 0$.

8.4.9. *Hint.* Represent $\int_0^\pi \frac{dx}{(\sin x)^k}$ as the sum of two integrals $\int_0^{\frac{\pi}{2}}\frac{dx}{(\sin x)^k} + \int_{\frac{\pi}{2}}^{\pi}\frac{dx}{(\sin x)^k}$; reduce the second integral to the first one by making the substitution $x = \pi - t$ and take advantage of the equivalence of $\sin x$ and x as $x \to 0$.

8.4.10. *Hint.* $\int_0^\infty \frac{\sin x\,(1-\cos x)}{x^s}dx = \int_0^{\pi/2}\frac{\sin x\,(1-\cos x)}{x^s}dx + \int_{\pi/2}^\infty \frac{\sin x\,(1-\cos x)}{x^s}dx$. The integrand of the first summand on the right side is an infinitely large quantity of order $s-3$ as $x \to 0$. By the special comparison test the first integral converges absolutely for $s - 3 < 1$, *ie*, $s < 4$, and diverges for $s \geq 4$. The second integral in the right side converges absolutely for $s > 1$, since the function $\sin x(1 - \cos x)$ is bounded. But if $0 < s \leq 1$, the second integral converges conditionally as the difference of two conditionally converging integrals $\int_{\pi/2}^{\infty} \frac{\sin x}{x^s}\,dx$ and $\int_{\pi/2}^{\infty} \frac{\sin x \cdot \cos x}{x^s}\,ds$ (see Problem 8.1.13).

8.4.11. ***Hint.*** Integral (2) can diverge. For example, let

$$\phi(x) = \begin{cases} 1, & 2n\pi \leq x \leq (2n+1)\,\pi, \\ -1, & (2n+1)\,\pi < x < (2n+2)\,\pi. \end{cases}$$

The integral $\int_0^{\infty} \frac{\sin x}{x}\,dx$ converges (see Problem 8.1.13). But $\int_0^{\infty} \frac{\sin x}{x}\,\phi(x)\,dx = \int_0^{\infty} \frac{|\sin x|}{x}\,dx$ diverges (see the same problem). But if the integral $\int_a^{\infty} f(x)\,dx$ converges absolutely, then the integral $\int_a^{\infty} f(x)\,\phi(x)\,dx$ also converges absolutely; if $|\phi(x)| < C$, then $|f(x)\,\phi(x)| < C|f(x)|$, and it remains to use the comparison theorem.

8.4.12. ***Hint.*** Transform the integral $f(x)$ into $f(x) = \int_{\pi/2}^{\pi/2} \ln \sin z\; dz$ by the substitution $y = \frac{\pi}{2} - z$. Taking into account that $\sin z = 2 \sin \frac{z}{2} \cdot \cos \frac{z}{2}$, reduce the above to the sum of three integrals.

8.4.13. ***Hint.*** Putting $u = \ln \cos x$, $\cos 2nx\,dx = dv$, integrate by parts and get the equality $I_n = \frac{1}{2n} \int_0^{\pi/2} \sin 2nx \frac{\sin x}{\cos x}\,dx, n \neq 0$. Since

$$\sin 2n\pi = \sin (2n-2)\,x \cdot \cos 2x + \sin 2x \cdot \cos (2n-2)\,x,$$

$$I_n = \frac{1}{2n}\left[-\int_0^{\pi/2} \sin (2n-2)\,x \frac{\sin x}{\cos x}\,dx\right.$$

$$\left.+ \int_0^{\pi/2} \sin(2n-2)\,x \cdot \sin 2x + dx + 2\int_0^{\pi/2} \sin^2 x \cos (2n-2)\,x\,dx\right]$$

Check by direct calculation that for $n \geq 2$ the second and the third summands equal zero, Therefore, for $n \geq 2$

$$I_n = -\frac{1}{2n} \int_0^{\pi/2} \sin (2n-2)\,x \frac{\sin x}{\cos x}\,dx = -\frac{n-1}{n} I_{n-1}.$$

Since $\quad I_1 = \frac{1}{2} \int_0^{\pi/2} \sin 2x \frac{\sin x}{\cos x}\,dx = \frac{\pi}{4}$ we have

$$I_2 = -\frac{1}{2} \cdot \frac{\pi}{4};\; I_3 = \frac{2}{3} \cdot \frac{1}{2} \cdot \frac{\pi}{4} = \frac{\pi}{3 \cdot 4}$$

and by induction, $I_n = (-1)^{n-1} \frac{\pi}{4n}$.